ECONOMIC GROWTH

McGraw-Hill Advanced Series in Economics

N. Gregory Mankiw, **Consulting Editor**

Economic Growth
    by Robert J. Barro and Xavier Sala-i-Martin

Advanced Macroeconomics
    by David Romer

ECONOMIC GROWTH

Robert J. Barro

Harvard University

Xavier Sala-i-Martin

Yale University

McGraw-Hill, Inc.

New York   St. Louis   San Francisco   Auckland   Bogotá   Caracas
Lisbon   London   Madrid   Mexico City   Milan   Montreal
New Delhi   San Juan   Singapore   Sydney   Tokyo   Toronto

This book was set in Times Roman by Publication Services, Inc.
The editors were Lucille H. Sutton and Scott D. Stratford;
the production supervisor was Denise L. Puryear.
The cover was designed by Carla Bauer.
Project supervision was done by Publication Services, Inc.
R. R. Donnelley & Sons Company was printer and binder.

Cover painting credit: Dalí, Salvador. *The Persistence of Memory* [Persistance de la mémoire]. 1931. Oil on canvas, $9\frac{1}{2} \times 13''$. The Museum of Modern Art, New York. Given anonymously. Photograph © 1995 The Museum of Modern Art, New York.

ECONOMIC GROWTH

This book is printed on recycled, acid-free
paper containing 10% postconsumer waste.

1 2 3 4 5 6 7 8 9 0 DOC DOC 9 0 9 8 7 6 5 4

ISBN 0-07-003697-7

Library of Congress Catalog Card Number: 94-73060

ABOUT THE AUTHORS

Robert J. Barro is Robert C. Waggoner Professor of Economics at Harvard University. He has a B.S. in physics from Caltech and a Ph.D. in economics from Harvard; he has previously held faculty positions at Rochester, Chicago, and Brown. He is also a contributing editor of *The Wall Street Journal,* a fellow of the Hoover Institution at Stanford, and a Research Associate of the National Bureau of Economic Research. In 1994–95, Barro was Houblon-Norman Research Fellow at the Bank of England. He is married to Judy Anne Barro and has four children.

Xavier Sala-i-Martin is an associate professor of economics at Yale University. He received his B.S. from Universitat Autonoma de Barcelona, and his Ph.D. from Harvard University. He is a Faculty Research Fellow of the National Bureau of Economic Research and a Research Associate of the Center for European Policy Research. In 1994–95, Sala-i-Martin was a visiting professor at the Universitat Pompeu Fabra (in Barcelona) and a consultant for the International Monetary Fund. In 1992, the graduate students at Yale honored him with the Distinguished Teacher Award for his classes on economic growth.

To My First Grandchild
—*Robert J. Barro*

A la Gubi i a la Schuxeta
—*Xavier Sala-i-Martin*

CONTENTS

Foreword   xv

Preface   xvii

Introduction   1

I.1   The Importance of Growth   1
I.2   Empirical Regularities about Economic Growth   5
I.3   A Brief History of Modern Growth Theory   9

1 Growth Models with Exogenous Saving Rates
   (The Solow–Swan Model)   14

1.1   The Basic Structure   14
1.2   The Neoclassical Model of Solow and Swan   16
       1.2.1   The Neoclassical Production Function   16
       1.2.2   The Fundamental Dynamic Equation for the Capital Stock   17
       1.2.3   The Steady State   19
       1.2.4   The Golden Rule of Capital Accumulation and Dynamic
                Inefficiency   19
       1.2.5   Transitional Dynamics   22
       1.2.6   Policy Experiments   24
       1.2.7   An Example: Cobb–Douglas Technology   25
       1.2.8   Absolute and Conditional Convergence   26
       1.2.9   Convergence and the Dispersion of Per Capita Income   31
       1.2.10   Technological Progress   32
       1.2.11   A Quantitative Measure of the Speed of Convergence   36
1.3   Models of Endogenous Growth   38
       1.3.1   The AK Model   39
       1.3.2   Endogenous Growth with Transitional Dynamics   41
       1.3.3   Constant-Elasticity-of-Substitution Production Functions   42
       1.3.4   The Leontief Production Function and the Harrod–Domar
                Controversy   46
       1.3.5   Growth Models with Poverty Traps   49

Appendix   Proofs of Various Propositions   52

Proof That Each Input Is Essential for Production with a Neoclassical
Production Function   52
Properties of the Convergence Coefficient in the Solow–Swan
Model   53
Proof That Technological Progress Must Be Labor Augmenting   54
Properties of the CES Production Function   55

Problems   56

**2 Growth Models with Consumer Optimization
(The Ramsey Model)**   59

2.1   Households   60
     2.1.1   Setup of the Model   60
     2.1.2   First-Order Conditions   63
2.2   Firms   67
2.3   Equilibrium   70
2.4   Alternative Environments   71
2.5   The Steady State   72
2.6   Transitional Dynamics   74
     2.6.1   The Phase Diagram   74
     2.6.2   The Shape of the Stable Arm   76
     2.6.3   Behavior of the Saving Rate   77
     2.6.4   The Paths of the Capital Stock and Output   79
     2.6.5   Speeds of Convergence   80

Appendix 2A   Log-Linearization of the Ramsey Model   87
Appendix 2B   Behavior of the Saving Rate   89
Appendix 2C   Proof That $\gamma_{\hat{k}}$ Declines Monotonically If
     the Economy Starts from $\hat{k}(0) < \hat{k}^*$ 90

Problems   92

**3 The Open Economy, Finite Horizons, and Adjustment
Costs**   96

3.1   An Open-Economy Version of the Ramsey Model   96
     3.1.1   Setup of the Model   96
     3.1.2   Behavior of a Small Economy's Capital Stock and Output   98
     3.1.3   Behavior of a Small Economy's Consumption and Assets   99
     3.1.4   The World Equilibrium   100
3.2   The World Economy with a Constraint on International Credit   101
     3.2.1   Setup of a Model with Physical and Human Capital   101
     3.2.2   The Closed Economy   102
     3.2.3   The Open Economy   103
3.3   Variations in Preference Parameters   108
3.4   Economic Growth in a Model with Finite Horizons   110
     3.4.1   Choices in a Model with Finite Horizons   110
     3.4.2   The Finite-Horizon Model of a Closed Economy   114
     3.4.3   The Finite-Horizon Model of an Open Economy   116

	3.5	Adjustment Costs for Investment	119
		3.5.1 The Behavior of Firms	119
		3.5.2 Equilibrium with a Given Interest Rate	122
		3.5.3 Equilibrium for a Closed Economy with a Fixed Saving Rate	125
	3.6	Some Conclusions	127

Appendix   Overlapping-Generations Models   128

Households   128
Firms   130
Equilibrium   130
The Steady State   131
The Golden Rule and Dynamic Efficiency   133
Dynamics   134
Altruism, Bequests, and Infinite Horizons   135

Problems   137

4   One-Sector Models of Endogenous Growth   140

4.1   The *AK* Model   141
   4.1.1   Behavior of Households   141
   4.1.2   Behavior of Firms   141
   4.1.3   Equilibrium   142
   4.1.4   Transitional Dynamics   142
   4.1.5   Determinants of the Growth Rate   143
4.2   A One-Sector Model with Physical and Human Capital   144
4.3   Models with Learning-By-Doing and Knowledge Spillovers   146
   4.3.1   Technology   146
   4.3.2   Equilibrium   148
   4.3.3   Pareto Nonoptimality and Policy Implications   149
   4.3.4   A Cobb–Douglas Example   150
   4.3.5   Scale Effects   151
4.4   Government and Growth   152
   4.4.1   The Public-Goods Model of Productive Government Services   152
   4.4.2   The Congestion Model of Productive Government Services   158
4.5   Transitional Dynamics in an Endogenous Growth Model   161
   4.5.1   A Cobb–Douglas Example   161
   4.5.2   A CES Example   164
4.6   Concluding Observations   166

Appendix   Conditions for Endogenous Growth in the
              One-Sector Model   167

Problems   169

**5   Two-Sector Models of Endogenous Growth
(With Special Attention to the Role of Human Capital)**   171

5.1   A One-Sector Model with Physical and Human Capital   172
   5.1.1   The Basic Setup   172
   5.1.2   The Constraint of Nonnegative Gross Investment   175

5.2	Different Technologies for Production and Education	179
	5.2.1 The Model with Two Sectors of Production	179
	5.2.2 The Uzawa–Lucas Model	182
	5.2.3 The Generalized Uzawa–Lucas Model	196
	5.2.4 The Model with Reversed Factor Intensities	197
5.3	Conditions for Endogenous Growth	198
5.4	Summary Observations	200

Appendix 5A Transitional Dynamics with Inequality Restrictions on Gross Investment in the One-Sector Model — 201

Appendix 5B Solution of the Uzawa–Lucas Model — 204

Appendix 5C The Model with Reversed Factor Intensities — 208

Problems — 210

6 Technological Change: Models with an Expanding Variety of Products — 212

6.1	Models with a Variety of Producer Products	213
	6.1.1 Production with a Fixed Number of Products	213
	6.1.2 Expansions in the Variety of Products	215
	6.1.3 Households and Market Equilibrium	218
	6.1.4 Determinants of the Growth Rate	220
	6.1.5 Pareto Optimality	220
	6.1.6 Erosion of Monopoly Power	223
	6.1.7 Romer's Model of Technological Change	226
6.2	Models with a Variety of Consumer Products	231
	6.2.1 Varieties of Consumer Goods	231
	6.2.2 A Comparison of Consumer Variety with Producer Variety	236
6.3	Concluding Observations	237

Problems — 238

7 Technological Change: Models with Improvements in the Quality of Products — 240

7.1	Sketch of the Model	241
7.2	Behavior of Firms	242
	7.2.1 Levels of Quality in the Production Technology	242
	7.2.2 The Incentive to Innovate	246
	7.2.3 The Behavior of the Aggregate Quality Index	251
	7.2.4 The Market Value of Firms	252
7.3	Households and Market Equilibrium	252
7.4	Innovation by the Leader	254
	7.4.1 The Leader as a Monopoly Researcher	255
	7.4.2 Research by Outsiders	257
7.5	Pareto Optimality	259
7.6	Summary Observations about Growth	262

Problems — 263

8   The Diffusion of Technology   265
  8.1   A Leader-Follower Model   266
        8.1.1   Behavior of Innovators in the Leading Country   267
        8.1.2   Behavior of Imitators in the Follower Country   268
        8.1.3   Variations in the Cost of Imitation   272
        8.1.4   Empirical Implications for Convergence   274
  8.2   Mutual Invention and Imitation   276
  8.3   Foreign Investment   276
  8.4   Leapfrogging   279
  8.5   Summary Observations about Diffusion and Growth   281
  Problems   281
9   Labor Supply and Population   285
  9.1   Migration in Models of Economic Growth   285
        9.1.1   Migration in the Solow–Swan Model   286
        9.1.2   Migration in the Ramsey Model   294
        9.1.3   The Braun Model of Migration and Growth   300
  9.2   Fertility Choice   308
        9.2.1   An Overlapping-Generations Setup   309
        9.2.2   The Model in Continuous Time   311
  9.3   Labor/Leisure Choice   321
  Appendix 9A   The Form of the Utility Function with
                 Consumption and Work Effort   326
  Problems   328
10 Data on Economic Growth, Growth Accounting   330
  10.1 Panel Data for Countries   330
  10.2 Long-term Data on GDP   332
  10.3 Regional Data Sets   341
        10.3.1 Data for U.S. States   341
        10.3.2 Data for European Regions   342
        10.3.3 Data for Canadian Provinces   344
        10.3.4 Data for Japanese Prefectures   345
  10.4 Growth Accounting   346
        10.4.1 General Setup   346
        10.4.2 Discrete Time and Variable Shares   347
        10.4.3 Measuring Input Shares and the Growth Rates
                of Inputs   348
        10.4.4 Results from Growth Accounting   350
        10.4.5 Extensions to Include R&D   351
        10.4.6 Limitations of Growth Accounting   352
11 Empirical Analysis of Regional Data Sets   382
  11.1 Two Concepts of Convergence   383
  11.2 Convergence across the U.S. States   387
        11.2.1 β Convergence   387
        11.2.2 Measurement Error   392
        11.2.3 σ Convergence   392

11.3	Convergence across Japanese Prefectures	393
	11.3.1 β Convergence	393
	11.3.2 σ Convergence across Prefectures	397
11.4	Convergence across European Regions	398
	11.4.1 β Convergence	398
	11.4.2 σ Convergence	400
11.5	Migration across the U.S. States	401
11.6	Migration across Japanese Prefectures	404
11.7	Migration across European Regions	407
11.8	Migration and Convergence	410
11.9	Conclusions	413

12 Empirical Analysis of a Cross Section of Countries 414

12.1	Losers and Winners from 1965 to 1985	415
12.2	The Empirical Analysis of Growth Rates	420
	12.2.1 Effects from State Variables	421
	12.2.2 Control and Environmental Variables	422
12.3	Regression Results for Growth Rates	424
	12.3.1 A Basic Regression	424
	12.3.2 Tests of Stability of Coefficients	436
	12.3.3 Additional Explanatory Variables	436
	12.3.4 World Bank Data on GDP	444
	12.3.5 Results from a Single Cross Section	445
12.4	Sources of Growth for Slow and Fast Growers	446
12.5	Empirical Analysis of the Investment Ratio	451
12.6	Empirical Analysis of Fertility and Health	452
	12.6.1 Results for Fertility	453
	12.6.2 Results on Health	454
12.7	Summary and Conclusions about Growth	455

Appendix on Mathematical Methods 462

1.1	Differential Equations	463
	1.1.1 Introduction	463
	1.1.2 First-Order Ordinary Differential Equations	464
	1.1.3 Systems of Linear Ordinary Differential Equations	471
1.2	Static Optimization	491
	1.2.1 Unconstrained Maxima	491
	1.2.2 Classical Nonlinear Programming: Equality Constraints	492
	1.2.3 Inequality Constraints: The Kuhn–Tucker Conditions	494
1.3	Dynamic Optimization in Continuous Time	498
	1.3.1 Introduction	498
	1.3.2 The Typical Problem	499
	1.3.3 Heuristic Derivation of the First-Order Conditions	500
	1.3.4 Transversality Conditions	503
	1.3.5 The Behavior of the Hamiltonian over Time	503
	1.3.6 Sufficient Conditions	503
	1.3.7 Infinite Horizons	504
	1.3.8 Example: The Neoclassical Growth Model	505

	1.3.9	Transversality Conditions in Infinite-Horizon Problems	507
	1.3.10	Summary of the Procedure to Find the First-Order Conditions	508
	1.3.11	Present-Value and Current-Value Hamiltonians	509
	1.3.12	Multiple Variables	510
1.4		Useful Results in Matrix Algebra: Eigenvalues, Eigenvectors, and Diagonalization of Matrices	510
1.5		Useful Results in Calculus	512
	1.5.1	Implicit Function Theorem	512
	1.5.2	Taylor's Theorem	513
	1.5.3	L'Hôpital's Rule	514
	1.5.4	Integration by Parts	515
	1.5.5	Fundamental Theorem of Calculus	515
	1.5.6	Rules of Differentiation of Integrals	516

References 518

Index 529

FOREWORD

The field of economic growth has reawakened. When I began studying economics almost two decades ago, the field of economic growth was dormant. The courses I took in macroeconomics included at most a brief section on long-run economic growth. And even that was at the end of the course. It was part of the material that the professor, always running behind schedule, never had time to cover in class.

Today, economic growth is central to the study of macroeconomics. Economists have come to understand that long-run growth is as important—perhaps even more important—than short-run fluctuations. The newspaper is filled with accounts of monthly changes in industrial production and retail sales. But these short-run changes have a relatively minor impact on economic well-being. Why GPD rose or fell a few percent over the last three months can be an intriguing question. Even more significant, however, is why the United States is so much richer than Nigeria or why growth in U.S. incomes over the past quarter-century has been slower than growth over the previous quarter-century.

Scholars choose the topics they study, however, based on more than the topics' importance. To a large extent, they choose topics based on their ability to say something novel. It is for this reason that the field of economic growth became dormant and then reawoke. Work on economic growth stopped in the 1960s because economists had nothing new to say. Twenty years later, a small group of economists began to explore alternative ways of explaining the large differences in income we observe across countries and over time. The new growth theory has highlighted ideas that played only a small role in the growth theory inherited from the past. Increasing returns, human capital, research and development, learning-by-doing, and externalities are now central to discussions of economic growth. At the same time, new data on economic growth have become available for a large sample of countries. These data have allowed the new research to include a healthy interplay between theory and empirics.

When the editors at McGraw-Hill asked me to help them assemble a series of advanced textbooks in economics, I had no doubt that a book on economic growth should be high on the agenda. Much had been learned and reported in academic journals. But no book was available to explain systematically all this material to the student. This book, the first in the McGraw-Hill series, fills that void. Moreover, this synthesis is presented by two of the most important scholars in this exploding field.

Economic growth comes largely from the accumulation of knowledge. This knowledge passes from one generation to the next in the form of textbooks. So, in a sense, this wonderful book by Robert Barro and Xavier Sala-i-Martin is not just about economic growth. It is itself part of the process of economic growth.

N. Gregory Mankiw
Harvard University
July 1994

PREFACE

Is there some action a government of India could take that would lead the Indian economy to grow like Indonesia's or Egypt's? If so, *what,* exactly? If not, what is it about the "nature of India" that makes it so? The consequences for human welfare involved in questions like these are simply staggering: Once one starts to think about them, it is hard to think about anything else. (Lucas [1988])

Economists have, in some sense, always known that growth is important. Yet at the core of the discipline, the study of economic growth languished after the late 1960s. Then, after a lapse of nearly two decades, this research became vigorous again in the mid-1980s. The impending tenth anniversary of this revival is a good time to assess the recent investigations and to place them in the context of earlier work. This unified approach brings out the contributions of the old and new research and also reveals areas in which knowledge is lacking. We attempt in some cases to fill the holes and in other cases to point out profitable directions for future work.

The research of the mid-1980s began with models of the determination of long-run growth, an area that is now called endogenous growth theory. Other recent research extended the older, neoclassical growth model, especially to bring out further the empirical implications of the theory. This book combines new results with expositions of the main research that appeared from the 1950s through the 1990s. The discussion stresses the empirical implications of the theories and the relation of these hypotheses to data and evidence. This combination of theory and empirical work is the most exciting aspect of the ongoing resurgence of work on economic growth.

The introduction motivates the study, brings out some key empirical regularities in the growth process, and provides a brief history of modern growth theory. Chapters 1–3 deal with the neoclassical growth model, from Solow–Swan in the 1950s, to Cass–Koopmans (and recollections of Ramsey) in the 1960s, to recent extensions. Chapters 4 and 5 cover the versions of endogenous growth theory that rely on forms of constant returns to reproducible factors. Chapters 6–8 explore recent models of technological change and R&D, including expansions in the variety and quality of products and the diffusion of knowledge. Chapter 9 allows for an endogenous determination of labor supply and population, including models of migration, fertility, and labor/leisure choice. Chapter 10 details the nature and availability of applicable data, and Chapters 11 and 12 discuss some empirical findings.

The material is written as a text at the level of first-year graduate students in economics. It is especially suitable for courses in macroeconomics, economic growth, and economic development. The authors developed and used the manuscript in second-year elective courses on economic growth and have used parts of the material in first-year, core graduate courses in macroeconomics. Other professors have already successfully used the manuscript for classes in macroeconomics, growth, and development.

Most of the chapters include problems that guide the students from routine exercises through suggestive extensions of the models. The level of mathematics includes differential equations and dynamic optimization, topics that are discussed in the mathematical appendix at the end of the book. For undergraduates who are comfortable with this level of mathematics, the book would work well for an advanced, elective course.

The lively pace of theoretical and empirical research on growth means that this version of the book will not remain up to date for many years. We therefore plan to revise as needed to maintain currency with developments in the field. Suggestions from readers—including notices of omissions of important contributions—would be appreciated. We have benefited in the preparation of this first edition from comments on the text or on related papers of ours by Philippe Aghion, Minna S. Andersen, Gary Becker, Olivier Blanchard, Juan Braun, Paul Cashin, Daniel Cohen, Michelle Connolly, Oded Galor, Zvi Griliches, Gene Grossman, Elhanan Helpman, Dale Jorgenson, Ken Judd, Jinill Kim, Michael Kremer, Phil Lane, Norman Loayza, Greg Mankiw, Casey Mulligan, Kevin M. Murphy, Pietro Peretto, Torsten Persson, Jordan Rappaport, Sergio Rebelo, Paul Romer, Michael Sarel, Etsuro Shioji, Chris Sims, B. Anna Sjögren, Nancy Stokey, Robert Tamura, Merritt Tilney, Aaron Tornell, Jaume Ventura, and Alwyn Young.

Robert J. Barro
Xavier Sala-i-Martin

ECONOMIC GROWTH

INTRODUCTION

I.1 THE IMPORTANCE OF GROWTH

The real per capita gross domestic product (GDP) in the United States grew by a
factor of 8.1 from $2244 in 1870 to $18,258 in 1990, all measured in 1985 dollars.
The increase in real per capita GDP corresponds to a growth rate of 1.75 percent per
year. This performance gave the United States the highest level of real per capita
GDP in the world in 1990 (with the possible exception of the United Arab Emirates,
an oil producer with a small population).[1]

To appreciate the consequences of apparently small differentials in growth
rates when compounded over long periods of time, we can calculate where the United
States would have been in 1990 if it had grown since 1870 at 0.75 percent per year,
one percentage point per year below its actual rate. A growth rate of 0.75 percent
per year is close to the rate experienced in the long run—from 1900 to 1987—by
India (0.64 percent per year), Pakistan (0.88 percent per year), and the Philippines
(0.86 percent per year). If the United States had begun in 1870 at a real per capita
GDP of $2244 and had then grown at a rate of 0.75 percent per year over the next
120 years, then its real per capita GDP in 1990 would have been $5519, only 2.5
times the value in 1870 and 30 percent of the actual value in 1990 of $18,258. Then,
instead of ranking first in the world in 1990, the United States would have ranked
37th out of 127 countries with data. To put it another way, if the growth rate had been
lower by just 1 percentage point per year, then the U.S. real per capita GDP in 1990
would have been close to that in Mexico and Hungary and would have been about
$1000 less than that in Portugal and Greece.

---

[1]The long-term data on GDP are in Tables 10.2 and 10.3 of Chapter 10. The cross-country information
for recent years is in Table 10.1. See Chapter 10 for sources and definitions.

Suppose, alternatively, that the U.S. real per capita GDP had grown since 1870 at 2.75 percent per year, 1 percentage point per year greater than the actual value. This higher growth rate is close to those experienced in the long run by Japan (2.95 percent per year from 1890 to 1990) and Taiwan (2.75 percent per year from 1900 to 1987). If the United States had still begun in 1870 at a real per capita GDP of $2244 and had then grown at a rate of 2.75 percent per year over the next 120 years, then its real per capita GDP in 1990 would have been $60,841—27 times the value in 1870 and 3.3 times the actual value in 1990 of $18,258. A real per capita GDP of $60,841 is well outside the historical experience of any country and may, in fact, be infeasible. We can say, however, that a continuation of the long-term U.S. growth rate of 1.75 percent per year implies that the United States will not attain a real per capita GDP of $60,841 until the year 2059.

The comparison of levels of real per capita GDP over a century involves multiples of as high as 20; for example, Japan's real per capita GDP in 1990 was about 20 times that in 1890. Comparisons of levels of real per capita GDP across countries at a point in time exhibit even greater multiples. Figure I.1 is a histogram for the log of real per capita GDP for 118 countries in 1960. The mean value corresponds to a real per capita GDP of $1470 (1985 U.S. dollars). The standard deviation of the log of real per capita GDP—a measure of the proportionate dispersion of real per capita GDP—is 0.90. This number means that a 1-standard-deviation band around the mean encompasses a range from 0.41 of the mean to 2.5 times the mean. The

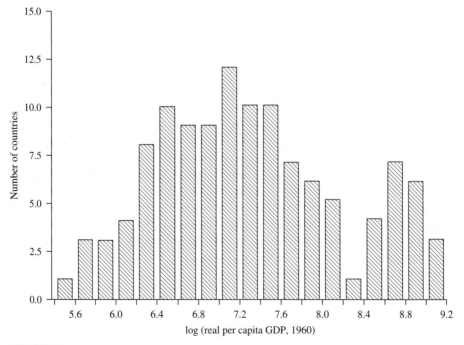

FIGURE I.1
Histogram for the log of real per capita GDP in 1960.

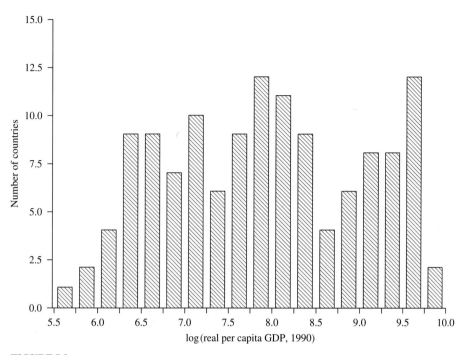

FIGURE I.2
Histogram for the log of real per capita GDP in 1990.

highest real per capita GDP of $9774 for the United States is 39 times the value of $249 for Ethiopia.

Figure I.2 shows a comparable histogram for 1990 for 129 countries. The mean here corresponds to a real per capita GDP of $2737, 1.9 times the value in 1960. The standard deviation of the log of real per capita GDP in 1990 is 1.11, implying a 1-standard-deviation band from 0.33 of the mean to 3.0 times the mean. Hence, the proportionate dispersion of real per capita GDP increased from 1960 to 1990. The highest value, $18,399 for the United States, is now 65 times the lowest value—$285 for Ethiopia.

If Ethiopia were to grow at the long-term U.S. rate of 1.75 percent per year, then it would take 239 years to reach the 1990 level of U.S. real per capita GDP. The required interval would still be 152 years if Ethiopia were to grow at the long-term Japanese rate of 2.75 percent per year.

For 114 countries, the average growth rate of real per capita GDP between 1960 and 1990 was 1.8 percent per year—nearly the same as the long-term U.S. rate—with a standard deviation of 1.8. Figure I.3 is a histogram of these growth rates; the range is from −2.1 percent per year for Iraq to 6.7 percent per year for South Korea. Thirty-year differences in growth rates of this magnitude have enormous consequences for standards of living. South Korea raised its real per capita GDP by a factor of 7.4 from $883 in 1960 (rank 83 out of 118 countries) to $6578 in 1990 (rank 35 of 129), while Iraq lowered its real per capita GDP by a factor of 0.5 from $3320 in 1960 (rank 23 of 118) to $1783 in 1990 (rank 82 of 129).

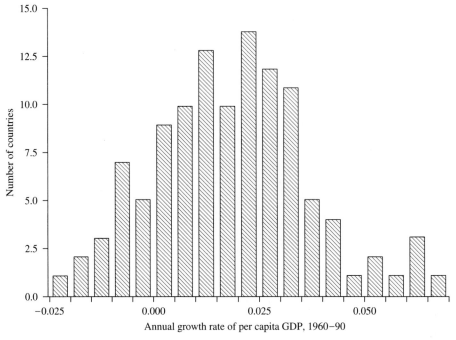

FIGURE I.3
Histogram for growth rates from 1960 to 1990.

A few other countries had growth rates from 1960 to 1990 that were nearly as high as South Korea's; those with rates above 5 percent per year were Singapore with 6.3 percent, Hong Kong with 6.2 percent, Taiwan with 6.1 percent, Botswana with 5.7 percent, Malta with 5.4 percent, and Japan with 5.4 percent. These countries increased their levels of real per capita GDP by a multiple of at least 5 over a single generation, that is, 30 years.

At the other end, 17 countries in addition to Iraq had negative growth rates of real per capita GDP from 1960 to 1990. The list, starting with the lowest rate, is Chad, Madagascar, Mozambique, Somalia, Zambia, Uganda, Guyana, Zaire, Nicaragua, Benin, Central African Republic, Haiti, Burundi, Ghana, Venezuela, Mauritania, and Niger. Thus, sub-Saharan African countries dominate the low-growth group; for the 39 sub-Saharan African countries with data, the mean growth rate from 1960 to 1990 was only 0.8 percent per year. That is, the typical country in sub-Saharan Africa increased its real per capita GDP by a factor of only 1.3 over 30 years.

If we want to understand why countries differ dramatically in standards of living (Figures I.1 and I.2), then we have to understand why countries experience such sharp divergences in long-term growth rates (Figure I.3). Even small differences in these growth rates, when cumulated over a generation or more, have much greater consequences for standards of living than the kinds of short-term business fluctuations that have typically occupied most of the attention of macro-economists. To put it another way, if we can learn about government policy options that have even small effects on the long-term growth rate, then we can contribute much more to improvements in standards of living than has been provided by the entire history of macroeconomic analysis of countercyclical policy and fine-tuning. Economic growth—the subject matter of this book—is the part of macroeconomics that really matters.

I.2 EMPIRICAL REGULARITIES ABOUT ECONOMIC GROWTH

Kaldor (1963) listed a number of stylized facts that he thought typified the process of economic growth:

1. Per capita output grows over time, and its growth rate does not tend to diminish.
2. Physical capital per worker grows over time.
3. The rate of return to capital is nearly constant.
4. The ratio of physical capital to output is nearly constant.
5. The shares of labor and physical capital in national income are nearly constant.
6. The growth rate of output per worker differs substantially across countries.[2]

Fact 6 accords with the cross-country data that we have already discussed. Facts 1, 2, 4, and 5 seem to fit reasonably well with the long-term data for currently developed countries. For discussions of the stability of the long-run ratio of physical capital to GDP in Japan, Germany, Italy, the United Kingdom, and the United States, see Maddison (1982, Chapter 3). For indications of the long-term stability of factor shares in the United States, see Denison (1974, Appendix J) and Jorgenson, Gollop, and Fraumeni (1987, Table 9.3). Young (1994) reports that factor shares were reasonably stable in four East-Asian countries—Hong Kong, Singapore, South Korea, and Taiwan—from the early or middle 1960s through 1990. Studies of seven developed countries—Canada, France, Germany, Italy, Japan, the Netherlands, and the United Kingdom—indicate that factor shares are similar to those in the United States (Christensen, Cummings, and Jorgenson [1980] and Dougherty [1991]). In some Latin-American countries considered by Elias (1990), the capital shares tend, however, to be higher than those in the United States.

---

[2]Kuznets (1973, 1981) brings out other characteristics of modern economic growth. He notes the rapid rate of structural transformation, which includes shifts from agriculture to industry to services. This process involves urbanization, shifts from home work to employee status, and an increasing role for formal education. He also argues that modern growth involves an increased role for foreign commerce and that technological progress implies reduced reliance on natural resources. Finally, he discusses the growing importance of government: "... the spread of modern economic growth placed greater emphasis on the importance and need for organization in national sovereign units ... The sovereign state unit was of critical importance as the formulator of the rules under which economic activity was to be carried on; as a referee ...; and as provider of infrastructure ..." (1981, p. 59).

Kaldor's claimed fact 3 on the stability of real rates of return appears to be heavily influenced by the experience of the United Kingdom; in this case, the real interest rate seems to have no long-run trend (see Barro [1987, Figures 4 and 7]). For the United States, however, the long-term data suggest a moderate decline of real interest rates (Barro [1993, Table 11.1]). Real rates of return in some fast-growing countries, such as South Korea and Singapore, are much higher than those in the United States but have declined over time (Young [1994]). Thus, it seems likely that Kaldor's hypothesis of a roughly stable real rate of return should be replaced by a tendency for returns to fall over some range as an economy develops.

We can use the data in Chapter 10 to assess the long-run tendencies of the growth rate of real per capita GDP. Tables 10.2 and 10.3 contain figures from Angus Maddison for 31 countries over periods of roughly a century. These numbers basically exhaust the available information about growth over very long time intervals.

Table 10.2 applies to 16 currently developed countries, the major countries in Europe plus the United States, Canada, and Australia. These data show an average per capita growth rate of 1.9 percent per year over roughly a century, with a breakdown by 20-year periods as follows:

Period	Growth rate (percent per year)	Number of countries
1870–1890	1.2	13
1890–1910	1.5	14
1910–1930	1.3	16
1930–1950	1.4	16
1950–1970	3.7	16
1970–1990	2.2	16

These numbers are consistent with Kaldor's proposition that the growth rate of real per capita GDP has no secular tendency to decline; in fact, the periods following World War II show growth rates well above the long-run average. The reduction in the growth rate from 3.7 percent per year in 1950–70 to 2.2 percent per year in 1970–90 corresponds to the often discussed *productivity slowdown*. It is apparent from the table, however, that the growth rate for 1970–90 is high in relation to the long-term history.

Table 10.3 contains figures for 15 currently less-developed countries in Asia and Latin America. In this case, the average long-run growth rate from 1900 to 1987 is 1.4 percent per year, and the breakdown into four subperiods is as follows:

Period	Growth rate (percent per year)	Number of countries
1900–1913	1.2	15
1913–1950	0.4	15
1950–1973	2.6	15
1973–1987	2.4	15

Again, the post–World War II period (here, 1950–87) shows growth rates well above the long-term average.

Table 10.1 contains information on real per capita GDP for over 100 countries from 1960 to 1990. We can use these data to extend the set of stylized facts that was provided by Kaldor. One pattern in the cross-country data is that the growth rate of real per capita GDP from 1960 to 1990 is essentially uncorrelated with the level of real per capita GDP in 1960 (see Chapter 12). In the terminology developed in Chapter 1, we refer to a tendency for the poor to grow faster than the rich as β convergence. Thus, the simple relationship between growth and the starting position for a broad cross section of countries does not reveal β convergence. This kind of convergence does appear if we limit attention to more homogeneous groups of economies, such as the U.S. states, regions of several European countries, and prefectures of Japan (see Barro and Sala-i-Martin [1991, 1992a, and 1992b] and Chapter 11). In these cases, the poorer places tend to grow faster than the richer ones. This behavior also appears in the cross-country data if we limit the sample to a relatively homogeneous collection of currently prosperous places, such as the OECD countries (see Baumol [1986] and DeLong [1988]).

We say in Chapter 1 that *conditional* β convergence applies if the growth rate of real per capita GDP is negatively related to the starting level of real per capita GDP after holding fixed some other variables, such as initial levels of human capital, measures of government policies, the propensities to save and have children, and so on. The broad cross-country sample—that is, the data set that does not show β convergence in an absolute sense—clearly reveals β convergence in this conditional context (see Barro [1991a]; Barro and Sala-i-Martin [1992a]; and Mankiw, Romer, and Weil [1992]). The rate of convergence is, however, only about 2 percent per year. Thus, it takes about 35 years for an economy to eliminate one-half of the gap between its initial real per capita GDP and its long-run or target level of real per capita GDP. (This target tends to grow over time.)

The results in Chapter 12 show that a number of variables are significantly related to the growth rate of real per capita GDP, once the starting level of real per capita GDP is held constant. For example, growth depends positively on the initial quantity of human capital in the form of educational attainment and health, negatively on the ratio of government consumption spending to GDP, and negatively on measures of distortions of markets and political instability. The ratio of gross investment to GDP is strongly positively correlated with the growth rate, but the timing evidence suggests that much of this association may reflect the reverse impact of growth prospects on the attractiveness of investment, rather than the favorable effect on growth from exogenous variations in the willingness to save. Similarly, Coe and Helpman (1993) demonstrate that investment in research and development (R&D) is highly correlated with productivity growth in a sample of 22 OECD countries (a group that has relatively satisfactory data on R&D expenditures). The direction of causation between R&D spending and growth has, however, not yet been established.

The cross-country evidence brings out a number of ways in which the government affects an economy's growth rate. Negative influences include the volume of consumption spending (and the associated level of taxation), distortions of international trade, and political instability. Positive influences involve the maintenance of institutions that sustain the rule of law, possibly policies that promote the development of financial institutions, and perhaps spending on some forms of public infrastructure. In most cases, the empirical work does not provide robust estimates for the effects of a specific governmental policy on growth, but it does show that the overall package of policies matters a lot. Thus, by affecting long-run growth rates, the government's actions can have major consequences for standards of living that we highlighted earlier. As a corollary, the relation between government policies and growth is a priority area for economic research.

The cross-sectional data also reveal regularities in the behavior of the ratio of gross investment to GDP. This ratio is positively related to initial human capital in the forms of educational attainment and health and is also positively correlated with the level of real per capita GDP. However, the correlation with real per capita GDP becomes virtually nil once the quantity of human capital is held constant. These observations suggest that the investment/GDP ratio would tend to rise over some range as a country develops and increases its human capital per person.

We can learn more about the patterns in the investment ratio from the long-run time-series data. Maddison (1992) provides long-term information for a few countries on the ratios of gross domestic investment to GDP and of gross national saving (the sum of domestic and net foreign investment) to GDP. (See Figures 10.5–10.15 and the sources discussed in Chapter 10.) Averages of the investment and saving ratios over 20-year intervals for the eight countries that have enough data for a long-period analysis are as follows:

Ratios to GDP of Gross Domestic Investment and Gross National Saving (%)

Period	Austrl.	Canada	France	India	Japan	Korea	U.K.	U.S.
1. Gross Domestic Investment								
1870–1889	16.5	16.0	12.8	—	—	—	9.3	19.8
1890–1909	13.7	17.2	14.0	—	14.0	—	9.4	17.9
1910–1929	17.4	19.8	—	6.4	16.6	5.1*	6.7	17.2
1930–1949	13.3	13.1	—	8.4	20.5	—	8.1	12.7
1950–1969	26.3	23.8	22.6	14.0	31.8	16.3†	17.2	18.9
1970–1989	24.9	22.8	23.2	20.2	31.9	29.1	18.2	18.7
2. Gross National Saving								
1870–1889	11.2	9.1	12.8	—	—	—	13.9	19.1
1890–1909	12.2	11.5	14.9	—	12.0	—	13.1	18.4
1910–1929	13.6	16.0	—	6.4	17.1	2.3*	9.6	18.9
1930–1949	13.0	15.6	—	7.7	19.8	—	4.8	14.1
1950–1969	24.0	22.3	22.8	12.2	32.1	5.9†	17.7	19.6
1970–1989	22.9	22.1	23.4	19.4	33.7	26.2	19.4	18.5

*1911–1929

†1951–1969

Note: See Chapter 10 for further discussion.

For an individual country, the table indicates that the time paths of domestic investment and national saving are usually similar. Domestic investment was, however, substantially higher than national saving (that is, borrowing from abroad was large) for Australia and Canada from 1870 to 1929, for Japan from 1890 to 1909, for the United Kingdom from 1930 to 1949, and for Korea from 1950 to 1969 (in fact, through the early 1980s). National saving was much higher than domestic investment (lending abroad was substantial) for the United Kingdom from 1870 to 1929 and for the United States from 1930 to 1949.

For the United States, the striking observation from the table is the stability over time of the ratios for domestic investment and national saving. The only exception is the relatively low values from 1930 to 1949, the period of the Great Depression and World War II. The United States is, however, an outlier with respect to the stability of its investment and saving ratios; the data for the other seven countries show a clear increase in these ratios over time. In particular, the ratios for 1950–1989 are, in all cases, substantially greater than those from before World War II.

The long-term data therefore indicate that the ratios to GDP of gross domestic investment and gross national saving tend to rise as an economy develops, at least over some range. This pattern in the long-run time series accords with the information that we have already discussed for the broad cross section of countries from 1960 to 1990. The assumption of a constant gross saving ratio, which appears in Chapter 1 in the Solow–Swan model, therefore misses this regularity in the data.

The cross-country data also reveal some regularities with respect to fertility rates and, hence, rates of population growth. For most countries, the fertility rate tends to decline with increases in real per capita GDP. For the poorest countries, however, the fertility rate may rise with real per capita GDP, as Malthus (1798) predicted. Even stronger relations exist between educational attainment and fertility. Except for the most advanced countries, female schooling is negatively related with the fertility rate, whereas male schooling is positively related with the fertility rate. The net effect of these forces is that the fertility rate—and the rate of population growth—tend to fall over some range as an economy develops. The assumption of an exogenous, constant rate of population growth—another key element of the Solow–Swan model—conflicts with this empirical pattern.

I.3 A BRIEF HISTORY OF MODERN GROWTH THEORY

Classical economists, such as Adam Smith (1776), David Ricardo (1817), and Thomas Malthus (1798), and, much later, Frank Ramsey (1928), Allyn Young (1928), Frank Knight (1944), and Joseph Schumpeter (1934), provided many of the basic ingredients that appear in modern theories of economic growth. These ideas include the basic approaches of competitive behavior and equilibrium dynamics, the role of diminishing returns and its relation to the accumulation of physical and human capital, the interplay between per capita income and the growth rate of population, the effects of technological progress in the forms of increased specialization of labor and discoveries of new goods and methods of production, and the role of monopoly power as an incentive for technological advance.

Our main study begins with these building blocks already in place and focuses on the contributions in the neoclassical tradition since the late 1950s. We use the neoclassical methodology and language and rely on concepts such as aggregate capital stocks, aggregate production functions, and utility functions for representative consumers (who often have infinite horizons). We also use modern mathematical methods of dynamic optimization and differential equations. These tools, which are described in an appendix at the end of this book, are familiar today to most first-year graduate students in economics.

From a chronological viewpoint, the starting point for modern growth theory is the classic article of Ramsey (1928), a work that was several decades ahead of its time. Ramsey's treatment of household optimization over time goes far beyond its application to growth theory; it is hard now to discuss consumption theory, asset pricing, or even business-cycle theory without invoking the optimality conditions that Ramsey (and Fisher [1930]) introduced to economists. Ramsey's intertemporally separable utility function is as widely used today as the Cobb–Douglas production function. The economics profession did not, however, accept or widely use Ramsey's approach until the 1960s.

Between Ramsey and the late 1950s, Harrod (1939) and Domar (1946) attempted to integrate Keynesian analysis with elements of economic growth. They used production functions with little substitutability among the inputs to argue that the capitalist system is inherently unstable. Since they wrote during or immediately after the Great Depression, these arguments were received sympathetically by many economists. Although these contributions triggered a good deal of research at the time, very little of this analysis plays a role in today's thinking.

The next and more important contributions were those of Solow (1956) and Swan (1956). The key aspect of the Solow–Swan model is the neoclassical form of the production function, a specification that assumes constant returns to scale, diminishing returns to each input, and some positive and smooth elasticity of substitution between the inputs. This production function is combined with a constant-saving-rate rule to generate an extremely simple general-equilibrium model of the economy.

One prediction from these models, which has been exploited seriously as an empirical hypothesis only in recent years, is conditional convergence. The lower the starting level of real per capita GDP, relative to the long-run or steady-state position, the faster is the growth rate. This property derives from the assumption of diminishing returns to capital; economies that have less capital per worker (relative to their long-run capital per worker) tend to have higher rates of return and higher growth rates. The convergence is conditional because the steady-state levels of capital and output per worker depend, in the Solow–Swan model, on the saving rate, the growth rate of population, and the position of the production function—characteristics that might vary across economies. Recent empirical studies indicate that we should include additional sources of cross-country variation, especially differences in government policies and in initial stocks of human capital. The key point, however, is that the concept of conditional convergence—a basic property of the Solow-Swan model—has considerable explanatory power for economic growth across countries and regions.

Another prediction of the Solow–Swan model is that, in the absence of continuing improvements in technology, per capita growth must eventually cease. This prediction, which resembles those of Malthus and Ricardo, also comes from the assumption of diminishing returns to capital. We have already observed, however, that positive rates of per capita growth can persist over a century or more and that these growth rates have no clear tendency to decline.

The neoclassical growth theorists of the late 1950s and 1960s recognized this modeling deficiency and usually patched it up by assuming that technological progress occurred in an exogenous manner. This device can reconcile the theory with a positive, possibly constant per capita growth rate in the long run, while retaining the prediction of conditional convergence. The obvious shortcoming, however, is that the long-run per capita growth rate is determined entirely by an element—the rate of technological progress—that is outside of the model. (The long-run growth rate of the level of output also depends on the growth rate of population, another element that is exogenous in the standard theory.) Thus, we end up with a model of growth that explains everything but long-run growth, an obviously unsatisfactory situation.

Cass (1965) and Koopmans (1965) brought Ramsey's analysis of consumer optimization back into the neoclassical growth model and thereby provided for an endogenous determination of the saving rate. This extension allows for richer transitional dynamics but tends to preserve the hypothesis of conditional convergence. The endogeneity of saving also does not eliminate the dependence of the long-run per capita growth rate on exogenous technological progress.

The equilibrium of the Cass–Koopmans version of the neoclassical growth model can be supported by a decentralized, competitive framework in which the productive factors, labor and capital, are paid their marginal products. Total income then exhausts the total product because of the assumption that the production function features constant returns to scale. Moreover, the decentralized outcomes are Pareto optimal.

The inclusion of a theory of technological change in the neoclassical framework is difficult, because the standard competitive assumptions cannot be maintained. Technological advance involves the creation of new ideas, which are partially nonrival and therefore have aspects of public goods. For a given technology—that is, for a given state of knowledge—it is reasonable to assume constant returns to scale in the standard, rival factors of production, such as labor, capital, and land. In other words, given the level of knowledge on how to produce, one would think that it is possible to replicate a firm with the same amount of labor, capital, and land and obtain twice as much output. But then, the returns to scale tend to be increasing if the nonrival ideas are included as factors of production. These increasing returns conflict with perfect competition. In particular, the compensation of nonrival old ideas in accordance with their current marginal cost of production—zero—will not provide the appropriate reward for the research effort that underlies the creation of new ideas.

Arrow (1962) and Sheshinski (1967) constructed models in which ideas were unintended by-products of production or investment, a mechanism described as learning-by-doing. In these models, each person's discoveries immediately spill over to the entire economy, an instantaneous diffusion process that might be technically feasible because knowledge is nonrival. Romer (1986) showed later that the competitive framework can be retained in this case to determine an equilibrium rate of technological advance, but the resulting growth rate would typically not be Pareto optimal. More generally, the competitive framework breaks down if discoveries depend in part on purposive R&D effort and if an individual's innovations spread only gradually to other producers. In this realistic setting, a decentralized theory of technological progress requires basic changes in the neoclassical growth model to incorporate models of imperfect competition.[3] These additions to the theory did not come until Romer's (1987, 1990) research in the late 1980s.

The work of Cass (1965) and Koopmans (1965) completed the basic neoclassical growth model. Thereafter, growth theory became excessively technical and steadily lost contact with empirical applications. In contrast, development economists, who are required to give advice to sick countries, retained an applied perspective and tended to use models that were technically unsophisticated but empirically useful. The fields of economic development and economic growth drifted apart, and the two areas became almost completely separated.

Probably because of its lack of empirical relevance, growth theory effectively died as an active research field by the early 1970s, on the eve of the rational-expectations revolution and the oil shocks. For about 15 years, macroeconomic research focused on short-term fluctuations. Major contributions included the incorporation of rational expectations into business-cycle models, improved approaches to policy evaluation, and the application of general-equilibrium methods to real business-cycle theory.

Since the mid-1980s, research on economic growth has experienced a new boom, beginning with the work of Romer (1986) and Lucas (1988). The motivation for this research was the observation (or recollection) that the determinants of long-run economic growth are crucial issues, far more important than the mechanics of business cycles or the countercyclical effects of monetary and fiscal policies. But a recognition of the significance of long-run growth is only a first step; to go further, one has to escape the straitjacket of the neoclassical growth model, in which the long-term per capita growth rate is pegged by the rate of exogenous technological progress. Thus, in one way or another, the recent contributions determine the long-run growth rate within the model; hence, the designation *endogenous-growth* models.

The initial wave of the new research—Romer (1986), Lucas (1988), Rebelo (1991)—built on the work of Arrow (1962), Sheshinski (1967), and Uzawa (1965) and did not really introduce a theory of technological change. In these models, growth may go on indefinitely because the returns to investment in a broad class of capital goods—which includes human capital—do not necessarily diminish as economies develop. (This idea goes back to Knight [1944].) Spillovers of knowledge across producers and external benefits from human capital are parts of this process, but only because they help avoid the tendency for diminishing returns to the accumulation of capital.

The incorporation of R&D theories and imperfect competition into the growth framework began with Romer (1987, 1990) and includes significant contributions by Aghion and Howitt (1992) and Grossman and Helpman (1991, Chapters 3 and 4). In these models, technological advance results from purposive R&D activity, and this activity is rewarded by some form of *ex-post* monopoly power. If there is

---

[3] Another approach is to assume that all of the nonrival research—a classic public good—is financed by the government through involuntary taxes; see Shell (1967).

no tendency for the economy to run out of ideas, then the growth rate can remain positive in the long run. The rate of growth and the underlying amount of inventive activity tend, however, not to be Pareto optimal because of distortions related to the creation of the new goods and methods of production. In these frameworks, the long-term growth rate depends on governmental actions, such as taxation, maintenance of law and order, provision of infrastructure services, protection of intellectual property rights, and regulations of international trade, financial markets, and other aspects of the economy. The government therefore has great potential for good or ill through its influence on the long-term rate of growth.

The new research also includes models of the diffusion of technology. Whereas the analysis of discovery relates to the rate of technological progress in leading-edge economies, the study of diffusion pertains to the manner in which follower economies share by imitation in these advances. Since imitation tends to be cheaper than innovation, the diffusion models predict a form of conditional convergence that resembles the predictions of the neoclassical growth model.

Another key exogenous parameter in the neoclassical growth model is the growth rate of population. A higher rate of population growth lowers the steady-state level of capital and output per worker and tends thereby to reduce the per capita growth rate for a given initial level of per capita output. The standard model does not, however, consider the effects of per capita income and wage rates on population growth—the kinds of effects stressed by Malthus—and also does not take account of the resources used up in the process of child rearing. Another line of recent research makes population growth endogenous by incorporating an analysis of fertility choice in the neoclassical model. The results are consistent, for example, with the empirical regularity that fertility rates tend to fall with per capita income over the main range of experience, but may rise with per capita income for the poorest countries. Additional work related to the endogeneity of labor supply in a growth context concerns migration and labor/leisure choice.

The clearest distinction between the growth theory of the 1960s and that of the 1980s and 1990s is that the recent research pays close attention to empirical implications and to the relation between theory and data. Some of this applied perspective involves amplification of the empirical implications of the older theory, notably the neoclassical growth model's prediction of conditional convergence. Other analyses apply more directly to the recent theories of endogenous growth, including the roles of increasing returns, R&D activity, human capital, and the diffusion of technology.

In this book we attempt to reflect the recent emphasis on the interplay between theory and applications. Thus, we stress the empirical implications of the various theories that we develop. We also include three chapters that are devoted entirely to data and empirical analyses.

The recent growth research has attracted interest from economists in a wide variety of fields. Conferences on growth have participation from specialists in macroeconomics, development, international economics, theory, history, econometrics, and industrial organization. We think that the effective combination of theory and empirical work will sustain this broad appeal and will allow growth theory to survive this time as a vibrant field. We do not expect the growth theory of the 1990s to suffer the same fate as the growth theory of the 1960s.

CHAPTER
1

GROWTH MODELS WITH EXOGENOUS SAVING RATES (THE SOLOW–SWAN MODEL)

1.1   THE BASIC STRUCTURE

All the models of growth that we discuss in this book have the same basic general-equilibrium structure. First, households (or families) own the inputs and assets of the economy, including ownership rights in firms, and choose the fractions of their income to consume and save. Each household determines how many children to have, whether to join the labor force, and how much to work. Second, firms hire inputs, such as capital and labor, and use these inputs to produce goods that they sell to households or other firms. Firms have access to a technology—which may evolve over time—that allows them to transform inputs into output. Third, markets exist on which firms sell goods to households or other firms and on which households sell the inputs to firms. The quantities demanded and supplied determine the relative prices of the inputs and the produced goods.

It is convenient in this initial chapter to use a simplified setup that excludes markets and firms. We can think of a composite unit—a household/producer like Robinson Crusoe—who owns the inputs and also manages the technology that transforms inputs into outputs. There are only two inputs, physical capital, $K(t)$, and labor, $L(t)$. The production function takes the form

$$Y(t) = F[K(t), L(t), t], \tag{1.1}$$

where $Y(t)$ is the flow of output produced at time t. The production function depends on time, t, to reflect the effects of technological progress: the same amount of capital and labor yields a larger quantity of output in 1995 than in 1895 if the technology employed in 1995 is superior.

We assume a one-sector production technology in which output is a homogeneous good that can be consumed, $C(t)$, or invested, $I(t)$, to create new units of physical capital, $K(t)$. One way to think about the one-sector technology is to draw an analogy with farm animals, which can be eaten or used as inputs to produce more farm animals. The literature on economic growth has used more inventive examples—with such terms as *shmoos, putty,* or *ectoplasm*—to reflect the easy transmutation of capital goods into consumables, and vice versa.

We assume in this chapter that the economy is closed: households cannot buy foreign goods or assets and cannot sell home goods or assets abroad. (Chapter 3 allows for an open economy.) In a closed economy, output equals income, and the amount invested equals the amount saved.

Let $s(\bullet)$ be the fraction of output that is saved—that is, the *saving rate*—so that $1 - s(\bullet)$ is the fraction of output that is consumed. Rational households choose the saving rate by comparing the costs and benefits of consuming today rather than tomorrow; this comparison involves preference parameters and variables that describe the state of the economy, such as the level of wealth and the interest rate. In Chapter 2, where we model this decision explicitly, we find that $s(\bullet)$ is a complicated function for which there are typically no closed-form solutions. To facilitate the analysis in this initial chapter, we assume that $s(\bullet)$ is given exogenously. The simplest function, the one assumed by Solow (1956) and Swan (1956) in their classic articles, is a constant, $s(\bullet) = s > 0$. We use this constant-saving-rate specification in this chapter because it brings out a large number of results in a clear way.

We assume that capital depreciates at the constant rate $\delta > 0$; that is, at each point in time, a constant fraction of the capital stock wears out and, hence, can no longer be used for production. (If we think of goods as farm animals, then a constant fraction of the animals dies at each moment, unrealistically independent of the average age of the stock.)

The net increase in the stock of physical capital at a point in time equals gross investment less depreciation:

$$\dot{K} = I - \delta K = s \cdot F(K, L, t) - \delta K, \tag{1.2}$$

where a dot over a variable, such as $\dot{K}$, denotes differentiation with respect to time, and $0 \leq s \leq 1$. Equation (1.2) determines the dynamics of K for a given technology and labor force. In the first sections of this chapter, we neglect technological progress; that is, we assume that $F(\bullet)$ is independent of t. This assumption will be relaxed later.

The labor force, L, varies over time because of population growth, changes in participation rates, and shifts in the amount of time worked by the typical worker. The growth of population reflects, in turn, the behavior of fertility, mortality, and migration. Chapter 9 allows for choices between work and leisure and also considers the effects from migration, fertility, and mortality on population. In this chapter, we simplify by assuming that population grows at a constant, exogenous rate, $\dot{L}/L = n \geq 0$, and that everyone works at a given intensity. If we normalize the number of people at time 0 to 1 and the work intensity per person also to 1, then the population and labor force at time t are equal to

$$L(t) = e^{nt}. \tag{1.3}$$

If $L(t)$ is given from Eq. (1.3) and technological progress is absent, then Eq. (1.2) determines the time paths of capital, K, and output, Y. In the next sections, we show that this behavior depends crucially on the properties of the production function, $F(\cdot)$. In fact, apparently minor differences in assumptions about $F(\cdot)$ can generate radically different theories of economic growth.

1.2   THE NEOCLASSICAL MODEL OF SOLOW AND SWAN

1.2.1   The Neoclassical Production Function

If we neglect technological progress, then the production function from Eq. (1.1) takes the form

$$Y = F(K, L). \tag{1.4}$$

We say that the production function is *neoclassical* if the following three properties are satisfied. First, for all $K > 0$ and $L > 0$, $F(\cdot)$ exhibits positive and diminishing marginal products with respect to each input:

$$\frac{\partial F}{\partial K} > 0, \qquad \frac{\partial^2 F}{\partial K^2} < 0$$

$$\frac{\partial F}{\partial L} > 0, \qquad \frac{\partial^2 F}{\partial L^2} < 0. \tag{1.5a}$$

Second, $F(\cdot)$ exhibits constant returns to scale:

$$F(\lambda K, \lambda L) = \lambda \cdot F(K, L) \text{ for all } \lambda > 0. \tag{1.5b}$$

Third, the marginal product of capital (or labor) approaches infinity as capital (or labor) goes to 0 and approaches 0 as capital (or labor) goes to infinity:

$$\lim_{K \to 0} (F_K) = \lim_{L \to 0} (F_L) = \infty$$

$$\lim_{K \to \infty} (F_K) = \lim_{L \to \infty} (F_L) = 0 \tag{1.5c}$$

These last properties are called *Inada conditions*, following Inada (1963).

The condition of constant returns to scale implies that output can be written as

$$Y = F(K, L) = L \cdot F(K/L, 1) = L \cdot f(k),$$

where $k \equiv K/L$ is the capital–labor ratio, $y \equiv Y/L$ is per capita output, and the function $f(k)$ is defined to equal $F(k, 1)$. This result means that the production function can be expressed in *intensive form* as

$$y = f(k). \tag{1.6}$$

We can use the condition $Y = L \cdot f(k)$ and differentiate with respect to K, for fixed L, and then with respect to L, for fixed K, to verify that the marginal products of the factor inputs are given by

$$\partial Y/\partial K = f'(k),$$
$$\partial Y/\partial L = [f(k) - k \cdot f'(k)]. \tag{1.7}$$

The Inada conditions imply $\lim_{k \to 0}[f'(k)] = \infty$ and $\lim_{k \to \infty}[f'(k)] = 0$.

We can show that the neoclassical properties, Eqs. (1.5a)–(1.5c), imply that each input is essential for production, that is, $F(0, L) = F(K, 0) = f(0) = 0$. The properties also imply that output goes to infinity as either input goes to infinity. See the appendix at the end of this chapter for proofs of these propositions.

One simple production function that is often thought to provide a reasonable description of actual economies is the Cobb–Douglas function,

$$Y = AK^\alpha L^{1-\alpha}, \tag{1.8}$$

where $A > 0$ is the level of the technology, and α is a constant with $0 < \alpha < 1$. The Cobb–Douglas function can be written in intensive form as

$$y = Ak^\alpha. \tag{1.9}$$

Note that $f'(k) = A\alpha k^{\alpha-1} > 0$, $f''(k) = -A\alpha(1-\alpha)k^{\alpha-2} < 0$, $\lim_{k \to \infty} f'(k) = 0$, and $\lim_{k \to 0} f'(k) = \infty$. Thus, the Cobb–Douglas form satisfies the properties of a neoclassical production function.

1.2.2 The Fundamental Dynamic Equation for the Capital Stock

We now analyze the dynamic behavior of the economy described by the neoclassical production function. The resulting growth model is called the Solow–Swan model, after the important contributions of Solow (1956) and Swan (1956).

The change in the capital stock over time is given by Eq. (1.2). If we divide both sides of this equation by L, then we get

$$\dot{K}/L = s \cdot f(k) - \delta k.$$

The right-hand side contains per capita variables only, but the left-hand side does not. We can write $\dot{K}/L$, as a function of k by using the condition

$$\dot{k} \equiv \frac{d(K/L)}{dt} = \dot{K}/L - nk,$$

where $n = \dot{L}/L$. If we substitute this result into the expression for $\dot{K}/L$ then we can rearrange terms to get

$$\dot{k} = s \cdot f(k) - (n + \delta) \cdot k. \qquad (1.10)$$

Equation (1.10) is the fundamental differential equation of the Solow–Swan model. This nonlinear equation depends only on k.

The term $n + \delta$ on the right-hand side of Eq. (1.10) can be thought of as the effective depreciation rate for the capital/labor ratio, $k \equiv K/L$. If the saving rate, s, were 0, then k would decline partly due to depreciation of K at the rate δ and partly due to growth of L at the rate n.

Figure 1.1 shows the workings of Eq. (1.10). The upper curve is the production function, $f(k)$. The term $s \cdot f(k)$, which appears in Eq. (1.10), looks like the production function except for the multiplication by the positive fraction s. Note from the figure that the $s \cdot f(k)$ curve starts from the origin (because $f[0] = 0$), has a positive slope (because $f'[k] > 0$), and gets flatter as k rises (because $f''[k] < 0$). The Inada conditions imply that the $s \cdot f(k)$ curve is vertical at $k = 0$ and becomes flat as k approaches infinity. The other term in Eq. (1.10), $(n + \delta) \cdot k$, appears in Fig. 1.1 as a straight line from the origin with the positive slope $n + \delta$.

Consider an economy with the initial capital stock per person $k(0) > 0$. Figure 1.1 shows that gross investment per person equals the height of the $s \cdot f(k)$ curve at this point. Consumption per person equals the vertical difference at this point between the $f(k)$ and $s \cdot f(k)$ curves.

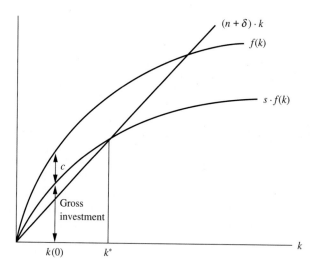

FIGURE 1.1
The Solow–Swan model. The curve for gross investment, $s \cdot f(k)$, is proportional to the production function, $f(k)$. Consumption per person equals the vertical distance between $f(k)$ and $s \cdot f(k)$. Effective depreciation (for k) is given by $(n + \delta) \cdot k$, a straight line from the origin. The change in k is given by the vertical distance between $s \cdot f(k)$ and $(n + \delta) \cdot k$. The steady-state level of capital, k^*, is determined at the intersection of the $s \cdot f(k)$ curve with the $(n + \delta) \cdot k$ line.

1.2.3   The Steady State

We define a *steady state* as a situation in which the various quantities grow at constant rates. In the Solow–Swan model, the steady state corresponds to $\dot{k} = 0$ in Eq. (1.10),[1] that is, to an intersection of the $s \cdot f(k)$ curve with the $(n + \delta) \cdot k$ line in Figure 1.1.[2] The corresponding value of k is denoted k^*. (We focus here on the intersection at $k > 0$ and neglect the one at $k = 0$.) Algebraically, k^* satisfies the condition

$$s \cdot f(k^*) = (n + \delta) \cdot k^*. \tag{1.11}$$

Since k is constant in the steady state, y and c are also constant at the values $y^* = f(k^*)$ and $c^* = (1 - s) \cdot f(k^*)$, respectively. Hence, in the neoclassical model, the per capita quantities k, y, and c do not grow in the steady state. The constancy of the per capita magnitudes means that the levels of variables—K, Y, and C—grow in the steady state at the rate of population growth, n.

Changes in the level of the technology, represented by shifts of the production function, $f(\bullet)$; in the saving rate, s; in the rate of population growth, n; and in the depreciation rate, δ; all have effects on the per capita *levels* of the various quantities in the steady state. In Fig. 1.1, for example, a proportional upward shift of the production function or an increase in s shifts the $s \cdot f(k)$ curve upward and thereby leads to an increase in k^*. An increase in n or δ moves the $(n + \delta) \cdot k$ line upward and leads to a decrease in k^*.

It is important to note that changes in the level of technology, the saving rate, the rate of population growth, and the depreciation rate do not affect the steady-state growth rates of per capita output, capital, and consumption, all of which are equal to 0. For this reason, the model as presently specified will not provide explanations of the determinants of long-run per capita growth.

1.2.4   The Golden Rule of Capital Accumulation and Dynamic Inefficiency

For a given production function and given values of n and δ, there is a unique steady-state value $k^* > 0$ for each value of the saving rate, s. Denote this relation by $k^*(s)$, with $dk^*(s)/ds > 0$. The steady-state level of per capita consumption is $c^* = (1 - s) \cdot f[k^*(s)]$. We know from Eq. (1.11) that $s \cdot f(k^*) = (n + \delta) \cdot k^*$; hence, we can write an expression for c^* as

$$c^*(s) = f[k^*(s)] - (n + \delta) \cdot k^*(s). \tag{1.12}$$

---

[1] We can show that k must be constant in the steady state. Divide both sides of Eq. (1.10) by k to get $\dot{k}/k = s \cdot f(k)/k - (n + \delta)$. The left-hand side is constant, by definition, in the steady state. Since s, n, and δ are all constants, it follows that $f(k)/k$ must be constant in the steady state. The time derivative of $f(k)/k$ equals $-\{[f(k) - kf'(k)]/k\} \cdot (\dot{k}/k)$. The expression $f(k) - kf'(k)$ equals the marginal product of labor and is positive. Therefore, as long as k is finite, $\dot{k}/k$ must equal 0 in the steady state.

[2] The intersection in the range of positive k exists and is unique because $f(0) = 0$, $n + \delta < \lim_{k \to 0}[s \cdot f'(k)] = \infty$, $n + \delta > \lim_{k \to \infty}[s \cdot f'(k)] = 0$, and $f''(k) < 0$.

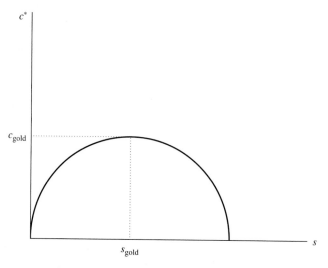

FIGURE 1.2

The golden rule of capital accumulation. The vertical axis shows the steady-state level of consumption per person that corresponds to each saving rate. The saving rate that maximizes steady-state consumption per person is called the Golden Rule saving rate and is denoted by s_{gold}.

Figure 1.2 shows the relation between c^* and s that is implied by Eq. (1.12). The quantity c^* is increasing in s for low levels of s and decreasing in s for high values of s. The quantity c^* attains its maximum when the derivative vanishes, that is, when $[f'(k^*) - (n + \delta)] \cdot dk^*/ds = 0$. Since $dk^*/ds > 0$, the term in brackets must equal 0. If we denote the value of k^* by k_{gold} that corresponds to the maximum of c^*, then the condition that determines k_{gold} is

$$f'(k_{gold}) = n + \delta. \tag{1.13}$$

The corresponding saving rate can be denoted as s_{gold}, and the associated level of steady-state per capita consumption is given by $c_{gold} = f(k_{gold}) - (n + \delta) \cdot k_{gold}$.

The condition in Eq. (1.13) is called the *golden rule of capital accumulation* (see Phelps [1966]). The source of this name is the biblical golden rule of conduct, which states, "do unto others as you would have others do unto you." In economic terms, the golden-rule result can be interpreted as "if we provide the same amount of consumption to members of each current and future generation—that is, if we do not provide less to future generations than to ourselves—then the maximum amount of per capita consumption is c_{gold}."

Figure 1.3 illustrates the workings of the golden rule. The figure considers three possible saving rates, s_1, s_{gold}, and s_2, where $s_1 < s_{gold} < s_2$. Consumption per person, c, in each case equals the vertical distance between the production function, $f(k)$, and the appropriate $s \cdot f(k)$ curve. For each s, the steady-state value k^* corresponds to the intersection between the $s \cdot f(k)$ curve and the $(n + \delta) \cdot k$ line. The steady-state per capita consumption, c^*, is maximized when $k^* = k_{gold}$ because the tangent to the production function at this point parallels the $(n + \delta) \cdot k$

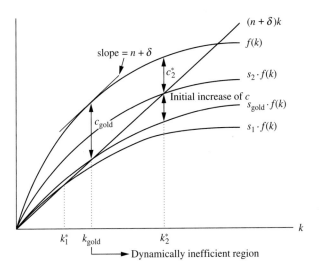

FIGURE 1.3
The golden rule and dynamic inefficiency. If the saving rate is above the golden rule ($s_2 > s_{gold}$ in the figure), then a reduction in s increases steady-state consumption per person and also raises consumption per person along the transition. Since c increases at all points in time, a saving rate above the golden rule is dynamically inefficient. If the saving rate is below the golden rule ($s_1 < s_{gold}$ in the figure), then an increase in s increases steady-state consumption per person but lowers consumption per person along the transition. The desirability of such a change depends on how households trade off current consumption against future consumption.

line. The saving rate that yields $k^* = k_{gold}$ is the one that makes the $s \cdot f(k)$ curve cross the $(n + \delta) \cdot k$ line at the value k_{gold}. Since $s_1 < s_{gold} < s_2$, we also see in the figure that $k_1^* < k_{gold} < k_2^*$.

One issue is whether some saving rates are better than others. We will be unable to select the best saving rate (or, indeed, to determine whether a constant saving rate is desirable) until we specify a detailed objective function, as we do in the next chapter. We can, however, argue in the present context that a saving rate that exceeds s_{gold} forever is inefficient because higher quantities of per capita consumption could be obtained at all points in time by reducing the saving rate.

Consider an economy, such as the one described by the saving rate s_2 in Fig. 1.3, for which $s_2 > s_{gold}$, so that $k_{gold}^* > k_2$ and $c_2^* < c_{gold}$. Imagine that, starting from the steady state, the saving rate is reduced permanently to s_{gold}. Figure 1.3 shows that per capita consumption, c—given by the vertical distance between the $f(k)$ and $s_{gold} \cdot f(k)$ curves—initially increases by a discrete amount. Then the level of c falls monotonically during the transition toward its new steady-state value, c_{gold}. Since $c_2^* < c_{gold}$, we conclude that c exceeds its previous value, c_2^*, at all transitional dates as well as in the new steady state. Hence, when $s > s_{gold}$, the economy is over-saving in the sense that per capita consumption at all points in time could be raised by lowering the saving rate. An economy that oversaves is said to be *dynamically inefficient*, because the path of per capita consumption lies below feasible alternative paths at all points in time.

If $s < s_{\text{gold}}$—as in the case of the saving rate s_1 in Figure 1.3—then the steady-state amount of per capita consumption can be increased by raising the saving rate. This rise in the saving rate would, however, reduce c currently and during part of the transition period. The outcome will therefore be viewed as good or bad depending on how households weigh today's consumption against the path of future consumption. We cannot judge the desirability of an increase in the saving rate in this situation until we make specific assumptions about how agents discount the future. We proceed along these lines in the next chapter.

1.2.5   Transitional Dynamics

The long-run growth rates in the Solow–Swan model are determined entirely by exogenous elements. Hence, the main substantive conclusions about the long run are negative, for example, that steady-state growth rates are independent of the saving rate and the level of the production function. The model does, however, have more interesting implications about transitional dynamics. This transition shows how an economy's per capita income converges toward its own steady-state value and to the per capita incomes of other economies.

Division of both sides of Eq. (1.10) by k implies that the growth rate of k is given by

$$\gamma_k \equiv \dot{k}/k = s \cdot f(k)/k - (n + \delta). \tag{1.14}$$

We use the symbol γ throughout the book to denote a growth rate of the variable designated by the subscript, in this case, k. Note that, at all points in time, the growth rate of the level of a variable equals the per capita growth rate plus n, for example,

$$\gamma_K = \gamma_k + n.$$

For subsequent purposes, we shall find it convenient to focus on the growth rate of k, as given in Eq. (1.14).

Equation (1.14) says that γ_k equals the difference between two terms, $s \cdot f(k)/k$ and $(n + \delta)$, which we plot versus k in Fig. 1.4. The first term is a downward-sloping curve,[3] which asymptotes to infinity at $k = 0$ and approaches 0 as k tends to infinity.[4] The second term is a horizontal line at $n + \delta$. The vertical distance between the curve and the line equals the growth rate of capital per person (from Eq. [1.14]), and the crossing point corresponds to the steady state. Since $n + \delta > 0$ and $s \cdot f(k)/k$ falls monotonically from infinity to 0, the curve and the line intersect once and only once. Hence (except for the trivial solution $k^* = 0$), the steady-state capital/labor ratio $k^* > 0$ exists and is unique.

---

[3]The derivative of $f(k)/k$ with respect to k equals $-[f(k) - kf'(k)]/k^2$. The expression in brackets equals the marginal product of labor, which is positive. Hence, the derivative is negative.

[4]Note that $\lim_{k \to 0}[s \cdot f(k)/k] = 0/0$. We can apply l'Hôpital's rule to get $\lim_{k \to 0}[s \cdot f(k)/k] = \lim_{k \to 0}[s \cdot f'(k)] = \infty$, from the Inada condition. Similarly, the Inada condition $\lim_{k \to \infty}[f'(k)] = 0$ implies $\lim_{k \to \infty}[s \cdot f(k)/k] = 0$.

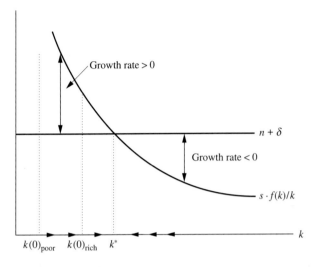

FIGURE 1.4
Dynamics of the Solow–Swan model. The growth rate of k is given by the vertical distance between the saving curve, $s \cdot f(k)/k$, and the effective depreciation line, $n + \delta$. If $k < k^*$, then the growth rate of k is positive, and k increases toward k^*. If $k > k^*$, then the growth rate is negative, and k falls toward k^*. Thus, the steady-state capital per person, k^*, is stable. Note that, along a transition from an initially low capital per person, the growth rate of k declines monotonically toward zero. The arrows on the horizontal axis indicate the direction of movement of $\hat{k}$ over time.

Figure 1.4 shows that to the left of the steady state, the $s \cdot f(k)/k$ curve lies above $n + \delta$. Hence, the growth rate of k is positive, and k rises over time. As k increases, γ_k declines and approaches 0 as k approaches k^*. (The $s \cdot f[k]/k$ curve gets closer to the $n + \delta$ line as k gets closer to k^*; hence, γ_k falls.) The economy tends asymptotically toward the steady state in which k—and, hence, y and c—do not change.

The source of these results is the diminishing returns to capital: when k is relatively low, the average product of capital, $f(k)/k$, is relatively high. By assumption, households save and invest a constant fraction, s, of this product. Hence, when k is relatively low, the gross investment per unit of capital, $s \cdot f(k)/k$, is relatively high. Capital per worker, k, effectively depreciates at the constant rate $n + \delta$. Consequently, the growth rate, $\dot{k}/k$, is also relatively high.

An analogous argument demonstrates that if the economy starts with $k(0) > k^*$, then the growth rate of k is negative, and k falls over time. (Note from Fig. 1.4 that for $k > k^*$, the $n + \delta$ line lies above the $s \cdot f(k)/k$ curve, and, hence, $\gamma_k < 0$.) The growth rate increases and approaches 0 as k approaches k^*. Thus, the system is globally stable: for any initial value, $k(0) > 0$, the economy converges to its unique steady state, $k^* > 0$.

We can also study the behavior of output along the transition. The growth rate of output per capita is given by

$$\gamma_y \equiv \dot{y}/y = f'(k) \cdot \dot{k}/f(k) = [k \cdot f'(k)/f(k)] \cdot \gamma_k. \tag{1.15}$$

The expression in brackets on the far right is often called the *capital share*, that is, the share of the rental income on capital in total income. We show in Chapter 2 that in a competitive equilibrium each unit of capital receives a rental equal to its marginal product, $f'(k)$. Hence, $k \cdot f'(k)$ is the income per person earned by owners of capital, and $k \cdot f'(k)/f(k)$—the term in brackets—is the share of this income in total income per person.

Equation (1.15) shows that the relation between γ_y and γ_k depends on the behavior of the capital share. In the Cobb–Douglas case (Eq. [1.9]), the capital share is the constant α, and γ_y is the fraction α of γ_k. Hence, the behavior of γ_y mimics that of γ_k.

More generally, we can substitute for γ_k from Eq. (1.14) into Eq. (1.15) to get

$$\gamma_y = s \cdot f'(k) - (n + \delta) \cdot \text{Sh}(k), \tag{1.16}$$

where $\text{Sh}(k) \equiv k \cdot f'(k)/f(k)$ is the capital share. If we differentiate with respect to k and combine terms, then we get

$$\partial \gamma_y / \partial k = [\frac{f''(k) \cdot k}{f(k)}] \cdot \gamma_k - \frac{(n + \delta)f'(k)}{f(k)} \cdot [1 - \text{Sh}(k)].$$

Since $0 < \text{Sh}(k) < 1$, the last term on the right-hand side is negative. If $\gamma_k \geq 0$, then the first term on the right-hand side is nonpositive, and hence, $\partial \gamma_y / \partial k < 0$. Thus, γ_y necessarily falls as k rises (and therefore as y rises) in the region in which $\gamma_k \geq 0$, that is, if $k \leq k^*$. If $\gamma_k < 0$ ($k > k^*$), then the sign of $\partial \gamma_y / \partial k$ is ambiguous for a general form of the production function, $f(k)$. However, if the economy is close to its steady state, then the magnitude of γ_k will be small and $\partial \gamma_y / \partial k < 0$ will surely hold even if $k > k^*$.

In the Solow–Swan model, which assumes a constant saving rate, the level of consumption per person is given by $c = (1 - s) \cdot y$. Hence, $\gamma_c = \gamma_y$ applies at all points in time in this model. Consumption, therefore, exhibits the same dynamics as output.

1.2.6 Policy Experiments

Suppose that the economy is initially in a steady-state position with the capital per person k_1^*. Imagine that the government then introduces some policy that raises the saving rate permanently from s_1 to a higher value s_2. Figure 1.5 shows that the $s \cdot f(k)/k$ schedule shifts to the right. Hence, the intersection with the $n + \delta$ line also shifts to the right, and the new steady-state capital stock, k_2^*, exceeds k_1^*.

How does the economy adjust from k_1^* to k_2^*? At $k = k_1^*$, the gap between the $s_1 \cdot f(k)/k$ curve and the $n + \delta$ line is positive, that is, saving is more than enough to generate an increase in k. As k increases, its growth rate, γ_k, falls and approaches 0 as k approaches k_2^*. The result, therefore, is that a permanent increase in the saving rate generates temporarily positive per capita growth rates. In the long run, the levels of k and y are permanently higher, but the per capita growth rates return to 0.

A permanent improvement in the level of the technology has similar, temporary effects on the per capita growth rates. If the production function, $f(k)$, shifts upward

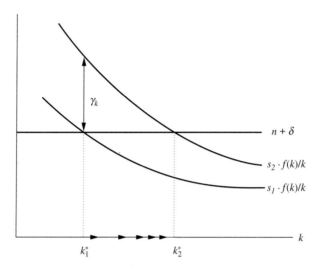

FIGURE 1.5
Effects from an increase in the saving rate. Starting from the steady-state capital per person k_1^*, an increase in s from s_1 to s_2 shifts the $s \cdot f(k)/k$ curve to the right. At the old steady state, investment exceeds effective depreciation, and the growth rate of k becomes positive. Capital per person rises until the economy approaches its new steady state at $k_2^* > k_1^*$.

in a proportional manner, then the $s \cdot f(k)/k$ curve shifts upward, just as in Figure 1.5. Hence, γ_k again becomes positive temporarily. In the long run, the permanent improvement in technology generates higher levels of k and y, but no changes in the per capita growth rates.

In Chapter 4, we observe that various kinds of government policies amount to differences in the level of the technology. For example, high tax rates on capital income, a failure to protect property rights, and various government regulations are equivalent to a poorer level of technology. (These policies may also influence the saving rate, s.) Thus, changes in these kinds of policies also have temporary, but not permanent, effects on growth rates in the Solow–Swan model.

1.2.7 An Example: Cobb–Douglas Technology

We can illustrate the results for the case of a Cobb–Douglas production function (Eq. [1.9]). The steady-state capital/labor ratio is determined from Eq. (1.11) as

$$k^* = [sA/(n + \delta)]^{1/(1-\alpha)}. \tag{1.17}$$

Note that, as we saw graphically for a more general production function, $f(k)$, k^* rises with the saving rate, s, and the level of technology, A, and falls with the rate of population growth, n, and the depreciation rate, δ. The steady-state output per capita is given by

$$y^* = A^{1/(1-\alpha)} \cdot [s/(n + \delta)]^{\alpha/(1-\alpha)}.$$

Thus, y^* is a positive function of s and A and a negative function of n and δ.

Along the transition, the growth rate of k is given from Eq. (1.14) by

$$\gamma_k = sAk^{-(1-\alpha)} - (n + \delta). \tag{1.18}$$

If $k(0) < k^*$, given by Eq. (1.17), then γ_k in Eq. (1.18) is positive. This growth rate declines as k rises and approaches 0 as k approaches k^*. Since $\gamma_y = \alpha \gamma_k$ (from Eq. [1.9]), the behavior of γ_y mimics that of γ_k. In particular, the lower $y(0)$, the higher γ_y.

1.2.8 Absolute and Conditional Convergence

Equation (1.14) implies that the derivative of γ_k with respect to k is negative:

$$\partial \gamma_k / \partial k = s \cdot [f'(k) - f(k)/k]/k < 0.$$

Other things equal, smaller values of k are associated with larger values of γ_k. An important question arises: does this result mean that economies with lower capital per person tend to grow faster in per capita terms? In other words, does there tend to be *convergence* across economies?

To answer these questions, consider a group of closed economies (say, isolated regions or countries) that are structurally similar in the sense that they have the same values of the parameters s, n, and δ and also have the same production function, $f(\cdot)$. Thus, the economies have the same steady-state values k^* and y^*. Imagine that the only difference among the economies is the initial quantity of capital per person, $k(0)$. These differences in starting values could reflect past disturbances, such as wars or transitory shocks to production functions. The model then implies that the less-advanced economies—with lower values of $k(0)$ and $y(0)$—have higher growth rates of k. The growth rate of y will also typically be higher in the more backward economies.[5]

Figure 1.4 distinguishes two economies, one with the low initial value, $k(0)_{poor}$, and the other with the high initial value, $k(0)_{rich}$. Since each economy has the same underlying parameters, the dynamics of k are determined in each case by the same $s \cdot f(k)/k$ and $n + \delta$ curves. Hence, the growth rate γ_k is unambiguously larger for the economy with the lower initial value, $k(0)_{poor}$. This result implies a form of convergence: regions or countries with lower starting values of the capital/labor ratio have higher per capita growth rates, γ_k, and tend thereby to catch up or converge to those with higher capital/labor ratios.

The hypothesis that poor economies tend to grow faster per capita than rich ones—without conditioning on any other characteristics of economies—is referred to as *absolute convergence*. This hypothesis receives only mixed reviews when confronted with data on groups of economies. We can look, for example, at the growth experience of a broad cross section of countries over the period 1960 to 1985. Figure 1.6 plots the average annual growth rate of real per capita GDP against the log of real per capita GDP at the start of the period, 1960, for 118 countries.[6] The growth

---

[5]This conclusion is unambiguous if the production function is Cobb–Douglas, if $k \leq k^*$, or if k is only a small amount above k^*.

[6]The data on real GDP, from Summers and Heston (1993), attempt to correct for differences in purchasing-power parity across countries. We discuss these data in Chapter 10.

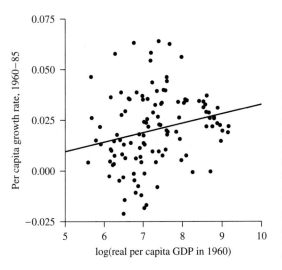

FIGURE 1.6
Convergence of GDP across countries: Growth rate versus initial level of real per capita GDP for 118 countries. For a sample of 118 countries, the average growth rate of GDP per capita from 1960 to 1985 (shown on the vertical axis) has little relation with the 1960 level of real per capita GDP (shown on the horizontal axis). The relation is actually slightly positive. Hence, absolute β convergence does not apply for a broad cross section of countries.

rates are essentially uncorrelated with the initial position; in fact, there is a slight tendency for the initially richer countries to grow faster in per capita terms. Thus, this sample rejects the hypothesis of absolute convergence.

The hypothesis fares better if we examine a more homogeneous group of economies. Figure 1.7 shows the results if we limit consideration to the 20 relatively advanced countries that were members of the OECD (Organization for Economic Cooperation and Development) at the beginning of the sample period, 1960. In this case, the initially poorer countries did experience significantly higher per capita growth rates.

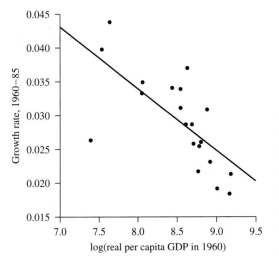

FIGURE 1.7
Convergence of GDP across OECD countries: Growth rate versus initial level of real per capita GDP for 20 OECD countries. If the sample is limited to the 20 original OECD countries, then the average growth rate of real per capita GDP from 1960 to 1985 is negatively related to the 1960 level of real per capita GDP. Hence, absolute β convergence applies for these OECD countries.

This type of result becomes more evident more strongly if we consider an even more homogeneous group, the continental U.S. states, each viewed as a separate economy. Figure 1.8 plots the growth rate of per capita personal income for each state from 1880 to 1990 against the log of per capita personal income in 1880.[7] Absolute convergence—the initially poorer states growing faster in per capita terms—holds clearly in this diagram.

We can accommodate the theory to the empirical observations on convergence if we allow for heterogeneity across economies, in particular, if we drop the assumption that all economies have the same parameters, and therefore, the same steady-state positions. If the steady states differ, then we have to modify the analysis to consider a concept of *conditional convergence*. The main idea is that an economy grows faster the further it is from its own steady-state value.

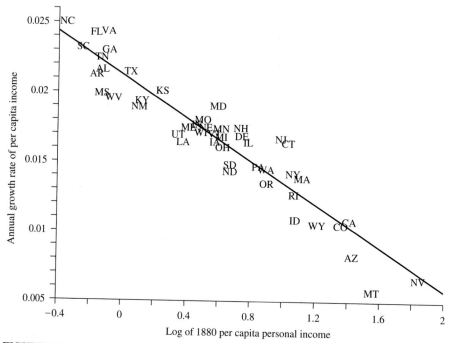

FIGURE 1.8

Convergence of personal income across U.S. states: 1880 personal income and income growth from 1880 to 1990. The relation between the growth rate of per capita personal income from 1880 to 1990 (shown on the vertical axis) is negatively related to the level of per capita income in 1880 (shown on the horizontal axis). Thus, absolute β convergence holds for the states of the United States.

---

[7]See Chapter 10 for a discussion of the data and Chapter 11 for more empirical results. There are 47 observations on U.S. states or territories. Oklahoma is omitted because 1880 preceded the Oklahoma land rush, and the data are consequently unavailable.

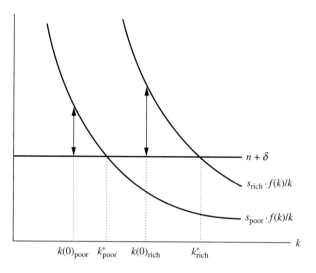

FIGURE 1.9
Conditional convergence. If a rich economy has a higher saving rate than a poor economy, then the rich
economy may be proportionately further from its steady-state position. In this case, the rich economy
would be predicted to grow faster per capita than the poor economy; that is, absolute β convergence
would not hold.

We illustrate the concept of conditional convergence in Figure 1.9 by considering two economies that differ in only two respects: first, they have different initial
stocks of capital per person, $k(0)_{\text{poor}} < k(0)_{\text{rich}}$, and second, they have different saving rates, $s_{\text{poor}} \neq s_{\text{rich}}$. Our previous analysis implies that differences in saving rates
generate differences in the same direction in the steady-state values of capital per
person, that is, $k^*_{\text{poor}} \neq k^*_{\text{rich}}$. (In Fig. 1.9, these steady-state values are determined by
the intersection of the $s_i \cdot f(k)/k$ curves with the common $n + \delta$ line.) We consider the
case in which $s_{\text{poor}} < s_{\text{rich}}$ and hence, $k^*_{\text{poor}} < k^*_{\text{rich}}$ because these differences likely
explain why $k(0)_{\text{poor}} < k(0)_{\text{rich}}$ applies at the initial date. (It is also true empirically,
as discussed in the introduction, that countries with higher levels of real per capita
GDP tend to have higher saving rates.)

The question is, Does the model predict that the poor economy will grow faster
than the rich one? If they have the same saving rate, then the per capita growth rate—
the distance between the $s \cdot f(k)/k$ curve and the $n + \delta$ line—would be larger for the
poor economy, and $\gamma_{\text{poor}} > \gamma_{\text{rich}}$ would apply. However, if the rich economy has a
higher saving rate, as in Fig. 1.9, then $\gamma_{\text{poor}} < \gamma_{\text{rich}}$ can hold. Hence, the model does
not predict convergence in all circumstances; a poor country may grow at a slower
rate than a rich one.

The neoclassical model does predict that each economy converges to its own
steady state and that the speed of this convergence relates inversely to the distance
from the steady state. In other words, the model predicts conditional convergence

in the sense that a lower starting value of real per capita income tends to generate a higher per capita growth rate, once we control for the determinants of the steady state.

Recall that the steady-state value, k^*, depends on the saving rate, s, the level of the production function, $f(\cdot)$, and on various government policies that effectively shift the position of the production function. The findings on conditional convergence suggest that we should hold constant these determinants of k^* in order to isolate the predicted inverse relationship between growth rates and initial positions.

Algebraically, we can illustrate the concept of conditional convergence by returning to the formula for γ_k in Eq. (1.14). One of the determinants of γ_k is the saving rate, s. We can use the steady-state condition from Eq. (1.11) to express s as follows:

$$s = (n + \delta) \cdot k^*/f(k^*).$$

If we replace s by this expression in Eq. (1.14), then γ_k can be expressed as

$$\gamma_k = (n + \delta) \cdot \left[\frac{f(k)/k}{f(k^*)/k^*} - 1 \right]. \tag{1.19}$$

Equation (1.19) is consistent with $\gamma_k = 0$ when $k = k^*$. For given k^*, the formula implies that a reduction in k, which raises the average product of capital, $f(k)/k$, increases γ_k. But a lower k matches up with a higher γ_k only if the reduction is relative to the steady-state value, k^*. In particular, $f(k)/k$ must be high relative to the steady-state value, $f(k^*)/k^*$. Thus, a poor country would not be expected to grow rapidly if its steady-state value, k^*, is as low as its current value, k.

The result in Eq. (1.19) suggests that we should look empirically at the relation between the per capita growth rate, γ_y, and the starting position, $y(0)$, after holding fixed variables that account for differences in the steady-state position, y^*. For a relatively homogeneous group of economies, such as the U.S. states, the differences in steady-state positions may be minor, and we would still observe the convergence pattern shown in Figure 1.8. For a broad cross section of 118 countries, however, as shown in Figure 1.6, the differences in steady-state positions would be substantial. Moreover, the countries with low starting levels, $y(0)$, are likely to be in this position precisely because they have low steady-state values, y^*, perhaps because of chronically low saving rates or persistently bad government policies that effectively lower the level of the production function. In other words, the per capita growth rate may have little correlation with $\log[y(0)]$, as in Figure 1.6, because $\log[y(0)]$ is itself uncorrelated with the gap from the steady state, $\log[y(0)/y^*]$. The perspective of conditional convergence indicates that this gap is the variable that matters for the subsequent per capita growth rate.

We show in Chapter 12 that the inclusion of variables that proxy for differences in steady-state positions makes a major difference in the results across the broad cross section of countries. When these additional variables are held constant, the relation between the per capita growth rate and the log of initial real per capita GDP becomes significantly negative, as predicted by the neoclassical model. In other words, the cross-country data support the hypothesis of conditional convergence.

1.2.9   Convergence and the Dispersion of Per Capita Income

Our concept of convergence is that economies with lower levels of per capita income (expressed relative to their steady-state levels of per capita income) tend to grow faster in per capita terms. This behavior is often confused with an alternative meaning of convergence, that the dispersion of real per capita income across a group of economies tends to fall over time. We show now that, even if absolute convergence holds in our sense, the dispersion of per capita income does not necessarily tend to decline over time.

Suppose that absolute convergence holds for a group of economies $i = 1, \ldots,$ N, where N is a large number. In discrete time, corresponding for example to annual data, the real per capita income for economy i can then be approximated by the process

$$\log(y_{it}) = a + (1 - b) \cdot \log(y_{i,t-1}) + u_{it}, \tag{1.20}$$

where a and b are constants, with $0 < b < 1$, and u_{it} is a disturbance term. The condition $b > 0$ implies absolute convergence because the annual growth rate, $\log(y_{it}/y_{i,t-1})$, is inversely related to $\log(y_{i,t-1})$. A higher coefficient b corresponds to a greater tendency toward convergence.[8] The disturbance term picks up temporary shocks to the production function, the saving rate, and so on. We assume that u_{it} has zero mean, the same variance σ_u^2 for all economies, and is independent over time and across economies.

One measure of the dispersion or inequality of per capita income is the sample variance of the $\log(y_{it})$:

$$D_t = \frac{1}{N} \cdot \sum_{i=1}^{N} [\log(y_{it}) - \mu_t]^2,$$

where μ_t is the sample mean of the $\log(y_{it})$. If there are a large number N of observations, then the sample variance is close to the population variance, and we can use Eq. (1.20) to derive the evolution of D_t over time:

$$D_t \approx (1 - b)^2 \cdot D_{t-1} + \sigma_u^2.$$

This first-order difference equation for dispersion has a steady state given by

$$D^* = \sigma_u^2 / [1 - (1 - b)^2].$$

Hence, the steady-state dispersion falls with b (the strength of the convergence effect), but rises with the variance σ_u^2 of the disturbance term. In particular, $D^* > 0$ even if $b > 0$, as long as $\sigma_u^2 > 0$.

---

[8]The condition $b < 1$ rules out a leapfrogging or overshooting effect, whereby an economy that starts out behind another economy would be predicted systematically to get ahead of the other economy at some future date. This leapfrogging effect cannot occur in the neoclassical model, but can arise in some models of technological adaptation that we discuss in Chapter 8.

The evolution of D_t can be expressed as

$$D_t = D^* + (1 - b)^2 \cdot (D_{t-1} - D^*) = D^* + (1 - b)^{2t} \cdot (D_0 - D^*), \quad (1.21)$$

where D_0 is the dispersion at time 0. Since $0 < b < 1$, D_t monotonically approaches its steady-state value, D^*, over time. Eq. (1.21) implies that D_t rises or falls over time depending on whether D_0 begins below or above the steady-state value.[9] Note especially that a rising dispersion is consistent with absolute convergence ($b > 0$).

These results about convergence and dispersion are analogous to Galton's fallacy about the distribution of heights in a population (see Quah [1993] and Hart [1994] for discussions). The observation that heights in a family tend to regress toward the mean across generations (a property analogous to our convergence concept for per capita income) does not imply that the dispersion of heights across the full population (a measure that parallels the dispersion of per capita income across economies) tends to narrow over time. Galton's fallacy is perhaps most obvious for the ordinal rankings of sports teams in a league. The dispersion of rankings is constant by definition. Our concept of convergence applies here to the tendency of weak teams to rebound toward the mean and of champions to revert to mediocrity. This convergence behavior is important in sports, yet it is obvious here that the dispersion of rankings cannot change no matter how strong the tendency toward convergence.

1.2.10 Technological Progress

CLASSIFICATION OF INVENTIONS. We have assumed thus far that the level of technology is constant over time. As a result, we found that all per capita variables were constant in the long run. This feature of the model is clearly unrealistic; in the United States, for example, the per capita growth rate has been positive for over two centuries. In the absence of technological progress, diminishing returns would have made it impossible to maintain per capita growth for so long just by accumulating more capital per worker. The neoclassical economists of the 1950s and 1960s recognized this problem and amended the basic model to allow the technology to improve over time. These improvements provided an escape from diminishing returns and thus enabled the economy to grow in per capita terms in the long run. We now explore how the model works when we allow for such technological advances.

Although some discoveries are serendipitous, most technological improvements reflect purposeful activity, such as research and development (R&D) carried out in universities and corporate or government laboratories. This research is sometimes financed by private institutions and sometimes by governmental agencies, such as the National Science Foundation. Since the amount of resources devoted to

---

[9]We could extend the model by allowing for temporary shocks to σ_u^2 or for major disturbances like wars or oil shocks that affect large subgroups of economies in a common way. In this extended model, the dispersion could depart from the deterministic path that we derived; for example, D_t could rise in some periods even if D_0 began above the steady-state value.

R&D depends on economic conditions, the evolution of the technology also depends on these conditions. This relation will be the subject of our analysis in Chapters 6–8. At present, we consider only the simpler case in which the technology improves exogenously.

The first issue is how to introduce exogenous technological progress into the model. This progress can take various forms. Inventions may allow producers to generate the same amount of output with either relatively less capital input or relatively less labor input, cases referred to as *capital-saving* or *labor-saving* technological progress, respectively. Inventions that do not save relatively more of either input are called *neutral,* or *unbiased.*

The definition of neutral technological progress depends on the precise meaning of capital saving and labor saving. Three popular definitions are due, respectively, to Hicks (1932), Harrod (1942), and Solow (1969).

Hicks says that a technological innovation is neutral (Hicks neutral) if the ratio of marginal products remains unchanged for a given capital/labor ratio. This property corresponds to a renumbering of the isoquants, so that Hicks-neutral production functions can be written as

$$Y = F(K, L, t) = T(t) \cdot F(K, L), \tag{1.22}$$

where $T(t)$ is an index of the state of the technology, and $\dot{T}(t) \geq 0$.

Harrod defines an innovation as neutral (Harrod neutral) if the relative input shares, $K \cdot F_K / L \cdot F_L$, remain unchanged for a given capital/output ratio. Robinson (1938) and Uzawa (1961) showed that this definition implied that the production function took the form

$$Y = F[K, L \cdot A(t)], \tag{1.23}$$

where $A(t)$ is an index of the technology, and $\dot{A}(t) \geq 0$. This form is called *labor-augmenting* technological progress because it raises output in the same way as an increase in the stock of labor.

Finally, Solow defines an innovation as neutral (Solow neutral) if the relative input shares, $L \cdot F_L / K \cdot F_K$, remain unchanged for a given labor/output ratio. This definition can be shown to imply a production function of the form

$$Y = F[K \cdot B(t), L], \tag{1.24}$$

where $B(t)$ is an index of the technology, and $\dot{B}(t) \geq 0$. Production functions of this form are called *capital augmenting* because a technological improvement increases production in the same way as an increase in the stock of capital.

THE NECESSITY FOR TECHNOLOGICAL PROGRESS TO BE LABOR AUGMENTING. Suppose that we consider only constant rates of technological progress. Then, in the neoclassical growth model, only labor-augmenting technological change turns out to be consistent with the existence of a steady state, that is, with constant growth rates of the various quantities in the long run. This result is proved in the appendix to this chapter.

If we want to consider models that possess a steady state, then we have to assume that technological progress takes the labor-augmenting form. Another approach, which would be substantially more complicated, would be to deal with models that lack steady states, that is, in which the various growth rates do not approach constants in the long run. However, one reason to stick with the simpler framework that possesses a steady state is that the long-term experiences of the United States and some other developed countries indicate that per capita growth rates can be positive and trendless over long periods of time (see Chapter 10). This empirical phenomenon suggests that a useful theory would predict that per capita growth rates approach constants in the long run; that is, the model would possess a steady state.

THE SOLOW–SWAN MODEL WITH LABOR-AUGMENTING TECHNOLOGICAL PROGRESS. We assume now that the production function includes labor-augmenting technological progress, as shown in Eq. (1.23), and that the technology term, $A(t)$, grows at the constant rate x. The condition for the change in the capital stock is

$$\dot{K} = s \cdot F[K, L \cdot A(t)] - \delta K.$$

If we divide both sides of this equation by L, then we can derive an expression for the change in k over time:

$$\dot{k} = s \cdot F[k, A(t)] - (n + \delta) \cdot k. \tag{1.25}$$

The only difference from Eq. (1.10) is that output per person now depends on the level of technology, $A(t)$.

Divide both sides of Eq. (1.25) by k to compute the growth rate:

$$\gamma_k = s \cdot F[k, A(t)]/k - (n + \delta). \tag{1.26}$$

As in Eq. (1.14), γ_k equals the difference between two terms, where the first term is the product of s and the average product of capital, and the second term is $n + \delta$. The only difference is that now, for given k, the average product of capital, $F[k, A(t)]/k$, increases over time because of the growth in $A(t)$ at the rate x. In terms of Fig. 1.4, the downward-sloping curve, $s \cdot F(\bullet)/k$, shifts continually to the right, and, hence, the level of k that corresponds to the intersection between this curve and the $n + \delta$ line also shifts continually to the right. We now compute the growth rate of k in the steady state.

By definition, the steady-state growth rate, γ_k^*, is constant. Since s, n, and δ are also constants, Eq. (1.26) implies that the average product of capital, $F[k, A(t)]/k$, is constant in the steady state. Because of constant returns to scale, the expression for the average product equals $F[1, A(t)/k]$ and is therefore constant only if k and $A(t)$ grow at the same rate, that is, $\gamma_k^* = x$.

Output per capita is given by

$$y = F[k, A(t)] = k \cdot F[1, A(t)/k].$$

Since k and $A(t)$ grow in the steady state at the rate x, the steady-state growth rate of y equals x. Moreover, since $c = (1 - s) \cdot y$, the steady-state growth rate of c also equals x.

To analyze the transitional dynamics of the model with technological progress, it will be convenient to rewrite the system in terms of variables that remain constant in the steady state. Since k and $A(t)$ grow in the steady state at the same rate, we can work with the ratio $\hat{k} \equiv k/A(t) = K/[L \cdot A(t)]$. The variable $L \cdot A(t) \equiv \hat{L}$ is often called the *effective amount of labor*—the physical quantity of labor, L, multiplied by its efficiency, $A(t)$. (The terminology *effective labor* is appropriate because the economy operates as if its labor input were $\hat{L}$.) The variable $\hat{k}$ is then the quantity of capital per unit of effective labor.

The quantity of output per unit of effective labor, $\hat{y} \equiv Y/[L \cdot A(t)]$, is given by

$$\hat{y} = F(\hat{k}, 1) \equiv f(\hat{k}). \tag{1.27}$$

Hence, we can again write the production function in intensive form if we replace y and k by $\hat{y}$ and $\hat{k}$, respectively. If we proceed as we did before to get Eqs. (1.10) and (1.14), but now use the condition that $A(t)$ grows at the rate x, then we can derive the dynamic equation for $\hat{k}$:

$$\gamma_{\hat{k}} = s \cdot f(\hat{k})/\hat{k} - (x + n + \delta). \tag{1.28}$$

The only difference between Eqs. (1.28) and (1.14), aside from the hats ($\hat{}$), is that the last term on the right-hand side includes the parameter x. The term $x + n + \delta$ is now the effective depreciation rate for $\hat{k} \equiv K/\hat{L}$. If the saving rate, s, were zero, then $\hat{k}$ would decline partly due to depreciation of K at the rate δ and partly due to growth of $\hat{L}$ at the rate $x + n$.

Since the steady-state growth rate of $\hat{k}$ is zero, the steady-state value $\hat{k}^*$ satisfies the condition

$$s \cdot f(\hat{k}^*) = (x + n + \delta) \cdot \hat{k}^*. \tag{1.29}$$

The transitional dynamics of $\hat{k}$ are qualitatively similar to those of k in the previous model. In particular, we can construct a picture like Fig. 1.4 in which the horizontal axis involves $\hat{k}$, the downward-sloping curve is now $s \cdot f(\hat{k})/\hat{k}$, and the horizontal line is at the level $x + n + \delta$, rather than $n + \delta$. The new construction is shown in Fig. 1.10. We can use this figure, as we used Fig. 1.4 before, to assess the relation between the initial value, $\hat{k}(0)$, and the growth rate, $\gamma_{\hat{k}}$.

In the steady state, the variables with hats—$\hat{k}$, $\hat{y}$, $\hat{c}$—are now constant. Therefore, the per capita variables—k, y, c—now grow in the steady state at the exogenous rate of technological progress, x.[10] The level variables—K, Y, C—grow accordingly in the steady state at the rate $n + x$, that is, the sum of population growth and technological change. Note that, as in the prior analysis that neglected technological progress, shifts to the saving rate or the level of the production function affect long-run levels—$\hat{k}^*$, $\hat{y}^*$, $\hat{c}^*$—but not steady-state growth rates. As before, these kinds of disturbances influence growth rates during the transition from an initial position, represented by $\hat{k}(0)$, to the steady-state value, $\hat{k}^*$.

---

[10]We always have the condition $\gamma_{\hat{k}} = \gamma_k - x$. Therefore, $\gamma_{\hat{k}} = 0$ implies $\gamma_k = x$, and similarly for γ_y and γ_c.

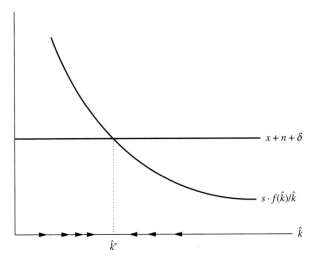

FIGURE 1.10
The Solow–Swan model with technological progress. The growth rate of capital per effective worker ($\hat{k} \equiv K/LA$) is given by the vertical distance between the $s \cdot f(\hat{k})/\hat{k}$ curve and the effective depreciation line, $x + n + \delta$. The economy is at a steady state when $\hat{k}$ is constant. Since A grows at the constant rate x, the steady-state growth rate of capital per person, k, also equals x.

1.2.11   A Quantitative Measure of the Speed of Convergence

It is important to know the speed of the transitional dynamics. If convergence is rapid, then we can focus on steady-state behavior, because most economies would typically be close to their steady states. Conversely, if convergence is slow, then economies would typically be far from their steady states, and, hence, their growth experiences would be dominated by the transitional dynamics.

We now provide a quantitative assessment of the convergence speed for the case of a Cobb–Douglas production function, shown in Eq. (1.9). (We generalize later to a broader class of production functions.) We can use Eq. (1.28) to determine the growth rate of $\hat{k}$ in the Cobb–Douglas case as

$$\gamma_{\hat{k}} = sA(\hat{k})^{-(1-\alpha)} - (x + n + \delta). \tag{1.30}$$

We shall find it useful to consider a log-linear approximation of Eq. (1.30) in the neighborhood of the steady state:

$$\gamma_{\hat{k}} = d[\log(\hat{k})]/dt \cong -\beta \cdot [\log(\hat{k}/\hat{k}^*)],$$
$$\beta = (1 - \alpha) \cdot (x + n + \delta). \tag{1.31}$$

The coefficient β, which comes from the log-linearization of Eq. (1.30) around the steady state, determines the speed of convergence from $\hat{k}$ to $\hat{k}^*$. See the appendix at the end of this chapter for the method of derivation and for further discussion of the convergence coefficient.

Before we consider the implications of Eq. (1.31), we will show that it applies also to the growth rate of $\hat{y}$. For a Cobb–Douglas production function, shown in Eq. (1.9), we have

$$\gamma_{\hat{y}} = \alpha \cdot \gamma_{\hat{k}},$$

$$\log(\hat{y}/\hat{y}^*) = \alpha \cdot \log(\hat{k}/\hat{k}^*).$$

If we substitute these formulas into Eq. (1.31), then we get

$$\gamma_{\hat{y}} \cong -(1 - \alpha) \cdot (x + n + \delta) \cdot [\log(\hat{y}/\hat{y}^*)], \qquad (1.32)$$

which has the same form as Eq. (1.31). That is, the convergence coefficient, β, for $\hat{y}$ is the same as that for $\hat{k}$.

The term $\beta = (1 - \alpha) \cdot (x + n + \delta)$ in Eq. (1.31) indicates how rapidly an economy's output per effective worker, $\hat{y}$, approaches its steady-state value, $\hat{y}^*$. For example, if $\beta = 0.05$ per year, then 5 percent of the gap between $\hat{y}$ and $\hat{y}^*$ vanishes in 1 year. The half-life of convergence—the time that it takes for half the initial gap to be eliminated—is thus about 14 years.[11] It would take about 28 years for three-quarters of the gap to vanish.

Consider what the theory implies quantitatively about the convergence coefficient, $\beta = (1 - \alpha) \cdot (x + n + \delta)$, in Eq. (1.31). One property is that the saving rate, s, does not affect the speed of convergence, β. This result reflects two offsetting forces that exactly cancel in the Cobb–Douglas case. First, given $\hat{k}$, a higher saving rate leads to greater investment and, therefore, to a faster speed of convergence. Second, a higher saving rate raises the steady-state capital intensity, $\hat{k}^*$, and thereby lowers the average product of capital in the vicinity of the steady state. This effect reduces the speed of convergence.

The convergence coefficient, β, in Eq. (1.31) is also independent of the level of the technology, A. Differences in A, like differences in s, have two offsetting effects on the convergence speed, and these effects exactly cancel in the Cobb–Douglas case.

To see the quantitative implications of the parameters that enter into Eq. (1.31), assume the benchmark values $x = 0.02$ per year, $n = 0.01$ per year, and $\delta = 0.05$ per year. These values appear reasonable, for example, for the U.S. economy. The long-term growth rate of real GDP, which is about 2 percent per year, corresponds in the theory to the parameter x. The rate of population growth in recent decades is about 1 percent per year, and the measured depreciation rate for the overall stock of structures and equipment is around 5 percent per year.

---

[11] Equation (1.32) is a differential equation in $\log[\hat{y}(t)]$ with the solution

$$\log[\hat{y}(t)] = (1 - e^{-\beta t}) \cdot \log(\hat{y}^*) + e^{-\beta t} \cdot \log[\hat{y}(0)].$$

The time t for which $\log[\hat{y}(t)]$ is halfway between $\log[\hat{y}(0)]$ and $\log(\hat{y}^*)$ satisfies the condition $e^{-\beta t} = \frac{1}{2}$. The half-life is therefore $\log(2)/\beta = 0.69/\beta$. Hence, if $\beta = 0.05$ per year, then the half-life is 14 years.

For given values of the parameters x, n, and δ, the convergence coefficient, β, in Eq. (1.31) is determined by the capital-share parameter, α. A conventional share for the gross income accruing to a narrow concept of physical capital (structures and equipment) is about $1/3$ (see Denison [1962], Maddison [1982], and Jorgenson, Gollop, and Fraumeni [1987]). If we use $\alpha = 1/3$, then Eq. (1.31) implies $\beta = 5.6$ percent per year, which implies a half-life of 12.5 years. In other words, if the capital share is $1/3$, then the neoclassical model predicts relatively short transitions.

Chapters 11 and 12 demonstrate that this predicted speed of convergence is much too high to accord with the empirical evidence. A convergence coefficient, β, in the range of 1.5 percent to 3.0 percent per year fits better with the data. For example, if $\beta = 2.0$ percent per year, then the half-life is about 35 years, and the time needed to eliminate three-quarters of an initial gap from the steady-state position is about 70 years. In other words, convergence speeds that are consistent with the empirical evidence imply that the time required for substantial convergence is typically on the order of several generations.

To accord with an observed rate of convergence of about 2 percent per year, the neoclassical model requires a much higher capital-share coefficient: for example, the value $\alpha = 0.75$, together with the benchmark values for the other parameters, implies $\beta = 2.0$ percent per year. Although a capital share of 0.75 is too high for a narrow concept of physical capital, this share is reasonable for an expanded measure that also includes human capital. Thus, with a broad concept of capital, the Solow–Swan model can generate the rates of convergence that have been observed empirically.

1.3   MODELS OF ENDOGENOUS GROWTH

In the mid-1980s, a group of growth theorists led by Paul Romer (1986) became increasingly dissatisfied with exogenously driven explanations of long-run productivity growth. This dissatisfaction motivated the construction of a class of growth models in which the key determinants of growth were endogenous to the model. The determination of long-run growth within the model, rather than by some exogenously growing variables like unexplained technological progress, is the reason for the name *endogenous growth*.

In Chapters 4 and 5, we study endogenous growth models in which agents optimally choose the amount of resources that they consume and save. In Chapters 6–8, we expand these ideas to allow for optimizing choices of the amount of resources devoted to R&D and, hence, to the improvements of technology. In the present section, however, we continue to assume a constant, exogenous saving rate, and we deal only with a fixed level of the technology. Despite these limitations, we are able to study a constant-saving-rate version of the simplest endogenous growth model, the *AK model*. Although this model is rudimentary, it is rich enough to show how the elimination of diminishing returns can lead to endogenous growth.

1.3.1 The *AK* Model

The key property of endogenous-growth models is the absence of diminishing returns to capital. The simplest version of a production function without diminishing returns is the *AK* function:[12]

$$Y = AK, \tag{1.33}$$

where A is a positive constant that reflects the level of the technology. The global absence of diminishing returns may seem unrealistic, but the idea becomes more plausible if we think of K in a broad sense to include human capital.[13] Output per capita is $y = Ak$, and the average and marginal products of capital are constant at the level $A > 0$.

If we substitute $f(k)/k = A$ in Eq. (1.14), then we get

$$\gamma_k = sA - (n + \delta).$$

We return here to the case of zero technological progress, $x = 0$, because we want to show that per capita growth can now occur in the long run even without exogenous technological change. For a graphical presentation, the main difference is that the downward-sloping curve, $s \cdot f(k)/k$, in Fig. 1.4 is replaced in Fig. 1.11 by the horizontal line at the level sA. Hence, γ_k is the vertical distance between the two

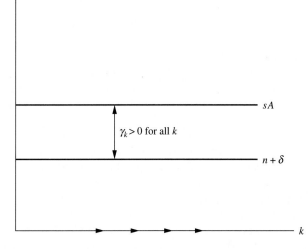

FIGURE 1.11
The *AK* Model. If the technology is *AK*, then the saving curve, $s \cdot f(k)/k$, is a horizontal line at the level sA. If $sA > n + \delta$, then perpetual growth of k occurs, even without technological progress.

---

[12] We think that the first economist to use a production function of the *AK* type was von Neumann (1937).

[13] Knight (1944) stressed the idea that diminishing returns might not apply to a broad concept of capital.

lines, sA and $n + \delta$. We depict the case in which $sA > (n + \delta)$, so that $\gamma_k > 0$. Since the two lines are parallel, γ_k is constant; in particular, it is independent of k. In other words, k always grows at the steady-state rate, $\gamma_k^* = sA - (n + \delta)$.

Since $y = Ak$, γ_y also equals γ_k^* at every point in time. In addition, since $c = (1 - s)y$, the growth rate of c equals γ_k^*. Hence, all the per capita variables in the model grow at the same rate, given by

$$\gamma = \gamma^* = sA - (n + \delta). \tag{1.34}$$

Note that an economy described by the AK technology can display positive long-run per capita growth without any technological progress. Moreover, the per capita growth rate shown in Eq. (1.34) depends on the behavioral parameters of the model, such as the saving rate and the rate of population growth. For example, unlike the neoclassical model, a higher saving rate, s, leads to a higher rate of long-run per capita growth, γ^*.[14] Similarly if the level of the technology, A, improves once and for all (or if the elimination of a governmental distortion effectively raises A), then the long-run growth rate is higher. Changes in the rates of depreciation, δ, and population growth, n, also have permanent effects on the per capita growth rate.

Unlike the neoclassical model, the AK formulation does not predict absolute or conditional convergence, that is, $\partial \gamma_y / \partial y = 0$ for all levels of y. This prediction is a substantial failing of the model, because conditional convergence appears to be an empirical regularity (see Chapters 11 and 12).

Consider a group of economies that are structurally similar in that the parameters s, A, n, and δ are the same. The economies differ only in terms of their initial capital stocks per person, $k(0)$, and, hence, in $y(0)$ and $c(0)$. Since the model says that each economy grows at the same per capita rate, γ^*, regardless of its initial position, the prediction is that all the economies grow at the same per capita rate. This conclusion reflects the absence of diminishing returns. Another way to see this result is to observe that the AK model is just a Cobb–Douglas model with a unit capital share, $\alpha = 1$. The analysis of convergence in the previous section showed that the speed of convergence was given in Eq. (1.31) by $\beta = (1 - \alpha) \cdot (x + n + \delta)$; hence, $\alpha = 1$ implies $\beta = 0$.

We mentioned that one way to think about the absence of diminishing returns to capital in the AK production function is to consider a broad concept of capital that encompassed physical and human components. In Chapter 5, we consider models that allow for these two types of capital.

Other approaches have been used to eliminate the tendency for diminishing returns in the neoclassical model. We study in Chapter 4 the notion of learning-by-doing, which was introduced by Arrow (1962) and used by Romer (1986). In these

---

[14]With the AK production function, we can never get the kind of inefficient oversaving that is possible in the neoclassical model. A shift at some point in time to a permanently higher s means a lower level of c at that point, but a permanently higher per capita growth rate, γ^*, and hence, higher levels of c after some future date. This change cannot be described as inefficient because it may be desirable or undesirable depending on how households discount future levels of consumption.

models, the experience with production or investment contributes to productivity. Moreover, the learning by one producer may raise the productivity of others through a process of spillovers of knowledge from one producer to another. In these models, a larger economy-wide capital stock (or a greater cumulation of the aggregate of past production) improves the level of the technology for each producer. Consequently, diminishing returns to capital may not apply in the aggregate, and increasing returns are even possible. In a situation of increasing returns, each producer's average product of capital, $f(k)/k$, tends to rise with the economy-wide value of k. Consequently, the $s \cdot f(k)/k$ curve in Figure 1.4 tends to be upward sloping, at least over some range, and the growth rate, γ_k, rises with k in this range. Thus, these kinds of models predict at least some intervals of per capita income in which economies tend to diverge. It is unclear, however, whether these divergence intervals are present in the data.

Another major idea in the endogenous-growth literature is that the level of the technology can be advanced by purposeful activity, such as R&D expenditures. This potential for endogenous technological progress may allow an escape from diminishing returns at the aggregate level, especially if the improvements in technique can be shared in a nonrival manner by all producers. This nonrivalry is plausible for advances in knowledge, that is, for new ideas. Models of this type were pioneered by Romer (1990) and Aghion and Howitt (1992); we consider them in Chapters 6–8.

1.3.2 Endogenous Growth with Transitional Dynamics

The *AK* model delivers endogenous growth by avoiding diminishing returns to capital in the long run. This particular production function also implies, however, that the marginal and average products of capital are always constant and, hence, that growth rates do not exhibit the convergence property. It is possible to retain the feature of constant returns to capital in the long run, while restoring the convergence property—an idea brought out in the paper by Jones and Manuelli (1992).[15]

Consider again the Equation for the growth rate of k from Eq. (1.14):

$$\gamma_k = s \cdot f(k)/k - (n + \delta). \tag{1.14}$$

If a steady state exists, then the associated growth rate, γ_k^*, is constant by definition. A positive steady-state value, γ_k^*, means that k grows without bound. Equation (1.14) implies that it is necessary and sufficient for γ_k^* to be positive to have the average product of capital, $f(k)/k$, remain above $(n + \delta)/s$ as k approaches infinity. In other words, if the average product approaches some limit, then $\lim_{k \to \infty}[f(k)/k] > (n + \delta)/s$ is necessary and sufficient for endogenous, steady-state growth.

If $f(k) \to \infty$ as $k \to \infty$, then an application of l'Hôpital's rule shows that the limits as k approaches infinity of the average product, $f(k)/k$, and the marginal

---

[15] See Kurz (1968) for a related discussion.

product, $f'(k)$, are the same. (We assume here that $\lim_{k\to\infty}[f'(k)]$ exists.) Hence, the key condition for endogenous, steady-state growth is that $f'(k)$ be bounded sufficiently far above 0:

$$\lim_{k\to\infty}[f(k)/k] = \lim_{k\to\infty}[f'(k)] > (n + \delta)/s > 0.$$

This inequality violates one of the standard Inada conditions in the neoclassical model, $\lim_{k\to\infty}[f'(k)] = 0$. Economically, the violation of this condition means that the tendency for diminishing returns to capital eventually ceases. In other words, the production function can exhibit diminishing or increasing returns to k when k is low, but the marginal product of capital must be bounded from below as k becomes large. A simple example, in which the production function converges asymptotically to the AK form, is

$$Y = F(K, L) = AK + BK^\alpha L^{1-\alpha}, \tag{1.35}$$

where $A > 0$, $B > 0$, and $0 < \alpha < 1$. Note that this production function is a combination of the AK and Cobb–Douglas functions. It exhibits constant returns to scale and positive and diminishing returns to labor and capital. However, one of the Inada conditions is violated because $\lim_{K\to\infty}(F_K) = A > 0$.

We can write the function in per capita terms as

$$y = f(k) = Ak + Bk^\alpha.$$

The average product of capital is given by

$$f(k)/k = A + Bk^{-(1-\alpha)},$$

which is decreasing in k, but approaches A as k tends to infinity.

The dynamics of this model can be analyzed with the usual expression for γ_k from Eq. (1.14):

$$\gamma_k = s \cdot f(k)/k - (n + \delta). \tag{1.14}$$

Figure 1.12 shows that the $s \cdot f(k)/k$ curve is downward sloping, and the line $n + \delta$ is horizontal. The difference from Fig. 1.4 is that, as k goes to infinity, the $s \cdot f(k)/k$ curve in Fig. 1.12 approaches the positive quantity sA, rather than 0. If $sA > n + \delta$, as assumed in the figure, then the steady-state growth rate, γ_k^*, is positive.

This model yields endogenous, steady-state growth, but also predicts conditional convergence, as in the neoclassical model. The reason is that the convergence property derives from the inverse relation between $f(k)/k$ and k, a relation that still holds in the model. Figure 1.12 shows that if two economies differ only in terms of their initial values, $k(0)$, then the one with the smaller capital stock per person will grow faster in per capita terms.

1.3.3 Constant-Elasticity-of-Substitution Production Functions

Consider as another example the production function (due to Arrow, et al. [1961]) that has a constant elasticity of substitution (CES) between labor and capital:

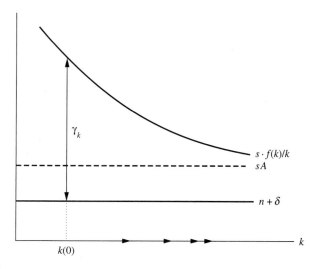

FIGURE 1.12
Endogenous growth with transitional dynamics. If the technology is $F(K, L) = AK + BK^\alpha L^{1-\alpha}$ then the growth rate of k is diminishing for all k. If $sA > n + \delta$, then the growth rate of k asymptotically approaches a positive constant, given by $sA - n - \delta$. Hence, endogenous growth coexists with a transition in which the growth rate diminishes as the economy develops.

$$Y = F(K, L) = A \cdot \left\{ a \cdot (bK)^\psi + (1 - a) \cdot [(1 - b) \cdot L]^\psi \right\}^{1/\psi}, \quad (1.36)$$

where $0 < a < 1$, $0 < b < 1$,[16] and $\psi < 1$. Note that the production function exhibits constant returns to scale for all values of ψ. The elasticity of substitution between capital and labor is $1/(1 - \psi)$ (see the appendix). As $\psi \to -\infty$, the production function approaches a fixed-proportions technology (discussed in the next section), $Y = \min[bK, (1 - b)L]$, where the elasticity of substitution is 0. As $\psi \to 0$, the production function approaches the Cobb–Douglas form, $Y = (\text{constant}) \cdot K^a L^{1-a}$, and the elasticity of substitution is 1 (see the appendix at the end of this chapter). For $\psi = 1$, the production function is linear, $Y = A \cdot [abK + (1 - a) \cdot (1 - b) \cdot L]$, so that K and L are perfect substitutes (infinite elasticity of substitution).

Divide both sides of Eq. (1.36) by L to get an expression for output per capita:

$$y = f(k) = A \cdot \left[a \cdot (bk)^\psi + (1 - a) \cdot (1 - b)^\psi \right]^{1/\psi}.$$

---

[16]The standard formulation does not include the terms b and $1 - b$. The implication then is that the shares of K and L in total product each approach one-half as $\psi \to -\infty$. In our formulation, the shares of K and L approach b and $1 - b$, respectively, as $\psi \to -\infty$.

The marginal and average products of capital are given respectively by

$$f'(k) = Aab^{\psi} \left[ab^{\psi} + (1 - a) \cdot (1 - b)^{\psi} \cdot k^{-\psi} \right]^{(1-\psi)/\psi},$$

$$f(k)/k = A \left[ab^{\psi} + (1 - a) \cdot (1 - b)^{\psi} \cdot k^{-\psi} \right]^{1/\psi}.$$

Thus, $f'(k)$ and $f(k)/k$ are each positive and diminishing in k for all values of ψ.

We can study the dynamic behavior of a CES economy by returning to the expression for γ_k from Eq. (1.14):

$$\gamma_k = s \cdot f(k)/k - (n + \delta). \tag{1.14}$$

If we graph versus k, then $s \cdot f(k)/k$ is a downwardly sloping curve, $n + \delta$ is a horizontal line, and γ_k is still represented by the vertical distance between the curve and the line. The behavior of the growth rate now depends, however, on the parameter ψ, which governs the elasticity of substitution between L and K.

Consider first the case $0 < \psi < 1$, that is, a high degree of substitution between L and K. The limits of the marginal and average products of capital in this case are

$$\lim_{k\to\infty}[f'(k)] = \lim_{k\to\infty}[f(k)/k] = Aba^{1/\psi} > 0,$$

$$\lim_{k\to 0}[f'(k)] = \lim_{k\to 0}[f(k)/k] = \infty.$$

Hence, the marginal and average products approach a positive constant, rather than 0, as k goes to infinity. In this sense, the CES production function with high substitution between the factors ($0 < \psi < 1$) looks like the example in Eq. (1.35) in which diminishing returns vanished asymptotically. We therefore anticipate that this CES model can generate endogenous, steady-state growth.

Figure 1.13 shows the results graphically. The $s \cdot f(k)/k$ curve is downward sloping, and it asymptotes to the positive constant $sAba^{1/\psi}$. If the saving rate is high enough so that $sAba^{1/\psi} > n + \delta$—as assumed in the figure—then the $s \cdot f(k)/k$ curve always lies above the $n + \delta$ line. In this case, the per capita growth rate is always positive, and the model generates endogenous, steady-state growth at the rate

$$\gamma^* = sAba^{1/\psi} - (n + \delta).$$

The dynamics of this model are similar to those described in Fig. 1.12.[17]

Assume now $\psi < 0$, that is, a low degree of substitution between L and K. The limits of the marginal and average products of capital in this case are

$$\lim_{k\to\infty}[f'(k)] = \lim_{k\to\infty}[f(k)/k] = 0,$$

$$\lim_{k\to 0}[f'(k)] = \lim_{k\to 0}[f(k)/k] = Aba^{1/\psi} < \infty.$$

---

[17]If $0 < \psi < 1$ and $sAba^{1/\psi} < n + \delta$, then the $s \cdot f(k)/k$ curve crosses $n + \delta$ at the steady-state value k^*, as in the standard neoclassical model of Fig. 1.4. Endogenous growth does not apply in this case.

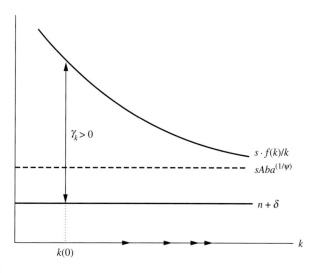

FIGURE 1.13
The CES model with 0< ψ <1 and $sAb \cdot a^{1/\psi} > n + \delta$. If the CES technology exhibits a high elasticity of substitution ($0 < \psi < 1$), then endogenous growth is possible if the parameters satisfy the inequality $sAb \cdot a^{1/\psi} > n + \delta$. Along the transition, the growth rate of k diminishes.

Since the marginal and average products approach 0 as k approaches infinity, the key Inada condition is satisfied, and the model does not generate endogenous growth. In this case, however, the violation of the Inada condition as k approaches 0 may cause problems. Suppose that the saving rate is low enough so that $sAba^{1/\psi} < n + \delta$. In this case, the $s \cdot f(k)/k$ curve starts at a point below $n + \delta$, and it converges to 0 as k approaches infinity. Figure 1.14 shows accordingly that the curve never crosses the $n + \delta$ line, and, hence, no steady state exists with a positive value of k. Since the growth rate γ_k is always negative, the economy shrinks over time, and k, y, and c all approach 0.[18]

Since the average product of capital, $f(k)/k$, is a negative function of k for all values of ψ, the growth rate γ_k is also a negative function of k. The CES model therefore always exhibits the convergence property: for two economies with identical parameters and different initial values, $k(0)$, the one with the lower value of $k(0)$ has the higher value of γ_k. When the parameters differ across economies, then the model predicts conditional convergence, as described before.

We can use the method developed earlier for the case of a Cobb–Douglas production function to derive a formula for the convergence coefficient in the

---

[18]If $\psi < 0$ and $sAba^{1/\psi} > n+\delta$, then the $s \cdot f(k)/k$ curve again intersects the $n+\delta$ line at the steady-state value k^*.

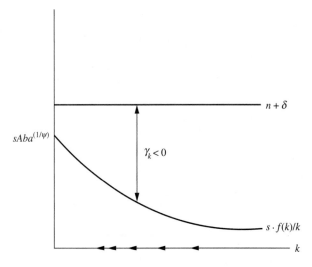

FIGURE 1.14
The CES model with $\psi < 0$ and $sAb \cdot a^{1/\psi} < n + \delta$. If the CES technology exhibits a low elasticity of substitution ($\psi < 0$), then the growth rate of k would be negative for all levels of k if $sAb \cdot a^{1/\psi} < n + \delta$.

neighborhood of the steady state. The result for a CES production function, which extends Eq. (1.33), is[19]

$$\beta = -(x + n + \delta) \cdot \left[1 - a \cdot \left(\frac{bsA}{x + n + \delta}\right)^{\psi}\right]. \tag{1.37}$$

For the Cobb–Douglas case, $\psi = 0$ and $a = \alpha$; hence, Eq. (1.37) reduces to Eq. (1.31). For $\psi \neq 0$, a new result is that β in Eq. (1.37) depends on s and A. If $\psi > 0$ (high substitutability between L and K), then the magnitude of β falls with sA, and vice versa if $\psi < 0$. The convergence coefficient, β, is independent of s and A only in the Cobb–Douglas case, $\psi = 0$.

1.3.4 The Leontief Production Function and the Harrod–Domar Controversy

A production function that was used prior to the neoclassical one is the Leontief (1941), or fixed-proportions, function,

$$Y = F(K, L) = \min(AK, BL), \tag{1.38}$$

---

[19]See Chua (1993) for additional discussion. The formula for β in Eq. (1.37) applies only for cases in which the steady-state level k^* exists. If $0 < \psi < 1$, then it applies for $bsAa^{1/\psi} < x + n + \delta$. If $\psi < 0$, then it applies for $bsAa^{1/\psi} > x + n + \delta$.

where $A > 0$ and $B > 0$ are constants. This specification, which corresponds to $\psi \to -\infty$ in the CES form in Eq. (1.36), was used by Harrod (1939) and Domar (1946). With fixed proportions, if the available capital stock and labor force happen to be such that $AK = BL$, then all workers and machines are fully employed. If K and L are such that $AK > BL$, then only the quantity of capital $(B/A) \cdot L$ is used, and the remainder remains idle. Conversely, if $AK < BL$, then only the amount of labor $(A/B) \cdot K$ is used, and the remainder is unemployed. The assumption of no substitution between capital and labor led Harrod and Domar to predict that capitalist economies would have undesirable outcomes in the form of perpetual increases in unemployed workers or machines. We provide here a brief analysis of the Harrod–Domar model using the tools developed earlier in this chapter.

Divide both sides of Eq. (1.38) by L to get output per capita:

$$y = \min(Ak, B).$$

For $k < B/A$, capital is fully employed, and $y = Ak$. Hence, Figure 1.15 shows that the production function in this range is a straight line from the origin with slope A. For $k > B/A$, the quantity of capital used is constant, and Y is the constant multiple B of labor, L. Hence, output per worker, y, equals the constant B, as shown by the horizontal part of $f(k)$ in the figure. Note that as k approaches infinity, the marginal product of capital, $f'(k)$, is zero. Hence, the key Inada condition is satisfied, and we do not expect this production function to yield endogenous, steady-state growth.

We can use the expression for γ_k from Eq. (1.14) to get

$$\gamma_k = s \cdot [\min(Ak,B)]/k - (n + \delta). \tag{1.39}$$

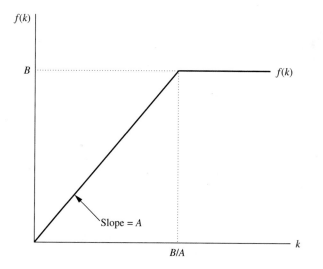

FIGURE 1.15
The Leontief production function in per capita terms. In per capita terms, the Leontief production function can be written as $y = \min(Ak, B)$. For $k < B/A$, output per capita is given by $y = Ak$. For $k > B/A$, output per capita is given by $y = B$.

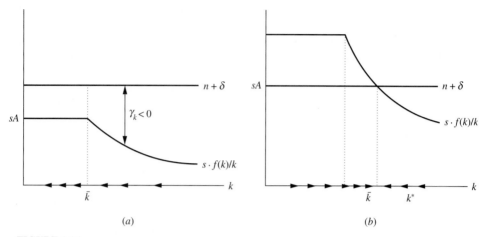

FIGURE 1.16
The Harrod–Domar model. In Panel (a), which assumes $sA < n + \delta$, the growth rate of k is negative for all k. Therefore, the economy approaches $k = 0$. In Panel (b), which assumes $sA > n+\delta$, the growth rate of k is positive for $k < k^*$ and negative for $k > k^*$, where k^* is the stable steady-state value. Since k^* exceeds B/A, a part of the capital stock always remains idle. Moreover, the quantity of idle capital grows steadily (along with K and L).

Figures 1.16a and 1.16b show that the first term, $s \cdot [\min(Ak, B)]/k$, is a horizontal line at sA for $k \le B/A$. For $k > B/A$, this term is a downward-sloping curve that approaches zero as k goes to infinity. The second term in Eq. (1.39) is the usual horizontal line at $n + \delta$.

Assume first that the saving rate is low enough so that $sA < n + \delta$, as depicted in Fig. 1.16a. The saving curve, $s \cdot f(k)/k$, then never crosses the $n+\delta$ line, so there is no positive steady-state value, k^*. Moreover, γ_k is always negative, so the economy shrinks in per capita terms, and k, y, and c all approach 0. The economy therefore ends up to the left of B/A and has permanent and increasing unemployment.

Suppose now that the saving rate is high enough so that $sA > n + \delta$, as shown in Fig. 1.16b. Since the $s \cdot f(k)/k$ curve approaches 0 as k tends to infinity, this curve eventually crosses the $n + \delta$ line at the point $k^* > B/A$. Therefore, if the economy begins at $k(0) < k^*$, then γ_k equals the constant $sA - n - \delta > 0$ until k attains the value B/A. At that point, γ_k falls until it reaches 0 at $k = k^*$. If the economy starts at $k(0) > k^*$, then γ_k is initially negative and approaches 0 as k approaches k^*.

Since $k^* > B/A$, the steady state features idle machines but no unemployed workers. Since k is constant in the steady state, the quantity K grows along with L at the rate n. Since the fraction of machines that are employed remains constant, the quantity of idle machines also grows at the rate n (yet households are nevertheless assumed to keep saving at the rate s).

The only way to reach a steady state in which all capital and labor are employed is for the parameters of the model to satisfy the condition $sA = n+\delta$. Since the four parameters that appear in this condition are all exogenous, there is no reason for the equality to hold. Hence, the conclusion from Harrod and Domar was that an economy would, in all probability, reach one of two undesirable outcomes: perpetual growth of unemployment or perpetual growth of idle machinery.

We know now that there are several implausible assumptions in the arguments of Harrod and Domar. First, the Solow–Swan model showed that Harrod and Domar's parameter A—the average product of capital—would typically depend on k, and k would adjust to satisfy the equality $s \cdot f(k)/k = n + \delta$ in the steady state. Second, the saving rate could adjust to satisfy this condition. In particular, if agents maximize utility (as we assume in the next chapter), then they would not find it optimal to continue to save at the constant rate s when the marginal product of capital was zero. This adjustment of the saving rate would rule out an equilibrium with permanently idle machinery.

1.3.5 Growth Models with Poverty Traps

One theme in the literature of economic development concerns *poverty traps*.[20] We can think of a poverty trap as a stable steady state with low levels of per capita output and capital stock. This outcome is a trap because, if agents attempt to break out of it, then the economy has a tendency to return to the low-level steady state.

We observed that the average product of capital, $f(k)/k$, declines with k in the neoclassical model. We also noted, however, that this average product may rise with k in some models that feature increasing returns, for example, in formulations that involve learning-by-doing and spillovers. One way for a poverty trap to arise is for the economy to have an interval of diminishing average product of capital that is followed by a range of rising average product. (Poverty traps also arise in some models with nonconstant saving rates; see Galor and Ryder [1989].)

Figure 1.17 is our usual growth diagram with an $s \cdot f(k)/k$ curve and the $n + \delta$ line. The important new feature is that the $s \cdot f(k)/k$ curve—which reflects the behavior of the average product, $f(k)/k$—has the familiar negative slope at low levels of k, but is then followed by a range with a positive slope. The solid line assumes that a negative slope for $s \cdot f(k)/k$ appears again at very high levels of k. The dashed portion assumes instead that $s \cdot f(k)/k$ asymptotes to a positive value that exceeds $n + \delta$, as in the model that we considered in Fig. 1.12.

One rationale that has been offered for the assumed pattern in $f(k)/k$ is that, at low levels of development, economies tend to focus on agriculture, a sector in which diminishing returns tend to prevail. As an economy develops, it typically concentrates more on industry and services, sectors that may involve ranges of increasing returns. In these ranges, the economy exploits the benefits from learning-by-doing and the division of labor. Eventually, these benefits may be exhausted, and the economy again encounters diminishing returns.

---

[20]See especially the *big-push* model of Lewis (1954). A more modern formulation of this idea appears in Murphy, Shleifer, and Vishny (1989).

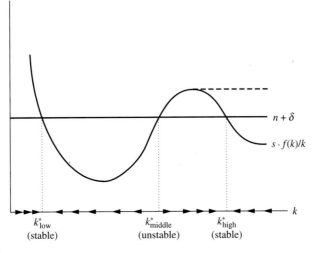

FIGURE 1.17

A poverty trap. The production function is assumed to exhibit diminishing returns to k when k is low, increasing returns for a middle range of k, and either constant or diminishing returns when k is high. The curve $s \cdot f(k)/k$ is therefore downward sloping for low values of k, upward sloping for an intermediate range of k, and downward sloping or horizontal for high values of k. The steady-state value k_{low}^* is stable and therefore constitutes a poverty trap for countries that begin with k between 0 and k_{middle}^*. If a country begins with $k > k_{middle}^*$, then it converges to k_{high}^* if diminishing returns to k ultimately set in. If the returns to capital are constant at high values of k, as depicted by the dashed portion of the curve then the country converges to positive long-run growth rate of k.

Figure 1.17 shows that the $s \cdot f(k)/k$ curve first crosses the $n + \delta$ line at the low steady-state value, k_{low}^*. This steady state has the properties that are familiar from the neoclassical model. In particular, $\gamma_k > 0$ for $k < k_{low}^*$ (the $s \cdot f(k)/k$ curve lies above the $(n + \delta)$ line), and $\gamma_k < 0$ (the $s \cdot f(k)/k$ curve lies below the $(n + \delta)$ line) at least in an interval of $k > k_{low}^*$. Hence, k_{low}^* is a stable steady state: it is a poverty trap in the sense described before.

Figure 1.17 assumes that the tendency for increasing returns in the middle range of k is strong enough so that the $s \cdot f(k)/k$ curve eventually rises to cross the $n + \delta$ line again at the steady-state value k_{middle}^*. This steady state is, however, unstable, because $\gamma_k < 0$ applies to the left, and $\gamma_k > 0$ holds to the right. Thus, if the economy begins with $k(0) < k_{middle}^*$, then its natural tendency is to return to the development trap at k_{low}^*, whereas if it manages somehow to get to $k(0) > k_{middle}^*$, then it tends to grow further to reach still higher levels of k.

The solid curve in Figure 1.17 applies if the economy's eventual tendency toward diminishing returns brings $s \cdot f(k)/k$ down enough to equal $n + \delta$ at the steady-state value k_{high}^*. This steady state, corresponding to a high level of per capita income but to zero long-term per capita growth, is familiar from our study of the neoclassical model. The dashed portion of the curve assumes instead that $s \cdot f(k)/k$ asymptotes to a value that exceeds $n + \delta$. In this case, the economy is capable of endogenous, steady-state growth, as in Figure 1.12. In any event, the key problem for a less-developed economy at the trap level k_{low}^* is how to get over the hump and thereby attain a high long-run level of per capita income or possibly a positive long-run per capita growth rate.

One empirical implication of the model described by Figure 1.17 is that there would exist a middle range of values of k—around k^*_{middle}—for which the growth rate γ_k is increasing in k and, hence, in y. That is, a divergence pattern should hold over this range of per capita incomes. Our reading of the evidence across countries, discussed in Chapter 12, does not support this hypothesis. These results are, however, controversial, so it may be worth bringing out some policy implications that would apply if the model were valid.

Imagine first that some rich country (such as the United States) or an international organization (such as the World Bank) donates a discrete quantity of capital to a country that begins at the low-level equilibrium, k^*_{low}. If this donation raises k to a level below k^*_{middle}, then the economy would still return over time to k^*_{low}. Thus, the economy would enjoy temporarily higher levels of income and consumption, but would not make a permanent escape from poverty. The implication is that a relatively small level of international assistance would not achieve long-run economic development.

A sufficiently large donation—which moves k above k^*_{middle}—would, however, place the economy on a path that leads eventually to the high-level steady state, k^*_{high}, or possibly to endogenous, steady-state growth. Thus, in this model, a relatively large quantity of foreign aid might allow an escape from the poverty trap.

Consider now a domestic policy that raises the saving rate. In the model, this change shows up as an upward shift in the entire $s \cdot f(k)/k$ curve in Figure 1.17. If the new curve still crosses the $n + \delta$ line at a low level of k, then the new point of crossing, $(k^*_{\text{low}})'$, is higher than k^*_{low}. Thus, the economy attains a somewhat higher steady-state level of per capita capital stock and income, but does not break away from the poverty trap. If, however, the increase in the saving rate is large enough so that the $s \cdot f(k)/k$ curve lies entirely above the $n + \delta$ line at low levels of k, then the economy escapes the trap and adjusts over time toward the high-level steady state, k^*_{high} (or possibly to endogenous, steady-state growth).

Note that the policy of high saving can help a country escape the poverty trap even if the high saving is only temporary. If the high saving rate is maintained long enough so that k surpasses the value k^*_{middle} shown in Figure 1.17 and if the saving rate is then lowered back to its initial value, then the economy would not revert back to the poverty trap. It would also work if the economy's temporarily high ratio of domestic investment to GDP is financed by international loans, rather than from domestic saving.

Finally, we note that a reduction in the population growth rate, n, has effects in this model that are analogous to those from increases in the saving rate. In particular, if the fall in n lowers the $n + \delta$ line enough—so that this line no longer intersects the $s \cdot f(k)/k$ curve at a low level of k—then the economy would escape the poverty trap.

Fundamentally, these policy conclusions depend on the idea that production involves a range of decreasing returns, followed by a range of increasing returns. This pattern creates a major hurdle—effectively, a large fixed cost—that the economy has to surmount before it can get on the path toward long-run economic development.

We do not know, however, of empirical evidence that supports the underlying pattern of decreasing/increasing returns. Therefore, these policy inferences are only speculative.

APPENDIX
PROOFS OF VARIOUS PROPOSITIONS

PROOF THAT EACH INPUT IS ESSENTIAL FOR PRODUCTION WITH A NEOCLASSICAL PRODUCTION FUNCTION

We noted in the main body of this chapter that the neoclassical properties for the production function imply that the two inputs, K and L, are each essential for production. To verify this proposition, note first that if $Y \to \infty$ as $K \to \infty$, then

$$\lim_{K \to \infty} \frac{Y}{K} = \lim_{K \to \infty} \frac{\partial Y}{\partial K} = 0,$$

where the first equality comes from l'Hôpital's rule and the second from the Inada condition. If Y remains bounded as K tends to infinity, then

$$\lim_{K \to \infty} (Y/K) = 0$$

follows immediately. We also know from constant returns to scale that, for any finite L,

$$\lim_{K \to \infty} (Y/K) = \lim_{K \to \infty} [F(1, L/K)] = F(1, 0),$$

so that $F(1, 0) = 0$. The condition of constant returns to scale then implies

$$F(K, 0) = K \cdot F(1, 0) = 0$$

for any finite K. We can show from an analogous argument that $F(0, L) = 0$ for any finite L. These results verify that each input is essential for production.

To demonstrate that output goes to infinity when either input goes to infinity, note that

$$F(K, L) = L \cdot f(k) = K \cdot [f(k)/k].$$

Therefore, for any finite K,

$$\lim_{L \to \infty} [F(K, L)] = K \cdot \lim_{k \to 0} [f(k)/k] = K \cdot \lim_{k \to 0} [f'(k)] = \infty,$$

where the last equalities follow from l'Hôpital's rule (because essentiality implies $f[0] = 0$) and the Inada condition. We can show from an analogous argument that $\lim_{K \to \infty} [F(K, L)] = \infty$. Therefore, output goes to infinity when either input goes to infinity.

PROPERTIES OF THE CONVERGENCE COEFFICIENT IN THE SOLOW–SWAN MODEL

Equation (1.31) is a log-linearization of Eq. (1.30) around the steady-state position. To obtain Eq. (1.31), we have to rewrite Eq. (1.30) in terms of $\log(\hat{k})$. Note that $\gamma_{\hat{k}}$ is the time derivative of $\log(\hat{k})$, and $(\hat{k})^{-(1-\alpha)}$ can be written as $e^{-(1-\alpha)\cdot\log(\hat{k})}$. The steady-state value of $sA(\hat{k})^{-(1-\alpha)}$ equals $x + n + \delta$. We can now take a first-order Taylor expansion of $\log(\hat{k})$ around $\log(\hat{k}^*)$ to get Eq. (1.31). See the appendix on mathematics at the end of the book for additional discussion. This result appears in Sala-i-Martin (1990) and in Mankiw, Romer, and Weil (1992).

In the present case—where the production function is Cobb–Douglas and the saving rate is constant—it is possible to get a closed-form solution for the exact time path of $\hat{k}$. Equation (1.30) can be written as

$$\left(\frac{d\hat{k}}{dt}\right) \cdot \hat{k}^{-\alpha} + (x + n + \delta) \cdot \hat{k}^{1-\alpha} = sA.$$

If we define $v \equiv \hat{k}^{1-\alpha}$, then we can transform the equation to

$$\left(\frac{1}{1-\alpha}\right) \cdot \left(\frac{dv}{dt}\right) + (x + n + \delta) \cdot v = sA,$$

which is a first-order, linear differential equation in v. The solution to this equation is

$$v \equiv \hat{k}^{1-\alpha} = \frac{sA}{(x + n + \delta)} + \left\{ [\hat{k}(0)]^{1-\alpha} - \frac{sA}{(x + n + \delta)} \right\} \cdot e^{-(1-\alpha)\cdot(x+n+\delta)\cdot t}.$$

This result means that the gap between $\hat{k}^{1-\alpha}$ and its steady-state value, $sA/(x+n+\delta)$, vanishes exactly at the constant rate $(1 - \alpha) \cdot (x + n + \delta)$, which is the expression for the convergence coefficient β in Eq. (1.31). We are grateful to Jaume Ventura for this result.

The true speed of convergence for $\hat{k}$ or $\hat{y}$ is not constant; it depends on the distance from the steady state. The growth rate of $\hat{y}$ can be written as

$$\gamma_{\hat{y}} = \alpha \cdot [s \cdot A^{1/\alpha} \cdot (\hat{y})^{-(1-\alpha)/\alpha} - (x + n + \delta)].$$

If we use the condition $\hat{y}^* = A[sA/(x + n + \delta)]^{\alpha/(1-\alpha)}$, then we can express the growth rate as

$$\gamma_{\hat{y}} = \alpha \cdot (x + n + \delta) \cdot [(\hat{y}/\hat{y}^*)^{-(1-\alpha)/\alpha} - 1].$$

The convergence coefficient is

$$\beta = -d\gamma_{\hat{y}}/d[\log(\hat{y})] = (1 - \alpha) \cdot (x + n + \delta) \cdot (\hat{y}/\hat{y}^*)^{-(1-\alpha)/\alpha}.$$

At the steady state, $\hat{y} = \hat{y}^*$ and $\beta = (1 - \alpha) \cdot (x + n + \delta)$, as in Eq. (1.31). More generally, β declines as $\hat{y}/\hat{y}^*$ rises.

PROOF THAT TECHNOLOGICAL PROGRESS MUST BE LABOR AUGMENTING

We mentioned in the text that technological progress must take the labor-augmenting form shown in Eq. (1.23) in order for the model to have a steady state with constant growth rates. To prove this result, we start by assuming a production function that includes labor-augmenting and capital-augmenting technological progress:

$$Y = F[K \cdot B(t), L \cdot A(t)], \tag{1A.1}$$

where if $B(t) = A(t)$, then the technological progress is Hicks neutral.

We assume that $A(t)$ and $B(t)$ grow at the constant rates $x \geq 0$ and $z \geq 0$, respectively. If we divide both sides of Eq. (1A.1) by K, then we can express output per unit of capital as

$$Y/K = e^{zt} \cdot F[1, L \cdot A(t)/K \cdot B(t)] = e^{zt} \cdot \varphi[(L/K) \cdot e^{(x-z)t}],$$

where $A(0)$ and $B(0)$ have been normalized to 1, and the function $\varphi(\cdot)$ is defined by $\varphi(\cdot) \equiv F[1, L \cdot A(t)/K \cdot B(t)]$. The population, L, grows at the constant rate n. If γ_K^* is the constant growth rate of K in the steady state, then the expression for Y/K can be written as

$$Y/K = e^{zt} \cdot \varphi[e^{(n+x-z-\gamma_K^*)t}]. \tag{1A.2}$$

Recall that the growth rate of K is given by

$$\gamma_K = s \cdot (Y/K) - \delta.$$

In the steady state, γ_K equals the constant γ_K^*, and hence, Y/K must be constant. There are two ways to get the right-hand side of Eq. (1A.2) to be constant. First, $z = 0$ and $\gamma_K^* = n + x$; that is, technological progress is solely labor augmenting, and the steady-state growth rate of capital equals $n + x$. In this case, the production function can be written in the form of Eq. (1.23).

The second way to get the right-hand side of Eq. (1A.2) to be constant is with $z \neq 0$, and the term $\varphi[e^{(n+x-z-\gamma_K^*)t}]$ exactly offsets the term e^{zt}. For this case to apply, the derivative of Y/K (in the proposed steady state) with respect to time must be identically 0. If we take the derivative of Eq. (1A.2), set it to 0, and rearrange terms, then we get

$$\varphi'(\chi) \cdot \chi/\varphi(\chi) = -z/(n + x - z - \gamma_K^*),$$

where $\chi \equiv e^{(n+x-z-\gamma_K^*)t}$, and the right-hand side is a constant. If we integrate out, then we can write the solution as

$$\varphi(\cdot) = (\text{constant}) \cdot \chi^{1-\alpha},$$

where α is a constant. This result implies that the production function can be written as

$$Y = (\text{constant}) \cdot (Ke^{zt})^\alpha \cdot (Le^{xt})^{1-\alpha} = (\text{constant}) \cdot K^\alpha \cdot (Le^{vt})^{1-\alpha},$$

where $\nu = [z\alpha + x(1-\alpha)]/(1-\alpha)$. In other words, if the rate of capital-augmenting technological progress, z, is nonzero and a steady state exists, then the production function must take the Cobb–Douglas form. Moreover, if the production function is Cobb–Douglas, then we can always express technological change as purely labor augmenting (at the rate ν above). The conclusion, therefore, is that the existence of a steady state implies that technological progress can be written in the labor-augmenting form.

Another approach to technological progress assumes that capital goods produced later—that is, in a more recent *vintage*—are of higher quality for a given cost. If quality improves in accordance with $T(t)$, then the equation for capital accumulation in this vintage model is

$$\dot{K} = s \cdot T(t) \cdot F(K, L) - \delta K, \tag{1A.3}$$

where K is measured in units of constant quality. This equation corresponds to Hicks-neutral technological progress given by $T(t)$ in the production function. The only difference from the standard specification is that output is $Y = F(K, L)$—not $T(t) \cdot F(K, L)$.

If we want to use a model that possesses a steady state, then we would still have to assume that $F(K, L)$ was Cobb–Douglas. In that case, the main properties of the vintage model turn out to be indistinguishable from those of the model that we consider in the text in which technological progress is labor augmenting (see Phelps [1962] and Solow [1969] for further discussion). One difference in the vintage model is that, although K and Y grow at constant rates in the steady state, the growth rate of K (in units of constant quality) exceeds that of Y. Hence, K/Y is predicted to rise steadily in the long run.

PROPERTIES OF THE CES PRODUCTION FUNCTION

The elasticity of substitution is a measure of the curvature of the isoquants. The slope of an isoquant is

$$\left.\frac{dL}{dK}\right|_{\text{isoquant}} = -\frac{\partial F(\cdot)/\partial K}{\partial F(\cdot)/\partial L}.$$

The elasticity is given by

$$\left[\frac{\partial(\text{slope})}{\partial(L/K)} \cdot \frac{L/K}{\text{slope}}\right]^{-1}.$$

For the CES production function shown in Eq. (1.36), the slope of the isoquant is

$$-(L/K)^{1-\psi} \cdot a \cdot b^{\psi}/[(1-a)(1-b)^{\psi}],$$

and the elasticity is $1/(1-\psi)$, a constant.

To compute the limit of the production function as ψ approaches 0, use Eq. (1.36) to get $\lim_{\psi \to 0}[\log(Y)] = \log(A) + 0/0$, which involves an indeterminate form. Apply l'Hôpital's rule to get

$$\lim_{\psi \to 0}[\log(Y)] = \log(A) + \left[\frac{a(bK)^{\psi} \cdot \log(bK) + (1-a)[(1-b)L]^{\psi} \cdot \log[(1-b)L]}{a(bK)^{\psi} + (1-a)[(1-b)L]^{\psi}}\right]\Bigg|_{\psi = 0}$$
$$= \log(A) + a \cdot \log(bK) + (1-a) \cdot \log[(1-b) \cdot L].$$

It follows that $Y = \tilde{A}K^a L^{1-a}$, where $\tilde{A} = Ab^a \cdot (1-b)^{1-a}$. That is, the CES production function approaches the Cobb–Douglas form as ψ tends to one.

PROBLEMS

1.1 Convergence.
    (a) Explain the differences among absolute convergence, conditional convergence, and a reduction in the dispersion of real per capita income across groups.
    (b) Under what circumstances does absolute convergence imply a decline in the dispersion of per capita income?

1.2 Forms of Technological Progress. Assume that the rate of exogenous technological progress is constant.
    (a) Show that a steady state can coexist with technological progress only if this progress takes a labor-augmenting form. What is the intuition for this result?
    (b) Assume that the production function is $Y = F[B(T) \cdot K, A(t) \cdot L]$, where $B(t) = e^{zt}$ and $A(T) = e^{xt}$, with $z \geq 0$ and $x \geq 0$. Show that if $z > 0$ and a steady state exists, then the production function must take the Cobb–Douglas form.

1.3 Dependence of the Saving Rate, Population Growth Rate, and Depreciation Rate on the Capital Intensity. Assume that the production function satisfies the neoclassical properties.
    (a) Why would the saving rate, s, generally depend on k? (Provide some intuition; the precise answer will be given in Chapter 2.)
    (b) How does the speed of convergence change if $s(k)$ is an increasing function of k? What if $s(k)$ is a decreasing function of k?
Consider now an AK technology.
    (c) Why would the saving rate, s, depend on k in this context?
    (d) How does the growth rate of k change over time depending on whether $s(k)$ is an increasing or decreasing function of k?
    (e) Suppose that the rate of population growth, n, depends on k. For an AK technology, what would the relation between n and k have to be in order for the model to predict convergence? Can you think of reasons why n would be related to k in this manner? (We analyze the determination of n in Chapter 9.)
    (f) Repeat part (e) in terms of the depreciation rate, δ. Why might δ depend on k?

1.4 Effects of a Higher Saving Rate. Consider this statement: "Devoting a larger share of national output to investment would help to restore rapid productivity growth and rising living standards." Under what conditions is the statement accurate?

1.5 Factor Shares. For a neoclassical production function, show that each factor of production earns its marginal product. Show that if owners of capital save all their income and workers consume all their income, then the economy reaches the golden rule of capital accumulation. Explain the results.

1.6 Human Capital in the Solow–Swan Model (Based on Mankiw, Romer, Weil [1992]). Assume that the production function is

$$Y = K^{\alpha} H^{\lambda} (AL)^{1-\alpha-\lambda},$$

where Y is output, K is physical capital, H is human capital, A is the level of technology, and L is labor. The parameters α and λ are positive, and $\alpha + \lambda < 1$. L and A grow at the constant rates n and x, respectively. Output can be used on a one-for-one basis for consumption or investment in either type of capital. Both types of capital depreciate at the rate δ. Assume that gross investment in physical capital is the fraction s_k of output and that gross investment in human capital is the fraction s_h of output.

(*a*) Obtain the laws of motion for physical and human capital per unit of effective labor.

(*b*) What are the steady-state values of physical capital, human capital, and output, all per unit of effective labor?

(*c*) This augmented Solow–Swan model can be tested empirically with cross-country data if we assume that all countries are in their steady states. Derive a log-linear regression equation for output per worker. What problems would arise in estimating this equation by ordinary least squares?

(*d*) Derive an equation for the growth rate of output per unit of effective labor. How does this equation look when expressed as a linear approximation in the neighborhood of the steady state? If $\alpha = 0.3$, $\lambda = 0.5$, $\delta = 0.05$, $n = 0.01$, and $x = 0.02$, then what is the rate of convergence near the steady state? Compare the convergence rate in this augmented Solow–Swan model with that in the standard Solow–Swan model.

(*e*) Use the result from part (*d*) to derive a regression equation for the average growth rate of output per worker, $(1/T) \cdot \log[y(t + T)/y(t)]$, where T is the length of the observation interval. What problems arise in the econometric estimation of the rate of convergence, for example, if the levels of technology differ across the countries?

1.7 Distortions in the Solow–Swan Model (Based on Easterly [1993]). Assume that output is produced by the CES production function,

$$Y = [(a_F K_F^{\eta} + a_I K_I^{\eta})^{\psi/\eta} + a_G K_G^{\psi}]^{1/\psi},$$

where Y is output; K_F is formal capital, which is subject to taxation; K_I is informal capital, which evades taxation; K_G is public capital, provided by government and used freely by all producers; $a_F, a_I, a_G > 0$; $\eta < 1$ and $\psi < 1$. Installed formal and informal capital differ in their location and form of ownership and, therefore, in their productivity.

Output can be used on a one-for-one basis for consumption or gross investment in the three types of capital. All three types of capital depreciate at the rate δ. Population is constant, and technological progress is nil.

Formal capital is subject to tax at the rate τ at the moment of its installation. Thus, the price of formal capital (in units of output) is $1 + \tau$. The price of a unit of informal capital is one. Gross investment in public capital is the fixed fraction s_G of tax revenues. Any unused tax receipts are rebated to households in a lump-sum manner. The sum of investment in the two forms of private capital is the fraction s of income net of taxes and transfers. Existing private capital can be converted on a one-to-one basis in either direction between formal and informal capital.

(a) Derive the ratio of informal to formal capital used by profit-maximizing producers.

(b) In the steady state, the three forms of capital grow at the same rate. What is the ratio of output to formal capital in the steady state?

(c) What is the steady-state growth rate of the economy?

(d) Numerical simulations show that, for reasonable parameter values, the graph of the growth rate against the tax rate, τ, initially increases rapidly, then reaches a peak, and finally decreases steadily. Explain this nonmonotonic relation between the growth rate and the tax rate.

CHAPTER

2

GROWTH MODELS WITH CONSUMER OPTIMIZATION (THE RAMSEY MODEL)

One shortcoming of the models that we analyzed in Chapter 1 is that the saving rate is exogenous and constant. In this chapter, we assume instead that the path of consumption and, hence, the saving rate are determined by optimizing households and firms that interact on competitive markets. We deal, in particular, with infinitely-lived households that choose consumption and saving to maximize their dynastic utility, subject to an intertemporal budget constraint. This specification of consumer behavior is a key element in the Ramsey growth model as constructed by Ramsey (1928) and refined by Cass (1965) and Koopmans (1965).

One finding will be that the saving rate is not constant in general, but is instead a function of the per capita capital stock, k. Thus, we modify the Solow–Swan model in two respects: first, we pin down the average level of the saving rate, and, second, we determine whether the saving rate rises or falls as the economy develops.

The average level of the saving rate is especially important for the determination of the levels of variables in the steady state. In particular, the optimizing conditions in the Ramsey model preclude the kind of inefficient oversaving that was possible in the Solow–Swan model.

The tendency for saving rates to rise or fall with economic development affects the transitional dynamics, for example, the speed of convergence to the steady state. If the saving rate rises with k, then the convergence speed is slower than that in the Solow–Swan model, and vice versa. We find, however, that even if the saving rate is rising, the convergence property still holds under fairly general conditions in the Ramsey model. That is, an economy still tends to grow faster in per capita terms when it is further from its own steady-state position.

We show that the Solow–Swan model with a constant saving rate is a special case of the Ramsey model; moreover, this case corresponds to reasonable parameter values. Thus, it was worthwhile to begin with the Solow–Swan model as a tractable approximation to the optimizing framework. We also note, however, that the empirical evidence suggests that saving rates typically rise with per capita income during the transition to the steady state. The Ramsey model is consistent with this pattern, and the model allows us to assess the implications of this saving behavior for the transitional dynamics. Moreover, the optimizing framework will be essential in later chapters when we extend the Ramsey model in various respects and consider the possible roles for government policy.

2.1   HOUSEHOLDS

2.1.1   Setup of the Model

The households in the economy provide labor services in exchange for wages, receive interest income on assets, purchase goods for consumption, and save by accumulating additional assets. Each household contains one or more adult, working members of the current generation. In making plans, these adults take account of the welfare and resources of their actual or prospective descendants. We model this intergenerational interaction by imagining that the current generation maximizes utility and incorporates a budget constraint over an infinite horizon. That is, although individuals have finite lives, we consider an immortal extended family. This setting is appropriate if altruistic parents provide transfers to their children, who give in turn to their children, and so on. The immortal family corresponds to finite-lived individuals who are connected via a pattern of operative intergenerational transfers that are based on altruism.[1]

The current adults expect the size of their extended family to grow at the rate n because of the net influences of fertility and mortality. In Chapter 9 we will study how rational agents choose their fertility by weighing the costs and benefits of rearing children. But at this point, we continue to simplify by treating n as exogenous and constant. We also neglect migration of persons, another topic explored in Chapter 9. If we normalize the number of adults at time 0 to unity, then the family size at time t—which corresponds to the adult population—is

$$L(t) = e^{nt}.$$

If $C(t)$ is total consumption at time t, then $c(t) \equiv C(t)/L(t)$ is consumption per adult person.

---

[1] See Barro (1974). We abstract from marriage, which generates interactions across family lines. See Bernheim and Bagwell (1988) for a discussion.

Each household wishes to maximize overall utility, U, as given by

$$U = \int_0^{\infty} u[c(t)] \cdot e^{nt} \cdot e^{-\rho t} \, dt. \tag{2.1}$$

This formulation assumes that the household's utility at time 0 is a weighted sum of all future flows of utility, $u(c)$. The function $u(c)$—often called the felicity function—relates the flow of utility per person to the quantity of consumption per person, c. We assume that $u(c)$ is increasing in c and concave—$u'(c) > 0$, $u''(c) < 0$.[2] The concavity assumption generates an eagerness to smooth consumption over time: households prefer a relatively uniform pattern to one in which c is very low in some periods and very high in others. We also assume that $u(c)$ satisfies Inada conditions: $u'(c) \to \infty$ as $c \to 0$, and $u'(c) \to 0$ as $c \to \infty$.

The multiplication of $u(c)$ in Eq. (2.1) by family size, $L = e^{nt}$, represents the adding up of utils for all family members alive at time t. The other multiplier, $e^{-\rho t}$, involves the rate of time preference, $\rho > 0$. A positive value of ρ means that utils are valued less the later they are received.[3] We assume $\rho > n$, which implies that U in Eq. (2.1) is bounded if c is constant over time.

One reason for ρ to be positive is that utils far in the future correspond to consumption of later generations. Suppose that, starting from a point at which the levels of consumption per person in each generation are the same, parents prefer a unit of their own consumption to a unit of their children's consumption. This parental "selfishness" corresponds to $\rho > 0$ in Eq. (2.1). In a fuller specification, we would also distinguish the rate at which individuals discount their own flow of utility at different points in time (for which $\rho = 0$ might apply) from the rate that applies over generations. Equation (2.1) assumes, only for reasons of tractability, that the discount rate within a person's lifetime is the same as that across generations.

It is also plausible that parents would have diminishing marginal utility with respect to the number of children. We could model this effect by allowing the rate of time preference, ρ, to increase with the population growth rate, n.[4] Because we treat n as exogenous, this dependence of ρ on n would not materially change the analysis in this chapter. We shall, however, consider this effect in Chapter 9, which allows for an endogenous determination of population growth.

---

[2] The results will be invariant with positive linear transformations of the utility function, but not with arbitrary positive, monotonic transformations. Thus, the analysis depends on a limited form of cardinal utility. See Koopmans (1965) for a discussion.

[3] Ramsey (1928) assumed $\rho = 0$. He then interpreted the optimizing agent as a social planner, rather than a competitive household, who chose consumption and saving for today's generation as well as for future generations. The discounting of utility for future generations ($\rho > 0$) was, according to Ramsey, "ethically indefensible." We work out an example with $\rho = 0$ in the mathematics chapter.

[4] One case common in the growth literature assumes that ρ rises one-to-one with n; that is, $\rho = \rho^* + n$, where ρ^* is the positive rate of time preference that applies under 0 population growth. In this case, utility at time t enters into Eq. (2.1) as $u(c)e^{-\rho^* t}$, which depends on per capita utility, but not on the size of the family at time t. This specification is used, for example, by Sidrauski (1967) and Blanchard and Fischer (1989, Chapter 2).

Households hold assets in the form of ownership claims on capital (to be introduced later) or as loans. Negative loans represent debts. We continue to assume a closed economy, so that no assets can be traded internationally. Households can lend to and borrow from other households, but the representative household will end up holding zero net loans in equilibrium. Because the two forms of assets, capital and loans, are assumed to be perfect substitutes as stores of value, they must pay the same real rate of return, $r(t)$. We denote the household's net assets per person by $a(t)$, where $a(t)$ is measured in real terms, that is, in units of consumables.

Households are competitive in that each takes as given the interest rate, $r(t)$, and the wage rate, $w(t)$, paid per unit of labor services. We assume that each adult supplies inelastically 1 unit of labor services per unit of time. (Chapter 9 considers a labor/leisure choice.) In equilibrium, the labor market clears and the household obtains the desired quantity of employment. That is, the model abstracts from "involuntary unemployment." Since each person works 1 unit of labor services per unit of time, the wage income per adult person equals $w(t)$. Total income per capita received by a household is the sum of labor income, $w(t)$, and financial or interest income (which can be positive or negative), $r(t) \cdot a(t)$.

The flow budget constraint for the household is

$$\dot{a} = w + ra - c - na. \qquad (2.2)$$

We omit time subscripts in Eq. (2.2) and in the subsequent analysis whenever no ambiguity results. The equation says that assets per person rise with per capita income, $w + ra$, fall with per capita consumption, c, and fall because of expansion of the population in accordance with the term na. (We can derive Eq. [2.2] by imposing the budget constraint in terms of the change in the level of assets, A, and then noting that, for given A, $a \equiv A/L$ falls at rate n due to population growth.)

If each household can borrow an unlimited amount at the going interest rate, $r(t)$, then it has an incentive to pursue a form of chain letter or Ponzi game. The household can borrow, say $1, to finance current consumption and then use future borrowings to roll over the principal and pay all of the interest. In this case, the household's debt grows forever at the rate of interest, $r(t)$. Since no principal ever gets repaid, today's added consumption of $1 is effectively free. Thus, a household that can borrow in this manner would be able to finance an arbitrarily high level of consumption in perpetuity.

To rule out chain-letter possibilities, we assume that the credit market imposes a constraint on the amount of borrowing. The appropriate restriction turns out to be that the present value of assets must be asymptotically nonnegative, that is,

$$\lim_{t \to \infty} \left\{ a(t) \cdot \exp\left[-\int_0^t [r(v) - n]dv \right] \right\} \geq 0. \qquad (2.3)$$

This constraint means that, in the long run, a household's debt per person (negative values of $a[t]$) cannot grow as fast as $r(t) - n$, so that the level of debt cannot grow as fast as $r(t)$. This restriction rules out the type of chain-letter finance that we described above. We show later how the credit-market constraint expressed in Eq. (2.3) emerges naturally from the market equilibrium.

The household's optimization problem is to maximize U in Eq. (2.1), subject to the budget constraint in Eq. (2.2), the stock of initial assets, $a(0)$, and the limitation on borrowing in Eq. (2.3). The inequality restrictions, $c(t) \geq 0$, would also apply. As $c(t)$ approaches 0, however, the Inada condition implies that the marginal utility of consumption becomes infinite. The inequality restrictions will therefore never bind, and we can safely ignore them.

2.1.2   First-Order Conditions

The mathematical methods for this type of dynamic optimization problem are discussed in the appendix on mathematics at the end of the book. We use these results here without further derivation. Begin with the present-value Hamiltonian,

$$J = u(c)e^{-(\rho-n)t} + v \cdot [w + (r - n)a - c], \tag{2.4}$$

where the expression in brackets equals $\dot{a}$ from Eq. (2.2). The variable v is the present-value shadow price of income. It represents the value of an increment of income received at time t in units of utils at time 0.[5] The first-order conditions for a maximum of U are

$$\frac{\partial J}{\partial c} = 0 \Longrightarrow v = u'(c)e^{-(\rho-n)t}, \tag{2.5}$$

$$\dot{v} = -\frac{\partial J}{\partial a} \Longrightarrow \dot{v} = -(r - n)v. \tag{2.6}$$

Eq. (2.6) is known as the Euler equation or the Ramsey rule of optimal saving. The transversality condition is

$$\lim_{t \to \infty}[v(t) \cdot a(t)] = 0. \tag{2.7}$$

THE EULER EQUATION. If we differentiate Eq. (2.5) with respect to time and substitute for v from this equation and for $\dot{v}$ from Eq. (2.6), then we get the basic condition for choosing consumption over time:

$$r = \rho - \left(\frac{du'/dt}{u'}\right) = \rho - \left[\frac{u''(c) \cdot c}{u'(c)}\right] \cdot (\dot{c}/c). \tag{2.8}$$

This equation says that households choose consumption so as to equate the rate of return, r, to the rate of time preference, ρ, plus the rate of decrease of the marginal utility of consumption, u', due to growing per capita consumption, c.

The interest rate, r, on the left-hand side of Eq. (2.8) is the rate of return to saving. The far right-hand side of the equation can be viewed as the rate of return to

---

[5]We could deal alternatively with the shadow price $ve^{(\rho-n)t}$. This shadow price measures the value of an increment of income at time t in units of utils at time t (see the discussion in the appendix on mathematics at the end of the book).

consumption. Agents prefer to consume today rather than tomorrow for two reasons. First, the term ρ appears because households discount future utility at this rate. Second, if $\dot{c}/c > 0$, then c is low today relative to tomorrow. Since agents like to smooth consumption over time—because $u''(c) < 0$—they would like to even out the flow by bringing some future consumption forward to the present. The second term on the far right picks up this effect. (Note that this term is negative if $\dot{c}/c < 0$.) If agents are optimizing, then Eq. (2.8) says that they have equated the two rates of return and are therefore indifferent at the margin between consuming and saving.

Another way to view Eq. (2.8) is that households would select a flat consumption profile, with $\dot{c}/c = 0$, if $r = \rho$. Households would be willing to depart from this flat pattern and sacrifice some consumption today for more consumption tomorrow—that is, tolerate $\dot{c}/c > 0$—only if they are compensated by an interest rate, r, that is sufficiently above ρ. The term $[(-u''(c) \cdot c)/(u'(c))] \cdot \dot{c}/c$ on the right-hand side of Eq. (2.8) gives the required amount of compensation. Note that the term in brackets is the magnitude of the elasticity of $u'(c)$ with respect to c. This elasticity, a measure of the concavity of $u(c)$, determines the amount by which r must exceed ρ. If the elasticity is larger in magnitude, then the required premium of r over ρ is greater for a given value of $\dot{c}/c$.

The magnitude of the elasticity of marginal utility, $[(-u''(c) \cdot c)/(u'(c))]$, is sometimes called the reciprocal of the elasticity of intertemporal substitution.[6] Equation (2.8) shows that to find a steady state in which r and $\dot{c}/c$ are constant, this elasticity must be constant asymptotically. We therefore follow the common practice of assuming the functional form

$$u(c) = \frac{c^{(1-\theta)} - 1}{(1 - \theta)}, \tag{2.9}$$

where $\theta > 0$, so that the elasticity of marginal utility equals the constant $-\theta$.[7] The elasticity of substitution for this utility function is the constant $\sigma = 1/\theta$. Hence,

---

[6]The elasticity of intertemporal substitution between consumption at times t_1 and t_2 is given by the reciprocal of the proportionate change in the magnitude of the slope of an indifference curve in response to a proportionate change in the ratio $c(t_1)/c(t_2)$. If we denote this elasticity by σ, then we get

$$\sigma = \left[\frac{c(t_1)/c(t_2)}{-u'[c(t_1)]/u'[c(t_2)]} \cdot \frac{d\{u'[c(t_1)]/u'[c(t_2)]\}}{d[c(t_1)/c(t_2)]} \right]^{-1},$$

where $-u'[c(t_1)]/u'[c(t_2)]$ is the magnitude of the slope of the indifference curve. If we let t_2 approach t_1, then we get the instantaneous elasticity,

$$\sigma = -u'(c)/[c \cdot u''(c)],$$

which is the inverse of the magnitude of the elasticity of marginal utility.

[7]The inclusion of the -1 in the formula is convenient because it implies that $u(c)$ approaches $\log(c)$ as $\theta \to 1$. (This result can be proven using l'Hôpital's rule.) The term $-1/(1 - \theta)$ can, however, be omitted without affecting the subsequent results, because the household's choices are invariant with respect to linear transformations of the utility function (see footnote 2).

this form is called the *constant intertemporal elasticity of substitution* (CIES) utility function. The higher θ, the more rapid is the proportionate decline in $u'(c)$ in response to increases in c and, hence, the less willing households are to accept deviations from a uniform pattern of c over time. As θ approaches 0, the utility function approaches a linear form in c; the linearity means that households are indifferent to the timing of consumption if $r = \rho$ applies.

The form of $u(c)$ in Eq. (2.9) implies that the optimality condition from Eq. (2.8) simplifies to

$$\dot{c}/c = (1/\theta) \cdot (r - \rho). \tag{2.10}$$

Therefore, the relation between r and ρ determines whether households choose a pattern of per capita consumption that rises over time, stays constant, or falls over time. A lower willingness to substitute intertemporally (a higher value of θ) implies a smaller responsiveness of $\dot{c}/c$ to the gap between r and ρ.

THE TRANSVERSALITY CONDITION. The transversality condition in Eq. (2.7) says that the value of the household's assets—which equals the quantity $a(t)$ times the shadow price $\nu(t)$—must approach 0 as time approaches infinity. If we think of infinity loosely as the end of the planning horizon, then the intuition is that optimizing agents do not want to have any valuable assets left over at the end.[8] Utility would increase if the assets, which are effectively being wasted, were used instead to raise consumption at some dates in finite time.

The shadow price ν evolves over time in accordance with Eq. (2.6). Integration of this equation with respect to time yields

$$\nu(t) = \nu(0) \cdot \exp\left\{ -\int_0^t [r(v) - n]dv \right\}.$$

The term $\nu(0)$ equals $u'[c(0)]$, which is positive because $c(0)$ is finite (if U is finite), and $u'(c)$ is assumed to be positive as long as c is finite.

If we substitute the result for $\nu(t)$ into Eq. (2.7), then the transversality condition becomes

$$\lim_{t \to \infty} \left\{ a(t) \cdot \exp\left[-\int_0^t [r(v) - n]dv \right] \right\} = 0. \tag{2.11}$$

This equation implies that the quantity of assets per person, a, does not grow asymptotically at a rate as high as $r - n$ or, equivalently, that the level of assets does not grow at a rate as high as r. It would be suboptimal for households to accumulate positive assets forever at the rate r or higher, because utility would increase if these assets were instead consumed in finite time.

---

[8]The interpretation of the transversality condition in the infinite-horizon problem as the limit of the corresponding condition for a finite-horizon problem is not always correct. See the appendix on mathematics at the end of the book.

In the case of borrowing, where $a(t)$ is negative, infinite–lived households would like to violate Eq. (2.11) by borrowing and never making payments for principal or interest. That is why we needed the constraint in Eq. (2.3) to rule out chain-letter finance, that is, schemes in which a household's debt grows forever at the rate r or higher. In order to borrow on this perpetual basis, households would have to find willing lenders; that is, other households that were willing to hold positive assets that grew at the rate r or higher. But we already know from the transversality condition that these other households will be unwilling to absorb assets asymptotically at this high a rate. Therefore, in equilibrium, each household will be unable to borrow in a chain-letter fashion. In other words, the inequality restriction shown in Eq. (2.3) is not arbitrary and would, in fact, be imposed in equilibrium by the credit market. Faced by this constraint, the best thing that optimizing households can do is to satisfy the condition shown in Eq. (2.11). That is, this equality holds whether $a(t)$ is positive or negative.

THE CONSUMPTION FUNCTION. The term $\exp[-\int_0^t r(v)dv]$, which appears in Eq. (2.11), is a present-value factor that converts a unit of income at time t to an equivalent unit of income at time 0. If $r(v)$ equaled the constant r, then the present-value factor would simplify to e^{-rt}. More generally we can think of an average interest rate between times 0 and t, defined by

$$\bar{r}(t) = (1/t) \cdot \int_0^t r(v)dv. \tag{2.12}$$

The present-value factor equals $e^{-\bar{r}(t)\cdot t}$.

Equation (2.9) determines the growth rate of c. To determine the level of c—that is, the consumption function—we have to use the flow budget constraint, Eq. (2.2), to derive the household's intertemporal budget constraint. We can solve Eq. (2.2) as a first-order linear differential equation in a to get an intertemporal budget constraint that holds for any time $T \geq 0$:[9]

$$a(T) \cdot e^{-[\bar{r}(T)-n]T} + \int_0^T c(t)e^{-[\bar{r}(t)-n]t}dt = a(0) + \int_0^T w(t)e^{-[\bar{r}(t)-n]t}\,dt,$$

where we used the definition of $\bar{r}(t)$ from Eq. (2.12). If we take the limit as $T \to \infty$, then the term on the far left vanishes (from the transversality condition in Eq. [2.11]), and the intertemporal budget constraint becomes

$$\int_0^\infty c(t)e^{-[\bar{r}(t)-n]t}dt = a(0) + \int_0^\infty w(t)e^{-[\bar{r}(t)-n]t}\,dt$$
$$= a(0) + \tilde{w}(0). \tag{2.13}$$

Hence, the present value of consumption equals wealth, defined as the sum of initial assets, $a(0)$, and the present value of wage income, denoted by $\tilde{w}(0)$.

---

[9]The methods for solving first-order linear differential equations with variable coefficients is discussed in the appendix on mathematics at the end of the book.

If we integrate Eq. (2.10) between times 0 and t and use the definition of $\bar{r}(t)$ from Eq. (2.12), then we find that consumption is given by

$$c(t) = c(0) \cdot e^{(1/\theta)[\bar{r}(t)-\rho]t}.$$

Substitution of this result for $c(t)$ into the intertemporal budget constraint in Eq. (2.13) leads to the consumption function at time 0:

$$c(0) = \mu(0) \cdot [a(0) + \tilde{w}(0)], \tag{2.14}$$

where $\mu(0)$, the propensity to consume out of wealth, is determined from

$$[1/\mu(0)] = \int_0^\infty e^{[\bar{r}(t)\cdot(1-\theta)/\theta - \rho/\theta + n]t} \, dt. \tag{2.15}$$

An increase in average interest rates, $\bar{r}(t)$, for given wealth, has two effects on the marginal propensity to consume in Eq. (2.15). First, higher interest rates increase the cost of current consumption relative to future consumption, an intertemporal-substitution effect that motivates people to shift consumption from the present to the future. Second, higher interest rates have an income effect that tends to raise consumption at all dates. The net effect of an increase in $\bar{r}(t)$ on $\mu(0)$ depends on which of the two forces dominates.

If $\theta < 1$, then $\mu(0)$ declines with $\bar{r}(t)$ because the substitution effect dominates. The intuition is that when θ is low, households care relatively little about consumption smoothing, and the intertemporal-substitution effect is large. Conversely, if $\theta > 1$, then $\mu(0)$ rises with $\bar{r}(t)$ because the substitution effect is relatively weak. Finally, if $\theta = 1$ (log utility), then the two effects exactly cancel, and $\mu(0)$ simplifies to $\rho - n$, which is independent of $\bar{r}(t)$. Recall that we assumed $\rho - n > 0$.

The effects of $\bar{r}(t)$ on $\mu(0)$ carry over to effects on $c(0)$ if we hold constant the wealth term, $a(0) + \tilde{w}(0)$. In fact, however, $\tilde{w}(0)$ falls with $\bar{r}(t)$ for a given path of $w(t)$. This third effect reinforces the substitution effect that we mentioned before.

2.2 FIRMS

Firms produce goods, pay wages for labor input, and make rental payments for capital input. Each firm has access to the production technology,

$$Y = F(K, L, t),$$

where Y is the flow of output, K is capital input (in units of commodities), L is labor input (in person-hours per year), and t, chronological time, represents the effect of exogenous technological progress. The function $F(\cdot)$ satisfies the neoclassical properties that were discussed in Chapter 1. In particular, Y exhibits constant returns to scale in K and L, and each input exhibits positive and diminishing marginal product.

We showed in Chapter 1 that a steady state coexists with technological progress at a constant rate only if this progress takes the labor-augmenting form. We therefore assume that the production function can be written as

$$Y = F(K, \hat{L}), \tag{2.16}$$

where $\hat{L} \equiv L \cdot A(t)$ is the effective amount of labor input, and $A(t)$, the level of the technology, grows at the constant rate $x \geq 0$. Hence, $A(t) = e^{xt}$, where we normalize the initial level of technology $A(0)$ to 1.

We shall find it convenient, as in Chapter 1, to work with variables that are constant in the steady state. Hence, we deal again with quantities per unit of effective labor:

$$\hat{y} \equiv Y/\hat{L} \qquad \text{and} \qquad \hat{k} \equiv K/\hat{L}.$$

The production function can then be written in intensive form, as in Eq. (1.27),

$$\hat{y} = f(\hat{k}), \tag{2.17}$$

where $f(0) = 0$. It can be readily verified that the marginal products of the factors are given by[10]

$$\partial Y/\partial K = f'(\hat{k}),$$
$$\partial Y/\partial L = [f(\hat{k}) - \hat{k} \cdot f'(\hat{k})]e^{xt}. \tag{2.18}$$

The Inada conditions, discussed in Chapter 1, imply $f'(\hat{k}) \to \infty$ as $\hat{k} \to 0$ and $f'(\hat{k}) \to 0$ as $\hat{k} \to \infty$.

We think of firms as renting the services of capital from the households that own the capital. (None of the results would change if the firms owned the capital, and the households owned shares of stock in the firms.) Hence, the firms' costs for capital are the rental payments, which are proportional to K. This specification implies that capital services can be increased or decreased without incurring any additional expenses, such as costs for installing machines or making other changes. We consider these kinds of adjustment costs in Chapter 3.

We assume, as in Chapter 1, a one-sector production model in which 1 unit of output can be used to generate 1 unit of household consumption, C, or 1 unit of additional capital, K. Therefore, as long as the economy is not at a corner solution in which all current output goes into consumption or new capital, the price of K in terms of C will be fixed at unity. Because C will be nonzero in equilibrium, we have to be concerned only with the possibility that none of the output goes into new capital; in other words, that gross investment is 0. Even in this situation, the price of K in terms of C would remain at unity if capital were reversible in the sense that the existing stocks could be consumed on a one-for-one basis. With reversible capital, the economy's gross investment can be negative, and the price of K in units of C stays at unity. Although this situation may apply to farm animals, economists usually assume that investment is irreversible. In this case, the price of K in units of C is 1 only if the constraint of nonnegative aggregate gross investment is non-binding in equilibrium. We maintain this assumption in the following analysis.

Let R be the rental price for a unit of capital services, and assume again that capital stocks depreciate at the constant rate $\delta \geq 0$. The net rate of return to a house-

---

[10]We can write $Y = \hat{L} \cdot f(\hat{k})$. Differentiation of Y with respect to K, holding fixed L and t, leads to $\partial Y/\partial K = f'(\hat{k})$. Differentiation of Y with respect to L, holding fixed K and t, leads to $\partial Y/\partial L = [f(\hat{k}) - \hat{k} \cdot f'(\hat{k})]e^{xt}$.

hold that owns a unit of capital is then $R - \delta$.[11] Recall that households can also receive the interest rate r on funds lent to other households. Since capital and loans are perfect substitutes as stores of value, we must have $r = R - \delta$ or, equivalently, $R = r + \delta$.

The representative firm's flow of net receipts or profit at any point in time is given by

$$\text{Profit} = F(K, \hat{L}) - (r + \delta) \cdot K - wL, \qquad (2.19)$$

that is, gross receipts from the sale of output, $F(K, \hat{L})$, less the factor payments, which are rentals to capital, $(r + \delta) \cdot K$, and wages to workers, wL. We assume that the firm seeks to maximize the present value of profits. Because the firm rents capital and labor services and has no adjustment costs, there are no intertemporal elements in the firm's maximization problem. That is, the problem of maximizing the present value of profits reduces here to a problem of maximizing profit in each period without regard to the outcomes in other periods. (The problem becomes intertemporal when we introduce adjustment costs for capital in Chapter 3.)

Consider a firm of arbitrary scale, say with level of effective labor input $\hat{L}$. Profit for this firm can be written as

$$\text{Profit} = \hat{L} \cdot [f(\hat{k}) - (r + \delta) \cdot \hat{k} - we^{-xt}]. \qquad (2.20)$$

A competitive firm, which takes r and w as given, maximizes profit for given $\hat{L}$ by setting

$$f'(\hat{k}) = r + \delta. \qquad (2.21)$$

That is, the firm chooses the ratio of capital to effective labor to equate the marginal product of capital to the rental price.

The resulting level of profit is positive, 0, or negative depending on the value of w. If profit is positive, then the firm could attain infinite profits by choosing an infinite scale. If the profit is negative, then the firm would contract its scale to 0. Therefore, in a full market equilibrium, w must be such that profit equals 0; that is, the total of the factor payments, $(r + \delta) \cdot K + wL$, just equals the gross receipts in Eq. (2.20). In this case, the firm is indifferent about its scale.

In order for profit to be 0, the wage rate has to equal the marginal product of labor corresponding to the value of $\hat{k}$ that satisfies Eq. (2.21):

$$[f(\hat{k}) - \hat{k} \cdot f'(\hat{k})]e^{xt} = w. \qquad (2.22)$$

It can be readily verified from substitution of Eqs. (2.21) and (2.22) into Eq. (2.20) that the resulting level of profit equals 0 for any value of $\hat{L}$. Equivalently, if the factor

---

[11]More generally, if the price of capital can change over time, then the real rate of return for owners of capital equals $R/P_k - \delta + (1 - \delta)(\dot{P}_k/P_k)$, where P_k is the price of capital in units of consumables. In the present case, where $P_k = 1$, the capital-gain term, which involves $\dot{P}_K/P_K$, vanishes, and the rate of return simplifies to $R - \delta$.

prices equal the respective marginal products, then the factor payments just exhaust the total output (a result that corresponds in mathematics to Euler's theorem). [12]

The model does not determine the scale of an individual, competitive firm that operates with a constant-returns-to-scale production function. The model will, however, determine the factor/input ratio, $\hat{k}$, as well as the aggregate level of production.

2.3 EQUILIBRIUM

We began with the behavior of competitive households that faced a given interest rate, r, and wage rate, w. We then introduced competitive firms that also faced given values of r and w. We can now combine the behavior of households and firms to analyze the structure of a competitive market equilibrium.

The representative household must end up with 0 net debt; therefore, the assets per adult person, a, equal the capital per worker, k. (Recall that the number of workers equals the number of adults, and each adult works 1 unit of labor services per unit of time.) The equality between k and a follows because all of the capital stock must be owned by someone in the economy; in particular, in this closed-economy model, all of the domestic capital stock must be owned by the domestic residents. If the economy were open to international capital markets, then the gap between k and a would correspond to the home country's net debt to foreigners. Chapter 3 considers an open economy, in which the net foreign debt can be nonzero.

The household's flow budget constraint in Eq. (2.2) determines $\dot{a}$. Use $a = k$, $\hat{k} = ke^{-xt}$, and the conditions for r and w in Eqs. (2.21) and (2.22) to get

$$\dot{\hat{k}} = f(\hat{k}) - \hat{c} - (x + n + \delta) \cdot \hat{k}, \qquad (2.23)$$

where $\hat{c} \equiv C/\hat{L} = ce^{-xt}$, and $\hat{k}(0)$ is given. Equation (2.23) is the resource constraint for the overall economy: the change in the capital stock equals output less consumption and depreciation, and the change in $\hat{k} \equiv K/\hat{L}$ also takes account of the growth in $\hat{L}$ at the rate $x + n$.

The differential equation (2.23) is the key relation that determines the evolution of $\hat{k}$ and, hence, $\hat{y} = f(\hat{k})$ over time. The missing element, however, is the determination of $\hat{c}$. If we knew the relation of $\hat{c}$ to $\hat{k}$ (or $\hat{y}$), or if we had another differential equation that determined the evolution of $\hat{c}$, then we could study the full dynamics of the economy.

In the Solow–Swan model of Chapter 1, the missing relation was provided by the assumption of a constant saving rate, which implied the linear consumption function, $\hat{c} = (1-s) \cdot f(\hat{k})$. In the present setting, the behavior of the saving rate is not

---

[12]Euler's theorem says that if a function $F(K, \hat{L})$ is homogeneous of degree 1 in K and $\hat{L}$, then

$$F(K, \hat{L}) = F_K \cdot K + F_{\hat{L}} \cdot \hat{L}.$$

This result can be proven using the equations $F(K, \hat{L}) = \hat{L} \cdot f(\hat{k}), F_K = f'(\hat{k}),$ and $F_{\hat{L}} = f(\hat{k}) - \hat{k} \cdot f'(\hat{k}).$

so simple, but we do know from household optimization that c grows in accordance with Eq. (2.10). If we use the conditions $r = f'(\hat{k}) - \delta$ and $\hat{c} = ce^{-xt}$, then we get

$$\dot{\hat{c}}/\hat{c} = \dot{c}/c - x = (1/\theta) \cdot [f'(\hat{k}) - \delta - \rho - \theta x]. \qquad (2.24)$$

This equation, together with Eq. (2.23), forms a system of two differential equations in $\hat{c}$ and $\hat{k}$. This system, together with the initial condition, $\hat{k}(0)$, and the transversality condition, determines the time paths of $\hat{c}$ and $\hat{k}$.

We can write the transversality condition in terms of $\hat{k}$ by substituting $a = k$ and $\hat{k} = ke^{-xt}$ into Eq. (2.11) to get

$$\lim_{t \to \infty} \left\{ \hat{k} \cdot \exp\left(- \int_0^t [f'(\hat{k}) - \delta - x - n]dv\right) \right\} = 0. \qquad (2.25)$$

We can interpret this result if we jump ahead to use the result that $\hat{k}$ tends asymptotically to a constant steady-state value $\hat{k}^*$, just as in the Solow-Swan model. The transversality condition in Eq. (2.25) therefore requires $f'(\hat{k}^*) - \delta$, the steady-state rate of return, to exceed $x + n$, the steady-state growth rate of K.

2.4 ALTERNATIVE ENVIRONMENTS

The analysis applies thus far to a decentralized economy with competitive households and firms. We can see from the setup of the model, however, that the same equations—and, hence, the same results—would emerge under some alternative environments. First, households could perform the functions of firms by employing adult family members as workers in accordance with the production process, $f(\hat{k})$. (This setup was assumed in Chapter 1.) Then Eq. (2.23) follows directly, and Eqs. (2.24) and (2.25) still apply to the maximization of utility. Thus, the separation of functions between households and firms is not central to the analysis.

We could also pretend that the economy was run by a benevolent *social planner* who dictates the choices of consumption over time and who seeks to maximize the utility of the representative family. (Despite its lack of realism, the device of the benevolent social planner will be useful in many circumstances for finding the economy's first-best outcomes.) If the planner has the same form of preferences as those assumed before—in particular, the same rate of time preference, ρ, and the same utility function, $u(c)$—then the solution will be the same as that for the decentralized economy.[13] Since a benevolent social planner with dictatorial powers will attain a Pareto optimum, the results for the decentralized economy—which coincide with those of the planner—must also be Pareto optimal.

---

[13]The planner's problem is to choose the path of c to maximize U in Eq. (2.1), subject to the economy's budget constraint in Eq. (2.23), the initial value $\hat{k}(0)$, and the inequalities $c \geq 0$ and $\hat{k} \geq 0$. The Hamiltonian for this problem is

$$J = u(c)e^{-\rho t} + v \cdot [f(\hat{k}) - ce^{-xt} - (x + n + \delta) \cdot \hat{k}].$$

The usual first-order conditions lead to Eq. (2.24), and the transversality condition leads to Eq. (2.25).

2.5 THE STEADY STATE

We now consider whether the equilibrium conditions, Eqs. (2.23), (2.24), and (2.25), are consistent with a steady state, that is, a situation in which the various quantities grow at constant rates. We show first that the steady-state growth rates of $\hat{k}$ and $\hat{c}$ must be zero, just as in the Solow-Swan model of Chapter 1.

Let $(\gamma_{\hat{k}})^*$ be the steady-state growth rate of $\hat{k}$, and $(\gamma_{\hat{c}})^*$ the steady-state growth rate of $\hat{c}$. In the steady state, Eq. (2.23) implies

$$\hat{c} = f(\hat{k}) - (x + n + \delta) \cdot \hat{k} - \hat{k} \cdot (\gamma_{\hat{k}})^*. \tag{2.26}$$

If we differentiate this condition with respect to time, then we find that

$$\dot{\hat{c}} = \dot{\hat{k}} \cdot \left\{ f'(\hat{k}) - [x + n + \delta + (\gamma_{\hat{k}})^*] \right\} \tag{2.27}$$

must hold in the steady state. The expression in the large brackets is positive from the transversality condition shown in Eq. (2.25). Therefore, $(\gamma_{\hat{k}})^*$ and $(\gamma_{\hat{c}})^*$ must be of the same sign.

If $(\gamma_{\hat{k}})^* > 0$, then $\hat{k} \to \infty$ and $f'(\hat{k}) \to 0$. Equation (2.24) then implies $(\gamma_{\hat{c}}) < 0$, an outcome that contradicts the result that $(\gamma_{\hat{k}})^*$ and $(\gamma_{\hat{c}})^*$ are of the same sign. If $(\gamma_{\hat{k}})^* < 0$, then $\hat{k} \to 0$ and $f'(\hat{k}) \to \infty$. Equation (2.24) then implies $(\gamma_{\hat{c}})^* > 0$, an outcome that again contradicts the result that $(\gamma_{\hat{k}})^*$ and $(\gamma_{\hat{c}})^*$ are of the same sign. Therefore, the only remaining possibility is $(\gamma_{\hat{k}})^* = (\gamma_{\hat{c}})^* = 0$. The result $(\gamma_{\hat{k}})^* = 0$ implies $(\gamma_{\hat{y}})^* = 0$. Thus, the variables per unit of effective labor, $\hat{k}$, $\hat{c}$, and $\hat{y}$, are constant in the steady state. This behavior implies that the per-capita variables, k, c, and y, grow in the steady state at the rate x, and the level variables, K, C, and Y, grow in the steady state at the rate $n + x$. These results on steady-state growth rates are the same as those in the Solow-Swan model, in which the saving rate was exogenous and constant.

The steady-state values for $\hat{c}$ and $\hat{k}$ are determined by setting the expressions in Eqs. (2.23) and (2.24) to zero. The solid curve in Fig. 2.1, which corresponds to $\hat{c} = f(\hat{k}) - (x + n + \delta) \cdot \hat{k}$, shows pairs of $(\hat{k}, \hat{c})$ that satisfy $\dot{\hat{k}} = 0$ in Eq. (2.23). Note that the peak in the curve occurs when $f'(\hat{k}) = \delta + x + n$, so that the interest rate, $f'(\hat{k}) - \delta$, equals the steady-state growth rate of output, $x + n$. This equality between the interest rate and the growth rate corresponds to the golden-rule level of $\hat{k}$ (as described in Chapter 1), because it leads to a maximum of $\hat{c}$ in the steady state. We denote by $\hat{k}_{gold}$ the value of $\hat{k}$ that corresponds to the golden rule.

Equation (2.24) and the condition $\dot{c}/c = 0$ imply

$$f'(\hat{k}^*) = \delta + \rho + \theta x. \tag{2.28}$$

This equation says that the steady-state interest rate, $f'(\hat{k}) - \delta$, equals the effective discount rate, $\rho + \theta x$.[14] The vertical line at $\hat{k}^*$ in Fig. 2.1 corresponds to this condition;

---

[14]The θx part of the effective discount rate picks up the effect from diminishing marginal utility of consumption due to growth of c at the rate x. See Eq. (2.8).

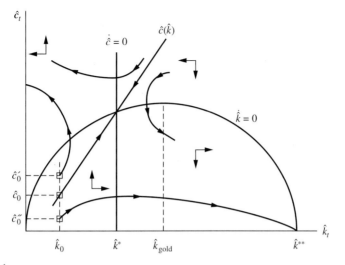

FIGURE 2.1
The phase diagram of the Ramsey model. The figure shows the transitional dynamics of the Ramsey model. The $\dot{\hat{c}} = 0$ and $\dot{\hat{k}} = 0$ loci divide the space into four regions, and the arrows show the directions of motion in each region. The model exhibits saddle-path stability. The stable arm is an upward-sloping curve that goes through the origin and the steady state. Starting from a low level of $\hat{k}$, the optimal initial $\hat{c}$ is low. Along the transition, $\hat{c}$ and $\hat{k}$ increase toward their steady-state values.

note that $\dot{\hat{c}} = 0$ holds at this value of $\hat{k}$ independently of the value of $\hat{c}$.[15] The key to the determination of $\hat{k}^*$ in Eq. (2.28) is the diminishing returns to capital, which make $f'(\hat{k}^*)$ a monotonically decreasing function of $\hat{k}^*$. Moreover, the Inada conditions— $f'(0) = \infty$ and $f'(\infty) = 0$—ensure that Eq. (2.28) holds at a unique positive value of $\hat{k}^*$.

Figure 2.1 shows the determination of the steady-state values, $(\hat{k}^*, \hat{c}^*)$, at the intersection of the vertical line with the solid curve. In particular, with $\hat{k}^*$ determined from Eq. (2.28), the value for $\hat{c}^*$ follows from setting the expression in Eq. (2.23) to 0 as

$$\hat{c}^* = f(\hat{k}^*) - (x + n + \delta) \cdot \hat{k}^*. \tag{2.29}$$

Note that $\hat{y}^* = f(\hat{k}^*)$ is the steady-state value of $\hat{y}$.

Consider the transversality condition in Eq. (2.25). Since $\hat{k}$ is constant in the steady state, this condition holds if the steady-state rate of return, $r^* = f'(\hat{k}^*) - \delta$, exceeds the steady-state growth rate, $x + n$. Equation (2.28) implies that this condition can be written as

$$\rho > n + (1 - \theta)x. \tag{2.30}$$

---

[15]Equation (2.24) indicates that $\dot{\hat{c}} = 0$ is also satisfied if $\hat{c} = 0$, that is, along the horizontal axis in Fig. 2.1.

If ρ is not high enough to satisfy Eq. (2.30), then the household's optimization problem is not well posed because infinite utility would be attained if c grew at the rate x.[16] We assume henceforth that the parameters satisfy Eq. (2.30).

In Fig. 2.1, the steady-state value, $\hat{k}^*$, was drawn to the left of $\hat{k}_{\text{gold}}$. This relation always holds if the transversality condition, Eq. (2.30), is satisfied. The steady-state value is determined from $f'(\hat{k}^*) = \delta + \rho + \theta x$,[17] whereas the golden-rule value comes from $f'(\hat{k}_{\text{gold}}) = \delta + x + n$. The inequality in Eq. (2.30) implies $\rho + \theta x > x + n$ and, hence, $f'(\hat{k}^*) > f'(\hat{k}_{\text{gold}})$. The result $\hat{k}^* > \hat{k}_{\text{gold}}$ follows from $f''(\hat{k}) < 0$.

The implication is that inefficient oversaving cannot occur in the optimizing framework, although it could arise in the Solow–Swan model with an arbitrary, constant saving rate. The reason is that if the typical infinitely-lived household were oversaving, then it would realize that it was not optimizing—that is, not satisfying the transversality condition—and would therefore shift to a path that entailed less saving. In contrast, the optimizing household does not save enough to attain the golden-rule value $\hat{k}_{\text{gold}}$. The impatience reflected in the effective discount rate, $\rho + \theta x$, makes it not worthwhile to sacrifice more of current consumption in order to reach the maximum of $\hat{c}$—that is, the golden rule value $\hat{c}_{\text{gold}}$—in the steady state.

The steady-state growth rates do not depend on parameters that describe the production function, $f(\cdot)$, or on the preference parameters ρ and θ that characterize households' attitudes about consumption and saving. These parameters do have long-run effects on levels of variables.

In Fig. 2.1, an increased willingness to save—represented by a reduction in ρ or θ—shifts the $\dot{\hat{c}} = 0$ schedule to the right and leaves the $\dot{\hat{k}} = 0$ schedule unchanged. These shifts lead accordingly to higher values of $\hat{c}^*$ and $\hat{k}^*$ and, hence, to a higher value of $\hat{y}^*$. Similarly, a proportional upward shift of the production technology or a reduction of the depreciation rate, δ, moves the $\dot{\hat{k}} = 0$ curve up and the $\dot{\hat{c}} = 0$ curve to the right. These shifts generate increases in $\hat{c}^*$, $\hat{k}^*$, and $\hat{y}^*$. An increase in x raises the effective time-preference term, $\rho + \theta x$, in Eq. (2.28) and also lowers the value of $\hat{c}^*$ that corresponds to a given $\hat{k}^*$ in Eq. (2.29). In Fig. 2.1, these changes shift the $\dot{\hat{k}} = 0$ schedule downward and the $\dot{\hat{c}} = 0$ schedule leftward and thereby reduce $\hat{c}^*$, $\hat{k}^*$, and $\hat{y}^*$. (Although $\hat{c}$ falls, utility rises because the increase in x raises the growth rate of c relative to that of $\hat{c}$.) Finally, the effect of n on $\hat{k}^*$ and $\hat{y}^*$ is nil if we hold fixed ρ. Equation (2.29) implies that $\hat{c}^*$ declines. If a higher n leads to a higher rate of time preference (for reasons discussed before), then an increase in n would reduce $\hat{k}^*$ and $\hat{y}^*$.

2.6 TRANSITIONAL DYNAMICS

2.6.1 The Phase Diagram

The Ramsey model, like the Solow–Swan model, is most interesting for its predictions about the behavior of growth rates and other variables along the transition path

---

[16]The appendix on mathematics at the end of the book considers some cases in which infinite utility can be handled.

[17]This condition is sometimes called the *modified golden rule*.

from an initial factor ratio, $\hat{k}(0)$, to the steady-state ratio, $\hat{k}^*$. Equations (2.23), (2.24), and (2.25) determine the path of $\hat{k}$ and $\hat{c}$ for a given value of $\hat{k}(0)$. The phase diagram in Fig. 2.1 shows the nature of the dynamics. (See the appendix on mathematics for a discussion of phase diagrams.)

Recall that the vertical line at $\hat{k}^*$ corresponds to the condition $\dot{\hat{c}} = 0$ in Eq. (2.24). This equation also implies that $\hat{c}$ is rising for $\hat{k} < \hat{k}^*$ (so the arrows point upward in this region) and falling for $\hat{k} > \hat{k}^*$ (where the arrows point downward).

Recall that the solid curve in Fig. 2.1 shows combinations of $\hat{k}$ and $\hat{c}$ that satisfy $\dot{\hat{k}} = 0$ in Eq. (2.23). This equation also implies that $\hat{k}$ is falling for values of $\hat{c}$ above the solid curve (so the arrows point leftward in this region) and rising for values of $\hat{c}$ below the curve (where the arrows point rightward).

The system exhibits saddle-path stability. Note, in particular, that the pattern of arrows in Fig. 2.1 is such that the economy can converge to the steady state if it starts in two of the four quadrants in which the two schedules divide the space. The saddle-path property can also be verified by linearizing the system of dynamic equations around the steady state and noting that the determinant of the characteristic matrix is negative (see Appendix 2A for details). This sign for the determinant implies that the two eigenvalues have opposite signs, an indication that the system is locally saddle-path stable.

The dynamic equilibrium follows the stable saddle path shown by the solid locus with arrows. Suppose, for example, that the initial factor ratio satisfies $\hat{k}(0) < \hat{k}^*$, as shown in Fig. 2.1. If the initial consumption ratio is $\hat{c}(0)$, as shown, then the economy follows the stable path toward the steady-state pair, $(\hat{k}^*, \hat{c}^*)$.

The two other possibilities are that the initial consumption ratio exceeds or falls short of $\hat{c}(0)$. If the ratio exceeds $\hat{c}(0)$, then the initial saving rate is too low for the economy to remain on the stable path. The trajectory eventually crosses the $\dot{\hat{k}} = 0$ locus. After that crossing, $\hat{c}$ continues to rise, $\hat{k}$ starts to decline, and the path hits the vertical axis in finite time, at which point $\hat{k} = 0$.[18] The condition $f(0) = 0$ implies $\hat{y} = 0$; therefore, $\hat{c}$ must jump downward to 0 at this point. Because this jump violates the first-order condition that underlies Eq. (2.24), these paths—in which the initial consumption ratio exceeds $\hat{c}(0)$—are not equilibria.

The final possibility is that the initial consumption ratio is below $\hat{c}(0)$. In that case, the initial saving rate is too high to remain on the saddle path, and the economy eventually crosses the $\dot{\hat{c}} = 0$ locus. After that crossing, $\hat{c}$ declines and $\hat{k}$ continues to rise. The economy converges to the point at which the $\dot{\hat{k}} = 0$ schedule intersects the horizontal axis. Note, in particular, that $\hat{k}$ rises above the golden-rule value, $\hat{k}_{\text{gold}}$, and asymptotically approaches a higher value of $\hat{k}$. Therefore, $f'(\hat{k}) - \delta$ falls below $x + n$ asymptotically, and the path violates the transversality condition given in Eq. (2.25). This violation of the transversality condition means that households are oversaving:

---

[18]We can verify from Eq. (2.23) that $\dot{\hat{k}}$ becomes more and more negative in this region. Therefore, $\hat{k}$ must reach 0 in finite time.

utility would increase if consumption were raised at earlier dates. Accordingly, paths in which the initial consumption ratio is below $\hat{c}(0)$ are not equilibria. This result leaves the stable saddle path as the only possibility.[19]

2.6.2 The Shape of the Stable Arm

The stable arm shown in Fig. 2.1 expresses the equilibrium $\hat{c}$ as a function of $\hat{k}$.[20] This relation is known in dynamic programming as a *policy function*: it relates the optimal value of a control variable, $\hat{c}$, to the state variable, $\hat{k}$. This policy function is an upward-sloping curve that goes through the origin and the steady-state position. Its exact shape depends on the parameters of the model.

Consider, as an example, the effects of the parameter θ on the shape of the stable arm. Suppose that the economy begins with $\hat{k}(0) < \hat{k}^*$, so that future values of $\hat{c}$ will exceed $\hat{c}(0)$. High values of θ indicate that households have a strong preference for smoothing consumption over time; hence, they will try hard to shift consumption from the future to the present. Therefore, when θ is high, the stable arm will lie close to the $\dot{\hat{k}} = 0$ schedule, as shown in Fig. 2.2. [21] The correspondingly low rate of investment suggests that the transition would take a long time.

Conversely, if θ is low, then households are more willing to postpone consumption in response to high rates of return. The stable arm in this case is flat and close to the horizontal axis for low values of $\hat{k}$ (see Fig. 2.2). The high levels of investment suggest that the transition is relatively quick, and as $\hat{k}$ approaches $\hat{k}^*$, households increase $\hat{c}$ sharply. It is clear from the diagram that linear approximations around the steady state will not capture these dynamics accurately.

We show in Appendix 2B for the case of a Cobb–Douglas technology, $\hat{y} = A\hat{k}^\alpha$, that $\hat{c}/\hat{k}$ is rising, constant, or falling in the transition from $\hat{k}(0) < \hat{k}^*$ depending on whether the parameter θ is smaller than, equal to, or larger than the capital share, α. It follows that the stable arm is convex, linear, or concave depending on whether θ is smaller than, equal to, or larger than α. (We argue later that $\theta > \alpha$ is the plausible case.) If $\theta = \alpha$, so that $\hat{c}/\hat{k}$ is constant during the transition, then the policy function has the simple closed-form solution, $\hat{c} = $ constant $\cdot \hat{k}$, where the constant turns out to be $(\delta + \rho)/\theta - (\delta + n)$.

---

[19]Similar results apply if the economy begins with $\hat{k}(0) > \hat{k}^*$ in Fig. 2.1. The only complication here is that, if capital is not reversible (cannot be uninstalled and consumed), then we should take account of the inequality constraint of nonnegative gross investment. This requirement, which corresponds to $\hat{c} \leq f(\hat{k})$, implies $\dot{\hat{k}} \geq -(x + n + \delta) \cdot \hat{k}$ in Eq. (2.23).

[20]The corresponding relation in the Solow–Swan model, $\hat{c} = (1 - s) \cdot f(\hat{k})$, was provided by the assumption of a constant saving rate.

[21]An increase in θ also implies a leftward shift of the $\dot{\hat{c}} = 0$ locus. For convenience, we neglect this effect in Figure 2.2.

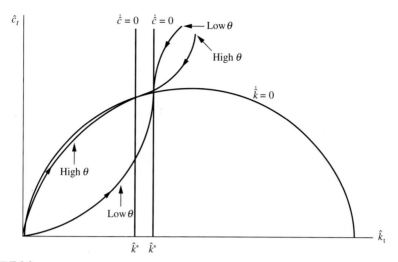

FIGURE 2.2
The slope of the saddle path. When θ is low, consumers do not mind large swings in consumption over time. Hence, they choose to consume relatively little when the capital stock is low (and the interest rate is high). The investment rate is high initially in this situation, and the economy approaches its steady state rapidly. In contrast, when θ is high, consumers are strongly motivated to smooth consumption over time. Hence, they initially devote most of their resources to consumption (the stable arm is close to the $\hat{k} = 0$ schedule) and little to investment. In this case, the economy approaches its steady state slowly.

2.6.3   Behavior of the Saving Rate

The gross saving rate, s, equals $1 - \hat{c}/f(\hat{k})$. The Solow–Swan model, discussed in Chapter 1, assumed that s was constant at an arbitrary level. In the Ramsey model with optimizing consumers, s can follow a complicated path that includes rising and falling segments as the economy develops and approaches the steady state.

Heuristically, the behavior of the saving rate is ambiguous because it involves the offsetting impacts from a substitution effect and an income effect. As $\hat{k}$ rises, the decline in $f'(\hat{k})$ lowers the rate of return, r, on saving. The reduced incentive to save—an intertemporal-substitution effect—tends to lower the saving rate as the economy develops. Second, the income per effective worker in a poor economy, $f(\hat{k})$, is far below the long-run or permanent income of this economy. Since households like to smooth consumption, they would like to consume a lot in relation to income when they are poor; that is, the saving rate would be low when $\hat{k}$ is low. As $\hat{k}$ rises, the gap between current and permanent income diminishes; hence, consumption tends to fall in relation to income, and the saving rate tends to rise. This force—an income effect—tends to raise the saving rate as the economy develops.

The transitional behavior of the saving rate depends on whether the substitution or income effect is more important. The net effect is ambiguous in general, and the path of the saving rate during the transition can be complicated. The results simplify, however, for a Cobb–Douglas production function. Appendix 2B shows for this case that, depending on parameter values, the saving rate falls monotonically, stays constant, or rises monotonically as $\hat{k}$ rises.

We show in Appendix 2B for the Cobb–Douglas case that the steady-state saving rate, s^*, is given by

$$s^* = \alpha \cdot (x + n + \delta)/(\delta + \rho + \theta x). \tag{2.31}$$

Note that the transversality condition, Eq. (2.30), implies $s^* < \alpha$ in Eq. (2.31), that is, the steady-state gross saving rate is less than the gross capital share. Appendix 2B shows that the transitional pattern for the saving rate depends on whether s^* is greater than, equal to, or less than $1/\theta$. See also Problem 2.3 at the end of the chapter for a graphical derivation of this result. If $s^* = 1/\theta$, then the saving rate is constant during the transition at the value $1/\theta$. Alternatively, if s^* is greater than (or less than) $1/\theta$, then the saving rate is always above (or below) $1/\theta$ and rises (or falls) throughout the transition, as shown in Fig. 2.3. For example, a high value of θ—which corresponds to a low willingness to substitute consumption intertemporally—makes it more likely that $s^* > 1/\theta$ will hold, in which case the saving rate will rise during the transition. This result follows because a higher θ weakens the substitution effect from the interest rate.

Although it is possible to have a constant saving rate in the optimizing framework, there is an important difference even in this case from the Solow–Swan model. The level of s in the Ramsey model is dictated by the underlying parameters and cannot be chosen arbitrarily. In particular, an arbitrary choice of s in the Solow–Swan model may generate results that are dynamically inefficient, whereas this outcome is not possible in the Ramsey model.

In a later discussion, we use the baseline values $\rho = 0.02$ per year, $\delta = 0.05$ per year, $n = 0.01$ per year, and $x = 0.02$ per year. If we also assume a conventional

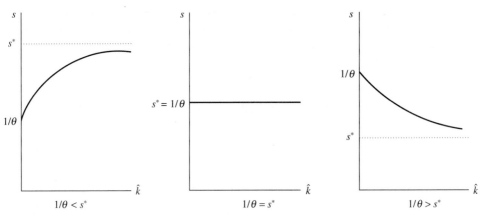

FIGURE 2.3
Behavior of the saving rate (in the Cobb–Douglas case). If the production function is Cobb–Douglas, then the transitional dynamics of the gross saving rate, s, is always monotonic. If the economy begins with a low value of $\hat{k}$, then the saving rate rises throughout if $s^* > 1/\theta$; it is constant if $s^* = 1/\theta$; and it falls throughout if $s^* < 1/\theta$. The steady-state saving rate, s^*, equals $\alpha \cdot (x + n + \delta)/(\rho + \theta x + \delta)$, which is less than α (from the transversality condition, $\rho + \theta x > x + n$).

capital share of $\alpha = 0.3$, then the value of θ that generates a constant saving rate is 17; that is, $s^* < 1/\theta$ applies and the saving rate falls—counterfactually—as the economy develops unless θ exceeds this high value.

We noted for the Solow–Swan model that the theory cannot fit the evidence about speeds of convergence unless the capital/share coefficient, α, is much larger than 0.3. Values in the neighborhood of 0.75 accord better with the empirical evidence, and these high values of α are reasonable if we take a broad view of capital to include the human components. We show in the following section that the findings about α still apply in the Ramsey growth model, which allows the saving rate to vary over time. If we assume $\alpha = 0.75$, along with the benchmark values of the other parameters, then the value of θ that generates a constant saving rate is 1.75. That is, the gross saving rate rises (or falls) as the economy develops if θ is greater (or less) than 1.75. If $\theta = 1.75$, then the gross saving rate is constant at the value 0.57. We have to interpret this high value for the gross saving rate by including in gross saving the various expenditures that expand or maintain human capital; aside from expenses for education and training, this gross saving would include portions of the outlays for food, health, and so on.

Our reading of the empirical evidence across countries (discussed in Chapter 12) is that the saving rate tends to rise to a moderate extent with per capita income during the transition. The Ramsey model can fit this pattern, as well as the observed speeds of convergence, if we combine the benchmark parameters with a value of α of around 0.75 and a value of θ somewhat above 2. The value of θ cannot be too much above 2 because then the steady-state saving rate, s^*, shown in Eq. (2.31) becomes too low. For example, the value $\theta = 10$ implies $s^* = 0.22$, which is too low for a broad concept that includes gross saving in the form of human capital.[22]

2.6.4 The Paths of the Capital Stock and Output

The stable arm shown in Fig. 2.1 shows that, if $\hat{k}(0) < \hat{k}^*$, then $\hat{k}$ and $\hat{c}$ rise monotonically from their starting values toward their steady-state values. The rising path of $\hat{k}$ implies that the rate of return, r, declines monotonically from its initial value, $f'[\hat{k}(0)] - \delta$, to its steady-state value, $\rho + \theta x$. Equation (2.24) and the path of decreasing r imply that the growth rate of per capita consumption, $\gamma_c \equiv \dot{c}/c$, falls monotonically. That is, the lower $\hat{k}(0)$ and, hence, $\hat{y}(0)$, the higher the initial value of γ_c.

We would also like to relate the initial per capita growth rates of capital and output, γ_k and γ_y, to the starting ratio, $\hat{k}(0)$. In Chapter 1, we referred to the negative

---

[22]For the United States, the ratio of real gross investment to real GDP averaged 0.21 from 1960 to 1990 (using figures from the *Citibase* data bank). But this concept of investment includes only purchases of equipment and structures by businesses and government plus purchases of residences by households. If we add the purchases of consumer durables by households to investment, then the ratio of gross investment to GDP averaged 0.29. An allowance for investment in human capital would make the ratio substantially greater.

relations between γ_k and $\hat{k}(0)$ and between γ_y and $\hat{y}(0)$ as convergence effects. We show in Appendix 2C, using the consumption function from Eqs. (2.14) and (2.15), that $\gamma_{\hat{k}}$ and, hence, γ_k decline monotonically as the economy develops and approaches the steady state. In other words, although the saving rate may rise during the transition, it cannot rise enough to eliminate the inverse relation between γ_k and $\hat{k}$. Thus, the endogenous determination of the saving rate does not eliminate the convergence property for $\hat{k}$.

We can take logs and derivatives of the production function in Eq. (2.17) to derive the growth rate of output per effective worker:

$$\gamma_{\hat{y}} \equiv \dot{\hat{y}}/\hat{y} = [\hat{k} \cdot f'(\hat{k})/f(\hat{k})] \cdot (\dot{\hat{k}}/\hat{k}), \tag{2.32}$$

that is, the growth rate of $\hat{k}$ is multiplied by the share of gross capital income in gross product. For a Cobb–Douglas production function, the share of capital income equals the constant α. Therefore, the properties of $\gamma_{\hat{k}}$ carry over immediately to those of $\gamma_{\hat{y}}$. This result applies more generally than in the Cobb–Douglas case unless the share of capital income rises fast enough as an economy develops to more than offset the fall in $\gamma_{\hat{k}}$.

2.6.5   Speeds of Convergence

LOG-LINEAR APPROXIMATIONS AROUND THE STEADY STATE. We want now to provide a quantitative assessment of the speed of convergence in the Ramsey model. We begin with a log-linearized version of the dynamic system for $\hat{k}$ and $\hat{c}$, Eqs. (2.23) and (2.24). This approach is an extension of the method that we used in Chapter 1 for the Solow–Swan model; the only difference here is that we have to deal with a two-variable system instead of a one-variable system. The advantage of this method is that it provides a closed-form solution for the convergence coefficient. The disadvantage is that it applies only as an approximation in the neighborhood of the steady state.

Appendix 2A examines a log-linearized version of Eqs. (2.23) and (2.24) when expanded around the steady-state position. The results can be written as

$$\log[\hat{y}(t)] = e^{-\beta t} \cdot \log[\hat{y}(0)] + (1 - e^{-\beta t}) \cdot \log(\hat{y}^*), \tag{2.33}$$

where $\beta > 0$. Thus, for any $t \geq 0$, $\log[\hat{y}(t)]$ is a weighted average of the initial and steady-state values, $\log[\hat{y}(0)]$ and $\log(\hat{y}^*)$, with the weight on the initial value declining exponentially at the rate β. The speed of convergence, β, depends on the parameters of technology and preferences. For the case of a Cobb–Douglas technology, the formula for the convergence coefficient (which comes from the log-linearization around the steady-state position) is

$$2\beta = \left\{ \zeta^2 + 4 \cdot \left(\frac{1-\alpha}{\theta}\right) \cdot (\rho + \delta + \theta x) \cdot \left[\frac{\rho + \delta + \theta x}{\alpha} - (n + x + \delta)\right] \right\}^{1/2} - \zeta, \tag{2.34}$$

where $\zeta = \rho - n - (1 - \theta) \cdot x > 0$. We discuss below the way that the various parameters enter into this formula.

Equation (2.33) implies that the average growth rate of per capita output, y, over an interval from an initial time 0 to any future time $T \geq 0$ is given by

$$(1/T) \cdot \log[y(T)/y(0)] = x + \frac{(1 - e^{-\beta T})}{T} \cdot \log[\hat{y}^*/\hat{y}(0)]. \qquad (2.35)$$

Hold fixed, for the moment, the steady-state growth rate, x, the convergence speed, β, and the averaging interval, T. Then Eq. (2.35) says that the average per capita growth rate of output depends negatively on the ratio of $\hat{y}(0)$ to $\hat{y}^*$. Thus, as in the Solow–Swan model, the effect of the initial position, $\hat{y}(0)$, is conditioned on the steady-state position, $\hat{y}^*$. In other words, the Ramsey model also predicts conditional rather than absolute convergence.

The coefficient that relates the growth rate of y to $\log[\hat{y}^*/\hat{y}(0)]$ in Eq. (2.35), $(1 - e^{-\beta T})/T$, declines with T for given β. If $\hat{y}(0) < \hat{y}^*$, so that growth rates decline over time, then an increase in T means that more of the lower future growth rates are averaged with the higher near-term growth rates. Therefore, the average growth rate, which enters into Eq. (2.35), falls as T rises. As $T \to \infty$, the steady-state growth rate, x, dominates the average; hence, the coefficient, $(1 - e^{-\beta T})/T$, approaches 0, and the average growth rate of y in Eq. (2.35) tends to x.

For a given T, a higher β implies a higher coefficient, $(1 - e^{-\beta T})/T$. (As $T \to 0$, the coefficient approaches β.) Equation (2.34) expresses the dependence of β on the underlying parameters. Consider first the case of the Solow–Swan model in which the saving rate is constant. As noted before, this situation applies if the steady-state saving rate, s^*, shown in Eq. (2.31) equals $1/\theta$ or, equivalently, if the combination of parameters $\alpha \cdot (\delta + n) - (\delta + \rho)/\theta - x \cdot (1 - \alpha)$ equals 0.

Suppose that the parameters take on the baseline values that we used in Chapter 1: $\delta = 0.05$ per year, $n = 0.01$ per year, and $x = 0.02$ per year. We also assume $\rho = 0.02$ per year to get a reasonable value for the steady-state interest rate, $\rho + \theta x$. As mentioned in a previous section, for these benchmark parameter values, the saving rate is constant if $\alpha = 0.3$ when $\theta = 17$ and if $\alpha = 0.75$ when $\theta = 1.75$.

With a constant saving rate, the formula for the convergence speed, β, simplifies from Eq. (2.34) to the result that applied in Eq. (1.33) for the Solow–Swan model:

$$\beta = (1 - \alpha) \cdot (x + n + \delta).$$

We noted in Chapter 1 that a match with the empirical estimate for β of roughly 0.02 per year requires a value for α around 0.75; that is, in the range in which the broad nature of capital implies that diminishing returns to capital set in slowly. Lower values of $x + n + \delta$ reduce the required value of α, but plausible values leave α well above the value of around 0.3, which would apply to a narrow concept of physical capital.

In the case of a variable saving rate, Eq. (2.34) determines the full effects of the various parameters on the convergence speed. The new element concerns the tilt of the time path of the saving rate during the transition. If the saving rate falls with $\hat{k}$, then the convergence speed would be higher than otherwise, and vice versa. For example, we found before that a higher value of the intertemporal-substitution parameter, θ, makes it more likely that the saving rate would rise with $\hat{k}$. Through this mechanism, a higher θ reduces the speed of convergence, β, in Eq. (2.34).

If the rate of time preference, ρ, increases, then the level of the saving rate tends to fall (see Eq. [2.31]). The effect on the convergence speed depends, however, not on the level of the saving rate, but on the tendency for the saving rate to rise or fall as the economy develops. A higher ρ tends to tilt downward the path of the saving rate. The effective time-preference rate is $\rho + \theta \cdot \dot{c}/c$. Because $\dot{c}/c$ is inversely related to $\hat{k}$, the effect of ρ on the effective time-preference rate is proportionately less the lower is $\hat{k}$. Therefore, the saving rate tends to decrease less the lower $\hat{k}$, and, hence, the time path of the saving rate tilts downward. A higher ρ tends accordingly to raise the magnitude of β in Eq. (2.34).

It turns out with a variable saving rate that the parameters δ and x tend to raise β, just as they did in the Solow–Swan model. The overall effect from the parameter n becomes ambiguous, but tends to be small in the relevant range.[23]

The basic result, which holds with a variable or constant saving rate, is that for plausible values of the other parameters, the model requires a high value of α—in the neighborhood of 0.75—to match the empirical estimates of the speed of convergence, β. We can reduce the required value of α to 0.5–0.6 if we assume very high values of θ (in excess of 10) along with a value of δ close to 0. We argued before, however, that very high values of θ make the steady-state saving rate too low, and values of δ near 0 are unrealistic. In addition, as we show later, values of α that are much below 0.75 generate counterfactual predictions about the transitional behavior of the interest rate and the capital/output ratio. We discuss in Chapter 3 how adjustment costs for investment can slow down the rate of convergence, but this extension does not change the main conclusions.

NUMERICAL SOLUTIONS OF THE NONLINEAR SYSTEM. We now assess the convergence properties of the model with a second approach, which uses numerical methods to solve the nonlinear system of differential equations. This approach avoids the approximation errors inherent in linearization of the model and provides accurate results for a given specification of the underlying parameters. The disadvantage is the absence of a closed-form solution. We have to generate a new set of answers for each specification of parameter values.

We can use numerical methods to obtain a global solution for the nonlinear system of differential equations. In the case of a Cobb–Douglas production function, the growth rates of $\hat{k}$ and $\hat{c}$ are given from Eqs. (2.23) and (2.24) as

$$\gamma_{\hat{k}} \equiv d[\log(\hat{k})]/dt = A \cdot (\hat{k})^{\alpha-1} - (\hat{c}/\hat{k}) - (x + n + \delta), \qquad (2.36)$$

$$\gamma_{\hat{c}} \equiv d[\log(\hat{c})]/dt = (1/\theta) \cdot [\alpha A \cdot (\hat{k})^{\alpha-1} - (\delta + \rho + \theta x)]. \qquad (2.37)$$

---

[23]Equation (2.34) implies that the effects on β are unambiguously negative for α and positive for δ. Our numerical computations indicate that the effects of the other parameters are in the directions that we mentioned as long as the other parameters are restricted to a reasonable range.

If we specified the values of the parameters $(A, \alpha, x, n, \delta, \rho, \theta)$, and knew the relation between $\hat{c}$ and $\hat{k}$ along the path—that is, if we knew the policy function $\hat{c}(\hat{k})$—then standard numerical methods for solving differential equations would allow us to solve out for the entire time paths of $\hat{k}$ and $\hat{c}$. The appendix on mathematics shows how to use a procedure called the *time-elimination method* to derive the policy function numerically. (See also Mulligan and Sala-i-Martin [1991]). We assume now that we have already solved this part of the problem.

Once we know the policy function, we can determine the paths of all the variables that we care about, including the convergence coefficient, defined by $\beta = -d(\gamma_{\hat{k}})/d[\log(\hat{k})]$. (In the Cobb–Douglas case, the convergence coefficient for $\hat{y}$ is still the same as that for $\hat{k}$.) Fig. 2.4 shows the relation between β and $\hat{k}/\hat{k}^*$ when we use our benchmark parameter values ($\delta = 0.05$, $x = 0.02$, $n = 0.01$, $\rho = 0.02$), $\theta = 3$, and $\alpha = 0.3$ or 0.75.[24] For either setting of α, β is a decreasing function of $\hat{k}/\hat{k}^*$, that is, the speed of convergence slows down as the economy approaches the steady state.[25] At the steady state, where $\hat{k}/\hat{k}^* = 1$, the values of β—0.082 if $\alpha = 0.3$ and 0.015 if $\alpha = 0.75$—are those implied by Eq. (2.34) for the log-linearization around the steady state.

If $\hat{k}/\hat{k}^* < 1$, then Fig. 2.4 indicates that β exceeds the values implied by Eq. (2.34). For example, if $\hat{k}/\hat{k}^* = 0.5$, then $\beta = 0.141$ if $\alpha = 0.3$ and 0.018 if $\alpha = 0.75$. If $\hat{k}/\hat{k}^* = 0.1$, then $\beta = 0.474$ if $\alpha = 0.3$ and 0.026 if $\alpha = 0.75$. Thus, if we use our preferred high value for the capital-share coefficient, $\alpha = 0.75$, then the convergence coefficient, β, remains between 1.5 percent and 3 percent for a broad range of $\hat{k}/\hat{k}^*$. This behavior accords with the empirical evidence discussed in Chapters 11 and 12; we find there that convergence coefficients do not seem to exceed this range even for economies that are very far from their steady states. In contrast, if we assume $\alpha = 0.3$, then the model incorrectly predicts extremely high rates of convergence when $\hat{k}$ is far below $\hat{k}^*$.

Since the convergence speeds rise with the distance from the steady state, the durations of the transition are shorter than those implied by the linearized model. We can use the results on the time path of $\hat{k}$ to compute the exact time that it takes to close a specified percentage of the initial gap from $\hat{k}^*$. Panel (a) of Fig. 2.5 shows how the gap between $\hat{k}$ and $\hat{k}^*$ is eliminated over time if the economy begins with $\hat{k}/\hat{k}^* = 0.1$ and if $\alpha = 0.3$ or 0.75. As an example, if $\alpha = 0.75$, then it takes 38 years to close 50 percent of the gap, compared with 45 years from the linear approximation.

Panel (b) in Fig. 2.5 displays the level of consumption, expressed as $\hat{c}/\hat{c}^*$; panel (c) the level of output, $\hat{y}/\hat{y}^*$; and panel (d) the level of gross investment, $\hat{i}/\hat{i}^*$. Note

---

[24]For a given value of $\hat{k}/\hat{k}^*$, the parameter A does not affect β in the Cobb–Douglas case.

[25]This relation does not hold in general. In particular, β can rise with $\hat{k}/\hat{k}^*$ if θ is very small and α is very large, for example, if $\theta = 0.5$ and $\alpha = 0.95$.

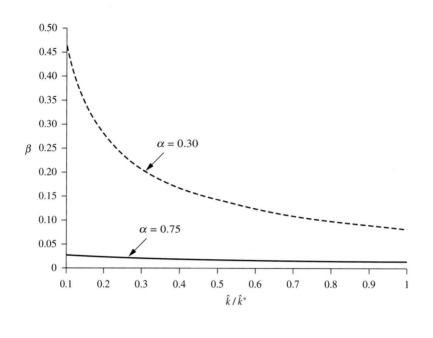

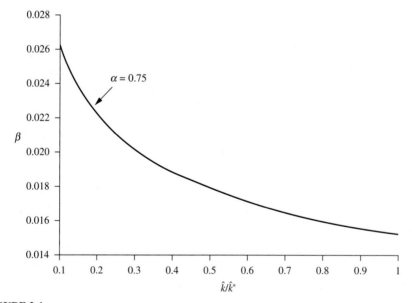

FIGURE 2.4
Numerical estimates of the speed of convergence in the Ramsey model. The exact speed of convergence (displayed on the vertical axis) is a decreasing function of the distance from the steady state, $\hat{k}/\hat{k}^*$ (shown on the horizontal axis). The analysis assumes a Cobb–Douglas production function, with results reported for two values of the capital share, $\alpha = 0.30$ and $\alpha = 0.75$. The change in the convergence speed during the transition is more pronounced for the smaller capital share. The value of the convergence speed, β, at the steady state ($\hat{k}/\hat{k}^* = 1$) is the value that we found analytically with a log-linear approximation around the steady state (Eq. [2.34]).

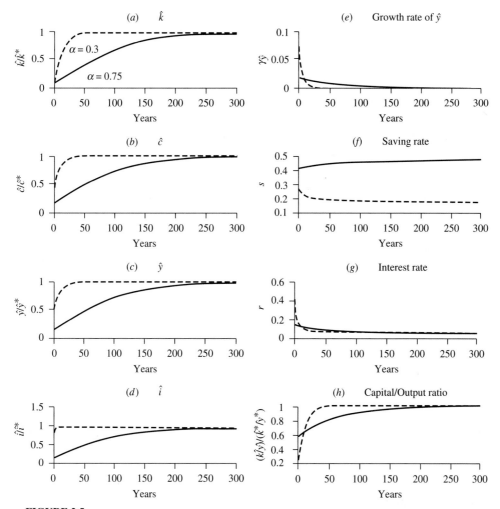

FIGURE 2.5
Numerical estimates of the dynamic paths in the Ramsey model. The eight panels display the exact dynamic paths of eight key variables: the values per unit of effective labor of the capital stock, consumption, output, and investment, the growth rate of output per effective worker, the saving rate, the interest rate, and the capital/output ratio. The first four variables and the last one are expressed as ratios to their steady-state values; hence, each variable approaches 1 asymptotically. The analysis assumes a Cobb–Douglas production technology, where the dotted line in each panel corresponds to $\alpha = 0.30$ and the solid line to $\alpha = 0.75$. The other parameters are reported in the text. The initial capital per effective worker is assumed in each case to be one-tenth of its steady-state value.

that for $\alpha = 0.75$, the paths of $\hat{c}/\hat{c}^*$ and $\hat{y}/\hat{y}^*$ are similar, because the gross saving rate and, hence, $\hat{c}/\hat{y}$ change only by small amounts in this case (see below).

Panel (*e*) shows the growth rate of $\hat{y}$. For $\alpha = 0.3$, the model has the counterfactual implication that the initial value of $\gamma_{\hat{y}}$ (corresponding to $\hat{k}/\hat{k}^* = 0.1$) is implausibly large, about 15 percent per year, which means that γ_y is about 17 percent per year. This kind of result led King and Rebelo (1993) to dismiss the transitional behavior of the Ramsey model as a reasonable approximation to actual growth experiences. We see, however, that for $\alpha = 0.75$, the model predicts more reasonably that $\gamma_{\hat{y}}$ would begin at about 3.5 percent per year, so that γ_y would be about 5.5 percent per year.

Panel (f) shows the gross saving rate, $s(t)$. We know from our previous analytical results for the Cobb–Douglas case that $s(t)$ falls monotonically when $\alpha = 0.3$ (given the assumed values of the other parameters) and rises monotonically when $\alpha = 0.75$. For $\alpha = 0.3$, the results are counterfactual in that the model predicts a fall in $s(t)$ as the economy develops from 0.28 at $\hat{k}/\hat{k}^* = 0.1$ to 0.22 at $\hat{k}/\hat{k}^* = 0.5$ and 0.18 at $\hat{k}/\hat{k}^* = 1$. The predicted levels of the saving rate are also unrealistically low for a broad concept of capital. In contrast, for $\alpha = 0.75$, the moderate rise in the saving rate as the economy develops fits well with the data. The saving rate rises in this case from 0.41 at $\hat{k}/\hat{k}^* = 0.1$ to 0.44 at $\hat{k}/\hat{k}^* = 0.5$ and 0.46 at $\hat{k}/\hat{k}^* = 1$. The predicted level of the saving rate is also reasonable if we take a broad view of capital.

Panel (g) displays the behavior of the interest rate, r. Note that the steady-state interest rate is $r^* = \rho + \theta x = 0.08$, and the corresponding marginal product is $f'(\hat{k}^*) = r^* + \delta = 0.13$. If we consider the initial position $\hat{k}(0)/\hat{k}^* = 0.1$, as in Fig. 2.5, then the Cobb–Douglas production function implies

$$f'[\hat{k}(0)]/f'(\hat{k}^*) = [\hat{k}(0)/\hat{k}^*]^{\alpha-1} = (10)^{1-\alpha}.$$

Hence, for $\alpha = 0.3$, we get $f'[\hat{k}(0)] = 5 \cdot f'(\hat{k}^*) = 0.55$. In other words, with a capital-share coefficient of around 0.3, the initial interest rate (at $\hat{k}[0]/\hat{k}^* = 0.1$) would take on the unrealistically high value of 60 percent. This counterfactual prediction about interest rates was another consideration that caused King and Rebelo (1993) to reject the transitional dynamics of the Ramsey model. However, if we assume our preferred capital-share coefficient, $\alpha = 0.75$, then we get $f'[\hat{k}(0)] = 1.8 \cdot f'(\hat{k}^*) = 0.23$, so that $r(0)$ takes on the more reasonable value of 18 percent.

The final panel in Fig. 2.5 shows the behavior of the capital/output ratio, $(\hat{k}/\hat{y})$, expressed in relation to $(\hat{k}^*/\hat{y}^*)$. Kaldor (1963) argues that this ratio changes relatively little during the course of economic development, and Maddison (1982, Chapter 3) supports this view. These observations pertain, however, to a narrow concept of physical capital, whereas our model takes a broad perspective to include human capital. The cross-country data show that places with higher real per capita GDP tend to have much larger ratios of human capital in the form of educational attainment to physical capital (see Judson [1993, Table 4]). This observation suggests that the ratio of human to physical capital would tend to rise during the transition to higher levels of real per capita GDP (see Chapter 5 for a theoretical discussion of this behavior). If the ratio of physical capital to output remains relatively stable, then the capital/output ratio for a broad measure of capital would increase during the transition.

With a Cobb–Douglas production function, the capital/output ratio is $\hat{k}/\hat{y} = (1/A) \cdot (\hat{k})^{(1-\alpha)}$. If $\alpha = 0.3$, then an increase in $\hat{k}$ by a factor of 10 would raise $\hat{k}/\hat{y}$ by a factor of 5, a shift that departs significantly from the observed variations in $\hat{k}/\hat{y}$ over long periods of economic development. In contrast, if $\alpha = 0.75$, then an increase in

$\hat{k}$ by a factor of 10 would raise $\hat{k}/\hat{y}$ by only a factor of 1.8. For a broad concept of capital, this behavior appears reasonable.

The main lesson from the study of the time paths in Fig. 2.5 is that the transitional dynamics of the Ramsey model with a conventional capital-share coefficient, α, of around 0.3 does not provide a good description of various aspects of economic development. For an economy that starts far below its steady-state position, the inaccurate predictions include an excessive speed of convergence, unrealistically high growth and interest rates, a rapidly declining gross saving rate, and large increases over time in the capital/output ratio. All of these shortcomings are eliminated if we take a broad view of capital and assume a correspondingly high capital-share coefficient, α, of around 0.75. This value of α, together with plausible values of the model's other parameters, generate predictions that accord well with the growth experiences that we study in Chapters 11 and 12.

APPENDIX 2A
LOG-LINEARIZATION OF THE RAMSEY MODEL

The system of differential equations that characterizes the Ramsey model is given from Eqs. (2.23) and (2.24) by

$$\dot{\hat{k}} = f(\hat{k}) - \hat{c} - (x + n + \delta) \cdot \hat{k},$$
$$\dot{\hat{c}}/\hat{c} = \dot{c}/c - x = (1/\theta) \cdot [f'(\hat{k}) - \delta - \rho - \theta x]. \tag{2A.1}$$

We now log-linearize this system for the case in which the production function is Cobb–Douglas, $f(\hat{k}) = A \cdot \hat{k}^\alpha$.

Start by rewriting the system from Eq. (2A.1) in terms of the logs of $\hat{c}$ and $\hat{k}$:

$$d[\log(\hat{k})]/dt = A \cdot e^{-(1-\alpha)\cdot\log(\hat{k})} - e^{\log(\hat{c}/\hat{k})} - (x + n + \delta),$$
$$d[\log(\hat{c})]/dt = (1/\theta) \cdot [\alpha A \cdot e^{-(1-\alpha)\cdot\log(\hat{k})} - (\rho + \theta x + \delta)]. \tag{2A.2}$$

In the steady state, where $d[\log(\hat{k})]/dt = d[\log(\hat{c})]/dt = 0$, we have

$$A \cdot e^{-(1-\alpha)\cdot\log(\hat{k}^*)} - e^{\log(\hat{c}^*/\hat{k}^*)} = (x + n + \delta),$$
$$\alpha A \cdot e^{-(1-\alpha)\cdot\log(\hat{k}^*)} = (\rho + \theta x + \delta). \tag{2A.3}$$

We take a first-order Taylor expansion of Eq. (2A.2) around the steady-state values determined by Eq. (2A.3):

$$\begin{bmatrix} d[\log(\hat{k})]/dt \\ d[\log(\hat{c})]/dt \end{bmatrix} =$$

$$\begin{bmatrix} \zeta & x + n + \delta - (\rho + \theta x + \delta)/\alpha \\ -(1-\alpha) \cdot (\rho + \theta x + \delta)/\theta & 0 \end{bmatrix} \cdot \begin{bmatrix} \log(\hat{k}/\hat{k}^*) \\ \log(\hat{c}/\hat{c}^*) \end{bmatrix}, \tag{2A.4}$$

where $\zeta \equiv \rho - n - (1 - \theta) \cdot x$. The determinant of the characteristic matrix equals

$$-[(\rho + \theta x + \delta)/\alpha - (x + n + \delta)] \cdot (\rho + \theta x + \delta) \cdot (1 - \alpha)/\theta.$$

Since $\rho + \theta x > x + n$ (from the transversality condition in Eq. [2.30]) and $\alpha < 1$, the determinant is negative. This condition implies that the two eigenvalues of the system have opposite signs, a result that implies saddle-path stability. (See the discussion in the mathematics appendix at the end of the book.)

To compute the eigenvalues, denoted by ϵ, we use the condition

$$\det \begin{bmatrix} \zeta - \epsilon & x + n + \delta - (\rho + \theta x + \delta)/\alpha \\ -(1 - \alpha)(\rho + \theta x + \delta)/\theta & \end{bmatrix} = 0.$$

(2A.5)

This condition corresponds to a quadratic equation in ϵ :

$$\epsilon^2 - \zeta \cdot \epsilon - [(\rho + \theta x + \delta)/\alpha - (x + n + \delta)] \cdot [(\rho + \theta x + \delta) \cdot (1 - \alpha)/\theta] = 0.$$

(2A.6)

This equation has two solutions:

$$2\epsilon = \zeta \pm \left[\zeta^2 + 4 \cdot \left(\frac{1 - \alpha}{\theta} \right) \cdot (\rho + \theta x + \delta) \cdot [(\rho + \theta x + \delta)/\alpha - (x + n + \delta)] \right]^{1/2},$$

(2A.7)

where ϵ_1, the root with the positive sign, is positive, and ϵ_2, the root with the negative sign, is negative. Note that ϵ_2 corresponds to $-\beta$ in Eq. (2.34).

The log-linearized solution for $\log(\hat{k})$ takes the form

$$\log[\hat{k}(t)] = \log(\hat{k}^*) + \psi_1 \cdot e^{\epsilon_1 t} + \psi_2 \cdot e^{\epsilon_2 t},$$

(2A.8)

where ψ_1 and ψ_2 are arbitrary constants of integration. Since $\epsilon_1 > 0$, $\psi_1 = 0$ must hold for $\log[\hat{k}(t)]$ to tend asymptotically to $\log(\hat{k}^*)$. ($\psi_1 > 0$ violates the transversality condition, and $\psi_1 < 0$ leads to $\hat{k} \to 0$, which corresponds to cases in which the system hits the vertical axis in Figure 2.1.) The other constant, ψ_2, is determined from the initial condition:

$$\psi_2 = \log[\hat{k}(0)] - \log(\hat{k}^*).$$

(2A.9)

If we substitute $\psi_1 = 0$, the value of ψ_2 from Eq. (2A.9), and $\epsilon_2 = -\beta$ into Eq. (2A.8), then we get the time path for $\log[\hat{k}(t)]$:

$$\log[\hat{k}(t)] = (1 - e^{-\beta t}) \cdot \log(\hat{k}^*) + e^{-\beta t} \cdot \log[\hat{k}(0)].$$

(2A.10)

Since $\log[\hat{y}(t)] = \log(A) + \alpha \cdot \log[\hat{k}(t)]$, the time path for $\log[\hat{y}(t)]$ is given by

$$\log[\hat{y}(t)] = (1 - e^{-\beta t}) \cdot \log(\hat{y}^*) + e^{-\beta t} \cdot \log[\hat{y}(0)],$$

(2A.11)

which corresponds to Eq. (2.33).

APPENDIX 2B
BEHAVIOR OF THE SAVING RATE

We again consider the transition in which $\hat{k}$ and $\hat{c}$ are rising over time. We assume here a Cobb–Douglas production function, so that $f(\hat{k}) = A\hat{k}^{\alpha}$. The gross saving rate, s, equals $1 - \hat{c}/f(\hat{k})$. In the steady state, $\dot{\hat{k}}$ in Eq. (2.23) and $\dot{\hat{c}}$ in Eq. (2.24) are each equal to 0. If we use these conditions together with $f(\hat{k})/\hat{k} = f'(\hat{k})/\alpha$, which holds in the Cobb–Douglas case, then we find that the steady-state saving rate is

$$s^* = \alpha \cdot (x + n + \delta)/(\rho + \theta x + \delta). \tag{2B.1}$$

The transversality condition in Eq. (2.30) implies $\rho + \theta x > x + n$ and, therefore, $s^* < \alpha$.

Since $s = 1 - \hat{c}/f(\hat{k})$, s moves in the direction opposite to the consumption ratio, $\hat{c}/f(\hat{k})$. Define $z \equiv \hat{c}/f(\hat{k})$ and differentiate the ratio to get

$$\gamma_z \equiv \dot{z}/z = \dot{\hat{c}}/\hat{c} - \frac{f'(\hat{k}) \cdot \dot{\hat{k}}}{f(\hat{k})} = \dot{\hat{c}}/\hat{c} - \alpha \cdot (\dot{\hat{k}}/\hat{k}), \tag{2B.2}$$

where the last term on the right follows in the Cobb–Douglas case. Substitution from Eqs. (2.23) and (2.24) into Eq. (2B.2) leads to

$$\gamma_z = f'(\hat{k}) \cdot [z(t) - (\theta - 1)/\theta] + (\delta + \rho + \theta x) \cdot (s^* - 1/\theta), \tag{2B.3}$$

where we used the condition, $f(\hat{k})/\hat{k} = f'(\hat{k})/\alpha$, which holds in the Cobb–Douglas case.

The behavior of z depends on whether s^* is greater than, equal to, or less than $1/\theta$. Suppose first that $s^* = 1/\theta$. Then $z(t) = (\theta - 1)/\theta$ is consistent with $\gamma_z = 0$ in Eq. (2B.3). In contrast, $z(t) > (\theta - 1)/\theta$ for some t would imply $\gamma_z > 0$ for all t, a result that is inconsistent with z approaching its steady-state value. Similarly, $z(t) < (\theta - 1)/\theta$ can be ruled out because it implies $\gamma_z < 0$ for all t. Therefore, if $s^* = 1/\theta$, then z is constant at the value $(\theta - 1)/\theta$, and, hence, the saving rate, s, equals the constant $1/\theta$. By analogous reasoning, we find that $s^* > 1/\theta$ implies $z(t) < (\theta - 1)/\theta$ for all t, whereas $s^* < 1/\theta$ implies $z(t) > (\theta - 1)/\theta$ for all t.

Differentiation of Eq. (2B.3) with respect to time implies

$$\dot{\gamma}_z = f''(\hat{k}) \cdot \dot{\hat{k}} \cdot [z(t) - (\theta - 1)/\theta] + f'(\hat{k}) \cdot \gamma_z \cdot z(t). \tag{2B.4}$$

Suppose now that $s^* > 1/\theta$, so that $z(t) < (\theta - 1)/\theta$ holds for all t. Then $\gamma_z > 0$ for some t would imply $\dot{\gamma}_z > 0$ in Eq. (2B.4) (because $f''(\hat{k}) < 0$, $f'(\hat{k}) > 0$, and $\dot{\hat{k}} > 0$). Therefore, $\gamma_z > 0$ would apply for all t, a result that is inconsistent with the economy's approaching a steady state. It follows if $s^* > 1/\theta$ that $\gamma_z < 0$, and, hence, $\dot{s} > 0$. By an analogous argument, $\gamma_z > 0$ and $\dot{s} < 0$ must hold if $s^* < 1/\theta$.

The results can be summarized as follows:

$$s^* = 1/\theta \text{ implies } s(t) = 1/\theta, \text{ a constant;}$$

$$s^* > 1/\theta \text{ implies } s(t) > 1/\theta \text{ and } \dot{s}(t) > 0; \text{ and}$$

$$s^* < 1/\theta \text{ implies } s(t) < 1/\theta \text{ and } \dot{s}(t) < 0.$$

These results are graphed in Fig. 2.3.

If we use the formula for s^* from Eq. (2B.1), then we find that $s^* \geq 1/\theta$ requires $\theta \geq (\rho + \theta x + \delta)/[\alpha \cdot (x + n + \delta)] > 1/\alpha$. Therefore, if $\theta \leq 1/\alpha$, then the parameters must be in the range in which $\dot{s} < 0$ applies throughout. In other words, if $\theta \leq 1/\alpha$, then the intertemporal-substitution effect is strong enough to ensure that the saving rate falls during the transition. However, for our preferred value of α in the neighborhood of 0.75, this inequality requires $\theta \leq 1.33$ and is unlikely to hold.

We can analyze the behavior of the consumption/capital ratio, $\hat{c}/\hat{k}$, in a similar way. The results are:

$$\theta = \alpha \text{ implies } \hat{c}/\hat{k} = (\delta + \rho)/\theta - (\delta + n), \text{ a constant;}$$

$$\theta < \alpha \text{ implies } \hat{c}/\hat{k} < (\delta + \rho)/\theta - (\delta + n) \text{ and } \hat{c}/\hat{k} \text{ rising over time; and}$$

$$\theta > \alpha \text{ implies } \hat{c}/\hat{k} > (\delta + \rho)/\theta - (\delta + n) \text{ and } \hat{c}/\hat{k} \text{ falling over time.}$$

APPENDIX 2C
PROOF THAT $\gamma_{\hat{k}}$ DECLINES MONOTONICALLY IF THE ECONOMY STARTS FROM $\hat{k}(0) < \hat{k}^*$

We need first to prove the following: $\hat{c}(0)$ declines if $r(v)$ increases over some interval for any $v \geq 0$. [26] Equations (2.14) and (2.15) imply

$$\hat{c}(0) = \frac{\hat{k}(0) + \int_0^\infty \hat{w}(t)e^{-[\bar{r}(t) - n - x]t}dt}{\int_0^\infty e^{[\bar{r}(t) \cdot (1-\theta)/\theta - \rho/\theta + n]t}dt}, \tag{2C.1}$$

where $\bar{r}(t)$ is the average interest rate between times 0 and t, as defined in Eq. (2.12). Higher values of $r(v)$ for any $0 \leq v \leq t$ raise $\bar{r}(t)$ and thereby reduce the numerator in Eq. (2C.1). Higher values of $r(v)$ raise the denominator if $\theta \leq 1$; therefore, the result follows at once if $\theta \leq 1$. Assume now that $\theta > 1$, so that the denominator decreases with an increase in $r(v)$. We know that $r(v) \cdot (1 - \theta)/\theta - \rho/\theta + n < 0$ if

---

[26] We are grateful to Olivier Blanchard for his help with this part of the proof.

$\theta > 1$ because $r(v)$ exceeds $\rho + \theta x$, the steady-state interest rate, which exceeds $x + n$ from the transversality condition. Therefore, the denominator in Eq. (2C.1) becomes proportionately more sensitive to $r(v)$ (in the negative direction) the larger the value of θ. Accordingly, if we prove the result for $\theta \to \infty$, then the result holds for all $\theta > 0$. Using $\theta \to \infty$, Eq. (2C.1) simplifies to

$$\hat{c}(0) = \frac{\hat{k}(0) + \int_0^\infty \hat{w}(t)e^{-[\bar{r}(t)-x-n]t}\, dt}{\int_0^\infty e^{-[\bar{r}(t)-n]t}\, dt}. \qquad (2C.2)$$

Equation (2C.2) can be rewritten as

$$\hat{c}(0) = \frac{\int_0^\infty \psi(t)e^{-[\bar{r}(t)-n-x]t}\, dt}{\int_0^\infty \phi(t)e^{-[\bar{r}(t)-n-x]t}\, dt}, \qquad (2C.3)$$

where $\psi(t) = \hat{k}(0)\cdot[r(t)-n-x]+\hat{w}(t)$ and $\phi(t) = e^{-xt}$. $\dot{\phi} < 0$ follows immediately and $\dot{\psi} > 0$ can be shown using the conditions $r(t) = f'[\hat{k}(t)] - \delta$, $\hat{w}(t) = f[\hat{k}(t)] - \hat{k}(t)\cdot f'[\hat{k}(t)]$, $\hat{k}(t) > \hat{k}(0)$, and $\dot{\hat{k}} > 0$. Therefore, an increase in $r(v)$ for $0 \le v \le t$, which raises $\bar{r}(t)$, has a proportionately larger negative effect on the numerator of Eq. (2C.3) than on the denominator. It follows that the net effect of an increase in $r(v)$ on $\hat{c}(0)$ is negative, the result that we need.

We can use this result to get a lower bound for $\hat{c}(0)$. Since $r(0) > \bar{r}(t)$, if we substitute $r(0)$ for $\bar{r}(t)$ and $\hat{w}(0)$ for $\hat{w}(t)$ in Eq. (2C.1), then $\hat{c}(0)$ must go down. Therefore[27]

$$\hat{c}(0)/\hat{k}(0) > [r(0) \cdot (1 - \theta)/\theta + \rho/\theta - n] \cdot \left[1 + \frac{\hat{w}(0)}{\hat{k} \cdot [r(0) - n - x]}\right]. \qquad (2C.4)$$

We shall use this inequality below.

The growth rate of $\hat{k}$ is given from Eq. (2.23) as

$$\gamma_{\hat{k}} = f(\hat{k})/\hat{k} - \hat{c}/\hat{k} - (n + x + \delta), \qquad (2C.5)$$

where we now omit the time subscripts. Differentiation of Eq. (2C.5) with respect to time yields

$$\dot{\gamma}_{\hat{k}} = -(\hat{w}/\hat{k}) \cdot \gamma_{\hat{k}} - d(\hat{c}/\hat{k})/dt,$$

where we used the condition $\hat{w} = f(\hat{k}) - \hat{k} \cdot f'(\hat{k})$. We want to show that $\dot{\gamma}_{\hat{k}} < 0$ holds in the transition during which $\hat{k}$ and $\hat{c}$ are rising. The formulas for $\hat{c}$ in Eq. (2.24) and $\hat{k}$ in Eq. (2.23) can be used to get

$$\dot{\gamma}_{\hat{k}} = -(\hat{w}/\hat{k}) \cdot \gamma_{\hat{k}} + (\hat{c}/\hat{k}) \cdot [\hat{w}/\hat{k} + [f'(\hat{k}) - \delta] \cdot (\theta - 1)/\theta + \rho/\theta - n - \hat{c}/\hat{k}].$$

$$(2C.6)$$

---

[27]The result follows from integration of the right-hand side of Eq. (2C.1) if $[r(0)\cdot(1-\theta)/\theta + \rho/\theta - n] > 0$. If this expression is nonpositive, then the inequality in Eq. (2C.4) holds trivially.

Hence, if $\hat{c}/\hat{k} \geq \hat{w}/\hat{k} + [f'(\hat{k}) - \delta] \cdot (\theta - 1)/\theta + \rho/\theta - n$, then $\dot{\gamma}_{\hat{k}} < 0$ follows from $\gamma_{\hat{k}} > 0$, Q.E.D. Accordingly, we now assume

$$\hat{c}/\hat{k} < \hat{w}/\hat{k} + [f'(\hat{k}) - \delta] \cdot (\theta - 1)/\theta + \rho/\theta - n. \tag{2C.7}$$

If we replace $\hat{c}/\hat{k}$ to the left of the brackets in Eq. (2C.6) by the right-hand side of the inequality in Eq. (2C.7), use the formula for $\gamma_{\hat{k}}$ from Eq. (2C.5), and replace $f(\hat{k})/\hat{k}$ by $\hat{w}/\hat{k} + f'(\hat{k})$, then we eventually get

$$\dot{\gamma}_{\hat{k}} < -(\hat{w}/\hat{k}) \cdot [f'(\hat{k}) - \delta - \rho - \theta x]/\theta + \left[\rho/\theta - n + [f'(\hat{k}) - \delta] \cdot (\theta - 1)/\theta \right]^2$$
$$+ \left[\rho/\theta - n + [f'(\hat{k}) - \delta] \cdot (\theta - 1)/\theta \right] \cdot (\hat{w} - \hat{c})/\hat{k}. \tag{2C.8}$$

If $\rho/\theta - n + [f'(\hat{k}) - \delta] \cdot (\theta - 1)/\theta \leq 0$, then we can use the inequality in Eq. (2C.7) to show $\dot{\gamma}_{\hat{k}} < 0$, Q.E.D. Therefore, we now assume

$$\rho/\theta - n + [f'(\hat{k}) - \delta] \cdot (\theta - 1)/\theta > 0. \tag{2C.9}$$

Given the inequality in Eq. (2C.9), we can use the lower bound for $\hat{c}/\hat{k}$ from Eq. (2C.4) in Eq. (2C.8) to get, after some manipulation,

$$\dot{\gamma}_{\hat{k}} < -\frac{(\hat{w}/\hat{k}) \cdot [f'(\hat{k}) - \delta - \rho - \theta x]^2}{[f'(\hat{k}) - \delta - n - x] \cdot \theta^2} < 0, \tag{2C.10}$$

where we used the condition $r = f'(\hat{k}) - \delta$. The expressions in parentheses in Eq. (2C.10) are each positive because $f'(\hat{k}) - \delta$ exceeds $\rho + \theta x$, the steady-state interest rate, which exceeds $n + x$ from the transversality condition. Therefore, $\dot{\gamma}_{\hat{k}} < 0$ follows, Q.E.D.

PROBLEMS

2.1 *Preclusion of Borrowing in the Ramsey Model.* Consider the household optimization problem in the Ramsey model. How do the results change if consumers are not allowed to borrow, only to save?

2.2 *Irreversibility of Investment in the Ramsey Model.* Suppose that the economy begins with $\hat{k}(0) > \hat{k}^*$. How does the transition path differ depending on whether capital is reversible (convertible back into consumables on a one-to-one basis) or irreversible?

2.3 *The Saving Rate in the Ramsey Model: A Graphical Approach.* Consider the two differential equations that characterize the dynamics of the Ramsey model, Eqs. (2.23) and (2.24). Assume that the production function is Cobb–Douglas, $\hat{y} = A\hat{k}^\alpha$.
   (a) Write down a differential equation for the growth rate of c/y. (Hint: use the equality $c/k = (c/y) \cdot A\hat{k}^{\alpha-1}$.)
   (b) Construct a phase diagram in $(c/y, \hat{k})$ space. What is the slope of the $\dot{\hat{k}} = 0$ schedule?
   (c) Why is the slope of the $(\dot{c}/y) = 0$ locus ambiguous? Under what conditions is this locus horizontal? What is the value of c/y for which this condition holds? What is the associated saving rate? When the $(\dot{c}/y) = 0$ locus is horizontal, what is the behavior of the saving rate along the transition from a low value of $\hat{k}(0)$?

(*d*) Under what conditions is the $(\dot{c}/y) = 0$ locus downward sloping? In this case, what is the behavior of c/y—and, hence, the saving rate—along the transition from a low value of $\hat{k}(0)$?

(*e*) Under what conditions is the $(\dot{c}/y) = 0$ locus upward sloping? What then is the behavior of c/y and the saving rate during the transition from a low value of $\hat{k}(0)$?

(*f*) Relate these findings to those discussed in Appendix 5B of this chapter.

2.4 *Exponential Utility.* Assume that infinite-horizon households maximize a utility function of the form of Eq. (2.1), where $u(c)$ is now given by the exponential form,

$$u(c) = -(1/\theta) \cdot e^{-\theta c}, \tag{1}$$

where $\theta > 0$. The behavior of firms is the same as in the Ramsey model, with zero technological progress.

(*a*) Relate θ to the concavity of the utility function and to the desire to smooth consumption over time. Compute the intertemporal elasticity of substitution. How does it relate to the level of per capita consumption, c?

(*b*) Find the first-order conditions for a representative household with preferences given by Eq. (1).

(*c*) Combine the first-order conditions for the representative household with those of firms to describe the behavior of $\hat{c}$ and $\hat{k}$ over time. (Assume that $\hat{k}(0)$ is below its steady-state value.)

(*d*) How does the transition depend on the parameter θ? Compare this result with the one in the model discussed in the text.

2.5 *End-of-the-World Model.* Suppose that the Ramsey model is the same as the one described in the text, except that everyone knows that the world will end deterministically at time $T > 0$.

(*a*) How does this modification affect the transition equations for $\hat{k}$ and $\hat{c}$ in Eqs. (2.23) and (2.24)?

(*b*) How does the modification affect the transversality condition?

(*c*) Use Fig. 2.1 to describe the new transition path for the economy.

(*d*) As T gets larger, how does the new transition path relate to the one shown in Fig. 2.1? What happens as T approaches infinity?

2.6 *Stone–Geary Preferences.* Assume that the usual conditions of the Ramsey model hold, except that the representative household's instantaneous utility function is modified from Eq. (2.9) to the Stone–Geary form:

$$u(c) = \frac{(c - \bar{c})^{1-\theta} - 1}{1 - \theta},$$

where $\bar{c} \geq 0$ represents the subsistence level of per capita consumption.

(*a*) What is the intertemporal elasticity of substitution for the new form of the utility function? If $\bar{c} > 0$, then how does the elasticity change as c rises?

(*b*) How does the revised formulation for utility alter the expression for consumption growth in Eq. (2.10)? Provide some intuition on the new result.

(*c*) How does the modification of utility affect the steady-state values $\hat{k}^*$ and $\hat{c}^*$?

(*d*) What kinds of changes are likely to arise for the transitional dynamics of $\hat{k}$ and $\hat{c}$ and, hence, for the rate of convergence? (This revised system requires numerical methods to generate exact results.)

2.7 *Land in the Ramsey Model.* Suppose that production involves labor, L, capital, K, and land, Λ, in the form of a constant-returns, C.E.S. function:

$$Y = A \cdot \left[a \cdot (K^\alpha L^{1-\alpha})^\psi + (1 - a) \cdot \Lambda^\psi \right]^{1/\psi},$$

where $A > 0$, $a > 0$, $0 < \alpha < 1$, and $\psi < 1$. Technological progress is absent, and L grows at the constant rate $n > 0$. The quantity of land, Λ, is fixed. Depreciation is 0. Income now includes rent on land, as well as the payments to capital and labor.

(a) Show that the competitive payments to factors again exhaust the total output.

(b) Under what conditions on ψ is the level of per capita output, y, constant in the steady state? Under what conditions does y decline steadily in the long run? What do the results suggest about the role of a fixed factor like land in the growth process?

2.8 *Alternative Institutional Environments.* We worked out the Ramsey model in detail for an environment of competitive households and firms.

(a) Show that the results are the same if households carry out the production directly and use family members as workers.

(b) Assume that a social planner's preferences are the same as those of the representative household in the model that we worked out. Show that if the planner can dictate the choices of consumption over time that the results are the same as those in the model with competitive households and firms. What does this result imply about the Pareto optimality of the decentralized outcomes?

2.9 *Money and Inflation in the Ramsey Model. (Based on Sidrauski [1967], Brock [1975], and Fischer [1979]).* Assume that the government issues fiat money. The stock of money, M, is denoted in dollars and grows at the rate μ, which may vary over time. New money arrives as lump-sum transfers to households. Households may now hold assets in the form of claims on capital, money, and internal loans. Household utility is still given by Eq. (2.1), except that $u(c)$ is replaced by $u(c, m)$, where $m \equiv M/PL$ is real cash balances and P is the price level (dollars per unit of goods). The partial derivatives of the utility function are $u_c > 0$ and $u_m > 0$. The inflation rate is denoted by $\pi \equiv \dot{P}/P$. Population grows at the rate n. The production side of the economy is the same as in the standard Ramsey model, with no technological progress.

(a) What is the representative household's budget constraint?

(b) What are the first-order conditions associated with the choices of c and m?

(c) Suppose that μ is constant in the long run and that m is constant in the steady state. How does a change in the long-run value of μ affect the steady-state values of c, k, and y? How does this change affect the steady-state values of π and m? How does it affect the attained utility, $u(c, m)$, in the steady state? What long-run value of μ would be optimally chosen in this model?

(d) Assume now that $u(c, m)$ is a separable function of c and m. In this case, how does the path of μ affect the transition path of c, k, and y?

2.10 *Fiscal Policy in the Ramsey Model. (Based on Barro [1974] and McCallum [1984]).* Consider the standard Ramsey model with infinite-horizon households, preferences given by Eqs. (2.1) and (2.9), population growth at rate n, a neoclassical production function, and technological progress at rate x. The government now purchases goods and services in the quantity G, imposes lump-sum taxes in the amount T, and has outstanding the quantity B of government bonds. The quantities G, T, and B—which can vary over time—are all measured in units of goods, and B starts at a given value, $B(0)$. Bonds are of infinitesimal maturity, pay the interest rate r, and are viewed by individual households as perfect substitutes for claims on capital or internal loans. (Assume that the government never defaults on its debts.) The government may provide public services that relate to the path of G, but the path of G is held fixed in this problem.

(a) What is the government's budget constraint?

(b) What is the representative household's budget constraint?

(c) Does the household still adhere to the first-order optimization condition for the growth rate of c, as described in Eq. (2.10)?

(d) What is the transversality condition and how does it relate to the behavior of B in the long run? What does this condition mean?

(e) How do differences in $B(0)$ or in the path of B and T affect the transitional dynamics and steady-state values of the variables c, k, y, and r? (If there are no effects, then the model exhibits *Ricardian equivalence*.)

2.11 *Government and Growth in the Ramsey Model.* Consider the household-production version of the Ramsey model. The government taxes output at the rate τ_Y, taxes labor at the rate τ_L (a lump-sum tax), provides per capita lump-sum transfers in the amount v, and purchases goods and services in the per capita amount g. The production function is Cobb–Douglas, and there is no technological progress. Thus, households maximize utility (given by Eqs. [2.1] and [2.9]), subject to the budget constraint,

$$\dot{k} = (1 - \tau_Y) \cdot Ak^\alpha - \tau_L - c - (n + \delta) \cdot k + v, \tag{1}$$

where $k(0)$ is given. Suppose that the government uses its goods and services to blow up Pacific islands, actions that neither provide utility nor enhance productivity. All of the government's remaining tax revenues are remitted to households as lump-sum transfers.

(a) What is the government's budget constraint?

(b) What are the household's first-order optimization conditions, assuming that the representative household takes τ_Y, τ_L, v, and g as given.

(c) Use a phase diagram in (k, c) space to show how the paths of k and c change when the government surprises people by permanently raising the values of τ_Y and g. What happens to the steady-state value of k?

(d) Redo part (c) for the case in which the government raises τ_L and g (without changing τ_Y). What happens to the steady-state value of k? Explain the differences from those in part (c).

(e) Redo part (c) for the case in which the government raises τ_L and v (without changing τ_Y and g). What happens to the steady-state value of k? Explain the differences from those in parts (c) and (d).

CHAPTER
3

THE OPEN ECONOMY, FINITE HORIZONS, AND ADJUSTMENT COSTS

In the closed-economy models of Chapters 1 and 2, domestic residents owned the entire stock of capital. Hence, for country i, the capital per worker, k_i, equaled the households' assets per person, a_i. We now extend the model to allow the economy to be open.

We begin by modifying the Ramsey model in a straightforward way to allow for mobility of goods across national borders and for international borrowing and lending. We find, however, that this modification leads to some paradoxical conclusions. Therefore, we consider in the remainder of the chapter some extensions—imperfections of world credit markets, nonconstant preference parameters, finite horizons, and adjustment costs for investment—that can generate more reasonable answers.

3.1 AN OPEN-ECONOMY VERSION OF THE RAMSEY MODEL

3.1.1 Setup of the Model

The world now contains many countries. For convenience, we think of one of these countries, country i, as domestic and view the others as foreign. Within any of the countries, the households and firms have the same forms of objectives and constraints as in the Ramsey model of Chapter 2.

Domestic and foreign claims on capital are assumed to be perfect substitutes as stores of value; hence, each must pay the same rate of return, r. Since loans and claims on capital in any country are still assumed to be perfect substitutes as stores of value, the variable r will be the single world interest rate.

Suppose that the domestic country has assets per person a_i and capital per person k_i. If k_i exceeds a_i, then the difference, $k_i - a_i$, must correspond to net claims by foreigners on the domestic economy. Conversely, if a_i exceeds k_i, then $a_i - k_i$ represents net claims by domestic residents on foreign economies. If we define d_i to be the domestic country's net debt to foreigners (foreign claims on the domestic country net of domestic claims on foreign countries), then

$$d_i = k_i - a_i. \tag{3.1}$$

Equivalently, domestic assets equal domestic capital less the foreign debt: $a_i = k_i - d_i$.

The current-account balance is the negative of the change in the aggregate foreign debt, $D_i = L_i d_i$, where L_i is country i's population and labor force. Therefore, if L_i grows at the rate n_i, then the per capita current-account balance for country i equals $-(\dot{d}_i + n_i d_i)$.[1]

The model still contains only one physical kind of good, but foreigners can buy domestic output, and domestic residents can buy foreign output. The only function of international trade in this model is to allow domestic production to diverge from domestic expenditure on consumption and investment. In other words, we consider the intertemporal aspects of international trade but neglect the implications for patterns of specialization in production.

We continue to assume that labor is immobile; that is, domestic residents cannot work abroad (or emigrate) and foreigners cannot work in the domestic country (or immigrate). Chapter 9 allows for migration.

The budget constraint for the representative household in country i is the same as that given in Eq. (2.2):

$$\dot{a}_i = w_i + (r - n_i) \cdot a_i - c_i. \tag{3.2}$$

The only new element is that r is the world interest rate.

We assume the same form of households' preferences as in Chapter 2 (Eqs. [2.1] and [2.9]). Therefore, the first-order condition for consumption is still the one shown in Eq. (2.10):

$$\dot{c}_i/c_i = (1/\theta_i) \cdot (r - \rho_i),$$

or, when expressed in terms of consumption per effective worker,

---

[1] Since D_i is the country's total foreign debt, the current-account balance equals $-\dot{D}_i$. The definition $d_i \equiv D_i/L_i$ and the condition $\dot{L}_i/L_i = n_i$ imply $-\dot{D}_i/L_i = -(\dot{d}_i + n_i d_i)$.

$$\dot{c}_i/\hat{c}_i = (1/\theta_i) \cdot (r - \rho_i - \theta_i x_i). \qquad (3.3)$$

The transversality condition again requires $a_i(t)$ to grow asymptotically at a rate less than $r - n_i$, as in Eq. (2.11).

The optimization conditions for firms again entail equality between the marginal products and the factor prices (Eqs. [2.21] and [2.22]):

$$f'(\hat{k}_i) = r + \delta_i, \qquad (3.4)$$

$$[f(\hat{k}_i) - \hat{k}_i \cdot f'(\hat{k}_i)] \cdot e^{x_i t} = w_i. \qquad (3.5)$$

If we substitute for w_i from Eq. (3.5) into Eq. (3.2) and use Eq. (3.4), then the change in assets per effective worker can be determined as

$$\dot{a}_i = f(\hat{k}_i) - (r + \delta_i) \cdot (\hat{k}_i - \hat{a}_i) - (x_i + n_i + \delta_i) \cdot \hat{a}_i - \hat{c}_i. \qquad (3.6)$$

Note from Eq. (3.1) that $(\hat{k}_i - \hat{a}_i) = \hat{d}_i$, which equals 0 for a closed economy. Equation (3.6) extends Eq. (2.23) to the case in which $\hat{d}_i \neq 0$.

3.1.2   Behavior of a Small Economy's Capital Stock and Output

If country i's economy is small in relation to the world economy, then the country's accumulation of assets and capital stocks has a negligible impact on the path of the world interest rate, $r(t)$. Therefore, we can treat the path of $r(t)$ as exogenous for country i. Given this path, Eqs. (3.4) and (3.5) determine the paths of $\hat{k}_i(t)$ and $w_i(t)$, without regard to the choices of consumption and saving by the domestic households. Given the time path for $w_i(t)$, Eqs. (3.3) and (3.6) and the transversality condition determine the paths of $\hat{c}_i(t)$ and $\hat{a}_i(t)$. Finally, the paths of $\hat{k}_i(t)$ and $\hat{a}_i(t)$ prescribe the behavior of the net foreign debt, $\hat{d}_i(t)$, from Eq. (3.1).

For simplicity, we now assume that the world interest rate equals a constant r. In effect, the world economy is in the kind of steady state that we considered before for a single closed economy. If country i were a closed economy, then its steady-state interest rate would be $\rho_i + \theta_i x_i$ (as in Chapter 2). We assume that $r \leq \rho_i + \theta_i x_i$ applies, because if $r > \rho_i + \theta_i x_i$, then the domestic economy would eventually accumulate enough assets to violate the small-country assumption that we made. We also assume $r > x_i + n_i$, that is, the world interest rate exceeds the steady-state growth rate that would apply in country i if the economy were closed. Otherwise, the present value of wages will turn out to be infinite and, hence, the attainable utility will be unbounded.

If r is constant, then Eq. (3.4) implies that $\hat{k}_i(t)$ equals a constant, denoted $(\hat{k}_i^*)_{\text{open}}$, which satisfies the condition $f'[(\hat{k}_i^*)_{\text{open}}] = r + \delta_i$. In other words, the speed of convergence from any initial value, $\hat{k}_i(0)$, to $(\hat{k}_i^*)_{\text{open}}$ is infinite. An excess of $(\hat{k}_i^*)_{\text{open}}$ over $\hat{k}_i(0)$ causes capital to flow in from the rest of the world so fast (at an infinite rate) that the gap disappears at once. Similarly, an excess of $\hat{k}_i(0)$ over $(\hat{k}_i^*)_{\text{open}}$ induces a massive outflow of capital. This counterfactual prediction of an infinite speed of convergence for $\hat{k}_i$ is one of the problematic implications of the open-economy version of the Ramsey model.

Recall that $\hat{k}_i^*$, the steady-state value for the closed-economy model of Chapter 2, satisfies the condition $f'(\hat{k}_i^*) - \delta = \rho_i + \theta_i x_i$. The condition $r \le \rho_i + \theta_i x_i$ implies $(\hat{k}_i^*)_{\text{open}} \ge \hat{k}_i^*$; that is, the steady-state capital intensity in the open economy is at least as high as in the closed economy.

Since $\hat{k}_i(t)$ is constant, $\hat{y}_i(t)$ is constant—that is, the speed of convergence from $\hat{y}_i(0)$ to $(\hat{y}_i^*)_{\text{open}}$ is infinite—and $y_i(t)$ grows at the constant rate x_i. Equation (3.5) implies that $w_i(t)$ also grows at the rate x_i. Therefore, the wage rate per unit of effective labor, $\hat{w}_i(t) = w_i(t) \cdot e^{-x_i^t}$, equals a constant, denoted $(\hat{w}_i^*)_{\text{open}}$.

3.1.3 Behavior of a Small Economy's Consumption and Assets

Equation (3.3) implies that consumption per effective worker, $\hat{c}_i(t)$, grows at the constant rate $(r - \rho_i - \theta_i x_i)/\theta_i \le 0$. If we use the form of the consumption function that we derived in Chapter 2 (Eqs. [2.14] and [2.15]), then $\hat{c}_i(t)$ can be written as

$$\hat{c}_i(t) = (1/\theta_i) \cdot [\rho_i - r \cdot (1-\theta_i) - n_i \theta_i] \cdot \left[\hat{a}_i(0) + \frac{(\hat{w}_i^*)_{\text{open}}}{r - x_i - n_i} \right] \cdot e^{[(r-\rho_i-\theta_i x_i)/\theta_i] \cdot t} \qquad (3.7)$$

The term in the first brackets on the right-hand side is positive from the conditions $\rho_i + \theta_i x_i \ge r$ and $r > x_i + n_i$.

If $r = \rho_i + \theta_i x_i$, then $\hat{c}_i(t)$ is constant. Otherwise—that is, if $r < \rho_i + \theta_i x_i$— $\hat{c}_i(t)$ asymptotically approaches 0. The domestic country borrows to enjoy a high level of consumption early on—because it is impatient in the sense that $\rho_i + \theta_i x_i > r$—but it pays the price later in the form of low consumption growth. Recall as a contrast that $\hat{c}_i(t)$ in a closed economy is constant asymptotically. The result that $\hat{c}_i$ tends to 0 if $r < \rho_i + \theta_i x_i$ is another problematic feature of the open-economy Ramsey model.

Equation (3.6) is a first-order linear differential equation in $\hat{a}_i(t)$. This equation, along with the formula for $\hat{c}_i(t)$ in Eq. (3.7) and the given initial value of assets, $\hat{a}_i(0)$, determines the time path of $\hat{a}_i(t)$ as

$$\hat{a}_i(t) = \left[\hat{a}_i(0) + \frac{(\hat{w}_i^*)_{\text{open}}}{r - x_i - n_i} \right] \cdot e^{[(r-\rho_i-\theta_i x_i)/\theta_i] \cdot t} - \frac{(\hat{w}_i^*)_{\text{open}}}{r - x_i - n_i}. \qquad (3.8)$$

The final term on the right-hand side is the present value of wage income, where $(r - x_i - n_i) > 0$ follows from the condition $r > x_i + n_i$.

If $r = \rho_i + \theta_i x_i$, then $\hat{a}_i(t)$ is constant. Otherwise—that is, if $r < \rho_i + \theta_i x_i$— the exponential term in Eq. (3.8), $e^{[(r-\rho_i-\theta_i x_i)/\theta_i] \cdot t}$, diminishes over time toward 0. Therefore, if $\hat{a}_i(0) > 0$, then $\hat{a}_i(t)$ eventually falls to 0, so that $\hat{d}_i(t)$ from Eq. (3.1) equals $(\hat{k}_i^*)_{\text{open}}$. Subsequently, $\hat{a}_i(t)$ becomes negative; that is, the domestic country becomes a debtor not only in the sense of not owning its capital stock but also of borrowing against the present value of its wage income as collateral. Asymptotically, $\hat{a}_i(t)$ approaches the final term in Eq. (3.8), $-[(\hat{w}_i^*)_{\text{open}}/(r - x_i - n_i)]$, so that $\hat{d}_i(t)$ approaches the positive constant $(\hat{k}_i^*)_{\text{open}} + [(\hat{w}_i^*)_{\text{open}}/(r - x_i - n_i)]$. In other words, an impatient country asymptotically mortgages all of its capital and all of its labor income. This counterfactual behavior of assets is yet another difficulty with the model.

3.1.4 The World Equilibrium

Suppose now that the world consists of a set of countries numbered $i = 1, \ldots, M$. We assume here that population growth, n_i, and the rate of technological progress, x_i, equal the same values, n and x, for all countries. In this case, the shares of each country's output, Y_i, in world output do not change over time.

Assume that the countries are ordered in terms of their effective rates of time preference, $\rho_i + \theta_i x$, with country 1 having the lowest value. We already showed that $\hat{c}_i(t)$ approaches 0 and $\hat{a}_i(t)$ approaches a negative number if $\rho_i + \theta_i x > r$. In contrast, if $\rho_i + \theta_i x < r$, then $\hat{c}_i(t)$ and $\hat{a}_i(t)$ would rise forever and country i's consumption would eventually exceed world output. Before this happened, the world interest rate would adjust downward; in particular, $\rho_i + \theta_i x \geq r$ must hold in the steady state for all countries. The only way to satisfy this condition and also to have the world capital stock owned by someone (so that the world capital stock equals world assets) is for r to equal $\rho_1 + \theta_1 x$, the term for the most patient country. Asymptotically, country 1 owns all the wealth in the sense of the claims on capital and the present value of wage income in all countries. All other countries own nothing (per unit of effective labor) in the long run.

Country 1's consumption grows asymptotically at the rate $n + x$, the same as the growth rate of world output. The ratio of country 1's consumption to world output approaches a positive constant, whereas the ratio for all other countries approaches 0.[2]

To summarize, the open-economy version of the Ramsey model generates several counterfactual results. The variables $\hat{k}_i$, $\hat{y}_i$, and $\hat{w}_i$ converge instantaneously to their steady-state values. In addition, for all but the most patient economy, $\hat{c}_i$ tends to 0, and $\hat{a}_i$ eventually becomes negative. The counterpart of these results is that net foreign claims and the current-account balance for the impatient economies become negative and large in magnitude in relation to GDP. Equivalently, the path of domestic expenditures on consumption and investment tends to evolve very differently from that of domestic production.

One way to think of some of the problematic results is in terms of the relation between the time-preference term, $\rho_i + \theta_i x$, and the interest rate, r_i, that country i faces. In the closed-economy framework of Chapter 2, r_i adjusts to equal $\rho_i + \theta_i x$ in the steady state, whereas in the open-economy model, r_i is pegged at the world interest rate, r. If $r_i < \rho_i + \theta_i x$, then the ratio of consumption to output asymptotically approaches 0. If $r_i > \rho_i + \theta_i x$, then the ratio of consumption to output would approach infinity, but before this happens the country ends up owning all the world's wealth, and the world interest rate adjusts to equal $\rho_i + \theta_i x$. This outcome applies to the most patient country, but all other countries end up eventually in the situation in which

---

[2] We would get similar results for a single country that comprises M family dynasties with differing values of the time-preference term, $\rho_i + \theta_i x$. Again, the most patient family ends up owning everything asymptotically. For families, this result would be tempered by imperfect inheritability of preference parameters and by marriage across dynasties. Similar considerations arise across countries, especially if we allow for migration of persons.

$r_i < \rho_i + \theta_i x$, so that the ratio of consumption to output approaches 0. To avoid this result, we need some mechanism to eliminate the gap between r_i and $\rho_i + \theta_i x$ for all countries, not just for the most patient country. That is, either r_i has to differ from r, or else the effective rate of time preference, $\rho_i + \theta_i x$, has to be variable. We begin by considering a model in which r_i diverges from r.

3.2 THE WORLD ECONOMY WITH A CONSTRAINT ON INTERNATIONAL CREDIT

Our first attempt to improve the predictions of the open-economy growth model involves the introduction of a constraint on international borrowing. In the previous section, we described an equilibrium in which an open economy eventually mortgages all of its capital and labor income, and the ratio of consumption to GDP approaches zero. Cohen and Sachs (1986) observe that the economy's residents would eventually default on their debts in this kind of equilibrium. As long as the penalty for default is limited to some fraction of domestic output or of the domestic capital stock, the residents (or their government) would, at some point, prefer default to remaining on the path in which the ratio of consumption to GDP approaches zero.

Since the inevitable default would presumably be foreseen by lenders, the path described before is not an equilibrium even before the time of default. In particular, the domestic residents in an impatient country would eventually reach a point at which they could not borrow the desired amount, $\hat{d}_i(t)$, at the world interest rate, r. We therefore want to reconsider the choices made by residents of an open economy when some constraints are imposed on their ability to borrow.

3.2.1 Setup of a Model with Physical and Human Capital

One tractable way to proceed is to distinguish two types of capital, one that serves well as collateral on foreign loans and another that does not serve as collateral. We can assume, for example, that human capital provides unacceptable security on loans, whereas at least some forms of physical capital are acceptable because the creditor can take possession of the object in the case of default.

We assume now that the production function involves the two kinds of capital:

$$\hat{y} = f(\hat{k}, \hat{h}) = A\hat{k}^\alpha \hat{h}^\eta, \tag{3.9}$$

where $\hat{k}$ is physical capital per unit of effective labor and $\hat{h}$ is human capital per unit of effective labor.[3] We use a Cobb–Douglas form of the production function,

---

[3]This analysis follows Barro, Mankiw, and Sala-i-Martin (1992). An alternative model, suggested by Cohen and Sachs (1986), sticks with one type of capital, k, but assumes that only a fraction ν, where $0 \le \nu \le 1$, of this capital serves as collateral on foreign loans. The results from this alternative framework are similar to those from the two-capital model, except that the two-capital model turns out to be simpler.

where α is the share of physical capital, η the share of human capital, and $0 < \alpha < 1$, $0 < \eta < 1$, and $0 < \alpha + \eta < 1$. The condition $0 < \alpha + \eta < 1$ ensures diminishing returns in the accumulation of broad capital, that is, for proportional changes in physical and human capital.

We maintain the assumption of a one-sector production technology in that units of output can now go on a one-to-one basis to consumption, additions to physical capital, or additions to human capital. (Chapter 4 deals further with this model, and Chapter 5 introduces a separate education sector that produces new human capital.) The budget constraint, an extension of Eq. (3.6), is

$$\dot{\hat{a}} = \dot{\hat{k}} + \dot{\hat{h}} - \dot{\hat{d}} = A\hat{k}^\alpha \hat{h}^\eta - (r + \delta) \cdot (\hat{k} + \hat{h} - \hat{a}) - (x + n + \delta) \cdot \hat{a} - \hat{c}, \quad (3.10)$$

where $\hat{a} = \hat{k} + \hat{h} - \hat{d}$, and we have dropped the country subscript i for convenience. We also assume that the depreciation rate, δ, is the same for both kinds of capital.

3.2.2   The Closed Economy

If we return for the moment to a closed economy, then $d = 0$ and $a = k + h$. The results on the growth process are then the same as those worked out in Chapter 2, except that we now explicitly take a broad view of capital to include physical and human components. Investors equate the marginal product of each type of capital to $r + \delta$, where r is the domestic interest rate. Given the Cobb–Douglas production function in Eq. (3.9), this condition implies that the ratio k/h is fixed at α/η.[4] In the steady state, the quantities of the two types of capital per unit of effective labor are constant at the values $\hat{k}^*$ and $\hat{h}^*$, respectively, where $\hat{k}^*/\hat{h}^* = \alpha/\eta$. If we start with $\hat{k}(0) < \hat{k}^*$ and $\hat{h}(0) < \hat{h}^*$, then the transition involves growth of $\hat{k}$, $\hat{h}$, and $\hat{y}$. As in our previous analysis, the growth rates fall during the transition.

In the Ramsey model of Chapter 2, the speed of convergence to the steady state depended on the capital share. That share equaled α in the Cobb–Douglas version of the model with one type of capital, but now equals $\alpha + \eta$ in the model with two kinds of capital. Except for the substitution of $\alpha + \eta$ for α, the results are identical to those from the model that we worked out in Chapter 2. In particular, the formula from Eq. (2.34) for the convergence coefficient, β, in the log-linearized model still applies if we replace α by $\alpha + \eta$:

$$2\beta = \left\{ \zeta^2 + 4 \cdot \left(\frac{1 - \alpha - \eta}{\theta} \right) \cdot (\rho + \delta + \theta x) \cdot \left[\frac{\rho + \delta + \theta x}{\alpha + \eta} - (n + x + \delta) \right] \right\}^{1/2} - \zeta,$$
$$(3.11)$$

where $\zeta = \rho - n - (1 - \theta) \cdot x > 0$. If we assume, for example, that $\alpha = 0.30$ and $\eta = 0.45$, then the findings about the speed of convergence coincide with those

---

[4]The economy jumps from an arbitrary starting ratio, $k(0)/h(0)$, to α/η if we allow both kinds of investment to be reversible so that units of k can be immediately converted into units of h and vice versa. If we constrain gross investment in each kind of capital to be nonnegative, then the transitional dynamics are more complicated. We explore these kinds of effects in Chapter 5.

from Chapter 2 for the case in which the capital share was 0.75. If we take our usual benchmark values for the other parameters—$n = 0.01$ per year, $x = 0.02$ per year, $\delta = 0.05$ per year, and $\rho = 0.02$ per year—and use $\theta = 3$, then the convergence coefficient is $\beta = 0.015$ per year.

3.2.3 The Open Economy

The distinction between the two kinds of capital becomes more interesting when we allow for an open economy and introduce the credit-market constraint. We now assume that the amount of foreign debt, d, can be positive but cannot exceed the quantity of physical capital, k. Physical capital can be used as collateral on foreign loans, but human capital and raw labor cannot.

We are assuming implicitly that domestic residents own the physical capital stock but may obtain part or all of the financing for this stock by issuing bonds to foreigners. The results would be the same if we allowed for direct foreign investment, in which case the foreigners would own part of the physical capital stock rather than bonds. The important assumption is that domestic residents cannot borrow with human capital or raw labor as collateral and that foreigners cannot own domestic human capital or raw labor.

There are various ways to motivate the borrowing constraint. Physical capital is more easily repossessed than human capital and is therefore more readily financed with debt. Physical capital is also more amenable to direct foreign investment: a person can own a factory but not someone else's stream of labor income. Finally, one can abandon the terms "physical capital" and "human capital" and recognize that not all investments can be financed through perfect capital markets. The key distinction between k and h in the present context is not the physical nature of the capital but whether the cumulated goods serve as collateral for borrowing on world markets.

We still assume that the world interest rate, r, is constant. We now assume also that $r = \rho + \theta x$, the steady-state interest rate that would apply if the domestic economy were closed. That is, the home economy is neither more nor less impatient than the world as a whole. (It is straightforward to extend to the case in which $r < \rho + \theta x$.)

The initial quantity of assets per effective worker is $\hat{k}(0) + \hat{h}(0) - \hat{d}(0)$, and the key consideration is whether this quantity is greater or less than the steady-state amount of human capital, $\hat{h}^*$. If $\hat{k}(0) + \hat{h}(0) - \hat{d}(0) \geq \hat{h}^*$, then the borrowing constraint is not binding and the economy jumps to the steady state. In contrast, if $\hat{k}(0) + \hat{h}(0) - \hat{d}(0) < \hat{h}^*$, then the constraint is binding—that is, $d = k$ applies—and we obtain some new results. We therefore focus on this situation.[5]

---

[5] If $r < \rho + \theta x$, then the domestic economy must eventually become constrained on the world credit market. Hence, our analysis of a debt-constrained economy applies at some time in the future even if not at the initial date. If $r > \rho + \theta x$, then the assumption of a small economy is violated eventually, and r would have to change.

Since physical capital serves as collateral, the net return on this capital, $f_k - \delta$, where f_k is the marginal product of capital, equals the world interest rate, r, at all points in time. The formula for f_k implied by the Cobb–Douglas production function in Eq. (3.9) therefore implies

$$\hat{k} = \alpha \hat{y}/(r + \delta). \tag{3.12}$$

Equation (3.12) ensures that the ratio of physical capital to GDP, k/y, will be constant throughout the transition to the steady state. In contrast, k/y would rise steadily during the transition for a closed economy. The rough constancy over time of k/y is one of Kaldor's (1963) stylized facts about economic development; see the discussion in the introductory chapter. The consistency of the credit-constrained open-economy model with this "fact" is therefore notable.[6]

The result for $\hat{k}$ from Eq. (3.12) can be combined with the production function from Eq. (3.9) to express $\hat{y}$ as a function of $\hat{h}$:

$$\hat{y} = B\hat{h}^\epsilon, \tag{3.13}$$

where $B \equiv A^{1/(1-\alpha)} \cdot [\alpha/(r + \delta)]^{\alpha/(1-\alpha)}$ and $\epsilon \equiv \eta/(1 - \alpha)$. The condition $0 < \alpha + \eta < 1$ implies $0 < \epsilon < \alpha + \eta < 1$. Thus, the reduced-form production function in Eq. (3.13) expresses $\hat{y}$ as a function of $\hat{h}$ with positive and diminishing marginal product. The convergence implications of this model are therefore similar to those of the closed economy—both models involve the accumulation of a capital stock under conditions of diminishing returns.

The budget constraint from Eq. (3.10) can be combined with the reduced-form production function from Eq. (3.13), the borrowing constraint $d = k$ (which implies $a = h$), and the condition $(r + \delta) \cdot \hat{k} = \alpha \hat{y}$ from Eq. (3.12), to get the revised budget constraint:

$$\dot{\hat{h}} = (1 - \alpha) \cdot B\hat{h}^\epsilon - (\delta + n + x) \cdot \hat{h} - \hat{c}. \tag{3.14}$$

Note that $\alpha B\hat{h}^\epsilon$, which subtracts from $B\hat{h}^\epsilon$ in the equation, corresponds to the flow of rental payments on physical capital, $(r + \delta)\hat{k}$ (see Eq. [3.12]). Since $d = k$, this term corresponds to the net factor payments to foreigners and therefore equals the difference (per unit of effective labor) between GNP and GDP. The GDP exceeds the GNP because the country is constrained on the international credit market and therefore has the positive foreign debt, $d = k$.

If we use the setting in which households produce goods directly, then they maximize utility (given in Eqs. [2.1] and [2.9]), subject to the budget constraint in Eq. (3.14) and a given initial stock of human capital, $\hat{h}(0) > 0$. (The value $\hat{h}(0)$

---

[6]The precise constancy of k/y in the model depends on the fixity of the world interest rate, r, and on the assumption that the production function is Cobb–Douglas. This production function implies that the average product of capital, y/k, is proportional to the marginal product. Since the marginal product of capital, net of depreciation, equals the fixed world interest rate, r, the average product, y/k, must be constant.

equals the given amount of initial assets, which was assumed to be less than $\hat{h}^*$.) The optimizing condition for consumption over time is

$$\dot{\hat{c}}/\hat{c} = (1/\theta) \cdot [(1 - \alpha) \cdot B\epsilon \hat{h}^{\epsilon-1} - (\delta + \rho + \theta x)], \tag{3.15}$$

where $(1 - \alpha) \cdot B\epsilon \hat{h}^{\epsilon-1} = B\eta \hat{h}^{\epsilon-1} = f_h$, the marginal product of human capital. Equation (3.15) corresponds to the usual formula in Eq. (3.3) if we think of r in that formula as the domestic rate of return, which equals $f_h - \delta$. Equations (3.14) and (3.15) and the usual transversality condition fully describe the transitional dynamics of this model.

Because we assumed $r = \rho + \theta x$, the steady state is the same as that for the closed economy that has physical and human capital. Hence, the opportunity to borrow on the world credit market does not influence the steady state but will turn out to affect the speed of convergence.[7]

The system described by Eqs. (3.14) and (3.15) and the transversality condition has the usual transitional dynamics. We can compare the results with those from the closed-economy model with capital goods k and h in which the total broad capital stock per worker is $k + h$ and the capital share is $\alpha + \eta$. The only differences are that Eq. (3.14) contains $(1 - \alpha) \cdot B$ as a proportional constant in the production function, the capital-stock variable is h rather than $k + h$, and the exponent on the capital stock is $\epsilon \equiv \eta/(1 - \alpha)$ rather than $\alpha + \eta$. Since ϵ and $\alpha + \eta$ are positive and less than 1—that is, both models feature diminishing returns—the dynamics of the models are essentially the same.

The formula for the convergence coefficient, β, coincides with that for the closed economy in Eq. (3.11), except that the capital-share parameter, $\alpha + \eta$, has to be replaced by $\epsilon \equiv \eta/(1 - \alpha)$. (Recall that the level of the production technology does not influence the rate of convergence.) Hence, the convergence coefficient for the credit-constrained open economy is given by

$$2\beta = \left\{ \zeta^2 + 4 \cdot \left(\frac{1 - \epsilon}{\theta} \right) \cdot (\delta + \rho + \theta x) \cdot \left[\frac{\delta + \rho + \theta x}{\epsilon} - (\delta + n + x) \right] \right\}^{1/2} - \zeta,$$

$$\tag{3.16}$$

where $\zeta = \rho - n - (1 - \theta) \cdot x > 0$. The coefficient determined from Eq. (3.16) is the same value that would arise in a closed economy that had the broad capital share ϵ, rather than $\alpha + \eta$. Since $\epsilon \equiv \eta/(1 - \alpha)$, it follows that $\epsilon < \alpha + \eta$ (using the condition $\alpha + \eta < 1$). *The credit-constrained open economy therefore behaves like a closed economy with a broad capital share that is less than $\alpha + \eta$.* Recall that the rate of convergence depends inversely on the capital share (because a smaller capital share

---

[7]If we had assumed $r < \rho + \theta x$—so that the home economy is more impatient than those of the rest of the world (see footnote 5)—then the availability of foreign borrowing would also affect the steady-state position. The open economy would have higher steady-state capital intensities, $\hat{h}^*$ and $\hat{k}^*$, than the closed economy.

means that diminishing returns set in more rapidly). The credit-constrained open economy therefore has a higher rate of convergence than the closed economy. Note, however, that $(\alpha + \eta) \to 1$ implies $\epsilon \to 1$ and, therefore, $\beta \to 0$ in Eq. (3.16). Thus, if diminishing returns to broad capital do not apply $(\alpha + \eta = 1)$, then the model still does not exhibit the convergence property.[8]

We can understand why the partially open economy converges faster than the closed economy by thinking about the tendency for diminishing returns to set in as human capital, $\hat{h}$, is accumulated. For given exponents of the production function, α and η, the key issue is the transitional behavior of the ratio, k/h. In the closed economy, k/h stays constant (at the value α/η), whereas in the open economy k/h falls during the transition (see below). That is, $\hat{k}$ is relatively high at the outset in an open economy because the availability of foreign finance makes it easy to acquire physical capital quickly. The fall in k/h over time causes diminishing returns to $\hat{h}$ to set in faster than otherwise; hence, the speed of convergence is greater in the open economy than in the closed economy.

Although the credit-constrained open economy converges faster than the closed economy, the speed of convergence is now finite for the open economy. If we use the values $\alpha = 0.30$ and $\eta = 0.45$, along with the benchmark values mentioned before for the other parameters, then the convergence coefficient implied by Eq. (3.16) is 0.025, compared with 0.015 for the closed economy. The value 0.025 conforms well with empirical estimates of convergence coefficients.

Recall that an open economy with perfect capital mobility converges at an infinite rate. Therefore, our finding is that an open economy with partial capital mobility looks much more like a closed economy than a fully open economy. Although we derived this result so far only for a particular set of values for α and η, the basic finding is much more general. If we raise α/η for given $\alpha + \eta$, then we increase the degree of capital mobility and thereby raise the convergence coefficient, β. For the benchmark values of the other parameters (including $\alpha + \eta = 0.75$), β rises from 0.015 at $\alpha/\eta = 0$ to 0.030 at $\alpha/\eta = 1$, 0.042 at $\alpha/\eta = 2$, and 0.053 at $\alpha/\eta = 3$. Therefore, if we use the benchmark values for the other parameters and assume that no more than half the total capital stock constitutes collateral for foreign borrowing $(\alpha/\eta \le 1)$, then the predicted convergence coefficient falls within the narrow range, 0.015 to 0.030 per year. This range accords well with empirical estimates.[9]

---

[8]If $\alpha = 0$, so that no capital constitutes collateral, then $\epsilon = \eta$ and β from Eq. (3.16) corresponds to the value from Eq. (3.11) for a closed economy (with capital share equal to η). If $\eta = 0$, so that all capital serves as collateral, then $\epsilon = 0$ and β from Eq. (3.16) becomes infinite, as in the open economy with perfect capital mobility.

[9]Barro, Mankiw, and Sala-i-Martin (1992) generalize the production function in Eq. (3.9) from a Cobb–Douglas form to a constant-elasticity-of-substitution (CES) specification. The degree of substitutability affects β—it turns out that β is higher if $\hat{k}$ and $\hat{h}$ are poorer substitutes in production. The main conclusion, however, is that β is confined to the narrow interval, (0.014, 0.035), for the usual benchmark parameters if $\alpha/\eta \le 1$. Thus, the theoretical predictions accord well with the empirical estimates of β even in this more general case.

The transition to the steady state involves a monotonic increase in human capital per effective worker, $\hat{h}$, from its initial value, $\hat{h}(0)$, to its steady-state value, $\hat{h}^*$. Equation (3.13) implies that the growth rate of $\hat{y}$ is ϵ times the growth rate of $\hat{h}$, where ϵ is between 0 and 1. The ratio h/y therefore rises steadily during the transition. Recall, however, that Eq. (3.12) implies that the ratio k/y is constant. Therefore, $\hat{k}$ grows at the same rate as $\hat{y}$, and the ratio of human to physical capital, h/k, increases during the transition. Note that, although physical capital serves fully as collateral, $\hat{k}$ nevertheless rises gradually toward its steady-state value, $\hat{k}^*$. The reason is the constraint of domestic saving on the accumulation of human capital and the complementarity between $\hat{h}$ and $\hat{k}$ in the production function. When $\hat{h}$ is low, the schedule for the marginal product of physical capital is low; hence, $\hat{k} < \hat{k}^*$ follows even though domestic producers can finance all acquisitions of physical capital with foreign borrowing. The gradual increase of human capital impacts positively on the marginal product of physical capital and leads thereby to an expansion of $\hat{k}$.

Foreign borrowing occurs only on loans secured by physical capital, and the interest rate on these loans is pegged at the world rate, r. We can also allow for a domestic credit market, although the setting with a representative domestic agent ensures that, in equilibrium, each person will not borrow. For loans that are secured by physical capital, the shadow interest rate on the domestic market must also be r. If we assume that human capital and raw labor do not serve domestically as collateral, then the shadow interest rate on the domestic market with these forms of security is infinity (or at least high enough to drive desired borrowing to zero), just as it is on the world market.

We might assume instead that human capital and raw labor serve as collateral for domestic borrowing but not for foreign borrowing. This situation would apply if the legal system enforces loan contracts based on labor income when the creditor is domestic, but not when the creditor is foreign.[10] In this case, the shadow interest rate on domestic lending, collateralized by labor income, equals the net marginal product of human capital. This net marginal product begins at a relatively high value (corresponding to the low starting stock, $\hat{h}[0]$) and then falls gradually toward the steady-state value, r. Thus, the transition features a decrease in the spread between this kind of domestic interest rate and the world rate, r. An example would be the curb market for informal lending in Korea (see Collins and Park [1989, p. 353]). The spread between curb-market interest rates and world interest rates was 30 to 40 percentage points in the 1960s and 1970s, but it fell by the mid-1980s to about 15 percentage points.

Another implication of the model is that, despite the existence of international borrowing and lending, the convergence properties of gross national product and

---

[10]If the foreign loans are made directly to the domestic government, then the collateral involves the security put up by the government. Domestic physical capital may then not serve well as collateral on foreign loans either—if the home government does not force itself to pay up—although it may work better on domestic loans (if the government enforces private loan contracts on the domestic market with physical capital as collateral).

gross domestic product are the same. As noted before, the net factor income from abroad (per unit of effective labor) is $-(r + \delta) \cdot \hat{k} = -\alpha \hat{y}$. Therefore,

$$\text{GNP (per unit of effective labor)} = \hat{y} - \alpha \hat{y} = \hat{y} \cdot (1 - \alpha). \qquad (3.17)$$

Since GNP is proportional to GDP, which corresponds to $\hat{y}$, the convergence rates for GNP and GDP are the same. This result suggests that data sets that involve GDP are likely to generate similar rates of convergence as those that involve GNP or measures of national income. Some confirmation of this prediction comes from the study of the U.S. states by Barro and Sala-i-Martin (1991): the rates of convergence are similar for gross state product per capita and state personal income per capita.

The model implies that the gap between GDP and GNP would be large for a credit-constrained open economy: roughly 20–25% of GDP for the parameter values assumed before. The current-account deficit, which equals the change in physical capital, is correspondingly large. It is unusual to find developing countries that have values this high for the GDP-GNP gap and the current-account deficit.[11] We can reconcile the theory with this observation by noting, first, that many developing countries are insufficiently productive to be credit constrained and, second, that the collateral for international debt may be substantially narrower than physical capital. If the coefficient α were less than 0.3, then the predicted ratios for the GDP-GNP gap and the current-account deficit would be correspondingly smaller.

The introduction of a credit constraint removes some of the counterfactual predictions from the open-economy model with perfect capital mobility, in particular, the speeds of convergence for the capital stock and output are no longer infinite. Consider, however, what happens if countries differ in their degree of impatience as represented by the combination of preference parameters, $\rho_i + \theta_i x$. With perfect capital markets, we found before that all but the most patient country follow a path in which $\hat{c}$ approaches 0. In the model with a credit constraint, the prediction is instead that all but the most patient country will eventually reach a situation in which the residents are effectively constrained on the international credit market (see footnote 5). This credit constraint implies that $\hat{c}$ approaches a positive constant, a more appealing asymptote than 0. The disturbing result, however, is that all countries except the most patient one must eventually be credit constrained. To avoid this result we have to consider models in which the effective rate of time preference, $\rho_i + \theta_i x$, is variable. The next sections consider models of this type.

3.3   VARIATIONS IN PREFERENCE PARAMETERS

We now consider whether some of the disturbing implications from the open-economy Ramsey model can be eliminated if we allow the preference parameters, ρ_i and θ_i, to vary. The idea, which comes from Uzawa (1968), is that the rate of time preference and the willingness to substitute consumption over time may depend on

---

[11]One counter-example is Singapore: its current-account deficit was between 10 and 20% of GDP throughout the 1970s (International Monetary Fund [1991]).

the level of a household's wealth or consumption and may therefore change as a_i and c_i change.

Return now to the open-economy model without credit restraints. A key property of this model is that countries with high values of the time-preference term, $\rho_i + \theta_i x > r$, follow a path in which $\hat{a}_i(t)$ becomes negative and $\hat{c}_i(t)$ declines toward zero. One way to avoid this unappealing result is to assume that $\rho_i + \theta_i x$ declines as $\hat{a}_i(t)$ and $\hat{c}_i(t)$ fall. In other words, countries or individuals would have to become more patient as they become poorer.

Uzawa (1968) obtains the desired result by assuming that ρ_i is a positive function of $c_i(t)$. This mechanism is unappealing, however, because it is counterintuitive that people would raise their rates of time preference as their levels of consumption rise.*

We could also get the desired result by assuming that people become less willing to substitute intertemporally—that is, θ_i increases—as the level of consumption rises. The usual assumption is, however, the opposite. We showed in Eq. (2.8) that the effective time-preference term involves the negative of the elasticity of marginal utility, $-u''(c) \cdot c/u'(c)$. In the specification that we have used thus far, the magnitude of this elasticity is constant and equal to θ_i. The form of the utility function is sometimes modified, however, to exhibit a variable elasticity by allowing for a subsistence level of consumption:

$$u(c_i) = \frac{(c_i - \bar{c}_i)^{(1-\theta_i)} - 1}{(1 - \theta_i)}, \tag{3.18}$$

where $\bar{c}_i > 0$ is the constant subsistence level. (This form is referred to as Stone–Geary, after Stone [1954] and Geary [1950–51].) Equation (3.18) implies that the magnitude of the elasticity of marginal utility is $\theta_i c_i/(c_i - \bar{c}_i)$, which equals θ_i when $\bar{c}_i = 0$, but is decreasing in c_i when $\bar{c}_i > 0$. This revised formulation of utility implies accordingly, that the effective time-preference term declines with $c_i(t)$; that is, the term moves in the wrong direction from the perspective of resolving the difficulties in the open-economy model.

More appealing results emerge from models that assume constant parameters ρ_i and θ_i for each country (or family) but that allow for effects from finite horizons. The first models of this type, due to Samuelson (1958) and Diamond (1965), assumed that people lived a fixed number of discrete periods, such as childhood and adulthood. The period of adulthood for one generation overlapped with the period of childhood for the next; hence, the customary designation overlapping-generations (OLG) model. Individuals in these models have finite horizons—because they live for only two periods and do not, by assumption, care about the welfare of their descendants—but the economy lasts forever. Although the OLG framework captures the effects of finite horizons, one shortcoming of this framework is that the equilibrium conditions turn out to be too cumbersome to carry out many of the comparative-statics exercises that we would like to consider.

---

*Mulligan (1993) argues that if the degree of altruism depends on the amount of time parents spend with their children, then people with high wages will be less altruistic because the opportunity cost of spending time with their children is high. It follows that rich people will have to have high discount rates.

Blanchard (1985) retained the essence of the finite-horizon idea in a more tractable framework by assuming that people die off randomly in accordance with a Poisson process. For present purposes, the key finding in his model is that *aggregate* consumption behaves as if each individual's time-preference term were positively related to $a_i(t)$. The results come, however, from the aggregation over individuals who are heterogeneous with respect to age (and, hence, with respect to assets and consumption) and not from variations in preference parameters for individuals. To get these results, we first set up Blanchard's framework, then apply it to a closed economy, and finally use it to extend our analysis of an open economy. The appendix contains an analysis of related OLG models.

3.4 ECONOMIC GROWTH IN A MODEL WITH FINITE HORIZONS

3.4.1 Choices in a Model with Finite Horizons

In the previous analysis, we assumed that family dynasties lasted forever so that households planned with an infinite horizon. We now want to allow for the possibility that the dynasty would terminate in finite time. This termination could reflect the death of adults who leave no descendants and therefore do not care about matters beyond their death. Alternatively, it could reflect the chance that finite-lived parents reach a position in which they are not connected to their children through a pattern of operative intergenerational transfers.

We think of "death" as the termination of a family dynasty, although this death need not correspond to anyone's literally dying. Let p be the probability of death per unit of time, so that a person (or household) born at time j is alive at time $t \geq j$ with probability $e^{-p \cdot (t-j)}$. A key assumption, which makes the aggregation tractable, is that p is invariant with age. This assumption is unrealistic if we think of the literal death of an individual, but is less troublesome in the context of the termination of a dynasty.

The probability of being dead at time t equals $1 - e^{-p \cdot (t-j)}$, so that the probability density for death at time t is the derivative of this expression, $pe^{-p \cdot (t-j)}$. The expected lifetime can be calculated from this probability density as $1/p$. Thus, a higher p lowers the expected lifetime and makes the finite-horizon effect more important.

We assume, as before, that population grows at the constant rate n, so that $L(t) = e^{nt}$ is the total population. The size of a cohort born at time t must then be $(p + n) \cdot e^{nt}$; that is, enough new people or households are born to replace those who die, pe^{nt}, and to provide for net growth, ne^{nt}.

The riskless interest rate on assets is again $r(t)$. We have to consider the disposition of assets for people or households who die. In the infinite-life model, these assets implicitly go to descendants in the form of intergenerational transfers. These transfers are motivated by altruistic linkages that are strong enough to keep people away from the corner solution of zero transfers. But the whole idea of "dying" in the finite-horizon model is that these linkages are not operative. We could assume that the assets go as unintended bequests to children or as unintended transfers to society as a whole. But if people are really unconcerned with events that occur after their deaths—which is the central idea in finite-horizon models–then they could do better by using markets for annuities. Also, if we allow people to die in debt without descendants to assume the debt, then lenders would require a rate of interest above r to cover the possibility that the borrower will die.

We follow Yaari (1965) and Blanchard (1985) by assuming that all loans are secured by life insurance. If a person lives, then he or she pays the interest rate r plus the life insurance premium on the loan. If the person dies in debt, then the life insurance pays off the loan. Because the probability of death per unit of time is p, the necessary premium is p. That is, the total rate paid on loans is $r + p$ if someone lives. From the perspective of a life insurance company, the premium at rate p just covers the expected payouts on policies for borrowers who die. Similarly, lenders can hold annuities that pay $r + p$ if the person lives and zero if the person dies. From the standpoint of an annuity company, the extra payout at rate p just balances the expected proceeds from the people who die. From the perspective of individuals with finite horizons, the rate of return on annuities (conditional on survival) of $r + p$ is more attractive than the riskless rate of return, r. Therefore, all assets would be held in the form of annuities.[12]

Since life insurance and annuity markets are fully exploited by a large population, the total of assets released by people who die, $p \cdot a(t)$, coincides with the extra return (above the riskless rate r) for the people who live. Insurance and annuity companies therefore break even, and we have accounted fully for the disposition of assets at death. It also follows that the relevant rate of return for surviving individuals— whether lenders or borrowers—is $r + p$, rather than r.

Let $c(j, v)$ be the consumption and $a(j, v)$ the assets at time v for a person born at time $j \leq v$. We assume that productivity is independent of age, so that the wage rate, $w(v)$, is the same for all $j \leq v$. Starting from the current time t, the household maximizes expected utility, given by

$$E_t U = E_t \left[\int_t^\infty \log[c(j, v)] \cdot e^{-\rho(v-t)} dv \right], \qquad (3.19)$$

where we have assumed $u(c) = \log(c)$, which corresponds to $\theta = 1$ in Eq. (2.9). Although log utility is convenient, we can readily generalize the steady-state results to cases in which $\theta \neq 1$. (The transitional dynamics is feasible, but cumbersome, if $\theta \neq 1$.)

The formulation in Eq. (3.19) differs from that in Eq. (2.1) of the Ramsey model by the omission of the population term, e^{nt}, as a multiple on per capita utility. The assumption in this finite-horizon model is that people give no weight to their descendants in the utility function or in the budget constraint, which we consider

---

[12]Economists sometimes dismiss this possibility by arguing that annuities are quantitatively not important in the real world, although private pensions and government pensions through social security are common. The limited use of annuities may, in any case, be an indication that the infinite-horizon model, which assumes altruistic linkages across generations, is a satisfactory framework. In this model, the demand for annuities is small, and the observed quantity of annuities would also be small.

below. Since $e^{-p(v-t)}$ is the probability of being alive at time v, conditioned on being alive at the earlier time t, the expected utility becomes

$$E_t U = \int_t^\infty \log[c(j, v)] \cdot e^{-(\rho+p)\cdot(v-t)} dv. \qquad (3.20)$$

Thus, $\rho + p$ is the effective rate of time preference in the context of an uncertain lifetime.

The flow budget constraint for the household is now

$$da(j, v)/dv = [r(v) + p] \cdot a(j, v) + w(v) - c(j, v). \qquad (3.21)$$

Each household maximizes expected utility in Eq. (3.20), subject to Eq. (3.21) and to the amount of initial assets, $a(j, t)$. The first-order condition for consumption is the same as that found before (Eq. [2.10] with $\theta = 1$) :

$$\frac{dc(j, t)/dt}{c(j, t)} = r - \rho. \qquad (3.22)$$

Note that the probability of death, p, cancels out because it impacts equally on the effective time-preference rate, $\rho + p$, and the rate of return, $r + p$.

The transversality condition is now

$$\lim_{v \to \infty} \left[e^{-[\bar{r}(t,v)+p]\cdot(v-t)} \cdot a(j, v) \right] = 0, \qquad (3.23)$$

where $\bar{r}(t, v)$ is the "average" interest rate between times t and v (see Eq. [2.12], which refers to the period between 0 and t). Eqs. (3.21) and (3.23) imply that the household's lifetime budget constraint is

$$\int_t^\infty c(j, v) \cdot e^{-[\bar{r}(t,v)+p]\cdot(v-t)} dv = a(j, t) + \tilde{w}(t), \qquad (3.24)$$

where $\tilde{w}(t) = \int_t^\infty w(v) \cdot e^{-[\bar{r}(v)+p]\cdot(v-t)} dv$ is the present value of wage income. Equation (3.24) corresponds to Eq. (2.13) in the infinite-horizon model.

We can also use Eqs. (3.22) and (3.24) to determine consumption as a function of "wealth":

$$c(j, t) = (\rho + p) \cdot [a(j, t) + \tilde{w}(t)], \qquad (3.25)$$

which corresponds to Eqs. (2.14) and (2.15) (with $\theta = 1$) in the infinite-horizon model. The simplification from log utility is that the marginal propensity to consume out of wealth is the constant $\rho + p$.

The aggregate variables, $C(t)$, $A(t)$, and $\tilde{W}(t)$, come from addition across the cohorts, indexed by the time of birth, $j \le t$. Each cohort is weighted by its size, which equals the initial size, $(p + n) \cdot e^{nj}$, multiplied by the fraction, $e^{-p\cdot(t-j)}$, that is still alive at time $t \ge j$. Therefore, aggregate consumption and assets are given by

$$C(t) = \int_{-\infty}^t c(j, t) \cdot (p + n) \cdot e^{nj} e^{-p(t-j)} dj, \qquad (3.26)$$

$$A(t) = \int_{-\infty}^t a(j, t) \cdot (p + n) \cdot e^{nj} e^{-p(t-j)} dj. \qquad (3.27)$$

Since wage rates are independent of age, the aggregate of the present value of wage income is

$$\tilde{W}(t) = \tilde{w}(t) \cdot e^{nt} = e^{nt} \cdot \int_{t}^{\infty} w(v) \cdot e^{-[\bar{r}(t,v)+p]\cdot(v-t)}dv. \qquad (3.28)$$

Since the propensity to consume out of wealth in Eq. (3.25) is $\rho + p$, which is independent of age, j, the aggregate relationship is the same as the individual one:

$$C(t) = (\rho + p) \cdot [A(t) + \tilde{W}(t)]. \qquad (3.29)$$

We want to use Eq. (3.29) to compute the aggregate analog to Eq. (3.22), which determines the change over time in individual consumption. The change over time in aggregate consumption, $\dot{C}$, depends on the change over time in aggregate wealth, $\dot{A} + \dot{\tilde{W}}$.

We can calculate $\dot{A}$ by differentiating Eq. (3.27) with respect to t. The result is

$$\dot{A} = r(t) \cdot A(t) + w(t) \cdot e^{nt} - C(t), \qquad (3.30)$$

where $w(t) \cdot e^{nt}$ is aggregate wages paid at time t. The derivation of Eq. (3.30) uses the individual budget constraint in Eq. (3.21) and the condition $a(j, j) = 0$; that is, individuals are born with zero assets. Note that the aggregate equation corresponds to the individual one in Eq. (3.21), except that the rate of return on total assets is r, whereas that on individual assets (for someone who survives) is $r + p$.

We can also compute the change in $\tilde{W}$ by differentiating Eq. (3.28) with respect to t. The result is

$$\dot{\tilde{W}} = [r(t) + p + n] \cdot \tilde{W}(t) - w(t) \cdot e^{nt}. \qquad (3.31)$$

The term on the far right equals aggregate wages, which are effectively the dividend paid on the asset stock $\tilde{W}(t)$. The first term on the right reflects the discounting of individual wages at the rate $r(t) + p$ (because wages vanish when a person dies) and the growth of population at the rate n.

We can use Eqs. (3.29)–(3.31) to determine the change over time in aggregate consumption, $\dot{C}$. The result, expressed in terms of the growth rate of per capita consumption, is[13]

$$\dot{c}/c = r(t) - \rho - (p + n) \cdot (\rho + p) \cdot a(t)/c(t). \qquad (3.32)$$

Note that $c(t)$ refers to aggregate consumption divided by aggregate population and not to the consumption of a surviving individual. The evolution of a surviving individual's consumption, $c(j, t)$, is given by Eq. (3.22).

The key new element in Eq. (3.32) is the term on the far right, $(p + n) \cdot (\rho + p) \cdot a(t)/c(t)$. Since $\rho + p$ is the propensity to consume out of wealth, $(\rho + p) \cdot a(t)$ is the consumption per person associated with $a(t)$. New people enter the economy at rate $p + n$. Because these new people arrive with zero assets, the inflow of these people

---

[13]For $\theta \neq 1$, this result turns out to generalize when $r(t)$ equals the constant r to $\dot{c}/c = (1/\theta) \cdot (r - \rho) - (1/\theta) \cdot [\rho + \theta p - (1 - \theta) \cdot r] \cdot (p + n) \cdot a(t)/c(t)$.

lowers the average consumption per person by the amount $(p + n) \cdot (\rho + p) \cdot a(t)$. Finally, the division by $c(t)$ gives the contribution of this term to the reduction in the growth rate of consumption per person, $\dot{c}/c$.

Note from the discussion that the crucial feature is the arrival of new persons (with zero assets) and not the departure of old persons. Thus, as Weil (1989) points out, the main results go through with infinite lifetimes ($p = 0$) if new people are born ($n > 0$). It is, however, crucial that the old people not care about the new ones in the manner of the altruistic linkages assumed in the infinite-horizon framework of Chapter 2. Thus, we can think of the new persons as unloved children and immigrants (as in Weil [1989]). We deal explicitly with immigrants in Chapter 9.

3.4.2 The Finite-Horizon Model of a Closed Economy

We consider again the model with one type of capital, k. For a closed economy, $\hat{a} = \hat{k}$, $f'(\hat{k}) = r + \delta$, and $\hat{w} = f(\hat{k}) - \hat{k} \cdot f'(\hat{k})$. The formula that determines $\dot{\hat{k}}$ is then the same as that in the infinite-horizon model (Eq. [2.23]):

$$\dot{\hat{k}} = f(\hat{k}) - \hat{c} - (x + n + \delta) \cdot \hat{k}. \qquad (3.33)$$

Equation (3.32) and the conditions $\hat{a} = \hat{k}$ and $r = f'(\hat{k}) - \delta$ imply

$$\dot{\hat{c}}/\hat{c} = f'(\hat{k}) - (\delta + \rho + x) - (p + n) \cdot (\rho + p) \cdot \hat{k}/\hat{c}. \qquad (3.34)$$

Figure 3.1 shows the phase diagram for $\hat{k}$ and $\hat{c}$. The solid curve, which corresponds to $\dot{\hat{k}} = 0$, is the same as the curve for the infinite-horizon model in Figure 2.1.

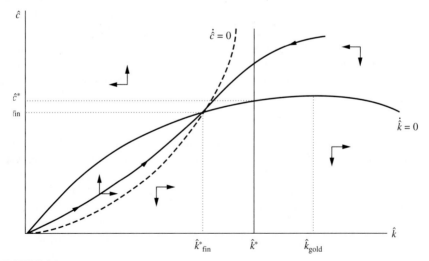

FIGURE 3.1
Dynamics in a finite-horizon closed economy. The $\dot{\hat{k}} = 0$ locus displays the usual inverse U-shape. The $\dot{\hat{c}} = 0$ locus goes through the origin, slopes upward, and asymptotes vertically at $\hat{k} = \hat{k}^*$. The shape of the stable arm and therefore the transitional dynamics of the model are similar to those of the Ramsey model.

The solid vertical line at $\hat{k}^*$, where $f'(\hat{k}^*) = \delta + \rho + x$, is the steady-state value in the infinite-horizon model (if $\theta = 1$). The term that involves $\hat{k}/\hat{c}$ in Eq. (3.34) effectively adds to the time-preference rate, ρ, if $p + n > 0$. The dashed curve in Figure 3.1, which shows the locus for $\dot{\hat{c}} = 0$, therefore lies everywhere to the left of the vertical line. As the ratio of $\hat{c}$ to $\hat{k}$ rises along the dashed curve, the size of the term that involves $\hat{k}/\hat{c}$ diminishes toward 0; therefore, the dashed curve asymptotically approaches the vertical line.

The steady-state values for the finite-horizon model of a closed economy, determined at the intersection of the solid and dashed curves, are denoted $\hat{k}_{fin}^*$ and $\hat{c}_{fin}^*$ in Figure 3.1. The important observation is that the higher effective rate of time preference leads to a higher marginal product of capital and therefore to a lower ratio of capital to effective labor, that is, $\hat{k}_{fin}^* < \hat{k}^*$. Correspondingly, the steady-state interest rate is higher than that for the infinite-horizon economy, $r_{fin}^* > r^* = \rho + x$,[14] consumption per effective worker is lower, $\hat{c}_{fin}^* < \hat{c}^*$.

The transition from an initial ratio, $\hat{k}(0)$, to $\hat{k}_{fin}^*$ is similar to the transition in the infinite-horizon model. If $\hat{k}(0) < \hat{k}_{fin}^*$, then $\hat{k}$ rises monotonically along the solid curve marked by the arrows in Figure 3.1. The dynamics of the other variables—$\hat{c}$, r, and the growth rates of $\hat{k}$, $\hat{y}$, and $\hat{c}$—is also similar to that in the infinite-horizon model.

Since $\hat{k}_{fin}^* < \hat{k}^*$, it follows that $\hat{k}_{fin}^* < \hat{k}_{gold}$—see Figure 3.1.[15] Hence, the asymptotic behavior of $\hat{k}$ in the finite-horizon model of a closed economy does not exhibit the kind of inefficient oversaving that can arise in the Solow–Swan model with an arbitrary saving rate. Diamond (1965) showed that oversaving can arise in a two-period overlapping-generations model of a closed economy. As our results (based on Blanchard [1985]) have shown, the feature of the Diamond model that generates the possibility of oversaving is not the finite horizons of individuals. Rather, the key difference from the model that we have just analyzed is the assumed life-cycle pattern of wage incomes. In the Diamond version of the OLG model, wages are positive in the first (working) period and zero in the second (retirement) period. Thus, the model assumes that wage income declines sharply over the life cycle, whereas the finite-horizon model that we have been considering assumes that wage income is invariant with age. A declining pattern of wage income with respect to age motivates additional saving; inefficient oversaving can emerge if this effect is very strong.

We can extend the finite-horizon model that we analyzed before to allow for a decline in productivity over the life cycle. (See Blanchard [1985] for an analysis of this situation.) If wage rates decline with age at the rate ω, then Eq. (3.34) is modified to

$$\dot{\hat{c}}/\hat{c} = f'(\hat{k}) - (\delta + \rho + x - \omega) - (p + n + \omega) \cdot (\rho + p) \cdot \hat{k}(t)/\hat{c}(t). \quad (3.35)$$

---

[14]We can use the formula in footnote 13 to show that this result still holds if $\theta \neq 1$, in which case $r^* = \rho + \theta x$. It is also possible to show that $r_{fin}^* < \rho + \theta x + p + n$.

[15]We used the condition $\rho > n$ to ensure $\hat{k}^* < \hat{k}_{gold}$ in the infinite-horizon model. We are still assuming that $\rho > n$ holds in the finite-horizon case.

The direct effect of ω in Eq. (3.35) subtracts from ρ and thereby effectively lowers the rate of time preference. Because of this encouragement to saving, $\hat{k}_{\text{fin}}^* > \hat{k}^*$ applies if ω is high enough. Moreover, for a still higher value of ω, the steady state exhibits inefficient oversaving: $\hat{k}_{\text{fin}}^* > \hat{k}_{\text{gold}}$.

Although inefficient oversaving is possible in the finite-horizon economy if wage income declines over the life cycle—that is, for sufficiently high ω—it is unclear in practice that we should even treat ω as positive. If we begin at the time of an individual's first job—say, age 18 or 21—then wage income *rises* substantially with age (and experience) for about 25 years and is relatively flat for the next 20–25 years (see Murphy and Welch [1990, p. 207]). Wage income then declines dramatically for the roughly 10 to 15–year span of retirement. Thus, the two-period overlapping-generations model ignores the interval of rising wage incomes and also errs in assuming that the retirement period is as long as the working span. Each of the errors works in the direction of overstating the life-cycle incentive to save.

To get a complete picture, we also have to decide how to treat the first 18–21 years that correspond to childhood and schooling. If we treat children as independent households, then the first 18–21 years of life feature wage incomes that are sharply below the lifetime average. The shortfall of current from expected future wage income impacts negatively on the aggregate desire to save; presumably, this effect would show up as children borrowing from their parents to finance consumption.

We can reasonably argue that minor children should not be treated as separate households.[16] But then the period of low wage income for children up to age 18 or 21 translates, for given parental wage income, into low per capita wage income of the family when the family contains dependent children. Therefore, the low level of children's wage income motivates parents to save less than otherwise during an interval of parental ages that corresponds typically to middle age. Thus, this effect combines with the influence of rising wage income of adults during much of their working span to offset the positive effect on saving from the existence of the retirement period.

The upshot of this discussion is that $\omega \approx 0$—a flat profile of the family's per capita wage income—may not be a bad first approximation for the purpose of analyzing the aggregate willingness to save. In that case, the analysis rules out the possibility of oversaving in the finite-horizon model of a closed economy.

3.4.3 The Finite-Horizon Model of an Open Economy

Consider now the finite-horizon model of an open economy with one type of capital, k, and with no constraint on borrowing. We omit the country subscript i for convenience. If the world interest rate, $r(t)$, equals the constant r, then the ratio of

---

[16]This argument is, however, more compelling in the infinite-horizon model in which parents' altruistic motives lead them to provide for their children's consumption. In the finite-horizon model, in which parents apparently do not care about their children, the rationale for parental support of minor children is harder to understand.

capital to effective labor in the domestic country equals the constant $(\hat{k}^*)_{\text{open}}$, where $f'[(\hat{k}^*)_{\text{open}}] = r + \delta$. Hence, this model still implies an infinite speed of convergence for $\hat{k}$ and $\hat{y}$. The behavior of $\hat{c}$ and $\hat{a}$ will, however, be more reasonable than before. Equation (3.6) gives the change in assets:

$$\dot{a} = f[(\hat{k}^*)_{\text{open}}] - (r + \delta) \cdot [(\hat{k}^*)_{\text{open}} - \hat{a}] - (x + n + \delta) \cdot \hat{a} - \hat{c} \qquad (3.36)$$

$$= (\hat{w}^*)_{\text{open}} + (r - x - n) \cdot \hat{a} - \hat{c},$$

where we used the condition $f[(\hat{k}^*)_{\text{open}}] = (\hat{w}^*)_{\text{open}} + (r + \delta) \cdot (\hat{k}^*)_{\text{open}}$. The behavior of household consumption from Eq. (3.32) implies

$$\dot{c}/\hat{c} = r - \rho - x - (p + n) \cdot (\rho + p) \cdot \hat{a}/\hat{c}. \qquad (3.37)$$

Figure 3.2 shows the phase diagram for $(\hat{a}, \hat{c})$ that is implied by Eqs. (3.36) and (3.37). Note that this diagram applies for a constant r; that is, we consider the dynamics for a small open economy when the world economy is in a steady state. The line for $\dot{a} = 0$, from Eq. (3.36), has a positive intercept (equal to $[\hat{w}^*]_{\text{open}}$) and a positive slope of $r - x - n$. The line for $\dot{c} = 0$, from Eq. (3.37), goes through the origin, and the sign of the slope equals the sign of $r - \rho - x$. This last term is positive in the finite-horizon model of a closed economy that we considered in the previous

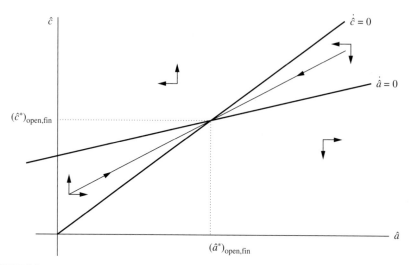

FIGURE 3.2
The phase diagram for a finite-horizon open economy (for a fixed interest rate). The diagram considers a small open economy that faces a fixed interest rate, given on world capital markets. The two loci are straight lines in this case, and the model exhibits saddle-path stability. If the economy starts with a low level of assets per effective person, then the transition features monotonically increasing levels of consumption and assets per effective person.

section. Now this term will be positive for any country that ends up holding positive assets in the steady state. Figure 3.2 shows the $\dot{c} = 0$ line with a positive slope that exceeds the slope of the $\dot{a} = 0$ line.[17]

Figure 3.2 shows the steady-state values for $\hat{c}$ and $\hat{a}$ in the finite-horizon open economy. In contrast with the infinite-horizon model, these steady-state values are positive and finite. This outcome is consistent with $\dot{c} = 0$ in Eq. (3.37) because the ratio $\hat{a}/\hat{c}$ adjusts so that the overall time-preference term, $\rho + x + (p+n) \cdot (\rho + p) \cdot \hat{a}/\hat{c}$, equals r. In other words, the key property is that the effective time-preference rate is an increasing function of $\hat{a}/\hat{c}$.

A higher value of ρ steepens the slope of the $\dot{c} = 0$ locus in Figure 3.2 (see Eq. [3.37]). That is, the locus pivots around the origin in a counterclockwise manner. The figure then implies that less-patient countries—with higher values of ρ—have lower steady-state values of $\hat{a}$ and $\hat{c}$. We can also verify from the figure that the steady-state values of $\hat{a}$ and $\hat{c}$ decline with increases in x, p, and n. (They also decline with θ if $\theta \neq 1$ is allowed.)

The steady-state value of $\hat{a}$ is positive for a range of parameter values; that is, the debt, $\hat{d}$, remains below the capital stock, $\hat{k}$. However, a sufficiently high value of ρ (or of x or θ) makes the slope of the $\dot{c} = 0$ locus negative, so that the steady-state value for $\hat{a}$ becomes negative. In other words, $\hat{d} > \hat{k}$ applies for sufficiently impatient economies. In these situations, borrowers use a part of the present value of wage income as collateral.

For a given r and a given array of parameter values for countries $i = 1, \ldots, M$, we can determine the corresponding array of $\hat{a}_i$ from Figure 3.2. We can also determine the array of $\hat{k}_i$ from the condition $f'(\hat{k}_i) = r + \delta_i$. In a full steady-state equilibrium, the world interest rate, r, is the value that equates the sum of the $\hat{a}_i$ (weighted by each country's effective labor force) to the sum of the $\hat{k}_i$ (similarly weighted).

The finite-horizon framework is attractive because economies with different underlying parameters can share a common capital market without the implication that $\hat{c}_i$ tends to zero for all but the most patient country. The model implies, however, that convergence rates of $\hat{k}_i$ and $\hat{y}_i$ would be infinite. To avoid this conclusion, we can combine the finite-horizon model with the analysis of credit constraints that we considered in the previous section. The results follow readily if we identify $\hat{k}_i$ with broad capital, $\hat{k}_i + \hat{h}_i$, in the model with a credit constraint.

For given $(\hat{k}_i^*)_{\text{open}}$, the countries that have high steady-state values of $\hat{a}_i$ in Figure 3.2 end up unconstrained on the credit market, whereas those with low values (and surely those with negative values) of $\hat{a}_i$ end up constrained. Thus, the countries with relatively high values of ρ_i, x_i, p_i, n_i, and θ_i tend to be credit constrained. In addition to the impatient countries—with high values of ρ_i and θ_i—the candidates for credit constraints therefore include those that grow rapidly in the steady state (high x_i and n_i) and those with high mortality rates (high p_i).

---

[17]If the slope of the $\dot{c} = 0$ locus is positive, but not greater than the slope of the $\dot{a} = 0$ locus, then we can show that $\hat{c}$ rises forever. This outcome is inconsistent with the fixed world interest rate, r.

The finite-horizon model of an open economy with credit constraints implies that $\hat{c}_i$ and $\hat{a}_i$ remain positive in all countries. Also, only some of the countries are credit constrained in the steady state. For these constrained countries, the convergence speeds for $\hat{k}_i$ and $\hat{y}_i$ in the neighborhood of the steady state are finite, as shown in the previous section. For the unconstrained countries, however, the convergence speeds for $\hat{k}_i$ and $\hat{y}_i$ are still infinite. To avoid this result, we have to introduce another feature, adjustment costs for investment.

3.5 ADJUSTMENT COSTS FOR INVESTMENT

We mentioned in Chapter 2 that adjustment costs for investment tend to slow down the economy's convergence to the steady state. Adjustment costs are the costs associated with the installation of capital. In an open economy, the presence of these costs implies that convergence of capital stocks and output would be less than instantaneous even if capital markets were perfect and households had infinite horizons. Thus, adjustment costs avoid some of the counterfactual results from the open-economy version of the Ramsey model.

If we distinguish between physical and human capital, then we anticipate that adjustment costs would be especially important for increases in human capital through the process of education. The learning experience fundamentally takes time, and attempts to accelerate the educational process are likely to encounter rapidly diminishing rates of return. We simplify the analysis in this section by thinking of a single type of capital good, which is a composite of physical and human capital. To assess the size of the adjustment cost, however, we should recall that the good consists partly of human capital, which is difficult to change rapidly.

3.5.1 The Behavior of Firms

We assume as in Chapter 2 that the production function is neoclassical:

$$Y = F(K, \hat{L}), \tag{3.38}$$

where $F(\bullet)$ satisfies the neoclassical properties (Eq. [1.5a]–[1.5c]) and $\hat{L} = Le^{xt}$ is the effective amount of labor input. Each firm i has access to the technology shown in Eq. (3.38); for convenience, we omit the subscript i.

We now find it convenient to think of the firm as owning its stock of capital, K, rather than renting it from households. The households will instead have a claim on the firm's net cash flows.

The change in the firm's capital stock is given by

$$\dot{K} = I - \delta K, \tag{3.39}$$

where I is gross investment. We assume that the cost in units of output for each unit of investment is 1 plus an adjustment cost, which is an increasing function of I in relation to K, that is,

$$\text{Cost of investment} = I \cdot [1 + \phi(I/K)], \tag{3.40}$$

where $\phi(0) = 0$, $\phi' > 0$, and $\phi'' \geq 0$. The assumption is that adjustment costs depend on gross investment, I, rather than net investment, $I - \delta K$.

Firms again pay the wage rate, w, for each unit of labor, L, and we neglect any adjustment costs associated with changes in L. The firm's net cash flow is given accordingly by

$$\text{Net cash flow} = F(K, \hat{L}) - wL - I \cdot [1 + \phi(I/K)]. \qquad (3.41)$$

The firm has a fixed number of equity shares outstanding, and the value of these shares at time 0 is determined on a stock market to be the amount $V(0)$. (If we normalize the number of shares to unity, then $V(0)$ is the price per share at time 0.) We assume that the net cash flow given in Eq. (3.41) is paid out as dividends to the shareowners.[18] Hence, $V(0)$ equals the present value of the net cash flows between times 0 and infinity, discounted in accordance with the market rate of return, $r(t)$. (The rate of return to holders of shares will then turn out to be $r(t)$ at each date.) The firm makes decisions to further the interests of the shareowners and seeks therefore to maximize $V(0)$.

We again define $\bar{r}(t)$ as the average interest rate between times 0 and t as in Eq. (2.12):

$$\bar{r}(t) \equiv (1/t) \cdot \int_0^t r(v)\, dv.$$

The firm's objective is then to choose L and I at each date to maximize

$$V(0) = \int_0^\infty e^{-\bar{r}(t)\cdot t} \cdot \left\{ F(K, \hat{L}) - wL - I \cdot [1 + \phi(I/K)] \right\} \cdot dt, \qquad (3.42)$$

subject to Eq. (3.39) and an initial value $K(0)$.

We can analyze this optimization problem by setting up the Hamiltonian

$$J = e^{-\bar{r}(t)\cdot t} \cdot \left\{ F(K, \hat{L}) - wL - I \cdot [1 + \phi(I/K)] + q \cdot (I - \delta K) \right\}, \qquad (3.43)$$

where q is the shadow price associated with $\dot{K} = I - \delta K$. We set up the current-value Hamiltonian so that q has the units of goods per unit of capital at time t; that is, q represents the current-value shadow price of installed capital in units of contemporaneous output. The present-value shadow price is then

$$v = q \cdot e^{-\bar{r}(t)\cdot t}.$$

---

[18]This setup is satisfactory if we allow for negative dividends—proportionate levies on shareowners—to finance negative net cash flows. We could instead allow firms to borrow at the interest rate, $r(t)$. The results would be the same as in the text if we introduced a borrowing constraint that ruled out chain-letter debt finance. (This constraint is the same as the one already imposed on households.) We could also allow firms to fund negative net cash flows by issuing new equity shares. The results would again be the same if we expressed the firm's objective as the maximization of the price per share of the shares that were already outstanding.

The maximization entails the standard first-order conditions, $\partial J/\partial L = \partial J/\partial I = 0$ and $\dot{\nu} = -\partial J/\partial K$, and the transversality condition, $\lim_{t \to \infty}(\nu K) = 0$. The first-order conditions can be expressed as

$$[f(\hat{k}) - \hat{k} \cdot f'(\hat{k})] \cdot e^{xt} = w, \tag{3.44}$$

$$q = 1 + \phi(\hat{i}/\hat{k}) + (\hat{i}/\hat{k}) \cdot \phi'(\hat{i}/\hat{k}), \tag{3.45}$$

$$\dot{q} = (r + \delta) \cdot q - [f'(\hat{k}) + (\hat{i}/\hat{k})^2 \cdot \phi'(\hat{i}/\hat{k})], \tag{3.46}$$

where we have used the intensive form of the production function, $f(\cdot)$, and written capital and gross investment as quantities per unit of effective labor, $\hat{k}$ and $\hat{i}$, respectively.[19]

Equation (3.44) is the usual equation of the marginal product of labor to the wage rate, a result that holds because no adjustment costs are attached to changes in labor input. Equation (3.45) indicates that the shadow value of installed capital, q, exceeds unity if $\hat{i} > 0$ because of the adjustment costs. The relation between q and $\hat{i}/\hat{k}$ is monotonically increasing because $\phi'(\hat{i}/\hat{k}) > 0$ and $\phi''(\hat{i}/\hat{k}) \geq 0$.[20]

Equation (3.46) can be rewritten as

$$r = (1/q) \cdot [f'(\hat{k}) + (\hat{i}/\hat{k})^2 \cdot \phi'(\hat{i}/\hat{k})] - \delta + \dot{q}/q.$$

This equation says that the market rate of return, r, is equated to the total rate of return from paying q to hold a unit of capital. This return on capital equals the marginal product, $f'(\hat{k})$, plus the marginal reduction in adjustment costs (when K rises for given I), all deflated by the cost of capital, q; less the depreciation of installed capital at rate δ; plus the rate of capital gain, $\dot{q}/q$. If adjustment costs were absent, so that $\phi(\hat{i}/\hat{k}) = \phi'(\hat{i}/\hat{k}) = 0$ and $q = 1$, then Eq. (3.46) would reduce to the conventional result, $r = f'(\hat{k}) - \delta$.

The transversality condition can be expressed as

$$\lim_{t \to \infty} \left[q\hat{k} \cdot e^{-[\bar{r}(t) - n - x] \cdot t} \right] = 0. \tag{3.47}$$

Thus, if q and $\hat{k}$ asymptotically approach constants (as they do), then the steady-state interest rate, r^*, must, as usual, exceed the steady-state growth rate, $n + x$.

Since the relation between q and $\hat{i}/\hat{k}$ in Eq. (3.45) is monotonically increasing, we can invert this relation to express $\hat{i}/\hat{k}$ as a monotonically increasing function of q :

$$\hat{i}/\hat{k} = \psi(q), \tag{3.48}$$

---

[19] For given w, r, q, and $\dot{q}$, Eqs. (3.44)–(3.46) ensure that all firms have the same values of $\hat{k}$ and $\hat{i}$. The relative size of each firm, $\hat{L}_i(t)/\hat{L}(t)$, is pinned down by its initial value, $\hat{L}_i(0)/\hat{L}(0)$; in particular, changes in relative size do not occur over time because of the adjustment costs for installing capital (if we assume that these costs must be paid even when a firm sells and buys used capital).

[20] This result requires only the weaker condition $2 \cdot \phi'(\hat{i}/\hat{k}) + (\hat{i}/\hat{k}) \cdot \phi''(\hat{i}/\hat{k}) > 0$.

where $\psi'(q) > 0$. Relations of the form of Eq. (3.48) have frequently been estimated empirically.[21] These empirical studies follow the suggestion of Brainard and Tobin (1968) and use the ratio of firms' market value to the capital stock, V/K, as a proxy for q. The ratio V/K is now called *average q*, whereas the shadow price of installed capital that appears in our theoretical analysis is called *marginal q*. The two concepts of q correspond, however, in our model.

To demonstrate the correspondence between marginal and average q, use Eqs. (3.46), (3.45), and (3.39) to get (after some manipulation)

$$d(qK)/dt = \dot{q}K + q\dot{K} = rqK - \hat{L} \cdot \left\{ f(\hat{k}) - we^{-xt} - \hat{i} \cdot [1 + \phi(\hat{i}/\hat{k})] \right\}.$$

This relation is a first-order, linear differential equation in qK and can be solved using $e^{-\bar{r}(t)\cdot t}$ as an integrating factor. If we use the transversality condition from Eq. (3.47) and the definition of V from Eq. (3.42), then we get

$$qK = V,$$

so that V/K (or average q) equals q (or marginal q). Hayashi (1982) shows that this result applies as long as the production function exhibits constant returns to scale.

3.5.2 Equilibrium with a Given Interest Rate

We now analyze the steady state and transitional dynamics when the interest rate, $r(t)$, is given exogenously. This setting applies to a single firm that takes as given the economy-wide interest rate or to a small open economy that takes as given the world interest rate. This last context corresponds to the first extension of the Ramsey model that we considered in this chapter. We found there that convergence of $\hat{k}$ and $\hat{y}$ to their steady-state values was instantaneous, but we now show that adjustment costs imply finite convergence speeds even when credit markets are perfect.

We simplify by assuming that the world interest rate, r, is constant, where $r > x + n$. We also specialize to the case in which the adjustment cost is proportional to $\hat{i}/\hat{k}$; that is,

$$\phi(\hat{i}/\hat{k}) = (b/2) \cdot (\hat{i}/\hat{k}), \tag{3.49}$$

so that $\phi'(\hat{i}/\hat{k}) = (b/2) > 0$. The parameter b expresses the sensitivity of the adjustment costs to the total amount invested. Higher values of b imply more adjustment costs per unit of $\hat{i}/\hat{k}$. This linear specification for $\phi(\bullet)$ is not necessary for the main results, but does simplify the exposition. If we substitute this form for $\phi(\bullet)$ into Eq. (3.45), then we get a linear relation between $\hat{i}/\hat{k}$ and q:

$$\hat{i}/\hat{k} = \psi(q) = (q - 1)/b. \tag{3.50}$$

[21]See, for example, von Furstenberg (1977), Summers (1981), and Blanchard, Rhee, and Summers (1993). Barro (1990a) estimates in first-difference form, so that the change in the investment ratio relates to the change in firms' market value. This change in market value was then approximated by the rate of return on the stock market.

Equations (3.39) and (3.50) imply that the change in $\hat{k}$ can be expressed as a function of q:

$$\dot{\hat{k}} = \hat{i} - (x + n + \delta) \cdot \hat{k} = [(q - 1)/b - (x + n + \delta)] \cdot \hat{k}. \qquad (3.51)$$

If we substitute for $\hat{i}/\hat{k}$ from Eqs. (3.49) and (3.50) into equation (3.46), then we can relate $\dot{q}$ to q and $\hat{k}$:

$$\dot{q} = (r + \delta) \cdot q - [f'(\hat{k}) + (q - 1)^2/2b]. \qquad (3.52)$$

Equations (3.51) and (3.52) form a two-dimensional system of differential equations in the state variable, $\hat{k}$, and the shadow price, q. We can use a phase diagram to analyze the steady state and transitional dynamics of this system. The phase diagram is drawn in $(\hat{k}, q)$ space in Figure 3.3.

The condition $\dot{\hat{k}} = 0$ implies from Eq. (3.51) (if $\hat{k} \neq 0$)

$$q = q^* = 1 + b \cdot (x + n + \delta). \qquad (3.53)$$

The steady-state value of q exceeds 1 because adjustment costs are borne in the steady state for the gross investment that replaces the capital that wears out at the rate δ. There is further depreciation of capital in efficiency units because $\hat{L}$ grows at the rate $x + \delta$. Equation (3.53) appears as the horizontal line $q = q^*$ in Figure 3.3. Equation (3.51) implies $\dot{\hat{k}} > 0$ for $q > q^*$ and $\dot{\hat{k}} < 0$ for $q < q^*$, as shown by the arrows.

The condition $\dot{q} = 0$ leads from Eq. (3.52) to the condition

$$(q - 1)^2 - 2b \cdot (r + \delta) \cdot q + 2b \cdot f'(\hat{k}) = 0. \qquad (3.54)$$

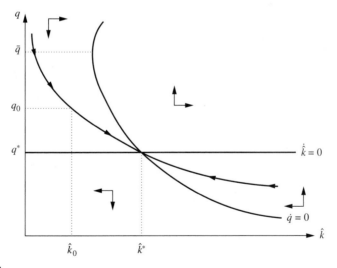

FIGURE 3.3
The phase diagram for the model with adjustment costs (assuming a fixed interest rate). The phase diagram is shown here in $(q, \hat{k})$ space, where q is the market value per unit of installed capital. The $\dot{\hat{k}} = 0$ locus is a horizontal line at q^*. The $\dot{q} = 0$ locus is downward sloping around the steady state. As q rises, the schedule becomes steeper, and the slope becomes positive when $q > 1 + b \cdot (r + \delta) > q^*$. The stable arm is downward sloping throughout. Hence, for low values of $\hat{k}$, $q > q^*$ applies. In this case, the transitional dynamics exhibit monotonic increases in $\hat{k}$ and monotonic decreases in q.

If we substitute $q = q^*$ from Eq. (3.53), then the steady-state value $\hat{k}^*$ must satisfy the condition

$$f'(\hat{k}^*) = r + \delta + b \cdot (x + n + \delta) \cdot [r + \delta - (1/2) \cdot (x + n + \delta)]. \quad (3.55)$$

Since $r > x + n$, Eq. (3.55) shows that the presence of adjustment costs, $b > 0$, raises $f'(\hat{k}^*)$ above the value, $r + \delta$, that would otherwise apply. Consequently, $\hat{k}^*$ is reduced by adjustment costs.

The slope of the relation between q and $\hat{k}$ along the $\dot{q} = 0$ locus is given from Eq. (3.54) by

$$\frac{dq}{d\hat{k}} = \frac{-b \cdot f''(\hat{k})}{(q - 1) - b \cdot (r + \delta)}.$$

The numerator is positive, and the denominator is negative if $q < 1 + b \cdot (r + \delta)$. This inequality must hold at the steady-state value, q^*, because $r > x + n$ (see Eq. [3.53]). Therefore, the $\dot{q} = 0$ locus is downward sloping, as shown in Figure 3.3, for $q \leq q^*$.[22] The slope is positive if $q > 1 + b \cdot (r + \delta) > q^*$. Equation (3.53) implies $\dot{q} < 0$ for values of $\hat{k}$ to the left of the $\dot{q} = 0$ locus and $\dot{q} > 0$ for values to the right of the locus. The arrows in the figure show these movements of q.

The system described in Figure 3.3 exhibits saddle-path stability. The stable arm is downward sloping, as shown by the solid line with arrows. Thus, if the economy begins at $\hat{k}(0) < \hat{k}^*$, then $q(0) > q^*$. The high market value of installed capital stimulates a great deal (but not an infinite amount) of investment; that is, $\hat{i}/\hat{k}$ is high when q is high in accordance with Eq. (3.50). The increase in $\hat{k}$ over time leads to decreases in q and, hence, to reductions in $\hat{i}/\hat{k}$. Eventually, q approaches q^*, $\hat{i}/\hat{k}$ approaches $x + n + \delta$, and $\hat{k}$ approaches $\hat{k}^*$.

The theory predicts that a poor economy (with $\hat{k}(0)$ well below $\hat{k}^*$) with access to world credit markets will have a high value of installed capital, q, and a high growth rate of the capital stock. We now quantify the implications about the speed of convergence for capital and output.

We can approximate Eqs. (3.51) and (3.52) as a linear system in $\log(\hat{k})$ and q in the vicinity of the steady state. We assume that the production function is Cobb–Douglas, $f(\hat{k}) = A\hat{k}^\alpha$, and we use familiar parameter values: $\alpha = 0.75$, $x = 0.02$/year, $n = 0.01$/year, and $\delta = 0.05$/year. We also assume that the world interest rate is $r = 0.06$/year, although the results are virtually the same if r is somewhat higher, say, $r = 0.08$/year.

Given these choices for the other parameters, the convergence coefficient, β, for $\hat{k}$ and $\hat{y}$ depends on the parameter b in the adjustment-cost function in Eq. (3.49). To think about reasonable values of this parameter, note that at the steady state, where $(\hat{i}/\hat{k})^* = x + n + \delta = 0.08$/year, the cost of a unit of capital is $1 + 0.04 \cdot b$. Also, Eq. (3.53) implies $q^* = 1 + 0.08 \cdot b$. Thus, $b = 1$ implies that $q^* = 1.08$ and

---

[22]This property can be shown to hold for any adjustment-cost function $\phi(\cdot)$ that satisfies $2 \cdot \phi'(\hat{i}/\hat{k}) + (\hat{i}/\hat{k}) \cdot \phi''(\hat{i}/\hat{k}) > 0$.

that the charge at the steady state for an incremental unit of capital is 1.04, whereas $b = 10$ implies that $q^* = 1.80$ and that the charge for extra capital is 1.40. The value $q^* = 1.80$ is high relative to the estimates of q reported by Blanchard, Rhee, and Summers (1993); their values never exceed 1.5. Thus, for physical capital, values of b as high as 10 imply unreasonably high costs of adjustment and tend thereby to generate counterfactually high values of q^*. In fact, since $q > q^*$ applies when $\hat{k} < \hat{k}^*$, the model would require b to be much less than 10 to ensure that $q > 1.5$ does not arise during the transition to the steady state.

The problem is that values of b much less than 10 imply an unrealistically high convergence coefficient, β. For the parameter values mentioned before, β falls from ∞ at $b = 0$ (our first model of an open economy) to 0.16 when $b = 1$, 0.11 when $b = 2$, and 0.09 when $b = 3$. The coefficient β does not fall to 0.05 until b exceeds 6 and does not fall to 0.03 until b equals 12.[23] In order to get β to fall to 0.03 at a lower value of b, we have to assume a capital-share coefficient, α, that is even greater than 0.75. For example, if $\alpha = 0.90$, then β falls to 0.03 when b equals 6.

We see two possible ways out of this difficulty. One is to argue that the adjustment costs associated with human capital are so great that b values of 10 or more—and the correspondingly high q values—are reasonable.[24] We do not know how to check this hypothesis from currently available information about the returns to human capital. The second possibility, which we followed before, is to drop the assumption that the economy can finance all of its investment at the fixed world interest rate, r. That is, we can combine the analysis of adjustment costs for investment with the closed-economy frameworks that we used in Chapters 1 and 2 or with the setting in this chapter in which only physical capital serves as collateral for foreign borrowing. We work out these results in the next section for the case in which adjustment costs for investment are added to the Solow–Swan model, that is, the framework from Chapter 1 in which the economy is closed and the gross saving rate is constant. The other contexts, which are left as exercises, have analogous implications.

3.5.3 Equilibrium for a Closed Economy with a Fixed Saving Rate

Gross investment expenditures, inclusive of adjustment costs, per effective worker are given by

$$\hat{i} \cdot [1 + \phi(\hat{i}/\hat{k})].$$

---

[23] As b tends to infinity, β approaches 0.025; that is, the convergence speed does not tend to zero as the adjustment-cost parameter becomes arbitrarily large. However, as b tends to infinity, the economy is approaching a steady-state value $\hat{k}^*$ that is tending to zero.

[24] Kremer and Thomson (1993) use an overlapping-generations framework in which young workers benefit from interactions with old, experienced workers in an apprentice-mentor context. Their framework effectively implies high adjustment costs for rapid increases in human capital.

In a closed economy, this expenditure corresponds to gross saving per effective worker. If we assume that this saving is the constant fraction s of gross output per worker, $f(\hat{k})$, then we have

$$s \cdot f(\hat{k})/\hat{k} = (\hat{i}/\hat{k}) \cdot [1 + \phi(\hat{i}/\hat{k})].$$

If we use the linear form for $\phi(\hat{i}/\hat{k})$ from Eq. (3.49) and the corresponding expression for $\hat{i}/\hat{k}$ from Eq. (3.50), then this result simplifies to

$$s \cdot f(\hat{k})/\hat{k} = (1/2b) \cdot (q^2 - 1). \tag{3.56}$$

If we use the Cobb–Douglas form of the production function, $f(\hat{k}) = A\hat{k}^{\alpha}$, solve out for q in terms of $\hat{k}$ from Eq. (3.56), and substitute the result into the expression for $\dot{\hat{k}}$ in Eq. (3.51), then we get a differential equation in $\hat{k}$:

$$\dot{\hat{k}}/\hat{k} = (1/b) \cdot \left\{ [1 + 2bsA \cdot \hat{k}^{\alpha-1}]^{1/2} - 1 \right\} - (x + n + \delta). \tag{3.57}$$

This result generalizes the formula from Eq. (1.30) for the Solow–Swan model to allow for adjustment costs. The Solow–Swan result applies if $b = 0.$[25]

We can, as usual, compute the convergence coefficient β by log-linearizing Eq. (3.57) around the steady state. The resulting formula for β is

$$\beta = (1 - \alpha) \cdot (x + n + \delta) \cdot \left[\frac{1 + (1/2) \cdot b \cdot (x + n + \delta)}{1 + b \cdot (x + n + \delta)} \right]. \tag{3.58}$$

Hence, if adjustment costs are absent ($b = 0$), then the formula for β reduces to that from the Solow–Swan model, $(1 - \alpha) \cdot (x + n + \delta)$ (see Eq. [1.31]). If $b > 0$, then Eq. (3.58) indicates that β in the adjustment-cost model is less than that in the Solow–Swan model and is a decreasing function of b. As b tends to infinity, β tends to $(1/2) \cdot (1 - \alpha) \cdot (x + n + \delta)$, that is, to one-half the value prescribed by the Solow–Swan model.

If we use the same parameter values as before ($\alpha = 0.75$, $x = 0.02$, $n = 0.01$, $\delta = 0.05$) and consider values of the adjustment-cost coefficient, b, that are much less than 10, then the major result is that adjustment costs do not have a large impact on the speed of convergence. For example, if $b = 0$ (the Solow–Swan case), then $\beta = 0.020$/year. For $b = 2$, we get $\beta = 0.019$, and for $b = 10$, we get $\beta = 0.016$. Thus, although the presence of adjustment costs slows down convergence, the magnitude of the effect tends to be small. As we mentioned before, to get more significant effects, we have to assume adjustment-cost coefficients that are so large that the implied value of q^*—and, moreover, of transitional values of q—exceed empirically observed values (at least for physical capital).

We can proceed in an analogous manner to allow for adjustment costs in the Ramsey model.[26] Instead of assuming a constant gross saving rate, we then use the familiar condition for household optimization, $\dot{c}/c = (1/\theta) \cdot (r - \rho)$. This analysis is

---

[25]We can use l'Hôpital's rule to show that, as b approaches zero, the formula in Eq. (3.57) reduces to that shown in Eq. (1.30).

[26]See Abel and Blanchard (1983) for an analysis of this model and Problem 3.3.

straightforward but cumbersome and turns out to lead to few new insights. In particular, we find that the presence of adjustment costs reduces the speed of convergence relative to that implied by the Ramsey model (Eq. [2.34]). But, as in the case of the Solow–Swan model, the quantitative effects are small if we assume an adjustment-cost coefficient, b, that is consistent with "reasonable" behavior of the shadow-price q.

3.6 SOME CONCLUSIONS

We began with the seemingly straightforward task of extending the Ramsey model to an open economy by allowing for international borrowing and lending. This extension led, however, to some counterfactual results: convergence speeds for capital stock and output were infinite and, except for the most patient country, consumption (per unit of effective labor) tended to zero and assets became negative. The most patient country asymptotically owned everything and consumed nearly all of the world's output.

We considered several modifications of the Ramsey model to eliminate these paradoxical findings. With imperfect international credit markets, the infinite speeds of convergence for capital and output would not apply to countries that were effectively constrained in their ability to borrow. Moreover, assets remained positive and consumption did not tend to zero in these countries. The particular model that we considered had, however, the counterfactual implication that all but the most patient country would eventually become credit constrained.

In a model where individuals have finite horizons and where new individuals come into the economy, the accumulation of assets effectively raises a country's rate of time preference. (Preference parameters are constant for individuals; the result comes from the aggregation over persons who differ with respect to levels of assets and consumption.) Therefore, even without credit-market constraints, the variation in the effective rate of time preference motivates the most patient country not to accumulate all the world's wealth. Similarly, the relatively impatient countries do not tend to zero consumption.

If we combine the finite-horizon framework with the model of imperfect credit markets, then the long-run equilibrium features a range of countries that are not effectively constrained in their ability to borrow and another range that are effectively constrained. The results are attractive in that many countries—with different preference parameters—are not constrained on the international credit market. In addition, the constrained countries exhibit finite speeds of convergence for capital stocks and output. One remaining problem, however, is that these speeds of convergence are still infinite for the unconstrained countries.

In the final section, we introduced adjustment costs for investment, costs that we thought would be especially important for the accumulation of human capital. These costs imply finite speeds of convergence for capital and output even if world capital markets are perfect and horizons are infinite. We argue, however, that adjustment costs cannot by themselves explain the slow speeds of convergence that are observed empirically, because the implied values of Brainard and Tobin's q would be counterfactually high. Moreover, the adjustment-cost model does not eliminate the puzzling behavior of consumption and assets in the open-economy setting.

We cannot argue at this stage that economists have settled on a fully satisfactory way to apply the Ramsey model to an open economy. The various pieces of analysis that we have gone through in this chapter do, however, get us closer to such a model. In particular, the combination of these pieces can account simultaneously for the observed slow convergence of capital stock and output, while avoiding counterfactual implications about the behavior of consumption and assets.

APPENDIX
OVERLAPPING-GENERATIONS MODELS

In the main text of this chapter, we considered a model of finite-horizon households that was developed by Blanchard (1985). His model is basically a tractable version of overlapping-generations (OLG) models, which were originated by Samuelson (1958) and Diamond (1965). This appendix describes the structure of OLG models and works out some implications of these models.

HOUSEHOLDS

The most popular OLG framework assumes that each person lives for only two periods. People work in the first period, when they are young, retire in the second period, when they are old, and then die off. To relate this setup to the real world, we have to think of a period as representing a generation, say 30 years. Since people consume in both periods of life, they have to pay for consumption in the second period by saving in the first period (if we do not allow for transfers from the government or from members of other generations).

We shall refer to the cohort that is born at time t as generation t. Members of this generation are young in period t and old in period $t + 1$. Therefore, during period t, the young of generation t overlap with the old of generation $t - 1$. At each point in time, members of only two generations are alive. The main justification for this assumption is that it simplifies the aggregation of consumption and other variables.[27]

Each person maximizes lifetime utility, which depends on consumption in the two periods of life. We make the crucial assumption that people do not care about events after their death; specifically, they are not altruistic toward their children and therefore do not provide bequests or other transfers to members of the next genera-

---

[27]In the Blanchard (1985) model, discussed in the text, the aggregate consumption function is simple because individuals of all ages have the same propensity to consume out of wealth. Aggregate consumption is therefore a simple function of aggregate wealth. In the OLG model, individuals of different generations have different propensities to consume and different levels of wealth. Aggregation is simple, however, because only two generations are alive at each point in time.

tion. We assume that the form of the lifetime utility function is a discrete-time analog to the one assumed in the Ramsey model:

$$U_t = \frac{c_{1t}^{1-\theta} - 1}{1 - \theta} + \left(\frac{1}{1 + \rho}\right) \cdot \left(\frac{c_{2t+1}^{1-\theta} - 1}{1 - \theta}\right), \qquad (3A.1)$$

where $\theta > 0$, $\rho > 0$, c_{1t} is consumption of generation t when young (that is, in period t), and c_{2t+1} is consumption of generation t when old (that is, in period $t + 1$).

Consider the lifetime of an individual born at time t. Since members of previous generations do not care about this person, we assume that he is born with no assets. He supplies one unit of labor inelastically while young and receives the wage income, w_t. He does not work when old. If s_t denotes the amount saved in period t, then the budget constraint for period t is

$$c_{1t} + s_t = w_t. \qquad (3A.2)$$

In period $t + 1$, the individual consumes the previous savings plus the accrued interest:

$$c_{2t+1} = (1 + r_{t+1}) \cdot s_t, \qquad (3A.3)$$

where r_{t+1} is the interest rate on one-period loans between periods t and $t + 1$. Equation (3A.3) incorporates the notion that, because individuals do not care about descendants, they choose to end up with zero assets when they die. If we allow for borrowing, $s_t < 0$, then we have to assume that the credit market imposes the constraint that people cannot die in debt.

Each individual treats w_t and r_{t+1} as given and then chooses c_{1t} and s_t (and, hence, c_{2t+1}) to maximize utility from Eq. (3A.1), subject to Eqs. (3A.2) and (3A.3). We can use Eqs. (3A.2) and (3A.3) to substitute out for c_{1t} and c_{2t+1} in the utility function in Eq. (3A.1) and then compute the first-order condition with respect to s, $\partial U / \partial s_t = 0$, to get

$$(s_t)^{-\theta} \cdot (1 + r_{t+1})^{1-\theta} = (1 + \rho) \cdot (w_t - s_t)^{-\theta}. \qquad (3A.4)$$

If we use Eqs. (3A.2) and (3A.3), then Eq. (3A.4) implies

$$c_{2t+1}/c_{1t} = [(1 + r_{t+1})/(1 + \rho)]^{1/\theta}. \qquad (3A.5)$$

This expression is the discrete-time counterpart of the usual relation from the Ramsey model, $\gamma_c = (1/\theta) \cdot (r - \rho)$ from equation (2.24).

Equation (3A.4) implies that the saving rate can be written as

$$s_t = w_t/\psi_{t+1}, \qquad (3A.6)$$

where $\psi_{t+1} \equiv \left[1 + (1 + \rho)^{1/\theta} \cdot (1 + r_{t+1})^{-(1-\theta)/\theta}\right] > 1$. The dependence of s_t on w_t and r_{t+1} can be described by

$$s_w \equiv \partial s_t/\partial w_t = 1/\psi_{t+1},$$

$$s_r \equiv \partial s_t/\partial r_{t+1} = \left(\frac{1 - \theta}{\theta}\right) \cdot \left[\frac{1 + \rho}{1 + r_{t+1}}\right]^{1/\theta} \cdot s_t/\psi_{t+1}.$$

Note that $0 < s_w < 1$, and $s_r > 0$ if $\theta < 1$, $s_r < 0$ if $\theta > 1$, and $s_r = 0$ if $\theta = 1$.

FIRMS

Firms have the usual neoclassical production function,

$$y_t = f(k_t), \tag{3A.7}$$

where $y_t \equiv Y_t/L_t$ and $k_t \equiv K_t/L_t$ are output and capital per worker. (We simplify by neglecting technological progress—that is, assume $x = 0$—because it does not affect the main points of this analysis.) Since each young person works one unit of time, the variable L_t is the total number of young people in the economy. Note that we assume that the capital stock in period t is productive in the same period; that is, there is no lag in the production and use of capital. The standard maximization of profit by competitive firms leads, as in Chapter 2, to the equation of net marginal products to factor prices:

$$w_t = f(k_t) - k_t \cdot f'(k_t), \tag{3A.8}$$

$$r_t = f'(k_t) - \delta, \tag{3A.9}$$

where δ is the depreciation rate.

EQUILIBRIUM

We assume a closed economy, so that households' assets—all owned at the start of a period by members of the old generation—equal the capital stock. Aggregate net investment equals total income minus total consumption:

$$K_{t+1} - K_t = w_t L_t + r_t K_t - c_{1t} L_t - c_{2t} L_{t-1}, \tag{3A.10}$$

where L_{t-1} is the number of people born at time $t - 1$, all of whom are old at time t. If we substitute for w_t and r_t from Eqs. (3A.8) and (3A.9) into Eq. (3A.10), then we get the economy's resource constraint:

$$K_{t+1} - K_t = F(K_t, L_t) - C_t - \delta K_t, \tag{3A.11}$$

where $C_t = c_{1t} L_t + c_{2t} L_{t-1}$ is aggregate consumption, that is, the sum of consumption by the young, $c_{1t} L_t$, and the old, $c_{2t} L_{t-1}$.

   If we substitute out for c_{1t} and c_{2t} in Eq. (3A.10) from Eqs. (3A.2) and (3A.3), then we get

$$K_{t+1} = s_t L_t,{}^{[28]} \tag{3A.12}$$

---

[28] Substitution from Eqs. (3A.2) and (3A.3) into Eq. (3A.10) yields the difference equation

$$K_{t+1} = s_t L_t + (1 + r_t) \cdot (K_t - s_{t-1} L_{t-1}).$$

We have to get the economy started off somehow, for example, with an initial capital stock, K_1, that is owned by the L_0 persons who are old in period 1. These old people consume the amount $c_{21} L_0 = (1 + r_1) \cdot K_1$. This condition, in conjunction with Eqs. (3A.2) and (3A.10), implies $K_2 = s_1 L_1$. The difference equation shown above then implies $K_{t+1} = s_t L_t$ for all $t \geq 2$.

that is, the savings of the young equals the next period's capital stock. This result holds because the old want to end up with no assets when they die (because they do not care about their descendants); hence, they sell all their capital stock to the young of the next generation. All of the capital owned by the old plus any net increase in capital must therefore be purchased by the young with their savings.

Note that the savings of period t become capital in period $t + 1$. If we think of a period as 30 years, then Eq. (3A.12) says that output that is not consumed becomes productive 30 years later. This unrealistic lag structure is an unfortunate by-product of overlapping-generations models with only two periods of life. The structure also means that we have to interpret the various rates—such as r_t and δ—as quantities per generation. For example, an interest rate of 6 percent per year corresponds to a value for r_t of 5.0, and a depreciation rate of 5 percent per year corresponds to a value for δ of 0.78.

Assume a constant rate of population growth, so that $L_{t+1}/L_t = 1 + n$. (A population growth rate of 1 percent per year corresponds to a value for n of 0.35.) We can express Eq. (3A.12) in per capita terms as

$$k_{t+1} \equiv K_{t+1}/L_{t+1} = s_t/(1 + n).$$

Substitution for s_t from equation (3A.6) into this result implies

$$k_{t+1} \cdot (1 + n) = w_t/\psi_{t+1}. \tag{3A.13}$$

If we replace ψ_{t+1} by the expression that appears below Eq. (3A.6), then we get

$$k_{t+1} \cdot (1 + n) \cdot \left\{ 1 + (1 + \rho)^{1/\theta} \cdot [1 + r(k_{t+1})]^{(\theta-1)/\theta} \right\} = w(k_t), \tag{3A.14}$$

where $r(k_{t+1})$ is given in Eq. (3A.9), and $w(k_t)$ is given in Eq. (3A.8).

Equation (3A.14) is a nonlinear difference equation in k_t; for every value of k_t, the equation implicitly determines the equilibrium value of k_{t+1}.[29] Therefore, for a given initial value of k_t, Eq. (3A.14) will prescribe the entire future path of capital stocks.

Equation (3A.14) can be solved in closed form only for special cases of the production and utility functions. For example, if utility is logarithmic ($\theta = 1$), then the expression in braces on the left-hand side of Eq. (3A.14) becomes $2 + \rho$. The difference equation then simplifies to

$$k_{t+1} = [f(k_t) - k_t \cdot f'(k_t)]/[(1 + n) \cdot (2 + \rho)]. \tag{3A.15}$$

THE STEADY STATE

To compute the steady-state capital intensity, let $k_{t+1} = k_t = k^*$ in Eq. (3A.14) to get

$$(1 + n) \cdot \left\{ 1 + (1 + \rho)^{1/\theta} \cdot [1 + f'(k^*) - \delta]^{(\theta-1)/\theta} \right\} = f(k^*)/k^* - f'(k^*). \tag{3A.16}$$

---

[29]This equilibrium value may or may not be unique; see below.

We can see the nature of the determination of k^* by specializing to a Cobb–Douglas production function, $f(k_t) = Ak_t^\alpha$. Equation (3A.16) simplifies in this case to

$$(1 + n) \cdot \left\{ 1 + (1 + \rho)^{1/\theta} \cdot [1 + \alpha A \cdot (k^*)^{\alpha-1} - \delta]^{(\theta-1)/\theta} \right\} = (1 - \alpha) \cdot A \cdot (k^*)^{\alpha-1}.$$

(3A.17)

If we define z^* to be the gross average product of capital—that is, $z^* \equiv A \cdot (k^*)^{\alpha-1}$; then Eq. (3A.17) can be rewritten as

$$(1 + n) \cdot \left\{ 1 + (1 + \rho)^{1/\theta} \cdot [1 + \alpha z^* - \delta]^{(\theta-1)/\theta} \right\} = (1 - \alpha) \cdot z^*. \quad (3A.18)$$

We determine z^* graphically in Fig. 3.4 by plotting the two sides of Eq. (3A.18) as functions of z^*. The right-hand side (RHS) of the equation is a straight line through the origin with slope $1-\alpha$. The shape of the left-hand side (LHS) depends on whether θ is equal to, less than, or greater than 1. These three cases are depicted in the three panels of the figure.

If utility is logarithmic, so that $\theta = 1$, then the left-hand side of Eq. (3A.18) is a horizontal line at $(1 + n) \cdot (2 + \rho) > 0$, as shown in panel (a) of Fig. 3.4. This line crosses the $(1 - \alpha) \cdot z^*$ line at a positive z^*, given by $(1 + n) \cdot (2 + \rho)/(1 - \alpha)$; hence, the steady-state capital stock exists and is unique. The solution for the steady-state capital intensity in this case is

$$k^* = \left[\frac{A \cdot (1 - \alpha)}{(1 + n) \cdot (2 + \rho)} \right]^{1/(1-\alpha)}. \quad (3A.19)$$

Panel (b) of Fig. 3.4 applies when $\theta < 1$. The left-hand side of Eq. (3A.18) is an inverse function of z^*. This function has a positive intercept, and it asymptotes to

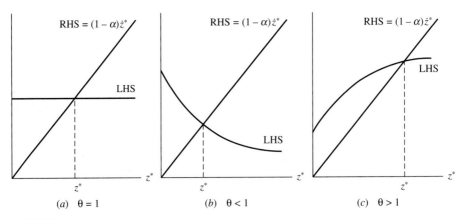

FIGURE 3.4
Determination of the steady state in the OLG model. Equation (3A.18) determines the steady-state gross average product of capital, z^*, in the overlapping-generations model with a Cobb–Douglas technology. In the figure, the straight line from the origin shows the right-hand side of the equation. The three panels plot the left-hand side of the equation for $\theta = 1$, $\theta < 1$, and $\theta > 1$. In each case, the steady state exists and is unique.

$1 + n$ as z^* goes to infinity. The intersection with the right-hand side, the straight line $(1 - \alpha) \cdot z^*$, therefore occurs at a unique, positive z^*. Hence, the steady-state capital stock exists and is unique.

Panel (c) of Fig. 3.4 applies if $\theta > 1$. The left-hand side of Eq. (3A.18) is an increasing function of z^*. The intercept is positive, and the slope diminishes monotonically toward 0 as z^* approaches infinity. The intersection with the right-hand side, the straight line $(1 - \alpha) \cdot z^*$, therefore again occurs at a unique, positive z^*.

THE GOLDEN RULE AND DYNAMIC EFFICIENCY

Consider now whether the overlapping-generations economy can generate the type of oversaving that may appear in the Solow–Swan model of Chapter 1. Recall that oversaving could arise in the Solow–Swan model only because it assumes an arbitrary saving rate; oversaving cannot arise in the Ramsey model of Chapter 2, in which infinite-lived households choose saving optimally. The surprising result in the OLG model is that oversaving can occur even though households choose saving optimally. This possibility exists because households have a finite horizon, corresponding to the two-period length of life, whereas the economy goes on forever.

To assess the possibility of oversaving, we first compute the capital intensity that yields a maximum of steady-state consumption per capita. At a point in time, aggregate consumption is $C_t \equiv c_{1t} \cdot L_t + c_{2t} \cdot L_{t-1}$. Since total population equals $L_t + L_{t-1}$, consumption per capita equals $C_t/(L_t + L_{t-1})$. Since $L_{t-1} = L_t/(1+n)$, this expression for consumption per capita is the multiple $(1 + n)/(2 + n)$ of consumption per worker, $c_t \equiv C_t/L_t$. Hence, maximization of consumption per capita is equivalent to maximization of consumption per worker.

To find the steady-state level of consumption per worker, we can divide both sides of Eq. (3A.11) by L_t to get

$$k_{t+1} \cdot (1 + n) - k_t = f(k_t) - c_t - \delta k_t. \tag{3A.20}$$

In a steady state, $k_{t+1} = k_t = k^*$, and the steady-state consumption per worker, c^*, is given by

$$c^* = f(k^*) - (n + \delta) \cdot k^*. \tag{3A.21}$$

The maximization of c^* therefore occurs at the value $k^* = k_g$ that satisfies $f'(k_g) = n + \delta$, that is, at the golden-rule value described in Chapter 1. It is easy to show that, even for simple functional forms for utility and production, the economy's steady-state value k^* may end up in the dynamically inefficient region where $k^* > k_g$.

Consider the case of log utility ($\theta = 1$) and Cobb–Douglas technology. We found in Eq. (3A.19) that the steady-state capital intensity is given in this case by $k^* = [(1-\alpha) \cdot A/(1+n) \cdot (2+\rho)]^{1/(1-\alpha)}$. In contrast, the golden-rule value is $k_{gold} = [\alpha A/(n + \delta)]^{1/(1-\alpha)}$. The condition for the steady-state capital intensity to exceed the golden-rule value (and, hence, for the economy to be in the dynamically inefficient region) is therefore

$$\frac{1 - \alpha}{(1 + n) \cdot (2 + \rho)} > \frac{\alpha}{n + \delta}. \tag{3A.22}$$

Thus, oversaving is more likely to occur if the rates of time preference, ρ, and population growth, n, are small—if the depreciation rate, δ, is large—and if the capital share, α, is small. Oversaving cannot occur if α is close to 1 (because wages are then close to 0, and young people have little capacity to save).

If we consider conventional parameter values, such as $n = 0.35$, $\rho = 0.82$, $\delta = 0.78$ (which correspond to respective annual rates of 0.01, 0.02, and 0.05), then the condition in (3A.22) becomes $\alpha < 0.32$. That is, inefficient oversaving occurs only if the capital share is one-third or less. We have argued before that a much higher capital share is reasonable if human capital is included. For example, if $\alpha = 0.8$, then oversaving does not arise with reasonable parameter values in this OLG framework.

DYNAMICS

The dynamics of the OLG economy come from Eq. (3A.14). Consider first the case of log utility ($\theta = 1$), as shown in Eq. (3A.15). If we also assume a Cobb–Douglas production function, $f(k) = Ak^\alpha$, then Eq. (3A.15) becomes

$$k_{t+1} = (1 - \alpha) \cdot Ak_t^\alpha / [(1 + n) \cdot (2 + \rho)] \equiv \Omega(k_t). \qquad (3A.23)$$

Figure 3.5 shows the relation between k_{t+1} and k_t, which we denote by $\Omega(k_t)$. The slope of $\Omega(k_t)$ is infinite at $k_t = 0$ and diminishes toward 0 as k_t approaches infinity. The function $\Omega(k_t)$ crosses the 45-degree line at the steady-state value, k^*. In this particular case, the capital stock monotonically approaches its unique steady-state

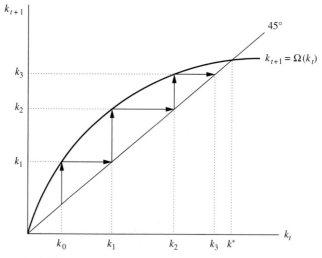

FIGURE 3.5
Dynamics in the OLG model. Equation (3A.23) prescribes the dynamics in the overlapping-generations model for the case of logarithmic utility and Cobb–Douglas technology. The function $\Omega(k_t)$, given in Eq. (3A.23) and shown in the figure, determines the value of k_{t+1} that corresponds to each value of k_t. If the economy begins at k_0, then it follows the sequence $k_1, k_2, \ldots$ shown in the figure.

value as time evolves. In other words, the steady state is stable. The reason is that the curve $\Omega(k_t)$ is always upward sloping, and it crosses the 45-degree line from above.

For general production and utility functions, the dynamics of the OLG economy can be complicated. It is possible to generate examples in which the $\Omega(k_t)$ curve is downward sloping when it crosses the 45-degree line. In these cases, the economy may display cycles.[30] The stability of the steady state is also not guaranteed.

ALTRUISM, BEQUESTS, AND INFINITE HORIZONS

The key assumption in the OLG model is that individuals have finite horizons in the sense that they do not care about their descendants. We now assume instead that people value their children's happiness (see Barro [1974]). If the altruistic linkage from parents to children is strong enough to generate intergenerational transfers— that is, if the typical person does not end up at a corner solution in which these transfers are zero—then the finite-horizon effect turns out to vanish. In particular, if intergenerational altruism is strong, then we return effectively to the Ramsey model of Chapter 2, in which horizons are infinite.

One way to allow for altruistic linkages across generations is to assume that a person born at time t derives utility from lifetime consumption and also from the prospective utility of children. For example, we could have

$$U_t = \frac{c_{1t}^{1-\theta} - 1}{1 - \theta} + \left(\frac{1}{1+\rho}\right) \cdot \left(\frac{c_{2t+1}^{1-\theta} - 1}{1 - \theta}\right) + \left(\frac{1+n}{(1+\rho) \cdot (1+\phi)}\right) \cdot U_{t+1} \quad (3A.24)$$

The first two terms on the right-hand side coincide with those from Eq. (3A.1) and represent the utility derived from consumption over the two periods of life. The term on the far right-hand side involves the prospective utility, U_{t+1}, of each immediate descendant. This utility will depend on the descendant's consumption in two periods of life and on the utility of descendants in the subsequent generation.

The term U_{t+1} in Eq. (3A.24) is multiplied by the number of descendants, $1 + n$, and is discounted by two terms. The first discount, $1 + \rho$, applies because the prospective utility arises one generation later and is, in this respect, comparable to own consumption when old, c_{2t+1}. The second discount, $1 + \phi$, arises because people may not count the anticipated utility of their children—derived in part from the children's prospective consumption—in the same way as their own consumption. Specifically, if $\phi > 0$, then parents are selfish in the sense that, if parent's consumption when old equals a child's consumption when young, then the parent prefers an additional unit of own old-period consumption to an added unit of a child's young-period consumption.

---

[30]The potential for cycles depends, however, on the discrete-time setup. For an individual family, this discreteness may be reasonable because it represents the length of a generation. At the aggregate level, however, the discreteness would be smoothed out by the adding up across families who differ in their positions in the life cycle. If the aggregated model involves a single state variable—such as the aggregate capital stock—then cycles would no longer materialize.

If we use Eq. (3A.24) repeatedly to substitute for U_{t+1}, U_{t+2}, and so on, then utility can be written as a forward, weighted sum of each generation's consumption when young and old:

$$U_t = \sum_{i=0}^{\infty} \left(\frac{1+n}{(1+\rho) \cdot (1+\phi)} \right)^i \cdot \left[\frac{c_{1t+i}^{1-\theta} - 1}{1-\theta} + \left(\frac{1}{1+\rho} \right) \cdot \left(\frac{c_{2t+1+i}^{1-\theta} - 1}{1-\theta} \right) \right]. \quad (3A.25)$$

In order for utility to be bounded when c_{1t+i} and c_{2t+i} are constant over time, we have to impose the condition $1 + n < (1 + \rho) \cdot (1 + \phi)$.

Let b_t be the intergenerational transfer received by each descendant born at time t. The amount transferred by each old person in period t is then $(1 + n) \cdot b_t$. The budget constraints for the two periods of life are revised accordingly from Eqs. (3A.2) and (3A.3) to

$$c_{1t} + s_t = w_t + b_t, \quad (3A.26)$$

$$c_{2t+1} + (1 + n) \cdot b_{t+1} = (1 + r_{t+1}) \cdot s_t. \quad (3A.27)$$

Note that we have set up the transfers so that they occur while the older generation is still alive and are therefore available to fund the young-period consumption of the next generation. One new element is that people have two sources of income when young: wage income and the transfers provided by their parents (if $b_t > 0$). People also have two ways to spend their resources when old: consumption and transfers to children.

A young person of generation t maximizes utility in Eq. (3A.25), subject to a given transfer b_t and to the constraints imposed by Eqs. (3A.26) and (3A.27) on each generation. We assume that the constraint $b_{t+i} \geq 0$ applies for all $i \geq 0$; that is, parents cannot require their children to provide transfers. If the restriction $b_{t+i} \geq 0$ is not binding for all $i \geq 0$, then the problem is straightforward; we deal here only with this case. (See Weil [1987] and Kimball [1987] for discussions of these restrictions and for an analysis of reverse transfers from children to parents.)

The specification of the utility function in Eq. (3A.25) implies that the form of the optimum problem does not change as old generations die and new ones are born. That is, the relative weighting on consumption in various periods does not change as new generations arrive. We can therefore pretend that the members of generation t can commit at time t to the choices that will be made by their descendants.

An easy way to get the first-order conditions is to use Eqs. (3A.26) and (3A.27) to substitute out for c_{1t}, c_{2t+1}, c_{1t+1}, and so on, in Eq. (3A.25) and then maximize over s_t and b_{t+1}. The resulting conditions can be expressed as

$$\frac{c_{2t+1}}{c_{1t}} = \left(\frac{1 + r_{t+1}}{1 + \rho} \right)^{1/\theta}, \quad (3A.28)$$

$$\frac{c_{2t}}{c_{1t}} = (1 + \phi)^{1/\theta}. \quad (3A.29)$$

Equation (3A.28) prescribes the allocation of consumption over a person's lifetime and has the same form as Eq. (3A.5). Equation (3A.29) relates parental consumption at time t to children's consumption at time t. These consumption levels differ only if the selfishness parameter, ϕ, is nonzero. In particular, if $\phi > 0$, then children consume less when they are young than parents consume when they are old.

Equations (3A.28) and (3A.29) can be combined to compute the evolution over time of consumption per worker, c_t :[31]

$$\frac{c_{t+1}}{c_t} = \frac{c_{1t+1}}{c_{1t}} = \frac{c_{2t+1}}{c_{2t}} = \left(\frac{1 + r_{t+1}}{(1 + \phi) \cdot (1 + \rho)}\right)^{1/\theta}. \tag{3A.30}$$

This result is the discrete-time counterpart to the standard solution for the change in c_t over time in the Ramsey model. The only difference is that the discount factor combines pure time preference, ρ, and the selfishness parameter, ϕ. The pure time effect can now be 0—that is, $\rho = 0$ is satisfactory—and the discount then reflects only the selfishness of parents ($\phi > 0$).

Equation (3A.30) can be combined with the economy's budget constraint in Eq. (3A.20) to determine the dynamics of k_t and c_t. An inspection of this system shows, however, that it is the discrete-time analog of the Ramsey model. Since the dynamic equations for k_t and c_t are the same as those in the Ramsey model—except for the shift to discrete time—the results are also the same. In particular, the steady state and dynamics are well behaved, and the equilibrium cannot be dynamically inefficient. Thus, if altruism is strong enough to ensure an interior solution for intergenerational transfers, then the OLG structure and finite lifetimes do not provide new insights about the evolution of the economy.

PROBLEMS

3.1 International Specialization and Diversification (Based on Ventura [1994]). Each small economy can produce two intermediate goods, X_1 and X_2, and a final good, Y, which can be used for consumption and investment. The production functions are

$$X_1 = (K_1)^{\alpha_1}(L_1)^{1-\alpha_1}, \tag{1}$$

$$X_2 = (K_2)^{\alpha_2}(L_2)^{1-\alpha_2}, \tag{2}$$

$$Y = (X_1)^{\alpha_3}(X_2)^{1-\alpha_3}, \tag{3}$$

where $\alpha_1, \alpha_2, \alpha_3 > 0$; K_1 and L_1 are the quantities of domestic capital and labor employed in the sector that produces X_1; K_2 and L_2 are the quantities employed in the sector that produces X_2; $K_1 + K_2 = K$; and $L_1 + L_2 = L$. The final output Y can be used, as usual, for C or for expansion of K. Total labor, L, is constant. Intermediate goods are tradable on world markets at the constant price p (in units of X_1 per unit of X_2). Final goods, Y, and units of C and K are not tradable internationally. There is no world credit market, so each country's sale or purchase of X_1 must equal its purchase or sale of X_2. In Eq. (3),

---

[31] The results for c_{1t} and c_{2t} in Eq. (3A.30) follow from Eqs. (3A.28) and (3A.29). The result for c_t holds because $c_t = [(1 + n)c_{1t} + c_{2t}]/(1 + n)$, and the ratio of c_{2t} to c_{1t} is the constant shown in Eq. (3A.29).

the quantities of X_1 and X_2 used to produce Y are the amounts produced domestically (from Eqs. [1] and [2]) plus the net quantity bought from abroad.

(a) For what range of $k \equiv K/L$ will the domestic economy be in the "diversification range" in which it produces both types of intermediate goods? Derive expressions for the rental rate on capital, R, and the wage rate, w, when k falls in the diversification range. (Note that, in the absence of factor mobility, factor-price equalization is achieved through the mobility of goods.)

(b) Assume that k increases, but not by enough to move the economy outside of the diversification range. Why does the increase in k not lead to diminishing returns? (Note: the results are an application of the Rybczinski [1955] theorem.)

(c) Suppose that infinite-horizon consumers solve the usual Ramsey optimization problem. Derive the laws of motion for c and k, assuming that p is constant.

(d) Suppose that the world consists of a large number of small countries, identical except for their values of $k(0)$. Furthermore, assume that all countries fall in the diversification range. Derive the world equilibrium path for p and obtain the laws of motion for the world's c and k. How do the results relate to those from part (c)?

3.2 International Credit Constraints (Based on Cohen and Sachs [1986]). Imagine that the domestic country, country i, can borrow on world credit markets at the constant real interest rate, r. The country can, however, borrow only up to a fraction $\lambda \geq 0$ of its capital stock, so that

$$d_i \leq \lambda k_i. \tag{1}$$

Since $d_i = k_i - a_i$ (Eq. [3.1]), Eq. (1) implies

$$a_i \geq (1 - \lambda) \cdot k_i. \tag{2}$$

Assume that the domestic economy has the usual infinite-horizon consumers with $\rho_i + \theta_i x_i > r$. The country also starts with sufficient assets, $a_i(0)$, so that Eq. (2) is not binding initially.

(a) What are the first-order optimization conditions if (2) is not binding? Relate these conditions to those discussed in Section 3.1.

(b) Argue that (2) becomes binding in finite time. Then use Eq. (3.6) to find an expression for $\hat{k}$ when (2) is binding. What is the expression for $\dot{c}/\hat{c}$ when (2) is binding? Provide economic intuition for this result for situations in which $\lambda = 1, \lambda = 0$, and $0 < \lambda < 1$.

(c) What is the steady-state value of $\hat{k}$, and how does this value depend on λ and r?

(d) How does the parameter λ affect the transitional dynamics?

3.3 Adjustment Costs in the Ramsey Model (Based on Abel and Blanchard [1983]). Consider the model of adjustment costs from Section 3.5 of the text. Assume that consumers have the usual Ramsey preferences. But, instead of assuming a constant interest rate, consider the equilibrium for a closed economy.

(a) Find an expression for $\dot{q}$ as a function of q, i/k, $\dot{c}/c$, and k.

(b) Use a phase diagram to work out the dynamics of i/k and k. (Note: it is easier to work with i/k than with q.)

3.4 End-of-the-World Model II. Suppose that the Ramsey model is the same as the one described in Chapter 2, except that utility is logarithmic ($\theta = 1$) and everyone thinks that the world will end with probability $p \geq 0$ per unit of time. That is, if the world exists at time t, then the probability that it will still exist at the future date T is $e^{-p \cdot (T-t)}$.

(a) What are the transition equations for $\hat{k}$ and $\hat{c}$? How do these equations relate to Eqs. (2.23) and (2.24) from Chapter 2 and to Eqs. (3.33) and (3.34) from the Blanchard (1985) model?

(*b*) Use a modification of Fig. 3.1 to describe the transition path for the economy.

(*c*) As *p* gets smaller, how does the transition path relate to the one shown in Fig. 2.1? What happens as *p* approaches 0?

3.5 Fiscal Policy in a Finite-Horizon Model. Reconsider Problem 2.7 in the context of the Blanchard (1985) model of a closed economy, as described in Section 3.4.2 of the text. Assume that $n = x = G = 0$, and begin with the case in which B is constant at the value $B(0)$.

(*a*) How do differences in $B(0)$ affect the economy's transition path and steady state?

(*b*) Suppose that B follows some path, but eventually approaches a constant. How does the path of B affect the economy's transition path and steady state?

CHAPTER

4

ONE-SECTOR
MODELS OF
ENDOGENOUS
GROWTH

In the Ramsey model, as in the Solow–Swan model, the steady-state per capita growth rate equals the rate of technological progress, x. These models take x to be exogenous. Thus, although they provide interesting frameworks for studying transitional dynamics, they are not helpful for understanding long-term growth of income per capita.

We mentioned in Chapter 1 that one way to construct a theory of endogenous growth is to eliminate the long-run tendency for capital to experience diminishing returns. We discussed as a simple example the AK model, in which the returns to capital are always constant, and we considered technologies in which the returns to capital diminished, but asymptotically approached a positive constant.

We begin our analysis in this chapter by combining the AK technology with optimizing behavior of households and firms. This framework generates endogenous growth, and the outcomes are Pareto optimal as in the Ramsey model. One difficulty, however, is that this kind of model is inconsistent with the empirical evidence on convergence.

We noted in Chapter 1 that a constant-returns production function at the aggregate level can reflect learning-by-doing and spillovers of knowledge. This kind of technology may support endogenous growth, but the outcomes tend not to be Pareto optimal because the spillovers constitute a form of externality. Hence, these models have possible implications for desirable government policy. We also examine models with governmentally provided public goods and show that they have analogous implications for growth and government policy.

140

At the end of the chapter, we analyze transitional dynamics in models with optimizing agents when the technology features returns to capital that diminish but asymptotically approach a positive constant. These models can combine the endogenous-growth features of AK models with the convergence behavior that we found in the Ramsey model. Thus, the empirical evidence on convergence may be consistent with these kinds of endogenous-growth models.

4.1 THE AK MODEL

4.1.1 Behavior of Households

We use the setup from Chapter 2 in which infinite-lived households maximize utility, as given by

$$ U = \int_0^\infty e^{-(\rho-n)t} \cdot \left[\frac{c^{(1-\theta)} - 1}{(1-\theta)} \right] dt, \tag{4.1} $$

subject to the constraint

$$ \dot{a} = (r - n) \cdot a + w - c, \tag{4.2} $$

where a is assets per person, r is the interest rate, w is the wage rate, and n is the growth rate of population. We again impose the constraint that rules out chain-letter debt finance:

$$ \lim_{t \to \infty} \left\{ a(t) \cdot \exp\left[-\int_0^t [r(v) - n]\, dv \right] \right\} \geq 0. \tag{4.3} $$

The conditions for optimization are again

$$ \gamma_c \equiv \dot{c}/c = (1/\theta) \cdot (r - \rho) \tag{4.4} $$

and the transversality condition,

$$ \lim_{t \to \infty} \left\{ a(t) \cdot \exp\left[-\int_0^t [r(v) - n]\, dv \right] \right\} = 0. \tag{4.5} $$

4.1.2 Behavior of Firms

The only departure from Chapter 2 is that firms have the linear production function,

$$ y = f(k) = Ak, \tag{4.6} $$

where $A > 0$. Equation (4.6) differs from the neoclassical production function in that the marginal product of capital is not diminishing ($f'' = 0$), and the Inada conditions are violated, in particular, $f'(k) = A$ as k goes to zero or infinity. The appendix at the end of this chapter shows more generally that the violation of the Inada condition $\lim_{k \to \infty}[f'(k)] = 0$ is the key element that underlies endogenous growth.

We noted in Chapter 1 that the global absence of diminishing returns to capital in Eq. (4.6) may seem unrealistic, but the idea becomes more plausible if we construe capital, K, broadly to encompass human capital, knowledge, public infrastructure, and so on. Subsequent sections of this chapter explore these interpretations in more detail.

The conditions for profit maximization again require the marginal product of capital to equal the rental price, $R = r + \delta$. The only difference here is that the marginal product of capital is the constant A; hence,

$$r = A - \delta. \tag{4.7}$$

Since the marginal product of labor is zero, the wage rate, w, is zero. (We can think of this zero wage rate as applying to raw labor, which has not been augmented by human capital.)

4.1.3   Equilibrium

We assume, as in Chapter 2, that the economy is closed, so that $a = k$ holds. If we substitute $a = k$, $r = A - \delta$, and $w = 0$ into Eqs. (4.2), (4.4), and (4.5), then we get

$$\dot{k} = (A - \delta - n) \cdot k - c, \tag{4.8}$$

$$\gamma_c = (1/\theta) \cdot (A - \delta - \rho), \tag{4.9}$$

$$\lim_{t \to \infty} \left\{ k(t) \cdot e^{-(A-\delta-n) \cdot t} \right\} = 0. \tag{4.10}$$

The striking aspect of Eq. (4.9) is that consumption growth does not depend on the stock of capital per person, k. In other words, if the level of consumption per capita at time 0 is $c(0)$, then consumption per capita at time t is given by

$$c(t) = c(0) \cdot e^{(1/\theta) \cdot (A-\delta-\rho) \cdot t}, \tag{4.11}$$

where the initial level of consumption, $c(0)$, remains to be determined.

We assume that the production function is sufficiently productive to ensure growth in c, but not so productive as to yield unbounded utility:

$$A > \rho + \delta > [(1 - \theta)/\theta] \cdot (A - \delta - \rho) + n + \delta. \tag{4.12}$$

The first part of this condition implies $\gamma_c > 0$. The second part, which is analogous to $\rho + \theta x > x + n$ in the model of Chapter 2, ensures that the attainable utility is bounded[1] and that the transversality condition holds.

4.1.4   Transitional Dynamics

We show now that the model has no transitional dynamics, that is, the growth rates γ_k and γ_y are constant and equal the growth rate γ_c shown in Eq. (4.9). If we substitute for $c(t)$ from Eq. (4.11) into Eq. (4.8), then we get

$$\dot{k} = (A - \delta - n) \cdot k - c(0) \cdot e^{(1/\theta) \cdot (A-\delta-\rho) \cdot t},$$

---

[1] To verify this result, substitute for $c(t)$ from Eq. (4.11) into the utility function to get $U = [1/(1-\theta)] \cdot \int_0^\infty e^{-(\rho-n) \cdot t} \cdot [c(0)^{1-\theta} \cdot e^{[(1-\theta)/\theta] \cdot (A-\delta-\rho) \cdot t} - 1] \, dt$. This integral converges to infinity unless $\rho - n > [(1-\theta)/\theta] \cdot (A - \delta - \rho)$. Add δ to both sides and rearrange this expression to get the second inequality in (4.12). The appendix on mathematics considers some cases in which unbounded utility can be handled.

which is a first-order, linear differential equation in k. The general solution of this equation is[2]

$$k(t) = \text{(constant)} \cdot e^{(A-\delta-n)\cdot t} + [c(0)/\varphi] \cdot e^{(1/\theta)\cdot(A-\delta-\rho)\cdot t}, \qquad (4.13)$$

where

$$\varphi \equiv (A - \delta) \cdot (\theta - 1)/\theta + \rho/\theta - n. \qquad (4.14)$$

Condition (4.12) implies $\varphi > 0$.

If we substitute for $k(t)$ from Eq. (4.13) into the transversality condition in Eq. (4.10), then we get

$$\lim_{t \to \infty} \left\{ \text{constant} + [c(0)/\varphi] \cdot e^{-\varphi t} \right\} = 0.$$

Since $\varphi > 0$, the second term inside the brackets converges toward 0. Hence, the transversality condition requires the constant to be 0. Equations (4.11) and (4.13) therefore imply

$$c(t) = \varphi \cdot k(t), {}^3 \qquad (4.15)$$

$$\gamma_k = \gamma_c = (1/\theta) \cdot (A - \delta - \rho). \qquad (4.16)$$

Since $y = Ak$, it also follows that $\gamma_y = \gamma_k = \gamma_c$. Thus, the model has no transitional dynamics: the variables $k(t)$, $c(t)$, and $y(t)$ begin, at the values $k(0)$, $c(0) = \varphi \cdot k(0)$, and $y(0) = A \cdot k(0)$, respectively, and all three variables then grow at the constant rate $(1/\theta) \cdot (A - \delta - \rho)$.

In the AK model, changes in the underlying parameters can affect levels and growth rates of variables. For example, a permanent increase in the rate of population growth, n, does not affect the per capita growth rates shown in Eq. (4.16), but it reduces the level of per capita consumption (see Eqs. [4.14] and [4.15]). Changes in A, ρ, and θ affect the levels and growth rates of c and k.

The gross saving rate is given by

$$s = (\dot{K} + \delta K)/Y = (1/A) \cdot (\gamma_k + n + \delta) = \left[\frac{A - \rho + \theta n + (\theta - 1) \cdot \delta}{\theta A} \right], \qquad (4.17)$$

where $\gamma_k = (1/\theta) \cdot (A - \delta - \rho)$. Thus, the gross saving rate is constant and, aside from n, depends on the same parameters that influence the per capita growth rate.

4.1.5 Determinants of the Growth Rate

A striking difference between the AK model and the neoclassical growth model of Chapter 2 concerns the determination of the long-run per capita growth rate. In the AK model, the long-run growth rate (which equals the short-run growth rate) depends in Eq. (4.16) on the parameters that determine the willingness to save and the

---

[2] See the appendix on mathematics for a discussion of this kind of first-order, linear differential equation.
[3] Note that this model yields a closed-form policy function for c.

productivity of capital. Lower values of ρ and θ, which raise the willingness to save, imply a higher per capita growth rate in Eq. (4.16) and a higher saving rate in Eq. (4.17). An improvement in the level of technology, A, which raises the marginal and average products of capital, also raises the growth rate and alters the saving rate. In a later section of this chapter, we show that changes in various kinds of government policies amount to shifts in A; that is, we can generalize the interpretation of the parameter A to go beyond literal differences in the level of the production function.

In contrast to the effects on long-run growth in the AK model, the Ramsey model of Chapter 2 implies that the long-run per capita growth rate is pegged at the value x, the exogenous rate of technological change. A greater willingness to save or an improvement in the level of technology shows up in the long run as higher levels of capital and output per effective worker, but in no change in the per capita growth rate.

The different results reflect the workings of diminishing returns to capital in the neoclassical model, and the absence of these diminishing returns in the AK model. Quantitatively, the extent of the difference depends on how rapidly diminishing returns set in, a characteristic that determines how quickly economies converge to the steady state in the neoclassical model. If diminishing returns set in slowly, then the convergence period is long. In this case, shifts in the willingness to save or the level of technology affect the growth rate for a long time in the neoclassical model, even if not forever. Thus, the distinction between the neoclassical and AK models is substantial if convergence is rapid, but becomes less serious if—as seems to be the case—convergence occurs slowly. If convergence is extremely slow, then the growth effects that appear in the AK model provide a satisfactory approximation to the effects on the average growth rate over a long interval in the neoclassical model.

We showed in Chapter 2 that the outcomes in the Ramsey model were Pareto optimal. We demonstrated this result by showing that the outcomes coincided with those that would be generated by a hypothetical social planner who had the same form of objective function as the representative household. It is straightforward to follow the same procedure here to prove that the equilibrium in the AK model is Pareto optimal.[4] This result makes sense because the elimination of diminishing returns in the production function—that is, the replacement of the neoclassical production function by the AK form—does not introduce any sources of market failure into the model.

4.2 A ONE-SECTOR MODEL WITH PHYSICAL AND HUMAN CAPITAL

We mentioned before that one interpretation of the AK model is that capital should be viewed broadly to include physical and human components. We now work out a simple model with human capital that makes this interpretation explicit.

---

[4]The planner chooses the path of c to maximize U in Eq. (4.1), subject to Eq. (4.8), $c(t) \geq 0$, and the given initial value $k(0)$.

Assume that the inputs to the production function are physical and human capital, K and H:

$$Y = F(K, H), \tag{4.18}$$

where $F(\cdot)$ exhibits the standard neoclassical properties, including constant returns to scale in K and H. This production function is similar to one used in Chapter 3, except that we previously assumed a Cobb–Douglas form with diminishing returns to scale in K and H. We can use the condition of constant returns to scale to write the production function in an intensive form:

$$Y = K \cdot f(H/K), \tag{4.19}$$

where $f'(H/K) > 0$.

Output can be used on a one-for-one basis for consumption, for investment in physical capital, or for investment in human capital. Hence, we assume that the one-sector technology applies to the production of human capital—that is, to education—as well as to the production of consumables and physical capital. (We introduce a separate education sector in Chapter 5.) The stocks of physical and human capital depreciate at the rates δ_K and δ_H, respectively. We assume that population, L, is constant, so that changes in H reflect only the net investment in human capital.

Let R_K and R_H be the rental prices paid by competitive firms for the use of the two types of capital. In the absence of barriers to entry, competition among firms will drive profits down to zero. Profit maximization and this zero-profit condition then imply (as in the discussion of Chapter 2) that the marginal product of each input equals its rental price:

$$\partial Y/\partial K = f(H/K) - (H/K) \cdot f'(H/K) = R_K,$$
$$\partial Y/\partial H = f'(H/K) = R_H. \tag{4.20}$$

Since the two types of capital are perfectly substitutable with each other and with consumables on the production side, the price of each type of capital would be fixed at unity.[5] Hence, the rates of return to owners of capital are $R_K - \delta_K$ and $R_H - \delta_H$, respectively, and each rate of return must be equal in equilibrium to the interest rate, r. If we use Eq. (4.20) and rearrange terms, then this equalization of rates of return implies

$$f(H/K) - f'(H/K) \cdot (1 + H/K) = \delta_K - \delta_H. \tag{4.21}$$

This condition determines a unique, constant value of H/K.[6]

---

[5] This result applies if the constraint of nonnegative gross investment in each type of capital is nonbinding or if units of old capital can, unrealistically, be consumed or converted into the other type of capital. We take explicit account of these kinds of constraints in Chapter 5.

[6] The expression on the left-hand side of Eq. (4.21) can be shown readily to be monotonically increasing in H/K. Moreover, this expression ranges from $-\infty$ to $+\infty$ as H/K goes from 0 to ∞. It follows that the solution for H/K exists and is unique.

If we define $A \equiv f(H/K)$, a constant, then Eq. (4.19) implies $Y = AK$. Thus, this model with two types of capital is essentially the same as the AK model that we analyzed in the previous section. We know from that analysis that the equilibrium features constant and equal growth rates of C, K, and Y.[7] (These growth rates equal the per capita growth rates because L is constant.) Since H/K is fixed, H grows at the same rate as the other variables.

The main conclusion from this simple case is that we can think of K as a proxy for a composite of capital goods that includes physical and human components. If we regard constant returns to the two kinds of capital as plausible, then the AK model may be a satisfactory representation of this broader model. We consider in Chapter 5 some additional effects that arise when we drop the assumptions of the one-sector model and assume that the production function for education differs from that for goods.

4.3 MODELS WITH LEARNING-BY-DOING AND KNOWLEDGE SPILLOVERS

4.3.1 Technology

The key to endogenous growth in the AK model is the absence of diminishing returns to the factors that can be accumulated. In the paper that revived the growth literature in the 1980s, Romer (1986) used Arrow's (1962) setup to eliminate the tendency for diminishing returns by assuming that knowledge creation was a side product of investment. A firm that increases its physical capital learns simultaneously how to produce more efficiently. This positive effect of experience on productivity is called learning-by-doing or, in this case, learning-by-investing.

We can illustrate the possibilities by considering a neoclassical production function with labor-augmenting technology for firm i,

$$Y_i = F(K_i, A_i L_i), \tag{4.22}$$

where L_i and K_i are the conventional inputs, and A_i is the index of knowledge available to the firm. The function $F(\cdot)$ satisfies the neoclassical properties that we detailed in Chapter 1 (Eqs. [1.5a]–[1.5c]): positive and diminishing marginal products of each input, constant returns to scale, and the Inada conditions. Technology is assumed to be labor augmenting so that a steady state exists when A_i grows at a constant rate. Unlike Chapter 2, however, we do not assume here that A_i grows exogenously at the rate x. Furthermore, for reasons that will become apparent later, we assume that the aggregate labor force, L, is constant.

---

[7]The growth rate in the present context is

$$\gamma = (1/\theta) \cdot (r - \rho) = (1/\theta) \cdot [f(H/K) - (H/K) \cdot f'(H/K) - \delta_K - \rho],$$

which does not equal $(1/\theta) \cdot (A - \delta_K - \rho)$ because if we define $A \equiv f(H/K)$, then r falls short of $A - \delta_K$ by the term $(H/K) \cdot f'(H/K)$.

We follow Arrow (1962), Sheshinski (1967), and Romer (1986) and make two assumptions about productivity growth. First, learning-by-doing works through each firm's investment. Specifically, an increase in a firm's capital stock leads to a parallel increase in its stock of knowledge, A_i. This process reflects Arrow's idea that knowledge and productivity gains come from investment and production, a formulation that was inspired by the empirical observation of large positive effects of experience on productivity in airframe manufacturing, shipbuilding, and other areas (see Wright [1936], Searle [1946], Asher [1956], and Rapping [1965]). This idea is supported more broadly by Schmookler's (1966) evidence that patents—a proxy for learning—closely follow investment in physical capital.

The second key assumption is that each firm's knowledge is a public good that any other firm can access at zero cost. In other words, once discovered, a piece of knowledge spills over instantly across the whole economy. This assumption implies that the change in each firm's technology term, $\dot{A}_i$, corresponds to the economy's overall learning and is therefore proportional to the change in the aggregate capital stock, $\dot{K}$.

On one level, the spillover assumption is natural because knowledge has a nonrival character: if one firm uses an idea, then it does not prevent others from using it. On the other hand, firms have incentives to maintain secrecy over their discoveries as well as formal patent protection for inventions. Knowledge about productivity improvements would therefore leak out only gradually, and innovators would retain competitive advantages for some time. In fact, in a decentralized setup, this individual advantage is essential to motivate any effort that is specifically directed at making discoveries. The type of interaction among firms that arises in this setup cannot, however, be adequately described by standard models of perfect competition, and we postpone a consideration of alternative approaches until Chapters 6 and 7. In this section, we make the extreme assumption that all discoveries are unintended by-products of investment and that these discoveries immediately become common knowledge. This specification allows us to retain the framework of perfect competition, although the outcomes will turn out not to be Pareto optimal.

The assumption here is that the spillovers of knowledge operate at the level of the overall economy. Alternative assumptions are that the spillovers apply to an industry, to a limited geographical area, within a particular political jurisdiction, and so on. The extent to which these spillovers apply will be crucial for the model's empirical implications.

If we combine the assumptions of learning-by-doing and knowledge spillovers, then we can replace A_i by K in Eq. (4.22) and write the production function for firm i as[8]

$$Y_i = F(K_i, K \cdot L_i). \tag{4.23}$$

If K and L_i are constant, then each firm faces diminishing returns to K_i as in the neoclassical model of Chapter 2. However, if each producer expands K_i, then K

---

[8]We neglect any baseline knowledge that producers have when no capital has ever been produced.

rises accordingly and provides a spillover benefit that raises the productivity of all firms. Moreover, Eq. (4.23) is homogeneous of degree one in K_i and K for given L_i; that is, there are constant returns to capital at the social level—when K_i and K expand together for fixed L. This constancy of the social returns to capital will yield endogenous growth.

A firm's profit can be written as

$$L_i \cdot [f(k_i, K) - (r + \delta) \cdot k_i - w], \tag{4.24}$$

where $f(\cdot)$ is the intensive form of the production function (see Eq. [4.23]), $r + \delta$ is the rental price of capital, and w is the wage rate. We assume, as usual, that each competitive firm takes these factor prices as given. We now also make the parallel assumption that each firm is small enough to neglect its own contribution to the aggregate capital stock and therefore treats K as given. Profit maximization and the zero-profit condition (as detailed in Chapter 2) then imply

$$\partial y_i/\partial k_i = f_1(k_i, K) = r + \delta,$$
$$\partial Y_i/\partial L_i = f(k_i, K) - k_i \cdot f_1(k_i, K) = w, \tag{4.25}$$

where $f_1(\cdot)$—the partial derivative of $f(k_i, K)$ with respect to its first argument, k_i—is the *private* marginal product of capital. In particular, this marginal product neglects the contribution of k_i to K and, hence, to aggregate knowledge.

In equilibrium, all firms make the same choices, so that $k_i = k$ and $K = kL$ apply. Since $f(k_i, K)$ is homogeneous of degree one in k_i and K, we can write the average product of capital as

$$f(k_i, K)/k_i = \tilde{f}(K/k_i) = \tilde{f}(L), \tag{4.26}$$

where $\tilde{f}(L)$—the function for the average product of capital—satisfies $\tilde{f}'(L) > 0$ and $\tilde{f}''(L) < 0$. Note that this average product is invariant with k, because the learning-by-doing and spillover effects eliminate the tendency for diminishing returns. The average product is, however, increasing in the size of the labor force, L. This last property is unusual and leads to scale effects that we discuss later.

The private marginal product of capital can be expressed from Eq. (4.26) as

$$f_1(k_i, K) = \tilde{f}(L) - L \cdot \tilde{f}'(L). \tag{4.27}$$

Hence, the private marginal product of capital is less than the average product, $\tilde{f}(L)$, and is invariant with k. Equation (4.27) implies also that the private marginal product of capital is increasing in L (because $\tilde{f}''(L) < 0$).

4.3.2   Equilibrium

We still assume a closed economy in which infinite-lived households maximize utility in the usual way. Therefore, the budget constraint is given by Eq. (4.2), the growth rate of per capita consumption by Eq. (4.4), and the transversality condition by Eq. (4.5). If we use the condition $r = f_1(k_i, K) - \delta$ and the form for the private marginal product of capital from Eq. (4.27), then Eq. (4.4) can be written as

$$\gamma_c = (1/\theta) \cdot [\tilde{f}(L) - L \cdot \tilde{f}'(L) - \delta - \rho]. \tag{4.28}$$

As in the *AK* model, this growth rate is constant (as long as *L* is constant). We assume that the parameters are such that the growth rate is positive but not large enough to yield infinite utility:

$$\tilde{f}(L) - L \cdot \tilde{f}'(L) > \rho + \delta > (1 - \theta) \cdot [\tilde{f}(L) - L \cdot \tilde{f}'(L) - \delta - \rho]/\theta + \delta. \quad (4.29)$$

This condition corresponds to (4.12) in the *AK* model.

If we substitute $a = k$ and the first-order conditions from Eq. (4.25) into the budget constraint of Eq. (4.2), then we get the accumulation equation for *k*:

$$\dot{k} = \tilde{f}(L) \cdot k - c - \delta k. \quad (4.30)$$

If we use this equation along with the transversality condition, then we can show that the model has no transitional dynamics: the variables *k* and *y* always grow at the rate γ_c shown in Eq. (4.28). Since the analysis is essentially the same as that for the *AK* model (Section 4.14), we leave this demonstration as an exercise.

4.3.3 Pareto Nonoptimality and Policy Implications

To see whether the outcomes are Pareto optimal, we follow our usual practice of comparing the decentralized solution with the results from a social-planner's problem. The planner maximizes the utility function shown in Eq. (4.1) (with *n* set to zero), subject to the accumulation constraint in Eq. (4.30). The key aspect of this optimization is that, unlike an individual producer, the planner recognizes that each firm's increase in its capital stock adds to the aggregate capital stock and, hence, contributes to the productivity of all other firms in the economy. In other words, the social planner *internalizes* the spillovers of knowledge across the firms.

To find the optimal choices of *c* and *k*, set up the Hamiltonian,

$$J = e^{-\rho t} \cdot (c^{1-\theta} - 1)/(1 - \theta) + \nu \cdot [\tilde{f}(L) \cdot k - c - \delta k].$$

The optimization involves the standard first-order conditions, $J_c = 0$ and $\dot{\nu} = -J_k$, and the transversality condition, $\lim_{t \to \infty} \nu k = 0$. We can manipulate the first-order conditions in the usual way to derive the condition for the growth rate of *c*:

$$\gamma_c \text{ (planner)} = (1/\theta) \cdot [\tilde{f}(L) - \delta - \rho]. \quad (4.31)$$

The social planner sets the growth rate of consumption in accordance with the average product of capital, $\tilde{f}(L)$, whereas the decentralized solution shown in Eq. (4.28) relates the growth rate to the private marginal product of capital, $\tilde{f}(L) - L \cdot \tilde{f}'(L)$. Since this private marginal product falls short of the average product, growth is too low in the decentralized equilibrium.

In the present model, the learning-by-doing and spillover effects exactly offset the diminishing returns that face an individual producer. Hence, the returns are constant at the social level, and the social marginal product of capital equals the average product, $\tilde{f}(L)$. Since the social planner internalizes the spillovers, this social marginal product appears as a determinant of the growth rate in Eq. (4.31). The decentralized solution in Eq. (4.28) dictates a lower growth rate because the individual producers do not internalize the spillovers; that is, they base decisions on the private marginal product, $\tilde{f}(L) - L \cdot \tilde{f}'(L)$, which falls short of the social marginal product.

The social optimum can be attained in a decentralized economy by subsidizing purchases of capital goods (an investment-tax credit). Alternatively, the government can generate the optimum by subsidizing production. These subsidies work in the model because they raise the private rate of return to investment and thereby tend to eliminate the excess of social over private returns. Of course, to avoid other distortions, the subsidies on capital or production would have to be financed with a lump-sum tax. These kinds of taxes are normally difficult to find, but in the current model—which contains no labor/leisure choice—a consumption tax would amount to a lump-sum tax.

4.3.4 A Cobb–Douglas Example

If the production function in Eq. (4.23) takes the Cobb–Douglas form, then output for firm i is given by

$$Y_i = A \cdot (K_i)^\alpha \cdot (KL_i)^{1-\alpha}, \tag{4.32}$$

where $0 < \alpha < 1$. If we substitute $y_i = Y_i/L_i, k_i = K_i/L_i$, and $k = K/L$, and then set $y_i = y$ and $k_i = k$, then the average product of capital is

$$y/k = \tilde{f}(L) = AL^{1-\alpha}, \tag{4.33}$$

a special case of Eq. (4.26). Note that Eq. (4.33) satisfies the general properties that y/k is invariant with k and increasing in L.

We can determine the private marginal product of capital by differentiating Eq. (4.32) with respect to K_i, while holding K and L fixed. If we then substitute $k_i = k$, then the result is

$$\partial Y_i/\partial K_i = A\alpha L^{1-\alpha}, \tag{4.34}$$

a special case of Eq. (4.27). In accordance with the general properties discussed before, the private marginal product of capital in Eq. (4.34) is invariant with k, increasing in L, and less than the average product shown in Eq. (4.33) (because $0 < \alpha < 1$).

If we substitute from Eq. (4.34) into Eq. (4.28), then we find that the decentralized growth rate is given by

$$\gamma_c = (1/\theta) \cdot (A\alpha L^{1-\alpha} - \delta - \rho).[9] \tag{4.35}$$

Substitution from Eq. (4.33) into Eq. (4.31) gives the social planner's growth rate as

$$\gamma_c \text{ (planner)} = (1/\theta) \cdot (AL^{1-\alpha} - \delta - \rho). \tag{4.36}$$

Since $\alpha < 1$, the decentralized growth rate is lower than the planner's growth rate.

---

[9]We assume that the parameters allow for positive growth and bounded utility; hence,

$$A\alpha L^{1-\alpha} > \rho + \delta > (1 - \theta) \cdot (A\alpha L^{1-\alpha} - \delta - \rho)/\theta + \delta,$$

a result that specializes (4.29).

The social optimum can be attained in the decentralized economy by introducing an investment-tax credit at the rate $1 - \alpha$ and financing it with a lump-sum tax. If buyers of capital pay only the fraction α of the cost, then the private return on capital corresponds to the social return. We can then show that the decentralized choices coincide with those of the social planner. Alternatively, the government could generate the same outcome by subsidizing production at the rate $(1 - \alpha)/\alpha$.

4.3.5 Scale Effects

The model implies a scale effect in that an expansion of the aggregate labor force, L, raises the per capita growth rate for the decentralized economy in Eq. (4.28) and for the social planner in Eq. (4.31). These results reflect, respectively, the positive effect of L on the private marginal product of capital, $\tilde{f}(L) - L \cdot \tilde{f}'(L)$, in Eq. (4.27) and on the average product, $\tilde{f}(L)$, in Eq. (4.26). Moreover, if the labor force grows over time, then the per capita growth rates would increase over time.[10]

If we can identify L with the aggregate labor force of a country, then the prediction is that countries with more workers tend to grow faster in per capita terms. The empirical results discussed in Chapter 12 for a large number of countries in the post–World War II period indicate that the growth rate of per capita GDP bears a weak positive relation to the size of the working-age population. (These results apply when the initial level of per capita GDP, the average person's education, and some other variables are held constant.) Thus, these findings do not reject a minor scale effect.

It is possible that the scale variable for spillovers, L, does not relate closely to aggregates measured at the country level. The relevant scale can, for example, be larger than the size of the domestic economy if producers benefit from knowledge accumulated in other countries. Kremer (1993) argues that the correct scale variable might be world population, and he provides some evidence from the long-run history that world population is positively correlated with productivity growth. Alternatively, if the free transmission of ideas is limited to close neighbors (either geographically or in terms of industry), then the appropriate scale may be smaller than the home economy. These caveats blur the empirical implications of the spillovers model and make difficult the testing of this model with macroeconomic data.

We derived the scale effect from a model that assumed learning-by-doing and spillovers of knowledge. These elements generate a scale effect on growth rates because they imply constant returns to K and increasing returns to K and L at the social level. A similar scale effect would result if this pattern of factor returns prevailed for other reasons. The learning-by-doing/spillovers model is special, however, in that it also implies constant returns to scale in the factors, K_i and L_i, that are chosen by an individual firm. If increasing returns applied at the level of a firm, then the model would be inconsistent with perfect competition, because firms would have an

---

[10]This result follows at once for γ_c, but γ_k and γ_y would not correspond to γ_c in an environment of growing L. Also, if L rises enough, then the condition for bounded utility in (4.29) must eventually be violated if $\theta < 1$.

incentive to grow arbitrarily large in order to benefit from the scale economy. We avoided this outcome by assuming that a firm's technology depended on the aggregate capital stock, K, and that each firm neglected its own contribution to this aggregate. This specification allows us to maintain the assumption of perfect competition, but it also implies that the competitive equilibrium is not Pareto optimal.

One way to eliminate the scale effect is to argue that the term A_i in Eq. (4.22) depends on the economy's average capital per worker, K/L, rather than the aggregate capital stock, K. For example, Lucas (1988) assumes that the learning and spillovers involve human capital and that each producer benefits from the *average* level of human capital in the economy, rather than from the *aggregate* of human capital. Thus, instead of thinking about the accumulated knowledge or experience of other producers, we have to think here about the benefit from interacting (freely) with the average person, who possesses the average level of skills and knowledge.

To analyze this model, we can let $A_i = K/L$ in Eq. (4.22) and then proceed as before. The only difference in the results is that the average product of capital and the private marginal product of capital no longer depend on L. For example, in the Cobb–Douglas case, the average product in Eq. (4.33) becomes A rather than $AL^{1-\alpha}$, and the private marginal product in Eq. (4.34) becomes $A\alpha$ rather than $A\alpha L^{1-\alpha}$. Since the formal analysis is the same as before, we leave the proof of these results as an exercise.

4.4   GOVERNMENT AND GROWTH

In the AK model, anything that changes the level of the baseline technology, A, affects the long-run per capita growth rate. We show in this section that various activities of government can be viewed as effects on the coefficient A and, hence, on the growth rate. The activities that we consider include the provision of infrastructure services, the protection of property rights, and the taxation of economic activity.

The governmental activities turn out to have effects on long-run growth rates because we are considering models that generate endogenous growth. We could, however, also include the effects from government in the Solow–Swan model of Chapter 1 or the Ramsey model of Chapter 2. In these contexts, changes in governmental activities would amount to shifts in the production function. Thus, these types of changes would affect the steady-state level of per capita output and would also affect per capita growth rates during the transition to the steady state.

4.4.1   The Public-Goods Model of Productive Government Services

We assume that the government purchases a portion of the private output and then uses these purchases to provide free public services to private producers.[11] The as-

---

[11]We could also allow for public consumption services as an influence on households' utility. If these services enter separably from c in the utility function, then these activities influence growth in the model only if the expenditures are financed by a distorting tax.

sumption that government buys a part of the private output, instead of engaging in public-sector production, amounts to the condition that the government's production function does not differ in form from each firm's production function.

Let G represent the total of government purchases. We begin with the standard approach to public goods, due to Samuelson (1954), in which G is nonrival and nonexcludable. Hence, each firm makes use of all of G, and one firm's use of the public good does not diminish the quantity available to others. Although this approach is standard, we believe that the activities to which this publicness applies are very limited. One minor example is the satisfaction that British people feel about the existence of the Queen of England (although the Queen probably does not enter into production functions). A more serious candidate for a significant public good is the knowledge that governments create by sponsoring research, for example, in the United States, through the National Science Foundation and the National Institutes of Health.

Although basic research may be an exception, we believe that most government expenditures are not well characterized as public goods and that a less conventional framework that allows for congestion of the government's services is applicable to a broader class of activities. We discuss this alternative model in the next section and show that it differs dramatically from the standard public-goods model with respect to scale effects and the implications for desirable public finance.

THE DECENTRALIZED ECONOMY. We assume, as in Barro (1990b), that the production function for firm i takes the Cobb–Douglas form,

$$Y_i = AL_i^{1-\alpha} \cdot K_i^{\alpha} \cdot G^{1-\alpha}, \tag{4.37}$$

where $0 < \alpha < 1$. This equation implies that production for each firm exhibits constant returns to scale in the private inputs, L_i and K_i. We assume that the aggregate labor force, L, is constant. For fixed G, the economy faces diminishing returns to the accumulation of aggregate capital, K, as in the Ramsey model of Chapter 2. If, however, G rises along with K, then Eq. (4.37) implies that diminishing returns will not arise; that is, the production function specifies constant returns in K_i and G for fixed L_i.[12] For this reason, the economy is capable of endogenous growth, as in the AK model studied earlier in this chapter. Note also that the form of the production function implies that the public services are complementary with the private inputs in the sense that an increase in G raises the marginal products of L_i and K_i.

If the exponent on G in Eq. (4.37) were less than $1-\alpha$, then diminishing returns to K_i and G would apply, and these diminishing returns would rule out endogenous growth. Conversely, if the exponent were greater than α, then growth rates would tend to rise over time. We are therefore focusing on the special case in which the exponent on G exactly equals $1-\alpha$, so that the constant returns to K_i and G imply that

---

[12]The formulation in Eq. (4.37) assumes that the flow of government purchases, G, enters into the production function. An alternate approach would include a stock of accumulated public capital.

the economy is capable of endogenous growth. This setting parallels the production function for the Romer model in Eq. (4.32), except that the aggregate capital stock, K, has been replaced by the quantity of public goods, G.

Suppose that the government runs a balanced budget financed by a proportional tax at rate τ on the aggregate of gross output:

$$G = \tau Y. \tag{4.38}$$

We assume that τ and, hence, the expenditure ratio, G/Y, are constant over time.

The firm's after-tax profit is

$$L_i \cdot [(1 - \tau) \cdot A \cdot k_i^\alpha \cdot G^{1-\alpha} - w - (r + \delta) \cdot k_i],$$

where $k_i \equiv K_i/L_i$, w is the wage rate, and $r + \delta$ is the rental rate. Profit maximization and the zero-profit condition now imply that the wage rate equals the *after-tax* marginal product of labor and that the rental rate equals the *after-tax* marginal product of capital. In particular, if we set $k_i = k$, then the rental price is given by

$$r + \delta = (1 - \tau) \cdot (\partial Y_i/\partial K_i) = (1 - \tau) \cdot \alpha A \cdot k^{-(1-\alpha)} \cdot G^{1-\alpha}. \tag{4.39}$$

We can use Eqs. (4.37) and (4.38) to get an expression for G:

$$G = (\tau A L)^{1/\alpha} \cdot k. \tag{4.40}$$

If we use this equation to substitute for G in Eq. (4.39), then we get

$$r + \delta = (1 - \tau) \cdot (\partial Y_i/\partial K_i) = \alpha A^{1/\alpha} \cdot (L\tau)^{(1-\alpha)/\alpha} \cdot (1 - \tau). \tag{4.41}$$

If L and τ are constant, then the after-tax marginal product—and, hence, the rate of return, r—is invariant with k and increasing with L. These results parallel our findings for the Romer model.

The after-tax marginal product of capital on the right-hand side of Eq. (4.41) plays the same role in the growth process that the constant A played in the AK model and that the constant private marginal product of capital played in the Romer model. There are no transitional dynamics, and the growth rates of c, k, and y all equal the same constant, γ. We can determine this constant from the expression for consumption growth in Eq. (4.4):[13]

$$\gamma = (1/\theta) \cdot [\alpha A^{1/\alpha} \cdot (L\tau)^{(1-\alpha)/\alpha} \cdot (1 - \tau) - \delta - \rho]. \tag{4.42}$$

The effects of government on growth involve two channels: the term $1 - \tau$ represents the negative effect of taxation on the after-tax marginal product of capital, and the term $\tau^{(1-\alpha)/\alpha}$ represents the positive effect of public services, G, on

---

[13] As in the AK and Romer models, we require some inequality conditions for the growth rate to be positive and for utility to be bounded. The former condition is $(1 - \tau) \cdot \partial Y_i/\partial K_i - \delta > \rho$, and the latter condition—which corresponds to the transversality condition—is $[(\theta - 1)/\theta] \cdot [(1 - \tau) \cdot \partial Y_i/\partial K_i - \delta] + \rho/\theta > 0$. The value for $(1 - \tau) \cdot \partial Y_i/\partial K_i$ is given in Eq. (4.41).

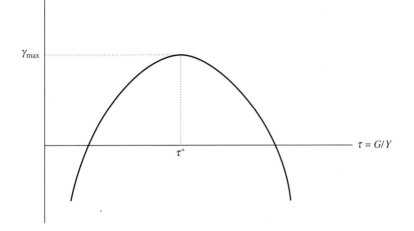

FIGURE 4.1
Government and growth. The relation between the size of the government, $\tau = G/Y$, and the per capita growth rate, γ, is U-shaped. At low values of τ, the positive effect of more G/Y on capital's marginal product dominate, and, hence, γ rises with τ. As τ rises, the adverse impact of distorting taxation becomes more important, and γ eventually reaches a peak. For still higher values of τ, the taxation effect dominates, and γ declines with τ.

this marginal product. Figure 4.1 shows the graph of γ from Eq. (4.42) against the government's spending share, $\tau = G/Y$. At low values of τ, the positive effect of G/Y on capital's marginal product dominates, and, hence, γ rises with τ. As τ rises, the adverse impact of distorting taxation becomes more important, and γ eventually reaches a peak. For still higher values of τ, the taxation effect dominates, and, hence, γ declines with τ.

The maximum of γ from Eq. (4.42) can be found by setting the derivative with respect to τ to 0. The result is

$$\tau = G/Y = 1 - \alpha. \tag{4.43}$$

To interpret this result, note that the marginal product of public services is given from Eq. (4.37) by[14]

$$\partial Y/\partial G = (1 - \alpha) \cdot (Y/G) = (1 - \alpha)/\tau.$$

The condition $\tau = 1 - \alpha$ therefore corresponds to the natural efficiency condition for the size of the government, $\partial Y/\partial G = 1$.[15]

---

[14]Equation (4.37) implies $\partial Y_i/\partial G = (1 - \alpha) \cdot Y_i/G$. The social marginal product of G is the sum over all firms i; that is, $\partial Y/\partial G = (1 - \alpha) \cdot Y/G$.

[15]The social cost of a unit of G is 1, and the benefit is $\partial Y/\partial G$. Therefore, $\partial Y/\partial G = 1$ equates the marginal cost to the marginal benefit.

In this model, a benevolent government would seek to maximize the utility attained by the representative household. Although the condition $\partial Y/\partial G = 1$ would be part of this utility maximization in a first-best environment, this condition would not necessarily hold in second-best situations in which taxes were distorting. Moreover, the maximization of utility would not, in general, correspond to the maximization of the growth rate, γ. It turns out, however, for a Cobb–Douglas production function (Eq. [4.37]) that the maximization of utility corresponds to the maximization of the growth rate and, as already demonstrated, that the maximization of the growth rate corresponds to $\partial Y/\partial G = 1$. We can prove these results by considering how the government would act to maximize the utility attained by the representative household.

The representative household's utility, given in Eq. (4.1), can be evaluated in closed form because c grows at the constant rate γ shown in Eq. (4.42). If we use $c(t) = c(0) \cdot e^{\gamma t}$ and carry out the integration, then the result is

$$U = \frac{1}{(1 - \theta)} \cdot \left\{ \frac{[c(0)]^{1-\theta}}{\rho - \gamma \cdot (1 - \theta)} - (1/\rho) \right\}, \tag{4.44}$$

where $\rho - \gamma \cdot (1 - \theta) > 0$ from the transversality condition (see footnote 13). Note that U increases with $c(0)$ and γ. The reason that the government may not wish, in general, to maximize γ is that an increase in γ entails a reduction in $c(0)$.

The initial level of consumption is $C(0) = Y(0) - G(0) - I(0)$, where $I = \dot{K} + \delta K$. We have the conditions $G(0) = \tau \cdot Y(0)$ and $I(0) = (\gamma + \delta) \cdot K(0)$. The production function in Eq. (4.37) implies

$$Y(0) = AL \cdot [k(0)]^\alpha \cdot [G(0)]^{1-\alpha} = A^{1/\alpha} \cdot (L\tau)^{(1-\alpha)/\alpha} \cdot K(0),$$

where we used the condition for $G(0)$ from Eq. (4.40). These results imply that the initial level of consumption per person is given by

$$c(0) = \left[A^{1/\alpha} \cdot (L\tau)^{(1-\alpha)/\alpha} \cdot (1 - \tau) - \gamma - \delta \right] \cdot k(0). \tag{4.45}$$

We can substitute this result into the expression for U in Eq. (4.44).

If we use the relation between γ and τ from Eq. (4.42), then we can determine U as a function of the policy variable, τ. A more convenient approach, however, uses Eq. (4.42) to solve for the term $\tau^{(1-\alpha)/\alpha} \cdot (1 - \tau)$ as a function of γ. If we substitute the result into the formula for $c(0)$ in Eq. (4.45) and substitute for $c(0)$ in the expression for U in Eq. (4.44), then we end up with an equation for U that depends on γ but not separately on τ. It is then straightforward to show that U is monotonically increasing in γ. Therefore, the maximization of U corresponds to the maximization of γ. Since we already showed that the maximization of γ entails $\tau = 1 - \alpha$, we conclude that $\tau = 1 - \alpha$ maximizes the utility attained by the representative household. We should stress that this result depends on the Cobb–Douglas specification of the production function in Eq. (4.37).

We have shown so far only that $\tau = 1 - \alpha$ is the government's best policy, given that the growth rate is determined by the decentralized choices of households and firms in accordance with Eq. (4.42). We want to see now whether the outcomes are Pareto optimal. As usual, we can check on Pareto optimality by considering the social planner's problem.

THE SOCIAL PLANNER'S PROBLEM. The planner chooses the time paths $G(t)$ and $c(t)$ to maximize U, as given in Eq. (4.1). This planner is constrained only by the production function in Eq. (4.37) and the budget constraint,

$$Y = AL \cdot k^\alpha \cdot G^{1-\alpha} = C + G + \dot{K} + \delta K.$$

(We have already assumed, correctly, that the planner assigns the same capital intensity, $k_i = k$, to each firm.) It is straightforward to set up a Hamiltonian expression to derive the conditions for dynamic optimization in the social planner's problem. Since the formal analysis is similar to that in the Romer model, we provide only a discussion of the results.

To begin, the social planner satisfies the condition $\partial Y/\partial G = 1$ and, hence, $G/Y = 1 - \alpha$. We already knew that this condition for the efficient size of the public sector would apply in a first-best environment, and the social planner always attains the first best.

The key distortion in the decentralized model is that individual investors take account of the private marginal product of capital, $(1 - \tau) \cdot \partial Y_i/\partial K_i$, which falls short of the social marginal product, $\partial Y_i/\partial K_i$, because of the tax rate, τ. This wedge between social and private returns leads to a shortfall of the growth rate, γ, given in Eq. (4.42), from the socially optimal rate, which is found by replacing $(1-\tau)\cdot\partial Y_i/\partial K_i$ with $\partial Y_i/\partial K_i$. Equivalently, the term $1 - \tau$ in Eq. (4.42) is replaced by 1. If we also set $G/Y = 1 - \alpha$, then the growth rate chosen by the social planner is given by

$$\gamma \text{ (social planner)} = (1/\theta) \cdot [(1 - \alpha) \cdot A^{1/(1-\alpha)} \cdot (L\alpha)^{\alpha/(1-\alpha)} - \delta - \rho]. \quad (4.46)$$

It is possible to generate the growth rate shown in Eq. (4.46)—and thereby the first-best outcomes—in a decentralized setup. First, the government sets $G/Y = 1 - \alpha$ to get the right quantity of public goods. Second, the government finances its expenditure with a lump-sum tax, that is, a tax with a marginal rate of zero with respect to production. In the present context, a consumption tax would amount to a lump-sum tax because the labor/leisure choice is not considered. However, the model in the next section questions the general wisdom of lump-sum taxation.

SCALE EFFECTS. The public-goods model of government services predicts scale effects that resemble those in the Romer model. In the present context, the economy benefits from a greater scale because the governmental services are assumed to be public goods, which can be spread costlessly over additional users.

An increase in scale, represented by L, raises the after-tax marginal product of capital in Eq. (4.41) and expands the social marginal product in a parallel way. A higher L leads accordingly to higher values of the decentralized growth rate in Eq. (4.42) and of the planner's growth rate in Eq. (4.46). A continuing expansion of L, due to population growth, would imply rising per capita growth rates. Thus, as in the Romer model, we had to assume zero population growth in order to study steady states.

As mentioned before, the cross-country data indicate that the per capita growth rate has, at most, a weak positive relation with the size of the working-age population. (Countries are a natural unit of observation here if we think that the benefits from the government's public goods extend only over the government's political jurisdiction.) The failure to detect more important scale effects likely means that most of the government's services do not have the nonrival character that is assumed in the model. We therefore now consider the alternative setting in which the government's services are subject to congestion. We shall show that this model has very different implications for scale effects and for desirable public finance.

4.4.2   The Congestion Model of Productive Government Services

PUBLIC SERVICES AS AN INPUT TO PRODUCTION. Many governmental activities, such as highways, water systems, police and fire services, and courts, are subject to congestion. For a given quantity of aggregate services, G, the quantity available to an individual declines as other users congest the facilities. For governmental activities that serve as an input to private production, we model this congestion (as in Barro and Sala-i-Martin [1992c]) by writing the production function for the ith producer as

$$Y_i = AK_i \cdot f(G/Y), \tag{4.47}$$

where $f' > 0$ and $f'' < 0$. The production process is AK modified by the term that involves public services: an increase in G *relative* to aggregate output, Y, expands Y_i for given K_i. Because of congestion, an increase in Y for given G lowers the public services available to each producer and therefore reduces Y_i. The formulation assumes that G has to rise in relation to total output, Y, in order to expand the public services available to each user. We could have assumed alternatively that G had to rise in relation to aggregate private capital, K, in order to raise the quantity of services. The results would be essentially the same under this specification.

For given G and Y, a firm's production exhibits constant returns with respect to the private input K_i. Hence, the competitive rental rate on capital will equal the after-tax marginal product of capital, and the payments to capital will exhaust the after-tax product. If G grows at the same rate as Y, then G/Y remains fixed, and the constant returns in K_i imply that the economy will generate endogenous growth, as in the AK model.

We assume as in Eq. (4.38) that the government levies the constant, proportionate tax rate τ on output, so that $G/Y = \tau$. The after-tax marginal product of capital is then given from Eq. (4.47) by

$$(1 - \tau) \cdot \partial Y_i / \partial K_i = (1 - \tau) \cdot A \cdot f(\tau) = r + \delta. \tag{4.48}$$

Note that, unlike the public-goods model, the after-tax marginal product and, hence, the rate of return, do not depend on the scale variable, L.

The growth rates of c, k, and y all equal the same constant, given from Eq. (4.4) by

$$\gamma = (1/\theta) \cdot [A \cdot (1 - \tau) \cdot f(\tau) - \delta - \rho]. \tag{4.49}$$

Since $f' > 0$ and $f'' < 0$, the relation between γ and τ looks again like that shown in Figure 4.1; in particular, γ rises with τ at low values of τ and falls with τ at high values of τ. Since the after-tax marginal product of capital is invariant with L (Eq. [4.48]), the growth rate is also independent of L.

Equation (4.49) implies that the choice of τ to maximize γ dictates $f(\tau) = (1 - \tau) \cdot f'(\tau)$, a condition that can be shown from Eq. (4.47) to imply the familiar efficiency condition for the size of government, $\partial Y/\partial G = 1$.[16] Moreover, this result now holds independently of the specific functional form for $f(\cdot)$.

Again we can work through the social planner's problem to assess the Pareto optimality of the decentralized outcomes. Since the methodology is the same as before, we provide only a discussion of the results.

Not surprisingly, the social planner satisfies the efficiency condition, $\partial Y/\partial G = 1$. A new result applies, however, to the comparison between the decentralized growth rate, γ, shown in Eq. (4.49) and the social-planner's growth rate. Suppose in the decentralized setup that the government sets G/Y to maximize γ, so that $\partial Y/\partial G = 1$ applies. In this case, the social planner's growth rate equals the decentralized rate, γ, even though the decentralized economy faces the proportional tax rate, τ, on production. In other words, unlike the public-goods model, in which a shift to a lump-sum tax would be Pareto improving, the proportionate tax on output now generates the social optimum. Moreover, a move to a lump-sum tax would be Pareto worsening: the economy would end up in this case with excessive growth.

The intuition for these results is straightforward. An individual producer's decision to expand capital, K_i, and hence, output, Y_i, contributes to total output, Y, and thereby increases congestion for a given aggregate of public services, G. With a lump-sum tax, the individual producer neglects these adverse external effects and therefore has too great an incentive to expand K_i and Y_i. To internalize the distortion, a producer who raises Y_i has to provide enough additional resources to maintain the public services available to others, that is, to keep G/Y constant. The required compensation is G/Y times the addition to Y. A tax rate, τ, at the rate G/Y provides exactly the right incentive to the individual producer and therefore results in a social optimum (if the size of the government, G/Y, is also determined to satisfy the condition $\partial Y/\partial G = 1$).

PUBLIC SERVICES AS AN INFLUENCE ON PROPERTY RIGHTS. minis1pt For public services like highways or water and power systems, it is natural to enter G/Y directly into the production function, as in Eq. (4.47).[17] Activities that maintain property rights, such as police services, courts, and national defense, can be viewed instead as affecting the probability that people retain the rights to their goods and thereby have an incentive to accumulate capital and produce.

---

[16]Equation (4.47) implies that the formula for the marginal product of public services is $\partial Y/\partial G = f'(\tau)/[f(\tau) + \tau \cdot f'(\tau)]$. An interior solution for the growth-maximizing τ is guaranteed if $f'(\tau) \to \infty$ as $\tau \to 0$ and $f'(\tau) \to 0$ as $\tau \to 1$.

[17]The government's participation in these areas has to be motivated from natural-monopoly arguments. Sala-i-Martin (1992) argues that transfer payments may also enhance productivity in some circumstances.

Suppose that the probability, p, of maintaining ownership in one's output is an increasing function of G/Y, that is, $p = p(G/Y)$, with $p' > 0$ and $p'' < 0$. For example, if G represents the aggregate expenditure on police, then the amount of protection for each individual depends on the ratio of G to the total amount of economic activity, Y, that the police have to guard. In some cases, it would be more natural to divide G by K, rather than by Y, but the results would be essentially the same.

If we neglect the direct productive effect of government services and assume that producers care only about the expected rate of return on investment, then Eq. (4.48) is modified to

$$(1 - \tau) \cdot A \cdot p(\tau) = r + \delta, \tag{4.50}$$

and Eq. (4.49) becomes

$$\gamma = (1/\theta) \cdot [A \cdot (1 - \tau) \cdot p(\tau) - \delta - \rho].^{18} \tag{4.51}$$

(We assume that the tax rate, τ, applies only to the part of gross output that is not stolen.) Equation (4.51) corresponds in form to Eq. (4.49)—with $p(\tau)$ replacing $f(\tau)$—and the conclusions are the same. In particular, the condition for maximizing γ is $p(\tau) = (1 - \tau) \cdot p'(\tau)$, and the resulting value of γ in Eq. (4.51) is Pareto optimal.[19]

It is controversial to treat national defense, a large part of government expenditures, as an activity that is subject to congestion in the sense that G enters relative to Y or K in the probability of maintaining property rights. Thompson (1976) argues, however, that Y and K represent the prize to potential foreign aggressors. If Y and K increase, then foreigners become more threatening if G does not change, and the government has to raise G roughly in proportion to Y and K to maintain a given state of national security. Thus, national defense is effectively subject to congestion in the same way as domestic services for police, fire, and so on.

It is interesting to compare the congestion model of government services with Romer's model of learning-by-doing with spillovers. In the congestion model, a tax on production is desirable because it internalizes the congestion. The same result would have held in the spillovers model if we had assumed that the spillovers conveyed a negative benefit (perhaps reflecting pollution of air or water). Since we assumed instead that production entailed an external benefit (essentially, negative congestion), we concluded that a subsidy to production was warranted. It is an unresolved empirical matter whether spillovers are typically positive or negative.

The main empirical predictions about government and growth come from the graph in Figure 4.1, a relation that holds for the various kinds of productive government services that we have considered. The predicted relation between the growth

---

[18] An alternative setup attaches the theft probability, $1 - p$, to the stock of capital rather than to the flow of output. In this alternative setting, $1 - p$ effectively adds to the depreciation rate in Eqs. (4.50) and (4.51). The results in this case are similar to those discussed in the text.

[19] The results are socially optimal if the utility of criminals does not count or if the resources that the criminals use up in their pursuit of crime equals the amount stolen (as occurs in some models of rent-seeking activity).

rate, γ, and the share of these services in GDP, G/Y, is not monotonic. The growth rate rises with G/Y when the government is small, but declines with G/Y when the government becomes too large.

4.5 TRANSITIONAL DYNAMICS IN AN ENDOGENOUS GROWTH MODEL

The models considered thus far in this chapter all lack any transitional dynamics. In particular, the prediction is that per capita growth rates would be independent of the initial levels of k and y. Thus, these models are inconsistent with the empirical evidence on convergence, as discussed in Chapters 11 and 12.

We showed in Chapter 1, in models that assume a constant saving rate, that it is possible to construct an endogenous growth model that exhibits transitional dynamics in which the convergence property holds. These results follow if we modify the technology to reintroduce diminishing returns to capital but also assume that capital's marginal product is bounded from below as the capital stock tends to infinity (so that the Inada condition at infinity is violated). We show in this section how this kind of technology can be combined with the type of household optimization that applies in the Ramsey model.

The technologies that we consider here take the form considered by Jones and Manuelli (1990),

$$Y = F(K, L) = AK + \Omega(K, L), \qquad (4.52)$$

where $\Omega(K, L)$ satisfies the properties of a neoclassical production function: positive and diminishing marginal products, constant returns to scale, and the Inada conditions (Eqs. [1.5a]–[1.5c]). Production functions of the form of Eq. (4.52) are not neoclassical only because they violate one of the Inada conditions, $\lim_{K\to\infty}[\partial Y/\partial K] = A > 0$. The AK part of the production function will deliver endogenous growth, whereas the $\Omega(K, L)$ part will generate the convergence behavior. To keep the dynamic analysis manageable, we limit the discussion to some specific functional forms for $\Omega(K, L)$.

4.5.1 A Cobb–Douglas Example

We begin with the production function that we considered in Chapter 1 (Eq. [1.37]):

$$Y = F(K, L) = AK + BK^\alpha \cdot L^{1-\alpha},$$

where $A > 0$, $B > 0$, and $0 < \alpha < 1$.[20] We can rewrite this function in per capita terms as

$$y = f(k) = Ak + Bk^\alpha. \qquad (4.53)$$

Note that $\lim_{k\to\infty}[f'(k)] = A > 0$.

---

[20] All of the results that we discuss in this section go through if L is replaced by $\hat{L}$, where $\hat{L} = Le^{xt}$. That is, we can allow for exogenous technological progress in the part of the production function that is subject to diminishing returns. If the parameter A grew steadily over time, then the model would not have a steady state.

The dynamic equations for k and c are the usual ones derived for the Ramsey model in Chapter 2 (Eqs. [2.23] and [2.24] with $x = 0$):

$$\gamma_k = f(k)/k - c/k - (n + \delta) = A + B \cdot k^{\alpha-1} - c/k - (n + \delta), \quad (4.54)$$

$$\gamma_c = (1/\theta) \cdot [f'(k) - \delta - \rho] = (1/\theta) \cdot [A + B\alpha \cdot k^{\alpha-1} - \delta - \rho]. \quad (4.55)$$

If the model generates endogenous growth—that is, $\gamma_k^* > 0$—then $k \to \infty$ as $t \to \infty$, and the terms involving $k^{\alpha-1}$ asymptotically become negligible. Therefore, the steady state looks exactly like the AK model, and the steady-state growth rates of c, k, and y are all given (from Eq. [4.16]) by

$$\gamma^* = (1/\theta) \cdot (A - \delta - \rho). \quad (4.56)$$

We assume $A > \delta + \rho$, so that $\gamma^* > 0$.[21] (If $A \leq \delta + \rho$, then $\gamma^* = 0$, just as in the standard Ramsey model discussed in Chapter 2.)

We could try to follow the approach from Figure 2.1 by constructing a phase diagram in (k, c) space. This method does not work, however, because k and c grow forever if $\gamma^* > 0$. A procedure that does work involves a transformation to variables that are constant in the steady state. We choose to study the evolution of the average product of capital, denoted by $z \equiv f(k)/k$, and the ratio of consumption to the capital stock, denoted by $\chi \equiv c/k$. Note that z is a *state-like variable* in that, like k, its value at a point in time is dictated by past investments and the evolution of L. Thus, if investment is finite and L has no jumps, then z and k cannot jump at a point in time. In contrast, χ is a *control-like variable* in that, like c, its value can jump at a point in time. (Such jumps will, however, not be optimal in the equilibria that we focus on.) Unlike k and c, the two new variables, z and χ, approach constants in the steady state.

We can use Eqs. (4.54) and (4.55) to derive a dynamic system in terms of the transformed variables, z and χ. The results can be written after a fair amount of algebra in the form

$$\dot{z} = -(1 - \alpha) \cdot (z - A) \cdot (z - \chi - n - \delta), \quad (4.57)$$

$$\dot{\chi} = \chi \cdot \left[(\chi - \varphi) - \frac{(\theta - \alpha)}{\theta} \cdot (z - A) \right], \quad (4.58)$$

where $\varphi \equiv (A - \delta) \cdot (\theta - 1)/\theta + \rho/\theta - n$. We require $\varphi > 0$ in order to satisfy the transversality condition. This condition also ensures that utility is finite when c grows at the rate γ^* shown in Eq. (4.56). It is clear from Eqs. (4.57) and (4.58) that $\dot{z} = \dot{\chi} = 0$ is consistent with $z = A$ and $\chi = \varphi$, which turn out to be the steady-state values of z and χ. (Note that $z = A$ means that, asymptotically, the AK part of the production function dominates the $BK^\alpha \cdot L^{1-\alpha}$ part.)

---

[21] We also continue to assume $\rho > n$, so that $A > \delta + \rho$ implies $A > \delta + n$. If the last inequality did not hold, then utility would be unbounded if c were constant over time.

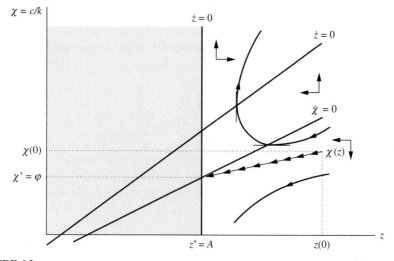

FIGURE 4.2

Transitional dynamics in an endogenous growth model (When $F[K, L] = AK + BK^{\alpha}L^{1-\alpha}$). The phase diagram is shown in (z, χ) space, where $z \equiv f(k)/k$ is the gross average product of capital and $\chi \equiv c/k$. The $\dot{\chi} = 0$ locus is a line with a slope that is less than one and is positive, as shown, if $\theta > \alpha$. There are two conditions that satisfy $\dot{z} = 0$. One is a vertical line at $z = A$, and the other is an upward-sloping line with unit slope. This line must cross the vertical line at A at a value of χ that exceeds χ^*. Since $z \equiv f(k)/k = A + Bk^{\alpha-1} > A$, the only steady state is the point at which the $\dot{\chi} = 0$ schedule intersects the vertical line, $z = A$. Since $z > z^*$ applies initially, then z and χ decline monotonically during the transition. (Note that the result on the path of χ depends on the assumption $\theta > \alpha$.)

Figure 4.2 shows the phase diagram in (z, χ) space. Equation (4.58) implies that the $\dot{\chi} = 0$ locus is (aside from $\chi = 0$) the straight line $\chi = \varphi - A \cdot (\theta - \alpha)/\theta + z \cdot (\theta - \alpha)/\theta$. The slope is less than 1 and is positive, as shown, if $\theta > \alpha$. If $\theta < \alpha$, then the line would have a negative slope. This case requires an unrealistically high degree of intertemporal substitution in that θ would have to be significantly below unity.

Equation (4.57) implies that $\dot{z} = 0$ if $z = A$ or if $\chi = z - n - \delta$. The former condition corresponds to the vertical line at A in Fig. 4.2. The latter condition is shown by the straight line with slope 1 and negative intercept. Note that the slope of this $\dot{z} = 0$ line must be steeper than that of the $\dot{\chi} = 0$ line, which has slope less than 1. (The inequality $A > \rho + \delta$ implies that the $\dot{z} = 0$ line intersects the vertical line at A at a value of χ that exceeds φ, as shown in the figure.)

Because $z = A + B \cdot k^{\alpha-1} > A$, the portions of Fig. 4.2 in which $z < A$ are irrelevant. We can therefore confine the analysis to the region in which $z \geq A$. Note from the figure that the $\dot{z} = 0$ and $\dot{\chi} = 0$ lines intersect in this region only at $z^* = A$ and $\chi^* = \varphi$, which are the steady-state values.

We now consider the transitional dynamics, starting from an initial position $z(0) > A$. The figure shows the stable arm that corresponds to the appropriately chosen initial value $\chi(0)$. Along this arm, the average product of capital, z, and the ratio of consumption to capital, χ, each decline monotonically.[22] The monotonic decline in z corresponds to the monotonic increase in k. The monotonic fall in χ depends on the assumption $\theta > \alpha$.[23] If we had assumed $\theta < \alpha$, then χ would have risen monotonically during the transition. (If $\theta = \alpha$, then $\chi = \varphi$, the steady-state value, throughout the transition.)

Capital's share of product is given by

$$k \cdot f'(k)/f(k) = (Ak + \alpha Bk^\alpha)/(Ak + Bk^\alpha),$$

which equals α if $A = 0$ and equals 1 if $B = 0$. If $A > 0$ and $B > 0$, then capital's share rises toward 1 and labor's share falls toward 0 as k increases without bound. This implication of the model would conflict with the data if we interpreted capital in the narrow sense of plant and equipment but is more reasonable if we add human capital. In this case, the implication is that the share of raw labor in total product falls toward 0 as the economy develops.

The most important aspect of the extended model is that it restores a transitional dynamics during which the average and marginal products of capital decline gradually toward the steady-state value, A. The falling productivity of capital tends to generate a decline over time in per capita growth rates; that is, the model again exhibits the convergence property that applies in the Ramsey model.

Appendix 2C showed that the growth rate of capital per person, $\dot{k}/k$, declines monotonically during the transition of the Ramsey model.[24] The proof relied on the diminishing marginal product of capital, $f''(k) < 0$, but not on the Inada condition, $\lim_{k\to\infty}[f'(k)] = 0$. Therefore, the convergence property of declining growth rates of capital per person applies immediately to the present model in which the production function is given by Eq. (4.53) or, more generally, by Eq. (4.52). This framework features the long-run growth properties of the AK model, together with the convergence behavior exhibited by the Ramsey model.

4.5.2   A CES Example

We now demonstrate that we can get similar results for endogenous growth and transitional dynamics if the production function takes a constant-elasticity-of-substitution (CES) form. We showed in Chapter 1 that endogenous growth is feasible

---

[22]We can rule out the unstable paths from the usual arguments. The paths that approach $\chi = 0$ and $z = A$ violate the transversality condition. Those that involve $\chi \to \infty$ and $z \to \infty$ entail running out of capital in finite time and therefore lead eventually to a discrete downward jump to zero consumption.

[23]Appendix 2B noted that c/k fell monotonically in the Ramsey model with a Cobb–Douglas technology if $\theta > \alpha$. This result still holds if the production function is modified to $f(k) = Ak + Bk^\alpha$, the case presently being considered.

[24]This result applies in the Ramsey model if the economy begins at $k(0) < k^*$. In the present case, k^* is effectively infinite, so that this inequality is never a constraint.

with a CES production function if the elasticity of substitution between the factors K and L is high. Specifically, we now assume that the technology is

$$Y = F(K, L) = A \cdot \left\{ a \cdot (bK)^\psi + (1 - a) \cdot [(1 - b) \cdot L]^\psi \right\}^{1/\psi}, \qquad (4.59)$$

where $0 < a < 1, 0 < b < 1$, and $0 < \psi < 1$, so that the elasticity of substitution, $1/(1 - \psi)$, is greater than 1.

The production function can be written in terms of per capita quantities as

$$y = f(k) = A \cdot \left[a \cdot (bk)^\psi + (1 - a) \cdot (1 - b)^\psi \right]^{1/\psi}. \qquad (4.60)$$

We showed in Chapter 1 that the marginal and average products of capital are positive and diminishing and have the following limits:

$$\lim_{k \to \infty} [f'(k)] = \lim_{k \to \infty} [f(k)/k] = Bba^{1/\psi},$$

$$\lim_{k \to 0} [f'(k)] = \lim_{k \to 0} [f(k)/k] = \infty.$$

In particular, since $f'(k)$ approaches a positive constant as k goes to infinity, the key Inada condition is violated, and the model may generate endogenous growth.

To make the analysis parallel with that in the previous section, we define the parameter A as

$$A \equiv Bba^{1/\psi}. \qquad (4.61)$$

With this definition, the CES production function (with $0 < \psi < 1$) is a special case of Eq. (4.52). If we define $\Omega(K, L) = F(K, L) - AK$, where $F(K, L)$ is the CES function in Eq. (4.59) and A is given by Eq. (4.61), then the function $\Omega(K, L)$ satisfies all of the neoclassical properties (Eqs. [1.5a]–[1.5c]), including the Inada conditions.

Since A is the limiting value of $f'(k)$, the previous analysis suggests that, in order to generate endogenous growth, the parameters of the model have to satisfy the condition $A > \delta + \rho$. This inequality will tend to hold when the level of technology, B, is high, when the elasticity of substitution (reflected in ψ) is high, and when the parameters a and b are large (the larger the values of a and b, the more important is capital in the production process).

The dynamic equations for k and c are again the ones derived for the Ramsey model in Chapter 2 (Eqs. [2.23] and [2.24] with $x = 0$):

$$\gamma_k = f(k)/k - c/k - (n + \delta),$$

$$\gamma_c = (1/\theta) \cdot [f'(k) - \delta - \rho].$$

We define $z \equiv f(k)/k$ and $\chi \equiv c/k$, as in the previous section, and can then work out the dynamic equations for z and χ as

$$\begin{aligned}
\dot{z}/z &= [(z/A)^{-\psi} - 1] \cdot (z - \chi - n - \delta), \\
\dot{\chi}/\chi &= (A/\theta) \cdot [(z/A)^{1-\psi} - 1] - (z - A) + (\chi - \varphi),
\end{aligned} \qquad (4.62)$$

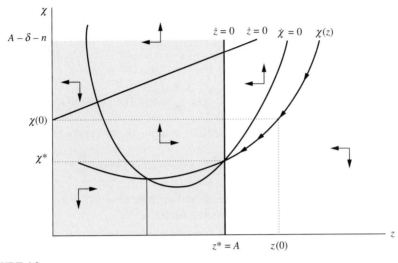

FIGURE 4.3
Transitional dynamics in an endogenous growth model when the production function is CES (with
$0 < \psi < 1$). The phase diagram is shown in (z, χ) space, as in Figure 4.2. We assume $\theta > 1 - \psi$. The
$\dot{\chi} = 0$ locus then displays a U-shape with a minimum to the left of A. The two $\dot{z} = 0$ loci cross at
$\chi = A - \delta - n$. The $\dot{\chi} = 0$ locus intersects the $z = A$ line below $A - \delta - n$. The steady state is given
accordingly by the intersection of the $\dot{\chi} = 0$ locus with the vertical line, $z = A$. Since the economy
begins with $z > z^*$, then the transition features monotonically decreasing values of z and χ. (Note: the
result on the path of χ depends on the assumption $\theta > 1 - \psi$.)

where $\varphi \equiv (A - \delta) \cdot (\theta - 1)/\theta + \rho/\theta - n > 0$, as before. The analysis again applies in
the region in which $z \geq A$, because $f(k)/k$ can never fall below A. The steady-state
position is again at $z^* = A$ and $\chi^* = \varphi$.

To analyze the dynamics of the model, we construct a phase diagram in (z, χ)
space in Figure 4.3. There are two lines (other than $z = 0$) that make $\dot{z} = 0$: a vertical
line at $z = A$ and an upward-sloping line with unit slope and intercept $-(n + \delta)$.
The two lines cross at $z = A$ and $\chi = A - \delta - n$.

The $\dot{\chi} = 0$ schedule is given (other than by $\chi = 0$) by the curve $\chi = \varphi +$
$(z - A) - (A/\theta) \cdot [(z/A)^{1-\psi} - 1]$. This curve is downward sloping for low values of z
and reaches a minimum at $z = A \cdot [(1 - \psi)/\theta]^{1/\psi}$. This minimum occurs to the left of
A, as shown, if $\theta > 1 - \psi$. Since $0 < \psi < 1$, this condition must hold if $\theta \geq 1$. (We
leave the case in which $\theta \leq 1 - \psi$ as an exercise.) As z goes to infinity, the slope of
the $\dot{\chi} = 0$ schedule approaches 1. This curve crosses the vertical line $z = A$ below
the point $A - \delta - n$ (if $A > \rho + \delta > n + \delta$, as we assume).

Figure 4.3 shows the stable, saddle path beginning from a value $z(0) > A$. The
variables z and χ decline monotonically during the transition, just as in the model discussed in the previous section. This transition again exhibits the convergence property, whereby γ_k declines as k rises (and z approaches A).

4.6 CONCLUDING OBSERVATIONS

This chapter shows that endogenous growth may arise if the returns to capital do
not fall in the long run below some positive, baseline value. The long-run growth

rate then depends on the level of the technology and the willingness to save. In some models, the effects from the level of technology can be generalized to include the extent of spillovers across producers, scale effects, and the influences of public services and taxation.

The simplest kinds of endogenous-growth models–which look like the *AK* model—are inconsistent with empirical observations on convergence. However, extended versions of endogenous-growth models combine the convergence behavior of the neoclassical growth model with the long-run growth properties of the *AK* model. These theories accord better with the empirical evidence on convergence.

APPENDIX
CONDITIONS FOR ENDOGENOUS GROWTH
IN THE ONE-SECTOR MODEL

In this chapter, we studied several models that could generate endogenous growth. The key property of these examples was that diminishing returns were not present, at least asymptotically, in the sense that the average and marginal products of capital had positive lower bounds. In particular, the Inada condition $\lim_{k\to\infty}[f'(k)] = 0$ was violated. We now discuss more generally the role of this condition in one-sector models of endogenous growth.

Consider a model without exogenous technological progress in which the dynamic equations are those from the Ramsey model of Chapter 2 (Eqs. [2.23] and [2.24]):

$$\gamma_k \equiv \dot{k}/k = f(k)/k - c/k - (n + \delta), \qquad (4A.1)$$

$$\gamma_c \equiv \dot{c}/c = (1/\theta) \cdot [f'(k) - \delta - \rho]. \qquad (4A.2)$$

If $f'(k)$ and γ_k asymptotically approach some finite limits, then the transversality condition from Eq. (2.25) can be expressed as

$$\lim_{t\to\infty}[f'(k) - \delta] > \lim_{t\to\infty}(\gamma_k + n); \qquad (4A.3)$$

that is, the asymptotic rate of return on capital, given on the left-hand side, exceeds the asymptotic growth rate of the capital stock, given on the right-hand side.

We define a steady state, as usual, as a situation in which the growth rates of the various quantities, K, Y, and C, are constant. In the steady states that we studied in Chapter 2, the growth rates of the quantities per unit of effective labor, such as $\gamma_{\hat{k}}$ and $\gamma_{\hat{c}}$, were 0, so that the per capita growth rates, γ_k and γ_c, equaled x, and the growth rates of levels, γ_K and γ_C, equaled $n + x$. Since we now assume $x = 0$, the per capita growth rates would be 0 in the steady states considered in Chapter 2. Hence, we want to consider what modifications of the technology will allow for steady states in which the per capita growth rates are positive constants, rather than 0, when $x = 0$.

Imagine that the steady-state per capita growth is positive, so that $\lim_{t\to\infty}(\gamma_k) \equiv \gamma_k^* > 0$. Since k then grows in the long run at a positive rate, $\lim_{t\to\infty}(k) = \infty$; that is, k rises without bound. The transversality condition in Eq. (4A.3) then requires

$$\lim_{k\to\infty}[f'(k)] > \gamma_k^* + n + \delta > n + \delta > 0. \tag{4A.4}$$

Note that the limit on the left-hand side of (4A.4) refers to $k \to \infty$, a situation that applies as $t \to \infty$ if k grows in the long run at a constant, positive rate.

The standard Inada condition, $\lim_{k\to\infty}[f'(k)] = 0$, rules out the inequality in (4A.4): that is why endogenous growth does not apply with a neoclassical production function. The model may, however, be able to generate positive long-term growth of k if capital's marginal product has a positive lower bound. We denote the asymptotic marginal product by $A > 0$; that is, we now assume

$$\lim_{k\to\infty}[f'(k)] = A > 0. \tag{4A.5}$$

The inequality in (4A.4) implies that $A > 0$ is not a sufficient condition to generate growth of k in the steady state. A necessary condition for γ_k^* to be positive is

$$A > n + \delta. \tag{4A.6}$$

Hence, the asymptotic rate of return to capital, $A - \delta$, must exceed the growth rate, n, of the capital stock that would obtain if k were constant in the steady state (as in the Ramsey model with $x = 0$).

If $\gamma_k^* > 0$, so that $\lim_{t\to\infty}(k) = \infty$ and, hence, $\lim_{t\to\infty}[f'(k)] = A$, then Eq. (4A.2) implies

$$(\gamma_c)^* = (1/\theta) \cdot (A - \delta - \rho). \tag{4A.7}$$

Therefore, $\gamma_c^* > 0$ requires

$$A > \delta + \rho. \tag{4A.8}$$

We showed in Chapter 2 that, when $x = 0$, the transversality condition required $\rho > n$. If this last inequality still holds—as we assume—then the inequality in (4A.8) implies the inequality in (4A.6). If the inequality in (4A.8) fails to hold, then the analysis of Chapter 2 still goes through–including the result $\gamma_k^* = 0$—even though the technology could physically support perpetual growth of k. The asymptotic rate of return on capital, $A - \delta$, is too low in this case for $\gamma_k^* > 0$ to be optimal. We assume henceforth that the inequality in (4A.8) is satisfied.

We now want to show that $\gamma_k^* = \gamma_c^*$. Equation (4A.1) implies

$$\gamma_k^* = \lim_{k\to\infty}[f(k)/k] - \lim_{k\to\infty}(c/k) - (n + \delta).$$

We know from l'Hôpital's rule (if $f[k]$ tends to infinity as k tends to infinity) that $\lim_{k\to\infty}[f(k)/k] = \lim_{k\to\infty}[f'(k)] = A$. Therefore,

$$\gamma_k^* = A - n - \delta - \lim_{k\to\infty}(c/k). \tag{4A.9}$$

If $\gamma_c^* > \gamma_k^*$, then $\lim_{k\to\infty}(c/k) = \infty$, which is obviously inconsistent with $\gamma_k^* > 0$ in Eq. (4A.9). If $\gamma_c^* < \gamma_k^*$, then $\lim_{k\to\infty}(c/k) = 0$, which implies $\gamma_k^* = A - n - \delta$.

This result implies $A - \delta = \gamma_k^* + n$, a violation of the transversality condition given in (4A.3). We can therefore rule out $\gamma_c^* < \gamma_k^*$.

The only remaining possibility is

$$\gamma_k^* = \gamma_c^* = (1/\theta) \cdot (A - \delta - \rho), \tag{4A.10}$$

where we used the formula for γ_c^* from Eq. (4A.7). This solution works if it satisfies the transversality condition shown in (4A.3), that is, if $A - \delta$ exceeds $\gamma_k^* + n$. The formula for γ_k^* in Eq. (4A.10) implies that the transversality condition can be written as

$$\varphi \equiv (A - \delta) \cdot (\theta - 1)/\theta + \rho/\theta - n > 0. \tag{4A.11}$$

This condition corresponds to (4.12) in the text. Equations (4A.9)–(4A.11) then imply

$$\lim_{k \to \infty} (c/k) = \varphi > 0. \tag{4A.12}$$

If we interpret A as the asymptotic value of $f'(k)$, then the conditions derived in this appendix are satisfied by all of the models that we discussed in this chapter. In particular, the steady-state per capita growth rate is given in Eq. (4A.10) and the steady-state level of c/k is given in Eq. (4A.12).

PROBLEMS

4.1 The AK Model as the Limit of the Neoclassical Model. Consider the neoclassical growth model discussed in Chapter 2. Imagine that the production function is Cobb–Douglas, $\hat{y} = A\hat{k}^\alpha$.

(a) How does an increase in α affect the transition equations for $\hat{k}$ and $\hat{c}$ in Eqs. (2.23) and (2.24). How, therefore, does the increase in α affect the $\dot{\hat{c}} = 0$ locus and the $\dot{\hat{k}} = 0$ locus in Fig. 2.1? How does it affect the steady-state values, $\hat{k}^*$ and $\hat{c}^*$?

(b) What happens, for example to $\hat{k}^*$, as α approaches 1? How does this result relate to the AK model that was discussed in this chapter?

4.2 Oversaving in the AK Model (Based on Saint Paul [1992]). We know from Chapter 1 that an economy oversaves if it approaches a steady state in which the rate of return, r, exceeds the growth rate. Suppose that the technology is $Y = AK$, and the ratio c/k approaches the constant $(c/k)^*$ in the steady state.

(a) Use Eq. (4.8) to determine the steady-state growth rate of K (and, hence, of Y and C). Can this steady-state growth rate exceed the interest rate, r, given in Eq. (4.7)? Is it possible to get oversaving if the economy approaches a steady state and the technology is $Y = AK$?

(b) Suppose that we combine the AK technology with the model of finite-horizon consumers of Blanchard (1985), as described in Section 3.4. Is it possible to get oversaving in this model? What if we combine the AK technology with an overlapping-generations model, as described in the appendix to Chapter 3?

4.3 Transitional Dynamics. Show that in the model of learning-by-doing with knowledge spillovers presented in Section 4.3 there is no transitional dynamics. That is, output and capital always grow at the constant consumption growth rate given in Eq. (4.28).

4.4 Spillovers from Average Capital per Worker. In the model presented in Section 4.3, assume that the firm's productivity parameter, A_i, depends on the economy's average capital per worker, K/L, rather than on the aggregate capital stock, K. The production function is assumed to be Cobb–Douglas:

$$Y_i = A \cdot (K_i)^\alpha \cdot [(K/L) \cdot L_i]^{1-\alpha}.$$

Derive the growth rates for the decentralized economy and for the social planner. Comment on how the scale effect discussed in Section 4.3 does not appear with this new specification.

4.5 Congestion of Public Services (Based on Barro and Sala-i-Martin [1992c]). In the congestion model discussed in Section 4.4.2, suppose that output for firm i is given by

$$Y_i = AK_i \cdot f(G/K),$$

that is, the congestion of public services involves G in relation to K, rather than Y. Retain the assumption that the government levies a constant, proportional tax at rate τ on output. How do the results change under this revised specification of congestion? Consider, in particular, the growth rates that arise in the decentralized economy and in the social planner's solution.

4.6 Adjustment Costs with an AK Technology (Based on Barro and Sala-i-Martin [1992c]). Imagine that firms face an AK technology, but that investment requires adjustment costs as described in Section 3.5. The unit adjustment-cost function is $\phi(i/k) = (b/2) \cdot (i/k)$, so that the total cost of purchasing and investment for 1 unit of capital is $1 + (b/2) \cdot (i/k)$. Producers maximize the present value of cash flows,

$$\int_0^\infty \left\{ AK - I \cdot [1 + (b/2) \cdot (I/K)] \right\} \cdot e^{-rt} \cdot dt,$$

where $r = A - \delta$. The maximization is subject to the constraint $\dot{K} = I - \delta K$.

(a) Set up the Hamiltonian and work out the first-order conditions for the representative firm. Find the relation between the interest rate and the growth rate of capital. Is this relation monotonic? Explain.

(b) Assume that consumers solve the usual infinite-horizon Ramsey problem, so that the growth rate of consumption relates positively to the interest rate. Suppose that the growth rate of consumption equals the growth rate of the capital stock. Does this condition pin down the growth rate? If not, can one of the solutions be ruled out from the transversality condition?

(c) Show that the growth rate of consumption equals the growth rate of the capital stock. What does this finding imply about the model's transitional dynamics? Explain.

4.7 Growth in a Model with Spillovers (Based on Romer [1986]). Assume that the production function for firm i is

$$Y_i = AK_i^\alpha \cdot L_i^{1-\alpha} \cdot K^\lambda,$$

where $0 < \alpha < 1, 0 < \lambda < 1$, and K is the aggregate stock of capital.

(a) Show that if $\lambda < 1 - \alpha$ and L is constant, then the model has transitional dynamics similar to those of the Ramsey model. What is the steady-state growth rate of Y, K, and C in this case?

(b) If $\lambda < 1 - \alpha$ and L grows at the rate $n > 0$, then what is the steady-state growth rate of Y, K, and C?

(c) Show that if $\lambda = 1 - \alpha$ and L is constant, then the steady state and transitional dynamics are like those of the AK model.

(d) What happens if $\lambda = 1 - \alpha$ and L grows at the rate $n > 0$?

CHAPTER
5

TWO-SECTOR MODELS OF ENDOGENOUS GROWTH (WITH SPECIAL ATTENTION TO THE ROLE OF HUMAN CAPITAL)

We showed in Chapter 4 that it was possible to obtain long-term per capita growth without exogenous technological progress if the returns to capital were constant asymptotically. We argued that this absence of diminishing returns might apply if we took a broad view of capital to include human, as well as physical, components. This chapter deals explicitly with models that distinguish between physical and human capital. More generally, the structure can be applied to various types of capital, including the kinds of accumulated knowledge that we shall study in Chapters 6 and 7.

We begin with a framework, similar to the one that we used to study an open economy in Chapter 3, in which physical and human capital are produced by identical production functions. In this setting, the output from the usual one-sector technology can be used on a one-for-one basis for consumption, investment in physical capital, and investment in human capital. New results arise, however, when we allow for the constraint that gross investment in physical and human capital must each be nonnegative. This constraint introduces effects on the growth process due to imbalances between the levels of physical and human capital: the growth rate of output is higher the larger the magnitude of the gap between the ratio of physical to human capital and the steady-state value of this ratio.

We next allow for the possibility that physical and human capital are produced by different technologies. Specifically, we focus on the empirically relevant case in which education—the production of new human capital—is relatively intensive in human capital as an input. This property holds, for example, in the model developed by Uzawa (1965) and used by Lucas (1988), in which existing human capital is the only input in the education sector. This modification of the production structure creates an asymmetry in the effect from imbalances between physical and human capital on the growth rate. The source of the asymmetry derives from the positive effect of the ratio of physical to human capital on the real wage rate (per unit of human capital) and, hence, on the opportunity cost of human capital devoted to education. In this setting, the growth rate for a broad concept of output still increases with the magnitude of the imbalance between physical and human capital if human capital is relatively abundant, but tends to fall with the magnitude of the imbalance if human capital is relatively scarce.

The presence of human capital may relax the constraint of diminishing returns to a broad concept of capital and can lead thereby to long-term per capita growth in the absence of exogenous technological progress. Hence, the production of human capital may be an alternative to improvements in technology as a mechanism to generate long-term growth. We should emphasize, however, some respects in which the accumulation of human capital differs from the creation of knowledge in the form of technological progress. If we think of human capital as the skills embodied in a worker, then the use of these skills in one activity precludes their use in another activity; hence, human capital is a rival good. Since people have property rights in their own skills, as well as in their raw labor, human capital is also an excludable good. In contrast, ideas or knowledge may be nonrival—in that they can be spread freely over activities of arbitrary scale—and may in some circumstances be nonexcludable. This distinction means that theories of technological progress—the subject of Chapters 6–8—differ in fundamental respects from the models of the accumulation of human capital that we consider in this chapter.

5.1   A ONE-SECTOR MODEL WITH PHYSICAL AND HUMAN CAPITAL

5.1.1   The Basic Setup

We assume a Cobb–Douglas production function that exhibits constant returns to physical and human capital, K and H:

$$Y = AK^\alpha H^{1-\alpha}, \tag{5.1}$$

where $0 \le \alpha \le 1$. We can think of human capital, H, as the number of workers, L, multiplied by the human capital of the typical worker, h. The assumption here is that the quantity of workers, L, and the quality of workers, h, are perfect substitutes in production in the sense that only the combination Lh matters for output. This specification means that a fixed number of bodies, L, will not be a source of diminishing returns because a doubling of K and h, for fixed L, leads to a doubling of Y.

We assume, only for convenience, that the total labor force, L, is fixed and, hence, that H grows only because of improvements in the average quality, h. Note also that Eq. (5.1) omits any technological progress.

Output can be used for consumption or investment in physical or human capital. We assume that the stocks of physical and human capital depreciate at the same rate, δ. The depreciation of human capital includes losses from skill deterioration and mortality, net of benefits from experience. (Different depreciation rates for physical and human capital can be introduced, but this generalization complicates the algebra without providing much additional insight.)

The economy's resource constraint is

$$Y = AK^{\alpha}H^{1-\alpha} = C + I_K + I_H, \tag{5.2}$$

where I_K and I_H are gross investment in physical and human capital, respectively. The changes in the two capital stocks are given by

$$\dot{K} = I_K - \delta K,$$
$$\dot{H} = I_H - \delta H. \tag{5.3}$$

We showed in Chapter 2 that we could deal equivalently with a model of distinct households and firms or with a setup in which households carry out production directly. If we use the formulation in which the households are the producers of goods, then the Hamiltonian expression (with zero population growth) is

$$J = u(C) \cdot e^{-\rho t} + \nu \cdot (I_K - \delta K) + \mu \cdot (I_H - \delta H) + \omega \cdot (AK^{\alpha}H^{1-\alpha} - C - I_K - I_H), \tag{5.4}$$

where ν and μ are shadow prices associated with $\dot{K}$ and $\dot{H}$, respectively, and ω is the Lagrange multiplier associated with the budget constraint from Eq. (5.2).[1] We use the usual specification of utility,

$$u(C) = (C^{1-\theta} - 1)/(1 - \theta).$$

Suppose that we neglect, for the moment, the inequality restrictions $I_K \geq 0$ and $I_H \geq 0$. Then the first-order conditions can be obtained in the usual manner by setting the derivatives of J with respect to C, I_K, and I_H to 0, equating ν and μ to $\partial J/\partial K$ and $\partial J/\partial H$, respectively, and allowing for the budget constraint in Eq. (5.2). If we simplify these conditions, then we obtain the familiar result for the growth rate of consumption:

$$\gamma_C = (1/\theta) \cdot [A\alpha \cdot (K/H)^{-(1-\alpha)} - \delta - \rho], \tag{5.5}$$

where $A\alpha \cdot (K/H)^{-(1-\alpha)} - \delta$ is the net marginal product of physical capital.

---

[1] We could equivalently write the Hamiltonian as

$$J = u(C)e^{-\rho t} + \nu \cdot (AK^{\alpha}H^{1-\alpha} - C - \delta K - I_H) + \mu \cdot (I_H - \delta H).$$

This formulation implicitly imposes the condition $I_K = AK^{\alpha}H^{1-\alpha} - C - I_H$, which involves the Lagrange multiplier ω in Eq. (5.4).

The second condition is that the net marginal product of human capital, $A \cdot (1 - \alpha) \cdot (K/H)^\alpha - \delta$, equals the net marginal product of physical capital. This equality,

$$A\alpha \cdot (K/H)^{-(1-\alpha)} - \delta = A \cdot (1 - \alpha) \cdot (K/H)^\alpha - \delta,$$

implies that the ratio of the two capital stocks is given by[2]

$$K/H = \alpha/(1 - \alpha). \tag{5.6}$$

This result for K/H implies that the net rate of return to physical and human capital is given by[3]

$$r^* = A\alpha^\alpha \cdot (1 - \alpha)^{(1-\alpha)} - \delta. \tag{5.7}$$

This rate of return is constant because the production function in Eq. (5.1) exhibits constant returns with respect to broad capital, K and H. Therefore, diminishing returns do not apply when K/H stays constant (Eq. [5.6]), that is, when K and H grow at the same rate.

If K/H is constant, then Eq. (5.5) implies that γ_C is constant and equal to

$$\gamma^* = (1/\theta) \cdot [A\alpha^\alpha \cdot (1 - \alpha)^{(1-\alpha)} - \delta - \rho], \tag{5.8}$$

where we substituted for K/H from Eq. (5.6). We assume that the parameters are so that $\gamma^* > 0$.

To see how this model relates to some previous analysis, we can substitute from Eq. (5.6) into the production function from Eq. (5.1) to get

$$Y = AK \cdot \left(\frac{1 - \alpha}{\alpha}\right)^{(1-\alpha)}.$$

Thus, the model is equivalent to the AK model that we studied in Chapter 4. We can use the method of analysis from that chapter to show that, if the transversality condition holds, then the growth rates of Y, K, and H must equal the growth rate of C.[4] That is, all quantities grow at the constant rate γ^* shown in Eq. (5.8).

The results for r^* and γ^* in Eqs. (5.7) and (5.8) are essentially the same as those obtained from the AK model developed in Chapter 4. That is, we have thus far made no meaningful distinction between a model with two types of capital, K and H, and a model with a single form of broad capital.

---

[2]The equality between net marginal products still holds if the depreciation rates on the two kinds of capital differ. This condition again determines K/H, but the solution cannot be written in general as a closed-form expression in terms of the underlying parameters.

[3]The rate of return, r, would apply on a competitive credit market if we introduced such a market into the model.

[4]The transversality condition is $r^* > \gamma^*$. Equations (5.7) and (5.8) imply that this condition can be expressed as $\rho > (1 - \theta) \cdot [A\alpha^\alpha \cdot (1 - \alpha)^{(1-\alpha)} - \delta]$.

5.1.2 The Constraint of Nonnegative Gross Investment

Suppose that the economy begins with the two capital stocks, $K(0)$ and $H(0)$. If the ratio $K(0)/H(0)$ deviates from the value $\alpha/(1 - \alpha)$ prescribed by Eq. (5.6), then the solution that we just found dictates discrete adjustments in the two stocks to attain the value $\alpha/(1-\alpha)$ instantaneously. This adjustment features an increase in one stock and a corresponding decrease in the other stock, so that the sum, $K + H$, does not change instantaneously.[5]

The difficulty with this solution is that it depends on the possibility of an infinite positive rate of investment in one form of capital and an infinite negative rate of investment in the other form. We must, in other words, assume that investments are reversible, so that old units of physical or human capital can be converted into the other type. More realistically, we should impose the inequality restrictions $I_K \geq 0$ and $I_H \geq 0$. One of the inequality constraints on gross investment is necessarily violated in the previous solution if $K(0)/H(0)$ differs from $\alpha/(1 - \alpha)$, because the discrete shift in the composition of capital at time zero requires negative gross investment (at an infinite rate) in one of the stocks. We therefore now reconsider the solution to the model in the presence of these inequality restrictions. The discussion in the text omits some details, which appear in Appendix 5A.

If $K(0)/H(0) < \alpha/(1 - \alpha)$—that is, if H is initially abundant relative to K—then the previous solution dictates a decrease in H and an increase in K at time zero. The desire to lower H by a discrete amount implies that the inequality $I_H \geq 0$ will be binding at time zero (and for a finite interval thereafter). When this restriction is binding, the household chooses $I_H = 0$; hence, the growth rate of H is given by $\dot{H}/H = -\delta$, and H follows the path

$$H(t) = H(0) \cdot e^{-\delta t} \qquad \text{for } t = 0, \ldots \qquad (5.9)$$

The agents realize that they have too much H in relation to K, but since it is infeasible to have negative gross investment in H, they allow H to depreciate at the exogenously given rate δ.

If $I_H = 0$, then the household's optimization problem can be written in terms of the simplified Hamiltonian expression,

$$J = u(C) \cdot e^{-\rho t} + \nu \cdot (AK^\alpha H^{1-\alpha} - C - \delta K), \qquad (5.10)$$

where ν multiplies the expression for $\dot{K}$ (when $I_H = 0$).[6] This setup is equivalent to the standard neoclassical growth model in which households choose consumption

---

[5] The sum $K + H$ can jump at a point in time only if C is plus or minus infinity. These extreme values of C are inconsistent with the first-order conditions for optimization because of the Inada conditions on the utility function ($u'[c] \to 0$ as $c \to \infty$ and $u'[c] \to \infty$ as $c \to 0$).

[6] We could equivalently write the Hamiltonian expression in a form that sets $I_H = 0$ in the last term on the right-hand side of Eq. (5.4):

$$J = u(C) \cdot e^{-\rho t} + \nu \cdot (I_K - \delta K) + \omega \cdot (AK^\alpha H^{1-\alpha} - C - I_K).$$

Equation (5.10) has already imposed the condition $I_K = AK^\alpha H^{1-\alpha} - C$.

and investment in a single form of capital, K, subject to exogenous technological progress that augments the quantity of the other input, here H. In the standard model, the other input, effective labor, grows at the rate x (with zero population growth), whereas in the present setting, the other input, H, grows at the rate $-\delta$.

The crucial difference from the standard neoclassical growth model is that K/H rises over time and reaches the value, $\alpha/(1-\alpha)$, shown in Eq. (5.6) in finite time. At this point, the net marginal products of physical and human capital are equal, and, hence, the constraint of nonnegative gross investment in human capital becomes nonbinding. The two capital stocks then grow forever at the rate γ^* shown in Eq. (5.8). We have already assumed that the parameters are such that $\gamma^* > 0$. Hence, the dynamics of the neoclassical growth model apply during the transition, but the long-run growth rate is positive (even without exogenous technological progress), because of the absence of diminishing returns to broad capital.

We know that the growth rates of H and Y equal $\gamma^* > 0$ in the steady state, where $K/H = \alpha/(1-\alpha)$. Prior to that time, $K/H < \alpha/(1-\alpha)$, and $I_H = 0$. We have shown in this situation that the dynamics of K and Y accord with the usual pattern from the neoclassical growth model (with a Cobb–Douglas technology). Hence, the analysis from Chapter 2 implies that the solution exhibits the convergence property in the sense that the growth rates, $\gamma_K \equiv \dot{K}/K$ and $\gamma_Y \equiv \dot{Y}/Y$, decline monotonically over time. Since the two growth rates fall monotonically toward $\gamma^* > 0$, they must be positive, but declining, during the transition. Thus, K/H rises monotonically over time, partly because H is declining (at the rate δ) and partly because K is increasing (at a rate that decreases toward γ^*). The increase in K/H implies that the net marginal product of physical capital—and, hence, the rate of return—falls monotonically.[7] This reduction in the rate of return corresponds in the usual way to a decline in γ_C.

The results imply that the growth rate of output, γ_Y, is inversely related to the ratio K/H as long as this ratio is below its steady-state value, $\alpha/(1-\alpha)$. The relation between γ_Y and K/H can be described as an *imbalance effect*. The greater the imbalance—that is, the further K/H is below its steady-state value—the higher the growth rate.

One reason for K/H to be low would be a war that destroyed a great deal of physical capital but left human capital relatively intact. The situations of Japan and Germany after World War II are examples. The theory predicts that output would grow at a high rate—well above the steady-state value γ^*—in this situation.

The results are analogous if the economy begins instead with a relative abundance of physical capital, $K(0)/H(0) > \alpha/(1-\alpha)$. This situation could arise, for

---

[7]The increase in K/H implies that the net marginal product of H rises over time. This net marginal product is, however, below that for physical capital. Hence, gross investment in H remains at its minimal value, 0. If we could observe a market price for existing units of H, then we would find that this price is below the replacement cost, 1, but rises toward 1 as K/H approaches $\alpha/(1-\alpha)$. The total rate of return from holding H—from capital gains and "dividends"—would then equal the net marginal product of K at each point in time. Thus, the net marginal product of K equals the single rate of return that would be observed on a credit market.

example, from an epidemic that killed people but did not destroy factories. In this case, the constraint $I_K \geq 0$ is binding. Hence, $I_K = 0$, and K grows at the rate $-\delta$. The choices of C and H are then governed by the conditions from the usual neoclassical growth model, except that the investment to be chosen involves H rather than K. In particular, γ_H and γ_Y decline monotonically toward the steady-state value, γ^*. The decline in K (at rate δ) and the rise in H (at a rate that diminishes toward γ^*) imply that K/H falls over time. The decrease in K/H lowers the net marginal product of H and thereby reduces the rate of return and the growth rate of consumption.[8]

The results imply that K/H and γ_Y are positively related in the region in which $K/H > \alpha/(1-\alpha)$. Thus, there is again an imbalance effect—the greater the imbalance, in the sense of the excess of K/H from its steady-state value, the higher the growth rate.

Figure 5.1 plots the growth rate, γ_Y, against K/H. The minimal growth rate, γ^*, corresponds to the steady-state ratio, $\alpha/(1-\alpha)$. On either side of the steady state, γ_Y rises with the magnitude of the gap between K/H and its steady-state value.

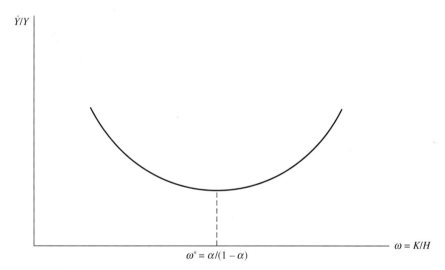

FIGURE 5.1
The imbalance effect in the one-sector model. The growth rate of output depends on the ratio between the two capital stocks, K/H. The minimal growth rate corresponds to the steady-state ratio, $(K/H)^* = \alpha/(1-\alpha)$. On either side of the steady state, the growth rate rises symmetrically with the magnitude of the gap between K/H and $(K/H)^*$.

---

[8]The behavior of rates of return is analogous to the case in which H is relatively abundant. The decrease in K/H implies that the net marginal product of K rises. This net marginal product is, however, below that for human capital, and gross investment in K remains at its minimal value, 0. The market price for existing units of K is below the replacement cost, 1, but rises toward 1 as K/H approaches $\alpha/(1-\alpha)$. The total rate of return from holding K—from capital gains and dividends—equals the net marginal product of H at each point in time. Thus, this net marginal product equals the single rate of return that would be observed on a credit market.

In the theory, a shortfall of physical capital—the situation in which K but not H is destroyed during a war—need not have a larger effect on the growth rate than a corresponding shortfall of human capital–caused, for example, by an epidemic that eliminated H but not K. There is little empirical evidence about the effects on growth from a sudden decline in human capital, but Hirshleifer's (1987, Chapters 1 and 2) discussion of the Black Death suggests that growth was not rapid in this situation. Thus, it may be that empirically an increase in K/H above its steady-state value has only a small positive effect, or possibly even a negative effect, on the growth rate.

One extension of the theory that would lead to asymmetric effects, from K/H below or above its steady-state value, is the type of adjustment cost for capital accumulation that we explored in Chapter 3. It is plausible that these adjustment costs would be much greater for H than for K; presumably, the educational process cannot be greatly accelerated without encountering a significant falloff in the rate of return from investment. In this case, a relative abundance of H would lead to substantial investment in K and, accordingly, to a high growth rate of output, but a corresponding relative abundance of K would have a much smaller effect on investment in H and, hence, on the growth rate of output. Figure 5.2 shows a case in which the minimal growth rate still occurs when K/H equals its steady-state value, $\alpha/(1-\alpha)$,[9] but the

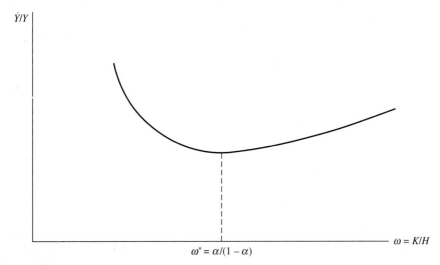

FIGURE 5.2
The imbalance effect with adjustment costs for human capital. We assume here that the adjustment costs for changing human capital are greater than those for changing physical capital. In this case, the sensitivity of the growth rate to K/H is larger in magnitude in the region in which $K/H < (K/H)^*$ (physical capital is relatively scarce) than in the region in which $K/H > (K/H)^*$ (human capital is relatively scarce).

---

[9]Some specifications of adjustment costs would affect the steady-state ratio of K to H, whereas others would not. See the discussion in Chapter 3.

slope in the region in which $K/H < \alpha/(1-\alpha)$ is much steeper in magnitude than that in the region in which $K/H > \alpha/(1-\alpha)$. This model predicts that an economy would recover much faster from a war that destroyed mainly K than from an epidemic that destroyed mainly H.

Another implication of adjustment costs for investment is that positive gross investment in both types of capital can occur when K/H deviates from its steady-state value, $\alpha/(1-\alpha)$. This outcome applies if the rates of return from each type of investment are high at low rates of investment and low at high rates of investment. The potential for positive gross investment outside of the steady state in both kinds of capital also arises in models in which the technology for producing goods, C and $\dot{K}$, differs from the technology for education, $\dot{H}$. We explore this idea in the next section.

5.2 DIFFERENT TECHNOLOGIES FOR PRODUCTION AND EDUCATION

5.2.1 The Model with Two Sectors of Production

We have assumed thus far that physical goods and education are generated by the same production functions. This specification neglects a key aspect of education; it relies heavily on educated people as an input. We should therefore modify the model to reflect the property that the production of human capital is relatively intensive in human capital. As already mentioned, this change in specification leads to different conclusions about the effects on growth from imbalances between physical and human capital.

We follow Rebelo (1991) and use the following setup with two Cobb–Douglas production functions:

$$Y = C + \dot{K} + \delta K = A \cdot (vK)^{\alpha} \cdot (uH)^{1-\alpha}, \tag{5.11}$$

$$\dot{H} + \delta H = B \cdot [(1-v) \cdot K]^{\eta} \cdot [(1-u) \cdot H]^{1-\eta}, \tag{5.12}$$

where Y is the output of goods (consumables and gross investment in physical capital); $A, B > 0$ are technological parameters; α ($0 \leq \alpha \leq 1$) and η ($0 \leq \eta \leq 1$) are the shares of physical capital in the outputs of each sector; and v ($0 \leq v \leq 1$) and u ($0 \leq u \leq 1$) are the fractions of physical and human capital, respectively, used in production. The corresponding fractions of physical and human capital used in education—that is, to generate human capital—are $1 - v$ and $1 - u$.

Equation (5.11) indicates that consumables, C, and investment in physical capital, $I_K = \dot{K} + \delta K$, are still perfect substitutes on the supply side. In other words, C and I_K come from a single output stream for goods.[10] If $\eta \neq \alpha$, then Eq. (5.12) implies that human capital is generated from a technology that differs from that for

---

[10]We could go further to allow for different factor intensities in the production of consumables and capital goods (the two-sector model used by Uzawa [1964] and Srinivasan [1964]) or in the production of different types of final products (see Ventura [1993]).

goods. (If $\eta = \alpha$, then the model is equivalent to the one-sector production setup that we considered in the previous section; see footnote 13, below.) As already mentioned, we view $\eta < \alpha$ as the empirically relevant case; that is, the education sector is relatively intensive in human capital, and the goods sector is relatively intensive in physical capital.[11] In fact, it is this feature of the model that may make it reasonable to identify "H" with human capital in the real world.

The forms of Eqs. (5.11) and (5.12) imply that the two production activities each exhibit constant returns to scale in the quantities of the two capital inputs. For this reason, the model will display endogenous steady-state growth of the type that we found in Chapter 4 in a one-sector model. In the steady state, v and u are constant, and C, K, H, and Y grow at the common rate, γ^*.

Measured output can be broadened to include gross investment in human capital, $\dot{H} + \delta H$, multiplied by an appropriate shadow price of human capital. (We discuss this shadow price later.) This broader measure of output will also grow at the rate γ^* in the steady state. Gross output as defined in the standard national accounts falls somewhere between the narrow and broad concepts, because this measured output includes a fraction of the gross investment in human capital. For example, gross product includes teacher salaries, but neglects the value of time foregone by students and also omits part of the value of time expended in on-the-job training. Kendrick (1976, Tables A-1 and B-2) made a rough estimate for the United States that one-half of gross investment in human capital was included in measured output.

We can embed the technologies shown in Eqs. (5.11) and (5.12) into the standard model of household optimization that we have considered before. The Hamiltonian expression can be written as[12]

$$J = u(C) \cdot e^{-\rho t} + v \cdot \left[A \cdot (vK)^{\alpha} \cdot (uH)^{1-\alpha} - \delta K - C \right]$$
$$+ \mu \cdot \left\{ B \cdot [(1 - v) \cdot K]^{\eta} [(1 - u) \cdot H]^{1-\eta} - \delta H \right\},$$

$$(5.13)$$

where v multiplies the expression for $\dot{K}$, and μ multiplies the expression for $\dot{H}$. If the inequality restrictions of nonnegative gross investment are not binding, then the solution satisfies the usual first-order conditions, which come from setting the derivatives of J with respect to C, v, and u to 0 and from the conditions $\dot{v} = -\partial J/\partial K$ and $\dot{\mu} = -\partial J/\partial H$.

If we manipulate the first-order conditions, then we get a familiar looking expression for the growth rate of consumption:

$$\gamma_C = (1/\theta) \cdot \left[A\alpha \cdot (vK/uH)^{-(1-\alpha)} - \delta - \rho \right]. \quad (5.14)$$

---

[11]We can interpret K and H more generally as two different types of capital goods, not necessarily physical and human capital. The assumption that the production of H is relatively intensive in H becomes more or less plausible depending on how H is interpreted.

[12]We can equivalently have v multiply $I_K - \delta K$ and μ multiply $I_H - \delta H$ and then introduce two Lagrange multipliers to correspond to the two equality constraints, $A \cdot (vK)^{\alpha} \cdot (uH)^{1-\alpha} = C + I_K$ and $B \cdot [(1 - v) \cdot K]^{\eta} \cdot [(1 - u) \cdot H]^{1-\eta} = I_H$. The formulation in Eq. (5.13) already imposes these equality constraints.

The term $A\alpha \cdot (vK/uH)^{-(1-\alpha)} - \delta$, the net marginal product of physical capital in the production of goods, equals the rate of return, r, in this model.

Physical capital must receive the same rate of return when allocated to either sector of production, and the same condition holds for human capital. These conditions lead to the following relation between v and u:

$$\left(\frac{\eta}{1-\eta}\right) \cdot \left(\frac{v}{1-v}\right) = \left(\frac{\alpha}{1-\alpha}\right) \cdot \left(\frac{u}{1-u}\right). \tag{5.15}$$

Equation (5.15) implies that v and u are positively related, with $v = 1$ when $u = 1$, and $v = 0$ when $u = 0$.[13] In other words, for given values of α and η, an expansion of goods production occurs via a simultaneous increase in the fraction of the two inputs, K and H, allocated to the goods sector.

Let $p \equiv \mu/v$ be the shadow price of human capital in units of goods. Equation (5.15) and the condition that the rates of return to K and H be equalized leads to a formula for p:

$$p \equiv \mu/v = (A/B) \cdot (\alpha/\eta)^{\eta} \cdot [(1-\alpha)/(1-\eta)]^{1-\eta} \cdot (vK/uH)^{\alpha-\eta}. \tag{5.16}$$

The price, p, equals the ratio of the marginal product of H in the goods sector (the wage rate) to its marginal product in the education sector. Equation (5.16) shows that this price depends only on the ratio of K employed in the goods sector, vK, to H employed in the goods sector, uH.

The formula for p enables us to calculate the broader concept of gross output that we mentioned before:

$$Q = Y + pB \cdot [(1-v) \cdot K]^{\eta} \cdot [(1-u) \cdot H]^{1-\eta}. \tag{5.17}$$

Note that broad output, Q, is the sum of narrow output, Y, and the value in units of goods of the gross investment in human capital, $pB \cdot [(1-v) \cdot K]^{\eta} \cdot [(1-u) \cdot H]^{1-\eta}$.

We can use Eq. (5.16) along with the first-order conditions for $\dot{\mu}$ and $\dot{v}$ to derive an expression for the growth rate of p. The result, after a significant amount of algebra, is

$$\gamma_p = A\phi^{\alpha/(\eta-\alpha)} \cdot \left[\alpha\phi^{1/(\alpha-\eta)} \cdot p^{(1-\alpha)/(\eta-\alpha)} - (1-\alpha) \cdot p^{\eta/(\alpha-\eta)}\right], \tag{5.18}$$

---

[13]If $\alpha = \eta$, then Eq. (5.15) implies $v = u$. If we substitute this result into Eqs. (5.11) and (5.12), then the production functions become

$$Y = AuK^{\alpha}H^{1-\alpha},$$

$$\dot{H} + \delta H = B \cdot (1-u) \cdot K^{\alpha}H^{1-\alpha}.$$

Broad output, Q, can be defined as

$$Q = Y + (A/B) \cdot (\dot{H} + \delta H) = AK^{\alpha}H^{1-\alpha},$$

where A/B is the constant price of H in units of Y; we can, in fact, define the units of H so that $A/B = 1$. With this definition, the economy's budget constraint is

$$Q = C + \dot{K} + \delta K + \dot{H} + \delta H.$$

The model is then equivalent to the one-sector version analyzed earlier in this chapter.

where $\phi \equiv (A/B) \cdot (\alpha/\eta)^{\eta} \cdot [(1 - \alpha)/(1 - \eta)]^{1-\eta}$. The key finding here is that the growth rate of p depends only on p, and not on any other variables.

If $\alpha \neq \eta$, then Eq. (5.16) determines a one-to-one relation between p and vK/uH. Equation (5.18) therefore implies that the growth rate of the ratio vK/uH depends only on the value of the ratio and not on any other variables.

The equation for the growth rate of vK/uH (derived from Eqs. [5.16] and [5.18]), the condition for γ_C in Eq. (5.14), the relation between u and v from Eq. (5.15), and the conditions for $\dot{K}$ and $\dot{H}$ from the budget constraints determine the behavior over time of u, v, C, K, and H. The variable v can be eliminated using Eq. (5.15). Since the production functions in Eqs. (5.11) and (5.12) exhibit constant returns to scale, the absolute levels of K, H, and C will not influence the dynamics, and the system can be written in terms of ratios of these variables. Thus, it is possible to express the model in terms of the variables $u, C/K$, and K/H. The steady state of this system involves constant values of $u, C/K$, and K/H. Hence, the growth rates of C, K, and H—as well as of Y and Q—are equal in the steady state.

The form of Eq. (5.18) has immediate implications for the nature of the dynamics. This relation is a differential equation in the single variable p. The equation can be readily shown to be stable $(\partial[\gamma_p]/\partial[p] < 0)$ if $\alpha > \eta$ and unstable $(\partial[\gamma_p]/\partial[p] > 0)$ if $\alpha < \eta$. (If $\alpha = \eta$, then the model is equivalent to the one-sector setup; see footnote 13.) Thus, if $\alpha > \eta$—the case that we regard as empirically relevant—then p converges monotonically to its steady-state value.

Since Eq. (5.16) relates p one-to-one to vK/uH, the monotonic convergence of p when $\alpha > \eta$ implies that vK/uH will also converge monotonically to its steady-state value. The ratio vK/uH determines the marginal product of physical capital in the production of goods. Therefore, r—equal to the net marginal product of physical capital in the production of goods—and γ_C—determined in Eq. (5.14)—will also converge monotonically to their steady-state values.

The rest of the model turns out to be difficult to analyze for the general situation in which $\alpha > \eta \geq 0$. We therefore begin with the special case in which $\eta = 0$, because it allows for a complete analytical description of the transitional dynamics. We then provide some results for the more general case, $\alpha > \eta > 0$. Finally, we address the case $\alpha < \eta$, although we regard this configuration of parameters as implausible.

5.2.2   The Uzawa–Lucas Model

THE BASIC FRAMEWORK. We now specialize to the model studied by Uzawa (1965) and Lucas (1988) in which the production of human capital involves no physical capital; that is, $\eta = 0$ in Eq. (5.12). This setting is the extreme case in which the education sector is relatively intensive in human capital ($\eta \leq \alpha$). Thus, by comparing the Uzawa–Lucas model with the one-sector framework—in which the relative intensities of physical and human capital are the same in each sector—we can bring out the main implications from the assumption about relative factor intensities. Appendix 5B contains the details of the Uzawa–Lucas model. We provide here a sketch of the results, starting with the case in which the nonnegativity constraints on gross investment in K and H are not binding.

The specification $\eta = 0$ implies $v = 1$; that is, since K is not productive in the education sector, all of it is used in the goods sector. The production functions from Eqs. (5.11) and (5.12) therefore simplify to

$$Y = C + \dot{K} + \delta K = AK^\alpha \cdot (uH)^{1-\alpha}, \tag{5.19}$$

$$\dot{H} + \delta H = B \cdot (1 - u) \cdot H. \tag{5.20}$$

We shall find it useful, as in Chapter 4, to express the system in terms of variables that will be constant in the steady state. A specification that facilitates the dynamic analysis involves the ratios $\omega \equiv K/H$ and $\chi \equiv C/K$. If we use these definitions along with Eqs. (5.19) and (5.20), then we get expressions for the growth rates of K and H:

$$\gamma_K = A \cdot u^{(1-\alpha)}\omega^{-(1-\alpha)} - \chi - \delta, \tag{5.21}$$

$$\gamma_H = B \cdot (1 - u) - \delta. \tag{5.22}$$

Hence, the growth rate of ω is given by

$$\gamma_\omega = \gamma_K - \gamma_H = A \cdot u^{(1-\alpha)}\omega^{-(1-\alpha)} - B \cdot (1 - u) - \chi. \tag{5.23}$$

The first-order conditions can be used to show that the growth rate of consumption is given by the familiar formula, $\gamma_C = (1/\theta) \cdot (r - \rho)$, where r equals the net marginal product of physical capital in the production of goods, $\alpha A \cdot u^{(1-\alpha)}\omega^{-(1-\alpha)} - \delta$. Therefore, the growth rate of consumption is given by

$$\gamma_C = (1/\theta) \cdot [\alpha A \cdot u^{(1-\alpha)}\omega^{-(1-\alpha)} - \delta - \rho]. \tag{5.24}$$

The growth rate of χ follows from Eqs. (5.24) and (5.21) as

$$\gamma_\chi = \gamma_C - \gamma_K = \left(\frac{\alpha - \theta}{\theta}\right) \cdot A \cdot u^{(1-\alpha)}\omega^{-(1-\alpha)} + \chi - (1/\theta) \cdot [\delta \cdot (1 - \theta) + \rho]. \tag{5.25}$$

Finally, Appendix 5B shows that Eqs. (5.18) and (5.16) imply that the growth rate of u is given by

$$\gamma_u = B \cdot (1 - \alpha)/\alpha + Bu - \chi. \tag{5.26}$$

STEADY-STATE ANALYSIS. Appendix 5B shows that the variables u, ω, and χ are constant in a steady state. If we define the combination of parameters

$$\varphi \equiv [\rho + \delta \cdot (1 - \theta)]/B\theta, \tag{5.27}$$

then the steady-state values, which correspond to $\dot{u} = \dot{\omega} = \dot{\chi} = 0$, are given by

$$\omega^* = (\alpha A/B)^{1/(1-\alpha)} \cdot [\varphi + (\theta - 1)/\theta],$$

$$\chi^* = B(\varphi + 1/\alpha - 1/\theta),$$

$$u^* = \varphi + (\theta - 1)/\theta. \tag{5.28}$$

The rate of return and the common growth rate of C, K, H, Y, and Q are given in this steady state by

$$r^* = B - \delta,$$

$$\gamma^* = (1/\theta)(B - \delta - \rho). \tag{5.29}$$

The usual transversality condition, $r^* > \gamma^*$, ensures that the values of ω^*, χ^*, and u^* shown in Eq. (5.28) are all positive. The condition $u^* < 1$ holds if $\gamma^* > 0$ in Eq. (5.29).

TRANSITIONAL DYNAMICS. The dynamic system for ω, χ, and u consists of Eqs. (5.23), (5.25), and (5.26). We shall find it convenient to work with a transformed system that replaces ω by the gross average product of physical capital in the production of goods, denoted by z:[14]

$$z \equiv Au^{(1-\alpha)}\omega^{-(1-\alpha)}. \tag{5.30}$$

The gross *marginal* product of physical capital equals αz, and the rate of return is $r = \alpha z - \delta$. Although the variable z is a combination of a state variable, ω, and a control variable, u, we show later that, in the equilibrium, z relates in a simple way to ω. In particular, we can determine the initial value $z(0)$ from the initial value $\omega(0)$.

The system given by Eqs. (5.23), (5.25), and (5.26) can be rewritten in terms of z, χ, and u as

$$\gamma_z = -(1-\alpha) \cdot (z - z^*), \tag{5.31}$$

$$\gamma_\chi = \left(\frac{\alpha - \theta}{\theta}\right) \cdot (z - z^*) + (\chi - \chi^*), \tag{5.32}$$

$$\gamma_u = B \cdot (u - u^*) - (\chi - \chi^*), \tag{5.33}$$

where z^* is the steady-state value of z. Equation (5.28) and the definition of z in Eq. (5.30) imply that this steady-state value is given by

$$z^* = B/\alpha. \tag{5.34}$$

Dynamics of the average product of physical capital, the rate of return, and the wage rate. Equation (5.31) is a one-variable differential equation, which determines the time path of z, the gross average product of physical capital. This equation can be solved in closed form to get

$$\left(\frac{z - z^*}{z}\right) = \left[\frac{z(0) - z^*}{z(0)}\right] \cdot e^{-(1-\alpha)\cdot z^* t}, \tag{5.35}$$

where $z(0)$ is the initial value of z. This equation shows that z adjusts monotonically from its initial value, $z(0)$, to its steady-state value, z^*. Figure 5.3 provides a graphical representation of this stability property.

---

[14]We could also work with the ratio vK/uH, which equals $(A\alpha/z)^{1/(1-\alpha)}$.

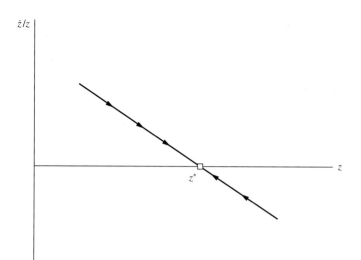

FIGURE 5.3
Stability of z, the gross average product of capital. Equation (5.31) from the Uzawa–Lucas model is a linear differential equation in z. When $z < z^*$, the growth rate of z is positive and z increases toward its steady-state value. The opposite pattern applies when $z > z^*$. Hence, the steady-state value, z^*, is stable.

Since the rate of return is $r = \alpha z - \delta$, the behavior of z determines the behavior of r. In particular, if $z(0) < z^*$, then $r(0) < r^*$, and r rises monotonically over time toward its steady-state value. These properties are all reversed if $z(0) > z^*$.

The wage rate, w, equals the marginal product of the human capital, uH, employed in the production of goods. The production function from Eq. (5.19) and the definition of z in Eq. (5.30) imply that this marginal product can be written as

$$w = A \cdot (1 - \alpha) \cdot u^{-\alpha} \omega^{\alpha} = A^{1/(1-\alpha)} \cdot (1 - \alpha) \cdot z^{-\alpha/(1-\alpha)}. \qquad (5.36)$$

Hence, if $z(0) < z^*$, then $w(0) > w^*$, and w falls monotonically over time toward its steady-state value. These properties are reversed if $z(0) > z^*$.

Dynamics of $\chi \equiv C/K$. The evolution of χ depends on the combination of parameters, $\alpha - \theta$, which appears as a determinant of γ_χ in Eq. (5.32). Since $\alpha \leq 1$ and we usually assume $\theta > 1$, then the inequality $\alpha < \theta$ is likely to hold in practice. Thus, we assume $\alpha < \theta$ in the main analysis.

We can treat Eqs. (5.31) and (5.32) as a two-dimensional system in z and χ and construct the usual type of phase diagram in (z, χ) space. (Note that the variable u does not appear in these equations.) The vertical line at z^* on the right side of Figure 5.4 corresponds to $\dot{z} = 0$ from Eq. (5.31). This equation also implies that z declines when $z > z^*$ and rises when $z < z^*$. Thus, the $\dot{z} = 0$ locus is stable, as shown in the figure.

Equation (5.32) implies that the $\dot{\chi} = 0$ locus satisfies the condition

$$\chi = \chi^* + \left(\frac{\theta - \alpha}{\theta}\right) \cdot (z - z^*). \qquad (5.37)$$

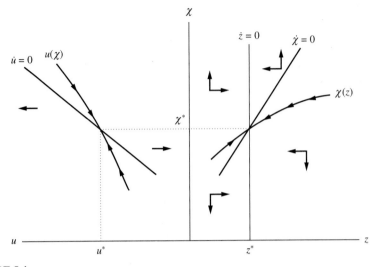

FIGURE 5.4
Dynamics of z, χ, and u in the Uzawa–Lucas model (when $\alpha < \theta$). The right side uses (z, χ) space to show the $\dot{z} = 0$ locus, the $\dot{\chi} = 0$ locus, and the dynamics of z and χ. The stable arm, $\chi(z)$, is upward sloping. The left side uses (u, χ) space to show the $\dot{u} = 0$ locus and the dynamics of u and χ. (Movements to the left correspond to higher values of u in this panel.) The stable arm, $u(\chi)$, is upward sloping. If $z(0) > z^*$, then $\chi(0) > \chi^*$ (from the right side) and $u(0) > u^*$ (from the left side). During the transition, z, χ, and u fall monotonically. (Note: the results on χ and u depend on the assumption $\alpha < \theta$.)

Since $\theta > \alpha$, this locus is linear and positively sloped, as shown on the right side of Figure 5.4. Moreover, the slope is less than 1, a property that we shall use later. Equation (5.32) implies that χ rises for points that lie above the $\dot{\chi} = 0$ locus and falls otherwise. That is, this locus is unstable, as shown in the figure.

The configuration of the two loci in the right side of Figure 5.4 implies that the stable, saddle path, denoted by $\chi(z)$, is upward sloping as shown. Thus, if $z(0) > z^*$, then $\chi(0) > \chi^*$, and z and χ decline monotonically over time toward their steady-state values. Conversely, if $z(0) < z^*$, then $\chi(0) < \chi^*$, and z and χ rise monotonically toward their steady-state values.

Dynamics of u, the fraction of human capital used in production. To ascertain the dynamics of u, use Eq. (5.33) to determine the $\dot{u} = 0$ locus as

$$u = u^* + (\chi - \chi^*)/B. \tag{5.38}$$

This locus is linear and upward sloping in (u, χ) space, as shown on the left side of Figure 5.4. (Movements to the left correspond to higher values of u). The stable, saddle path for u is denoted by $u(\chi)$ in the figure. Note that, if $z(0) > z^*$, so that $\chi(0) > \chi^*$, then $u(0) > u^*$. (It can be verified from the figure that $u(0) \leq u^*$ or $u(0)$ lying to the left of the $\dot{u} = 0$ locus would cause u to diverge over time from u^*.)

To sum up, we have shown that, if $\alpha < \theta$, then $z(0) > z^*$ implies $\chi(0) > \chi^*$ and $u(0) > u^*$—with z, χ, and u all decreasing monotonically toward their steady-state values. Conversely, if $z(0) < z^*$, then $\chi(0) < \chi^*$ and $u(0) < u^*$—with z, χ, and u all increasing monotonically toward their steady-state values.

Dynamics when $\alpha \geq \theta$. We can use the same approach to deal with cases in which $\alpha \geq \theta$. Since we do not regard these cases as empirically relevant, we just indicate the results and leave the derivations as exercises. If $\alpha > \theta$, then the results for χ and u are the reverse of those found before. For example, if $z(0) > z^*$, then $\chi(0) < \chi^*$ and $u(0) < u^*$. The monotonic fall in z over time is then associated with monotonic increases in χ and u.

If $\alpha = \theta$, then $\chi(0) = \chi^*$ and $u(0) = u^*$. That is, in this knife-edge case, the variables χ and u remain fixed at their steady-state values throughout the transition from $z(0)$ to z^*.

The relation between z, the gross average product of physical capital, and the state variable, $\omega \equiv K/H$. Return now to the case in which $\alpha < \theta$. To finish the dynamic analysis, we have to relate the behavior of z—and, hence, of χ and u—to the behavior of the state variable, ω. In particular, we want to make use of the initial condition that ω begins at $\omega(0)$.

Appendix 5B shows that $z(0)$ and $\omega(0)$ are inversely related, with $z(0) \gtreqless z^*$ as $\omega(0) \lesseqgtr \omega^*$. In other words, the gross average product of physical capital, z, is high initially if ω, the ratio of K to H, is low initially, and vice versa.

As an example, if ω starts above its steady-state value—a situation in which human capital is scarce relative to physical capital—then z, the average product of physical capital, and r, the rate of return, start at low values and then rise monotonically toward their steady-state positions. We also know in this situation that the wage rate, w, starts above its steady-state value and then declines, whereas χ and u start below their steady-state values and then increase. The behavior of u means that relatively little human capital is allocated initially to the production of goods and relatively more is allocated to education. Over time, the allocation shifts toward production and away from education. These results are all reversed if ω begins below its steady-state value.

Policy functions for χ and u. We can summarize the results for χ and u in terms of policy functions. Figure 5.5 shows that the choices of χ and u are each downward-sloping functions of ω.[15] (We draw a single curve here for both variables only for convenience.) Thus, if we think again of a country that starts with a relative scarcity of human capital—$\omega > \omega^*$—then ω falls over time, while χ and u rise. Thus, the country initially allocates relatively little to consumption ($\chi \equiv C/K$ is low), but it spends a lot of time on education ($1 - u$ is high).

Transitional behavior of growth rates. We consider now how the dynamics of ω, z, χ, and u relate to the transitional behavior of growth rates. We consider, in particular, whether imbalances between K and H—that is, excesses or shortfalls of ω from ω^*—lead to higher or lower growth rates of the various quantities in the model.

---

[15]Figure 5.4 applies if $\alpha < \theta$. The policy functions are positively sloped if $\alpha > \theta$ and flat if $\alpha = \theta$.

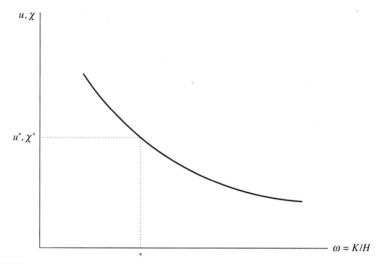

FIGURE 5.5
Policy functions for u and χ (when $\alpha < \theta$). The policy functions relate the optimal values of the control variables, u and $\chi \equiv C/K$, to the state variable, $\omega \equiv K/H$. When $\alpha < \theta$, the policy functions are each downwardly sloping. (The figure shows one curve only for convenience.) If $\alpha = \theta$, then the policy functions would be flat, and if $\alpha > \theta$, then the functions would be upward sloping.

The growth rate of consumption. If the economy begins with relatively low physical capital, $\omega < \omega^*$, then the interest rate, r, declines monotonically toward its steady-state value, $B - \delta$. This fall in r implies a decline in γ_C. Conversely, if $\omega > \omega^*$, then r and γ_C rise steadily during the transition. If we graph γ_C versus ω, then we determine a downward-sloping curve, as shown in the upper panel of Figure 5.6.

Recall that, in the one-sector model with inequality constraints on gross investment, the relation between γ_C and ω was described by a U-shaped curve of the form shown in Figure 5.1. Imbalances between K and H in either direction led therefore to a higher growth rate of consumption. In contrast, in the range of the Uzawa–Lucas model in which inequality constraints on gross investment in K and H are not binding, an imbalance that involves a shortfall of $K(\omega < \omega^*)$ implies a higher value of γ_C, whereas an imbalance that involves a shortfall of $H(\omega > \omega^*)$ implies a lower value of γ_C.

The growth rates of human and physical capital. The transitional behavior of the growth rates of other variables is more complicated. Appendix 5B demonstrates that we can manipulate the formulas for γ_z, γ_χ, and γ_u from Eqs. (5.31)–(5.33) and use the condition for γ_C from Eq. (5.24) to get expressions for the growth rates of H and K:

$$\gamma_H = \gamma^* - B \cdot (u - u^*), \tag{5.39}$$

$$\gamma_K = \gamma^* + (z - z^*) - (\chi - \chi^*), \tag{5.40}$$

where γ^* is the steady-state growth rate, $(1/\theta) \cdot (B - \delta - \rho)$, given in Eq. (5.29).

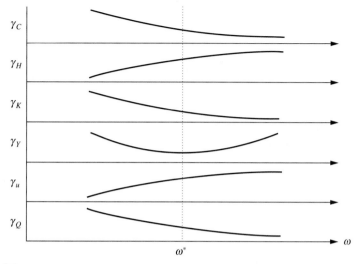

FIGURE 5.6
Patterns for growth rates in the Uzawa–Lucas model. The figure shows the behavior of the growth rates of consumption, human capital, physical capital, goods output (Y), the fraction of capital devoted to goods production (u), and broad output (Q). These variables are all related to $\omega \equiv K/H$. (Note: the minimal value of γ_Y can occur to the right or left of the steady-state value, ω^*.)

If $\alpha < \theta$, as we have been assuming, then Fig. 5.5 shows that $u - u^*$ is monotonically declining in ω. Hence, Eq. (5.39) implies that γ_H is monotonically increasing in ω. A rise in the relative quantity of physical capital increases the growth rate of human capital. This property is shown in the second panel of Figure 5.6.

Recall that $z - z^*$—the deviation of the average product of capital from its steady-state value—is monotonically decreasing in ω. This effect tends to make γ_K fall with ω in accordance with Eq. (5.40). Figure 5.5 shows, however, that $\chi - \chi^*$ is monotonically decreasing in ω, and this effect offsets the tendency for γ_K to decline.[16]

Figure 5.7 provides a graphical approach to the determination of γ_K. We begin by reproducing the saddle path, denoted $\chi(z)$, from the right side of Figure 5.4. Note that this curve is positively sloped, but flatter than the $\dot{\chi} = 0$ locus, at least in the neighborhood of the steady state. Recall also from Eq. (5.37) that the slope of the $\dot{\chi} = 0$ locus is positive but less than 1. Therefore, the slope of the $\chi(z)$ curve must also be less than 1 in the neighborhood of the steady state.

We can use Eq. (5.40) to construct isogrowth lines, that is, loci for z and χ that correspond to constant values of γ_K. The equation implies that these loci are linear with slope equal to one. Figure 5.7 shows several isogrowth lines, where those that lie further to the right—with higher values of z—correspond to higher values of γ_K.

---

[16]If $\alpha \geq \theta$, then $\chi - \chi^*$ is either monotonically increasing in z or constant. It follows unambiguously in this case that γ_K is monotonically decreasing in ω.

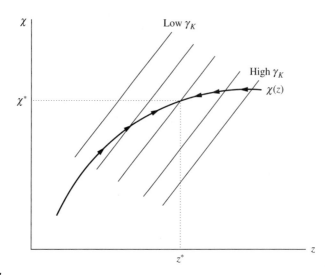

FIGURE 5.7
Determination of γ_K, the growth rate of physical capital. In the vicinity of the steady state, the isogrowth lines are steeper than the saddle path, $\chi(z)$. The isogrowth lines that lie farther to the right correspond to higher values of γ_K. Therefore, γ_K is positively related to z in the vicinity of the steady state. The inverse relation between z and ω implies that γ_K is inversely related to ω.

We know also that the slope of these lines exceeds the slope of the $\chi(z)$ curve, at least in the neighborhood of the steady state (because in this region the $\chi(z)$ curve has slope less than 1).

Figure 5.7 shows that γ_K is positively related to z in the vicinity of the steady state. Hence, γ_K is negatively related to ω in this region. In other words, if $\omega(0) < \omega^*$, then as ω rises over time, the fall in $z - z^*$ dominates the fall in $\chi - \chi^*$ in terms of the effects on γ_K in Eq. (5.40).

We have found through numerical simulations that the inverse relation between γ_K and ω holds for a broad range of ω around its steady-state position (see Mulligan and Sala-i-Martin [1993]). That is, the fall in $z - z^*$ dominates the fall in $\chi - \chi^*$ for a wide array of parameter values that we have considered.[17] Thus, the model implies that a higher ratio of physical to human capital, ω, is associated with a lower growth rate of physical capital, γ_K. We show this property in the third panel of Figure 5.6.

The growth rate of Y, the output of goods. The quantity of goods produced (in the form of consumables and physical capital) is given from Eq. (5.19) by $Y = AK^{\alpha} \cdot (uH)^{1-\alpha}$. We can therefore use the expressions for γ_H and γ_K from Eqs. (5.39)

---

[17]We find numerically that the inverse relation between γ_K and ω may reverse at very high values of ω. However, for very high (or very low) values of ω, the inequality constraints on gross investment become binding (see below). If we examine only the range of ω for which these constraints are not operative, then our numerical results indicate that γ_K is decreasing in ω for all parameter values that we have considered.

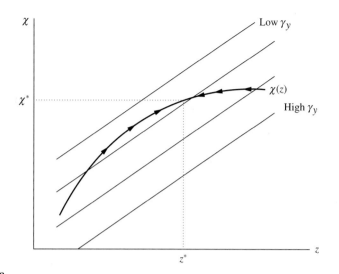

FIGURE 5.8
Determination of γ_Y, the growth rate of goods output. In the vicinity of the steady state, the isogrowth lines could be steeper or flatter than the saddle path, $\chi(z)$. The growth rate γ_Y is therefore ambiguously related to z and ω. Note that the $\chi(z)$ curve comes from the right side of Fig. 5.4 and applies when $\alpha < \theta$.

and (5.40), along with the formula for γ_u from Eq. (5.33), to determine the growth rate of Y:

$$\gamma_Y = \gamma^* + \alpha \cdot (z - z^*) - (\chi - \chi^*). \tag{5.41}$$

We can analyze γ_Y by a procedure that parallels our treatment of γ_K. Equation (5.41) implies that isogrowth lines for γ_Y in (z, χ) space are linear with slope $\alpha < 1$. Several of these lines appear in Fig. 5.8; note that lines further to the right are associated with higher growth rates. The difference from the previous case is that the isogrowth lines are not necessarily steeper than the $\chi(z)$ curve in the neighborhood of the steady state. Thus, the relation of γ_Y to z is ambiguous in the vicinity of the steady state. We conclude that γ_Y may either rise or fall with ω.[18]

Our numerical results verify these findings and show that the relation between γ_Y and ω tends to be U-shaped, as depicted by the fourth panel of Fig. 5.6. The minimum of γ_Y can occur either to the left or right of the steady state; that is, γ_Y can be either rising or falling with ω in the neighborhood of the steady state.

Suppose, for example, that we fix α at 0.5, use our standard values for some parameters that we have considered before ($\rho = 0.02, n = 0.01, \delta = 0.05$), and set $B = 0.11$ to get a steady-state rate of return, $B - \delta$, of 0.06. (The steady-state growth rate, $(1/\theta) \cdot (B - \delta - \rho)$, then equals 0.02 if $\theta = 2$.) For this specification of parameters, the minimum of γ_Y occurs at the steady-state value of ω if $\theta = 3.5$,

---

[18] If $\alpha \geq \theta$, then $\chi - \chi^*$ is either increasing in ω or constant. Hence, γ_Y is then unambiguously decreasing in ω.

to the left of the steady state if $\theta > 3.5$, and to the right of the steady state if $\theta < 3.5$. (Note that, if the minimum of γ_Y occurs to the left of the steady state, then γ_Y is increasing with z in the vicinity of the steady state, and vice versa.) Thus, the imbalance effect can be symmetric, with higher growth rates of output emerging if either K or H is in relatively short supply, or asymmetric, with growth rates rising with one type of imbalance and falling with the other type in the neighborhood of the steady state.

The growth rate of broad output, Q. Broad output, Q, is defined in Eq. (5.17) (recall that $\eta = 0$ now applies). If we use the formula for μ/ν from Eq. (5.16) and the expressions for γ_Y from Eq. (5.41), γ_H from Eq. (5.39), and γ_u from Eq. (5.33), then the growth rate of Q can be computed as

$$\gamma_Q = \gamma_Y - \gamma_u \cdot (1 - \alpha)/(1 - \alpha + \alpha u). \tag{5.42}$$

We have already discussed the determination of γ_Y. Therefore, to analyze γ_Q, we have to study the behavior of γ_u.

Equation (5.33) implies that isogrowth lines for γ_u are linear with slope equal to that of the $\dot{u} = 0$ locus, which appears on the left side of Fig. 5.4. Figure 5.9 shows several of these isogrowth lines; those farther to the left (for higher values of u) correspond to higher values of γ_u. If $z(0) > z^*$, corresponding to $\omega(0) < \omega^*$, then $u(0) > u^*$ and $\chi(0) > \chi^*$. The economy therefore moves downward along the $u(\chi)$ curve shown in Fig. 5.9 toward lower values of u and χ. The figure also shows that γ_u goes up; that is, as z increases, γ_u rises from a negative value toward its steady-state value of 0. We show this behavior in the fifth panel of Figure 5.6.

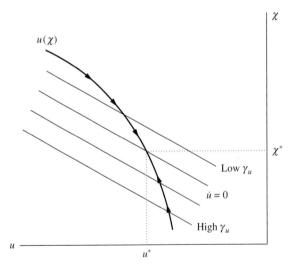

FIGURE 5.9
Determination of γ_u. In the vicinity of the steady state, the isogrowth lines are flatter than the saddle path, $\chi(u)$. The isogrowth lines that lie farther to the upper right correspond to lower values of γ_u. Therefore, γ_u is negatively related to χ—and, hence, to z—around the steady state. The inverse relation between z and ω implies that γ_u is positively related to ω.

Return now to the formula for γ_Q in Eq. (5.42). As ω rises, γ_u increases (as was just shown) and u declines. Therefore, the term on the far right of the equation tends to generate an inverse relation between γ_Q and ω.

The formula for γ_Q also contains γ_Y, which tends to be U-shaped versus ω (see Fig. 5.6), with the minimum occurring to the left or the right of the steady state. Our numerical results show, however, that γ_Q is downward sloping versus ω for a broad range of ω.[19] That is, the new term on the far right of Eq. (5.42) is strong enough to eliminate the U-shape for the parameter values that we have considered. The bottom panel of Figure 5.6 therefore shows γ_Q as a monotonically decreasing function of ω.

Summary of dynamics in the Uzawa–Lucas model. The Uzawa–Lucas model provides a perspective on the effects of imbalances between K and H that differs from that in the one-sector model. In the one-sector model, larger imbalances between K and H in either direction raise the growth rates of output and consumption. Note that, in the one-sector model, output includes consumables plus both forms of capital. Therefore, we should compare the growth rate of output in the one-sector context with the growth rate of broad output in the Uzawa–Lucas model.

In the Uzawa–Lucas model, γ_C is always inversely related to ω, and γ_Q tends to be inversely related to ω (see Fig. 5.6). Hence, these growth rates tend to rise with the amount of the imbalance between human and physical capital if human capital is abundant relative to physical capital ($\omega < \omega^*$), but they tend to fall with the amount of the imbalance if human capital is relatively scarce ($\omega > \omega^*$). The model predicts accordingly that an economy would recover faster in response to a war that destroyed mainly physical capital than to an epidemic that destroyed mainly human capital.

The underlying source of the new results is the assumption that the education sector is relatively intensive in human capital. If $\omega > \omega^*$, for example, then the marginal product of human capital in the goods sector is high, and growth would be expected to occur mainly because of the high growth rate of human capital. The high level of ω implies, however, a high wage rate and therefore a high cost of operation for the sector, education, which is relatively intensive in human capital. In other words, this effect motivates people to allocate human capital to production of goods, rather than to education, the sector that produces the relatively scarce factor, H. This effect tends accordingly to retard the economy's growth rate when ω rises above ω^*.

Behavior of the saving rate. We discussed in Chapter 2 the behavior of the gross saving rate in the one-sector Ramsey model. If the production function was Cobb–Douglas, then the saving rate fell monotonically, stayed constant, or rose

---

[19] As mentioned in footnote 17, very low or very high values of ω cause the inequality constraints on gross investment to become operative. If we examine only the range of ω for which these constraints are not binding, then our numerical results indicate that γ_Q, like γ_K, is decreasing in ω for all parameter values that we have considered.

monotonically during the transition depending on whether a particular combination of parameters was positive, zero, or negative (see Appendix 2B). We also noted that if we assumed a high capital share of approximately 0.75, corresponding to a broad notion of capital, then reasonable parameter values were consistent with a roughly constant gross saving rate.

A similar analysis can be applied to the Uzawa–Lucas model with a Cobb–Douglas form of the production function for goods. Suppose that we define gross saving to be the portion of the output of goods, Y, that is not consumed. That is, we take narrow definitions that exclude the production of human capital from output and saving. We can then show (following a procedure analogous to that in Appendix 2B) that the transitional behavior of the saving rate is determined as follows:

$$\Psi = -B \cdot (1 - \alpha)/\alpha + \delta - (\rho + \delta)/\theta \begin{cases} > 0 & \implies ds/d\omega > 0 \\ = 0 & \implies s = 1 - \alpha \cdot (\theta - 1)/\theta, \\ < 0 & \implies ds/d\omega < 0. \end{cases} \quad (5.43)$$

The condition for a constant saving rate, $\Psi = 0$, is now difficult to satisfy. First, Eq. (5.43) implies that $\alpha\delta > B \cdot (1 - \alpha)$ must hold to get $\Psi = 0$. For the parameter values that we assumed before, $\delta = 0.05$ and $B = 0.11$, this condition implies $\alpha > 0.69$. Since α is supposed to refer now only to physical capital, this inequality is unlikely to be satisfied. Second, the transversality condition for the model—the steady-state rate of return, $B - \delta$, exceeds the steady-state growth rate, $(1/\theta) \cdot (B - \delta - \rho)$—can be used to show that Ψ can equal 0 only if $(1/\theta) + (1/\alpha) > 2$. This condition requires, in particular, $\theta > 1/\alpha$. Thus, if a low value of α worked in the first inequality, then a constant saving rate would require a high value of θ.

If the saving rate were constant during the transition, then its value, $s = 1 - \alpha(\theta - 1)/\theta$, would be very high unless α is close to 1 and θ is high. For example, if $\alpha = 0.5$ and $\theta = 2$, then $s = 0.75$. Since saving corresponds here only to the part of goods output that goes into physical capital—and does not include investment in human capital—this high value of s is unrealistic.

Reasonable values of the parameters, including a value of α well below 1, correspond to $\Psi < 0$ and, hence, $ds/d\omega < 0$ in Eq. (5.43). Consider a less-developed country that starts with a relative scarcity of human capital, so that $\omega > \omega^*$. The model predicts that this country's gross saving rate (defined as the fraction of goods output that is not consumed) would start out low and then rise as the economy approaches its steady state. This behavior accords with some evidence described in Chapter 12.

INEQUALITY RESTRICTIONS ON GROSS INVESTMENT. In the one-sector model that we analyzed in the first part of this chapter, one of the inequality constraints for nonnegative gross investment was binding if the initial value of $\omega \equiv K/H$ departed from its steady-state value. In particular, $\omega < \omega^*$ implied that gross investment in human capital was set to zero, whereas $\omega > \omega^*$ implied that gross investment in physical capital was set to zero. In the Uzawa–Lucas model, the inequality constraints are not binding for a range of ω around its steady-state value, and the dynamics that we have considered thus far applies in this range. However, if ω starts sufficiently below or above its steady-state value, then an inequality restriction on gross investment becomes operative.

If $\alpha < \theta$, as we assume, then u and ω are inversely related as shown in Fig. 5.5. If ω is far enough below ω^*, then the restriction $u \leq 1$ binds; that is, if K is sufficiently in short supply relative to H, then gross investment in H is set to zero. In this case, H grows at the constant rate $-\delta$, and the situation parallels the usual one-sector growth model in which output can be used for either C or K. We know that the growth rates of C, K, and Y are inversely related to ω in this range. Hence, in Fig. 5.6, the downward-sloping curves for γ_C and γ_K and the downward-sloping portion of the curve for γ_Y apply even when ω is low enough for the restriction $u \leq 1$ to bind.

We can determine numerically how far ω has to fall below ω^* for the inequality constraint $u \leq 1$, and, hence, $\dot{H} + \delta H \geq 0$, to become operative. For the parameter values mentioned before, including $\alpha = 0.5$ and $\theta = 2$, ω has to decline to 5 percent of ω^* to make the restriction bind. Similar conclusions apply if we allow the parameters to depart somewhat from our preferred values.[20] Thus, the results indicate that we can satisfactorily neglect the restriction $u \leq 1$ for a wide range of ω below ω^*.

A sufficient increase in ω above ω^* causes the restriction $\dot{K} + \delta K \geq 0$ to bind. That is, if K is sufficiently abundant relative to H, then gross investment in K is set to zero.[21] In this case, K grows at the constant rate $-\delta$, and all of the output is used for consumption. The household's only decision here is the allocation of H between production (u) and education ($1 - u$). This framework amounts to a two-sector model in which consumables are produced by one technology and capital (H) with another technology. The only difference from standard two-sector models of this type (such as Uzawa [1964] and Srinivasan [1964]) is that the consumables sector involves diminishing returns, whereas the capital-goods (H) sector features constant returns.

Appendix 5B shows that the growth rates of C and Y are constant in the Uzawa–Lucas model when the restriction $\dot{K} + \delta K \geq 0$ is operative. That is, if ω is high enough for the constraint of nonnegative physical investment to bind, then γ_C and γ_Y, as well as γ_K, are invariant with ω. In Fig. 5.6, the graphs of γ_C, γ_Y, and γ_K therefore become horizontal for high enough ω.

The behavior of the other growth rates depends on the dynamics of u. In particular, even if $\alpha < \theta$, the policy function for u need not be downward sloping versus ω (as it was in Fig. 5.5) when the restriction $\dot{K} + \delta K \geq 0$ is operative. If u were inversely related to ω in the restricted range, then γ_H and γ_Q would rise with ω

---

[20]If $\alpha \geq \theta$, then the constraint $u \leq 1$ never binds.

[21]If $\alpha < \theta$, then u declines with ω as shown in Fig. 5.5. A sufficient increase in ω would cause the inequality $u \geq 0$ to bind. However, the restriction $C \geq 0$ never binds because $u'(c) \to \infty$ as $c \to 0$. Therefore, as ω increases, the inequality $\dot{K} + \delta K \geq 0$ becomes operative before the inequality $u \geq 0$. We also find numerically that the restriction $\dot{K} + \delta K \geq 0$ becomes binding for high enough ω even if $\alpha \geq \theta$.

in this range. In contrast, if u were positively related to ω, then γ_H and γ_Q would fall with ω. This last outcome turns out to hold unambiguously if $\theta \leq 1$, but either result can apply if $\theta > 1$.

We have found numerically (how high ω has to be) for the constraint of non-negative physical investment to bind. For the parameter values mentioned before, ω has to be almost five times ω^* for the constraint to become operative. Similar conclusions apply if we allow the parameters to differ somewhat from our preferred values. Hence, the results indicate that we can satisfactorily neglect the restriction $\dot{K} + \delta K \geq 0$ for a wide range of ω above ω^*.

For reasonable parameter values, the range of ω over which the inequality constraints do not bind—from 5 percent of ω^* to 5 times ω^* for our favored parameter values—appears to be wide relative to the ranges of the K/H ratio that are likely to prevail empirically. It therefore seems reasonable to focus on the empirical implications that derive from interior solutions to the model, that is, from the graphs shown in Figs. 5.5 and 5.6.

5.2.3 The Generalized Uzawa–Lucas Model

The generalized form of the Uzawa–Lucas model maintains the assumption that education is relatively intensive in human capital, $\eta < \alpha$, but allows for the presence of physical capital in the education sector, $\eta > 0$. We already observed from Eqs. (5.16) and (5.18) for the case $\eta < \alpha$ that vK/uH—the ratio of physical capital employed in production to human capital employed in production—converges monotonically to its steady-state value. This result implies that the rate of return, r, and the growth rate of consumption, γ_C, converge monotonically to their steady-state values. Thus, these results are the same as those for the Uzawa-Lucas case, $\eta = 0$.

The difference from before is that we cannot simplify the dynamic system to a two-dimensional setup and therefore cannot construct phase diagrams of the form presented in Fig. 5.4. Moreover, we cannot demonstrate in general that the policy functions for χ and u are monotonically related to ω[22] or that the growth rates of K, H, Y, and Q behave qualitatively as they did before.

We have carried out simulations in which α is set at 0.4 and the parameter η is varied between 0 and 0.4. We assume familiar values for the other parameters; a representative case is $\delta = 0.05$, $\rho = 0.02$, $n = 0.01$, and $\theta = 3$. For $\eta = 0$, we set $B = 0.13$, so that the steady-state interest rate is 0.08 and the steady-state per-capita growth rate is 0.02. The patterns for the various growth rates when $\eta = 0$ then correspond to those shown in Fig. 5.6. As we raise η, we adjust B so as to maintain the steady-state interest and growth rates.[23]

---

[22]We have found from simulations that u can be nonmonotonically related to $\omega \equiv K/H$, but only for strange values of the underlying parameters. We have also found cases with odd parameter values in which the policy function for χ can slope in the direction opposite to that for u—a result that cannot hold when $\eta = 0$.

[23]We normalize to set $A = 1$ throughout.

As η approaches α, the simulations show that the policy functions for u and χ continue to be monotonically and inversely related to ω, as shown in Fig. 5.5 for the case in which $\eta = 0$ (see, however, footnote 22). We find also that the qualitative behavior of the various growth rates remains as shown in Fig. 5.6, except that higher values of η tend to make γ_Y slope upward in the vicinity of the steady state. Thus, these numerical results suggest that, if we assume "reasonable" values of the underlying parameters, then the main qualitative results of the Uzawa–Lucas model are likely to be maintained when we drop the unrealistic assumption that the education sector has no inputs of physical capital ($\eta = 0$). In particular, our previous discussion of the effects from imbalances between K and H is likely to remain valid.

Another difference in the generalized model is that the range in which the inequality restrictions $u \leq 1$ and $\dot{K} + \delta K \geq 0$ are not binding narrows as η rises toward α. This result makes sense because we know from our previous analysis of the one-sector model that this range compresses to 0 when $\eta = \alpha$. If we make the reasonable assumption that η is much less than α—even if η is now positive—then we still find there exists a broad range of values of ω around the steady state for which the inequality constraints are not binding.

5.2.4 The Model with Reversed Factor Intensities

We have dealt thus far with environments in which the education sector is relatively intensive in human capital, that is, $\alpha > \eta \geq 0$. This section considers briefly the implications of reversed factor intensities, $\alpha < \eta$. We spend little time on this case because the assumption that education is relatively intensive in physical capital is implausible. (If we were to interpret K and H not as physical and human capital, but in some alternative way, then the reversed factor intensities might apply.)

We observed before that the condition $\alpha < \eta$ implies that Eq. (5.18) is an unstable differential equation in the variable $p \equiv \mu/\nu$. (This equation applies as long as inequality restrictions on gross investment are not operative.) Hence, any departure of p from its steady-state value would be magnified over time. This unstable behavior would then be transmitted to the ratio $\nu K/uH$ (from Eq. [5.16]). Recall that this ratio determines the marginal product of physical capital in the production of goods and therefore determines r and γ_C. The unstable behavior of $\nu K/uH$ would be transmitted accordingly to r and γ_C. Since these explosive outcomes will conflict with household optimization, we focus on the case in which p equals its steady-state value at all points in time.

The constancy of p implies that the ratio $\nu K/uH$ is constant (from Eq. [5.16]). Hence, r and γ_C are also constant throughout the transition to the steady state.

Appendix 5C shows that the growth rate of broad output, γ_Q, is also constant and equal to γ_C. Thus, we get the surprising result that the growth rates of C and Q do not vary as the state variable $\omega \equiv K/H$ changes (in the range in which inequality restrictions are not binding). In other words, the imbalance effect does not operate on these growth rates when the factor intensities are reversed.

The constancy of vK/uH, γ_C, and γ_Q makes it easy to assess the dynamics of the variables u, χ, γ_H, and γ_K. Appendix 5C shows that each of these variables adjusts monotonically toward its steady-state value as the state variable, ω, adjusts toward its steady-state value. The slopes of the variables in relation to ω are all unambiguous and are negative for u and χ, positive for γ_H, and negative for γ_K.

5.3 CONDITIONS FOR ENDOGENOUS GROWTH

We have worked thus far with models in which constant returns to scale apply in the sectors for goods and education; that is, we assumed production functions of the forms of Eqs. (5.11) and (5.12). (The Uzawa–Lucas model, expressed in Eqs. [5.19] and [5.20], is the special case in which the education sector uses only human capital as an input, that is, $\eta = 0$.) These production functions imply that diminishing returns do not arise when physical and human capital grow at the same rate. Thus, in the steady state, rates of return remain constant, and the economy can grow at a constant rate. Following Mulligan and Sala-i-Martin [1993] we now consider whether more general specifications of the production functions are consistent with positive growth in the steady state, that is, with endogenous growth.

We modify Eqs. (5.11) and (5.12) to

$$Y = C + \dot{K} + \delta K = A \cdot (vK)^{\alpha_1} \cdot (uH)^{\alpha_2}, \qquad (5.44)$$

$$\dot{H} + \delta H = B \cdot [(1 - v) \cdot K]^{\eta_1} \cdot [(1 - u) \cdot H]^{\eta_2}. \qquad (5.45)$$

Thus, we retain Cobb–Douglas forms of the production functions, but we allow the sums $\alpha_1 + \alpha_2$ and $\eta_1 + \eta_2$ to depart from unity, so that constant returns to scale need not apply.

If a sector exhibits diminishing returns, say $\alpha_1 + \alpha_2 < 1$, then we can remain within the usual competitive framework if we add to the production function a factor such as raw labor or land that is in fixed aggregate supply. If this factor has an exponent of $1 - \alpha_1 - \alpha_2$, then constant returns again apply at the level of an individual producer. The important consideration is that diminishing returns, $\alpha_1 + \alpha_2 < 1$, apply to the factors that can be accumulated.

The model can also have increasing returns, say $\alpha_1 + \alpha_2 > 1$, within a competitive setup if we introduce the types of spillover effects that we considered in Chapter 4. For example, for the production of Y, an individual firm's inputs of K and H could have exponents α_1 and $1 - \alpha_1$, respectively, so that constant returns apply for an individual firm. The economy's aggregate of H could then appear as an additional input in the production function (as in Lucas [1988]) with an exponent of $\alpha_1 + \alpha_2 - 1$, where $\alpha_2 > 1 - \alpha_1$. The key consideration here is that increasing returns, $\alpha_1 + \alpha_2 > 1$, apply to the factors that can be accumulated by the overall economy.[24]

---

[24]We observed in Chapter 4 that the presence of these kinds of spillovers implies that the competitive outcomes will generally not be Pareto optimal. Thus, these models tend to have roles for government intervention, basically to subsidize the activities with positive spillovers. In extreme situations, in which

Suppose that we look for a steady state in which u and v are constant, and C, Y, K, and H grow at constant, but not necessarily equal, rates. (Unless u or v approach 0, we cannot allow u and v to grow at constant rates because of the constraints $0 \le v \le 1$ and $0 \le u \le 1$). If we divide Eq. (5.45) by H and then take logs and derivatives with respect to time, then we get

$$\eta_1 \gamma_K^* + (\eta_2 - 1) \cdot \gamma_H^* = 0, \tag{5.46}$$

where γ^* denotes the steady-state growth rate of the variable indicated by the subscript.

If we divide Eq. (5.44) by K and take logs and derivatives, then we get

$$\left(\frac{C/K}{C/K + \gamma_K^* + \delta} \right) \cdot (\gamma_C^* - \gamma_K^*) = (\alpha_1 - 1) \cdot \gamma_K^* + \alpha_2 \gamma_H^*. \tag{5.47}$$

We can show that $\gamma_C^* = \gamma_K^*$ from the arguments that we used in Chapter 4. (If $\gamma_C^* > \gamma_K^*$, then γ_K^* as computed from Eq. (5.44) tends to $-\infty$. If $\gamma_C^* < \gamma_K^*$, then $\gamma_K^* = r$, the net marginal product of K in the goods sector. This equality violates the transversality condition.) Equation (5.47) then simplifies to

$$(\alpha_1 - 1) \cdot \gamma_K^* + \alpha_2 \gamma_H^* = 0. \tag{5.48}$$

We can use the condition $\gamma_Y^* = \alpha_1 \gamma_K^* + \alpha_2 \gamma_H^*$ implied by Eq. (5.44) along with Eq. (5.48) to show that $\gamma_Y^* = \gamma_K^*$. Thus, the variables C, K, and Y must all grow at the same rate in the steady state.

Equations (5.46) and (5.48) form a system of two linear homogeneous equations with two unknowns, γ_K^* and γ_H^*. This system has a solution other than $\gamma_K^* = \gamma_H^* = 0$ only if the characteristic matrix of the coefficients is 0. This condition requires the parameters to satisfy

$$\alpha_2 \eta_1 = (1 - \eta_2) \cdot (1 - \alpha_1). \tag{5.49}$$

Equation (5.49) is the key condition that must hold if the model is to deliver endogenous growth at positive, constant rates.

One example that satisfies Eq. (5.49) is the case that we have already considered of constant returns in each sector: $\alpha_1 + \alpha_2 = 1$ and $\eta_1 + \eta_2 = 1$. In this situation, $\gamma_H^* = \gamma_K^*$, so that the ratio K/H is constant in the steady state. Equation (5.49) can, however, be satisfied in other ways.

---

the spillovers are very large, multiple equilibria are possible, and the equilibria can typically be ranked by the Pareto criterion. Suppose, as an example, that an individual's return to education depends positively on the average education level of the population. Then, in one kind of equilibrium, everyone gets education, because when most people are educated, the remaining people find it advantageous also to be educated. In another kind of equilibrium, no one receives education, because when most people are not educated, the remaining people find it desirable not to be educated. We have not explored the class of models with multiple equilibria because the amount of spillovers required to generate this multiplicity seems to be unrealistically large. Moreover, from a positive standpoint, models that do not select among the possible equilibria are incomplete. For analyses of these types of models—and for more favorable appraisals of them—see Krugman (1991), Matsuyama (1991), Benhabib and Farmer (1991), Boldrin and Rustichini (1993), Chamley (1992), and Xie (1992).

If $\eta_1 = 0$ and $\eta_2 = 1$—the case assumed by Uzawa (1965) and Lucas (1988)—then Eq. (5.49) holds for any values of α_1 and α_2. Thus, if education is linear in H, then all variables can grow in the steady state even if the production of goods involves diminishing returns to scale, $\alpha_1 + \alpha_2 < 1$. Lucas highlighted a spillover benefit from aggregate human capital that led to the condition $\alpha_1 + \alpha_2 > 1$ (see footnote 24). Our results show that this condition is consistent with, but not essential for, endogenous growth. If $\eta_1 = 0$ and $\eta_2 = 1$, as Lucas also assumed, then this model can generate endogenous growth even if no human-capital spillovers are present.

Equation (5.48) implies, if $\alpha_1 \neq 1$,

$$\gamma_K^* = \left(\frac{\alpha_2}{1 - \alpha_1} \right) \cdot \gamma_H^*.$$

Hence, $\gamma_K^* \lessgtr \gamma_H^*$ as $\alpha_1 + \alpha_2 \lessgtr 1$. Thus, although all quantities can grow at constant rates when $\eta_1 = 0$ and $\eta_2 = 1$, the ratios K/H, Y/H, and C/H do not approach constant values unless $\alpha_1 + \alpha_2 = 1$.

For another example, assume that $\alpha_i, \eta_i > 0$ for $i = 1, 2$. If $\alpha_1 + \alpha_2 < 1$, then Eq. (5.49) can be satisfied if $\eta_1 + \eta_2 > 1$. Analogously, $\alpha_1 + \alpha_2 > 1$ can be paired with $\eta_1 + \eta_2 < 1$. In other words, diminishing returns to scale in one sector can be offset by the appropriate degree of increasing returns in the other sector. If $\alpha_1 + \alpha_2 < 1$, then $\gamma_K^* < \gamma_H^*$, and vice versa.

Finally, Eq. (5.49) is also satisfied if $\alpha_1 = 1$ and $\alpha_2 = 0$. This specification corresponds to the AK model studied in Chapter 4. In this specification, human capital serves no purpose; it does not help to produce goods and also does not appear in the utility function. Hence, optimizing agents would not accumulate any H, and all of K would be allocated to the production of goods ($v = 1$ in Eqs. [5.44] and [5.45]).

If we want endogenous growth and also want K and H to grow at the same rate in the steady state, then Eq. (5.49) can be satisfied only if each sector exhibits constant returns to scale, $\alpha_1 + \alpha_2 = 1$ and $\eta_1 + \eta_2 = 1$, that is, the specification in Eqs. (5.11) and (5.12). Since the alternative in which K/H rises or falls forever seems implausible, we assumed in the main discussion in this chapter that constant returns held in each sector.

5.4   SUMMARY OBSERVATIONS

We extended the AK model from Chapter 4 to allow for two sectors, one that produced consumables, C, and physical capital, K, and another that created human capital, H. If the sectors have the same factor intensities, then the main new results about growth come from the restriction that gross investment in each type of capital good must be nonnegative. This restriction generates an imbalance effect, whereby the growth rate of output rises with the magnitude of the gap between the ratio K/H and its steady-state value.

The assumption of equal factor intensities neglects a key aspect of education; it relies heavily on educated people as an input. We therefore modified the structure to specify that the production of human capital is relatively intensive in human capital. This change in specification alters the conclusions about the imbalance effect. The growth rate of output (defined broadly to include the production of new human capital) tends to rise with the extent of the imbalance if human capital is relatively abundant, but to decline with the extent of the imbalance if human capital is relatively scarce. These results imply that an economy would recover rapidly in reaction to a war that destroyed primarily physical capital, but would rebound only slowly from an epidemic that eliminated mainly human capital.

APPENDIX 5A
TRANSITIONAL DYNAMICS WITH INEQUALITY
RESTRICTIONS ON GROSS INVESTMENT
IN THE ONE-SECTOR MODEL

Suppose that $K(0)/H(0) > \alpha/(1 - \alpha)$. Recall that in this case the household wants to reduce K and raise H by discrete amounts, so that the inequality restriction $I_K \geq 0$ will be binding. Hence, $I_K = 0$ and $\dot{K}/K = -\delta$. In this situation, the household's problem amounts to maximizing utility, subject to this path for K and to the constraint $\dot{H} = Y - C - \delta H$. The Hamiltonian for this problem is

$$J = u(C) \cdot e^{-\rho t} + \nu \cdot [AK^\alpha H^{1-\alpha} - \delta H - C], \qquad (5A.1)$$

where $u(C) = (C^{1-\theta} - 1)/(1 - \theta)$. The first-order conditions, $\partial J/\partial C = 0$ and $\dot{\nu} = -\partial J/\partial H$, lead in the usual way to the condition for the growth rate of consumption:

$$\gamma_C = (1/\theta) \cdot [A \cdot (1 - \alpha) \cdot (K/H)^\alpha - \delta - \rho], \qquad (5A.2)$$

where $A \cdot (1 - \alpha) \cdot (K/H)^\alpha - \delta$ is the net marginal product of H. This condition and the budget constraint,

$$\dot{H} = AK^\alpha H^{1-\alpha} - \delta H - C,$$

along with $K(t) = K(0) \cdot e^{-\delta t}$, determine the paths of C, H, and K.

We can proceed as in Chapter 4 by defining two variables, $\omega \equiv K/H$ and $\chi \equiv C/K$, that will be constant in the steady state. The conditions for $\dot{C}$ and $\dot{H}$ can be used to get the transition equations for z and χ:

$$\gamma_\omega = -A\omega^\alpha + \chi\omega, \qquad (5A.3)$$

$$\gamma_\chi = (1/\theta) \cdot [A \cdot (1 - \alpha) \cdot \omega^\alpha - \rho] + \delta \cdot (\theta - 1)/\theta. \qquad (5A.4)$$

Figure 5.10 shows the phase diagram in (ω, χ) space. The condition $\dot{\omega} = 0$ implies $\chi = A\omega^{-(1-\alpha)}$, the downward-sloping curve in the figure. A value of χ above (below) the curve corresponds to $\dot{\omega} > 0$ ($\dot{\omega} < 0$). These directions of motion are shown by the arrows in the figure.

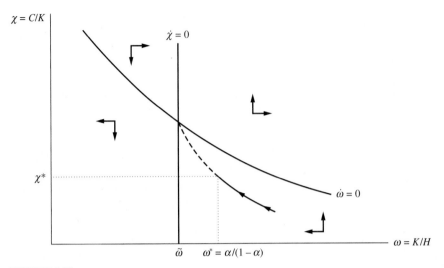

FIGURE 5.10
Phase diagram for the one-sector model when $\omega > \omega^*$. The dynamics shown in this figure apply when $\omega \equiv K/H > \omega^* = \alpha/(1 - \alpha)$. When $\omega > \omega^*$, the economy moves along the saddle path in the direction of the "hypothetical target," $\tilde{\omega}$. During the transition, $\chi \equiv C/K$ rises monotonically and ω falls monotonically. The economy reaches ω^* in finite time (before it reaches $\tilde{\omega}$). At this point, the inequality constraint that gross investment in K cannot be negative is no longer binding. The variables K and H then grow together at a constant, positive rate.

The condition $\dot{\chi} = 0$ requires

$$\omega = \left[\frac{\rho + \delta \cdot (1 - \theta)}{A \cdot (1 - \alpha)} \right]^{1/\alpha} \equiv \tilde{\omega}. \tag{5A.5}$$

We assume $\rho + \delta \cdot (1 - \theta) \geq 0$, so that $\tilde{\omega}$ is well defined and nonnegative, but this condition is not required for the analysis. A value of ω above (below) $\tilde{\omega}$ corresponds to $\dot{\chi} > 0$ ($\dot{\chi} < 0$), as shown by the arrows in the figure. (If $\rho + \delta \cdot (1 - \theta) < 0$, then $\dot{\chi} > 0$ applies for all $\chi \geq 0$.)

The figure shows $\tilde{\omega} < \omega^* = \alpha/(1 - \alpha)$, the ratio of K to H that applies in the long run in the absence of effective inequality constraints on gross investment. The formula for $\tilde{\omega}$ implies that this condition corresponds to $\rho + \delta < A\alpha^\alpha \cdot (1 - \alpha)^{1-\alpha}$, a result that holds from the assumption $\gamma^* > 0$ in Eq. (5.8).

The dynamics shown in Fig. 5.10 are relevant for $\omega > \omega^*$, the condition that causes $I_K \geq 0$ to be a binding constraint. The figure shows that, in this region, χ rises monotonically and ω falls monotonically along the stable, saddle path. The variable ω is effectively heading along this path toward the target $\tilde{\omega}$, but reaches ω^* in finite time before it gets close to $\tilde{\omega}$. From that point on, the constraint of nonnegative gross investment in K is no longer binding, and ω remains at ω^*, rather than continuing along the saddle path.

The results are analogous if $K(0)/H(0) < \alpha/(1 - \alpha)$. The condition $I_H \geq 0$ is then binding, and $\dot{H}/H = -\delta$. The transition equations for ω and χ are

$$\gamma_\omega = A\omega^{-(1-\alpha)} - \chi, \tag{5A.6}$$

$$\gamma_\chi = -A \cdot \left(\frac{\theta - \alpha}{\theta}\right) \cdot \omega^{-(1-\alpha)} + \chi + \delta \cdot (\theta - 1)/\theta - \rho/\theta. \tag{5A.7}$$

Figure 5.11 shows the phase diagram for the case in which $\alpha < \theta$. The condition $\dot\omega = 0$ corresponds to $\chi = \omega^{-(1-\alpha)}$. The condition $\dot\chi = 0$ corresponds to

$$\chi = A \cdot \left(\frac{\theta - \alpha}{\theta}\right) \cdot \omega^{-(1-\alpha)} - \delta \cdot (\theta - 1)/\theta + \rho/\theta. \tag{5A.8}$$

The $\dot\chi = 0$ locus slopes downward, as shown, if $\alpha < \theta$. This locus must be less negatively sloped than the $\dot\omega = 0$ locus (but the $\dot\chi = 0$ locus would be positively sloped if $\alpha > \theta$). The $\dot\omega = 0$ and $\dot\chi = 0$ loci intersect at the value $\hat\omega$, which can be shown (from the condition $\gamma^* > 0$) to exceed $\omega^* = \alpha/(1 - \alpha)$.

The dynamics shown in Fig. 5.11 apply if $\omega < \omega^*$. The figure shows that, in this region, χ declines monotonically and ω rises monotonically along the stable, saddle path. (If $\alpha > \theta$, then χ falls monotonically, and if $\alpha = \theta$, then χ remains constant.) The variable ω is effectively heading toward the target $\hat\omega$, but reaches ω^* in finite time before it gets close to $\hat\omega$. From there on, the constraint on nonnegative gross investment is no longer binding, and ω remains at ω^* (rather than continuing further along the saddle path).

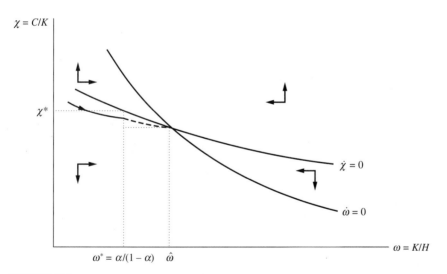

FIGURE 5.11
Phase diagram for the one-sector model when $\omega < \omega^*$. The dynamics shown in this figure apply when $\omega \equiv K/H < \omega^* = \alpha/(1 - \alpha)$. When $\omega < \omega^*$, the economy moves along the saddle path in the direction of the "hypothetical target," $\hat\omega$. During the transition, $\chi \equiv C/K$ falls monotonically and ω rises monotonically. The economy reaches ω^* in finite time (before it reaches $\hat\omega$). At this point, the inequality constraint that gross investment in H cannot be negative is no longer binding. The variables K and H then grow together at a constant, positive rate.

APPENDIX 5B
SOLUTION OF THE UZAWA–LUCAS MODEL

The Hamiltonian expression for this model is given by

$$J = u(C) \cdot e^{-\rho t} + v \cdot [AK^\alpha \cdot (uH)^{1-\alpha} - C - \delta K] + \mu \cdot [B \cdot (1-u) \cdot H - \delta H].$$

(5B.1)

The term in the first set of brackets equals $\dot{K}$, and the term in the second set of brackets equals $\dot{H}$. If we define $\omega \equiv K/H$ and $\chi \equiv C/K$, then the growth rates of K and H are given by

$$\gamma_K = Au^{1-\alpha} \cdot \omega^{-(1-\alpha)} - \chi - \delta,$$

(5B.2)

$$\gamma_H = B \cdot (1-u) - \delta.$$

(5B.3)

The growth rate of ω is therefore given by

$$\gamma_\omega = \gamma_K - \gamma_H = Au^{1-\alpha} \cdot \omega^{-(1-\alpha)} - \chi - B \cdot (1-u).$$

(5B.4)

The first-order conditions, $\partial J/\partial C = 0$ and $\partial J/\partial u = 0$, lead respectively to

$$u'(C) = ve^{\rho t},$$

(5B.5)

$$\mu/v = (A/B) \cdot (1-\alpha) \cdot u^{-\alpha}\omega^\alpha.$$

(5B.6)

The condition $\dot{v} = -\partial J/\partial K$ implies

$$\dot{v}/v = -A\alpha \cdot u^{1-\alpha} \cdot \omega^{-(1-\alpha)} + \delta.$$

(5B.7)

The condition $\dot{\mu} = -\partial J/\partial H$ implies

$$\dot{\mu}/\mu = -(v/\mu) \cdot A \cdot (1-\alpha) \cdot u^{1-\alpha}\omega^\alpha - B \cdot (1-u) + \delta.$$

If we substitute for v/μ from Eq. (5B.6) and simplify, then the result is

$$\dot{\mu}/\mu = -B + \delta.$$

(5B.8)

We can differentiate Eq. (5B.5) with respect to time and use $u(C) = (C^{1-\theta} - 1)/(1-\theta)$ and the expression for $\dot{v}/v$ in Eq. (5B.7) to get the usual equation for consumption growth:

$$\gamma_C = (1/\theta) \cdot [A\alpha \cdot u^{1-\alpha} \cdot \omega^{-(1-\alpha)} - \delta - \rho].$$

(5B.9)

This result corresponds to Eq. (5.24). The growth rate of χ can then be determined from Eqs. (5B.9) and (5B.2) to get the formula given in Eq. (5.25):

$$\gamma_\chi = \gamma_C - \gamma_K = \left(\frac{\alpha-\theta}{\theta}\right) \cdot Au^{1-\alpha} \cdot \omega^{-(1-\alpha)} + \chi - (1/\theta) \cdot [\delta \cdot (1-\theta) + \rho].$$

(5B.10)

If we differentiate Eq. (5B.6) with respect to time and use the formulas for $\dot{v}/v$ from Eq. (5B.7), $\dot{\mu}/\mu$ from Eq. (5B.8), and γ_ω from Eq. (5B.4), then we get, after simplifying,

$$\gamma_u = B \cdot (1 - \alpha)/\alpha + Bu - \chi. \tag{5B.11}$$

This result appears in Eq. (5.26). Equations (5B.4), (5B.10), and (5B.11) form a system of three differential equations in the variables ω, χ, and u, where the state variable ω begins at some value $\omega(0)$.

The steady state of this system can be found readily by setting the three time derivatives to zero. If we define the combination of parameters as in the text,

$$\varphi \equiv [\rho + \delta \cdot (1 - \theta)]/B\theta,$$

then the results are

$$\omega^* = (\alpha A/B)^{1/(1-\alpha)} \cdot [\varphi + (\theta - 1)/\theta],$$

$$\chi^* = B \cdot (\varphi + 1/\alpha - 1/\theta), \tag{5B.12}$$

$$u^* = \varphi + (\theta - 1)/\theta.$$

These values are given in Eq. (5.28). The steady-state rate of return, which equals the net marginal product of K in the goods sector and the net marginal product of H in the education sector, is

$$r^* = B - \delta.$$

The corresponding steady-state growth rate of Y, C, K, and H is

$$\gamma^* = (1/\theta) \cdot (B - \delta - \rho).$$

The values for r^* and γ^* are shown in Eq. (5.29).

Define z to be the gross average product of physical capital:

$$z \equiv Au^{1-\alpha} \cdot \omega^{-(1-\alpha)}.$$

The steady-state value of z can be determined from Eq. (5B.12) to be $z^* = B/\alpha$. The system of three differential equations as expressed in Eqs. (5B.4), (5B.10), and (5B.11) can then be rewritten as

$$\gamma_\omega = (z - z^*) - (\chi - \chi^*) + B \cdot (u - u^*), \tag{5B.13}$$

$$\gamma_\chi = \left(\frac{\alpha - \theta}{\theta}\right) \cdot (z - z^*) + (\chi - \chi^*), \tag{5B.14}$$

$$\gamma_u = B \cdot (u - u^*) - (\chi - \chi^*). \tag{5B.15}$$

The definition of z implies

$$\gamma_z = (1 - \alpha) \cdot (\gamma_u - \gamma_\omega) = -(1 - \alpha) \cdot (z - z^*). \tag{5B.16}$$

The results for γ_z, γ_χ, and γ_u are in Eqs. (5.31)–(5.33).

Equation (5B.16) can be integrated to get Eq. (5.35):

$$\frac{z - z^*}{z} = \left[\frac{z(0) - z^*}{z(0)}\right] \cdot e^{-(1-\alpha)\cdot z^* t},$$

where $z(0)$ is the initial value of z. This equation can be rewritten to solve for z as

$$z = z^* \cdot z(0) / \left\{ z^* \cdot e^{-(1-\alpha)\cdot z^* t} + z(0) \cdot [1 - e^{-(1-\alpha)\cdot z^* t}] \right\}. \tag{5B.17}$$

Equation (5B.17) implies $z \to z^*$ as $t \to \infty$. If $z(0) > z^*$, then $\dot{z} < 0$ and $z > z^*$ for all t, whereas if $z(0) < z^*$, then $\dot{z} > 0$ and $z < z^*$ for all t.

We now look for the characteristics of the stable path of χ and u, that is, the path along which χ approaches χ^* and u approaches u^*. Assume $z(0) > z^*$, so that $z - z^*$ declines monotonically over time. Equation (5B.14) can then be written as

$$\gamma_\chi = (\chi - \chi^*) + \left(\frac{\alpha - \theta}{\theta}\right) \cdot \Omega(t), \tag{5B.18}$$

where $\Omega(t) = z - z^*$ is a monotonically decreasing function of time. If $\alpha < \theta$, then the term on the right of Eq. (5B.18) is negative but declining in magnitude over time. If $\chi \le \chi^*$ for some finite t, then the equation implies $\dot{\chi} < 0$ for all subsequent t. Since the magnitude of $\dot{\chi}$ asymptotically exceeds some finite lower bound, χ would diverge from χ^* and reach the value of 0 in finite time. The stable path therefore features $\chi > \chi^*$ for all t. If $\dot{\chi} \ge 0$ for some t, then Eq. (5B.18) implies $\dot{\chi} > 0$ for all subsequent t (because the negative term on the right decreases in size over time). Hence, χ would diverge from χ^* and approach infinity. The stable path therefore involves $\dot{\chi} < 0$ for all t.

The conclusions are analogous if we assume $\alpha > \theta$ or begin with $z(0) < z^*$. The columns for $\chi - \chi^*$ and $\dot{\chi}$ in Table 5A.1 summarize the results.

Equation (5B.15) determines the behavior of u, given the behavior of χ. Suppose, for example, that $z(0) > z^*$ and $\alpha < \theta$, so that $\chi > \chi^*$ and $\dot{\chi} < 0$. If $u \le u^*$ for some t, then Eq. (5B.15) implies $\dot{u} < 0$ for all subsequent t. Therefore, u diverges from u^* and approaches 0. The stable path therefore features $u > u^*$ for all t. If $\dot{u} \ge 0$ for some t, then $\dot{u} > 0$ for all subsequent t, because the term $-(\chi - \chi^*)$ in Eq. (5B.15) is negative and decreasing in size over time. Therefore, $\dot{u} < 0$ holds for all t. The behavior of $u - u^*$ and $\dot{u}$ are shown for the various sign combinations of $z(0) - z^*$ and $\alpha - \theta$ in Table 5A.1.

TABLE 5A.1
Transitional Behavior of χ and u

$z(0) - z^*$	$\alpha - \theta$	$\chi - \chi^*$	$\dot{\chi}$	$u - u^*$	$\dot{u}$
> 0	< 0	> 0	< 0	> 0	< 0
> 0	> 0	< 0	> 0	< 0	> 0
$= 0$	$--$	$= 0$	$= 0$	$= 0$	$= 0$
< 0	< 0	< 0	> 0	< 0	> 0
$--$	$= 0$	$= 0$	$= 0$	$= 0$	$= 0$

We want to show now how the starting value $z(0) - z^*$ relates to the starting value of the state variable, ω. If we use Eq. (5B.14) to substitute for $\chi - \chi^*$ in the formula for γ_ω in Eq. (5B.13), then we get

$$\gamma_\omega = (\alpha/\theta) \cdot (z - z^*) - \gamma_\chi + B \cdot (u - u^*). \qquad (5B.19)$$

Suppose $\alpha \leq \theta$ and $z(0) > z^*$. In this case, the conditions $z - z^* > 0$, $\dot\chi \leq 0$, and $u - u^* \geq 0$ imply $\gamma_\omega > 0$ in Eq. (5B.19). Hence, the system can be on the stable path only if $\omega(0) < \omega^*$. Moreover, ω then rises monotonically from $\omega(0)$ toward ω^* (because $\gamma_\omega > 0$). Hence, the monotonic decline in z corresponds to a monotonic rise in ω. This result implies that a lower starting value of the state variable, $\omega(0)$, is associated with a higher initial value $z(0)$. By similar reasoning, $z(0) < z^*$ corresponds to $\omega(0) > \omega^*$, and $z(0) = z^*$ to $\omega(0) = \omega^*$.

To deal with the case in which $\alpha > \theta$, substitute for $u - u^*$ from Eq. (5B.15) into Eq. (5B.13) to get

$$\gamma_\omega = (z - z^*) + \gamma_u. \qquad (5B.20)$$

We can use this equation when $\alpha > \theta$ to show that $z(0) > z^*$ ($z[0] < z^*$) corresponds to $\omega(0) < \omega^*$ ($\omega[0] > \omega^*$).

We conclude that $z(0) \gtreqless z^*$ corresponds to $\omega(0) \lesseqgtr \omega*$ for all configurations of α and θ. Moreover, a smaller $\omega(0)$ matches up with a higher $z(0)$. Thus, z is high or low initially depending only on whether physical capital is scarce or abundant relative to human capital. We can use this result along with the findings in Table 5A.1 to draw policy functions for χ and u as functions of ω. These results appear in Fig. 5.5.

The rate of return, r, equals the net marginal product of physical capital in the production of goods, which equals $\alpha z - \delta$. Therefore, r moves together with z and inversely with ω. Equation (5B.9) implies that the growth rate of C is given by

$$\gamma_C = (1/\theta) \cdot (\alpha z - \delta - \rho). \qquad (5B.21)$$

Since γ_C moves directly with z, it moves inversely with ω.

The growth rate of K is given by

$$\gamma_K = \gamma_C - \gamma_\chi = (1/\theta) \cdot (\alpha z - \delta - \rho) - \gamma_\chi,$$

where we substituted for γ_C from Eq. (5B.21). If we substitute for γ_χ from Eq. (5B.18) and use the formulas $z^* = B/\alpha$ and $\gamma^* = (1/\theta) \cdot (B - \delta - \rho)$, then we get

$$\gamma_K = \gamma^* + (z - z^*) - (\chi - \chi^*), \qquad (5B.22)$$

the formula that appears in Eq. (5.40).

The growth rate of H is given by

$$\gamma_H = \gamma_K - \gamma_\omega.$$

If we substitute for γ_K from Eq. (5A.30) and for γ_ω from Eq. (5B.21), then we can simplify to get

$$\gamma_H = \gamma* - B \cdot (u - u^*), \qquad (5B.23)$$

the formula that appears in Eq. (5.39).

Since $Y = AK^\alpha \cdot (uH)^{1-\alpha}$, the growth rate of output is given by

$$\gamma_Y = \alpha \cdot \gamma_K + (1 - \alpha) \cdot (\gamma_u + \gamma_H).$$

If we substitute for γ_K from Eq. (5B.22), for γ_u from Eq. (5B.15), and for γ_H from Eq. (5B.23), then we get

$$\gamma_Y = \gamma^* + \alpha \cdot (z - z^*) - (\chi - \chi^*), \tag{5B.24}$$

the formula that appears in Eq. (5.41).

Broad output is given by

$$Q = Y + (\mu/\nu) \cdot B \cdot (1 - u) \cdot H = AK^\alpha \cdot (uH)^{1-\alpha} + (\mu/\nu) \cdot B \cdot (1 - u) \cdot H,$$

where μ/ν, the shadow price of human capital in units of goods, is given in Eq. (5A.14). If we substitute out for μ/ν, then we get

$$Q = Y \cdot (1 - \alpha + \alpha u)/u.$$

Hence, the growth rate of broad output is given by

$$\gamma_Q = \gamma_Y - \gamma_u \cdot (1 - \alpha)/(1 - \alpha + \alpha u), \tag{5B.25}$$

the formula given in Eq. (5.42).

For alternative treatments of the Uzawa–Lucas model, see Faig (1991) and Caballe and Santos (1993).

APPENDIX 5C
THE MODEL WITH REVERSED FACTOR INTENSITIES

We consider here the production structure from Eqs. (5.11) and (5.12) with the condition $\alpha < \eta$. Let $p \equiv \mu/\nu$ be the value of H in units of goods. We noted in the text that Eq. (5.18) is an unstable differential equation in p and that p always equals its steady-state value, which is given by

$$p = p^* = \psi^{1/(\alpha-\eta)} \cdot \left(\frac{\alpha}{1-\alpha}\right)^{(\alpha-\eta)/(1-\alpha+\eta)}, \tag{5C.1}$$

where

$$\psi \equiv \left(\frac{A}{B}\right) \cdot \left(\frac{\alpha}{\eta}\right)^\eta \cdot \left(\frac{1-\alpha}{1-\eta}\right)^{1-\eta}.$$

Equation (5.16) implies accordingly that $\nu K/uH$ always equals its steady-state value.

$$\frac{\nu K}{uH} = \left(\frac{\nu K}{uH}\right)^* = \left[\psi \cdot \left(\frac{\alpha}{1-\alpha}\right)\right]^{1/(1-\alpha+\eta)}. \tag{5C.2}$$

The rate of return and the growth rate of consumption are then constants, given by

$$r = r^* = \alpha A \cdot \left[\left(\frac{\nu K}{uH}\right)^*\right]^{\alpha-1} - \delta, \tag{5C.3}$$

$$\gamma_C = \gamma^* = (1/\theta) \cdot (r^* - \rho). \tag{5C.4}$$

We now show that full wealth, $K + pH$, and full output, $Q \equiv Y + p \cdot (\dot{H} + \delta H)$, always grow at the rate γ^*, that is, at the same rate as C. The analysis of consumer optimization from Chapter 2 applies if we think of households as earning the rate of return r on their full wealth, $K + pH$. (The wage rate on raw labor is 0 in this setting.) Equations (2.14) and (2.15) showed that consumption is a multiple of full wealth; moreover, the multiple is constant here because r is constant. Consequently, $K + pH$ grows at the same rate, γ^*, as C.

The Hamiltonian expression from Eq. (5.13) can be written as

$$J = u(C) \cdot e^{-\rho t} + \nu \cdot (Q - C) - \nu \delta \cdot (K + pH), \qquad (5C.5)$$

where

$$u(C) = \frac{C^{1-\theta} - 1}{1 - \theta}.$$

We can verify from the first-order conditions for optimization that $\dot{J} = \partial J / \partial t = -\rho \cdot u(C) \cdot e^{-\rho t}$. If we differentiate the right-hand side of Eq. (5C.5) with respect to time, use the first-order condition $\nu = C^{-\theta} e^{-\rho t}$, and simplify, then we get

$$(\dot{\nu}/\nu - \delta) \cdot [C + \delta \cdot (K + pH)] + \delta Q = (\dot{\nu}/\nu) \cdot Q + \dot{Q}.$$

If we use $\dot{\nu}/\nu = -(\rho + \theta \cdot \dot{C}/C)$ and rearrange terms, then we get a formula for the growth rate of Q:

$$\gamma_Q = (\delta + \rho + \theta \gamma_C) \cdot \left\{ 1 - \left(\frac{1}{Q} \right) \cdot [C + \delta \cdot (K + pH)] \right\}. \qquad (5C.6)$$

Since γ_C is constant and $K + pH$ is a constant, positive multiple of C, Eq. (5C.6) expresses γ_Q as a negative, linear function of C/Q.

One solution to Eq. (5C.6) is $\gamma_Q = \gamma_C = \gamma^*$, so that C/Q is the constant $(C/Q)^*$. Alternatively, if $C/Q < (C/Q)^*$, then Eq. (5C.6) implies $\gamma_Q > \gamma^*$ and $C/Q \to 0$, whereas $C/Q > (C/Q)^*$ implies $\gamma_Q < \gamma^*$ and $C/Q \to \infty$. Therefore, the stable path features $\gamma_Q = \gamma^*$ at all times.

If we use the relation between u and v from Eq. (5.15), then Eq. (5C.2) allows us to write u as a function of $\omega \equiv K/H$:

$$u = \frac{\eta \cdot (1 - \alpha)}{(\eta - \alpha)} - \left[\frac{\alpha \cdot (1 - \eta)}{(vK/uH)^* \cdot (\eta - \alpha)} \right] \cdot \omega. \qquad (5C.7)$$

Hence, the policy function for u is a closed-form, linear, negative function of ω. Since the intercept exceeds 1, Eq. (5C.7) determines a range of ω for which the indicated value of u is in the interior, $u \in (0, 1)$. The form of the equation implies that the width of this range diminishes to 0 as $\beta - \alpha$ approaches 0.

We can use the relation $v = (vK/uH)^* \cdot (u/\omega)$ along with Eq. (5C.7) to derive a formula for v:

$$v = -\frac{\alpha \cdot (1 - \beta)}{\beta - \alpha} + \left[\frac{\beta \cdot (1 - \alpha)}{\beta - \alpha} \right] \cdot \left[\left(\frac{vK}{uH} \right)^* \right] \cdot \left(\frac{1}{\omega} \right). \qquad (5C.8)$$

Hence, v is a positive, linear function of $1/\omega$ and therefore a decreasing function of ω. We can also verify that the solution for v is in the interior; that is, $v \in (0, 1)$, when $u \in (0, 1)$. (This result follows readily from Eq. [5.15].)

Equations (5.12) and (5.15) imply that the growth rate of H is given by

$$\gamma_H = B \cdot \left[\frac{\eta \cdot (1 - \alpha)}{\alpha \cdot (1 - \eta)} \right]^{\eta} \cdot \left[\left(\frac{vK}{uH} \right)^* \right]^{\eta} \cdot (1 - u) - \delta.$$

If we substitute for u from Eq. (5C.7), then we get

$$\gamma_H = -a_1 + a_2 \cdot \omega, \tag{5C.9}$$

where $a_1 > 0$, $a_2 > 0$ are constants. Thus, γ_H is a positive, linear function of ω.

Since full wealth, $K + pH$, grows at the constant rate γ^*, we have

$$\gamma^* = \left(\frac{\omega}{\omega + p} \right) \cdot \gamma_K + \left(\frac{p}{\omega + p} \right) \cdot \gamma_H.$$

Hence, the growth rate of K is given by

$$\gamma_K = \gamma^* + (\gamma^* - \gamma_H) \cdot (p/\omega).$$

If we substitute for γ_H from Eq. (5C.9), then we get

$$\gamma_K = \gamma^* - a_2 \cdot p + p \cdot (\gamma^* + a_1)/\omega. \tag{5C.10}$$

Thus, γ_K is a positive, linear function of $1/\omega$ and therefore an inverse function of ω. We can also use Eq. (5C.10) to determine a range of ω for which the inequality restriction $\gamma_K + \delta \geq 0$ is not binding.

To ascertain the dynamics of $\chi \equiv C/K$, note that the condition $Y = C + \dot{K} + \delta K$ implies

$$\chi = Av \cdot \left[\left(\frac{vK}{uH} \right)^* \right]^{\alpha - 1} - \delta - \gamma_K.$$

If we substitute for v from Eq. (5C.8) and for γ_K from Eq. (5C.10), then we get

$$\chi = \text{constant} + \left\{ A \cdot \left[\frac{\eta \cdot (1 - \alpha)}{\eta - \alpha} \right] \cdot \left[\left(\frac{vK}{uH} \right)^* \right]^{\alpha} - p \cdot (\gamma^* + a_1) \right\} \cdot \left(\frac{1}{\omega} \right), \tag{5C.11}$$

where $-a_1$ is the constant term in the expression for γ_H in Eq. (5C.9). If we substitute for a_1 and use the expression for p from Eq. (5C.1), then we can use the transversality condition—$r^* > \gamma^*$ in Eqs. (5C.3) and (5C.4)—to show that the term in the braces in Eq. (5C.11) is positive. Hence, χ is a positive, linear function of $1/\omega$ and therefore a negative function of ω.

PROBLEMS

5.1 A C.E.S. Production Function with Physical and Human Capital. Consider the C.E.S. production function in terms of physical capital, K, and human capital, H:

$$Y = A \cdot \left\{ a \cdot (bK)^{\psi} + (1 - a) \cdot [(1 - b) \cdot H]^{\psi} \right\}^{1/\psi}, \tag{1}$$

where $0 < a < 1, 0 < b < 1, \psi < 1$. Output can be used on a one-for-one basis for consumption and for investment in K and H. The depreciation rate for each type of capital is δ. Households have the usual infinite-horizon preferences, as in the Ramsey model. Assume initially that there are no irreversibility constraints on K and H, so that gross investment in either form of capital can be negative.

(a) Set up the Hamiltonian and find the first-order conditions.

(b) What is the optimal relation between K and H? Substitute this relation into Eq. (1) to get a relation between Y and K. What does this "reduced-form" production function look like?

(c) What is the steady-state value of the ratio of physical to human capital, $(K/H)^*$?

(d) Describe the behavior of the economy over time if the initial condition is such that $K(0)/H(0) < (K/H)^*$. What are the instantaneous rates of investment in each type of capital at time 0?

(e) Suppose that the inequality restrictions $I_K \geq 0$ and $I_H \geq 0$ apply. How do these constraints affect the dynamics if the economy begins with $K(0)/H(0) < (K/H)^*$?

5.2 Adjustment Costs for Human and Physical Capital. Consider the model from Section 5.1 in which consumables and physical and human capital are produced by the same technology. Imagine, however, that there are adjustment costs for changes in the two types of capital. The unit adjustment costs, analogous to the formulation discussed in Section 3.5 are $(b_K/2) \cdot (I_K/K)$ for K and $(b_H/2) \cdot (I_H/H)$ for H. Assume that the depreciation rates for each types of capital are 0.

(a) Discuss the parameters b_K and b_H. Which one would likely be larger?

(b) Suppose that $b_K = b_H$. Discuss the short-run dynamics if the economy begins with $K(0)/H(0) < (K/H)^*$. What if $K(0)/H(0) > (K/H)^*$?

(c) Suppose now that $b_K < b_H$. Redo part (b), and comment on the main differences in the results.

5.3 Externalities in Human Capital (Based on Lucas [1988]). The production function for the ith producer of goods is

$$Y_i = A \cdot (K_i)^\alpha \cdot (H_i)^\lambda \cdot H^\epsilon,$$

where $0 < \alpha < 1, 0 < \lambda < 1, 0 \leq \epsilon < 1$. The variables K_i and H_i are the inputs of physical and human capital used by firm i to produce goods, Y_i. The variable H is the economy's average level of human capital; the parameter ϵ represents the strength of the external effect from average human capital to each firm's productivity. Output from the goods sector can be used as consumables, C, or as gross investment in physical capital, I_K. Physical capital depreciates at the rate δ. The production function for human capital is

$$(I_H)_j = BH_j,$$

where H_j is the human capital employed by the jth producer of human capital. Human capital also depreciates at the rate δ. Households have the usual infinite-horizon preferences, as in the Ramsey model, with rate of time preference ρ and intertemporal-substitution parameter θ. Consider first a competitive equilibrium in which producers of Y and H act as perfect competitors.

(a) What is the steady-state growth rate of C, Y, and K? How does the answer depend on the size of the human-capital externality, that is, the parameter ϵ?

(b) What is the steady-state growth rate of H? Under what circumstances does H grow at the same rate as K in the steady state?

(c) How would the social planner's solution differ from the competitive one?

CHAPTER

6

TECHNOLOGICAL CHANGE: MODELS WITH AN EXPANDING VARIETY OF PRODUCTS

In Chapters 4 and 5, we studied models of endogenous growth in which diminishing returns to a broad concept of capital did not apply, at least asymptotically. This absence of diminishing returns meant that long-term per capita growth was feasible in the absence of technological progress. A different view is that the mere accumulation of capital—even a broad concept that includes human capital—cannot sustain growth in the long run because this accumulation must eventually encounter a significant decline in the rate of return. This view implies that we have to look to technological progress—continuing advances in methods of production and types and qualities of products—in order to escape from diminishing returns in the long run.

The exogenous rate of technological progress, x, determined the steady-state per capita growth rate in the Solow–Swan and Ramsey models in Chapters 1 and 2. In this and the next chapter, we describe recent theoretical advances that endogenize this process of technological improvement; that is, these models explain the origin of the parameter x. These theories therefore determine how government policies and other factors influence an economy's long-term per capita growth rate.

This chapter considers models in which technological progress shows up as an expansion of the number of varieties of producer and consumer products. We think of a change in this number as a basic innovation, akin to opening up a new industry. Of course, the identification of the state of technology with the number of varieties of products should be viewed as a metaphor; it selects one aspect of technical advance and thereby provides a tractable framework to study long-term growth.

The next chapter uses another metaphor in which progress shows up as quality improvements for an array of existing kinds of products. These quality enhancements represent the more or less continuous process of upgrading that occurs within an established industry. Thus, the approach in the next chapter should be viewed as complementary with the analysis of variety in this chapter.

6.1 MODELS WITH A VARIETY OF PRODUCER PRODUCTS

6.1.1 Production with a Fixed Number of Products

We follow Spence (1976), Dixit and Stiglitz (1977), Ethier (1982), and Romer (1987, 1990) by writing the production function for firm i as

$$Y_i = A \cdot L_i^{1-\alpha} \cdot \sum_{j=1}^{N} (X_{ij})^\alpha, \qquad (6.1)$$

where $0 < \alpha < 1$, Y_i is output, L_i is labor input, and X_{ij} is the employment of the jth type of specialized intermediate good.[1] The production function specifies diminishing marginal productivity of each input, L_i and X_{ij}, and constant returns to scale in all inputs together.

The additively separable form for the $(X_{ij})^\alpha$ means that the marginal product of intermediate good j is independent of the quantity employed of intermediate good j'. In this sense, a new type of product is neither a direct substitute for nor a direct complement with the types that already exist. We think that this specification is reasonable on average for breakthrough innovations, the kinds of changes that we wish to model in this chapter. In a particular case, a new product j may substitute for an existing good j' (that is, reduce the marginal product of $X_{j'}$) or complement the good (raise the marginal product of $X_{j'}$). But the independence of marginal products may hold in the average situation. This assumption of independence is important because it implies that discoveries of new types of goods do not tend to make any existing types obsolete.

---

[1]The basic approach to the benefits from variety comes from Spence (1976), although he dealt with consumer preferences and wrote utility as an integral over the various types (his equation [45]), rather than a sum. Dixit and Stiglitz (1977) refined Spence's analysis and used a form analogous to Eq. (6.1) to express consumer preferences over a variety of goods. Ethier (1982) applied this representation to inputs of production. Romer (1987, 1990) used Ethier's model with a variety of productive inputs in the context of technological change and economic growth.

In contrast, for the quality improvements that we study in the next chapter, a reasonable specification is that a good of superior quality is a close substitute for a good of lesser quality. This assumption means that the goods of lesser quality tend to become obsolete when the new, better kinds are invented.

In Eq. (6.1), the marginal product of each type of intermediate good, $\partial Y_i/\partial X_{ij}$, is infinite at $X_{ij} = 0$ and then diminishes as X_{ij} rises. If N types of goods are available at finite prices at the current time, then the firm will be motivated to use all N types.

Technological progress takes the form of expansions in N, the number of specialized intermediate goods available. To see the effect from an increase in N, suppose that the intermediate goods can be measured in a common physical unit and that all are employed in the same quantity, $X_{ij} = X_i$ (which turns out to be true in equilibrium). The quantity of output is then given from Eq. (6.1) by

$$Y_i = A \cdot L_i^{1-\alpha} \cdot N \cdot X_i^{\alpha} = A \cdot L_i^{1-\alpha} \cdot (NX_i)^{\alpha} \cdot N^{1-\alpha}. \qquad (6.2)$$

For given N, Eq. (6.2) implies that production exhibits constant returns to scale in L_i and NX_i, the total quantity of intermediate inputs. For given quantities of L_i and NX_i, the term $N^{1-\alpha}$ in Eq. (6.2) indicates that Y_i increases with N. This effect, which captures a form of technological progress, reflects the benefit from spreading a given total of intermediates, NX_i, over a wider range, N. The benefit arises because of the diminishing returns to each of the X_{ij} individually.

For fixed L_i, Eq. (6.2) implies that an expansion of intermediates, NX_i, encounters diminishing returns if it occurs through an increase in X_i (that is, in all of the X_{ij}) for given N. Diminishing returns do not arise, however, if the increase in NX_i takes the form of a rise in N for given X_i. Thus, technological change in the form of continuing increases in N avoids the tendency for diminishing returns. This property of the production function provides the basis for endogenous growth.

We shall find it convenient to think of the number of varieties, N, as continuous rather than discrete. This assumption is unrealistic if we view N as literally the number of kinds of intermediate goods employed, although the error would be small if N is large. More generally, N should be viewed as a tractable proxy for the technological complexity of the typical firm's production process or, alternatively, for the average degree of specialization of the factors employed by the typical firm. This broader notion of N would be continuous rather than discrete.[2]

We assume that the goods, Y_i, produced by all firms are physically identical. We also retain the assumptions of the one-sector production model in that Y, the ag-

---

[2]We could justify the continuous nature of N formally by shifting from the sum over a discrete number of types in Eq. (6.1) to an integral over a continuum of types:

$$Y_i = A \cdot (L_i)^{1-\alpha} \cdot \int_0^N [X_i(j)]^{\alpha} \, dj,$$

where j is the continuous index of type and N is the range of types available. We would get essentially the same results if we used this formulation instead of Eq. (6.1).

gregate of the outputs Y_i, can be used in a perfectly substitutable manner for various purposes. Specifically, this output can be used for consumption, for the production of intermediates, X_j, and later for the research and development (*R&D*) needed to invent new types of intermediates (that is, to expand N). We measure all prices in units of the homogeneous flow of goods, Y.

We could model the X_{ij} as service flows from durable goods. Firms would then rent the underlying capital goods, K_{ij}, and the total quantity of capital rented by firm i, $K_i = \sum_{j=1}^{N} K_{ij}$, would look like the capital input employed by firm i in our previous models. If we took this approach, then we would end up with a model with two state variables: the aggregate quantity of capital, K, and the number of varieties of goods, N. The model would then be similar to those studied in Chapter 5.

We shall find it more convenient to assume that the X_{ij} represent purchases of nondurable goods and services. This model and the one with durable intermediates turn out to yield similar insights about the determinants of technological change and economic growth. The model with nondurable inputs is simpler because it involves only a single state variable, the number of products, N.

The profit for a producer of final goods is

$$Y_i - wL_i - \sum_{j=1}^{N} P_j X_{ij},$$

where w is the wage rate, and P_j is the price of intermediate j. These producers are competitive and therefore take w and the prices P_j as given. Hence, we get the usual equations between factor prices and marginal products, and the resulting profit is zero.

The production function in Eq. (6.1) implies that the marginal product of the jth intermediate good is given by

$$\partial Y_i / \partial X_{ij} = A\alpha \cdot L_i^{1-\alpha} \cdot X_{ij}^{\alpha-1}. \tag{6.3}$$

The equation of this marginal product to P_j therefore implies

$$X_{ij} = L_i \cdot (A\alpha/P_j)^{1/(1-\alpha)}. \tag{6.4}$$

The equality between w and the marginal product of labor implies

$$w = (1 - \alpha) \cdot (Y_i/L_i). \tag{6.5}$$

6.1.2 Expansions in the Variety of Products

At a point in time, the technology exists to produce N varieties of intermediate goods. An expansion of the number N requires a technological advance in the sense of an invention or adaptation that permits the production of the new kind of intermediate good. We assume that this advance requires purposive effort in the form of research and development. A realistic description of this research process would include uncertainty about the quantity of resources required to generate an invention and about the success of the invention. We simplify the analysis, however, by assuming that it takes a deterministic amount of effort to generate a successful new product. (Chapter 7 considers a model in which the research process is subject to uncertainty.)

The deterministic framework for the invention of new products ultimately generates a smooth path for aggregate economic growth. Randomness in the discovery of new products eliminates the smoothness at the aggregate level and thereby induces variations of the growth rate around the long-term path. These variations would look like the fluctuations that occur in real business-cycle models. (See, for example, Kydland and Prescott [1982] and McCallum [1989].) Since we are primarily interested here in the determinants of long-term growth, we assume a deterministic R&D process in which the cyclical elements are not present.

We assume that the cost to create a new type of product is fixed at η units of Y.[3] The cost therefore does not depend on the number of goods, N, that have already been invented. The tendency to run out of new ideas suggests that the cost would rise with N. But if the concepts already discovered make it easier to come up with new ideas, then the cost could fall with N.[4] We assume here that these effects roughly cancel so that the cost of inventing a new good does not change over time. This assumption turns out to be consistent with a constant growth rate of aggregate output.

In order to motivate research, successful innovators have to be compensated in some manner. The basic problem is that the creation of a new idea or design, say for intermediate good j, is costly, but could then be used in a nonrival way by all potential producers of good j. That is, one producer's use of the design would not affect the output that could be generated for given inputs by other producers who use the design. It would be efficient *ex post* to make the existing discoveries freely available to all producers, but this practice fails to provide the *ex ante* incentives for further inventions. A tradeoff arises, as in the usual analysis of patents, between restrictions on the use of existing ideas and the rewards to inventive activity.

We assume that the inventor of good j retains a perpetual monopoly right over the production and sale of the good, X_j, that uses his or her design.[5] The flow of monopoly rentals will then provide the incentive for invention. The monopoly rights could be enforced through explicit patent protection or through secrecy. It would, in either case, be realistic to assume that the inventor's monopoly position lasts only for a finite time or erodes gradually over time. We consider this extension later in this chapter.

---

[3] We are, in other words, applying the assumptions of the one-sector production model to the use of output for R&D. Rivera-Batiz and Romer (1991) use this specification in one of their models.

[4] The assumption that the cost of inventing a new product declines is equivalent to the assumption that the cost is constant but that new products are more productive per unit than the old ones. Chapter 7 considers a model in which the new goods are more productive than the old goods.

[5] We assume for convenience that the inventor of the jth design is also the producer of the jth intermediate good. We would get the same results if we assumed instead that the inventor charged a royalty for the use of the design by competitive producers of goods.

Suppose that, once invented, an intermediate good of type j costs one unit of Y to produce.[6] The present value of the returns from discovering the jth intermediate good is then

$$V(t) = \int_t^\infty (P_j - 1) \cdot X_j \cdot e^{-\bar{r}(v,t) \cdot (v-t)} \, dv, \tag{6.6}$$

where X_j is the total quantity produced at each date, and $\bar{r}(v, t) \equiv [1/(v - t)] \cdot \int_t^v r(\omega) d\omega$ is the average interest rate between times t and v. If the interest rate equals a constant, r—which turns out to be true in the equilibrium—then the present-value factor simplifies to $e^{-r \cdot (v-t)}$. The equation shows that the fixed cost η for discovering a new good can be recouped only if the sales price, P_j, exceeds the marginal cost of production, 1, for at least part of the time after date t.

The monopolist sets the price P_j at each date to maximize $(P_j - 1) \cdot X_j$, where

$$X_j = \sum_i X_{ij} = (A\alpha/P_j)^{1/(1-\alpha)} \cdot \sum_i L_i = L \cdot (A\alpha/P_j)^{1/(1-\alpha)}$$

is the aggregate of the quantity demanded over the producers i from Eq. (6.4). (Since there are no state variables on the production side and no intertemporal elements in the demand function, the producer of X_j just selects P_j to maximize the flow of monopoly profit at each date.) The expression to maximize is therefore

$$(P_j - 1) \cdot L \cdot (A\alpha/P_j)^{1/(1-\alpha)},$$

and the solution for the monopoly price is

$$P_j = P = 1/\alpha > 1. \tag{6.7}$$

Hence, the price P_j is constant over time and the same for all intermediate goods j.

The monopoly price is the markup $1/\alpha$ on the marginal cost of production, 1. The price is the same for all goods j because the cost of production is the same for all goods and each good enters symmetrically into the production function in Eq. (6.1).

If we substitute for P_j from Eq. (6.7) into Eq. (6.4), then we can determine the aggregate quantity produced of each good:

$$X_j = X = L \cdot A^{1/(1-\alpha)} \cdot \alpha^{2/(1-\alpha)}. \tag{6.8}$$

The quantity X_j is the same for all goods and at all points in time (if L is constant).

If we substitute for P_j and X_j from Eqs. (6.7) and (6.8) into Eq. (6.6) and take the constant terms outside the integral, then the inventor's net present value at time t is given by

$$V(t) = L \cdot A^{1/(1-\alpha)} \cdot \left(\frac{1 - \alpha}{\alpha}\right) \cdot \alpha^{2/(1-\alpha)} \cdot \int_t^\infty e^{-\bar{r}(v,t) \cdot (v-t)} \, dv. \tag{6.9}$$

---

[6]We are, in other words, using the assumptions of the one-sector production model for the use of output as intermediate goods.

We assume that there is free entry into the business of being an inventor so that anyone can pay the R&D cost η to secure the net present value, $V(t)$, shown in Eq. (6.9). If $V(t) > \eta$, then an infinite amount of resources would be channeled into R&D at time t; hence, $V(t) > \eta$ cannot hold in equilibrium. If $V(t) < \eta$, then no resources would be devoted at time t to R&D, and, therefore, the number of goods, N, would not change over time.[7] We focus the main discussion on equilibria with positive R&D and, hence, growing N at all points in time. In these cases, $V(t) = \eta$ holds in Eq. (6.9) for all t; that is,

$$\eta = L \cdot A^{1/(1-\alpha)} \cdot \left(\frac{1-\alpha}{\alpha}\right) \cdot \alpha^{2/(1-\alpha)} \cdot \int_{t}^{\infty} e^{-\bar{r}(v,t)\cdot(v-t)}dv.$$

Everything except the integral in the above equation is assumed to be constant. The equation can therefore hold for all t only if the integral is constant, a condition that requires the interest rate, $r(t)$, to equal a constant, r.[8] The integral then simplifies to $1/r$. Hence, the condition $V(t) = \eta$ requires

$$r = (L/\eta) \cdot A^{1/(1-\alpha)} \cdot \left(\frac{1-\alpha}{\alpha}\right) \cdot \alpha^{2/(1-\alpha)}. \tag{6.10}$$

The underlying technology and market structure peg the rate of return at the value shown in Eq. (6.10) (assuming that the underlying growth rate of N is positive). The situation therefore parallels the one in the AK model of Chapter 4, in which the technology and incentives to invest pegged the rate of return at the value $A - \delta$.

The marginal $(N + 1^{st})$ intermediate good, which is just about to be discovered, generates a present value of monopoly profits that just covers the R&D cost, η. That is, $V(t) = \eta$ in Eq. (6.9). Since old and new products receive the same flow of monopoly profits, the present value of the profits for each existing intermediate good must also equal η. Hence, η is the market value of a firm that possesses the blueprint to produce one of the intermediate goods, and the aggregate market value of these firms is ηN. (Recall that firms own no capital, because there are no durable goods in the model.)

6.1.3 Households and Market Equilibrium

We assume, as usual, that households maximize utility over an infinite horizon:

$$U = \int_{0}^{\infty} \left(\frac{c^{1-\theta} - 1}{1 - \theta}\right) \cdot e^{-\rho t} \, dt, \tag{6.11}$$

where the rate of population growth, n, is 0. Households earn the rate of return r on assets and receive the wage rate w on the fixed aggregate quantity L of labor. In a

---

[7]The number of inventions, N, is not reversible. That is, it is impossible to forget some of the existing designs and thereby get a rebate on the R&D expenditures that went into the discovery of those designs. If N were reversible in this sense, then $V(t) = \eta$ would have to hold at all points in time.

[8]This result can be demonstrated by differentiating the integral, $I = \int_{t}^{\infty} e^{-\bar{r}(v,t)\cdot(v-t)} \, dv$, with respect to t. The result is $0 = dI/dt = -1 + r(t) \cdot I$. Therefore, $r(t) = r$, and $I = 1/r$.

closed economy, the total of households' assets equals the market value of the firms, ηN.[9] Saving equals investment, $\eta \dot{N}$, which equals the resources expended on R&D.

The key condition from households' optimization is the familiar expression for the growth rate of consumption:[10]

$$\gamma_C = (1/\theta) \cdot (r - \rho).$$

If we substitute for r from Eq. (6.10), then we get

$$\gamma = (1/\theta) \cdot \left[(L/\eta) \cdot A^{1/(1-\alpha)} \cdot \left(\frac{1-\alpha}{\alpha} \right) \cdot \alpha^{2/(1-\alpha)} - \rho \right]. \qquad (6.12)$$

We use the symbol γ, rather than γ_C, because this growth rate turns out to apply to the number of designs, N, and to total output, Y, as well as to aggregate consumption, C.

Equation (6.12) is valid only if the underlying parameters lead to $\gamma \geq 0$ in the equation. If $\gamma < 0$ were indicated, then potential inventors have insufficient incentive to expend resources on R&D and, hence, N stays constant. The growth rate, γ, then equals zero. We assume henceforth that $\gamma \geq 0$ applies in Eq. (6.12).

The present model, like the AK model, exhibits no transitional dynamics.[11] The number of varieties of goods, N, starts at some value $N(0)$ and then grows at the constant rate γ shown in Eq. (6.12). The level of aggregate output is determined from Eqs. (6.2) and (6.8) as

$$Y = A \cdot L^{1-\alpha} \cdot X^{\alpha} N = A^{1/(1-\alpha)} \cdot \alpha^{2\alpha/(1-\alpha)} \cdot LN. \qquad (6.13)$$

Thus, for fixed L, Y grows at the same rate as N.

The level of consumption, C, must satisfy the economy's budget constraint:

$$C = Y - \eta\gamma N - NX,$$

where $\eta\gamma N = \eta \dot{N}$ is the amount of resources devoted to R&D, and NX is the amount expended on intermediate goods. If we substitute for Y from Eq. (6.13), for γ from Eq. (6.12), and for X from Eq. (6.8), then we can simplify to get

$$C = (N/\theta) \cdot \left\{ L \cdot A^{1/(1-\alpha)} \cdot (1-\alpha) \cdot \alpha^{2\alpha/(1-\alpha)} \cdot [\theta - \alpha \cdot (1-\theta)] + \eta\rho \right\}. \qquad (6.14)$$

Equation (6.14) verifies that, for fixed L, C and N grow at the same rate, γ, shown in Eq. (6.12).[12]

---

[9]Since the factor prices equal the respective marginal products—Eqs. (6.4) and (6.5)—the households' aggregate income, $wL + r\eta N$, can be shown to equal the economy's net product, $Y - NX$.

[10]Recall that population and the labor force, L, are constant in the present model. The growth rate of consumption therefore equals the growth rate of per capita consumption.

[11]We demonstrate here that an equilibrium exists with no transitional dynamics. A proof that no other equilibria are possible can be constructed along the lines followed in Chapter 4. We leave this proof as an exercise.

[12]The transversality condition is $r > \gamma$. (Recall that population growth, n, equals zero.) Since $\gamma = (1/\theta) \cdot (r - \rho)$, the transversality condition can be written as $r \cdot (1 - \theta) < \rho$. Substitution for r from Eq. (6.10) leads to the inequality $(1 - \theta) \cdot L \cdot A^{1/(1-\alpha)} \cdot \alpha \cdot (1 - \alpha) \cdot \alpha^{2\alpha/(1-\alpha)} < \rho\eta$. This condition guarantees that the expression for the level of C in Eq. (6.14) is positive.

6.1.4   Determinants of the Growth Rate

Consider now the determinants of the growth rate, γ, shown in Eq. (6.12). The households' preference parameters, ρ and θ, and the level of the production technology, A, enter essentially in the same way as they did in the AK model, which we considered in Chapter 4. A greater willingness to save—lower ρ and θ—and a better technology—higher A—raise the growth rate.

A new effect involves the cost of inventing a new product, η. A decrease in η raises the rate of return, r, in Eq. (6.10) and therefore raises the growth rate, γ, in Eq. (6.12).

The model also contains a scale effect: a larger labor endowment, L, raises γ in Eq. (6.12). This scale effect is similar to those that arose in the model of learning-by-doing with spillovers and in the model of public goods in Chapter 4.[13] The present model has a scale effect because a new product, which costs η to invent, can be used in a nonrival manner across the entire economy. The larger the economy—represented by L—the lower the cost of an invention per unit of L (or Y). The cost of carrying out R&D per unit of economic activity is effectively η/L. An increase in L therefore has the same effect on γ in Eq. (6.12) as an equiproportionate decrease in η.

We already observed in Chapter 4 that scale effects are not supported empirically if we identify scale with the size of a country's population or economic activity. Countries may, however, not be the proper unit for measuring scale in the present context. The scale that matters in the model has two aspects: first, it involves the total of production over which a new idea can be used in a nonrival manner, and, second, it measures the scope of the inventor's property rights. If ideas flow readily across borders, then countries do not define the proper units in the first context. (We consider the diffusion of technology in Chapter 8.) Countries may also be inappropriate in the second context if patent protection applies internationally or if a monopoly position can be sustained worldwide by secrecy.

If the world operated as a single unit with respect to the flow of ideas and the maintenance of property rights, then L would be identified with world population or an aggregate of world economic activity. The model would then predict a positive relation between world per capita growth and the levels of world population or the aggregate of world output. See Kremer (1993) for an argument that this hypothesis may be correct.

6.1.5   Pareto Optimality

THE SOCIAL PLANNER'S PROBLEM. We now demonstrate that the outcomes in the decentralized economy are not Pareto optimal. We can, as usual, assess Pareto optimality by comparing the previous results—specifically, the growth rate γ shown

---

[13] As in these earlier models, the economy does not tend toward a steady state with constant per capita growth if we allow for growth in population, L, at a positive rate.

in Eq. (6.12)—with the results from the parallel problem for a hypothetical social planner.

The social planner seeks to maximize the utility of the representative household, as given in Eq. (6.11). The planner is constrained only by the economy's budget constraint:

$$Y = AL^{1-\alpha} \cdot NX^\alpha = C + \eta\dot{N} + NX. \tag{6.15}$$

We use the same production function as in Eq. (6.1), but we have already imposed the conditions $X_{ij} = X$ for all firms i and intermediate products j. We can readily show by optimizing with respect to each of the X_{ij} that the planner satisfies these conditions for efficient production. The right-hand side of Eq. (6.15) comprises the three possible uses of output: consumption, R&D, and intermediate goods.

The Hamiltonian expression for the social planner's problem can be written as

$$J = u(c) \cdot e^{-\rho t} + v \cdot (1/\eta) \cdot [AL^{1-\alpha} \cdot NX^\alpha - Lc - NX], \tag{6.16}$$

where the shadow price v applies to $\dot{N}$, and we substituted the condition $C = Lc$. The control variables are c and X, and the state variable is N.

The contrast with the decentralized solution involves the determination of X, the quantity of intermediates, and γ, the growth rate of N. The usual optimization conditions for the social planner lead to the formulas for X and γ:

$$X \text{ (social planner)} = LA^{1/(1-\alpha)} \cdot \alpha^{1/(1-\alpha)}, \tag{6.17}$$

$$\gamma \text{ (social planner)} = (1/\theta) \cdot \left[(L/\eta) \cdot A^{1/(1-\alpha)} \cdot \left(\frac{1-\alpha}{\alpha} \right) \cdot \alpha^{1/(1-\alpha)} - \rho \right]. \tag{6.18}$$

The choice of X in Eq. (6.17) implies that the level of output is

$$Y \text{ (social planner)} = A^{1/(1-\alpha)} \cdot \alpha^{\alpha/(1-\alpha)} \cdot LN. \tag{6.19}$$

In comparison with the social planner's choice in Eq. (6.17), the decentralized solution for X in Eq. (6.8) is multiplied by $\alpha^{1/(1-\alpha)} < 1$. Hence, the decentralized economy allocates fewer resources than the social planner to intermediates and therefore ends up with a lower level of output (Eq. [6.13] versus Eq. [6.19]). This gap represents the static efficiency loss from monopoly.

In the decentralized solution for the growth rate, Eq. (6.12), the first term inside the large brackets is the multiple $\alpha^{1/(1-\alpha)} < 1$ of the corresponding term for the social planner in Eq. (6.18). Recall that this term in Eq. (6.12) corresponded to the private rate of return, r, as given in Eq. (6.10). Thus, the decentralized economy has a lower growth rate than the planned economy, and the lower growth rate corresponds to a shortfall of the private rate of return from the rate of return implicitly used by the social planner. This social rate of return is the first term inside the brackets in Eq. (6.18):

$$r \text{ (social planner)} = (L/\eta) \cdot A^{1/(1-\alpha)} \cdot \left(\frac{1-\alpha}{\alpha} \right) \cdot \alpha^{1/(1-\alpha)}. \tag{6.20}$$

We encountered some models in Chapter 4 in which the private rate of return on investment differed from the social rate of return. In the model of learning-by-doing with spillovers, the gap reflected the uncompensated benefits that one producer conveyed to others. In the model with public goods, the gap resulted from the taxation of output. Other models featured negative externalities, for example, from congestion or pollution. In these cases, the private rate of return on investment exceeded the social return.

The model with inventions of new products and monopoly rights in these inventions generates a gap between social and private returns from a different source. The underlying distortion is the monopoly pricing of intermediates: the price P in Eq. (6.7) is the multiple $1/\alpha$ of the marginal cost of production, 1. The government could induce the private sector to attain the social optimum in a decentralized setting if it could engineer a tax-subsidy policy—a form of "industrial policy"—that induced marginal-cost pricing without eliminating the appropriate incentive for inventors to create new types of products.

SUBSIDIES TO PURCHASES OF INTERMEDIATE GOODS. Suppose that the economy is decentralized, but the government uses a lump-sum tax to finance a subsidy on the purchase of all varieties of intermediate goods. If the subsidy is at the rate $1 - \alpha$, then the producers of Y pay only αP for each unit of X. The demand, X_{ij} in Eq. (6.4), rises accordingly by the factor $(1/\alpha)^{1/(1-\alpha)}$. The equilibrium price P is still the multiple $1/\alpha$ of marginal cost, 1, but the equilibrium quantity, X in Eq. (6.8), is multiplied by the factor $(1/\alpha)^{1/(1-\alpha)}$ and thereby coincides with the social planner's choice in Eq. (6.17). This result follows because the user price of X, net of the public subsidy, equals 1.

The expansion of the quantity of intermediates, X, provides a static and a dynamic gain in efficiency. In a static context, with fixed N, the monopoly pricing implies that the marginal product of X exceeds its cost of production, 1, and therefore that the economy fails to maximize the goods available for consumption. If more output were allocated to X, then the expansion of Y on a more than one-for-one basis means that consumption could rise. The government's subsidy to purchases of X allows the economy to secure this static gain.

The higher level of X also has a dynamic effect that involves the incentive to expand N over time. The increase in the quantity of intermediates, X_j in Eq. (6.9), raises the flow of monopoly profit by the factor $(1/\alpha)^{1/(1-\alpha)}$. This increase in profit raises the rate of return, r, in Eq. (6.10) by the same factor; hence, the private rate of return coincides with the social rate of return, given in Eq. (6.20). It follows that the decentralized growth rate equals the social planner's growth rate, shown in Eq. (6.18). Thus, the public subsidy provides a dynamic gain in that N now grows at the efficient rate.

The result that the static and dynamic inefficiencies from monopoly can be eliminated with a single policy instrument depends on the underlying form of the production function in Eq. (6.1). In more general models, two instruments would be required. We show in a later section that, even if we maintain the form of Eq. (6.1), two policy instruments are required to attain a Pareto optimum if an inventor's monopoly position does not last forever.

SUBSIDIES TO FINAL PRODUCT. The government could also induce the private economy to attain the social optimum if it stimulated the demand for intermediates by subsidizing production. The required subsidy rate on output, Y_i, is $(1 - \alpha)/\alpha$, so that producers receive $1/\alpha$ units of revenue for each unit of goods produced.

SUBSIDIES TO RESEARCH. One policy that seems natural but that fails to achieve the social optimum in this model is a subsidy to research and development. If the government absorbs part of the cost of R&D, then a potential inventor lowers the net cost of research, η, accordingly in Eq. (6.10). This change can raise the privately chosen values of r and γ to equal the social planner's values. The problem is that the quantity of intermediates, X in Eq. (6.8), is still wrong from a social perspective due to monopoly pricing. Thus, although the economy grows at the "right" rate, it fails to achieve static efficiency because it allocates insufficient resources to intermediates for given N.

Although various governmental tax-subsidy policies can work in the model to improve allocations, the successful execution of these industrial policies would be difficult. The government not only has to subsidize the right things—basically the demands for the goods that are monopoly priced—but then has to finance the scheme with a nondistorting tax. If the tax were levied on output, then the scheme would be self-defeating. Moreover, in a more realistic model, the required subsidy would have to vary across factors of production or final products; in other words, the government would have to pick winners in an omniscient and benevolent manner. The next section illustrates this problem by allowing for a distinction between monopolized and competitive goods.

6.1.6   Erosion of Monopoly Power

Return now to the decentralized economy. We assumed before that the inventor of each intermediate good retained a perpetual monopoly over its use. More realistically, this position would erode over time as competitors learned about the new product (or new technique) and imitated it or created close substitutes. The temporary nature of patent protection would also matter in some areas.

A tractable way to model the gradual erosion of monopoly power is to assume that goods transform from monopolized to competitive with a probability that is generated from a Poisson process.[14] That is, if intermediate good j is presently monopolized, then this good becomes competitive in the next interval dT with probability $p \cdot dT$, where $p \geq 0$. Thus, if a good is invented at time t and is initially monopolized, then the probability of it still being monopolized at the future date $v \geq t$ is $e^{-p \cdot (v-t)}$. (The parameter p works just like the death probability that we used in the finite-horizon model of Chapter 3.)

---

[14]See Judd (1985) for a discussion of an analogous model.

A monopolized intermediate good sells as before at the markup price, $1/\alpha$. The quantity demanded of each monopolized intermediate, X^m, is still given by Eq. (6.8):

$$X^m = LA^{1/(1-\alpha)} \cdot \alpha^{2/(1-\alpha)}. \qquad (6.21)$$

In a monopolized state, the flow of profit is $[(1 - \alpha)/\alpha] \cdot X^m$, whereas, in a competitive state, the flow of profit is 0. The expected present value from the discovery of an (initially monopolized) intermediate good at time t is therefore a modification of Eq. (6.9) to include the probability term, $e^{-p \cdot (v-t)}$:

$$E[V(t)] = LA^{1/(1-\alpha)} \cdot \left(\frac{1-\alpha}{\alpha}\right) \cdot \alpha^{2/(1-\alpha)} \cdot \int_t^\infty e^{-[p + \bar{r}(v,t)] \cdot (v-t)} \, dv. \qquad (6.22)$$

We assume that potential inventors care only about the expectation $E[V(t)]$.[15] The free-entry condition with positive R&D therefore entails $E[V(t)] = \eta$, so that

$$\frac{\eta \alpha/(1-\alpha)}{L \cdot A^{1/(1-\alpha)} \cdot \alpha^{2/(1-\alpha)}} = \int_t^\infty e^{-[p + \bar{r}(v,t)] \cdot (v-t)} \, dv.$$

Since the left-hand side is constant, it follows that $r(t)$ equals the constant r (see footnote 8). Carrying out the integration implies that r must satisfy[16]

$$r + p = (L/\eta) \cdot A^{1/(1-\alpha)} \cdot \left(\frac{1-\alpha}{\alpha}\right) \cdot \alpha^{2/(1-\alpha)}. \qquad (6.23)$$

The result in Eq. (6.23) modifies Eq. (6.10) only by the addition of the parameter p on the left-hand side. Therefore, the temporary nature of the monopoly position lowers r from its previous value by the amount p. Recall also that the rate of return shown in Eq. (6.10) was already below the social rate of return given in Eq. (6.20). Consequently, the temporary nature of an innovator's monopoly position creates an even larger gap between the social and private rates of return. The reason is that, from a social perspective, the gain from a discovery is permanent, whereas, from a private standpoint, the reward is now temporary.

The constant rate of return determined in Eq. (6.23) implies, as usual, a constant growth rate of consumption:[17]

$$\gamma_C = (1/\theta) \cdot [(L/\eta) \cdot A^{1/(1-\alpha)} \cdot \left(\frac{1-\alpha}{\alpha}\right) \cdot \alpha^{2/(1-\alpha)} - p - \rho]. \qquad (6.24)$$

The growth rate of the number of intermediates, N, and the level of output, Y, no longer generally equals γ_C; to study these other growth rates, we have to analyze the breakdown of N into monopolized and competitive parts.

Let N^c be the number of intermediates that have become competitive, so that $N - N^c$ is the number that remain monopolized. The quantity produced of each

---

[15]This result is consistent with individual risk aversion because the risks are purely idiosyncratic and the ownership of firms is diversified.

[16]Equation (6.23) applies only if the next condition, Eq. (6.24), indicates $\gamma_C \geq 0$. Otherwise, $\gamma_C = 0$ and $r = \rho$.

[17]If Eq. (6.24) indicates $\gamma_C < 0$, then a corner solution applies with $\gamma_C = \gamma_N = \gamma_Y = 0$.

monopolized intermediate is the amount X^m shown in Eq. (6.21). For each competitive good, which is priced at marginal cost, 1, the quantity produced follows from Eq. (6.4) as

$$X^c = LA^{1/(1-\alpha)} \cdot \alpha^{1/(1-\alpha)} > X^m. \tag{6.25}$$

The level of aggregate output can be computed from Eqs. (6.1), (6.21), and (6.25) as

$$Y = A^{1/(1-\alpha)} \cdot \alpha^{2\alpha/(1-\alpha)} \cdot LN \cdot [1 + (N^c/N) \cdot (\alpha^{-\alpha/(1-\alpha)} - 1)]. \tag{6.26}$$

Hence, for given N, Y exceeds the quantity shown in Eq. (6.13) if $N^c > 0$ (because $0 < \alpha < 1$). Moreover, Y rises with N^c/N for given N; this effect represents the static gain from shifting from monopoly to competition in the provision of the existing intermediate goods.

Since each monopolized good becomes competitive with the probability p per unit of time, the change in N^c over time can be approximated (if $N - N^c$ is large) by

$$\dot{N^c} \approx p \cdot (N - N^c). \tag{6.27}$$

Finally, the model is closed by using the economy's budget constraint to determine the level of C :

$$C = Y - \eta \dot{N} - N^c X^c - (N - N^c) \cdot X^m; \tag{6.28}$$

that is, consumption equals output, Y, less R&D spending, $\eta \dot{N}$, less production of competitive intermediates, $N^c X^c$, less production of monopolized intermediates, $(N - N^c) \cdot X^m$.

The model contains two state variables, N and N^c, and features a transitional dynamics in which the ratio N^c/N approaches its steady-state value, $(N^c/N)^*$. In this respect, the model resembles the two-sector framework discussed in Chapter 5 in which the ratio of the two types of capital goods, K/H, adjusts gradually toward $(K/H)^*$. In the present context, the transitional analysis is cumbersome, and we limit attention to the characteristics of the steady state.

In the steady state, N, N^c, Y, and C all grow at the rate γ_C shown in Eq. (6.24). That is, $\gamma^* = \gamma_C$ is the steady-state growth rate of all the quantities. Equation (6.27) implies accordingly

$$(N^c/N)^* = \frac{p}{\gamma^* + p}. \tag{6.29}$$

Thus, the competitive fraction rises with the rate, p, at which goods become competitive and falls with the rate, γ^*, at which new (monopolized) intermediates are discovered.

If we substitute for N^c/N from Eq. (6.29) into Eq. (6.26), then we can determine a formula for output in the steady state:

$$Y^* = A^{1/(1-\alpha)} \cdot \alpha^{2\alpha/(1-\alpha)} \cdot LN \cdot \left[1 + \left(\frac{p}{\gamma^* + p}\right) \cdot \left(\alpha^{-\alpha/(1-\alpha)} - 1\right)\right]. \tag{6.30}$$

(Note that Y^* grows at the same rate as N.) If $p = 0$, so that $(N^c/N)^* = 0$ (see Eq. [6.29]), then the expression for Y^* is the same as that shown in Eq. (6.13) for the pure monopoly model. If $p \to \infty$—so that intermediates become competitive instantly and, hence, $(N^c/N)^* = 1$—then the formula for Y^* approaches the social planner's expression in Eq. (6.19). The difficulty, however, is that $p \to \infty$ also implies $\gamma^* = 0$.[18] In other words, if p had always been infinite, then nothing would ever have been invented, and N in Eq. (6.29) would equal the endowed value, $N(0)$, which predates any purposive R&D activity.

In the pure monopoly model, we showed that the social optimum can be attained if the government uses a lump-sum tax to finance a subsidy at the rate $1 - \alpha$ on purchases of intermediate goods. In the present context, this subsidy has to be limited to purchases of the monopolized intermediates. The selection of which goods to subsidize is feasible in the model—because goods can be observed to be either completely monopolized or completely competitive—but would be a challenge in practice.

In any event, a subsidy at the rate $1 - \alpha$ on the monopolized intermediates does not attain the social optimum because the term p still leaves a gap between the social rate of return (equation [6.20]) and the private rate of return (Eq. [6.23] with $\alpha^{2/(1-\alpha)}$ replaced by $\alpha^{1/(1-\alpha)}$). To reach the social optimum, the government would also have to subsidize research spending to raise the private rate of return on R&D by the amount p. In other words, two policy instruments are now required—one that encourages production of the monopolized intermediates and another that stimulates R&D.

The government can also affect the parameter p directly by attempting to curb monopoly power, for example, through anti-trust enforcement or limitations on patent protection. An increase in p involves the usual tradeoff that appears in models of optimal patent policy—the static gain from increased competition versus the dynamic loss from too low a rate of growth of new products (see, for example, Reinganum [1989]).[19] This analysis is difficult because it encounters time-consistency problems: the government would like to eliminate all existing monopoly power—make the N existing products available at a competitive price—but then promise protection of property rights over future inventions. Such promises tend, of course, not to be credible. One possible way to proceed is to assume that the government commits itself not to change the probability p for existing products, but can choose this probability for goods that are yet to be invented. This analysis has not yet been fully worked out.

6.1.7 Romer's Model of Technological Change

Return now to the setting in which the intermediate goods are permanently monopolized ($p = 0$). This model is similar to the one constructed by Romer (1990), but

---

[18]A large value of p implies $r < 0$ in Eq. (6.23) and $\gamma_C < 0$ in Eq. (6.24). The equilibrium is then the corner solution in which inventors spend 0 on R&D (because they cannot spend a negative amount), so that N stays constant and $\gamma^* = 0$.

[19]In the present setting, a reduced rate of innovation constitutes a social loss. In other contexts, such as the model considered in Chapter 7, a reduced rate of innovation may be desirable.

differs in the specification of the R&D costs.[20] We assumed a one-sector production model in which R&D is one of the uses of the flow of current output, Y. The cost of R&D was therefore a fixed amount, η, in units of Y. The underlying assumption was that the technology that uses research to create new products or ideas has the same factor intensities as the technologies that generate consumables and intermediate goods. Rivera-Batiz and Romer (1991) describe this specification as the lab-equipment model of R&D.

Romer (1990) assumes instead that the invention of a new product requires a specified amount of human capital, rather than output, Y, and that human capital is in fixed aggregate supply. We get the same kind of results if we assume that an invention requires a specified amount of raw labor, L, the input that is in fixed aggregate supply in our model.

Romer's idea is that the research sector is relatively intensive in human capital. It seems reasonable, however, that the intermediate inputs, X_j, would also contribute something to this sector. After all, these intermediates would include computers and other types of "lab equipment" that make researchers more productive. The extreme assumption that R&D uses only a fixed resource like L must therefore be regarded as a tractable approximation to the idea that R&D is intensive in human capital relative to the sectors that produce consumables and intermediate goods.

If R&D requires a fixed quantity of L, then the cost of R&D in units of goods depends on the wage rate, w. Equations (6.5) and (6.13) imply that the wage rate is given by

$$w = A^{1/(1-\alpha)} \cdot (1 - \alpha) \cdot \alpha^{2\alpha/(1-\alpha)} \cdot N. \tag{6.31}$$

Hence, growth of N at the rate γ leads to growth of w at the rate γ.

If the invention of a new product requires a fixed quantity of L, then the growth of w at the rate γ implies that η, the R&D cost in units of goods, rises at the rate γ. This rise in η means that new inventions eventually are not worth the expense; hence, N would approach a constant, and the growth rate, γ, would approach 0. Thus, if we modified the setup to peg the R&D cost in units of L, then the model would no longer generate endogenous growth.

Romer's (1990) model generates endogenous growth because of another difference in specification from our setup. He assumes that the cost of inventing a new product declines as society accumulates more ideas, represented by the number of products, N. Specifically, the assumption is that the R&D cost is proportional to w/N. Since w is proportional to N in Eq. (6.31), the end result is that the cost of inventing a new product remains constant over time in units of goods. Thus, this specification is consistent with a constant growth rate, γ, of N and Y.

Although the growth rate is constant in equilibrium, the determination of this growth rate in a decentralized economy involves a new type of externality: an individual's decision to conduct R&D and therefore to expand N reduces the required

---

[20]Romer (1990) treats the intermediate goods as infinite-lived durables, rather than nondurables, but this difference does not affect the main results.

amount of labor needed for subsequent inventions. Current research therefore has a positive spillover on the productivity of future research. The failure of the decentralized economy to compensate researchers for this spillover benefit constitutes another form of distortion. A government policymaker who seeks to guide the decentralized economy therefore has to worry about this spillover effect in addition to the monopoly pricing of intermediate goods.

We now provide the formal structure and solution of the Romer model. Because the analytical methods are basically the same as those considered earlier in this chapter, we omit some of the details.

The production function for firm i is again given by Eq. (6.1), and the demand function for X_{ij} is still given by Eq. (6.4). If η/N is the quantity of labor required to invent a new product, then the cost of an invention in units of goods is $w\eta/N$, where w is the wage rate, which equals the marginal product of labor.

The present value, $V(t)$, for an inventor at time t is now equated to $w\eta/N$, rather than η.

Monopoly pricing still dictates the markup formula for P in Eq. (6.7). The quantity of each intermediate is modified from Eq. (6.8) to

$$X = (L - L_R) \cdot A^{1/(1-\alpha)} \cdot \alpha^{2/(1-\alpha)}, \tag{6.32}$$

where L_R is the part of the aggregate labor force, L, that is employed in the research sector. Thus, X depends on the total quantity of labor, $L - L_R$, that is employed in the production of goods. The formula for X implies that the present value for an inventor is

$$V(t) = (L - L_R) \cdot A^{1/(1-\alpha)} \cdot \left(\frac{1-\alpha}{\alpha}\right) \cdot \alpha^{2/(1-\alpha)} \cdot (1/r).$$

The wage rate, w, equals $\partial Y_i/\partial L_i$, which corresponds to the expression given in Eq. (6.31). (This formula is correct even though X in Eq. (6.32) depends on $L - L_R$ rather than L.) The cost of an invention is therefore

$$w\eta/N = \eta A^{1/(1-\alpha)} \cdot (1 - \alpha) \cdot \alpha^{2\alpha/(1-\alpha)}.$$

The condition $V(t) = w\eta/N$—which must hold if N is growing for all t—then implies

$$r = \alpha \cdot (L - L_R)/\eta. \tag{6.33}$$

A single invention requires η/N units of labor. The change in N is given accordingly by

$$\dot{N} = L_R \cdot (N/\eta)$$

or, in other words,

$$\gamma = \dot{N}/N = L_R/\eta. \tag{6.34}$$

We can use the condition $\gamma = (1/\theta) \cdot (r - \rho)$—which applies because C and N again grow at the same rate—in conjunction with Eqs. (6.33) and (6.34) to get the solutions for the decentralized economy:

$$\gamma = (\alpha L/\eta - \rho)/(\theta + \alpha),$$

$$r = \alpha \cdot (\theta L/\eta + \rho)/(\theta + \alpha), \qquad (6.35)$$

$$L_R = (\alpha L - \eta\rho)/(\theta + \alpha).$$

The result for the growth rate, γ, is in many respects similar to that obtained in Eq. (6.12) for the decentralized economy when the R&D cost was fixed in terms of goods rather than labor. The similarities are first, γ is higher if households are more willing to save (lower ρ or θ); second, γ is higher if η, the cost of R&D, is lower; and third, there is a scale effect in that γ is higher if L is higher. In Romer's version of the model, we would interpret L as human capital rather than raw labor.

One difference in the results is that γ in Eq. (6.35) is independent of the productivity parameter, A, that appears in the production function for goods (Eq. [6.1]). This result follows only because we assumed that the research sector used no intermediate goods as inputs. If intermediates entered as productive inputs in this sector (even if less intensively than in the goods sector), then an increase in A would raise γ.

To clarify the distortions in the Romer model we can consider the social planner's problem. The social planner seeks to maximize the representative household's utility, subject to the constraints

$$Y = A \cdot (L - L_R)^{(1-\alpha)} \cdot NX^\alpha = C + NX,$$

$$\dot{N} = NL_R/\eta.$$

The control variables are C, X, and L_R, and the state variable is N. If we invoke the usual optimization conditions, then we find that the solutions are

$$X \text{ (social planner)} = (L - L_R) \cdot A^{1/(1-\alpha)} \cdot \alpha^{1/(1-\alpha)},$$

$$\gamma \text{ (social planner)} = (1/\theta) \cdot (L/\eta - \rho), \qquad (6.36)$$

$$L_R \text{ (social planner)} = (1/\theta) \cdot (L - \rho\eta).$$

The choice of γ in Eq. (6.36) corresponds to an implicit social rate of return of L/η.

The social planner's growth rate in Eq. (6.36) exceeds the decentralized growth rate in Eq. (6.35). The gap between the growth rates reflects the excess of the social planner's choice of L_R over the privately determined value of L_R. The improper allocation of labor between production $(L - L_R)$ and research (L_R) reflects the underlying distortions: monopoly pricing and research spillovers. To clarify the nature of these distortions, we can consider the policies that would cause the decentralized outcomes to coincide with the Pareto-optimal choices made by the social planner.

A policymaker can again neutralize the direct effect of monopoly pricing by using a lump-sum tax to subsidize the purchase of intermediate goods at the rate $1 - \alpha$. This subsidy would equate the privately chosen X to the social planner's value shown in Eq. (6.36) *if the values of L_R were the same*. Since these values are not the same, the choices of X will still diverge. The subsidy at rate $1 - \alpha$ for purchases of intermediate goods raises the decentralized values of the rate of return and the growth rate above the values shown in Eq. (6.35).[21] The increase in the growth rate corresponds to an expansion of L_R; nevertheless, the value of L_R remains below the social planner's value shown in Eq. (6.36). This remaining shortfall of L_R reflects the research spillovers that have yet to be internalized.

The elimination of the remaining distortion requires another form of subsidy, one that applies directly to research. The required rate of subsidy on R&D spending turns out to be $(1/\theta) \cdot [1 - (\rho\eta/L)]$. This subsidy provides a sufficient incentive for research so that the decentralized growth rate coincides with the social planner's choice shown in Eq. (6.36).[22] Equivalently, the private rate of return becomes $r = L/\eta$, the rate of return that was used implicitly by the social planner in the determination of γ.

The call for a subsidy to research because of positive spillovers is analogous to the argument for a subsidy on purchases of capital goods or output in the model with positive spillovers in production in Chapter 4. We noted in that model that spillovers in production could be negative as well as positive and, hence, that a tax would sometimes be more desirable than a subsidy. The research sector is perhaps more compelling as an area in which spillovers would typically be positive and significant: ideas are fundamentally nonrival and flow readily across researchers, and discoveries often build on the breakthroughs made by predecessors. A successful subsidy policy is nevertheless difficult to implement because it requires the government to identify promising areas of research that have substantial spillover benefits, and it assumes that the necessary public finance will not have distorting influences that outweigh the benefits from the internalization of the spillovers.

The next chapter brings out another potential drawback from research subsidies: the private benefit from innovation can be too high because it includes the transfer of rents from an existing monopolist to the innovator. This kind of effect can also arise in models in which competitive researchers race to discover a new product or process (see Reinganum [1989] for a survey).

---

[21] If the subsidy is at the rate σ, then the quantity demanded of the jth intermediate good is modified from Eq. (6.4) to $X_j = (L - L_R) \cdot [A\alpha/P(1 - \sigma)]^{1/(1-\alpha)}$. If we substitute the monopoly-pricing formula, $P = 1/\alpha$, then $\sigma = 1 - \alpha$ would equate X_j to the social planner's value of X shown in Eq. (6.36), if L_R equaled the social planner's value. Since the subsidy at rate $1 - \alpha$ affects X_j, it modifies the wage rate from Eq. (6.31) to $w = A^{1/(1-\alpha)} \cdot (1 - \alpha) \cdot \alpha^{\alpha/(1-\alpha)} \cdot N$. If we substitute the new values of X and w into the free-entry condition, $V(t) = \eta$, then we can determine the growth rate to be $\gamma = [1/(1+\theta)] \cdot [(L/\eta) - \rho]$, which can be shown to exceed the value shown in Eq. (6.35), but to fall short of the social planner's value shown in Eq. (6.36).

[22] If R&D expenditures are subsidized at the rate σ', then the effective cost of R&D becomes $\eta \cdot (1 - \sigma')$. If we also use the results for X and w described in footnote 21, then the free-entry condition, $V(t) = 0$, can be shown to imply that the decentralized growth rate is $\gamma = [(L/\eta) - \rho \cdot (1 - \sigma')]/[1 + \theta \cdot (1 - \sigma')]$. We can then show that $\sigma' = (1/\theta) \cdot [1 - (\rho\eta/L)]$ equates this growth rate to the social planner's value shown in Eq. (6.36).

6.2 MODELS WITH A VARIETY OF CONSUMER PRODUCTS

Spence (1976) originally applied his model to a variety of consumer products, and this setting has been used to study technological change and economic growth by Grossman and Helpman (1991, Ch. 3). We now introduce a variety of consumer goods into the utility function in a manner that parallels the treatment of a variety of intermediate products in the production function, Eq. (6.1). Our final conclusion, however, is that this extension does not generate new insights and that the framework with producer intermediates is more straightforward.

6.2.1 Varieties of Consumer Goods

We have assumed thus far that household i's utility depends on its consumption, c_i. We now assume that consumer goods come in numerous varieties and that the household cares about an index of these varieties, given by

$$\tilde{c}_i = \left[\sum_{j=1}^{M} (c_{ij})^\epsilon \right]^{1/\epsilon}, \tag{6.37}$$

where c_{ij} is household i's consumption of goods of type j, M is the number of types available at the current time, and $0 < \epsilon \leq 1$. Equation (6.37) implies that a doubling of each of the c_{ij}, for given M, doubles the index, $\tilde{c}_i$. The index increases with each of the c_{ij} individually, but at a nonincreasing rate. A higher ϵ signifies that the goods are better substitutes in consumption; $\epsilon = 1$ corresponds to the standard case in which the index, $\tilde{c}_i$, equals the household's total consumption, $c_i = \sum_{j=1}^{M} c_{ij}$.

The household's utility is now given by

$$U_i = \int_0^\infty \left[\frac{(\tilde{c}_i)^{1-\theta} - 1}{1 - \theta} \right] \cdot e^{-\rho t} \, dt. \tag{6.38}$$

To see the nature of the utility function with a variety of consumer goods, suppose that the c_{ij} are measured in a common physical unit and that the quantities consumed of each type are the same, $c_{ij} = c_i/M$. The flow of utility, which appears inside the integral, can then be written as

$$[M^{(1-\epsilon)\cdot(1-\theta)/\epsilon} \cdot c_i^{(1-\theta)} - 1]/(1 - \theta).$$

If M is constant, then this formulation is equivalent to the standard one without varieties, and the parameter θ again governs a household's willingness to substitute its total consumption, c_i, over time. For given c_i, the effect of an increase in the number of varieties is given by the derivative of the above expression with respect to M:

$$[(1 - \epsilon)/\epsilon] \cdot M^{[(1-\epsilon)\cdot(1-\theta)/\epsilon - 1]} \cdot c_i^{(1-\theta)} > 0.$$

Thus, the formulation captures the idea that consumers like variety. In the model with producer intermediates, the parallel idea is that variety is productive.

We assume, as before, that the invention of a new product—an increase in M—requires η units of goods. The inventor retains a perpetual monopoly in the production of the associated nondurable consumer good, C_j. The marginal cost of production of each consumer good is 1, and the producer selects the consumer price, P_j, to maximize the flow of monopoly profit. The choice of P_j depends on the form of the households' demand function for C_j. We now consider the form of this demand function.

We can set up a Hamiltonian expression to assess the household's maximization of utility:

$$J = \left\{ \frac{\left[\sum_{j=1}^{M} (c_{ij})^{\epsilon} \right]^{(1-\theta)/\epsilon} - 1}{(1-\theta)} \right\} \cdot e^{-\rho t} + \nu \cdot \left[w + ra - \sum_{j=1}^{M} P_j c_{ij} \right], \quad (6.39)$$

where a is assets per person, and the expression in brackets at the far right equals $\dot{a}$. The new element is that the household chooses an array of consumptions, c_{ij}, when faced at each date by a corresponding array of prices, P_j.

If we compute the first-order optimization condition with respect to c_{ij} and divide it by the corresponding condition with respect to c_{ik}, then we get

$$c_{ij}/c_{ik} = (P_j/P_k)^{-1/(1-\epsilon)}$$

for all $j, k = 1, \ldots, M$. We can use this result to derive the consumer's demand function for the jth good:

$$c_{ij} = \left\{ \frac{\sum_{k=1}^{M} P_k c_{ik}}{\sum_{k=1}^{M} (P_k)^{-\epsilon/(1-\epsilon)}} \right\} \cdot (P_j)^{-1/(1-\epsilon)}. \quad (6.40)$$

The ratio of sums is roughly the household's total expenditure in relation to the number of goods.

We assume that the number of products, M, is sufficiently large so that the producer of good j can neglect the effect of P_j on the households' total spending per variety of good, that is, on the ratio of sums given in Eq. (6.40). Consumer demand then has the constant elasticity $-1/(1 - \epsilon)$ with respect to P_j. (Since $0 < \epsilon \leq 1$, the magnitude of the elasticity of demand exceeds one.) The monopoly producer of good j determines the profit-maximizing consumer price in the same way as in the model with a variety of intermediate products. The result, which parallels Eq. (6.7), is a markup on the unit marginal cost of production:

$$P_j = 1/\epsilon. \quad (6.41)$$

Since the prices of all consumer goods are equal and the goods enter symmetrically into the utility function, the quantities consumed are the same: $c_{ij} = c_i/M$. We can use the remaining optimization conditions associated with the Hamiltonian in Eq. (6.39) to determine the evolution of c_i over time. The first condition is

$$\nu P = M^{(1-\epsilon) \cdot (1-\theta)/\epsilon} \cdot (c_i)^{-\theta} \cdot e^{-\rho t}.$$

This condition comes from setting the derivative of J with respect to c_{ij} equal to zero and then substituting $c_{ij} = c_i/M$ for all goods j. The second condition is the usual one associated with the state variable a:

$$\dot{\nu} = -r\nu.$$

We can use the two conditions together to determine

$$\dot{c}_i/c_i = (1/\theta) \cdot \left\{ r - \rho + \left[\frac{(1 - \epsilon) \cdot (1 - \theta)}{\epsilon} \right] \cdot (\dot{M}/M) \right\}. \qquad (6.42)$$

Since c_i represents the consumer's aggregate consumption, the growth rate of any of the individual varieties is given by

$$(\dot{c_i/M})/(c_i/M) = \dot{c}_i/c_i - (\dot{M}/M) = (1/\theta) \cdot [r - \rho - \frac{(\theta + \epsilon - 1)}{\epsilon} \cdot (\dot{M}/M)]. \quad (6.43)$$

We now consider the incentives for invention. The net present value, $V(t)$, for an inventor of a new consumer good at time t is the same as in Eq. (6.6), except that X_j is replaced by C_j, the aggregate sales of the jth consumer good. If r is constant, then the free-entry condition is

$$\eta \geq [(1 - \epsilon)/\epsilon] \cdot \int_t^\infty C_j e^{-r \cdot (v - t)} \, dv, \qquad (6.44)$$

where we substituted $P_j = 1/\epsilon$ from Eq. (6.41). The condition in Eq. (6.44) holds with equality if $\dot{M} > 0$. In this case, C_j is constant and given by

$$C_j = C/M = r\eta\epsilon/(1 - \epsilon), \qquad (6.45)$$

where C is aggregate consumption. (The analogous condition held in the model with intermediate inputs; see Eqs. [6.8] and [6.10].)

If C_j is constant and population is constant, then the consumption of good j by individual i, $c_{ij} = c_i/M$, must also be constant; hence, the growth rate of c_i/M, shown in Eq. (6.43), is 0. If we set the right-hand side of this equation to 0 and assume $\theta + \epsilon \neq 1$, then we get an expression for the growth rate of aggregate consumption:

$$\dot{C}/C = \dot{M}/M = \frac{\epsilon}{(\theta + \epsilon - 1)} \cdot (r - \rho). \qquad (6.46)$$

Note that all of the growth in C occurs through expansions of variety, M, and none through increases in the quantity consumed of each type, C/M.

We assume now that $\theta + \epsilon > 1$. (Since $\epsilon > 0$, this inequality must hold if $\theta \geq 1$.) If $\theta + \epsilon > 1$, then Eq. (6.46) relates the growth rate of consumption in the familiar positive way to $r - \rho$. The only difference from the standard model with one type of consumer good is that the coefficient on $r - \rho$ is $\epsilon/(\theta + \epsilon - 1)$, rather than $1/\theta$. If $\epsilon = 1$—so that variety does not matter and only the total of consumption, $\sum_{j=1}^{M} c_{ij}$, enters into utility—then the coefficient is again $1/\theta$.

The possibilities for endogenous growth depend on the production side of the model. In the simplest case, aggregate output, Y, is constant. That is, the quantity of labor, L, is given, and productivity does not change through capital accumulation, exogenous technological progress, or expansions in the variety of intermediate inputs. This economy cannot, by construction, exhibit growth in Y, but we want to examine whether it can sustain growth in M. If M were to grow at a positive rate in the steady state, then the flow of utility would rise continually. In effect, the expansion of variety would steadily decrease the cost of utils in terms of goods. Output deflated by a suitable price index—the cost of utils in terms of goods—would then be growing even though output was constant in a physical sense.

The given total of output, Y, can be allocated to R&D expenditure, $\eta \dot{M}$, or to aggregate consumption, $C = M \cdot (C/M)$, where C/M is the quantity produced of each variety. In the steady state, r is constant and, therefore, C/M is constant (see Eq. [6.45]). If we conjecture $r > \rho$ in the steady state, then C and M would rise at the constant rate $\gamma > 0$ in accordance with Eq. (6.46). The increase in C means that fewer resources are available for R&D and, hence, that $\dot{M}/M$ must fall, which is a contradiction. Thus, a situation with $r > \rho$ cannot be a steady state.

If the economy begins with a low value of M in relation to L, then $r > \rho$ and $\dot{M} > 0$ would apply initially if the resources required for R&D were not too large. The economy then approaches a steady state in which $r = \rho$, M is constant, R&D outlays are zero, and all of the given output, Y, goes to consumption, C. This model therefore cannot sustain positive growth of M in the steady state.

A one-time increase in L has a scale effect in the model. In the steady state, $r = \rho$ and $C = Y$ apply. C/M is pegged at the value shown in Eq. (6.45). Therefore, the one-time increases in L and Y lead to an equiproportionate increase in M in the steady state. Each household ends up with the same total of consumption, C/L, but the composition changes to less of each type, C/LM, and a greater number of varieties, M. The form of the utility function (Eqs. [6.37] and [6.38]) implies that households like this exchange; that is, the level of utility rises for each household.

The source of the scale effect is the same as that in the model with producer intermediates: a larger L means that the fixed cost of inventing a new product can be spread over a larger market. The difference is that the scale variable affects the level of well-being, not the growth rate, in the steady state.

It is worth noting that the outcomes are Pareto optimal in this model despite the monopoly pricing of the consumer goods. The markup over marginal cost of each price, P_j, by the factor $1/\epsilon$ does not affect the relative prices of the goods. Thus, there are no distortions that involve the composition of demand;[23] such distortions would arise if some of the goods were produced competitively. Monopoly pricing affects the price of consumption relative to leisure because the wage rate is determined competitively. No distortions arise in this context, however, because the quantity of labor supplied, L, is assumed to be unresponsive to price changes.

We showed before, with a fixed total output, Y, that M could grow in the steady state only if the cost of R&D in units of goods declined over time. We can relate this

---

[23]The model with producer intermediates was different because the monopoly pricing affected the price of intermediate goods relative to the value of producer output. Hence, the demand for intermediate goods was distorted in that model.

finding to the earlier model with producer intermediates if we think of the various costs in terms of utils rather than goods. We already observed that expansions of M reduce the cost of utils in terms of goods; that is, the economy gets more efficient at producing utils. If the cost of R&D were pegged in units of utils, rather than goods, then an increase in M would lower the cost of R&D in terms of goods. Growth in M could then occur in the steady state.

The specification in which the R&D cost is pegged in terms of utils parallels the first model that we constructed earlier to analyze producer intermediates. In that case, an expansion of the number of varieties, N, made the economy more efficient at using labor to produce goods. Since η, the cost of R&D, was pegged in terms of goods, the economy also became more efficient at using labor to carry out research. It was therefore feasible for N to grow in the steady state even though labor was in fixed aggregate supply. Similarly, in the present model, if the cost of R&D were pegged in units of utils, then M could grow in the steady state even though aggregate output was constant. The meaning of pegging the R&D cost in terms of utils is, however, unclear.

Grossman and Helpman (1991, Ch. 3) obtain growth of M in the steady state in this framework because they introduce Romer's (1990) spillover effect in the research sector. An increase in the number of varieties, M, lowers the cost of inventing the next good. Specifically, the assumption is that the R&D cost is η/M in units of goods. We sketch the results for this case and leave the details as an exercise.

In the steady state, $\dot{M}/M$ equals the constant γ. The quantity of resources devoted to research is constant in this situation—although the flow of new products, $\dot{M}$, rises along with M, this effect is exactly offset by the fall in the required outlay, η/M, per good invented. Since total output, Y, and the R&D expenditure are constant, the aggregate of consumer spending, C, is also constant. This result means that the quantity consumed of each type, C/M, falls at the rate γ in the steady state. (Equation [6.45] does not apply because the cost of R&D, represented by η in the equation, is not constant over time.) Each consumer has a constant total consumption, C/L, but experiences a steady increase in variety, M, and therefore enjoys a greater flow of utility over time. Thus, income grows steadily in terms of its command over utility, although output is constant in a physical sense.

This model has the same type of externality in the research sector that appeared in Romer's model of intermediate goods. The attainment of a Pareto optimum therefore requires a subsidy to research. The difference from the model with producer intermediates is that it is unnecessary to eliminate the effects from monopoly pricing of the consumer goods. This monopoly markup is not distorting for the reasons already discussed.

Another way to generate steady-state growth is to return to the case in which the R&D cost, η, is fixed in units of goods, but to reintroduce a production technology that allows for continuing growth of output, Y. Suppose, for example, that the production function is $Y = AK$. This technology pegs the rate of return at $r = A - \delta$. Equation (6.45) determines the constant amount produced of each variety, C/M, and Eq. (6.46) prescribes the growth rate, γ, of C and M. In this situation, aggregate consumption grows only because of new products; the quantity consumed of each of the existing products stays constant over time. The outcomes are Pareto optimal because there is no research spillover, and the monopoly pricing of the consumer goods creates no distortion. (The monopoly pricing works like a consumption tax: it does not affect the rate of return to investment and therefore does not influence the accumulation of capital.)

We could also combine the model of varieties of producer intermediates with the model of varieties of consumer goods. The key result for present purposes is that the model of producer intermediates pegs the steady-state rate of return, r, at the value shown in Eq. (6.10). This given value of r determines the steady-state growth rate, γ, from Eq. (6.46), just as in the AK model. In the steady state, Y, C, M, and N all grow at the rate γ; that is, the available varieties of the consumer and producer goods grow at the same rate.[24]

6.2.2   A Comparison of Consumer Variety with Producer Variety

Fundamentally, the only final good is the flow of utility, and the quantities of producer and consumer goods can both be thought of as intermediates that help to produce the final good. Therefore, the models of expanding variety for producer and consumer goods must be ultimately similar stories about the sources of technological change. The different results in the models relate to different assumptions about the structure of costs.

We can conclude, however, that the introduction of varieties of consumer goods adds little to the understanding of the growth process. If there are no sources of growth on the production side, then a continuing expansion of the varieties of consumer products occurs only if the cost of R&D in terms of goods declines steadily. This assumption about the R&D technology seems implausible, and the properties of the resulting equilibrium are unappealing. In particular, the total quantity of consumer goods stays constant, the quantity of any given variety declines, and the number of types increases. This picture does not accord well with observed economic growth over long periods: expanding variety does occur, but this kind of growth seems to be accompanied by increases in the quantities of goods of a given type.

If we allow for growth on the production side, then we can analyze the expansion of varieties on the consumer side as part of the story. The general nature of the equilibrium is, however, similar to the one in models that assume a single type of consumer good. The possibilities for growth hinge on the same issues—especially the avoidance of diminishing returns in production—that we stressed in earlier models. We therefore still have to think about technological progress in production or about the possibility that a broad concept of capital can be accumulated,

---

[24]This model contains two state variables, M and N. If the ratio M/N does not start at its steady-state value, then the economy experiences transitional dynamics in which the growth rate and interest rate depart from their steady-state values. The nature of the dynamics is similar to that discussed for models with two types of capital goods in Chapter 5.

at least asymptotically, without encountering diminishing returns. The potential for an expanding variety of consumer products is not an alternative way to explain the long-term growth of output.

6.3 CONCLUDING OBSERVATIONS

We modeled technological progress as an expansion of the variety of intermediate goods used by producers. Researchers are motivated by the prospect of monopoly profits to expend resources to discover new types of goods. In the particular setting that we considered—production exhibits constant returns to the number of types of goods, and the cost structure entails a fixed outlay of goods for each invention—the economy is capable of generating endogenous growth. The rate of growth depends on various characteristics of preferences and technology, including the willingness to save, the level of the production function (which could include effects from taxation or other government policies), the cost of R&D, and the scale of the economy (measured by the quantity of a fixed factor, such as raw labor or human capital).

The resulting growth rate—and the related choices about the quantities of intermediate goods to use in production—are generally not Pareto optimal. We discussed the possibilities for improving on outcomes by means of tax and subsidy schemes. Although these possibilities exist in the model, we are skeptical that these kinds of industrial policies would work in richer, more realistic contexts. Satisfactory outcomes typically require the government to have too much information (and to act in a benevolent manner).

The equilibrium growth rate in the model corresponds to the exogenous rate of technological change, x, in the Solow–Swan and Ramsey models of Chapters 1 and 2. Thus, the analysis endogenizes the parameter x and therefore fills in a significant gap in the theories. For example, if the diffusion of ideas from one country to another is very rapid, then the model explains why the technology in all countries would improve. Thus, the model can explain why the long-term growth rate of the world's real per capita GDP would be positive.

The model explains less well why the rates of technological change would differ across countries. If we assume that ideas do not flow at all across international borders, then the model would predict how each economy would carry out its own R&D and make its own discoveries. We would then predict an important scale effect on per capita growth: larger countries would perform better because they could afford more readily the fixed costs of innovations (which could then be used in a nonrival way within the country). The predicted scale effect conflicts with empirical observations, and the likely source of difficulty is the assumption that knowledge does not flow across international borders. We can improve on the cross-country predictions by allowing for a positive, but finite, cost for one country to imitate or learn the technological advances that were made in other countries. We make this extension in Chapter 8.

We have said a great deal about convergence behavior in some of the preceding chapters, so it is worth commenting about convergence properties in the present setting. As it stands, the model is like the AK framework of Chapter 4 and is therefore inconsistent with convergence; in particular, the growth rate is independent of the level of per capita product.

It is not difficult to extend the model in ways that preserve the long-run growth properties, but introduce elements of convergence. Suppose, for example, that we consider a single isolated economy, but allow the intermediate inputs to be durable, like the capital in previous models. Our conjecture is that, if the quantity of capital, K, is low in relation to N (which represents the level of the technology), then the rate of return and growth rate would tend to be high. That is, convergence effects would show up as a negative relation between the growth rate and the ratio K/N. This relation would also tend to show up across countries if technology—that is, N—is determined at the world level, but capital is imperfectly mobile. The main point is that the empirical evidence on convergence would not reject the general approach to technogical progress that we developed in this chapter and extend in the next chapter.

PROBLEMS

6.1 Transitional Dynamics in the Varieties Model. We showed in the text that an equilibrium exists in which N, Y, and C grow at the same constant rate, and the rate of return, r, is constant.

  (a) Show that there are no other equilibria; that is, the model has no transitional dynamics. (Hint: consider the analysis of a related situation in Chapter 4.)

  (b) Suppose that the growth rate shown in Eq. (6.12) is negative. What is the equilibrium in this case? What condition on the underlying parameters implies that this situation applies?

6.2 Alternative Specifications of the R&D Technology. We assumed in the first model in the text that the cost of inventing a new product was a fixed amount, η, of goods.

  (a) How does the analysis differ if the cost of invention is instead a fixed quantity of labor input, L? Is it plausible that the R&D technology would be relatively intensive in L?

  (b) How does the analysis differ if the goods cost of invention, η, declines with the number, N, of goods that have previously been discovered? Is it reasonable that an increase in N would reduce the cost of invention? What new distortion arises if the cost of invention declines with N?

6.3 Policy Implications of the Varieties Model. Consider the first model of varieties of producer intermediates, for which the economy's equilibrium growth rate is given in Eq. (6.12).

  (a) Show that the government can ensure a first-best equilibrium if it uses a lump-sum tax to finance the appropriate subsidy of the intermediate goods. What rate of subsidy is required? In a richer model, why would it be difficult to carry out the required form of policy?

  (b) Can the government ensure a first-best solution if it relies solely on a subsidy to R&D (financed again by a lump-sum tax)? Explain the answer. What modifications to the model would make it important for the government to subsidize research?

6.4 Intermediate Inputs as Durables. Suppose that the intermediate inputs, X_{ij}, are infinite-lived durable goods. New units of these durables can be formed from one unit of final output. The inventor of the jth type of intermediate good charges the rental price R_j, and the competitive producers of final goods treat R_j as given.

(a) How is R_j determined?

(b) In the steady state, what is the quantity, X_j, of each type of intermediate good?

(c) What is the steady-state growth rate of the economy? How does this answer differ from the one discussed in the text for the case in which the intermediate inputs were perishable goods?

(d) If the intermediate goods are durables, then what kinds of dynamic effects arise in the transition to the steady state?

6.5 The Duration of Monopoly Positions. Consider the model in which the monopolized intermediate goods become competitive with the probability p per unit of time.

(a) How do differences in p affect the steady-state properties of the model?

(b) What kinds of policy interventions by the government would lead to a first-best outcome in this model? In particular, is it possible to reach the first best solely by subsidizing purchases of the monopolized intermediate goods?

(c) If the government can influence p through various instruments (such as anti-trust enforcement and patent protection), then what are the model's implications about desirable policies?

6.6 Scale Effects.

(a) Why does the varieties model of technological change exhibit a scale effect in the sense that the growth rate rises with the aggregate quantity of raw labor, L? Is it reasonable to identify L empirically with a country's population?

(b) What happens in the model if population, L, grows at a constant positive rate?

(c) What types of modifications to the model would eliminate the scale effects?

CHAPTER 7

TECHNOLOGICAL CHANGE: MODELS WITH IMPROVEMENTS IN THE QUALITY OF PRODUCTS

The last chapter modeled technological progress as an increase in the number of types of products, N. In this chapter, we hold N constant, but allow for improvements in the quality or productivity of each type. We can think of increases in N as basic innovations that amount to dramatically new kinds of goods or methods of production. In contrast, increases in the quality of the existing products involve a continuing series of improvements and refinements of goods and techniques. Thus, the analysis of this chapter complements the discussion in Chapter 6.

Figure 7.1 shows the basic setup. Intermediate goods come in N varieties, arrayed along the horizontal axis. In Chapter 6, N could increase over time, but now we treat it as fixed. The leading-edge quality of each type of intermediate good is currently at the level shown on the vertical axis. We specify later the precise meaning of the ladder numbers indicated on this axis. Since the process of quality improvement turns out to occur at different rates (and in a random manner), the figure shows that the levels currently attained vary in an irregular way across the sectors.

For the analysis of basic innovation in Chapter 6, we assumed that the new types of intermediate inputs did not interact directly with the old ones. (We used the Spence [1976]/Dixit-Stiglitz [1977] functional form in which these inputs entered in an additively separable manner.) Therefore, the introduction of a new kind of good did not make any old goods obsolete.

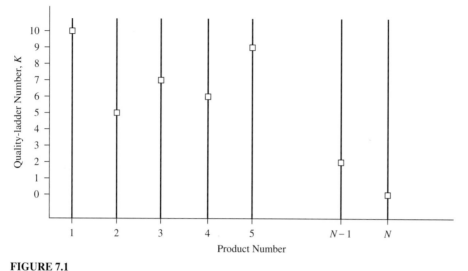

FIGURE 7.1
Quality ladders and product varieties. The horizontal axis shows the number of types of products, and the vertical axis shows the quality rung currently attained in each sector.

In contrast, when a product or technique is improved, the new good or method tends to displace the old one. That is, it is natural to model different quality grades for a good of a given type as close substitutes. We make the extreme assumption that the different qualities of a particular type of intermediate input are perfect substitutes; hence, the discovery of a higher grade turns out to drive out completely the lower grades. For this reason, successful researchers along the quality dimension tend to eliminate the monopoly rentals of their predecessors, the process of "creative destruction" described by Schumpeter (1934) and Aghion and Howitt (1992). This feature of the model in this chapter is the key distinction from the framework constructed in the previous chapter.

7.1 SKETCH OF THE MODEL

Before we get into the technical details, we provide a sketch of the structure of the model that we shall develop to analyze improvements in quality. Producers of the final product again use N varieties of intermediate inputs, but N is now constant. Each type of intermediate good has a quality ladder along which improvements can occur. Improvements build on the currently best technology and derive from efforts by researchers. A successful researcher retains exclusive rights over the use of his or her improved intermediate good.

At each point in time, the knowledge exists to produce an array of qualities of each type of intermediate good. We assume, however, a type of equilibrium in which only the leading-edge quality is actually produced in each sector and used by final-goods producers to generate output.

The researcher who has a monopoly over the use of the latest technology receives a flow of profit. We begin with a model in which the latest innovator is a different person from the previous innovator, so that a research success terminates the predecessor's flow of profit. Therefore, in considering how many resources to devote to research, entrepreneurs consider the size of the profit flow and its likely duration. This duration is random, because it depends on the uncertain outcomes from the research efforts by competitors.

The temporary nature of an inventor's monopoly position brings in two considerations that differentiate the present model from the one with perpetual monopoly rights in Chapter 6. First, the shorter the expected duration of the monopoly, the smaller the anticipated payoff from R&D; this is a distortion because the advances are permanent from a social perspective. (This force also appears in Chapter 6 for the model in which the intermediate goods become competitive over time.) Second, part of the reward from successful research is the creative-destruction effect that involves the transfer of monopoly rentals from the incumbent innovator to the newcomer. Since this transfer has no social value, this second force constitutes an excessive incentive for R&D. We show that the second element is larger than the first, because the two terms are basically the same, except that the second element comes earlier in time. Hence, the net effect is an increase in the private return from research relative to the social return.

In a later section, we assume that the industry leader has a cost advantage in research. If the cost advantage is large enough, then the leader carries out all the research, and the results are similar to those discussed in Chapter 6. In particular, the leader regards innovations as permanent and does not give any credit for the expropriation of his or her own monopoly rentals. If the leader's cost advantage in research is smaller, then the leader still carries out all the research, but the intensity of this research is the amount required to deter entry by outsiders. The equilibrium rate of return and growth rate then turn out to coincide with the values that prevail when research is done by outsiders. We comment at the end about implications for policy.

7.2 BEHAVIOR OF FIRMS

7.2.1 Levels of Quality in the Production Technology

We modify the production function for firm i from Eq. (6.1) to

$$Y_i = AL_i^{1-\alpha} \cdot \sum_{j=1}^{N} (\tilde{X}_{ij})^{\alpha}, \tag{7.1}$$

where, as before, L_i is labor input and $0 < \alpha < 1$. The new element is that $\tilde{X}_{ij}$ is the *quality-adjusted* amount employed of the jth type of intermediate good.

The potential grades of each intermediate good are arrayed along a quality ladder with rungs spaced proportionately at interval $q > 1$.[1] We normalize so that each good begins—when first invented—at quality 1. The subsequent rungs are at

---

[1]This setup follows the models of Aghion and Howitt (1992) and Grossman and Helpman (1991, Ch. 4).

the levels q, q^2, and so on. Thus, if κ_j improvements in quality have occurred in sector j, then the available grades in the sector are 1, q, q^2, ..., $(q)^{\kappa_j}$. Increases in the quality of goods available in a sector—that is, rises in κ_j—result from the successful application of research effort, to be described later. These improvements must occur sequentially, one rung at a time.

Let X_{ijk} be the quantity used by the ith firm of the jth type of intermediate good of quality rung k. The rung k corresponds to quality q^k, so that $k = 0$ refers to quality 1, $k = 1$ to quality q, and so on. Thus, if κ_j is the highest quality level available in sector j, then the quality-adjusted input from this sector is given by

$$\tilde{X}_{ij} = \sum_{k=0}^{\kappa_j} (q^k \cdot X_{ijk}). \tag{7.2}$$

The assumption in Eq. (7.2) is that the quality grades within a sector are perfect substitutes as inputs to production. The overall input from a sector, $\tilde{X}_{ij}$, is therefore the quality-weighted sum of the amounts used of each grade, $q^k \cdot X_{ijk}$.

In Chapter 6, quality improvements were not considered, and $\kappa_j = 0$ applied in each sector. In this case, Eq. (7.2) implies $\tilde{X}_{ij} = X_{ij0}$, and technological advances would arise in Eq. (7.1) only from increases in N. Since N is now fixed, we are assuming implicitly that all of the existing types of intermediate goods were discovered sometime in the (distant) past. But we allow κ_j to evolve over time in each sector in response to the R&D effort aimed at quality improvement in that sector.

Figure 7.2 shows a possible path for the evolution of the leading-edge quality in sector j. The best quality available equals 1 at time t_0, rises to q (rung 1) at time t_1, to q^2 (rung 2) at time t_2, to q^k (rung k) at time t_k, and so on. Thus, $t_{k+1} - t_k$ is

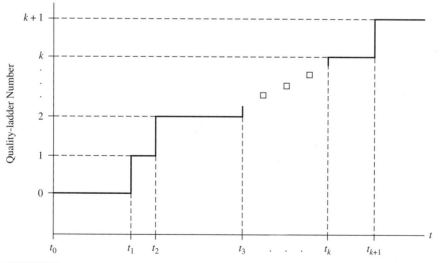

FIGURE 7.2

A quality ladder in a single sector. Over time, the quality-ladder position in a single sector either stays constant or jumps discretely to the next rung. The timing of the jumps is stochastic because it depends on the uncertain outcomes from research effort.

the interval over which the best quality is q^k for $k = 0, 1, \ldots, \kappa_j - 1$. The figure shows intervals of differing length for each value of k; these lengths are random in the model developed below.

The researcher responsible for each quality improvement in sector j retains a monopoly right to produce the jth intermediate good at that quality level. In particular, if the quality rungs $k = 1, \ldots, \kappa_j$ have been reached, then the kth innovator is the sole source of intermediate goods with the quality level q^k.[2]

The intermediate good is nondurable and entails a unit marginal cost of production (in terms of output, Y). That is, the cost of production is the same for all qualities q^k, where $k = 0, \ldots, \kappa_j$. Thus, the latest innovator has an efficiency advantage over the prior innovators in the sector, but will eventually be at a disadvantage relative to future innovators.

Suppose for the moment that only the best existing quality of intermediate good j—with quality level $(q)^{\kappa_j}$—is available currently for production. (The other grades will turn out not to be used in equilibrium.) The marginal product of this good can be computed from equations (7.1) and (7.2) as

$$\partial Y_i/\partial X_{ij\kappa_j} = A\alpha \cdot L_i^{1-\alpha} \cdot (q)^{\alpha\kappa_j} \cdot (X_{ij\kappa_j})^{\alpha-1}. \tag{7.3}$$

If units of the leading-edge good are priced at $P_{j\kappa_j}$ and if no other quality grades of good j are available, then the implied demand function (from the aggregate of profit-maximizing, final-goods producers) can be written as

$$X_{j\kappa_j} = L \cdot [A\alpha \cdot (q)^{\alpha\kappa_j}/P_{j\kappa_j}]^{1/(1-\alpha)}. \tag{7.4}$$

This result corresponds to Eq. (6.4) if $\kappa_j = 0$.

The leading-edge producer acts as a monopolist in this environment, and profit maximization leads to the same markup formula as in Eq. (6.7):

$$\text{Monopoly pricing} \Longrightarrow P_{j\kappa_j} = P = 1/\alpha. \tag{7.5}$$

Hence, the monopoly price is again constant over time and across sectors.

The aggregate quantity produced of the jth intermediate good—all of leading-edge quality—can be determined from Eq. (7.4) as

$$\text{Monopoly pricing} \Longrightarrow X_{j\kappa_j} = LA^{1/(1-\alpha)} \cdot \alpha^{2/(1-\alpha)} \cdot (q)^{\kappa_j\alpha/(1-\alpha)}. \tag{7.6}$$

Since $\kappa_j = 0$ in the model of Chapter 6, this quantity was constant over time and across sectors (see Eq. [6.8]). The evolution of κ_j over time in each sector and the divergences of the κ_j across the sectors will lead now to variations in $X_{j\kappa_j}$ over time and across sectors.

Suppose now that goods from quality rungs below κ_j are also available for production in sector j. We assume in this section that the κ_jth innovator, who has the rights to produce the best known quality, was not also the $(\kappa_j - 1)$th innovator, who

---

[2]Since this model does not consider the initial discovery of a type of product, we have to assume that goods of quality 1 (rung 0) can be produced by anyone. The treatment of these lowest quality goods will not be an issue if substantial quality improvements have already occurred in each sector.

can produce the next best quality. If the leading-edge producer charges the monopoly price shown in Eq. (7.5) and if this price is high enough, then the producer of the next lowest grade will be able to make positive profits by producing.

Recall from Eq. (7.2) that the different quality grades are perfect substitutes, but are weighted by their respective grades. Thus, each unit of the leading-edge good is equivalent to $q > 1$ units of the next best good. It follows that if the highest grade is priced at $P_{j\kappa_j}$, then a good of the next lowest grade could be sold at most at the price $(1/q) \cdot P_{j\kappa_j}$, the one below that at the price $(1/q^2) \cdot P_{j\kappa_j}$, and so on. If $(1/q) \cdot P_{j\kappa_j}$ is less than the unit marginal cost of production, then the next best grade (and, moreover, all of the lower quality grades) cannot survive.

Equation (7.5) shows that the leading-edge producer's monopoly price is $1/\alpha$, a price that would allow the next best producer to price at most at $1/(\alpha q)$, the one below that at $1/(\alpha q^2)$, and so on. If $1/(\alpha q)$ is less than one, then the next best producer (and all lower quality producers) cannot compete against the leader's monopoly price. Therefore, the condition $\alpha q > 1$ implies that monopoly pricing will prevail. This inequality will hold if q, the spacing between quality improvements, is large enough; the lower grades are then immediately driven out of the market even though the leading good is priced at the monopoly level. In this case, only the best available quality, κ_j, of each type of intermediate good is produced and used as an input by final-goods producers. The price and quantity of type j are then given by Eq. (7.5) and (7.6).

If $\alpha q \leq 1$, then we can follow Grossman and Helpman (1991, Ch. 4) by assuming that the providers of intermediate goods of a given type engage in Bertrand price competition. In this case, the quality leader employs a limit-pricing strategy; that is, the leader sets a price that is sufficiently below the monopoly price so as to make it just barely unprofitable for the next best quality to be produced.[3] This limit price is given by

$$\text{Limit pricing} \implies P_{j\kappa_j} = q. \tag{7.7}$$

If the leader prices at $q - \epsilon$, where ϵ is an arbitrarily small positive amount, then the producer of the next best quality can charge at most $1 - \epsilon/q$, a price that results in negative profit. The lower quality goods are therefore again driven out of the market. A comparison of Eqs. (7.7) and (7.5) shows that, if $\alpha q \leq 1$—the condition for limit pricing to prevail—then the limit price is no larger than the monopoly price.

The total quantity produced (of the highest quality) when limit pricing applies is given by

$$\text{Limit pricing} \implies X_{j\kappa_j} = LA^{1/(1-\alpha)} \cdot (\alpha/q)^{1/(1-\alpha)} \cdot (q)^{\kappa_j \alpha/(1-\alpha)}. \tag{7.8}$$

A comparison of Eq. (7.8) and (7.6) shows that, if $\alpha q \leq 1$, then the quantity produced under limit pricing is at least as large as the amount that would have been produced under monopoly.

---

[3]Grossman and Helpman (1991, Ch. 4) effectively assume $\alpha = 0$, so that the magnitude of the elasticity of demand is 1, and the monopoly price shown in Eq. (7.5) is infinite. Since the inequality $\alpha q \leq 1$ must hold in this situation, monopoly pricing cannot apply in their model.

The monopoly formulas in Eq. (7.5) and (7.6) apply if $\alpha q \geq 1$, and the limit-pricing formulas in Eq. (7.7) and (7.8) hold if $\alpha q \leq 1$. Either way, price is a fixed markup on the marginal cost of production, and only the best available quality of each type of intermediate good is actually produced in each sector and used by final-goods producers. We assume in the main discussion that $\alpha q \geq 1$, so that the monopoly formulas in Eqs. (7.5) and (7.6) apply. The main results are similar, however, if $\alpha q < 1$, so that limit pricing prevails.[4]

We can use the results to rewrite the production function from Eq. (7.1) as

$$Y_i = AL_i^{1-\alpha} \cdot \sum_{j=1}^{N} (q)^{\alpha \kappa_j} \cdot (X_{ij\kappa_j})^{\alpha}, \tag{7.9}$$

where $X_{ij\kappa_j}$ is the ith firm's input of the jth intermediate from the highest available quality rung, κ_j. We can, in other words, ignore any goods of less than leading-edge quality.

If we substitute the quantity $X_{ij\kappa_j}$ from Eq. (7.6) (with L_i appearing instead of L) and aggregate over the firms i, then we get an expression for aggregate output,

$$Y = A^{1/(1-\alpha)} \cdot \alpha^{2\alpha/(1-\alpha)} \cdot L \cdot \sum_{j=1}^{N} q^{\kappa_j \alpha/(1-\alpha)}. \tag{7.10}$$

Since L and N are constants, the key to growth of Y in this model is expansions of the quality-ladder positions κ_j in the various sectors.

We can define an aggregate quality index,

$$Q \equiv \sum_{j=1}^{N} q^{\kappa_j \alpha/(1-\alpha)}, \tag{7.11}$$

so that

$$Y = A^{1/(1-\alpha)} \cdot \alpha^{2\alpha/(1-\alpha)} \cdot LQ. \tag{7.12}$$

The index Q is a combination of the various κ_j's, and increases in the κ_j's affect aggregate output to the extent that they raise Q.

We also note from aggregation of Eq. (7.6) across the sectors that total quantity of intermediates produced, denoted by X, is proportional to Q:

$$X = A^{1/(1-\alpha)} \cdot \alpha^{2/(1-\alpha)} \cdot LQ. \tag{7.13}$$

We now consider the determinants of changes in the κ_j's.

7.2.2   The Incentive to Innovate

THE FLOW OF MONOPOLY PROFIT.   Innovation in a sector takes the form of an improvement in quality by the multiple q. The κ_jth innovator in sector j raises the

---

[4]Limit pricing applies, in any case, only if successive innovators are different persons. We argue later that the leader tends to do all of the innovating, in which case the limit-pricing results are not relevant.

quality from $q^{\kappa_j - 1}$ to q^{κ_j}. This innovator will be able to price in accordance with Eq. (7.5) and sell the quantity of intermediate goods given by Eq. (7.6). The flow of profit associated with quality rung κ_j equals $(P - 1) \cdot X_{j\kappa_j}$ and is therefore given by

$$\pi_{j\kappa_j} = LA^{1/(1-\alpha)} \cdot \left(\frac{1 - \alpha}{\alpha} \right) \cdot \alpha^{2/(1-\alpha)} \cdot q^{\kappa_j \alpha/(1-\alpha)}. \tag{7.14}$$

The profit shown in Eq. (7.14) applies when a sector's highest quality rung is κ_j. Thus, this profit accrues from the time of the κ_jth quality improvement, t_{κ_j}, until the time of the next improvement by a competitor, t_{κ_j+1}. (Recall that the κ_jth and $[\kappa_j + 1]$th innovators are assumed to be different persons.) The interval over which the κ_jth innovation is in the forefront is therefore

$$T_{j\kappa_j} = t_{\kappa_j+1} - t_{\kappa_j}.$$

If the interest rate is the constant r—as will be true in equilibrium—then the present value (evaluated at time t_{κ_j}) of the profit from the κ_jth innovation in sector j is given by

$$V_{j\kappa_j} = \pi_{j\kappa_j} \cdot [1 - \exp(-rT_{j\kappa_j})]/r. \tag{7.15}$$

This present value, which represents the prize for the κ_jth innovation, depends positively on $\pi_{j\kappa_j}$ and $T_{j\kappa_j}$. Since we know $\pi_{j\kappa_j}$, we now have to determine the duration, $T_{j\kappa_j}$, to determine $V_{j\kappa_j}$.

THE DURATION OF MONOPOLY PROFIT. We denote by $Z_{j\kappa_j}$ the flow of resources (in units of Y) expended by the aggregate of potential innovators in sector j when the highest quality-ladder number reached in that sector is κ_j. The higher $Z_{j\kappa_j}$ is, the larger probability, $p_{j\kappa_j}$, per unit of time of a successful innovation, that is, an increase in the ladder number from κ_j to $\kappa_j + 1$. Specifically, we assume

$$p_{j\kappa_j} = Z_{j\kappa_j} \cdot \phi(\kappa_j), \tag{7.16}$$

so that, for given κ_j, the probability of success is proportional to the overall research effort, $Z_{j\kappa_j}$.[5] We assume also that the probability of success declines for given effort with the complexity of the project, represented by the ladder number, κ_j, that is, $\phi'(\kappa_j) < 0$.

Equation (7.16) specifies a Poisson process in which the probability per unit of time of success, $p_{j\kappa_j}$, depends for given κ_j only on current R&D effort by all researchers in the sector and not on the history of research or other variables.

---

[5]The linearity in $Z_{j\kappa_j}$ means that the marginal contribution of R&D effort to the probability of success, $\partial p/\partial Z_{j\kappa_j}$, equals the average contribution, $p/Z_{j\kappa_j}$. That is, the research process is *not* being modeled as a congestible resource, like a fishing pond, in which an individual's expected return declines with the aggregate level of investment. For this reason, a researcher is indifferent to entry by additional researchers or to changes in the effort levels by his or her competitors. The model therefore does not have the property of some patent-race formulations in which—for congestion reasons—the overall level of research tends to be too high from a social perspective (see Reinganum [1989] for a survey of these models).

Recall that we also assumed a Poisson process for the case in Chapter 6 in which an innovator's monopoly position was temporary.

The randomness of R&D success implies that progress will occur unevenly in a single sector; usually nothing happens, but on rare occasions the productivity jumps by a discrete amount. We assume, however, that individual sectors are small and that the probabilities of research success across sectors are independent. The Law of Large Numbers then implies that the jumpiness in microeconomic outcomes is not transmitted to the macroeconomic variables: the adding up across a large number of independent sectors N leads to a smooth path for the aggregate quality index Q, shown in Eq. (7.11), and therefore for aggregate economic growth. Thus, as in Chapter 6, the analysis abstracts from the aggregate fluctuations that are the focus of real business-cycle models.[6]

Define $G(\tau)$ to be the cumulative probability density function for $T_{j\kappa_j}$, that is, the probability that $T_{j\kappa_j} \leq \tau$. The change in $G(\tau)$ with respect to τ represents the probability per unit of time that the innovation occurs at τ. In order for an innovation to happen at τ, it must first not have occurred earlier, an outcome that has probability $1 - G(\tau)$. Then, conditional on a discovery not having happened yet, the probability of one occurring is $p_{j\kappa_j}$ per unit of time. Hence, the derivative of $G(\tau)$ is

$$dG/d\tau = [1 - G(\tau)] \cdot p_{j\kappa_j}. \qquad (7.17)$$

We assume that $p_{j\kappa_j}$ is constant over the interval, $(t_{\kappa_j}, t_{\kappa_j+1})$; that is, the research effort, $Z_{j\kappa_j}$, and, hence, the probability of success, $p_{j\kappa_j}$, do not vary over time between innovations in a sector. (These conditions hold in equilibrium.) Since $p_{j\kappa_j}$ is constant over time, we can readily solve the differential Eq. (7.17). If we use the boundary condition, $G(0) = 0$, then the result is

$$G(\tau) = 1 - \exp(-p_{j\kappa_j}\tau).$$

The probability density function can then be found from differentiation of the cumulative density:

$$g(\tau) = G'(\tau) = p_{j\kappa_j} \cdot \exp(-p_{j\kappa_j}\tau). \qquad (7.18)$$

Equation (7.15) shows the present value of profit, $V_{j\kappa_j}$, from the κ_jth innovation for a given duration, $T_{j\kappa_j}$. Equation (7.18) gives the probability density for $T_{j\kappa_j}$. The expected present value of profit, computed at time t_{κ_j}, is therefore

$$E(V_{j\kappa_j}) = (\pi_{j\kappa_j}/r) \cdot p_{j\kappa_j} \cdot \int_0^\infty (1 - e^{-r\tau}) \cdot \exp(-p_{j\kappa_j}\tau)\,d\tau.$$

The integral can be evaluated to get

$$E(V_{j\kappa_j}) = \pi_{j\kappa_j}/(r + p_{j\kappa_j}).$$

---

[6]We could get similar results for aggregate growth if we assumed that innovation occurred deterministically in a single sector; that is, the application of a given level of R&D effort generated a quality improvement after a known interval of time. The aggregation would then depend, however, on how the R&D effort and, hence, the innovations were synchronized across the sectors. The framework with a Poisson success probability in each sector is much more manageable.

If we substitute for $\pi_{j\kappa_j}$ from Eq. (7.14), then we get

$$E(V_{j\kappa_j}) = LA^{1/(1-\alpha)} \cdot \left(\frac{1-\alpha}{\alpha}\right) \cdot \alpha^{2/(1-\alpha)} \cdot [q^{\kappa_j\alpha/(1-\alpha)}]/(r + p_{j\kappa_j}). \quad (7.19)$$

Equation (7.19) shows the expected reward from making the κ_jth innovation. Note that the uncertainty that underlies $E(V_{j\kappa_j})$ involves the duration of the monopoly position, that is, the randomness of the time of success of the $(\kappa_j + 1)$th innovator. We have not yet considered the additional uncertainty that innovators face *ex ante* because of the randomness of the success of their own research efforts.

DETERMINATION OF R&D EFFORT. We now consider how the prize for successful research, $E(V_{j\kappa_j})$, determines the quantity of R&D effort, $Z_{j\kappa_j}$, and thereby the probability of success, $p_{j\kappa_j}$. We assume that potential innovators care only about the expected value shown in Eq. (7.19) and not about the randomness of the return. This assumption can be satisfactory even if individuals are risk averse because each R&D project is small and has purely idiosyncratic uncertainty.[7]

The cost of research per unit of time is $Z_{j\kappa_j}$, and this effort results in the probability $p_{j\kappa_j}$ per unit of time of success, where $p_{j\kappa_j} = Z_{j\kappa_j} \cdot \phi(\kappa_j)$ from Eq. (7.16). The expected reward per unit of time for pursuing the $(\kappa_j + 1)$th innovation is $p_{j\kappa_j} \cdot E(V_{j,\kappa_j+1})$. Hence, the expected flow of net profit, $\Pi_{j\kappa_j}$, from research in a sector that is currently at quality rung κ_j is $p_{j\kappa_j} \cdot E(V_{j,\kappa_j+1}) - Z_{j\kappa_j}$, which equals

$$\Pi_{j\kappa_j} = Z_{j\kappa_j} \qquad (7.20)$$

$$\cdot \left[\phi(\kappa_j) \cdot LA^{1/(1-\alpha)} \cdot \left(\frac{1-\alpha}{\alpha}\right) \cdot \alpha^{2/(1-\alpha)} \cdot [q^{(\kappa_j+1)\cdot\alpha/(1-\alpha)}]/(r + p_{j,\kappa_j+1}) - 1\right].$$

We again assume free entry into the research business. Hence, if $Z_{j\kappa_j} > 0$, then $\Pi_{j\kappa_j} = 0$ must hold. The term $Z_{j\kappa_j}$ then cancels out in Eq. (7.20), and the free-entry condition can be written as

$$r + p_{j,\kappa_j+1} = LA^{1/(1-\alpha)} \cdot \left(\frac{1-\alpha}{\alpha}\right) \cdot \alpha^{2/(1-\alpha)} \cdot \phi(\kappa_j) \cdot [q^{(\kappa_j+1)\cdot\alpha/(1-\alpha)}]. \quad (7.21)$$

Note that the right-hand side depends on κ_j, but does not differ otherwise across sectors.

Equation (7.21) implies that the probability of innovation would generally vary with κ_j because of two offsetting effects. The term $q^{(\kappa_j+1)\cdot\alpha/(1-\alpha)}$ appears because the expected reward from an innovation is increasing in κ_j (see Eq. [7.19]). This effect arises because the quantity of intermediates sold (Eq. [7.6]) increases with quality and, hence, with κ_j. The second term, $\phi(\kappa_j)$, reflects the assumption that innovations in a sector are increasingly difficult, that is, $\phi'(\kappa_j) < 0$.

---

[7]We have to assume that research projects are carried out by syndicates that are large enough to diversify the risk. The syndicates cannot be so large, however, that they would internalize the distortions that are present in the model.

If the first effect dominates, then the rate of return to R&D is higher the more advanced a sector. The more advanced sectors will then tend to grow faster than less advanced sectors, and the growth rate of the overall economy will rise over time as the average value of κ_j increases. In other words, R&D features a form of increasing returns, and this property creates a pattern of divergence for growth rates.

In contrast, if the second effect dominates, then more advanced sectors will tend to grow relatively slowly, and the growth rate of the overall economy will fall over time. In this case, R&D exhibits a form of decreasing returns, and this relation generates the kind of convergence behavior that we found in the Ramsey model.

Finally, if the two forces exactly offset, then all sectors will tend to grow at the same rate, and the growth rate of the overall economy will be constant over time. In this case, R&D exhibits constant returns. This case therefore features endogenous, steady-state growth, and we can compare the results to those from previous models of endogenous growth, such as the AK model of Chapter 4 or the framework with an expanding variety of producer intermediates in Chapter 6.

Equation (7.21) shows that the balance between the two forces depends on the form of $\phi(\kappa_j)$. A specification that makes the two effects exactly offset is

$$\phi(\kappa_j) = (1/\zeta) \cdot q^{-(\kappa_j+1)\cdot\alpha/(1-\alpha)}, \tag{7.22}$$

where recall that $p_{j\kappa_j} = Z_{j\kappa_j} \cdot \phi(\kappa_j)$ in Eq. (7.16). The parameter $\zeta > 0$ represents the cost of research; a higher ζ lowers the probability of success for given values of $Z_{j\kappa_j}$ and κ_j. In the model of expanding variety of producer intermediates in Chapter 6, the parameter η was the comparable measure of the cost of research.

The term on the far right-hand side of Eq. (7.22), $q^{-(\kappa_j+1)\cdot\alpha/(1-\alpha)}$, indicates the negative effect of a project's complexity (represented by $\kappa_j + 1$) on the probability of success. This particular form cancels out the term on the far right-hand side of Eq. (7.21). For that reason, p_{j,κ_j+1} is invariant with κ_j.

If we substitute from Eq. (7.22) into Eq. (7.21), then the free-entry condition becomes

$$r + p = (L/\zeta) \cdot A^{1/(1-\alpha)} \cdot \left(\frac{1-\alpha}{\alpha}\right) \cdot \alpha^{2/(1-\alpha)}, \tag{7.23}$$

where we substitute $p = p_{j,\kappa_j+1}$ because the probability is now constant (across sectors and over time in a given sector).[8] This formula coincides (after the replacement of η by ζ) with the result from Chapter 6 (Eq. [6.23]) for the model in which intermediate goods became competitive with the probability p per unit of time.[9]

---

[8]Equation (7.21) determines the probabilities that correspond to the *next* quality rung in each sector, p_{j,κ_j+1}. In the equilibrium, the current relative spending on R&D across sectors can differ from the amount that corresponds to the constant p (Eq. [7.24] below) by a random term.

[9]For the case of limit pricing (Eqs. [7.7] and [7.8]), the result in Eq. (7.23) is modified to

$$r + p = (L/\zeta) \cdot A^{1/(1-\alpha)} \cdot (q-1) \cdot (\alpha/q)^{1/(1-\alpha)}.$$

This result applies if $\alpha q \leq 1$ and reduces to Eq. (7.23) if $\alpha q = 1$.

The right-hand side of Eq. (7.23) represents the rate of return from research (the expected flow of profit per unit of research effort). The key, however, is that a successful researcher maintains this return only until the time of the next innovation. The rate of return must therefore cover the ordinary rate of return, r, plus the premium for the probability, p, per unit of time that a competitor will succeed and thereby drive the incumbent out of business.

Equation (7.23) implies that the probability of an innovation per unit of time is

$$p = (L/\zeta) \cdot A^{1/(1-\alpha)} \cdot \left(\frac{1-\alpha}{\alpha}\right) \cdot \alpha^{2/(1-\alpha)} - r. \tag{7.24}$$

If r is constant over time, then p is also constant (as well as the same for all sectors).

The amount of resources devoted to R&D in sector j is $Z_{j\kappa_j} = p/\phi(\kappa_j)$. If we use Eqs. (7.22) and (7.24) to substitute for $\phi(\kappa_j)$ and p, then we get

$$Z_{j\kappa_j} = q^{(\kappa_j+1)\cdot\alpha/(1+\alpha)} \cdot \left[LA^{1/(1-\alpha)} \cdot \left(\frac{1-\alpha}{\alpha}\right) \cdot \alpha^{2/(1-\alpha)} - r\zeta\right]. \tag{7.25}$$

Hence, more advanced sectors—with higher κ_j—have a larger quantity of research devoted to them. The probability of success is, however, independent of κ_j because Eq. (7.22) implies that correspondingly more effort is required in a more advanced sector to generate the same probability.

The aggregate of R&D spending, denoted by Z, is

$$Z \equiv \sum_{j=1}^{N} Z_{j\kappa_j} = Q \cdot q^{\alpha/(1-\alpha)} \cdot \left[LA^{1/(1-\alpha)} \cdot \left(\frac{1-\alpha}{\alpha}\right) \cdot \alpha^{2/(1-\alpha)} - r\zeta\right], \tag{7.26}$$

where Q is the aggregate quality index, as shown in Eq. (7.11). Hence, Z is proportional to Q for a given value of r.

7.2.3 The Behavior of the Aggregate Quality Index

The level of aggregate output, Y in Eq. (7.12), the aggregate resources expended on intermediates, X in Eq. (7.13), and the total expenditure on R&D, Z in Eq. (7.26), are all constant multiples of the aggregate quality index, Q. (We assume here that r is constant, a condition that will hold in equilibrium.) Hence, the growth rates of these quantities are all equal to the growth rate of Q:

$$\gamma_Y = \gamma_X = \gamma_Z = \gamma_Q.$$

To understand growth in this model, we therefore have to explain the changes over time in Q.

Recall the definition of Q from Eq. (7.11):

$$Q \equiv \sum_{j=1}^{N} q^{\kappa_j \alpha/(1-\alpha)}. \tag{7.11}$$

In sector j, the term $q^{\kappa_j \alpha/(1-\alpha)}$ does not change if no innovation occurs, but rises to $q^{(\kappa_j+1)\cdot \alpha/(1-\alpha)}$ in the case of a research success. The proportionate change in this term due to a success is $q^{\alpha/(1-\alpha)} - 1$, and the probability per unit of time of a success is the value p shown in Eq. (7.24). Since p is the same for all sectors, the expected proportionate change in Q per unit of time is given by

$$E(\Delta Q/Q) = p \cdot (q^{\alpha/(1-\alpha)} - 1). \tag{7.27}$$

If the number of sectors, N, is large, then the Law of Large Numbers implies that the average growth rate of Q measured over any finite interval of time will be close to the expression shown on the right-hand side of Eq. (7.27). We assume, in particular, that N is large enough to treat Q as differentiable, with $\dot{Q}/Q$ nonstochastic and equal to the right-hand side of Eq. (7.27). If we substitute for p from Eq. (7.24), then we get the growth rate of Q:

$$\gamma_Q = \left[(L/\zeta) \cdot A^{1/(1-\alpha)} \cdot \left(\frac{1-\alpha}{\alpha} \right) \cdot \alpha^{2/(1-\alpha)} - r \right] \cdot [q^{\alpha/(1-\alpha)} - 1]. \tag{7.28}$$

Equation (7.28) shows that, to determine the growth rate of Q—and, hence, the growth rates of Y, X, and Z—we have to pin down the rate of return, r. To determine r, we have to bring in the behavior of households as consumers. We first analyze the market value of firms, then consider the choices of households (who own the firms), and finally deal with the equilibrium conditions that allow us to determine r and γ_Q.

7.2.4   The Market Value of Firms

Since goods below leading-edge quality are not produced, the only firm with market value in each sector is the one that possesses the rights over the latest (κ_jth) innovation. The market value of this innovation, $E(V_{j\kappa_j})$, is given by Eq. (7.19). If we substitute for $r + p$ from Eq. (7.23), then the formula becomes

$$E(V_{j\kappa_j}) = \zeta \cdot q^{\kappa_j \alpha/(1-\alpha)}. \tag{7.29}$$

The expression on the right-hand side represents the (expected) cost of generating the κ_jth innovation (taking account of Eq. [7.22]). Note that the more advanced a sector—the higher κ_j—the greater the market value of the leading-edge firm.

The aggregate market value of firms, denoted by V, is the sum of Eq. (7.29) over the N sectors:

$$V = \zeta \cdot \sum_{j=1}^{N} q^{\kappa_j \alpha/(1-\alpha)} = \zeta Q. \tag{7.30}$$

The total market value of firms is therefore a constant multiple of Q.

7.3   HOUSEHOLDS AND MARKET EQUILIBRIUM

We assume that each household maximizes the usual expression for utility,

$$U = \int_0^\infty \left(\frac{c^{1-\theta} - 1}{1-\theta} \right) \cdot e^{-\rho t} \, dt, \tag{7.31}$$

where c is consumption per person, and the rate of population growth, n, is 0. Households earn the rate of return r on assets and receive the wage rate w (equal to the marginal product of labor) on the fixed aggregate quantity L of labor. In a closed economy, the total of households' assets equals the market value of firms, ζQ, as shown in Eq. (7.30).[10] The key condition that we need from household optimization is, as usual, the one for the growth rate of consumption:

$$\gamma_C = (1/\theta) \cdot (r - \rho), \tag{7.32}$$

where C is aggregate consumption.

To apply the result in Eq. (7.32), we have to use our previous analysis to derive an expression for C, the level of consumption. The economy's overall resource constraint is

$$C = Y - X - Z,$$

where Y is given in Eq. (7.12); X, the total spending on intermediates, is given in Eq. (7.13); and Z, the total spending on R&D, is given in Eq. (7.26). Since Y, X, and Z are all constant multiples of Q, C is also a constant multiple of Q. In particular, if we make the substitutions for Y, X, and Z, then we get[11]

$$C = \left[A^{1/(1-\alpha)} \cdot (1 - \alpha^2) \cdot \alpha^{2\alpha/(1-\alpha)} \cdot L - p\zeta \cdot q^{\alpha/(1-\alpha)} \right] \cdot Q. \tag{7.33}$$

Since the expression in brackets is constant (if p is constant), C grows at the same rate as Q.

The variables Y, X, Z, C, and Q all grow at the same rate, which we can denote by γ. Equation (7.28), which derived from the behavior of firms as producers, gives one expression for γ as a function of r. Equation (7.32), which came from the behavior of households as consumers, provides another expression for γ as a function of r. In a market equilibrium, the value of r is such as to equate the two expressions for the growth rate. The resulting values of r and γ are constants and therefore constitute the steady-state values. The solutions are

$$r = \frac{\rho + \theta \cdot [q^{\alpha/(1-\alpha)} - 1] \cdot \left[(L/\zeta) \cdot A^{1/(1-\alpha)} \cdot \left(\frac{1-\alpha}{\alpha} \right) \cdot \alpha^{2/(1-\alpha)} \right]}{1 + \theta \cdot [q^{\alpha/(1-\alpha)} - 1]}, \tag{7.34}$$

$$\gamma = \frac{[q^{\alpha/(1-\alpha)} - 1] \cdot \left[(L/\zeta) \cdot A^{1/(1-\alpha)} \cdot \left(\frac{1-\alpha}{\alpha} \right) \cdot \alpha^{2/(1-\alpha)} - \rho \right]}{1 + \theta \cdot [q^{\alpha/(1-\alpha)} - 1]}. \tag{7.35}$$

---

[10] The wage rate equals the marginal product of labor, which can be computed from Eq. (7.1). We can use this condition to show that the households' aggregate income, $wL + r\zeta Q$, equals a concept of net product that takes account of capital losses, $Y - X - p\zeta Q$, where X is aggregate spending on intermediates (Eq. [7.13]) and $p\zeta Q$ is the capital loss from destruction of the market value of superseded innovations. Household saving, $\zeta \dot{Q}$, equals income less consumption, $Y - X - p\zeta Q - C$. The economy's resource constraint is $Y = C + X + Z$, where Z is aggregate spending on R&D. Household saving therefore equals $Z - p\zeta Q$; that is, net investment equals R&D spending less the capital loss due to destruction of existing market value.

[11] The transversality condition, $r > \gamma$ in the following, ensures that the expression for C in Eq. (7.33) is positive.

We assume that the parameters are such that γ is positive (so that the free-entry condition in Eq. [7.21] actually holds with equality), and $r > \gamma$ applies (to satisfy the transversality condition).[12] Equation (7.27) implies that the equilibrium value of p is the expression for γ in Eq. (7.35) divided by the term $(q^{\alpha/(1-\alpha)} - 1)$:

$$p = \frac{\left[(L/\zeta) \cdot A^{1/(1-\alpha)} \cdot \left(\frac{1-\alpha}{\alpha}\right) \cdot \alpha^{2/(1-\alpha)} - \rho\right]}{[1 + \theta \cdot (q^{\alpha/(1-\alpha)} - 1)]}. \tag{7.36}$$

The results are like those from the varieties model of Chapter 6 in that no transitional dynamics exist.[13] The single state variable is now the aggregate quality index, Q. Given an initial value, $Q(0)$, the variables Q, Y, X, Z, and C all grow at the constant rate γ shown in Eq. (7.35). The interest rate, r, is the constant value shown in Eq. (7.34).

Although the mean growth rate of output in each sector j is also γ, the realized growth depends on the random outcomes of research efforts. In particular, the relative quality positions of the sectors and, hence, the relative amounts spent on intermediate goods and R&D evolve in a random walk–like fashion. At a point in time, the realized quality positions across the sectors will therefore exhibit an irregular pattern, as suggested by Figure 7.1.

Many of the properties of the solution for the growth rate in Eq. (7.35) are similar to those from Eq. (6.12) for the model with expanding variety. Specifically, γ in Eq. (7.35) is higher if people are more willing to save (lower ρ and θ), if the technology for producing goods is better (higher A), if the cost of doing research is lower (lower ζ), and if the scale of the economy is larger (higher L). A new result is that the growth rate rises with q, the step size between innovations.[14]

7.4   INNOVATION BY THE LEADER

The results derived in the previous section predict a continual leapfrogging in leadership positions in an industry. Since the incumbent does no research, he or she is replaced on top at the time of the next quality improvement by an outside competitor, who is subsequently replaced by another outsider, and so on.

In the real world, most improvements in the quality of existing products seem to be made by industry leaders. This outcome likely arises because the leaders typically have the best information about the current technology and other advantages that

---

[12]Equations (7.34) and (7.35) imply that the condition for $r > \gamma$ is $\rho > (1 - \theta) \cdot [1 - q^{-\alpha/(1-\alpha)}] \cdot [(L/\zeta) \cdot A^{1/(1-\alpha)} \cdot \left(\frac{1-\alpha}{\alpha}\right) \cdot \alpha^{2/(1-\alpha)}]$. The condition for $\gamma > 0$ in Eq. (7.35) is $\rho < (L/\zeta) \cdot A^{1/(1-\alpha)} \cdot \left(\frac{1-\alpha}{\alpha}\right) \cdot \alpha^{2/(1-\alpha)}$.

[13]We have shown here only that an equilibrium exists with no transitional dynamics. A proof that no other equilibria are possible can be constructed along the lines followed in Chapter 4.

[14]If the cost of research is specified as an increasing function of q, then we can also use the model to determine q.

effectively reduce their research costs.[15] We therefore want to investigate whether a change in specification about research costs will improve the model's predictions about research by insiders.

We begin with a setting in which outsiders are precluded from research; hence, the industry leader acts as a monopolist with respect to the choice of research intensity. Next we allow for research by outsiders, but at a cost that exceeds that for insiders. We show that the monopoly research outcome applies if the leader's cost advantage in R&D is sufficiently great. Otherwise, the probability of research success coincides with the value from our previous analysis. We now predict, however, that the research will be carried out by the (low-cost) insider, rather than the (high-cost) outsiders.

7.4.1 The Leader as a Monopoly Researcher

Suppose that the incumbent's research technology takes the form of Eqs. (7.16) and (7.22):

$$ p_{j\kappa_j} = (Z_{j\kappa_j}/\zeta_\ell) \cdot q^{-(\kappa_j+1)\cdot\alpha/(1-\alpha)}, \tag{7.37} $$

where ζ_ℓ is the cost parameter for the industry leader. We assume that the leader's cost may be smaller than that for competitors, $\zeta_\ell \leq \zeta$.

Suppose, for the moment, that the leader is the *only* source of research in a sector; that is, outsiders are prohibited from conducting research. This setup differs from the previous one in two respects: the leader regards all quality improvements as permanent and does not value the transfer of monopoly rentals from his or her predecessor (that is, from himself or herself). We therefore have to compute the present value of the leader's net receipts in this new environment.

Let $Z_{j\kappa_j}$ be the level of research effort, $p_{j\kappa_j}$ the resulting probability of success per unit of time, and $\pi_{j\kappa_j}$ the flow of monopoly profit, which is still given by Eq. (7.14):

$$ \pi_{j\kappa_j} = LA^{1/(1-\alpha)} \cdot \left(\frac{1-\alpha}{\alpha}\right) \cdot \alpha^{2/(1-\alpha)} \cdot q^{\kappa_j\alpha/(1-\alpha)}. \tag{7.14} $$

Let $V_{j\kappa_j}$ be the present value of the leader's net receipts.

The expectation, $E(V_{j\kappa_j})$, can be broken into two parts. The first part is the present value of the net earnings, $\pi_{j\kappa_j} - Z_{j\kappa_j}$, up to the time of the next quality improvement. These earnings accrue, as before, over an interval of random length $T_{j\kappa_j}$. The present value of this flow has the same form as Eq. (7.15):

$$ (\pi_{j\kappa_j} - Z_{j\kappa_j}) \cdot [1 - \exp(-rT_{j\kappa_j})]/r. $$

---

[15]Current technological leaders—companies or countries—are less likely to have a cost advantage for the discovery of entirely new products, as considered in Chapter 6. See Brezis, Krugman, and Tsiddon (1993) for this argument.

The probability density for $T_{j\kappa_j}$ is again given by Eq. (7.18):

$$g(\tau) = p_{j\kappa_j} \cdot \exp(-p_{j\kappa_j}\tau). \tag{7.18}$$

Therefore, the expected present value of the first part of $E(V_{j\kappa_j})$ is

$$\left(\frac{\pi_{j\kappa_j} - Z_{j\kappa_j}}{r}\right) \cdot p_{j\kappa_j} \cdot \int_0^\infty (1 - e^{-r\tau}) \cdot \exp(-p_{j\kappa_j}\tau) \cdot d\tau = (\pi_{j\kappa_j} - Z_{j\kappa_j})/(r + p_{j\kappa_j}).$$

The second part of $E(V_{j\kappa_j})$ covers the period after the time of the next quality improvement, $T_{j\kappa_j}$. The expected present value starting from that date is $E(V_{j\kappa_{j+1}})$, but we have to discount this term by the factor $\exp(-rT_{j\kappa_j})$. Therefore, if we again use the probability density for $T_{j\kappa_j}$ from Eq. (7.18), then we can evaluate this second part as

$$E(V_{j\kappa_{j+1}}) \cdot p_{j\kappa_j} \cdot \int_0^\infty e^{-r\tau} \cdot \exp(-p_{j\kappa_j}\tau) \cdot d\tau = p_{j\kappa_j} \cdot E(V_{j\kappa_{j+1}})/(r + p_{j\kappa_j}).$$

If we combine the two parts, then we get

$$E(V_{j\kappa_j}) = \left(\frac{1}{r + p_{j\kappa_j}}\right) \cdot [\pi_{j\kappa_j} - Z_{j\kappa_j} + p_{j\kappa_j} \cdot E(V_{j,\kappa_{j+1}})]. \tag{7.38}$$

We can use Eq. (7.37) to substitute out for $Z_{j\kappa_j}$ in Eq. (7.38). The result is

$$E(V_{j\kappa_j}) = \left(\frac{1}{r + p_{j\kappa_j}}\right) \cdot \left[\pi_{j\kappa_j} - \zeta_\ell \cdot q^{(\kappa_j+1)\cdot\alpha/(1-\alpha)} \cdot p_{j\kappa_j} + p_{j\kappa_j} \cdot E(V_{j\kappa_{j+1}})\right].$$

Thus, $E(V_{j\kappa_j})$ depends on $p_{j\kappa_j}$ and some other terms, including $E(V_{j\kappa_{j+1}})$, that are independent of $p_{j\kappa_j}$. The monopolist would choose $p_{j\kappa_j}$ (by selecting the R&D effort, $Z_{j\kappa_j}$) to maximize $E(V_{j\kappa_j})$. If we set the derivative of $E(V_{j\kappa_j})$ with respect to $p_{j\kappa_j}$ to 0 to get the first-order condition, then the result can be written as

$$E(V_{j,\kappa_{j+1}}) - E(V_{j\kappa_j}) = \zeta_\ell \cdot q^{(\kappa_j+1)\cdot\alpha/(1-\alpha)} = Z_{j\kappa_j}/p_{j\kappa_j}, \tag{7.39}$$

where the last equality uses Eq. (7.37).

The result in Eq. (7.39) differs from the free-entry condition in the previous setup ($\Pi_{j\kappa_j} = 0$ in Eq. [7.20]) in two respects. First, the term $Z_{j\kappa_j}/p_{j\kappa_j}$ is now equated to the increment in present value, $E(V_{j,\kappa_{j+1}}) - E(V_{j\kappa_j})$, rather than to the full present value, $E(V_{j,\kappa_{j+1}})$, because the leader does not value the expropriation of his or her own monopoly profit. Second, the term $E(V_{j\kappa_j})$ is calculated differently from before because it considers that the leadership position is permanent, rather than temporary.

To see this last property, substitute the result for $E(V_{j\kappa_{j+1}})$ from Eq. (7.39) into Eq. (7.38) and also substitute for $Z_{j\kappa_j}$ from Eq. (7.37) to get

$$E(V_{j\kappa_j}) = \pi_{j\kappa_j}/r. \tag{7.40}$$

The term on the right-hand side is the present value yielded by a permanent stream of profit of size $\pi_{j\kappa_j}$. (Since the stream is permanent, the discount rate is r, rather than $r + p_{j\kappa_j}$.)

If we substitute from Eq. (7.40) into Eq. (7.39) and use Eq. (7.14) to substitute out for $\pi_{j\kappa_j}$, then we get a condition for r. The resulting value, denoted r_ℓ, is the equilibrium rate of return for an environment in which the research in all sectors is carried out by the industry leader:[16]

$$r_\ell = (L/\zeta_\ell) \cdot A^{1/(1-\alpha)} \cdot \left(\frac{1-\alpha}{\alpha}\right) \cdot \alpha^{2/(1-\alpha)} \cdot [1 - q^{-\alpha/(1-\alpha)}]. \qquad (7.41)$$

The corresponding growth rate (of Q and the other quantities) is given as usual from $\gamma_\ell = (1/\theta) \cdot (r_\ell - \rho)$.

Recall that the rate of return in the previous model satisfies the condition (from Eq. [7.23])

$$r = (L/\zeta) \cdot A^{1/(1-\alpha)} \cdot \left(\frac{1-\alpha}{\alpha}\right) \cdot \alpha^{2/(1-\alpha)} - p. \qquad (7.42)$$

This expression includes p on the right-hand side, although we could also substitute the equilibrium value for p from Eq. (7.36). The result for r_ℓ in Eq. (7.41) differs from the solution for r in Eq. (7.42) in three ways. First, $\zeta_\ell \leq \zeta$ tends to make $r_\ell \geq r$. Second, r falls with p in Eq. (7.42) because the private return to an innovation is temporary. This force tends to make $r_\ell > r$. Finally, Eq. (7.41) includes the term $[1 - q^{-\alpha/(1-\alpha)}] < 1$, because the leader weighs only the increment in present value from a research success. This term tends to make $r_\ell < r$.

If we use Eq. (7.36) to substitute out for p in Eq. (7.42), then we get the equilibrium value for r, as expressed in Eq. (7.34). If $\zeta_\ell = \zeta$, so that the leader has no cost advantage in research, then we can use Eqs. (7.41) and (7.34) to show $r_\ell < r$.[17] The difference between the rates of return involves two offsetting forces: $r_\ell < r$ because no weight is given to the expropriation of the existing monopoly rentals, but $r_\ell > r$ because innovations are viewed as permanent. The net effect is unambiguous because the two forces are essentially the same, except that they differ in sign and one comes earlier than the other. The extraction of the monopoly rent is the amount taken from one's predecessor. The treatment of an innovation as temporary is equivalent to ignoring the rents that will be taken by one's followers. The terms are the same in magnitude, except for two considerations: the later term is higher because of growth of the economy at the rate γ, but is smaller in present value because of discounting at the rate r. The relation $r > \gamma$—the transversality condition—implies that the first term dominates, so that $r_\ell < r$ must hold.

7.4.2 Research by Outsiders

Suppose now that we allow outside competitors, as well as the leader, to carry out research. If $\zeta = \zeta_\ell$, then Eqs. (7.41) and (7.34) imply $r_\ell < r$; that is, outsiders view

---

[16]If $r < r_\ell$, where r_ℓ is given in Eq. (7.41), then the derivative of $E(V_{j\kappa_j})$ with respect to $p_{j\kappa_j}$ is positive, so that the leader would like to carry out an infinite amount of research. If $r > r_\ell$, then the derivative is negative, so that no research is carried out, and the economy does not grow. An equilibrium with positive growth therefore requires $r = r_\ell$.

[17]The proof requires the transversality condition, $r > \gamma$, given in footnote 12.

research more favorably than the leader. The probability of success, p, and the expected growth rate of quality in each sector are therefore higher than the values that would be determined by a leader who had exclusive rights to do research.

These results do not mean that all research will be conducted by outsiders. Given the competitors' willingness to carry out enough research to generate a probability of success p, the leader would have to accept this probability of an innovation as a constraint given by the existence of the outside competition. (The constraint is effective here because leaders would otherwise determine a lower probability.) For a given success probability—and, hence, a given expected duration of the currently leading technology—the rate of return from research for the leader is exactly the same as that for outsiders (when $\zeta = \zeta_\ell$). Although the leader does not consider the extraction of the existing monopoly rentals as part of the return from successful research, he or she does count as a return the prevention of the loss of these rentals to an outsider. Thus, when $\zeta = \zeta_\ell$, the solutions that we obtained before are valid—for r in Eq. (7.34), γ in Eq. (7.35), and p in Eq. (7.36)—but it is a matter of indifference whether the research is done by leaders or outsiders.[18]

Now we make the more realistic assumption $\zeta_\ell < \zeta$; that is, incumbents have a cost advantage in improving and refining the existing types of products. We noted before that $r_\ell < r$ applies when $\zeta_\ell = \zeta$, but Eq. (7.41) shows that a reduction in ζ_ℓ raises r_ℓ. There exists a critical value $\tilde{\zeta}$ such that $\zeta_\ell < \tilde{\zeta}$ implies $r_\ell > r$. If the leader's cost advantage in research in each sector is large enough so that $\zeta_\ell < \tilde{\zeta}$, then the existence of the outside competitors does not constrain the incumbent's choice of research intensity. Hence, $\zeta_\ell < \tilde{\zeta}$ implies that the equilibrium rate of return equals the value r_ℓ shown in Eq. (7.41), and the growth rate is given correspondingly by $\gamma_\ell = (1/\theta) \cdot (r_\ell - \rho)$.[19] Note that the computations that underlie these solutions for r_ℓ and γ_ℓ treat innovations as permanent and do not attach any value to the taking of the existing monopoly rentals.

Consider now the range $\tilde{\zeta} < \zeta_\ell < \zeta$. In this case, the cost advantage for leaders is not sufficient to ignore the outside competition. The equilibrium is then an analog to limit pricing—research intensities and the corresponding probability of success are just sufficient to deter outsiders from entering the research business. In particular, the limit success probability is the value p shown in Eq. (7.36). In this equilibrium, the industry leaders conduct all the research, but the solutions for r and γ are the same as those that arise when outsiders do all the research (Eqs. [7.34] and [7.35], respectively).[20]

---

[18]This statement is correct if monopoly pricing prevails in either case.

[19]This equilibrium determines the aggregate spending on R&D and the economy's overall growth rate. The allocation of R&D across the sectors is indeterminate, however, because all rates of return to research by leaders equal r_ℓ and are independent of the amount invested. See footnote 8 for an analogous indeterminacy in the model in which outsiders carry out all of the research.

[20]The only difference from before is that the amount spent on research, Z, is smaller because it depends on the research cost for leaders, ζ_ℓ, rather than for outsiders, ζ. The level of consumption, C, in Eq. (7.33) is correspondingly higher.

Thus, on the one hand, we no longer predict the pattern of leapfrogging in which every innovation goes along with the replacement of the industry leader by an outsider. But, on the other hand, the values of r and γ are the same as those predicted by the leapfrogging model. The results are as if researchers were seeking the incumbent's rentals and anticipating that their successes would only be temporary.

7.5 PARETO OPTIMALITY

We can again assess the Pareto optimality of the decentralized equilibria by comparing them with the solution to the social planner's problem. The social planner seeks to maximize the expression for utility in Eq. (7.31), subject to the economy's resource constraint,

$$Y = AL^{1-\alpha} \cdot \sum_{j=1}^{N} (q^{\kappa_j} \cdot X_{j\kappa_j})^\alpha = C + \sum_{j=1}^{N} (X_{j\kappa_j} + Z_j) = C + X + Z. \tag{7.43}$$

The first part of the equation says that total output depends on the quality levels, q^{κ_j}, and the quantities employed, $X_{j\kappa_j}$, of the leading-edge intermediates in each sector. (We have already used the result here that the optimizing social planner would not produce and use any intermediate goods of less than leading-edge quality.) The next part of the equation indicates that output can be used for consumption, C, intermediates, X, and R&D effort, Z.

The planner's problem is also constrained by the R&D technology. We assume that the probability of a research success in sector j, which has attained the quality rung κ_j, is again given from Eq. (7.37) by

$$p_{j\kappa_j} = (1/\zeta_\ell) \cdot Z_{j\kappa_j} \cdot q^{-(\kappa_j+1)\cdot\alpha/(1-\alpha)}. \tag{7.37}$$

We enter the leader's research cost, ζ_ℓ, which we assume is no larger than the cost for outsiders, because the social planner would assign the research activity to the low-cost researcher.

It is convenient first to work out the planner's choice of $X_{j\kappa_j}$—which is a static problem—and then use the result to write out a simplified Hamiltonian expression. We can show that the first-order condition for maximizing U with respect to the choice of $X_{j\kappa_j}$ implies

$$X_{j\kappa_j} \text{ (social planner)} = LA^{1/(1-\alpha)} \cdot \alpha^{1/(1-\alpha)} \cdot q^{\kappa_j\alpha/(1-\alpha)}. \tag{7.44}$$

Recall that the choice in a decentralized economy is

$$X_{j\kappa_j} = LA^{1/(1-\alpha)} \cdot \alpha^{2/(1-\alpha)} \cdot q^{\kappa_j\alpha/(1-\alpha)}. \tag{7.6}$$

The social planner's choice of $X_{j\kappa_j}$ relates to the decentralized choice in the usual manner: monopoly pricing implies that the privately chosen quantity is smaller than the socially chosen amount (by the multiple $\alpha^{1/(1-\alpha)}$).

Substitution for $X_{j\kappa_j}$ from Eq. (7.44) into Eq. (7.43) gives an expression for aggregate output:

$$Y \text{ (social planner)} = A^{1/(1-\alpha)} \cdot \alpha^{\alpha/(1-\alpha)} \cdot LQ, \tag{7.45}$$

where $Q = \sum_{j=1}^{N} q^{\kappa_j \alpha/(1-\alpha)}$ is the same aggregate quality index that we considered for the decentralized economy (see Eq. [7.11]). The level of output for a decentralized economy is

$$Y = A^{1/(1-\alpha)} \cdot \alpha^{2\alpha/(1-\alpha)} \cdot LQ. \tag{7.12}$$

Therefore, for given Q, the social planner's level of output exceeds the decentralized value. This result reflects the decentralized economy's failure to achieve static efficiency by choosing a high enough quantity of intermediate goods, $X_{j\kappa_j}$, in each sector. Equation (7.45) also implies that the social planner's growth rate of Y equals the growth rate of Q.

If the social planner applies the research effort $Z_{j\kappa_j}$ to sector j, then the expected change in Q per unit of time is given by

$$E(\Delta Q) = \sum_{j=1}^{N} p_{j\kappa_j} \cdot [q^{(\kappa_j+1)\cdot\alpha/(1-\alpha)} - q^{\kappa_j \alpha/(1-\alpha)}].$$

Substitution for $p_{j\kappa_j}$ from Eq. (7.37) simplifies the expression to

$$E(\Delta Q) = [1 - q^{-\alpha/(1-\alpha)}] \cdot (Z/\zeta_\ell). \tag{7.46}$$

Thus, the expected change in Q—and, hence, in Y—depends only on the aggregate of R&D spending, Z, and not on the manner in which this spending is spread across the sectors. We again assume that the number of sectors is large enough so that we can treat Q as differentiable; hence, we use Eq. (7.46) to represent the actual change, $\dot{Q}$.

We can use the results to write the social planner's Hamiltonian expression as

$$J = \left(\frac{c^{1-\theta}-1}{1-\theta}\right) \cdot e^{-\rho t} + v \cdot \left[LA^{1/(1-\alpha)} \cdot \left(\frac{1-\alpha}{\alpha}\right) \cdot \alpha^{1/(1-\alpha)} \cdot Q - Z - cL\right]$$
$$+ \mu \cdot [1 - q^{-\alpha/(1-\alpha)}] \cdot (Z/\zeta_\ell). \tag{7.47}$$

The Lagrange multiplier v applies to the resource constraint. This constraint comes from Eq. (7.43) after substitution for Y from Eq. (7.45). The shadow price μ attaches to the expression for $\dot{Q}$ from Eq. (7.46).

Note that the Hamiltonian in Eq. (7.47) depends on the aggregate outlay for R&D, Z, but not on the distribution of this spending across the sectors. This property means that the relative allotments of R&D across the sectors are indeterminate.[21]

We can now use our familiar methods to derive the dynamic-optimization conditions for the choices of c and Z in Eq. (7.47). The first-order conditions and the transition equation for Q lead to the social planner's growth rate:

$$\gamma \text{ (social planner)} = (1/\theta) \cdot \left\{ \left(\frac{L}{\zeta_\ell}\right) \cdot A^{1/(1-\alpha)} \cdot \left(\frac{1-\alpha}{\alpha}\right) \cdot \alpha^{1/(1-\alpha)} \cdot [1 - q^{-\alpha/(1-\alpha)}] - \rho \right\}. \tag{7.48}$$

---

[21]This indeterminacy reflects the lack of diminishing returns to research in each sector. This kind of indeterminacy also applied in the decentralized frameworks; see footnotes 8 and 19.

The implicit social rate of return, which corresponds to the expression in the large brackets that precedes the term $-\rho$, is therefore

$$r \text{ (social planner)} = \left(\frac{L}{\zeta_\ell}\right) \cdot A^{1/(1-\alpha)} \cdot \left(\frac{1-\alpha}{\alpha}\right) \cdot \alpha^{1/(1-\alpha)} \cdot [1 - q^{-\alpha/(1-\alpha)}]. \quad (7.49)$$

The planner's rate of return can be readily compared with the return r_ℓ (from Eq. [7.41]) that applies when industry leaders have a monopoly in research. The rate r_ℓ is lower than the social rate of return by the multiple $\alpha^{1/(1-\alpha)}$ because of the familiar effect from the monopoly pricing of the intermediate goods. (Recall that the decentralized quantity of intermediates, $X_{j\kappa_j}$, in Eq. [7.6] falls short of the social planner's quantity in Eq. [7.44] by the factor $\alpha^{1/(1-\alpha)}$.) The gap in rates of return corresponds to an excess of the planner's growth rate over the decentralized growth rate. The appropriate subsidy on the purchases of intermediate goods would eliminate the discrepancy in rates of return and growth rates in the manner familiar from Chapter 6. This subsidy also removes the static inefficiency that results from the economy's failure to employ a sufficient quantity of intermediate goods.

The rate of return r_ℓ prevails in the decentralized economy if leaders have a sufficient cost advantage in research ($\zeta_\ell \leq \tilde{\zeta}$ in the previous discussion). Otherwise, the rate of return is the value r shown in Eq. (7.34). The spread between the social rate of return and r adds $r_\ell - r$ to the gap between the social rate and r_ℓ, a gap that we have already discussed.

Recall that $r_\ell < r$ because of two offsetting effects: the rate r is higher because it counts the expropriation of the predecessor's monopoly profit, but is lower because it views the benefits from an innovation as temporary. We discussed before why the first effect was larger, so that $r_\ell < r$ on net. This result implies that the difference between the social rate of return and r is smaller than the difference between the social rate and r_ℓ. Hence, the gap between the planner's growth rate and the decentralized growth rate is also not as large as before. It is even possible that the privately determined rate of return and growth rate would exceed the planner's values. This result applies if the effect from the monopoly pricing of the intermediates is less important than the gap between r and r_ℓ (which reflects the net effect from the seeking of monopoly profit).

We already mentioned that the appropriate subsidy to the purchase of intermediates would remove the distortions from monopoly pricing. The additional distortions that arise when the private rate of return is r (given in Eq. [7.34]) can be eliminated if a scheme is implemented—in the spirit of Coase (1960)—that effectively endows industry leaders with property rights over their monopoly profits. This scheme would require innovators to compensate their immediate predecessor for the loss of rental income. An innovator in sector j then raises the cost of innovation to include the required compensation to the current leader, but also raises the prospective reward to include the anticipated compensation from the next innovator. The first part of the scheme causes the innovator to count only the net change in the flow of monopoly rentals as a contribution; that is, the incentive to seek the existing rents is eliminated. The second part motivates the innovator to view his or her contribution as lasting forever, rather than just until the next innovation. As usual, however, the successful implementation of this kind of policy becomes problematic in a richer model; for example, in contexts where quality improvements are hard for a policy-maker to evaluate.

The internalization just described occurs automatically in the model if the leaders have a monopoly position in research, so that the private rate of return is the value r_ℓ. Thus, one way to reach the first best in this framework is to preclude research by outsiders! This provision reduces the incentive to innovate, but only to the appropriate extent. This method works, however, only if the effects of monopoly pricing have already been neutralized through the appropriate tax-subsidy policy. If these tax-subsidy policies are infeasible, then the prevention of research by followers is likely to worsen the outcomes in this model.

We can summarize the model's conclusions about welfare as follows:

1. The decentralized rate of return and growth rate coincide with the social planner's choices if the effects of monopoly pricing are eliminated (for example, by implementing the appropriate subsidy to the purchase of intermediates) and if innovators are forced to compensate their immediate predecessor for the loss of monopoly rentals. This compensation scheme effectively institutes the claim on these monopoly rentals as a formal property right.

2. If the effects of monopoly pricing are eliminated, but no compensation is awarded to predecessors, then the decentralized values for the rate of return and the growth rate *exceed* the social planner's values. The failure to compensate one's predecessor makes the private rewards to innovation too high, whereas the failure to receive compensation later goes the other way. The net effect from this rent seeking is unambiguous, however, because the distortions are essentially the same except that the second one occurs later.

3. If there are no interventions—so that the effects of monopoly pricing are not eliminated and no compensation is paid to one's predecessor—then the decentralized values for the rate of return and the growth rate may be higher or lower than the social planner's values. We already know from Chapter 6 that monopoly pricing causes the decentralized rate of return and growth rate to fall short of the socially optimal values. This element is now offset by the net effect from rent seeking, a force that makes the private rate of return too high.

7.6 SUMMARY OBSERVATIONS ABOUT GROWTH

The quality improvements studied in this chapter represent ongoing refinements of products and techniques, whereas the expansions of variety considered in the previous chapter describe basic innovations. From a modeling standpoint, one distinction between the two kinds of technological progress is that goods of higher quality are close substitutes for those of lesser quality, so that quality enhancements tend to make the old goods obsolete. In contrast, we assumed that discoveries of new kinds of products were not (on average) direct substitutes or complements for the existing types; therefore, innovation did not tend to drive out the old varieties. One consequence of this distinction is that, in a decentralized economy, the R&D effort aimed at quality improvements may be too high (because of the incentive to seek the monopoly rents of incumbents), whereas the effort aimed at basic innovations tends to be too low.

Another difference in specification is that the costs of quality improvements for insiders tend to be smaller than those for outsiders. Hence, we argued that the insiders would tend, in equilibrium, to carry out most of the research that underlies the regular process of product refinement. In contrast, insiders are unlikely to have a cost advantage in breakthrough research, basically because there are no insiders for this activity. Therefore, dramatically new innovations are unlikely to come from existing industry leaders.

The two types of technological progress that we have studied have similar predictions about the determination of growth rates. In both cases, growth is higher if the willingness to save is greater, the level of technology is higher, and the cost of R&D is lower. Both formulations also predict scale effects, represented in the models by the quantity of a fixed factor like raw labor or human capital.

PROBLEMS

7.1 The Step Size between Innovations. Suppose that the cost of doing research, $Z_{j\kappa_j}$, is a function, $Z(q)$, of the step size, q, between innovations. (We continue to assume here that q is known with certainty.) Assume that the function $Z(\cdot)$ satisfies $Z' > 0$ and $Z'' > 0$.
   (a) What value of q will be determined in equilibrium, say in the model in which the leader's cost advantage in R&D is sufficiently great to neglect the potential research of outsiders?
   (b) Under what conditions is the previous answer consistent with the assumption that the leader can neglect the potential research by outsiders?

7.2 Monopoly Rights in Research. Suppose that the government maintains the monopoly position of industry leaders by precluding research by outsiders. Under what conditions will such a policy be welfare enhancing? What problems would arise in practice in the pursuit of this kind of policy?

7.3 The Industry Leader as the Exclusive Researcher. Assume that the industry leader's cost parameter for research in quality improvements, ζ_ℓ, is less than that for outsiders, ζ.
   (a) Under what conditions will the leader carry out all of the research on quality improvements in equilibrium? Would the results be different for breakthrough research, rather than quality refinements?
   (b) Under what conditions will the equilibrium research intensity on quality improvements be independent of the outsiders' potential to carry out research? Describe the nature of the interaction for the case in which the outsiders' potential research matters for the equilibrium. Is there a sense in which more competition raises the economy's growth rate?
   (c) Suppose that the condition for monopoly pricing, $\alpha q \geq 1$, is *not* satisfied (for the environment in which the leader and the immediate predecessor are different agents). How do the results change in this circumstance?

7.4 Alternative Relations between the Probability of Research Success and the Research Intensity. Suppose that the dependence of the probability of research success in sector j, $p_{j\kappa_j}$, on the total R&D effort in the sector, $Z_{j\kappa_j}$, is modified from Eq. (7.16) to

$$p_{j\kappa_j} = (Z_{j\kappa_j})^\epsilon \cdot \phi(\kappa_j),$$

where $\epsilon > 0$ and $\phi(\kappa_j)$ is still given by Eq. (7.22). Each researcher's probability of success per unit of time is $p_{j\kappa_j}$ multiplied by the researcher's share of the total R&D effort in sector j.

(a) Consider the free-entry condition for R&D in sector j. How does the condition differ from the one obtained by setting Eq. (7.20) to 0, the result that applies when $\epsilon = 1$?

(b) What new kind of distortion arises if $\epsilon < 1$? (Hint: consider the analogy of a fishing pond that has free entry and is subject to congestion.)

(c) What happens if $\epsilon > 1$?

(d) Discuss how equilibrium research intensities in each sector are determined for a setting in which $\epsilon \neq 1$. (The technical details of this problem have not yet been worked out.)

7.5 Alternative Relations between the Probability of Research Success and the Quality-Ladder Position. Suppose that Eq. (7.16) still describes the dependence of the probability of research success in sector j, $p_{j\kappa_j}$, on the total research effort in the sector, $Z_{j\kappa_j}$, and the quality-ladder position, κ_j. Assume, however, that the function $\phi(\kappa_j)$ differs from the one shown in Eq. (7.22).

(a) If the magnitude of $\phi'(\kappa_j)$ is larger than that prescribed by Eq. (7.22) for all values of κ_j, then how do the results change?

(b) If the magnitude of $\phi'(\kappa_j)$ is smaller than that prescribed by Eq. (7.22) for all values of κ_j, then how do the results change?

(c) Suppose that the magnitude of $\phi'(\kappa_j)$ were smaller than that prescribed by Eq. (7.22) for small values of κ_j but larger in magnitude for large values of κ_j. What would the results look like in this case?

CHAPTER

8

THE DIFFUSION
OF TECHNOLOGY

In the Solow–Swan model of Chapter 1, the tendency for convergence across economies derived from the diminishing returns to capital. The higher rate of return on capital in poor economies—or at least in economies that were further below their own steady-state positions—generated a faster rate of per capita growth. We showed in the Ramsey model of Chapter 2 how this tendency would be modified by the behavior of the saving rate. The convergence rate was faster or slower depending on whether poor economies tended to save a higher or lower fraction of their incomes. Then we found in Chapter 3 that the international mobility of capital among open economies tended to speed up the process of convergence.

In the models developed in Chapters 4 and 5, economies could sustain positive per capita growth in the steady state if the returns to a broad concept of capital, which includes human capital, were constant. If the returns to broad capital diminish for awhile, but are roughly constant asymptotically, then economies exhibit convergence behavior, but also feature endogenous growth in the long run. (We discussed in Chapter 1 some technological specifications that had this character.) We also examined in Chapter 5 how imbalances between physical and human capital affected the transitional dynamics. Economies that began with a high ratio of human to physical capital would grow especially fast. Thus, the endogenous growth theories that rely on constant long-run returns to broad capital are consistent with a rich transitional dynamics, which can include convergence-type behavior.

In the models of Chapters 6 and 7, long-term growth arose if R&D investments—the source of technological progress in these models—exhibited constant returns. We have not yet discussed whether these theories are consistent with the empirical evidence on convergence. In a multi-economy setting, the key issue here is how rapidly the discoveries made in leading economies diffuse to follower economies.

265

We shall find in this chapter that, if the diffusion of technology occurs gradually, then we get another reason to predict a pattern of convergence across economies.

We study technological diffusion in the context of the model of variety of intermediate products from Chapter 6.[1] We would, however, get similar results if we examined the type of quality improvements that we introduced in Chapter 7. The main idea here is that follower countries tend to catch up to the leaders because imitation and implementation of discoveries are cheaper than innovation. This mechanism tends to generate convergence even if diminishing returns to capital or to R&D do not apply.

8.1 A LEADER-FOLLOWER MODEL

We begin with the spread of technology from a leading economy, called country 1, to a follower economy, called country 2. We use the setup from Chapter 6 in which the level of technology corresponds to the number of varieties of intermediate products, N_1, that have been discovered by the technological leader. Researchers in country 1 expend effort to invent these products, and they are initially used to produce final goods in country 1.

Country 2 does not invent intermediate goods, but instead imitates or adapts the products that have been discovered and used in country 1. The use of one of these products in country 2 requires some effort for adaptation to a different environment. We think of this effort as a cost of imitation. This cost is like the R&D outlay that we considered in Chapter 6, except that the cost of imitation is typically less than the cost of invention. We assume here that imitators pay no fees to foreign inventors; hence, agents in country 1 do not receive any compensation for the use of their innovations in country 2. In a later section, we consider a different setup in which the adaptation of a technology to country 2 involves foreign investment by country 1.

Final goods are tradable across countries and are exchanged at a single world price. In contrast, the intermediate products do not flow freely across international borders. We assume that the final-goods producers in country 2 can use a particular intermediate good only if a local expert is available to oversee the installation and use of this good. The inventor of a new type of product—who is also the monopolistic provider of the good—performs this service in country 1. The good becomes available for use in country 2 only if someone first expends resources to adapt the good to this environment.

Some success stories of economic development involve the absorption of technological expertise from abroad in ways that correspond roughly to our theoretical setup. Young (1989, Ch. 6) argues that many entrepreneurs in Hong Kong learned businesses as production workers, serving effectively as apprentices to foreign

---

[1]The previous theoretical research on technological diffusion that we build on includes Nelson and Phelps (1966), Krugman (1979), Jovanovic and Lach (1991), Grossman and Helpman (1991, Chs. 11, 12), and Segerstrom (1991).

managers. The locals subsequently used this knowledge to establish their own enterprises. In Singapore, entry into several leading-edge industries, such as electronics and financial services, depended on substantial foreign investment and expertise. ·This foreign involvement was actively encouraged by the Singaporean government (Young [1992]). Foreign investments in China from Hong Kong and in Mexico from the United States have been important in facilitating the flow of knowledge about advanced manufacturing techniques (Romer [1993]). In Mauritius, the dramatic growth of garment manufacturing entailed the importation of foreign entrepreneurs, who trained and supervised the local workers. These foreigners, principally from Hong Kong, were attracted by an export processing zone that featured a number of favorable government policies, including low taxes and guaranteed low wages (see Gulhati and Nallari [1990], Bowman [1991], and Romer [1992]).

8.1.1 Behavior of Innovators in the Leading Country

The model for the innovator in country 1 is the same as that worked out in the first part of Chapter 6. If N_1 intermediate goods have been discovered, then the quantity Y_1 of final goods produced by the representative firm in country 1 is given by

$$Y_1 = A_1 \cdot L_1^{1-\alpha} \cdot \sum_{j=1}^{N_1}(X_{1j})^{\alpha}, \tag{8.1}$$

where $0 < \alpha < 1$, A_1 is a productivity parameter, L_1 is the quantity of labor input, and X_{1j} is the quantity of nondurable input of type j. We assume that population and, hence, the aggregate labor input, L_1, are constant. Recall also that the parameter A_1 can represent various aspects of government policy—such as taxation, provision of public services, and maintenance of property rights—as well as the level of technology.

The cost of production of each intermediate input, X_{1j}, is unity, and each good is sold, as in Chapter 6, at the monopoly price, $P = 1/\alpha$. By equating the marginal product of X_{1j} to the price, we obtain the quantity of each type:

$$X_{1j} = (A_1)^{1/(1-\alpha)} \cdot \alpha^{2/(1-\alpha)} \cdot L_1. \tag{8.2}$$

Substitution from Eq. (8.2) into Eq. (8.1) implies that the level of output per worker in country 1 is

$$y_1 \equiv Y_1/L_1 = (A_1)^{1/(1-\alpha)} \cdot \alpha^{2\alpha/(1-\alpha)} \cdot N_1. \tag{8.3}$$

Output per worker, y_1, increases with the productivity parameter, A_1, and the number of products, N_1. The wage rate, w_1, equals a firm's marginal product of labor and is the multiple $1 - \alpha$ of y_1.

Equation (8.2) implies that the flow of monopoly profit from sales of the jth intermediate good in country 1 is

$$\pi_{1j} = \left(\frac{1-\alpha}{\alpha}\right) \cdot (A_1)^{1/(1-\alpha)} \cdot \alpha^{2/(1-\alpha)} \cdot L_1. \tag{8.4}$$

The present value of profit for the jth innovator is π_{1j}/r_1, where r_1 is the rate of return in country 1. (This rate of return will be constant in equilibrium, just as it was in Chapter 6.) The free-entry condition equates this present value to the cost, η, of inventing a new product. (We assume that a positive amount of innovation occurs in the equilibrium and, hence, that the equilibrium growth rate is positive. In this case, the free-entry condition holds as an equality.) Rearrangement of the free-entry condition implies that r_1 is given by

$$r_1 = (L_1/\eta) \cdot (\frac{1-\alpha}{\alpha}) \cdot (A_1)^{1/(1-\alpha)} \cdot \alpha^{2/(1-\alpha)}. \tag{8.5}$$

The usual consumer-optimization condition implies that the growth rate of consumption, C_1, is given by $\gamma_1 = (1/\theta) \cdot (r_1 - \rho)$. (We assume here that the preference parameters, ρ and θ, do not vary across countries.) If we substitute for r_1 from Eq. (8.5), then the growth rate is

$$\gamma_1 = (1/\theta) \cdot \left[(L_1/\eta) \cdot (\frac{1-\alpha}{\alpha}) \cdot (A_1)^{1/(1-\alpha)} \cdot \alpha^{2/(1-\alpha)} - \rho \right]. \tag{8.6}$$

As in Chapter 6, country 1 is always in a steady state with the quantities N_1, Y_1, and C_1 all growing at the constant rate γ_1.

8.1.2   Behavior of Imitators in the Follower Country

The production function for the representative firm in country 2 is

$$Y_2 = A_2 \cdot L_2^{1-\alpha} \cdot \sum_{j=1}^{N_2} (X_{2j})^\alpha, \tag{8.7}$$

where $N_2 \le N_1$ is the number of products that are available for use in country 2. We focus on the adaptation to country 2 of the products that were discovered by innovators in country 1, but some of the N_2 varieties may have been discovered previously in country 2. We do not allow here for any new discoveries in country 2, and we assume that the N_2 products available in country 2 are a subset of the N_1 goods known in country 1.[2] In other words, we do not allow for innovation in country 2 or imitation in country 1.

The productivity parameter, A_2, and the aggregate labor input, L_2, may differ from the corresponding parameters for country 1. Differences between A_2 and A_1 could, as already mentioned, reflect differences in government policies. The total labor input represents the scale over which an intermediate good can be utilized

---

[2]We do not explain how country 2 learned to produce its first type of good. The problem is that Eq. (8.7) implies that country 2 produces nothing if it lacks access to all varieties of intermediate products. The same difficulty arises for country 1's initial innovation and for the discoveries of products in the model of Chapter 6. Given the form of the production function, we have to assume that people always knew how to produce at least one type of intermediate good.

in production. Thus, the gap between L_2 and L_1 reflects the differences in scale of the two economies.

The adapter of the jth intermediate product in country 2 is assumed to receive a perpetual monopoly over the production and sale of this good in that country. Hence, the treatment of imitation in country 2 parallels the setup for innovation in country 1. (We could assume, as discussed in Chapter 6, that the imitator's monopoly power diminishes over time; for example, the good becomes available at a competitive price with the probability p per unit of time. This alternative specification would not change the basic results that we obtain.)

The model of imitation in country 2 parallels the one for innovation in country 1, except that country 2's cost of imitation, denoted by ν, replaces the cost of innovation, η. We assume $0 < \nu < \eta$—imitation is costly, but less expensive than innovation—but we reconsider later the assumption that ν is constant.

A crucial assumption here is that the costs of imitation are nontrivial; that is, innovations cannot be transferred to other locations at negligible cost. Mansfield, Schwartz, and Wagner (1981, pp. 908–909) studied the cost of imitation in the United States for 48 product innovations that were made in the chemical, drug, electronics, and machinery industries. They found that the cost of imitation averaged 65% of the cost of innovation. The ratio of costs varied substantially, however, across the products; only half of the ratios were between 40% and 90%.

Griliches (1957) found in U.S. regional data that the time at which hybrid corn was introduced and the rate at which this innovation spread depended on measures of the cost of absorption and the eventual profitability of the new technology. The date of introduction tended to be sooner the more similar an area's preferred hybrids were to those developed initially in the corn belt (the location to which most of the early research on hybrid corn was directed). The rate of absorption was faster the greater the market size and the larger the potential improvement in crop yields.

Teece (1977) examined the cost of technology transfer across countries for multinational firms. For 26 cases in chemicals, petroleum refining, and machinery, he found that the cost averaged 19% of total project expenditures. He also found that the transfer cost declined with measures of experience with the technology being transferred, but did not depend on the level of economic development in the recipient country. In contrast, Nelson and Phelps (1966) conjectured that ν would be lower the more abundant human capital is in the receiving location, and some of the empirical results discussed in Chapter 12 support this viewpoint. In any case, the results of Mansfield, Schwartz, and Wagner (1981) and Teece (1977) suggest that the transfer cost, ν, would typically be significant.

The price of each intermediate good in country 2 is again the monopoly markup $1/\alpha$ on the unit cost of production. The quantity of each type is given by

$$X_{2j} = (A_2)^{1/(1-\alpha)} \cdot \alpha^{2/(1-\alpha)} \cdot L_2, \tag{8.8}$$

a result that parallels Eq. (8.2).

The formula for output per worker in country 2 is analogous to that shown for country 1 in Eq. (8.3):

$$y_2 \equiv Y_2/L_2 = (A_2)^{1/(1-\alpha)} \cdot \alpha^{2\alpha/(1-\alpha)} \cdot N_2. \tag{8.9}$$

The wage rate, w_2, is the multiple $1 - \alpha$ of y_2. Equations (8.9) and (8.3) imply that the ratio of the per-worker products for the two countries, y_2/y_1, depends positively on the ratio of the productivity parameters, specifically on $(A_2/A_1)^{1/(1-\alpha)}$, and on the fraction of products that have been imitated, N_2/N_1. The ratio of wage rates, w_2/w_1, depends on the same terms.

The flow of profit from sales of the jth intermediate good in country 2 takes the same form as Eq. (8.4):

$$\pi_{2j} = \left(\frac{1 - \alpha}{\alpha}\right) \cdot (A_2)^{1/(1-\alpha)} \cdot \alpha^{2/(1-\alpha)} \cdot L_2. \tag{8.10}$$

The free-entry condition for imitation in country 2 equates the present value of this profit to the cost of imitation, ν. (We assume that country 2's equilibrium growth rate is positive—in particular, that imitation occurs in the equilibrium—so that the free-entry condition holds with equality.)

The free-entry condition for country 2 is complicated because the rate of return, r_2, will not generally be constant. Specifically, if N_2 grows faster than N_1, then country 2 eventually exhausts the pool of innovations that can be imitated; at that point, the rate of return in country 2 surely declines. This end-point condition generally affects the entire time path of the rate of return. However, if the time at which the pool of innovations is exhausted is far in the future, then this consideration will have only a minor effect, and the rate of return, r_2, will be nearly constant.

If r_2 is (approximately) constant, then the free-entry condition equates the present value of profit, π_{2j}/r_2, to the cost, ν, of imitation. The formula for π_{2j} from Eq. (8.10) therefore implies that r_2 is given by

$$r_2 = (L_2/\nu) \cdot \left(\frac{1 - \alpha}{\alpha}\right) \cdot (A_2)^{1/(1-\alpha)} \cdot a^{2/(1-a)}. \tag{8.11}$$

We assume here that the two countries do not participate in a common capital market and, hence, that r_2 can diverge from r_1, given in Eq. (8.5).

The rate of return, r_2, determines the growth rate in the usual way:

$$\gamma_2 = (1/\theta) \cdot \left[(L_2/\nu) \cdot \left(\frac{1 - \alpha}{\alpha}\right) \cdot (A_2)^{1/(1-\alpha)} \cdot \alpha^{2/(1-\alpha)} - \rho \right]. \tag{8.12}$$

Country 2 is in a steady state in the sense that γ_2 prescribes the constant growth rate of N_2, Y_2, and C_2. Recall, however, that this result is an approximation that neglects the fact that country 2 will eventually exhaust the pool of potential imitations if $\gamma_2 > \gamma_1$.

If the two countries have the same values of A_i and L_i, then the condition $\nu < \eta$ ensures $\gamma_2 > \gamma_1$ (see Eqs. [8.6] and [8.12]). That is, the follower country would grow faster because imitation is cheaper than innovation. More generally, $\gamma_2 > \gamma_1$ applies if ν is sufficiently below η; specifically

$$\gamma_2 > \gamma_1 \text{ if } \nu/\eta < (L_2/L_1) \cdot (A_2/A_1)^{1/(1-\alpha)}. \tag{8.13}$$

Thus, country 2 grows faster unless it is strongly disadvantaged with respect to its productivity parameter, A_2, or its size, L_2. The inequality in (8.13) also implies that r_2 in Eq. (8.11) exceeds r_1 in Eq. (8.5). (Recall that the preference parameters, ρ and θ, are assumed to be the same in the two countries.)

If $\gamma_2 > \gamma_1$, then N_2, the number of designs known in country 2, grows faster than N_1, the number known in country 1. The number N_2 eventually rises to equal N_1; thereafter, country 2 cannot grow at a faster rate than country 1 by imitating country 1's innovations. (Some observers would say that Japan as country 2 has reached this point in relation to the United States as country 1.) The change in N_2—through imitation—would then be constrained to equal the change in N_1.[3] Hence, once country 2 learned all of country 1's designs, the two countries would grow at the same rate. Country 1 then continues to innovate, and country 2 immediately imitates the results. (If we had assumed that imitation takes time, as well as goods, then the imitation would occur with a lag, and a gap between country 1 and country 2 would persist forever.[4])

This model of the diffusion of technology implies a form of convergence, even though diminishing returns do not apply to innovation in country 1 or to imitation in country 2. The follower country, with $N_2 < N_1$, grows at a faster rate than the leader if the inequality in (8.13) holds.

The results do not provide a full description of the transition from a high growth rate, $\gamma_2 > \gamma_1$—where γ_2 is nearly constant when N_2 is far below N_1—to the lower growth rate, $\gamma_2 = \gamma_1$—which must hold when $N_2 = N_1$. Our conjecture is that the equilibrium entails a gradually declining path of γ_2 and r_2, but this analysis has not yet been worked out.

If the productivity parameters, A_2 and A_1, are the same, then Eqs. (8.3) and (8.9) imply $y_2 < y_1$ when $N_2 < N_1$. The wage rate, w_2, is correspondingly below w_1. If $A_2 = A_1$, then $y_2 = y_1$ and $w_2 = w_1$ apply when $N_2 = N_1$. In contrast, if $A_2 < A_1$, then y_2 and w_2 would converge to levels that were lower, respectively, than y_1 and w_1. (However, the inequality shown in [8.13] limits the extent to which A_2 can fall short of A_1 if country 2 is to grow faster than country 1 during the transition.) If $A_2 > A_1$, then y_2 and w_2 would converge to levels that were higher, respectively, than y_1 and w_1. That is, the imitating country might eventually do better than the leader in terms of the levels of per capita product and wage rate. In any event, although the countries eventually grow at the same rate, they need not converge to the same levels of output per worker and wage rate.

---

[3]If imitators know that they can pay ν to copy one of country 1's innovations, then the rate of return from imitation would be too high in this situation to satisfy the free-entry condition. We could assume that J potential followers engage in an imitation race in which each entrant pays ν and then receives the probability $1/J$ of gaining the monopoly right to use the copy in country 2. The number J would be determined to satisfy the free-entry condition (if we ignore the integer restriction on J). Let $(\gamma_2)^*$ be the growth rate and $(r_2)^*$ the rate of return in this equilibrium. We know that $(\gamma_2)^* = (1/\theta) \cdot [(r_2)^* - \rho] = \gamma_1$. Therefore, if the parameters ρ and θ are the same in the two countries, then $(r_2)^* = r_1$, given in Eq. (8.5).

[4]Jovanovic and Lach (1991) construct a model that includes a time lag for imitation. Mansfield, Schwartz, and Wagner (1981, p. 909) find in their sample of 48 innovations that the ratio of the time required for imitation to that for innovation averaged 70 percent. The lag with which advances become known in an industry appears to be brief. For example, Mansfield (1985) reports that 70% of product innovations are familiar to rival companies within a year. Caballero and Jaffe (1993) reach similar conclusions from their use of patent citation data (references in patent documents to previous patents upon which the current discovery builds) to measure the time required for ideas to influence other researchers. They find that the diffusion is rapid with a mean lag between one and two years.

8.1.3   Variations in the Cost of Imitation

The results obtained thus far depend on the absence of diminishing returns to innovation and imitation. One way to defend the assumed constancy of returns to innovation is to argue that the number of potential discoveries—the number of products in the present context—is unlimited (see Romer [1992] for a discussion). Since an infinite number of potential inventions exist, it is possible, first, that the contribution of each new product to output would not decline with the number already discovered and, second, that the cost of inventing the next product would not rise with this number.

The situation is different, however, for imitation. The set of products that can be copied by a follower is limited at any point in time to the finite number that have been discovered by leaders but have not yet been imitated. If we allow for elements of heterogeneity across countries, then some inventions made by a leader, such as country 1, would turn out to be more readily adaptable and potentially more productive for a follower, such as country 2. Therefore, the larger the set that the follower can choose from—that is, the greater the gap between the leader and the follower—the higher tends to be the return from the most promising project that is available for imitation.

We can represent this idea formally by assuming that country 2's cost of imitation, ν, is an increasing function of the ratio of N_2 to N_1 :

$$\nu = \psi(N_2/N_1), \tag{8.14}$$

where $\psi' > 0$ and $\psi'' \geq 0$. We assume that $\psi(1)$ is large enough to deter complete imitation—that is, not all inventions will be copied asymptotically in the equilibrium—and that $\psi(0)$ is small enough to motivate a positive amount of imitation (see, however, footnote 2).

Country 2's growth rate, γ_2 from Eq. (8.12), would equal country 1's growth rate, γ_1 from Eq. (8.6), if the cost of innovation, ν, equaled

$$\nu^* = \eta \cdot (L_2/L_1) \cdot (A_2/A_1)^{1/(1-\alpha)}. \tag{8.15}$$

Thus, $\nu^* = \eta$ if $A_2 = A_1$ and $L_2 = L_1$.

Given the properties of the function ψ, we can use Eq. (8.14) to determine the unique ratio of N_2 to N_1 that corresponds to the cost ν^* shown in Eq. (8.15):

$$(N_2/N_1)^* = \phi[\eta \cdot (L_2/L_1) \cdot (A_2/A_1)^{1/(1-\alpha)}], \tag{8.16}$$

where the function ϕ is the inverse of the function ψ from Eq. (8.14). The properties of ψ imply $\phi' > 0$, $\phi'' \leq 0$, and $0 < (N_2/N_1)^* < 1$.

If $N_2/N_1 = (N_2/N_1)^*$, then the two countries would be in a steady state in which N_2 and N_1 grow at the same rate (of innovation and imitation, respectively). Since the ratio N_2/N_1 then remains constant, the form of Eq. (8.14) implies that ν stays constant at the value ν^*. Equation (8.12) therefore prescribes the constant growth rate, $\gamma_2 = \gamma_1$, that prevails in country 2. Thus, even if the countries differ by productivity parameters, A_i, and size, L_i, the process of technological diffusion implies that the follower country will grow in the long run at the same rate as the leader. This result will also hold if the economies differ in their preference parameters, ρ_i and θ_i, which determine the willingness to save.

If $\rho_2 = \rho_1$ and $\theta_2 = \theta_1$, as we have been assuming, then the equalization of growth rates in the steady state implies that the rates of return must also be equal. That is, the long-run value of r_2, given in Eq. (8.11), equals the value r_1 shown in Eq. (8.5).[5] Thus, even without a global capital market, the diffusion of technology equalizes the rates of return in the steady state. (The rates of return would not be the same, however, if the economies differ in their preference parameters, ρ_i and θ_i.)

If $N_2/N_1 < (N_2/N_1)^*$, then Eq. (8.14) implies $\nu < \nu^*$. The lower cost of innovation tends to raise r_2 above r_1 and thereby to raise γ_2, the growth rate of N_2, above γ_1.[6] Hence, if country 2 begins with $N_2/N_1 < (N_2/N_1)^*$, then N_2/N_1 tends to rise over time, ν tends thereby to increase, and γ_2 tends to decline toward its steady-state value, γ_1. The process works in reverse if country 2 begins with $N_2/N_1 > (N_2/N_1)^*$.

This model delivers a familiar kind of convergence behavior: country 2 grows faster the further below it is from its steady-state position, that is, the lower N_2/N_1 compared to $(N_2/N_1)^*$. We can write this result as a log-linear approximation in the form

$$\gamma_2 \approx \gamma_1 - \mu \cdot \log\left[\frac{N_2/N_1}{(N_2/N_1)^*}\right]. \qquad (8.17)$$

The positive parameter μ, which determines the speed of convergence, depends on the properties of the function ψ in Eq. (8.14). Note that $\gamma_2 = \gamma_1$ if $N_2/N_1 = (N_2/N_1)^*$, and γ_2 rises as N_2/N_1 falls, *for a given value of* $(N_2/N_1)^*$.

We can use Eqs. (8.3) and (8.9) to express the convergence result in terms of levels of per capita product. The ratio of per capita products is given by

$$y_2/y_1 = (A_2/A_1)^{1/(1-\alpha)} \cdot (N_2/N_1). \qquad (8.18)$$

In the steady state, where $N_2/N_1 = (N_2/N_1)^*$, the ratio of per capita products is

$$(y_2/y_1)^* = (A_2/A_1)^{1/(1-\alpha)} \cdot (N_2/N_1)^*, \qquad (8.19)$$

where $(N_2/N_1)^*$ is increasing in L_2/L_1 and A_2/A_1 from Eq. (8.16). We can replace the ratio of N_2/N_1 to $(N_2/N_1)^*$ in Eq. (8.17) by the corresponding ratio for per capita products to get

$$\gamma_2 \approx \gamma_1 - \mu \cdot \log\left[\frac{y_2/y_1}{(y_2/y_1)^*}\right]. \qquad (8.20)$$

---

[5]Recall that we derived Eq. (8.11) from a free-entry condition that assumed a constant rate of return. Hence, this assumption is appropriate in the steady state in this model.

[6]We can show from the free-entry condition for imitation that $r_2 = (\pi_{2j}/\nu) + \epsilon \cdot (\gamma_2 - \gamma_1)$, where π_{2j} is the flow of monopoly profit shown in Eq. (8.10) and ϵ is the elasticity of ν with respect to N_2/N_1. If we think of ν as the price of a claim on a design, then the first term in the expression for r_2 is analogous to the real flow of dividends on this claim, and the second term corresponds to the capital gain due to the change in ν over time. An increase in N_2/N_1 tends to raise ν and thereby to reduce r_2. We have, however, been unable to work out sufficient conditions for γ_2 to fall monotonically as N_2/N_1 rises.

Equation (8.20) implies a form of conditional convergence: the growth rate γ_2 declines with y_2/y_1 for given values of $(y_2/y_1)^*$ and γ_1. Equations (8.19) and (8.16) imply that $(y_2/y_1)^*$ is an increasing function of A_2/A_1 and L_2/L_1. Thus, for given values of y_2/y_1 and γ_1, a follower economy grows faster if A_2/A_1 and L_2/L_1 are higher, that is, if the follower's level of technology and government policies are more favorable relative to those in the leading economy and if the follower has a relatively larger scale. These effects reflect the positive effects of A_2 and L_2 on the incentive to introduce new products into economy 2.

We can consider a group of follower countries, $i = 2, 3, \ldots,$ with associated levels of per capita product y_i. Unless the values of A_i and L_i are the same, the poorer places may not grow faster—that is, absolute convergence need not hold. We have to condition the observed values of y_i on A_i and L_i (or on observable proxies for these variables) to isolate the predicted inverse relation between the growth rate and the initial level of per capita product.

These results on conditional convergence do not depend on diminishing returns to capital or innovation, but do require a form of diminishing returns in imitation. The key assumption is that, for a given stock of inventions, the cost of imitation rises as the number of goods already copied increases.

8.1.4   Empirical Implications for Convergence

One question to consider is whether the type of conditional convergence that arises in this model of technological diffusion can be distinguished empirically from the type that appeared in standard models of a closed economy, say in the Solow–Swan and Ramsey models of Chapters 1 and 2. In these earlier models, the log-linearization around the steady state implies that the growth rate of per capita product for country i can be approximated as

$$\gamma_i \approx x - \beta \cdot \log(\hat{y}_i/\hat{y}_i^*), \qquad (8.21)$$

where x is the rate of labor-augmenting technological progress, $\beta > 0$ is the speed of convergence, $\hat{y}_i$ is output per effective worker, and $\hat{y}_i^*$ is the steady-state value of $\hat{y}_i$. We assume in Eq. (8.21) that x and β are the same for all countries. The observable variable y_i is related to $\hat{y}_i$ in accordance with

$$\log(\hat{y}_i) = \log(y_i) - xt,$$

where t is chronological time. If we substitute this formula into Eq. (8.21), then we get

$$\gamma_i \approx x - \beta \cdot \log(y_i) + \beta \cdot \log(\hat{y}_i^*) + \beta xt. \qquad (8.22)$$

In a cross section of countries for a given time period, βxt is a constant that adds to the constant x in Eq. (8.22). Suppose that we have observable variables for each country that proxy satisfactorily for variations in $\hat{y}_i^*$ (in Chapter 12, we use measures of government policy, demographic factors, investment ratios, and other variables). Then we can run a regression in the form of Eq. (8.22) to obtain an estimate of the coefficient β.

Equation (8.20), from the diffusion model, implies that the growth rate for follower country i is determined by

$$\gamma_i \approx \gamma_1 - \mu \cdot \log(y_i) + \mu \cdot \log(y_1) + \mu \cdot \log[(y_i/y_1)^*], \qquad (8.23)$$

where economy 1 represents the world technological leader. More generally, country 1 would refer to an array of leading economies that lagging economies can copy in various sectors. In a cross section of follower countries for a given time period, γ_1 and y_1 are constants. Suppose that we have observable variables that proxy for variations in $(y_i/y_1)^*$; operationally, these variables would be the same as those that we mentioned before as proxies for variations in $\hat{y}_i^*$. Then we can run a regression in the form of Eq. (8.23) to get an estimate of the coefficient μ. This estimate would coincide with the one for β implied by Eq. (8.22). Thus, in a single cross section, the models are indistinguishable.

We may be able to discriminate between the models if we have a panel data set, which contains variation in the variable y_1 over time. The key to the distinction is that Eq. (8.23) implies that the growth effect from $\log(y_i)$ is conditioned on the leader's value, $\log(y_1)$. If we hold fixed the steady-state ratio $(y_i/y_1)^*$, then an increase in $\log(y_1)$ slows down economy i's growth rate for a given value of $\log(y_i)$. In contrast, Eq. (8.22) says that economy i's growth rate does not depend on $\log(y_1)$.[7]

The operational difficulty, however, is that Eq. (8.22) includes another term, βxt, that varies over time. This term picks up the effects of exogenous technological change, and we have to filter the observable variable $\log(y_i)$ for this effect in order to isolate the convergence effect. Thus, in practice, the discrimination between the two theories requires us to distinguish the changes over time in $\log(y_1)$ in Eq. (8.23) from the time trend, βxt, in Eq. (8.22). Since $\log(y_1)$—identified with the per capita product of some technologically leading countries—would not be precisely a time trend, it appears that the separation between the two theories would be feasible.

Several problems arise in the implementation of this idea. First, the variable $\log(y_1)$ is intended to represent the level of technology in the leading economies. Short-term fluctuations in output—due to elements that are not present in the growth models—make it difficult to isolate the underlying level of technology from the available data. In addition, it would not be satisfactory to look only at the world's most advanced economy, such as the United States, as a representation of country 1.

Second, the assumption in Chapters 1 and 2 that labor-augmenting technological change occurred at a constant rate, x, was merely a technical convenience. Even if technological advances are exogenous, there is no reason for them to occur at an even rate. The cumulated level of technology would, instead, evolve randomly. But in this case the exogenous level of technology that arises with no effort in all economies (the xt term) cannot be distinguished from the level of technology that has been attained in the leading economies (represented by the $\log[y_1]$ term).

---

[7]Chua (1993, Chs. 2, 3) argues that spillover effects across countries can lead to a dependence of country i's growth rate on country j's variables. Thus, he provides another reason why γ_i would depend on $\log(y_j)$. Chua's analysis does not, however, place special emphasis on the world's technological leaders, represented by country 1 in the diffusion model.

It seems that any hope of discriminating between the models has to rely on the theory of how technology evolves in the leading countries, along the lines of the models developed in Chapters 6 and 7. These implications can potentially be distinguished from the hypothesis that technological improvements are exogenous. This approach has, however, not yet been implemented.

8.2   MUTUAL INVENTION AND IMITATION

We have assumed, thus far, that country 2 never innovates and, hence, that country 1 never has anything to imitate. Suppose now that country 2 can also invent a new product at cost η, the same value that applies to country 1. If $\nu < \eta$, then imitation is cheaper than innovation for country 2. Thus, if the starting value of N_2/N_1 is such that $\nu < \eta$ (from Eq. [8.14]), then country 2 engages initially only in imitation, as in the setting that we already analyzed. As N_2/N_1 increases, ν rises toward the value ν^* shown in Eq. (8.15). If $\nu^* < \eta$—that is, if $(L_2/L_1) \cdot (A_2/A_1)^{1/(1-\alpha)} < 1$— then country 2 never finds it advantageous to innovate, and the equilibrium takes the form assumed before in which country 1 is always the leader, and country 2 is always the follower.

If $\nu^* > \eta$—that is, if $(L_2/L_1) \cdot (A_2/A_1)^{1/(1-\alpha)} > 1$—then N_2/N_1 and, hence, ν eventually get high enough so that researchers in country 2 find it advantageous to allocate part of their R&D spending to innovation. We assume now that the products discovered in country 2 are different from those discovered in country 1; the absence of duplication seems reasonable if there really is an infinite number of potential products that can be invented.

The innovations by country 2 create a pool of new products that can be imitated by country 1. Some amount of imitation then becomes attractive for country 1, because the cost of imitation would be low if none of country 2's discoveries had yet been copied by country 1. The two countries therefore devote part of their R&D budgets for a while to imitation and part to innovation. The condition $(L_2/L_1) \cdot (A_2/A_1)^{1/(1-\alpha)} > 1$ implies, however, that country 2 will innovate at a faster rate than country 1. The increasing pool of material to copy eventually lowers the cost of imitation sufficiently so that researchers in country 1 will find it desirable to channel all of their R&D outlays to imitation. This response lowers the pool of innovations that are available for country 2 to copy and therefore tends to drive up the cost of imitation in country 2. Thus, researchers in country 2 eventually choose to allocate all of their R&D outlays to innovation. In the long run, the two countries switch roles: country 2 becomes the pure leader and country 1 the pure follower. In general, the country with the higher combination of parameters, $L_i \cdot A_i^{1/(1-\alpha)}$, assumes the role of innovator in the long run. (The model can sustain a mixing of innovation and imitation in the long run within a country only if each country has the same values of $L_i \cdot A_i^{1/(1-\alpha)}$.)

8.3   FOREIGN INVESTMENT

We now consider the role of foreign investment in the process of technological diffusion. We return, for convenience, to the first model in which country 1 as the leader faces the constant cost of innovation, η, and country 2 as the follower faces the constant cost of imitation, ν, where $0 < \nu < \eta$. (We could, however, use the model in which the cost of imitation depends on the number of innovations that have already been implemented in country 2.) We assume that the inequality in (8.13) holds, so that $\gamma_2 > \gamma_1$ and $r_2 > r_1$ when $N_2 < N_1$.

In this setting, the innovators from country 1 retained no property rights over the use of their designs in country 2. We now assume instead that the innovators from country 1 have perpetual monopoly rights over the use of their goods as intermediate inputs for production in country 2. This situation would apply if countries fully respected the intellectual property rights of foreigners, a major topic in the ongoing GATT (General Agreement on Tariffs and Trade) negotiations. In the model, these intellectual property rights make it infeasible for researchers in country 2 to devote resources to imitation (without paying a fee to country 1). We also assume for now that entrepreneurs in country 2 do not find it worthwhile to innovate. Hence, all of the innovation and adaptation stem from the efforts of entrepreneurs from country 1.

An innovator from country 1 must pay a cost beyond the initial R&D outlay, η, to transfer and adapt his or her product for use in country 2. (The cost estimates provided by Teece [1977], which we discussed earlier, apply directly to this situation.) We think of the transfer cost as a lump-sum entry charge for foreign investment and represent it by ν, the symbol that we used before for the cost of imitation. The cost may be lower than before because the innovator would be better suited than other entrepreneurs to the process of adapting a discovery for use in other countries. Locals would have some advantages related to familiarity with language, customs, and so on, but the foreigners can, if desired, hire or license domestic residents.

Suppose that country 2 was previously closed to foreign investment and had not experienced much imitation of country 1's inventions. If country 2 were suddenly opened up to foreign investment, then the number N_1 of known products from country 1 would greatly exceed the number N_2 that were available in country 2. The rate of return to foreign investment—that is, adaptation of products for use in country 2—would be given by the formula for r_2 in Eq. (8.11). This rate of return exceeds the rate of return to innovation, given by the expression for r_1 in Eq. (8.5). (Recall that we are assuming that the inequality in [8.13] is satisfied.) Since the model assumes no diminishing returns to adaptation or innovation, the researchers from country 1 would initially devote all of their R&D outlays to foreign investment in country 2.

The backlog of unadapted products is eventually eliminated—that is, N_2 reaches N_1—and the rate of return r_2 from pure adaptation becomes unavailable. The researchers from country 1 are then motivated to direct R&D expenditures to the discovery of new products, that is, to expand N_1. The rate of return to innovation now exceeds the value for r_1 shown in Eq. (8.5), however, because an entrepreneur knows that a successful product can also be adapted at the cost ν for use under conditions of monopoly in country 2. If the inequality in (8.13) holds, then this adaptation is immediately worthwhile.

The total flow of monopoly profits from the discovery of a new product in country 1 and the simultaneous adaptation of this product to country 2 is now the sum of the flows shown in Eqs. (8.4) and (8.10):

$$\pi_{1j} = \left(\frac{1-\alpha}{\alpha}\right) \cdot \alpha^{2/(1-\alpha)} \cdot \left[(A_1)^{1/(1-\alpha)} \cdot L_1 + (A_2)^{1/(1-\alpha)} \cdot L_2\right]. \qquad (8.24)$$

The assumption underlying Eq. (8.24) is that the intermediate inputs used to produce goods in country 1 operate through the technology in Eq. (8.1)—with productivity parameter A_1—whereas those used to produce goods in country 2 operate through the technology in Eq. (8.7)—with productivity parameter A_2. In other words, foreign investment makes more of the intermediate inputs available to country 2, but does not affect the productivity parameter that governs the production process in country 2. This assumption is appropriate, for example, if the parameter A_2 represents local government policies—such as taxation, provision of public services, and maintenance of property rights—that apply equally to all producers.

An innovator now pays the total cost $\eta + \nu$ to secure the flow of monopoly profit shown in Eq. (8.24). The free-entry condition implies accordingly that the rate of return in country 1 is given by

$$r_1 = \left(\frac{1-\alpha}{\alpha}\right) \cdot \alpha^{2/(1-\alpha)} \cdot \left[\frac{(A_1)^{1/(1-\alpha)} \cdot L_1 + (A_2)^{1/(1-\alpha)} \cdot L_2}{\eta + \nu}\right]. \qquad (8.25)$$

The inequality in (8.13) implies that this rate of return exceeds the value for r_1 in Eq. (8.5).

The constant rate of return in Eq. (8.25) corresponds to a steady state in which the various quantities—N_1, Y_1, C_1, N_2, Y_2, and C_2—all grow at the rate γ_1, given as usual by $\gamma_1 = (1/\theta) \cdot (r_1 - \rho)$. This steady state features a simultaneous flow of new products, N_1, and adapted versions of these products, $N_2 = N_1$. Since r_1 is higher than before, the growth rate exceeds the value γ_1 from Eq. (8.6) obtained in the original model with no foreign investment.

Foreign investment—that is, property rights over product adaptations for use in foreign countries—eliminates some of the distortions that were present in the first model. To begin, foreign investment gets around the capital-market imperfection that allowed for a divergence between the rates of return, r_1 and r_2, that prevailed in the two countries. In effect, the property rights over the use of designs in another country provide the collateral for foreign investment. The implicit assumption in the original model was that households from country 1 were unwilling to loan funds to investors in country 2, even though the rate of return r_2 that these investors would be willing to pay exceeded the rate of return r_1 available to savers in country 1.

Second, in the initial model, innovators in country 1 neglected the spillover benefit that they provided to country 2 by providing a pool of discoveries that could be adapted (without compensation) for use in country 2. This effect is internalized in the model with foreign investment because innovators take account of the profit flow, π_{2j}, that they receive by paying the adaptation cost, ν. The elimination of this distortion causes the increase in the rate of return, r_1, and the growth rate, γ_1. Thus, the model demonstrates why the international guarantee of intellectual property rights can have some desirable effects.

The equilibrium from the model with foreign investment would be Pareto optimal if the familiar distortion due to monopoly pricing is eliminated. In the present case, the removal of this distortion requires a subsidy to the purchase of durable inputs (or to the production of goods) in both countries. The execution of this subsidy involves the usual difficulties associated with distorting public finance and with picking technological winners. These difficulties are now compounded by the necessity to provide subsidies in more than one country.

8.4 LEAPFROGGING

The models discussed in this and some other chapters feature convergence in the sense that initially lagging economies tend to grow faster. From the standpoint of the diffusion of technology, the force that underlies convergence is that, at least over some range, the cost of imitation is smaller than the cost of innovation. We also mentioned a case in which a country that was initially technologically backward would eventually become the innovator. This result depended, however, on the assumption that the initially backward place happened to have a better productivity parameter, A_i—perhaps because its government policies were more conducive to economic activity—or a larger scale, L_i. There was nothing about backwardness, *per se*, that led to the prediction that the laggard would eventually become the leader. Moreover, once the initial follower became the leader, the model did not predict that the positions would change again in the future.

Some researchers argue that the benefits from backwardness are strong enough to generate not only a convergence effect, but also a tendency for *leapfrogging* (see Brezis, Krugman, and Tsiddon [1993]). In this case, for a pair of countries, the hypothesis is that the technological follower at an initial date will systematically become the leader at some future time. Examples are supposed to include the English passing the Dutch by the 1700s, the United States and Germany overtaking England in the late 1800s, and perhaps Japan surpassing the United States by the end of the 1900s.[8]

If we add random disturbances to a model that contains the convergence force, then we can readily generate the prediction that the leader will eventually be overtaken by someone. Suppose, for example, that the growth process for economy i is described in discrete time (years) by

$$\log(y_{it}/y_{i,t-1}) = \text{constant} + (1 - e^{-\beta}) \cdot \log(\hat{y}^*/\hat{y}_{i,t-1}) + u_{it}, \qquad (8.26)$$

where the convergence speed, $\beta > 0$, and the steady-state position, $\hat{y}^*$, are assumed to be the same in all places. The random term, u_{it}, has 0 mean, the same variance σ^2 for all economies, and is serially and cross-sectionally independent. The deterministic part of Eq. (8.26) generates the type of absolute convergence that can arise in the Solow–Swan and Ramsey models or in the model of diffusion of technology from this chapter. The random term adds Brownian motion to this convergence process.

---

[8]An interesting, unresolved empirical question is whether leapfrogging applies to professional sports teams. One force that goes in this direction is the new-player draft; teams typically get to pick in inverse relation to their past performance.

Equation (8.26) predicts absolute convergence (a place that starts behind tends to grow faster) and that the initial leader will eventually be overtaken by someone (because of the random terms). However, for any pair of economies i and j for which $y_{i0} \geq y_{j0}$, the expectations will satisfy $E(y_{it}) \geq E(y_{jt})$ for all $t > 0$. That is, the benefits from backwardness are not strong enough to imply that a particular follower will systematically move ahead of the current leader at some future date; in this sense, the model does not predict leapfrogging. This simple model also shows that the eventual fall from leadership of the Dutch, the English, and perhaps the Americans is not sufficient to demonstrate that leapfrogging exists. These events could merely be a manifestation of the leader being eventually surpassed by someone, an outcome that is predicted by the convergence model with Brownian motion, as described by Eq. (8.26).

It is possible to generate leapfrogging in theoretical models if the leading producer has a stake in the currently best technology and if there exist potential technologies that are eventually more productive. For example, Brezis, Krugman, and Tsiddon (1993) assume that the country with the current technological lead has learned through experience to be highly productive with the existing techniques. The leader's knowledge is assumed not to be accessible by other countries, and the returns from experience are diminishing within each country. Fundamentally new technologies appear occasionally; these new approaches offer the potential of higher productivity, but not until substantial learning-by-doing has occurred. As a consequence, the adoption of the new technique may be unattractive for the current leader—who has the option to continue with the old method of production at a currently high level of productivity—but may be worthwhile for a laggard. Since the new technology is more productive in the long run, the follower eventually becomes the leader, hence, the leapfrogging effect.[9]

A force that makes leapfrogging less probable is that the leader's familiarity with the current state of the art makes it easier to generate technological improvements. (We used this idea in Chapter 7 to show that quality improvements on existing types of products tend to be made by the industry leaders.) This advantage of incumbency is probably most powerful for incremental advances in technique, rather than for radical changes or the discovery of entirely new products. For that reason, Brezis, Krugman, and Tsiddon (1993) assume that " 'normal' technical change is likely to proceed largely through learning by doing, and will tend to occur most rapidly in those countries with established advantages in technologically progressive sectors." They then assume, however, that this advantage of leadership does not apply to major breakthroughs, which "require that nations start fresh." Hence, in their framework, leapfrogging takes the form of fundamental changes in methods of production.

An alternative view is that countries that are familiar with the best technology are particularly productive at basic research.[10] This perspective likely explains why

---

[9]Jovanovic and Nyarko (1994) develop a more general model of learning in which this leapfrogging effect can occur.

[10]Ohyama and Jones (1993) point out that the key issue is whether the current technological leader has a *comparative* advantage in R&D.

virtually all of the major technological breakthroughs seem to have occurred in a handful of the principal developed countries.[11] This force tends to cement leadership positions and therefore makes it less likely that leapfrogging will apply.

8.5   SUMMARY OBSERVATIONS ABOUT DIFFUSION AND GROWTH

The diffusion of technology from leading economies to followers involves costs of imitation and adaptation. We assume that these costs are lower than those for innovation when very little has yet been copied, but rise as the pool of uncopied ideas gets smaller. This cost structure implies a form of diminishing returns to imitation and thereby tends to generate a pattern of convergence. Follower countries tend to grow faster the greater the gap from the leaders. This process is, however, conditional, in that the growth rate depends, for a given technological gap, on government policies and other variables that influence the rate of return to imitation in a follower economy.

In the steady state, the leading and following countries grow at the same rate. Thus, equalization of growth rates occurs in the long run even if countries differ in costs of R&D, levels of productivity, and the willingness to save. If the countries have the same preferences about saving (that is, equal parameters ρ_i and θ_i), then the equalization of growth rates implies that rates of return are also the same in the steady state. Hence, even without a global capital market, the diffusion of technology can equate the rates of return across countries in the long run.

In some cases, technological diffusion involves imitation by local entrepreneurs of products or ideas developed elsewhere. This process is costly, but often escapes any fees paid to the inventor of the good or method of production. In other cases, the diffusion occurs via foreign investment. This foreign involvement tends to speed diffusion if the costs of adapting a good or technique are smaller for agents who are more familiar with how the new idea operates in the country of origin. In addition, the honoring of intellectual property rights across international borders helps to provide the proper incentive for discoveries of new goods and techniques in the leading economies. For this reason, the institution of these rights tends to raise the long-term growth rate in leading *and* following economies.

PROBLEMS

8.1 Pareto Optimality in the Leader-Follower Model. Consider the leader-follower model described in Section 8.1 of this chapter.

(*a*) Discuss the distortions that lead to Pareto nonoptimal outcomes. How do the distortions differ from those present in the one-country varieties model of Chapter 6?

---

[11] In pre modern times, the dominant technological leader was China. See Temple (1986). For a discussion in the context of recent theories of endogenous growth, see Young (1990).

(*b*) What policies could be implemented to ensure Pareto optimality?

(*c*) Suppose that the leading country has a decentralized equilibrium with no government intervention. Would it ever be optimal for the government of the following country to subsidize innovation in the leading country?

8.2 Rates of Return in the Leader-Follower Model. Consider again the leader-follower model from section 8.1 of this chapter.

(*a*) Are the rates of return constant in the two countries? Which rate of return is higher?

(*b*) What happens if the leader and follower countries join in a common, perfect credit market?

8.3 Convergence in the Leader-Follower Model.

(*a*) In the model of section 8.1 of this chapter, discuss whether the two countries converge to the same levels of per capita output and wage rate. Discuss whether they converge to a common growth rate of per capita output.

(*b*) Is it possible for the country with an initially lower level of per capita output to become the country with the higher level of per capita output? Is it possible to get another switch later on in the relative levels of per capita output? What are the implications for leapfrogging?

(*c*) Can the countries switch roles at some point in terms of innovation and imitation?

(*d*) What are the implications of the model for absolute and relative convergence?

8.4 The Model with a Variable Cost of Imitation. Consider the model of section 8.1.3 in which the cost of imitation is an increasing function of the ratio of the number of designs known in the imitating country, N_2, to the number known in the innovating country, N_1.

(*a*) Discuss the determination of the steady-state ratio, $(N_2/N_1)^*$. What are the growth rates and rates of return in this steady state?

(*b*) How do the rate of return and the growth rate of per capita output behave in country 2 during the transition to the steady state? (These results have not been fully worked out.)

(*c*) What are the implications of the model for absolute and relative convergence?

8.5 Different Theories of Convergence. Contrast the results on convergence from the diffusion theories with those from the Ramsey model. Is it feasible to distinguish the theories empirically? If so, how?

8.6 Foreign Investment.

(*a*) Discuss the role of foreign investment in the context of the diffusion models.

(*b*) Does the potential for foreign investment in the imitating economy, country 2, benefit the agents of the innovating economy, country 1?

(*c*) Does the potential for foreign investment benefit the agents of the imitating economy, country 2?

8.7 Leapfrogging.

(*a*) Discuss the concept of leapfrogging and demonstrate how it differs from absolute convergence.

(*b*) Does the Ramsey model of Chapter 2 (augmented to allow for random shocks to the technology) preclude leapfrogging? Is this model inconsistent with the observation that an economy that is initially lagging in technological sophistication becomes the leader at a later date?

8.8 Innovation and Technology Transfer. (Based on Krugman [1979]). Consider a two-country world (North and South) with M types of consumer goods. These goods cannot be stored but can be traded across countries. Each country has L consumer-workers with instantaneous utility functions given by

$$U = \left(\sum_{i=1}^{M} (c_i)^{\theta} \right)^{1/\theta},$$

where $0 < \theta < 1$ and c_i is the amount of good i consumed. There are two kinds of goods, old ones and new ones. At a point in time, M_o of the M goods are old, and $M_n = M - M_o$ are new. The technology for producing old goods is common property, so that they can be produced in the North or the South. The technology for producing new goods is freely accessible in the North, but is unavailable in the South. It takes one unit of labor to produce one unit of any good, and all goods are produced under conditions of perfect competition.

Normalize the price of each old good to 1 and let P_n be the price of each new good. (Note that the price of all old goods must be the same, and the price of all new goods must be the same.) Let w_N and w_S be the wage rates in the North and South, respectively. Define τ to be the terms of trade for the North, that is, the ratio of the prices of goods produced in the North to those produced in the South.

(a) How does τ depend on w_N and w_S? How does y, the ratio of the North's per capita income to the South's per capita income, depend on w_N and w_S?

(b) Let $\sigma \equiv M_n/M_o$. Derive the pattern of specialization in the world economy as a function of σ. Use this result to relate w_N, w_S, τ, and y to σ.

(c) Let $\dot{M} = iM$ describe the rate of innovation in the North, where i is exogenous. Let $\dot{M}_O = tM_n$ describe the rate of technological transfer, where t is exogenous. Find the steady-state value of σ and its law of motion. How does the world pattern of specialization change over time? What happens to y over time?

(d) Define the set of initial conditions under which convergence applies, that is, $\dot{y} < 0$. In this model, is convergence equivalent to the long-run equalization of incomes, that is, $y^* = 1$?

8.9 Technology Choice and Overtaking (Based on Ohyama and Jones [1993]). Consider a two-country world with a single, nonstorable good. Each country has L consumer-workers with linear preferences and rate of time preference $\rho > 0$. There is a traditional technology, characterized by

$$q_i^T = A_i \cdot (1 - \theta_i)$$

for $i = 1, 2$, where $1 - \theta_i$ is the share of the labor force used in the traditional technology in country i. Country 1 is the current technological leader, in the sense that $A_1 > A_2$.

At time 0, a new technology appears with the following characteristics:

$$q_i^N = B_i \theta_i,$$

$$B_i = B + \lambda \cdot \int_0^t q_i^N \cdot d\tau,$$

where B is a constant with $0 < B < A_i$, and λ is another constant with $0 < \lambda < \rho$. The new technology is less productive initially ($B < A_i$), but exhibits learning-by-doing ($\lambda > 0$).

(a) Assume that the technologies are mutually exclusive within a country, so that θ_i must equal 0 or 1. Under what conditions will the new technology be adopted, and by which country? Is it possible to observe leapfrogging? If so, calculate the time T that it takes for country 2 to overtake country 1?

(b) Assume now that the technologies can be operated simultaneously within each country, so that $0 \leq \theta_i \leq 1$. At time 0, each country chooses a value for θ_i and is then constrained to maintain it forever. Will we ever observe partial adoption? Discuss whether leapfrogging is possible and, if so, characterize T.

(c) Assume now that there are one-time costs of switching from the traditional to the new technology, and these costs are given by $c(\theta_i) = c\theta_i/(1 - \theta_i)$, where $c > 0$ is a constant. Under what conditions will we observe partial adoption? Discuss whether leapfrogging is possible and, if so, characterize T.

(d) (difficult) Finally, assume that θ_i can be set at different values at each point in time. Assume again that there are no costs of switching from the old to the new technology. Describe the dynamics of θ_i and output. Discuss whether leapfrogging is possible and, if so, characterize T. Redo the analysis for the case in which the one-time cost of switching is $c(\theta_i)$.

LABOR
SUPPLY AND
POPULATION

In previous chapters, we assumed that population and the labor force grew together at the exogenous rate n. We now modify this assumption in various respects. First, we consider the possibility of immigration and emigration in response to economic opportunities. This process alters population and the labor force for given fertility and mortality. Second, we introduce choices about fertility, another channel that allows for an endogenous determination of population and the labor force. Finally, we allow for variations in work effort. That is, we relax the equality between labor force and population.

9.1 MIGRATION IN MODELS
OF ECONOMIC GROWTH

The migration of persons is one mechanism for change in an economy's population and labor supply. This migration or labor mobility is analogous to the capital mobility that we explored in Chapter 3. Whereas capital tends to move from places with low rates of return to those with high rates of return, labor tends to move from economies with low wage rates or other unfavorable characteristics to those with high wage rates or other favorable elements. We found before that capital mobility tends to speed up an economy's convergence toward its steady-state position, and we shall find that labor mobility typically works in a similar way.

Migration differs in some respects from changes in natural population growth, that is, differences between births and deaths. First, in the case of migration, gains in population for the destination economy represent corresponding losses for the source economy. Thus, we have to consider immigration and emigration as two sides of a single process.

Second, unlike newly born persons, migrants come with accumulated human capital. Since a movement of a person entails the movement of this human capital, labor mobility or migration implies some degree of capital mobility. Newborns also differ from migrants in that the residents of an economy tend to care about the newborns——that is, about their children——but not about the migrants. This difference in linkages with the existing population implies differences in the way that population growth interacts with saving behavior and, hence, with rates of economic growth.

A convenient starting point for the study of migration and growth is the Solow–Swan model, which assumes a closed economy and an exogenous, constant saving rate. The extension to incorporate migration means that economies are opened to some extent; that is, the migration process implies some degree of mobility of raw labor and human capital. Although the analysis allows for a feedback from economic growth to wage rates to the rate of migration, the underlying optimization problem for migrants is not considered at this point. That is, the model just postulates a functional form for a migration function.

We next extend the analysis to the Ramsey framework in which saving behavior reflects household optimization. This extension assumes that the representative household determines the path of consumption without regard to the welfare of immigrants. This model continues to use a postulated form for the migration function.

Finally, we present a model that allows for capital mobility and assumes that migration rates are determined by household optimization. In this setting, we can analyze how changes in the costs or benefits associated with moving affect the dynamic paths of migration and growth.

9.1.1 Migration in the Solow–Swan Model

THE MODEL WITH MIGRATION. This section introduces migration into the Solow–Swan model of a closed economy. Thus, we allow for mobility of persons but assume that the economy is closed with respect to foreign goods and assets; that is, we make the unrealistic assumption that people are more mobile than physical capital. Although this assumption is extreme, the analysis does bring out some effects of migration on the growth process. A later section allows for capital mobility.

Let $M(t)$, which can be positive or negative, be the flow of migrants into the domestic economy and $\kappa(t)$ the quantity of capital that each migrant brings along. Since we assume that capital cannot move by itself, the quantity of capital that each migrant carries brings in a degree of capital mobility.

Migrants typically do not carry much physical capital (machines and buildings), but may possess substantial amounts of human capital. We find it convenient here not to distinguish among the different forms of capital (as we did in Chapters 4 and 5) and to deal instead with a single broad concept of capital that encompasses physical and human forms. Therefore, κ corresponds to the quantity of this broad capital that accompanies each migrant.[1]

The domestic population and labor force, $L(t)$, grow due to fertility net of mortality at the constant rate n. The overall growth rate of the domestic population is therefore

$$\dot{L}/L = n + M/L = n + m, \tag{9.1}$$

where $m \equiv M/L$ is the net migration rate. We have omitted time subscripts for convenience.

The change in the domestic capital stock is given by

$$\dot{K} = s \cdot F(K, \hat{L}) - \delta K + \kappa M, \tag{9.2}$$

where s is the constant gross saving rate. The new element is that κM—the capital brought by immigrants or taken by emigrants—contributes to $\dot{K}$. The growth rate of capital per effective worker can be determined from Eqs. (9.1) and (9.2) as

$$\gamma_{\hat{k}} = s \cdot f(\hat{k})/\hat{k} - (x + n + \delta) - m \cdot [1 - (\hat{\kappa}/\hat{k})]. \tag{9.3}$$

Recall that $x + n + \delta$ is the effective depreciation rate for capital in models without migration, that is, the rate of decline in $\hat{k}$ due to growth of effective labor at the rate $x + n$ and to depreciation of the capital stock at the rate δ. (See, for example, Eq. [1.30] in the Solow–Swan model.) This effective depreciation rate is now augmented by a migration term, $m \cdot [1 - (\hat{\kappa}/\hat{k})]$. The overall term would therefore be the same as in previous models if $m = 0$ or if $\hat{\kappa} = \hat{k}$ at all points in time.

Since migrants bring little physical capital, $\hat{\kappa} < \hat{k}$ would apply unless the human capital per migrant were substantially greater than that per worker in the domestic economy.[2] If $\hat{\kappa} < \hat{k}$, then the migration term, $m \cdot [1 - (\hat{\kappa}/\hat{k})]$, adds to the effective depreciation rate if $m > 0$ and subtracts from it if $m < 0$. If migrants come with no capital, $\hat{\kappa} = 0$, then the migration rate, m, adds one-to-one to the natural population growth rate, n, in Eq. (9.3). If we think of n as corresponding to the birth of children, then this result makes sense because we treat children as beginning life with no human capital.[3]

If $m > 0$, then the quantity $\hat{\kappa}$ is the capital per effective worker carried by each immigrant. This quantity would be related to the total capital per effective worker that prevails in the immigrant's place of origin. Hence, the quantity $\hat{\kappa}/\hat{k}$ would decline as $\hat{k}$ rises. (We neglect the possibility that a change in $\hat{k}$ alters the selection of immigrants with respect to their capital $\hat{\kappa}$.) Moreover, if we assume that the typical

---

[1] In this model, the migrants cannot maintain any financial claims on foreign-source income. People who move relinquish or consume all capital that they cannot carry with them.

[2] If $m > 0$, then we have to compare the capital of immigrants with that of persons in the receiving economy. If $m < 0$, then the comparison is between emigrants and persons in the sending economy.

[3] In contrast, death implies the loss of a person's human capital. We have, however, simplified the model by treating the depreciation of physical and human capital as the constant multiple δ of the existing stocks of capital.

foreign country is close to its steady-state position, then we can treat $\hat{\kappa}$ as roughly constant over time.

If $m < 0$, then $\hat{\kappa}$ represents the capital per effective worker of each emigrant.[4] In this case, $\hat{\kappa}/\hat{k}$ is likely to be roughly constant; that is, $\hat{\kappa}/\hat{k}$ would not change as $\hat{k}$ rises.

THE MIGRATION FUNCTION. In a later section, we work out a model in which the migration rate responds positively to the present value of domestic wage rates, compared to the present value in other economies. For given conditions elsewhere, a higher value of $\hat{k}$ raises the domestic wage rate and tends accordingly to increase the migration rate, m.[5]

In the present setting, we postulate a positive relation between m and $\hat{k}$, as shown in Fig. 9.1. The assumption is that conditions that affect wage rates per unit of effective labor in other economies do not change as $\hat{k}$ changes. We also hold constant

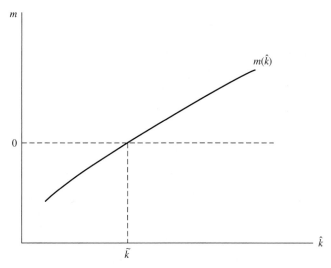

FIGURE 9.1
The migration rate. For given conditions in other economies, a higher value of $\hat{k}$ raises the domestic wage rate and tends accordingly to increase the net migration rate, m. The value $\tilde{k}$ is the quantity of capital per effective worker that yields a 0 net migration rate.

---

[4]We assume that immigration and emigration do not occur simultaneously, so that net and gross migration coincide. More generally, heterogeneity in human capital or other variables would cause gross flows to exceed net flows.

[5]With no capital mobility, however, a higher $\hat{k}$ also reduces the domestic rate of return on capital, including the human capital that the migrants bring with them. We assume that the effect from the higher wage rate is dominant.

any domestic or foreign amenities that enter into households' utility functions. Note that the value denoted $\tilde{k}$ in the figure corresponds to zero net migration.

An experiment that we would like to consider is a shift of the migration function, $m(\hat{k})$. The migration theory that we consider later relates these shifts to changes in the costs or benefits associated with moving. For example, a reduction of wage rates or a worsening of amenities in foreign countries makes migration to the domestic country more attractive and therefore shifts the function $m(\hat{k})$ upward. The slope of the function depends, among other things, on the relation between the cost of moving (for the marginal migrant) and the volume of migration. If this cost increases rapidly with the number of migrants, then a change in $\hat{k}$ has only a small effect on migration; that is, the curve $m(\hat{k})$ is relatively flat.

Define the overall migration term that appears on the right-hand side of Eq. (9.3) as

$$\xi(\hat{k}) \equiv m(\hat{k}) \cdot [1 - (\hat{\kappa}/\hat{k})], \tag{9.4}$$

so that the growth rate of $\hat{k}$ is given by

$$\gamma_{\hat{k}} = s \cdot f(\hat{k})/\hat{k} - [x + n + \delta + \xi(\hat{k})]. \tag{9.5}$$

The effective depreciation rate, $x + n + \delta + \xi(\hat{k})$, includes the term $\xi(\hat{k})$ on a one-to-one basis. The $m(\hat{k})$ part of $\xi(\hat{k})$ in Eq. (9.4) adds to the growth rate of effective labor and thereby to $x + n$. The $-m(\hat{k}) \cdot (\hat{\kappa}/\hat{k})$ part of $\xi(\hat{k})$ is the negative of the effect of the migrants' human capital on the growth rate of the domestic capital stock. This inflow of human capital subtracts from the effective depreciation rate.

If $m(\hat{k}) > 0$, then we argued before that we could treat $\hat{\kappa}$ as independent of $\hat{k}$. In this case, the effect of $\hat{k}$ on $\xi(\hat{k})$ is given from Eq. (9.4) by

$$\xi'(\hat{k}) = m'(\hat{k}) \cdot [1 - (\hat{\kappa}/\hat{k})] + m(\hat{k}) \cdot \hat{\kappa}/(\hat{k})^2.$$

Thus, $\xi'(\hat{k}) > 0$ follows from $m'(\hat{k}) > 0$, $\hat{\kappa} < \hat{k}$, and $m(\hat{k}) > 0$.

If $m(\hat{k}) < 0$, then we argued that we could treat $\hat{\kappa}/\hat{k}$ as constant. In this case, $\xi'(\hat{k}) > 0$ follows from Eq. (9.4) because of $m'(\hat{k}) > 0$ and $\hat{\kappa} < \hat{k}$. Thus, we assume that $\xi'(\hat{k}) > 0$ holds whether the migration rate is positive or negative. It follows that a higher $\hat{k}$ raises the effective depreciation term, $x + n + \delta + \xi(\hat{k})$, in Eq. (9.5). In contrast, this term was independent of $\hat{k}$ in earlier models.

THE STEADY STATE. Figure 9.2 is our standard form of a growth diagram. The $s \cdot f(\hat{k})/\hat{k}$ curve is downward-sloping as usual because of the diminishing average product of capital. The horizontal line at $x + n + \delta$ has now been replaced by the upward-sloping curve, $x + n + \delta + \xi(\hat{k})$. If $\hat{k} = \tilde{k}$, then $m(\hat{k}) = 0$ (see Fig. 9.1) and $\xi(\hat{k}) = 0$ (see Eq. [9.4]). Therefore, the height of the effective-depreciation curve at $\tilde{k}$ is $x + n + \delta$. If $\hat{k} > \tilde{k}$, then $m(\hat{k}) > 0$, and the effective-depreciation curve lies above $x + n + \delta$. Conversely, if $\hat{k} < \tilde{k}$, then the curve lies below $x + n + \delta$. We have drawn the curves in Fig. 9.2 so that the intersection occurs at a point $\hat{k}^*$ that exceeds $\tilde{k}$.

The steady state corresponds to the intersection of the $s \cdot f(\hat{k})/\hat{k}$ and $x + n + \delta + \xi(\hat{k})$ curves at the point $\hat{k}^*$. Given the way that we drew the curves, so that $\hat{k}^* > \tilde{k}$, $m^* > 0$ and the domestic economy is a recipient of migrants in the steady state. That

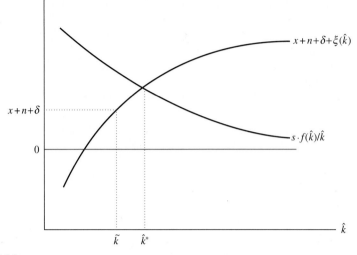

FIGURE 9.2

The Solow–Swan model with migration. The positive response of net migration to the wage rate implies that the rate of population growth is a positive function of $\hat{k}$. Hence, the effective depreciation term in the Solow–Swan model becomes upward sloping. The steady state is determined by the intersection of the saving curve, $s \cdot f(\hat{k})/\hat{k}$, with the effective depreciation curve, $x + n + \delta + \xi(\hat{k})$. For any value of $\hat{k}$, the growth rate of $\hat{k}$ is given by the vertical distance between these two curves.

is, the economy remains in the steady state as a perpetual receiver of migrants (or would persist as a sender of migrants if $\hat{k}^* < \tilde{k}$).[6]

We can use Fig. 9.2 to assess the effects of changes in various parameters on the steady-state values. For example, an increase in s or a permanent improvement of the production function shifts the $s \cdot f(\hat{k})/\hat{k}$ curve upward and leads thereby to increases in $\hat{k}^*$ and m^*. The higher value of m^* arises because the shift raises the steady-state wage rate per unit of effective labor and thereby makes the domestic economy more attractive to foreigners.

If conditions worsen in other economies, then the migration function, $m(\hat{k})$, would shift upward in Fig. 9.1. This change shifts the curve for effective depreciation, $x + n + \delta + \xi(\hat{k})$, in Fig. 9.2 in a similar manner (see the expression for $\xi(\hat{k})$ in Eq. [9.4]). Hence, $\hat{k}^*$ falls and m^* rises. Thus, an expansion of the supply of immigrants lowers the steady-state capital intensity in the domestic economy. This result follows because the immigrants come with relatively little capital.

TRANSITIONAL DYNAMICS AND CONVERGENCE. To assess the speed of convergence implied by Eq. (9.5), we follow our usual practice and assume a Cobb–

---

[6]The migration theory that we consider in a later section assumes that a higher level of population congests some fixed factor, such as land. This congestion implies that the steady-state migration rate is zero for each economy (if the natural population growth rate, n, is also zero in each economy in the steady state).

Douglas production function, $f(\hat{k}) = A\hat{k}^{\alpha}$. We also approximate the $\xi(\hat{k})$ function from Eq. (9.4) in a log-linear form:

$$\xi(\hat{k}) \equiv m(\hat{k}) \cdot [1 - (\hat{\kappa}/\hat{k})] = b \cdot [\log(\hat{k}/\hat{k}_{\text{world}})], \qquad (9.6)$$

where $b \geq 0$ and $\hat{k}_{\text{world}}$ represents the average capital intensity in other economies. Equation (9.6) implies that $\xi(\hat{k}) = 0$ if the domestic economy has the same capital intensity as the rest of the world—because the incentive to migrate would then be nil (if we neglect differences in amenities or in forms of production functions). We treat $\hat{k}_{\text{world}}$ as a constant; that is, we assume that the world is (on average) in the steady state.

The key element for the convergence analysis will be the size of the parameter b. To see what this parameter represents, differentiate Eq. (9.6) with respect to $\log(\hat{k})$ to get[7]

$$b = \partial\xi(\hat{k})/\partial[\log(\hat{k})] = [1 - (\hat{\kappa}/\hat{k})] \cdot \partial m(\hat{k})/\partial[\log(\hat{k})]. \qquad (9.7)$$

This equation shows that, if $\hat{\kappa} < \hat{k}$, then b depends positively on the sensitivity of migration to $\log(\hat{k})$. We noted before that if the cost of moving (for the marginal migrant) increases rapidly with the number of migrants, then the function $m(\hat{k})$ in Fig. 9.1 will be relatively flat. In this case, the coefficient b will be small. For a limiting case in which the cost of moving rises extremely rapidly with m, b is close to 0, $\xi(\hat{k})$ is therefore near 0, and the effective-depreciation term in Eq. (9.5) is approximately $x + n + \delta$, as in our earlier models.

For a given sensitivity of migration to $\log(\hat{k})$, the coefficient b declines if $\hat{\kappa}/\hat{k}$ rises. In particular, if $\hat{\kappa} = \hat{k}$, then $b = 0$, and the effective depreciation term is again $x + n + \delta$.

If we log-linearize the differential Eq. (9.5) around its steady-state position, then we can compute the speed of convergence to the steady state as

$$\beta = (1 - \alpha) \cdot (x + n + \delta) + b + b \cdot (1 - \alpha) \cdot \log(\hat{k}^*/\hat{k}_{\text{world}}). \qquad (9.8)$$

This formula reduces to the Solow–Swan value (Eq. [1.33]) if $b = 0$.

If we consider the typical economy, for which $\hat{k}^* = \hat{k}_{\text{world}}$, and assume $b > 0$, then Eq. (9.8) shows that the potential for migration raises the convergence coefficient, β, above the Solow–Swan value by the amount b. To assess the size of b, we use some empirical results on the determinants of migration.

Barro and Sala-i-Martin (1991) and Braun (1993) used data from the U.S. states, the regions of Japan, and five European countries (France, Germany, Italy, Spain, and the United Kingdom) to estimate the sensitivity of within-country migration to differentials in per capita income. The regression coefficient for the net migration rate on the log of initial per capita income or product averaged 0.012 per year (see Chapter 11 for details).

---

[7]For $m < 0$, we hold fixed $\hat{\kappa}/\hat{k}$ to get equation (9.7). For $m > 0$, if we hold fixed $\hat{\kappa}$, then the equation would have the additional term $m(\hat{k}) \cdot (\hat{\kappa}/\hat{k})$ on the right-hand side. Equation (9.7) is then an approximation that is satisfactory when $m(\hat{k})$ is relatively small.

The sensitivity of international migration to income differentials tends to be smaller than that for regions within a country. For example, Hatton and Williamson (1992) examine the behavior of migration from 11 European countries to the United States from 1850 to 1913. Their regression coefficients, based on responses of immigration to proportional differentials in wage rates, averaged 0.008 per year.

To relate these results to the coefficient b, we can use the Cobb–Douglas relation, $\log(\hat{y}) = \log(A) + \alpha \cdot \log(\hat{k})$, along with Eq. (9.7), to get

$$b = \alpha \cdot [1 - (\hat{\kappa}/\hat{k})] \cdot \partial m/\partial[\log(\hat{y})]. \tag{9.9}$$

The empirical estimates suggest that $\partial m/\partial[\log(\hat{y})]$ is about 0.012 per year for regions of countries and about 0.008 per year across countries. We have argued before (in Chapters 1 and 2) that a coefficient α of around 0.75 is reasonable for a broad concept of capital. Therefore, we have to specify the ratio $\hat{\kappa}/\hat{k}$ to pin down the coefficient b in Eq. (9.9).

Dolado, Goria, and Ichino (1993, Table 2) examine the composition of immigration for 1960–87 to nine developed countries—Australia, Belgium, Canada, Germany, the Netherlands, Sweden, Switzerland, the United Kingdom, and the United States. They observe that the educational attainment of immigrants averaged about 80 percent of that of natives, assuming that the schooling of immigrants did not differ systematically from the average schooling in their countries of origin. Chiswick (1978, Table 1) finds for U.S. census data in 1970 that the school attainment of foreign-born men was 91 percent of that of natives. Borjas (1992, Table 1.4) reports from U.S. census data that the schooling of foreign-born men rose from 79 percent of natives in 1940 to 82 percent in 1950, 87 percent in 1960, 94 percent in 1970, and 93 percent in 1980.

For international immigration, we take 80 percent as a typical value for the ratio of immigrants' to natives' human capital. If immigrants carry no physical capital and if the ratio of human to total capital in the domestic economy is 5/8—the value that we specified in Chapter 5—then $\hat{\kappa}/\hat{k}$ is 0.5 (0.8 times 5/8).

For migration within a country, the ratio of immigrants' to natives' human capital is likely to be higher than that for international migration. For example, Borjas, Bronars, and Trejo (1992) find for young U.S. males in 1986 that immigrants to a state averaged 3 percent more years of education than the average of natives of the state.[8] If we assume that this ratio is 100 percent, then $\hat{\kappa}/\hat{k}$ is 0.62.

In the context of regions of a country, we use $\hat{\kappa}/\hat{k} = 0.62$ and $\partial m/\partial[\log(\hat{y})] = 0.012$ per year. If we assume $\alpha = .75$, then we find that b is around 0.003 per year. In the international context, we use $\hat{\kappa}/\hat{k} = 0.5$ and $\partial m/\partial[\log(\hat{y})] = 0.008$ per year. If we assume $\alpha = 0.75$, then we get that b is again around 0.003 per year. The results are similar in the two contexts because the higher value of $\partial m/\partial[\log(\hat{y})]$ in the regional setting is offset by the higher value of $\hat{\kappa}/\hat{k}$.

---

[8]This information comes from a supplementary table that was provided to us by Steve Trejo.

For the other parameter values that we have assumed previously ($x = 0.02$, $n = 0.01$, $\delta = 0.05$), the Solow–Swan value for β when $\alpha = 0.75$ is 0.020. The value for β implied by Eq. (9.8) is higher than the Solow–Swan value by the amount b; that is, β would be around 0.023 in the cross-region and international contexts. Therefore, the inclusion of migration suggests, first, a small increase—by roughly 10 percent—in the convergence speed and, second, that convergence coefficients estimated across regions within countries would not differ greatly from those estimated across countries. This prediction accords with the findings of Barro and Sala-i-Martin (1992a), who report that estimated (conditional) convergence rates across regions of countries are only slightly higher than those across countries.

A lower value of $\hat{\kappa}/\hat{k}$ raises b in Eq. (9.9) and thereby increases the convergence coefficient, β. The predictions about convergence would therefore differ for an economy that is receiving migrants, $m > 0$, from one that is sending migrants, $m < 0$. Since the receivers tend to have higher capital intensities than the senders, the value of $\hat{\kappa}/\hat{k}$ tends to be lower for the receivers. Hence, the propensity to migrate raises the speed at which destination economies approach their steady states relative to the speed for source economies. It is even possible, as discussed below, that migration would lower the speed of convergence for the sending economies.

The potential to migrate raises the speed of convergence because we assumed $b > 0$. If the migration rate responds positively to income—that is, if $\partial m / \partial [\log(\hat{y})] > 0$—then the coefficient b in Eq. (9.9) would be negative if $\hat{\kappa}/\hat{k} > 1$. This case could arise if migrants possess human capital that is substantially greater than the average in their home economies.

For destination economies, where $m > 0$, the condition $\hat{\kappa}/\hat{k} \geq 1$ seems implausible. The immigrants would not only have to possess more human capital than the average person in the receiving location, but this gap in human capital would also have to more than offset the immigrants' failure to carry a significant amount of nonhuman capital. This condition is unlikely to be satisfied because, as already noted, immigrants tend to have less human capital than the residents of the receiving economy.

For source economies, where $m < 0$, the condition $\hat{\kappa}/\hat{k} \geq 1$ is conceivable, but still unlikely. For migration across regions of a country, the usual view—expressed, for example, by Greenwood (1975)—is that more educated persons are more likely to migrate. Borjas, Bronars, and Trejo (1992, Tables 2 and 4) quantify this effect for young men in the United States in 1986. Their figures imply that migrants averaged 2 percent more years of schooling than the average of native persons from their states of origin. This small excess of human capital would, however, be offset by the migrants' failure to carry physical capital (if we continue to assume that physical capital is not perfectly mobile across the U.S. states).

Hatton and Williamson (1992, p. 4) observe that European emigrants from 1850 to 1913 were typically unskilled, so that $\hat{\kappa}/\hat{k} < 1$ would hold even for human capital for the sending countries in these cases. For poorer countries, it is plausible that persons with relatively high human capital would be more inclined to migrate, a phenomenon often described as a *brain drain*. This situation is especially likely to apply to the return of settlers from crumbling empires, as in the case of the British from India, the French from Algeria, and the Portuguese from Mozambique. In some cases, this force may be great enough to more than offset the migrants' failure to carry much nonhuman capital. Thus, the potential to migrate would, in these cases, slow down the speed of convergence for economies that are senders of immigrants.

A new result when $b > 0$ is that β in Eq. (9.8) increases with $\hat{k}^*$ for given values of the other parameters. The reason is that a higher $\hat{k}^*$ implies a higher steady-state migration rate, m^*, and, hence, a faster speed of convergence in the neighborhood of the steady state. Recall, for example, that a permanent improvement in the production function or an increase in the domestic economy's saving rate, s, raises $\hat{k}^*$. We find now that these changes also increase the speed of convergence, β. In contrast, β was invariant with the level of the production function or the saving rate in the Solow–Swan model.

If we assume perfect labor mobility—that is, let the cost of migration approach 0—then $\partial m/\partial[\log(\hat{y})]$ becomes infinite. Therefore, if $\hat{\kappa} < \hat{k}$, then the coefficient b becomes infinite in Eq. (9.9). Equation (9.8) implies accordingly that β becomes infinite; that is, perfect labor mobility generates an infinite speed of convergence. This result corresponds to the effect of perfect capital mobility, as studied in Chapter 3.

Finally, consider the effect of the capital-share coefficient, α, on the speed of convergence. The usual result is that an increase in α implies a smaller tendency of capital to experience diminishing returns. The convergence speed therefore declines and tends to 0 as α tends to 1; that is, the convergence property does not appear in the AK model, which we studied in Chapter 4.

The form for the convergence coefficient, β, in Eq. (9.8) exhibits this standard inverse relation between β and α for a given coefficient b. (We assume here that $\hat{k}^* = \hat{k}_{world}$, so that the last term on the right-hand side of Eq. [9.8] is zero.) Equation (9.9) shows how b is determined. For a given value of $\partial m/\partial[\log(\hat{y})]$, b increases with α, an effect that would offset the inverse relation between β and α. However, we also have to consider the effect of α on $\partial m/\partial[\log(\hat{y})]$.

In the Cobb–Douglas case, the wage rate per unit of effective labor is $\hat{w} = (1 - \alpha) \cdot A\hat{k}^{\alpha}$, which is proportional to $\hat{y}$. As α rises, the share of income represented by wages (on raw labor) declines. We therefore anticipate that $\partial m/\partial[\log(\hat{y})]$ would also decline, because the benefit from moving raw labor from one place to another becomes smaller. Thus, it is unclear, on net, whether b rises or falls with α. However, as α approaches 1, $\hat{w}$ approaches 0, and $\partial m/\partial[\log(\hat{y})]$ would tend to 0 (because the benefit from moving raw labor becomes nil). This result means that b approaches 0 as α approaches 1 and, hence, that the coefficient β in Eq. (9.8) also tends to 0 as α approaches 1. Thus, even with migration, the model does not exhibit the convergence property if diminishing returns to capital are absent.

9.1.2 Migration in the Ramsey Model

In Chapter 2, we used the Ramsey framework of household optimization to extend the Solow–Swan model to the context of a variable saving rate. The major change in the results involved the transitional behavior of the saving rate; for example, if saving rates turned out to rise during the course of economic development, then the speed of convergence was reduced relative to that implied by the Solow–Swan model. The Ramsey model also had some implications for the level of the saving rate and, hence, for the levels of variables in the steady state. In particular, the potential for inefficient oversaving, which was present in the Solow–Swan model, could not arise in the Ramsey setting.

We now apply the Ramsey formulation to the version of the Solow–Swan model that includes migration. The new results involve the interaction between migration and the choices of saving rates. These results concern the transitional behavior of saving and, hence, the speed of convergence and also involve the level of the saving rate and, hence, some characteristics of the steady state. The principal findings about the role of migration in the growth process do not differ, however, from those already presented for the Solow–Swan model.

SETUP OF THE RAMSEY MODEL WITH MIGRATION. The framework that we use is a modification of Weil's (1989) extension of the Blanchard (1985) model and is formally similar to the study of finite-horizon households that we carried out in Chapter 3. We now assume, however, that the domestic residents consist of immortal families, as in the Ramsey model; that is, $p = 0$ in the context of the Blanchard model. The size of each family grows at the constant, exogenous rate n.

Migrants again enter the economy at the rate $m(t)$, and each migrant comes with the quantity of capital $\kappa(t)$, presumably mainly in the form of human capital.[9] A key assumption is that, unlike the children of the existing residents, no one cares about the immigrants. That is, their consumption does not appear as an argument in the utility functions of the residents.[10]

Let $L(t)$ be the total domestic population at time t, given by

$$L(t) = L(0) \cdot e^{nt} \cdot \exp\left[\int_0^t m(v)dv\right], \tag{9.10}$$

so that the flow of migrants at time t is $m(t) \cdot L(t)$. The $L(0)$ inhabitants at time 0 represent identical "natives," who arrived all at once in the manner of the Oklahoma land rush of the 1890s.[11] The population at later dates then consists partly of descendants of natives and partly of immigrants and their descendants. We normalize henceforth by setting $L(0) = 1$.

---

[9]As before, migrants cannot maintain any financial claims on foreign-source income.

[10]The analysis works also for emigration, $m(t) < 0$, if the domestic residents do not care about the people who leave. For example, if migration takes the form of the departure of an entire extended family, then it is natural to assume that the remaining families do not care about those who left. The problem is more complicated if family members migrate to other places and then send home remittances or receive funding from those who remain in the domestic economy.

[11]We have to get the domestic population started off in some manner. For dates $t > 0$ that are far in the future, the precise way that things begin does not matter much. For further discussion, see Braun (1993).

Immigrant households are indexed by their vintage $j \geq 0$ of arrival in the country. For native families, we set $j = 0-$, that is, these families arrived in the country sometime before time 0.

OPTIMIZATION CONDITIONS AND AGGREGATION OF THE RESULTS. Households of each vintage j maximize utility, as given at time t by

$$U(j, t) = \int_t^\infty \left\{ \log[c(j, v)] \cdot e^{-(\rho-n)\cdot(v-t)} \right\} dv, \qquad (9.11)$$

where $c(j, v)$ is the consumption per person for households of vintage j at time v. We assume log utility, as in Chapter 3, to simplify the aggregation over immigrants of differing vintages.

The analysis in Chapter 2 implies that each household's maximization of utility, subject to its budget constraint, dictates the following conditions:

$$\dot{c}(j, t)/c(j, t) = r(t) - \rho, \qquad (9.12)$$

$$\dot{a}(j, t) = [r(t) - n] \cdot a(j, t) + w(t) - c(j, t), \qquad (9.13)$$

$$c(j, t) = (\rho - n) \cdot [a(j, t) + \tilde{w}(t)], \qquad (9.14)$$

where $a(j, t)$ is assets per person, $w(t)$ is the wage rate (the same for all persons), and $\tilde{w}(t)$ is the per capita present value of future wages, as given by

$$\tilde{w}(t) = \int_t^\infty w(v) \cdot e^{n(v-t)} \cdot e^{-\bar{r}(v,t)\cdot(v-t)} \cdot dv, \qquad (9.15)$$

where $\bar{r}(v, t) \equiv [1/(v - t)] \cdot \int_t^v r(v)dv$ is the average interest rate between times t and v. We also have the usual transversality condition, which requires the present value of assets to tend asymptotically to 0.

The method for studying aggregate consumption and assets is essentially the same as that used for the finite-horizon economy in Chapter 3; therefore, we provide only a sketch of the analysis. Aggregate consumption at time t is found by summing (integrating) over the vintages $j(0 \leq j \leq t)$ of immigrants:

$$C(t) = \int_0^t \left[c(j, t) \cdot m(j) \cdot L(j) \cdot e^{n(t-j)} \right] dj + e^{nt} \cdot c(0-, t)$$
$$= e^{nt} \cdot \int_0^t \left\{ c(j, t) \cdot m(j) \cdot \exp\left[\int_0^j m(v)dv \right] \right\} dj + e^{nt} \cdot c(0-, t), \qquad (9.16)$$

where $m(j) \cdot L(j)$ is the initial size of immigrant vintage j, we used the formula for $L(j)$ from Eq. (9.10), and the final term represents the consumption of native families. The result for aggregate assets is similar:

$$A(t) = e^{nt} \cdot \int_0^t \left\{ a(j, t) \cdot m(j) \cdot \exp\left[\int_0^j m(v)dv \right] \right\} dj + e^{nt} \cdot a(0-, t). \qquad (9.17)$$

The aggregate of the present value of wage income is given from Eq. (9.15) by

$$\tilde{W}(t) = L(t) \cdot \tilde{w}(t) = e^{nt} \cdot \exp\left[\int_0^t m(v)dv \right] \cdot \int_t^\infty w(v)e^{n(v-t)} \cdot e^{-\bar{r}(v,t)\cdot(v-t)} \cdot dv. \qquad (9.18)$$

The changes over time in $A(t)$ and $\tilde{W}(t)$ come from differentiation of Eqs. (9.17) and (9.18) as

$$\dot{A}(t) = \kappa(t) \cdot m(t) \cdot L(t) + r(t) \cdot A(t) - C(t)$$

$$+ w(t) \cdot e^{nt} \cdot \left\{ 1 + \int_0^t m(j) \cdot \exp\left[\int_0^j m(v)dv \right] dj \right\}, \tag{9.19}$$

$$\dot{\tilde{W}}(t) = [r(t) + m(t)] \cdot \tilde{W}(t) - w(t) \cdot L(t). \tag{9.20}$$

To get Eq. (9.19), we used the individual family's budget constraint in Eq. (9.13) and the condition $a(t, t) = \kappa(t)$; that is, immigrant families arrive with per capita assets $\kappa(t)$.

Equation (9.14) implies $\dot{C}(t) = (\rho - n) \cdot [\dot{A}(t) + \dot{\tilde{W}}(t)]$. If we use Eqs. (9.19) and (9.20) and the condition $A(t) = K(t)$, then we eventually get an expression for the growth rate of per capita consumption:

$$\gamma_c = r(t) - \rho - m(t) \cdot (\rho - n) \cdot [k(t) - \kappa(t)]/c(t), \tag{9.21}$$

where $c(t) = C(t)/L(t)$. This relation reduces to the standard Ramsey result (with log utility) if $m(t) = 0$ or if $\kappa(t) = k(t)$. If $m(t) > 0$ and $\kappa(t) < k(t)$, then the inflow of migrants reduces per capita consumption in accordance with the last term on the right-hand side of Eq. (9.21). In this sense, a higher flow of migrants, $m(t)$, works like an increase in ρ. This effect is analogous to the inflow of children in the Blanchard (1985) model (the term $p + n$ in Eq. [3.32]) because, as Weil (1989) points out, immigrants are just like Blanchard's unloved children.

STEADY STATE AND DYNAMICS OF THE MODEL. As in the Ramsey model, the dynamics can be expressed as a system of differential equations in $\hat{k}$ and $\hat{c}$. The equation for the growth rate of $\hat{k}$, analogous to Eq. (9.3) in the Solow–Swan context, is

$$\gamma_{\hat{k}} = f(\hat{k})/\hat{k} - \hat{c}/\hat{k} - (x + n + \delta) - m \cdot [1 - (\hat{\kappa}/\hat{k})]. \tag{9.22}$$

The equation for the growth rate of $\hat{c}$ comes from Eq. (9.21):

$$\gamma_{\hat{c}} = f'(\hat{k}) - (x + \rho + \delta) - m \cdot (\rho - n) \cdot (\hat{k} - \hat{\kappa})/\hat{c}. \tag{9.23}$$

We again use the specification for migration that we assumed in Eq. (9.6) for the Solow–Swan model:

$$m \cdot [1 - (\hat{\kappa}/\hat{k})] = b \cdot [\log(\hat{k}/\hat{k}_{\text{world}})], \tag{9.6}$$

where $\hat{k}_{\text{world}}$ is constant. If we substitute this form for migration into Eqs. (9.22) and (9.23), then we can use our usual methods to work out a phase diagram in $(\hat{k}, \hat{c})$ space and use this diagram to analyze the steady state and the transitional dynamics.

Equations (9.23) and (9.6) imply that, if $\hat{c} \neq 0$, then the $\dot{\hat{C}} = 0$ locus is given by

$$f'(\hat{k}) = \delta + \rho + x + \frac{(\rho - n) \cdot b \cdot \log(\hat{k}/\hat{k}_{\text{world}})}{\hat{c}/\hat{k}}. \tag{9.24}$$

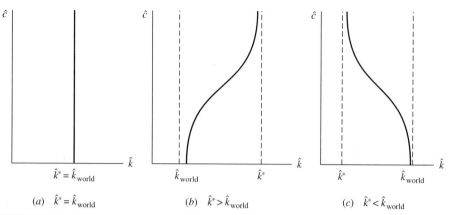

FIGURE 9.3
The shape of the $\dot{\hat{c}} = 0$ locus in the Ramsey model with migration. The shape of the $\dot{\hat{c}} = 0$ locus depends on the relation between $\hat{k}^*$ and $\hat{k}_{world}$. If $\hat{k}^* = \hat{k}_{world}$, then the locus is vertical, as shown in panel (a). If $\hat{k}^* > \hat{k}_{world}$, then the locus is upward sloping (b), and if $\hat{k}^* < \hat{k}_{world}$, then the locus is downward sloping (c).

This condition differs from the standard one in Chapter 2 by the inclusion of the last term on the right-hand side. Let $\hat{k}^*$ be the steady-state value for the model that excludes migration, that is, the value that satisfies $f'(\hat{k}^*) = \delta + \rho + x$. Then the appearance of the $\dot{\hat{c}} = 0$ locus depends on the relation between $\hat{k}^*$ and $\hat{k}_{world}$. If $\hat{k}^* = \hat{k}_{world}$, as would be true for the typical economy if $\hat{k}_{world}$ is the average steady-state value for the world, then the locus is a vertical line at $\hat{k}^*$, as shown in panel (a) of Fig. 9.3. The locus therefore coincides in this case with the standard one from the model without migration (see Fig. 2.1).

If the domestic economy would be attractive to immigrants in the no-migration steady state—that is, if $\hat{k}^* > \hat{k}_{world}$—then the locus looks as shown in panel (b) of Fig. 9.3. In particular, $\hat{k}_{world} < \hat{k} < \hat{k}^*$, $\hat{c}$ approaches 0 as $\hat{k}$ tends to $\hat{k}_{world}$, and $\hat{c}$ approaches infinity as $\hat{k}$ tends to $\hat{k}^*$. Finally, if $\hat{k}^* < \hat{k}_{world}$, then the locus looks as shown in panel (c) of the figure, with $\hat{k}^* < \hat{k} < \hat{k}_{world}$.

Equations (9.22) and (9.6) imply that the $\dot{\hat{k}} = 0$ locus is determined by

$$\hat{c} = f(\hat{k}) - (x + n + \delta) \cdot \hat{k} - b \cdot \log(\hat{k}/\hat{k}_{world}) \cdot \hat{k} \qquad (9.25)$$

This condition also differs from the standard one in Chapter 2 by the inclusion of the last term on the right-hand side. If $\hat{k} < \hat{k}_{world}$, then $\hat{c}$ is higher than before for a given value of $\hat{k}$, whereas if $\hat{k} > \hat{k}_{world}$, then $\hat{c}$ is lower than before. Otherwise, the shape of the locus, shown in Fig. 9.4, is similar to the standard one shown in Fig. 2.1.

Figure 9.4 uses the vertical $\dot{\hat{c}} = 0$ locus from panel (a) of Fig. 9.3, the case that corresponds to $\hat{k}^* = \hat{k}_{world}$. The steady-state value of $\hat{k}$, denoted by $(\hat{k}^*)_{mig.}$, then equals $\hat{k}^*$. This result follows because $(\hat{k}^*)_{mig.} = \hat{k}_{world}$ implies $m^* = 0$ (from equation [9.6]). Thus, for the typical economy, the steady-state capital intensity is unaffected by the potential for migration, and the steady-state migration rate is 0.

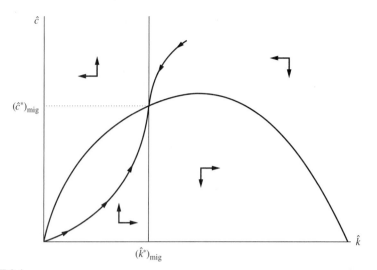

FIGURE 9.4
The phase diagram for the Ramsey model with migration. This diagram considers the case in which $\hat{k}^* = \hat{k}_{world}$, so that the $\dot{\hat{c}} = 0$ locus is vertical, as shown in panel (a) of Fig. 9.3. The $\dot{\hat{k}} = 0$ locus has the usual inverse u-shape. The steady-state $\hat{k}^*$ exhibits 0 net migration because we assumed $\hat{k}^* = \hat{k}_{world}$. The model exhibits the usual saddle-path stability. If the economy begins at a low value of $\hat{k}$, then $\hat{k}$ and $\hat{c}$ rise monotonically during the transition. Net migration is negative throughout this transition, but asymptotically approaches the steady-state value of 0.

If $\hat{k}^* > \hat{k}_{world}$, as in panel (*b*) of Fig. 9.3, then the $\dot{\hat{k}} = 0$ locus intersects the $\dot{\hat{c}} = 0$ locus at a point where $\hat{k}_{world} < (\hat{k}^*)_{mig.} < \hat{k}^*$ and $m^* > 0$. Thus, if the domestic economy would be attractive to immigrants in its no-migration steady state, then the opening up to migration leads to a steady state with positive immigration and, consequently, a reduced capital intensity (because migrants bring relatively little capital with them). These conclusions are reversed if $\hat{k}^* < \hat{k}_{world}$, as in panel (*c*) of Fig. 9.3. In this case, $\hat{k}^* < (\hat{k}^*)_{mig.} < \hat{k}_{world}$ and $m^* < 0$.

The model is saddle-path stable, as usual, and the phase diagram in Fig. 9.4 can be used to show the directions of motion. To assess the implications for the speed of convergence, we follow our usual procedure and use a Cobb–Douglas production function, $f(\hat{k}) = A\hat{k}^\alpha$. We can substitute this functional form into Eqs. (9.22) and (9.23) and then log-linearize the system around its steady-state position. Since this procedure is familiar, we leave the details as an exercise and just note that the convergence coefficient turns out to be given by

$$2\beta = \left\{ \zeta^2 + 4b \cdot (\rho - n) + 4(1 - \alpha)(\rho + \delta + x)\left[\frac{\rho + \delta + x}{\alpha} - (n + x + \delta)\right] \right\}^{1/2} - \zeta,$$
(9.26)

where $\zeta = \rho - n - b$. The result from the standard Ramsey model of Chapter 2 (Eq. [2.34]) corresponds to Eq. (9.26) if $b = 0$ (and $\theta = 1$).

We can readily verify from equation (9.26) that β rises with b. That is, as in the Solow-Swan model, a greater propensity to migrate raises the convergence speed (if $\hat{\kappa} < \hat{k}$). To assess this effect quantitatively, we use our usual parameter values, $\alpha = .75$, $x = 0.02$, $n = 0.01$, $\delta = 0.05$, and $\rho = 0.02$. For these values, the convergence coefficient, β, implied by Eq. (9.26) would be 0.025 if $b = 0$. (This relatively high value of β applies because log utility—$\theta = 1$—implies a higher intertemporal elasticity of substitution than we usually assume.) We mentioned before that estimates of migration propensities and of the ratio $\hat{\kappa}/\hat{k}$ suggest that b would be around 0.003 in the context of regions of a country or in an international setting. Eq. (9.26) implies that these values of b raise β from 0.025 in the model without migration to 0.027. This minor effect of migration on the convergence speed is similar to that found in the Solow-Swan model.

9.1.3.   The Braun Model of Migration and Growth

The theories of migration and growth that we have considered thus far have two major shortcomings. First, the flows of migrants are determined by a postulated migration function and not by households' optimizing choices of whether to move. Second, the only capital mobility in the models derives from the migrants' carrying of human capital.

Braun (1993) works out several models in which migration reflects optimizing decisions and in which varying degrees of capital mobility are assumed. A key simplifying assumption in his analysis is the existence of a perfect world credit market, which offers the same real interest rate to residents of all economies. In this case, the choice of whether to migrate depends only on comparisons across economies of paths of wage rates (and of amenities), but not on differences in rates of return.

Braun makes some alternative assumptions about the mobility of physical capital. In one model, it is perfectly mobile across economies, and, in another model, the changes in an economy's stock of capital entail adjustment costs of the type that we studied in Chapter 3. To bring out the main ideas in a tractable setting, we work out the case in which physical capital is perfectly mobile, and we consider the situation of a small economy that faces a given, constant world real interest rate.

If we use our usual constant-returns-to-scale production functions and assume that the levels of the technology are the same in all countries, then labor would never move if the migration of people is costly and the movements of capital are free. If the levels of technology differ, then people (and capital) tend to flow toward the better places. In fact, if natural population growth rates are 0, then the cost function for migration that we specify later implies that only the economy with the best technology would remain populated in the long run. The introduction of adjustment costs for investment does not invalidate this conclusion, because workers and capital still flow continually toward the best location.

To avoid this result, we introduce a form of diminishing returns to scale in each economy. In particular, we adopt Braun's (1993) assumption that an increase in an economy's population congests a natural resource, such as land or a good that is freely accessible to residents but is available in fixed supply and is subject to congestion. This effect leads to a steady-state distribution of the world's population and implies that no location ever gets depopulated. We assume, however, a functional form that allows for steady-state growth if the standard form of labor-augmenting technological progress occurs at a constant, exogenous rate.

SETUP OF THE MODEL. The domestic economy and all other economies have access to a Cobb–Douglas production function,

$$Y = AK^\alpha \cdot (\hat{L})^{1-\alpha} \cdot (R/L)^\lambda, \tag{9.27}$$

where $\hat{L} \equiv Le^{xt}$ is the effective labor input and $x \geq 0$ is the rate of exogenous, labor-augmenting technological progress in all economies. The new element in Eq. (9.27) is the input R, a constant that represents a natural resource to which residents of the domestic economy have free access. This good is, however, subject to congestion in that the per capita magnitude, R/L, enters into the production function. We assume $0 < \lambda < 1 - \alpha$, so that the overall returns to K and L are diminishing for fixed R, but the social marginal product of L is positive.

We could treat R in Eq. (9.27) as land, although the incentives to migrate would be affected if we introduced a competitively determined rental price that users of land had to pay. We could also view R as a governmentally provided service that was provided to residents in fixed aggregate supply and at no user charge. The incentives to migrate would, however, be affected by the nature of the public finance. For example, a head tax or a fee for immigration would reduce the incentive for foreigners to move to the economy. We study an environment in which taxes and fees are not levied.

A competitive individual producer views R/L as given (because the L in this term represents the aggregate population of the economy) and chooses the inputs, K and L, subject to a usual constant-returns production function. The factor prices will therefore equal the respective private marginal products, and the factor payments will exhaust the total domestic product. The wage rate equals the private marginal product of labor and is given from Eq. (9.27) by

$$w = (1 - \alpha) \cdot A\hat{k}^\alpha \cdot (R/L)^\lambda \cdot e^{xt}, \tag{9.28}$$

where $\hat{k} \equiv K/\hat{L}$.

The rental price of capital is $r + \delta$, where r is the world real interest rate, which is independent of choices made in the small domestic economy. We treat r as a constant, with $r > x$; that is, the world economy is in a steady state in which the transversality condition is satisfied.[12] Producers in the domestic economy equate the private marginal product of capital, determined from Eq. (9.27), to the rental price:

$$\alpha A \cdot (\hat{k})^{\alpha-1} \cdot (R/L)^\lambda = r + \delta.$$

---

[12]We simplify by assuming that the world's population growth rate is zero. The natural population growth rate in the world could be zero, and migration between the world and the domestic economy has a negligible effect on the world's population growth rate.

This condition determines the capital intensity in the domestic economy as

$$\hat{k} = \left[\frac{\alpha A \cdot (R/L)^{\lambda}}{r + \delta} \right]^{1/(1-\alpha)}. \tag{9.29}$$

If we substitute for $\hat{k}$ from Eq. (9.29) into Eq. (9.28), then the formula for the domestic wage rate becomes

$$w = \left[\frac{(1-\alpha) \cdot A^{1/(1-\alpha)} \cdot \alpha^{\alpha/(1-\alpha)} \cdot (R/L)^{\lambda/(1-\alpha)}}{(r + \delta)^{\alpha/(1-\alpha)}} \right] \cdot e^{xt}. \tag{9.30}$$

Hence, the domestic wage rate is high relative to that offered elsewhere if the domestic economy has a relatively large per capita quantity of natural resources, R/L, or a relatively high level of technology, A. Recall also that some forms of government policies can be represented by the parameter A.

THE DECISION TO MIGRATE. Since we assume perfect capital mobility and neglect any differences in amenities that enter into utility functions, people will evaluate locations solely in terms of wage rates. Suppose that we think of the world economy as offering the single wage rate, w_{world}. The benefit from a permanent move at time t from the world to the domestic economy is the present value of the wage differential:

$$B(t) \equiv \int_{t}^{\infty} [w(v) - w_{world}] \cdot e^{-r \cdot (v-t)} dv. \tag{9.31}$$

If we define $\hat{B}(t) \equiv B(t) \cdot e^{-xt}$, then the time derivative of $\hat{B}(t)$ is given from Eq. (9.31) by

$$\dot{\hat{B}}(t) = -[\hat{w}(t) - \hat{w}_{world}] + (r - x) \cdot \hat{B}(t), \tag{9.32}$$

where $\hat{w}(t) = w(t) \cdot e^{-xt}$ and $\hat{w}_{world} = w_{world} \cdot e^{-xt}$. Since we have already assumed that the world economy is in a steady state, $\hat{w}_{world}$ is constant.

We assume, without loss of generality, that $\hat{w}(t) \geq \hat{w}_{world}$. This condition turns out to imply $\hat{w}(v) \geq \hat{w}_{world}$ and, hence, $\hat{B}(v) \geq 0$ for all $v \geq t$. Any migration that occurs will therefore always be in the direction toward the domestic economy. The situation is reversed if $\hat{w}(t) \leq \hat{w}_{world}$.

We simplify by assuming that the natural rate of population growth in the domestic economy is 0. Then, if $M(t) \geq 0$ denotes the flow of migrants at time t from the world to the domestic economy, the growth rate of the domestic population is

$$\gamma_L \equiv \dot{L}(t)/L(t) = M(t)/L(t). \tag{9.33}$$

The key matter now is to specify the costs of migration. The cost incurred by each migrant is assumed to be an increasing function of $M(t)/L(t)$. This specification is reasonable if, for example, the expenses for finding a job or a house increase with the number of new searchers in relation to the population of the receiving location.[13]

---

[13]The key property is that the cost of moving for the marginal mover rises with the number of movers. This relation would also hold if there were heterogeneity with respect to moving costs. The persons

The cost is assumed to show up as a quantity of work time foregone, so that, for a given value of $M(t)/L(t)$, the cost in units of output is proportional to the world wage rate, w_{world}, that the migrants would have earned in their original locations. Hence, the amount paid by each migrant takes the form

$$\text{cost of moving} = \eta[M(t)/L(t)] \cdot w_{world}, \tag{9.34}$$

where we assume $\eta' > 0$ and $\eta'' \geq 0$. We also simplify the analysis by assuming $\eta(0) = 0$; that is, we ignore any fixed expenses associated with transportation and related outlays and assume accordingly that the cost per migrant goes to 0 as the flow of migrants goes to 0 (see Braun [1993] for further discussion).

As people move to the domestic economy, R/L falls, and w falls accordingly in Eq. (9.30). If enough people have moved to equate w to w_{world}, then the incentive to migrate would be eliminated. (If the domestic technology parameter, A, is the same as the world A, then the equality in wage rates arises when the domestic value of R/L equals the world value of R/L.) At the point of equal wage rates, the domestic economy is in a steady state in which migration is zero; population, L, is constant; and the capital intensity, $\hat{k}$, is also constant. The condition $\eta(0) = 0$ implies that the system actually approaches this steady state, because if $w > w_{world}$, then $B > 0$, and people would be motivated to move at zero cost. Thus, more people migrate, and the domestic population changes as long as $w > w_{world}$. (If we had assumed $\eta(0) > 0$, then a positive gap between domestic and world wage rates would persist in the steady state.)

Since the world economy is not depopulated in the steady state,[14] we know that some of the world's inhabitants will never move to the domestic economy, that is, some of these people do not exercise the option to migrate. If people are identical and if they all optimize, then some of them can end up in equilibrium with a zero net benefit from migration only if they all end up with a zero net benefit. Hence, the equilibrium entails enough migration at each date so that the benefits and costs of moving are equated:

$$B(t) = \eta[M(t)/L(t)] \cdot w_{world} \tag{9.35}$$

for all t. This equation still holds if we replace $B(t)$ by $\hat{B}(t)$ on the left and w_{world} by the constant $\hat{w}_{world}$ on the right.

We can compute the flow of migrants at each date and therefore the growth rate of the domestic population by inverting Eq. (9.35):

$$\gamma_L = M(t)/L(t) = \psi[\hat{B}(t)/\hat{w}_{world}], \tag{9.36}$$

---

with lower costs would move sooner, and the cost of moving would therefore rise at the margin with the number of movers (although in this case with the cumulated number, rather than with the current flow).

[14]This condition holds because a large decrease in world population would significantly raise the world value of R/L and thereby increase w_{world}. The form for the wage rate in Eq. (9.28), which also applies for the world, implies that the equality between w and w_{world} must occur before population reaches 0 in the domestic or the world economy.

where we use Eq. (9.33), and the function ψ is the inverse of the function η in Eq. (9.34). Since $\eta' > 0$ and $\eta'' \geq 0$, the function η is one-to-one, and the inverse function ψ is well-defined and one-to-one. The function ψ satisfies the conditions $\psi' > 0$ and $\psi'' \leq 0$. The assumption $\eta(0) = 0$ implies $\psi(0) = 0$.

In our discussions of the Solow–Swan and Ramsey models, we postulated a migration function in Fig. 9.1 in which the migration rate, $m = M/L$, varied positively with $\hat{w}$ and, hence, with $\hat{k}$. We noted that this function assumed that conditions elsewhere, represented now by $\hat{w}_{\text{world}}$, were held constant. The main difference between the postulated function and the present one is that the former relation involved only the current wage rate per unit of effective labor, $\hat{w}$, whereas the latter relation involves the entire path of effective wage rates as they enter into the benefit expression, $\hat{B}$.

THE DYNAMIC SYSTEM, THE STEADY STATE, AND THE TRANSITIONAL DYNAMICS. The dynamic system can be written in terms of the variables L and $\hat{B}$, where L is the single state variable. The two dynamic equations come from Eqs. (9.32) and (9.36):

$$\dot{\hat{B}} = -(\hat{w} - \hat{w}_{\text{world}}) + (r - x) \cdot \hat{B}, \tag{9.32}$$

$$\gamma_L = \psi(\hat{B}/\hat{w}_{\text{world}}), \tag{9.36}$$

where $\hat{w}_{\text{world}}$ and r are constants, and $\hat{w}$ varies inversely with L in accordance with Eq. (9.30):

$$\hat{w} = \left[\frac{(1 - \alpha) \cdot A^{1/(1-\alpha)} \cdot \alpha^{\alpha/(1-\alpha)} \cdot (R/L)^{\lambda/(1-\alpha)}}{(r + \delta)^{\alpha/(1-\alpha)}} \right]. \tag{9.37}$$

Figure 9.5 uses Eqs. (9.32) and (9.36) to construct a phase diagram in $(L, \hat{B})$ space. Equation (9.36) and the properties of the ψ function, including $\psi(0) = 0$, imply that $\dot{L} = 0$ corresponds (if $L \neq 0$) to $\hat{B} = 0$. The equation also implies (because $\psi' > 0$) that L rises if $\hat{B} > 0$ and falls if $\hat{B} < 0$.

Equation (9.32) implies that $\dot{\hat{B}} = 0$ corresponds to a positive, linear relation between $\hat{B}$ and $\hat{w}$. Since $\hat{w}$ is inversely related to L in equation (9.37), the relation between $\hat{B}$ and L is also inverse, as shown in Fig. 9.5. Since $r > x$, values of $\hat{B}$ above the curve imply $\dot{\hat{B}} > 0$, and values below the curve imply $\dot{\hat{B}} < 0$.

The figure shows that the steady state involves $L = L^*$, a constant, and $\hat{B}^* = 0$. Equation (9.32) implies $\hat{w}^* = \hat{w}_{\text{world}}$, and Eq. (9.37) determines the value L^* that satisfies this equality. In particular, L^* rises with A and increases proportionately with R.

The system is saddle-path stable, and Figure 9.5 shows the directions of motion. If the domestic economy starts with $L < L^*$, then $\hat{B} > 0$, and L rises over time. The resulting decline in $\hat{w}$ leads to a fall in $\hat{B}$ and, hence, to a decrease in the migration rate. Over time, the migration rate falls steadily and approaches 0 as L tends to L^*.

We can determine the speed of convergence to the steady state in the usual way by linearizing in the neighborhood of the steady state. In this case, the system

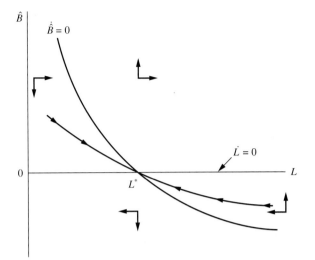

FIGURE 9.5
The phase diagram when migration is a choice variable. The dynamics of the model can be expressed in terms of the present value of the benefits from moving, $\hat{B}$, and the domestic population, L. The system is saddle-path stable, and the stable arm is downward sloping. Thus, a low initial population is associated with high benefits from net migration toward the domestic economy and, consequently, with a high net migration rate, m. As population increases, the net benefit from migration diminishes. In the steady state, the net benefit, $\hat{B}$, is 0, and population, L, is constant.

is described by Eqs. (9.32) and (9.36), and the linearization is in terms of $\hat{B}$ (relative to its steady-state value of 0) and $\log(L/L^*)$. The migration rate, which equals the growth rate of L, is given by

$$M/L = \gamma_L \approx \beta \cdot \log(L^*/L), \qquad (9.38)$$

where the convergence coefficient, β, is given by

$$2\beta = \left[(r-x)^2 + \frac{4\lambda \cdot \psi'(0)}{1-\alpha} \right]^{1/2} - (r-x). \qquad (9.39)$$

Equation (9.39) shows that the key determinant of the convergence speed is $\psi'(0)$, the sensitivity of the migration rate in the vicinity of the steady state to the relative benefit from moving, $\hat{B}/\hat{w}_{\text{world}}$ (see Eq. [9.36]). The greater this sensitivity, the faster is the speed of convergence. Recall that the function ψ is the inverse of the function η, which relates the cost of moving to the migration rate in Eq. (9.34). The slope $\psi'(0)$ is the reciprocal of $\eta'(0)$; therefore, the more rapidly migration costs rise with the volume of migration the smaller is the responsiveness of the migration rate to the relative benefit, $\hat{B}/\hat{w}$, and, hence, the slower is the speed of convergence.

The convergence speed for L is also the convergence speed for y. To see this, use the production function from Eq. (9.27) and the expression for $\hat{k}$ in Eq. (9.29) to derive a formula for $\hat{y}$:

$$\hat{y} = \left[\frac{A^{1/(1-\alpha)} \cdot \alpha^{\alpha/(1-\alpha)} \cdot (R/L)^{\lambda/(1-\alpha)}}{(r+\delta)^{\alpha/(1-\alpha)}} \right]. \qquad (9.40)$$

This formula is the same as that for $\hat{w}$ in Eq. (9.37), except for the multiple $1 - \alpha$ in the expression for $\hat{w}$. The result for $\hat{y}$ implies

$$\log(\hat{y}/\hat{y}^*) = [\lambda/(1 - \alpha)] \cdot \log(L^*/L); \tag{9.41}$$

that is, $\hat{y}$ is above its steady-state value when L is below its steady-state value, and vice versa. Equation (9.40) also implies that the growth rate of $\hat{y}$ is given by

$$\gamma_{\hat{y}} = -[\lambda/(1 - \alpha)] \cdot \gamma_L. \tag{9.42}$$

We can use Eq. (9.42) along with Eqs. (9.38) and (9.41) to get a familiar-looking convergence equation for $\hat{y}$:

$$\gamma_{\hat{y}} = -\beta \cdot \log(\hat{y}/\hat{y}^*). \tag{9.43}$$

Thus, the growth rate of $\hat{y}$ is inversely related to the level of $\hat{y}$, and the speed of convergence, β, is given by Eq. (9.39).

Recall that we discussed earlier some empirical findings on net migration rates. These findings relate the migration rate to differentials in per capita income or product. We can write Eq. (9.38) in this form if we use Eq. (9.41) to transform from $\log(L^*/L)$ to $\log(\hat{y}/\hat{y}^*)$ to get

$$M/L = \gamma_L \approx [\frac{\beta \cdot (1 - \alpha)}{\lambda}] \cdot \log(\hat{y}/\hat{y}^*). \tag{9.44}$$

We can look at Eqs. (9.43) and (9.44) as a system of two equations that involve the growth rate of output and the migration rate. Suppose that we examine a group of economies for which we can assume that the parameters α and λ are the same. Then, places with a higher $\psi'(0)$—that is, with a greater sensitivity of the migration rate to the relative benefit, $\hat{B}/\hat{w}_{world}$, and, hence, with a smaller tendency for the cost of moving to rise with the migration rate—have a higher value of β. Therefore, these places have a larger responsiveness of the migration rate to differentials in per capita product in Eq. (9.44) *and* a faster speed of convergence for per capita output in accordance with Eq. (9.43).

Braun (1993) tested the hypothesis that a high migration-rate sensitivity tended to go along with a high speed of convergence for per capita product or income. He used information on within-country migration and convergence for the U.S. states and the regions of five European countries (France, Germany, Italy, Spain, and the United Kingdom) and Japan. That is, he effectively compared seven estimates of migration-rate sensitivities with the corresponding seven estimates of convergence coefficients for per capita output or income. Although the number of data points is small, the results provide some support for the underlying theory because the places with greater migration-rate sensitivities tended also to have higher convergence rates. See Chapter 11 for a discussion of this evidence.

DYNAMICS OF THE WORLD ECONOMY. In the previous analysis, we assumed that the world economy was in a steady state with a constant wage rate per unit of effective labor, $\hat{w}_{world}$, and an associated constant capital intensity, which we can denote by $\hat{k}_{world}$. We described a dynamic process for migration whereby the domestic economy's effective wage rate, $\hat{w}$, approached the constant world value, $\hat{w}_{world}$. If the domestic economy has the same level of technology, A, as the world, then $\hat{k}$ tends correspondingly toward the constant $\hat{k}_{\text{world}}$.

More generally, we could allow for a transitional dynamics in which $\hat{k}_{\text{world}}$ approaches its steady-state value, $(\hat{k}_{\text{world}})^*$. Then, for economy i, the changes over time in $\hat{k}_i$ can be broken into two parts: first, the adjustment of $\hat{k}_i$ toward $\hat{k}_{\text{world}}$, and, second, the adjustment of $\hat{k}_{\text{world}}$ toward $(\hat{k}_{\text{world}})^*$.

Braun (1993) works out an analysis of this type in which the world consists of only two regions, $i = 1, 2$. Migration is possible between the regions at the cost specified in Eq. (9.34). For the world economy—that is, for the aggregate of the two regions—the evolution of the capital stock and consumption per effective worker, $\hat{k}_{\text{world}}$ and $\hat{c}_{\text{world}}$, are similar to that in the Ramsey model of Chapter 2. This process implies a gradual adjustment of $\hat{k}_{\text{world}}$ to its steady-state value, $(\hat{k}_{\text{world}})^*$, and the speed of convergence depends on the same parameters that mattered in the Ramsey setting.[15]

At the same time, people migrate toward the region with a higher wage rate, and this movement tends to reduce per capita output in the high-wage region and to raise per capita output in the low-wage region. The speed of this process involves a convergence coefficient that is determined as in Eq. (9.39). In particular, a higher value of $\psi'(0)$—the sensitivity of the migration rate to the benefit from moving—implies a higher convergence rate. If the underlying technology parameters, A_i, are the same in the two regions, then the migration process implies a convergence of region's i's output per effective worker, $\hat{y}_i$, toward the world level, $\hat{y}_{\text{world}}$. (Otherwise, $\hat{y}_i$ converges toward a value that is either above or below $\hat{y}_{\text{world}}$.)

The growth rate of each region's output per effective worker can be approximated by

$$\gamma_{\hat{y}_i} = -\beta \cdot \log(\hat{y}_i/\hat{y}_{\text{world}}) - \mu \cdot \log[\hat{y}_{\text{world}}/(\hat{y}_{\text{world}})^*], \qquad (9.45)$$

where β is given in Eq. (9.39), and μ is determined by a Ramsey model of the world economy. Equation (9.45) combines a cross-sectional effect that involves the elimination of differences between the economies with a time-series effect that involves the adjustment of the world economy to its steady-state position. If we consider a cross section of data for a single time period, then the relative growth rates would depend inversely on the initial relative positions, $\hat{y}_i/\hat{y}_{\text{world}}$, and would involve the coefficient β. In contrast, if we examine time-series data on the world variable $\hat{y}_{\text{world}}$, then the growth rate would vary negatively with $\hat{y}_{\text{world}}/(\hat{y}_{\text{world}})^*$ and would involve the coefficient μ. In a panel setting, the growth rate for each economy depends on $\hat{y}_i/\hat{y}_{\text{world}}$ and $\hat{y}_{\text{world}}/(\hat{y}_{\text{world}})^*$ and involves both coefficients, β and μ.[16]

---

[15] In the neighborhood of the steady state, the rate of convergence for the world economy turns out to be independent of parameters that determine the speed of the migration process. This result holds because wage rates are equalized in the steady state; hence, shifts of persons from one economy to the other do not affect world output or the rate of return in the vicinity of the steady state.

[16] If a panel estimation includes dummy variables for each time period, then the term that involves μ would be picked up by these variables. In this case, the estimated convergence effect would involve only the coefficient β.

IMPERFECT CAPITAL MOBILITY. In the present setting, an economy's speed of convergence toward the world economy involves the coefficient β in Eq. (9.39), which reflects only the gradual migration of persons. If we had assumed less than complete capital mobility, then the forces that influenced convergence in some of our previous models would also have affected β. For example, if investment entails adjustment costs or if capital markets are imperfect, then these elements would influence the speed of convergence.

It is straightforward to allow for adjustment costs for investment if we retain the framework of perfect capital markets (see Braun [1993]). These adjustment costs can be introduced in the way discussed in Chapter 3. The main new finding is that the convergence coefficient, β, is higher if the sensitivity of the adjustment cost to the quantity of investment is smaller.

The analysis is more complicated if credit markets are imperfect. The rate of return then differs across the economies, and the decision to migrate would be based on this difference along with the gap in wage rates. We also have to keep track of ownership of assets in various places, and the behavior of consumption is correspondingly more complicated. The results that we obtained before in the settings of the Solow–Swan and Ramsey models apply when capital flows are entirely absent, except for the human capital carried by migrants.

9.2 FERTILITY CHOICE

For Malthus (1798), the effects of economic factors on fertility and mortality were a central element in the theory of economic development. His ideas have, however, exerted little influence on modern theories of economic growth, probably because he predicted incorrectly that rising prosperity would lead inevitably to increased population growth. The empirical evidence indicates that, except for very poor countries or households, increases in per capita income tend to reduce fertility.

Although empirical studies have not confirmed Malthus's specific predictions, these studies have typically found important linkages from economic variables—such as per capita income, wage rates, levels of female and male education, and urbanization—to fertility and mortality (see Wahl [1985], Behrman [1990], Schultz [1989], and Barro and Lee [1994]). Thus, the empirical findings firmly reject the notion that the natural growth rate of population is exogenous with respect to economic growth.

Despite Malthus's theoretical precedent and the empirical evidence, most modern theories of economic growth have assumed that the rate of population growth is an exogenous constant. For example, in our presentations of the Solow–Swan and Ramsey models in Chapters 1 and 2, different settings for the rate of population growth, n, mattered for the growth process, but we did not consider feedback from the growth process to the rate of population growth. We have allowed in this chapter for endogenous responses of population through migration, but have not yet considered variations in the natural growth rate of population.

In this section, we construct a growth model in which economic development influences family choices about the number of children and, hence, the fertility rate.

We want, in particular, to design a model that mimics some of the major empirical findings, especially the negative relation between fertility and per capita income except at very low levels of per capita income.

Since our framework neglects migration and treats the mortality rate as an exogenous constant, the theory of fertility corresponds to a theory of the rate of population growth. We could extend the analysis to introduce migration, as before, and we could also allow for feedback from economic growth to the state of health and, hence, to mortality rates. These important extensions are left for future research.

9.2.1 An Overlapping-Generations Setup

We begin with the approach of Becker and Barro (1988) and Barro and Becker (1989), in which parents and children are linked through altruism. Parental decisions about numbers of children are made jointly with choices about consumption and intergenerational transfers. Children are costly to produce and raise, but the addition to utility–as viewed by the parents–may be sufficient to justify these costs. If the marginal utility attached to children diminishes with their number, or if the child-rearing cost increases with the number, then the model determines the fertility rate from a standard first-order condition. The choice of the quantity of children also interacts with the determination of their quality, as represented in the model by the amounts of consumption and capital stock allocated to each person.

Becker and Barro (1988) use an overlapping-generations (OLG) framework in which people live for two periods, childhood and adulthood. (See the appendix to Chapter 3 for a discussion of OLG frameworks.) Marriage is not considered, and a single adult of generation i has n_i children. The utility function takes the form,

$$U_i = u(c_i, n_i) + Y(n_i) \cdot n_i U_{i+1}, \tag{9.46}$$

where the subscript i is the period in which a person is an adult, U_i is the adult's utility, c_i is consumption per adult person during adulthood, and n_i is the number of children per adult. The term $u(c_i, n_i)$ represents the utils generated during adulthood from consumption and the presence of children. (This formulation does not distinguish the consumption of children during their childhood from that of their parents.)

The last term on the right-hand side of Eq. (9.46) represents the utils that adults obtain by considering the prospective happiness of their children when the children become adults. The term U_{i+1} is the utility that each child will attain as an adult. This utility is also determined by Eq. (9.46), with all variables updated by one period. We assume that children are identical and are treated equally by parents, so that all attain the same utility U_{i+1}. (This egalitarian treatment will apply if everyone has the same utility function, $u[\cdot]$, and if this utility is a concave function of the resources provided to each child.)

The function $Y(n_i)$ in Eq. (9.46) represents the degree of altruism that parents attach to each child's utility; hence, $Y(n_i)$ multiplies the "aggregate" utility attained by the next generation, $n_i U_{i+1}$. The assumed properties are $Y(n_i) > 0$ (parents value their children's happiness), $Y'(n_i) < 0$ (a form of diminishing marginal utility of children), and $Y(1) < 1$. The last property implies that, if the number of children per adult equals one, then parents are selfish in the sense that they value a unit of $u(c_i, 1)$ more than a unit of $u(c_{i+1}, 1)$.[17]

Becker and Barro (1988) assume that the altruism function takes a constant-elasticity form,

$$Y(n_i) = Y \cdot (n_i)^{-\epsilon}, \qquad (9.47)$$

where $\epsilon > 0$ and $0 < Y < 1$. The parameter Y represents the degree of altruism between parents and children that applies when $n_i = 1$. The notion of parents liking children is captured by $Y > 0$, and the idea of parental selfishness is reflected in $Y < 1$. The condition $\epsilon > 0$ yields diminishing marginal utility in the number of children in the sense that $Y(n_i)$ declines with n_i.

If we use Eqs. (9.46) and (9.47), then we can write U_i as a forward, weighted sum of the $u(c_j, n_j)$ for each generation starting with the ith:

$$U_i = \sum_{j=i}^{\infty} Y^{j-i} \cdot (N_j)^{1-\epsilon} \cdot u(c_j, n_j), \qquad (9.48)$$

where N_j is the number of adult descendants in generation j. This number equals 1 when $j = i$ (that is, when we start from the perspective of a single adult) and equals the product of the various n_j for $j > i$:

$$N_i = 1; N_j = \prod_{k=i}^{j-1}(n_k), \qquad \text{for } j = i+1, i+2, \ldots \qquad (9.49)$$

In previous settings, we assumed a functional form for $u(c)$ that implied a constant elasticity of marginal utility, $u'(c)$, with respect to c. We now make the parallel assumption that the functional form for $u(c_j, n_j)$ implies constant elasticities of marginal utility with respect to c_j and n_j :

$$u(c_j, n_j) = [c_j \cdot (n_j)^{\phi}]^{1-\theta}/(1-\theta), \qquad (9.50)$$

where $\phi > 0$ and $\theta > 0$. We also assume $\phi \cdot (1-\theta) < 1$ to get diminishing marginal utility with respect to n_j. If we define

$$\psi \equiv (1-\epsilon)/(1-\theta),$$

where we assume $\psi > 0$,[18] and substitute the form for $u(c_j, n_j)$ from Eq. (9.50) into Eq. (9.48), then we get

$$U_i = \sum_{j=i}^{\infty} Y^{j-i} \cdot \{[(N_j)^{\psi} \cdot c_j \cdot (n_j)^{\phi}]^{1-\theta} - 1\}/(1-\theta). \qquad (9.51)$$

---

[17]In terms of the discussion of altruism in the appendix to Chapter 3, the term Y combines pure time preference (the term that involves ρ) with the attitude toward children. We can think of the pure rate of time preference, ρ, as 0 in the present context.

[18]The condition $\psi > 0$ implies $\epsilon < 1$ if $\theta < 1$, as in the case considered by Becker and Barro (1988). The present formulation also allows $\epsilon > 1$ if $\theta > 1$. If $\theta = 1$, then $\epsilon = 1$ must hold for ψ to be finite.

Note that the condition $\epsilon > 0$ implies $\psi \cdot (1-\theta) < 1$. We added the term -1 inside the large brackets, so that, as θ tends to 1, the expression inside the integral approaches the log-utility form:

$$U_i = \sum_{j=i}^{\infty} Y^{j-i} \cdot [\psi \cdot \log(N_j) + \log(c_j) + \phi \cdot \log(n_j)]. \tag{9.52}$$

(If we let θ approach 1, then we can derive Eq. [9.52] from Eq. [9.51] by using l'Hôpital's rule.)

We can complete the model as in Becker and Barro (1988) by specifying a cost for having and raising children and by introducing an intergenerational budget constraint. This constraint relates a parent's intergenerational transfer to each child to the parent's initial assets, the amounts of wage and asset income, and the expenditures on child rearing and consumption. The adults in each generation then choose consumption and fertility to maximize U_i in Eq. (9.51), subject to the intertemporal budget constraint. The analysis is straightforward if the solutions for intergenerational transfers are interior; that is, if parents always opt for positive transfers. We then do not have to consider that the environment likely precludes negative transfers in the sense of debts left for children. We do not carry out the details of this analysis here, because we prefer to work instead with a continuous-time version of the model.

9.2.2 The Model in Continuous Time

The overlapping-generations setup is useful for a study of fertility choice because the length of the period has an important meaning. It represents the average spread in age between parents and children; that is, the length of a generation. For aggregate purposes, however, we would have to add up across families who, at a given point in time, have children of varying ages. (To some extent, this distribution of child ages also applies to an individual family.) Moreover, the restriction to an integer number of children, a condition that holds for a single household, would be smoothed out in the aggregation across heterogeneous families.

These considerations suggest that it would not be useful to work out an individual family's choice problem in a discrete-time setup and then apply the findings directly to the behavior of economy-wide variables. The results that we would get from the underlying discreteness in time—which may include a potential to cycle around the steady state—would reflect the failure to add up appropriately across households. Thus, we either have to carry out the aggregation explicitly or else use as an approximation a continuous-time representation for the behavior of the typical household. The continuous-time approach lacks realism at the level of a family—for example, it neglects integer restrictions on the number of children—but may nevertheless be satisfactory for a study of economy-wide variables.

We now use the results from the previous section to modify the continuous-time model of infinite-lived households that we introduced in the Ramsey model in Chapter 2. The infinite horizon is natural here because it represents the altruistic linkage from parents to children to the children's children and so on. The rate of time preference, $\rho > 0$, in the Ramsey formulation corresponds to the degree of intergenerational altruism, $Y < 1$, in the overlapping-generations model. Two new elements are that time preference also depends on the number of children and that child rearing uses up resources.

BIRTHS AND DEATHS. In the discrete-period model, a new generation of finite size is born each period, and each person lives for two periods, childhood and adulthood. In the continuous-time formulation, we instead treat births and deaths as continuous flows.

Let $n \geq 0$ be a family's birth rate, treated as a choice variable at every point in time, and $d > 0$ the mortality rate. For reasons of tractability, we do not allow d to depend on a family's age structure. We also do not allow d to depend on family or public expenditures on medical care, sanitation, and so on, although these influences on the mortality rate would be an important extension of the model. The size of the family, N, changes continuously in accordance with

$$\dot{N} = (n - d) \cdot N. \tag{9.53}$$

The variable N will now be an additional state variable for households.

THE UTILITY FUNCTION. We use the formulation of household utility from the discrete-time model in Eq. (9.48) to modify the standard continuous-time representation from Eq. (2.1) to

$$U = \int_0^\infty \frac{e^{-\rho t}}{1 - \theta} \cdot \left\{ [N^\psi c \cdot (n - d)^\phi]^{1-\theta} - 1 \right\} \cdot dt. \tag{9.54}$$

The term $e^{-\rho t}$ corresponds to the altruism factor, Y^{j-i}, in Eq. (9.48). Equation (9.54) includes the net growth rate of population, $n - d$, rather than the gross fertility rate, n. If we think of d as representing infant mortality, then $n - d$ refers to surviving children, the variable that would plausibly appear in the utility function.[19]

CHILD-REARING COSTS. The birth and rearing of each child costs an amount η. We think of η as expended entirely at the time of birth, although a more realistic model would recognize that these expenditures arise over a long period of child development. We attempt to get around this shortcoming by thinking of η as a large single outlay that represents the present value of expenditures for each child. Since nN is the number of births per unit of time, ηnN is the total of expenditures on child rearing, and ηn is the amount expended per capita.

A key issue is the relation of the cost η to other variables, such as the value of parents' time and measures of child quality, which correspond in the model to

---

[19]The model is not rich enough for the mortality rate to depend on age. However, the household's choices would not be affected if we entered a factor like $d^{-\iota}$, where $\iota > 0$, multiplicatively with $N^\psi \cdot c \cdot (n - d)^\phi$ in Eq. (9.54). This factor could perhaps capture the disutility associated with adult mortality.

consumption and capital stock per person, c and k.[20] If η represents only purchases of market goods and services, then the cost of rearing a child declines relative to per capita income as the economy grows. In this case, the fertility rate, n, tends—counterfactually—to rise as the economy develops.

Becker (1991) and others argue that child rearing is intensive in parental time, especially in the mother's time in societies in which women are the primary providers of child care.[21] In other words, the productivity advances that apply to market goods and services because of capital accumulation and technological progress are not thought to apply very much to the raising of children. In this case, the cost η tends to rise with parents' wage rates or with other measures of the opportunity costs of parental time. Greater educational attainment of adults (especially of women) tends in this case to raise η. More generally, η increases with the per capita quantities of human and physical capital, represented by the variable k in the model.

To introduce a linkage between η and parents' wage rates, we would have to allow for alternative uses of parental time; for example, for choices between time spent producing goods and time spent raising children. (The next section deals with the related choice between work and leisure.) This extension leads to technical complexity in the form of nonlinearities. Since the main idea involves a positive relation between η and k, we proceed instead by postulating a linear relation,

$$\eta = b_0 + bk, \tag{9.55}$$

where $b_0 \geq 0$ and $b \geq 0$. The b_0 part represents the goods cost of child rearing, and the bk part represents the part of the cost that increases with the capital intensity.

The specification in Eq. (9.55) turns out to be especially simple if we assume $b_0 = 0$, because the per capita child-rearing cost, $\eta n = bnk$, then combines with the term nk that has appeared all along as a negative term in the household's budget constraint (see Eq. [2.23]). We discuss later some results for specifications that include the goods cost, b_0.

THE FAMILY'S BUDGET CONSTRAINT. We assume that each family member receives the same wage rate, w. (More realistically, we would like to allow a dependence of w on age, so that children would not start immediately to earn wages.) The family's assets earn the rate of return r.

---

[20]We treat the child-rearing cost as proportional to the number of children. The setup cost for a family to have its first child suggests that there might be a range in which the cost per child diminishes with the number of children. Eventually, however, the costs would increase more than linearly with the number, because the bearing of more children implies that the spacing between births gets inconveniently short or that the parents are very old when they have the children.

[21]See Galor and Weil (1993) for a recent emphasis on this element in the context of growth models. Becker, Murphy, and Tamura (1990) also stress the linkage between human capital and the costs of child rearing.

Let c and k be the family's per capita consumption and assets, respectively. (We have, for convenience, already imposed the closed-economy condition that per capita assets, a, equals k.) The budget constraint can then be expressed as

$$\dot{k} = w + (r - n + d) \cdot k - bnk - c, \qquad (9.56)$$

where we used the form for the child-rearing cost, η, from Eq. (9.55) with b_0 set to 0. We assume, as usual, that each household takes as given the path of the wage rate, w, and the rate of return, r.[22] The change from the standard formulation is the inclusion of the per capita outlay on child-rearing, bnk.

OPTIMIZATION CONDITIONS. The household's optimization problem is to choose the path of the control variables c and n to maximize U in Eq. (9.54). This maximization problem is subject to the initial assets $k(0)$; the transition equations for the two state variables, N and k, given by Eqs. (9.53) and (9.56), the inequalities $c \geq 0$ and $n \geq 0$ (which will never bind because of the form of the utility function in Eq. [9.54]); and the usual restriction that rules out chain-letter behavior for debt (if we allow $k < 0$).

We can set up the Hamiltonian expression,

$$J = \frac{e^{-\rho t}}{1 - \theta} \cdot \left\{ [N^{\psi} c \cdot (n - d)^{\phi}]^{1-\theta} - 1 \right\} + v \cdot [w + (r + d) \cdot k - (1 + b) \cdot nk - c]$$
$$+ \mu \cdot (n - d) \cdot N, \qquad (9.57)$$

where v and μ are the shadow prices associated with the two state variables, k and N. Since the restrictions $c \geq 0$ and $n \geq 0$ will never bind (because the marginal utilities approach infinity as c and n tend to 0 and $d \geq 0$, respectively), the household satisfies the usual first-order conditions obtained from setting $\partial J/\partial c = \partial J/\partial n = 0$, $v = -\partial J/\partial k$, and $\dot{\mu} = -\partial J/\partial N$.[23] The results simplify considerably for the case of log utility, $\theta = 1$, and we concentrate our analysis on this situation.

The conditions $\partial J/\partial c = 0$ and $\dot{v} = -\partial J/\partial k$ can be manipulated in the usual way to get an expression for the growth rate of c:

$$\dot{c}/c = (1/\theta) \cdot \left\{ r - \rho - (n - d) \cdot [1 - \psi \cdot (1 - \theta)] - nb + \phi \cdot (1 - \theta) \cdot \dot{n}/(n - d) \right\} \quad [24]$$

---

[22]We assume, however, that the child-rearing cost, η, depends on the household's own assets, k, rather than on the economy-wide capital per person, and that the household's choice problem therefore internalizes the relation between η and k. The analysis is somewhat different if η depends only on economy-wide variables, perhaps through a relation between η and the wage rate.

[23]The one possible problem is that children may be so cheap to produce that it would be attractive to borrow enough to make n arbitrarily large. This difficulty does not arise if the cost parameter b is big enough to ensure that the variable Ω—defined below to equal $(1 + b) \cdot k/c - \phi/(n - d)$—is always positive.

[24]In the standard Ramsey analysis considered in Chapter 2, n is an exogenous constant and $b = 0$, so that the growth rate of c is given by

$$\dot{c}/c = (1/\theta) \cdot \left\{ r - \rho - (n - d) \cdot [1 - \psi \cdot (1 - \theta)] \right\}.$$

This result simplifies in the case of log utility, $\theta = 1$, to

$$\dot{c}/c = r - \rho - (n - d) - bn. \tag{9.58}$$

With $\theta = 1$, population growth, $n - d$, effectively adds to the time-preference rate, ρ (see footnote 22 for a comparison with the standard Ramsey model). In addition, the term bn subtracts from r because a higher k raises child-rearing costs, given by bnk.

We shall find it useful to define a new variable Ω as follows:

$$\Omega \equiv (1 + b) \cdot k/c - \phi/(n - d).$$

We can then use the conditions $\partial J/\partial c = \partial J/\partial n = 0$ to get

$$\mu = e^{-\rho t} \cdot N^{\psi(1-\theta)-1} \cdot c^{1-\theta} \cdot (n - d)^{\phi(1-\theta)} \cdot \Omega. \tag{9.59}$$

If we differentiate this expression for μ with respect to time and use the condition $\dot{\mu} = -\partial J/\partial N$ to substitute out for $\dot{\mu}$, then we eventually get

$$\dot{\Omega} = -\psi + (\Omega/\theta) \cdot \left\{ \rho - (1 - \theta) \cdot [r - (1 - \psi) \cdot (n - d) - nb + \phi \cdot \dot{n}/(n - d)] \right\}.$$

If $\theta = 1$, then this differential equation simplifies to

$$\dot{\Omega} = -\psi + \Omega\rho,$$

which is unstable. That is, if $\Omega(0)$ departs from its steady-state value, ψ/ρ, then Ω moves over time toward $\pm\infty$. Since these unstable paths violate the transversality condition associated with N,[25] optimizing behavior dictates that Ω equal ψ/ρ at

---

(*Footnote 24, continued*) The standard analysis also assumes that $\psi \cdot (1 - \theta)$, which equals $1 - \epsilon$, is unity, so that the formula becomes

$$\dot{c}/c = (1/\theta) \cdot (r - \rho).$$

The specification $\psi \cdot (1 - \theta) = 1$ (or, equivalently, $\epsilon = 0$) implies, however, that the marginal contribution of N to the flow of utility (for given c and n) is negative if $\theta > 1$ and becomes of unbounded magnitude as θ approaches 1. For that reason, Becker and Barro (1988) and Barro and Becker (1989) dealt only with the case $\theta < 1$. We assume here that ψ is positive and finite, in which case the marginal contribution of N to the flow of utility is also positive and finite.

[25] The differential equation for Ω has the general solution,

$$\Omega = \psi/\rho + [\Omega(0) - \psi/\rho] \cdot e^{\rho t}.$$

The condition for μ in Eq. (9.59) simplifies when $\theta = 1$ to $\mu N = \Omega e^{-\rho t}$. Substitution of the solution for Ω into this expression for μN leads to

$$\mu N = e^{-\rho t} \cdot (\psi/\rho) + \Omega(0) - \psi/\rho.$$

Therefore, the transversality condition associated with N— $\lim_{t \to \infty}(\mu N) = 0$—is satisfied only if $\Omega(0) = \psi/\rho$. In this case, $\dot{\Omega} = 0$ for all t, and Ω always equals its steady-state value, ψ/ρ.

every point in time. The definition of Ω then implies that the fertility rate always satisfies the condition[26]

$$n = d + \frac{\phi\rho \cdot (c/k)}{\rho \cdot (1 + b) - \psi \cdot (c/k)}. \tag{9.60}$$

Equation (9.60) indicates that the fertility rate, n, varies one-to-one with the mortality rate, d, for given values of the parameters ϕ, ψ, b, and ρ, and for a given value of the variable c/k. Higher values of ϕ and ψ raise the marginal utility associated respectively with n and N (see Eq. [9.54]) and thereby raise the chosen value of n. A higher value of b increases the cost of child rearing and tends accordingly to reduce n. A higher value of ρ deters investment (in N) and therefore tends to lower n.

The variable c/k expresses the ratio of the income effect on the demand for children, represented by c, to the cost of children, which depends linearly on k through the term $(1 + b) \cdot nk$ in the budget constraint shown in Eq. (9.56). Hence, an increase in c/k goes along with a rise in n. This result means that n moves in the same direction as c/k during the transition to the steady state.

TRANSITIONAL DYNAMICS AND THE STEADY STATE. The dynamic model consists of the expressions for $\dot{k}$ and $\dot{c}/c$ in Eqs. (9.56) and (9.58) and the relation for n in Eq. (9.60). The equations for $\dot{k}$ and $\dot{c}/c$ involve w and r, which are determined in the usual way by the production function. We assume, as usual, that labor input, L, and population, N, coincide (which means that children are not distinguished in this respect from adults), that labor-augmenting technological progress occurs at the constant rate $x \geq 0$, and that the production function has the Cobb–Douglas form,

$$\hat{y} = A\hat{k}^{\alpha},$$

where $0 < \alpha < 1$, $\hat{k} \equiv K/\hat{L}$, and $\hat{y} \equiv Y/\hat{L}$. If capital depreciates at the constant rate δ, then the profit-maximizing behavior of competitive firms implies the usual formulas,

$$r = \alpha A\hat{k}^{\alpha-1} - \delta, w = (1 - \alpha) \cdot A\hat{k}^{\alpha} \cdot e^{xt}. \tag{9.61}$$

It is convenient to express the system in terms of the transformed variables

$$\chi \equiv c/k \text{ and } z \equiv A\hat{k}^{\alpha-1},$$

where z is the gross average product of capital. Equations (9.56) and (9.58) can then be used along with Eq. (9.61) to get the transition equation for χ:

$$\dot{\chi}/\chi = -\rho - (1 - \alpha) \cdot z + \chi. \tag{9.62}$$

---

[26] A condition analogous to Eq. (9.60) also arises if the child-rearing cost, η, depends linearly on the wage rate, w. The right-hand side of the equation is then somewhat more complicated because it involves w/k as well as c/k.

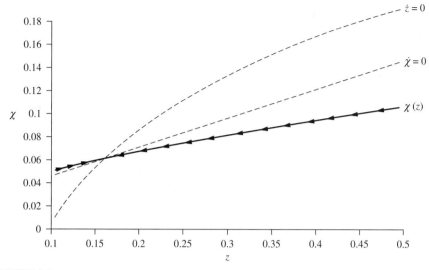

FIGURE 9.6
Phase diagram for the fertility model in (z, χ) space. The fertility model exhibits saddle-path stability. In (z, χ) space, the stable arm is upward sloping. Therefore, if the economy begins with a high gross average product of capital, z, then z and $\chi \equiv c/k$ decline monotonically during the transition.

If we substitute for n from Eq. (9.60) and use Eqs. (9.56) and (9.61), then we get the transition equation for z:

$$\dot{z}/z = -(1 - \alpha) \cdot \left[z - \delta - bd - x - \chi - \frac{\phi \rho \chi \cdot (1 + b)}{\rho \cdot (1 + b) - \psi \chi} \right]. \qquad (9.63)$$

Figure 9.6 uses Eqs. (9.62) and (9.63) to construct a phase diagram in (z, χ) space. The curves shown correspond to a particular specification of the underlying parameters:

$$\alpha = 0.75, \delta = 0.05, \rho = 0.02, x = 0.02,$$

$$\qquad (9.64)$$

$$d = 0.01, b = 1, \psi = 0.2, \phi = 0.2.$$

The first row contains values that are familiar from previous discussions. In the second row, we assume a mortality rate, d, of 0.01 per year. The settings for b, ψ, and ϕ are more arbitrary, and we discuss below the dependence of the answers on variations in these parameters. In any event, the general appearance of the phase diagram is not very sensitive to these choices.

The locus for $\dot{\chi} = 0$ from Eq. (9.62) is a positively sloped straight line with intercept ρ. This locus is unstable; that is, $\dot{\chi}/\chi$ rises with χ for a given z.

Equation (9.63) implies that the $\dot{z} = 0$ locus is positively sloped and stable; that is, $\dot{z}/z$ declines with z for a given χ. The relation between χ and z along this locus is the solution to a quadratic equation, which has two real, positive roots for a range of "reasonable" parameters. The larger root turns out always to lie above the $\dot{\chi} = 0$ locus. The locus for $\dot{z} = 0$ shown in Fig. 9.6 corresponds to the smaller root.

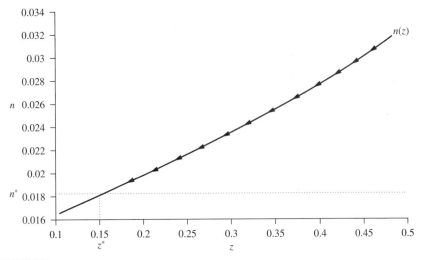

FIGURE 9.7

Transitional behavior of the fertility rate. If the economy begins with a high gross average product of capital, z, then as z declines—along the saddle path shown in Fig. 9.6—the fertility rate, n, falls toward its steady-state value. Quantitatively, for the assumed parameter values, if z begins at 0.3 (correspond to a rate of return of 0.25), then n starts at 0.023 and falls gradually toward its steady-state value of 0.018.

The intersection of the two loci determines the steady-state values, z^* and χ^*. Once these values are known, we can use Eq. (9.60) to compute n^*. The steady-state interest rate can be calculated from the relation

$$r^* = \alpha z^* - \delta.$$

Figure 9.6 shows that the stable, saddle path is positively sloped in (z, χ) space. Therefore, if the economy begins with $z(0) > z^*$ (that is, $\hat{k}[0] < \hat{k}^*$), then z and χ fall monotonically toward their steady-state positions.[27]

Equation (9.60) implies that n is positively related to $\chi \equiv c/k$ along the transition path. Therefore, the declining path of χ in Fig. 9.6 corresponds to a declining path of n. Figure 9.7 shows the relation between n and z during the transition. (Once we know the relation between χ and z from Fig. 9.6, we can use the relation between n and χ from Eq. [9.60] to determine n as a function of z.) As z decreases, n falls monotonically toward its steady-state value. That is, with a given mortality rate, d, the fertility rate declines steadily as the economy develops.

The result that fertility falls as per capita product rises accords with empirical findings for countries, as discussed in Chapter 12. The one exception in the data is that fertility and per capita GDP seem to be positively related at extremely low levels of per capita GDP—up to about $800 (in 1985 U.S. dollars). This initially rising

---

[27]Recall that χ fell monotonically during the transition to the steady state in the Ramsey model if $\theta > \alpha$ (see the appendix to Chapter 2). Since $\theta = 1$ in the present context, the monotonic decline of χ is not surprising.

segment of the relation between fertility and per capita product tends to appear in the theory if we introduce a goods cost of child rearing along with the cost that rises linearly with k. The goods cost introduces a force—an income effect—that generates a positive relation between fertility and per capita product. Moreover, since the goods cost is relatively more important in poor countries, the net positive relation between fertility and per capita product tends to appear only at low levels of per capita product.

We can allow for a goods cost of child rearing by letting the intercept b_0 in Eq. (9.55) be nonzero. Although our analytical procedure does not go through when the expression for the child-rearing cost contains a positive intercept, we can use numerical methods to work out the dynamics of this revised model. Specifically, we provide detailed results for the case $b_0 = 50$. If we maintain the parameter values, including $b = 1$, that we used to construct Figs. 9.6 and 9.7, then a value $b_0 = 50$ means, when $n = 0.02$ and $\hat{k}$ is one-tenth of $\hat{k}^*$, that the goods cost of raising a child is about one-sixteenth of total output (if the parameter A in the production function is set to equal 1).

We find numerically that the specification $\eta = 50 + bk$ leads to the phase diagram in (z, χ) space that is shown in Fig. 9.8.[28] The associated relation between n and

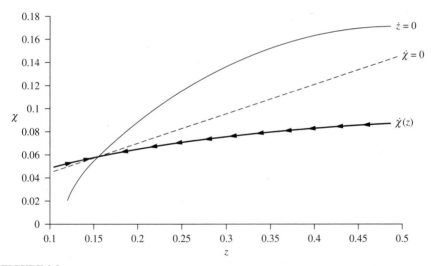

FIGURE 9.8
Phase diagram in (z, χ) space with a goods cost of child rearing. This figure modifies Fig. 9.6 to include a goods cost of child rearing. If the economy begins with a high gross average product of capital, z, then z and $\chi \equiv c/k$ still decline monotonically during the transition.

---

[28]These results assume that the goods cost, which starts at 50, rises at the rate $x = 0.02$ per year along with exogenous technological progress. Since x represents labor-augmenting technological change, the quality of children effectively improves over time even if k is constant. The assumption that the intercept term rises at rate x means that the goods cost of producing a child of standardized quality remains constant over time. Note that if we assumed instead that the intercept remain fixed at 50, then the goods cost would asymptotically become negligible relative to the cost that depends on k.

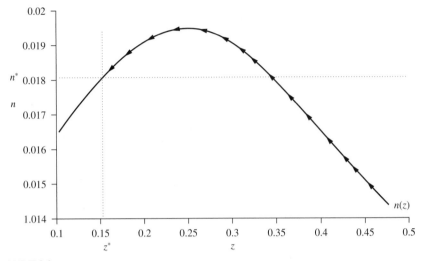

FIGURE 9.9
Transitional behavior of the fertility rate with a goods cost of child rearing. This figure modifies
Fig. 9.7 to include a goods cost of child rearing. If the economy starts with a high gross average product
of capital, z, then as z declines along the saddle path shown in Fig. 9.8, the fertility rate can now adjust
in a nonmonotonic fashion. In contrast with Fig. 9.7, the fertility rate can rise for awhile and then decline
later to approach its steady-state value. This behavior corresponds to the tendency of fertility rates to
rise with per capita income for the poorest countries, but to fall with per capita income in the main range
of experience.

z appears in Fig. 9.9. The interesting feature of Fig. 9.9, in comparison with Fig. 9.7,
is that n now rises as z falls for very high values of z (that is, for very low values
of $\hat{k}$). Thus, the extended model can be consistent with the observation that fertility
rises with per capita product for very poor countries, but falls with per capita product
in the main range of experience.

Table 9.1 returns to the specification with $b_0 = 0$ to show how the steady-state
values n^* and r^* depend on the settings of the parameters ϕ, ψ, d, and b. For the
baseline parameters, the results are $n^* = 0.018$ and $r^* = .067$. Increases in ϕ or
ψ raise the benefit from children and thereby increase n^*. For example, n^* rises to
0.030 if ϕ or ψ increase to 0.4 (the exact correspondence does not apply generally).
The value n^* falls to 0.014 if ϕ declines to 0.1 and to 0.017 if ψ decreases to 0.1.
Since $\dot{c}/c = x$ in the steady state, we can use Eq. (9.58) to think about the relation
between n^* and r^*. For given values of ρ, b, and d, r^* moves by the factor $1 + b$ in
the same direction as n^*. Therefore, Table 9.1 shows that an increase in ϕ or ψ leads
to a rise in r^*.

For a given c/k, Eq. (9.60) shows that n moves one-to-one with the mortality
rate, d. Because an increase in d turns out to raise $(c/k)^*$, the full effect of d on n^* is
slightly greater than one-to-one. For example, if d increases from 0.01 to 0.02, then
Table 9.1 shows that n^* rises from 0.0183 to 0.0291. Since the change in the rate of
population growth, $n^* - d$, is small, Eq. (9.58) implies that r^* still moves in the same

TABLE 9.1
Effects of Parameter Variations on n^* and r^*

Parameter specification	n^*	r^*
baseline	0.0183	0.067
$\phi = 0.4$	0.0300	0.090
$\phi = 0.1$	0.0139	0.058
$\psi = 0.4$	0.0300	0.090
$\psi = 0.1$	0.0168	0.064
$d = 0.02$	0.0291	0.078
$d = 0$	0.0076	0.055
$b = 0.5$	0.0226	0.064
$b = 2$	0.0152	0.076

Note: The baseline specification is $\alpha = 0.75, \delta = 0.05, \rho = 0.02, x = 0.02, d = 0.01, b = 1, \psi = 0.2, \phi = 0.2$. The table shows the effect on the steady-state values n^* and r^* when the designated parameter is changed to the value indicated while all other parameters remain at their baseline settings.

direction as n^*, but roughly by the factor b. The table shows accordingly that a rise in d leads to an increase in r^*.

An increase in the cost parameter b leads to a decline in n^*. For example, Table 9.1 shows that if b rises to 2, then n^* decreases to 0.015, whereas if b falls to 0.5, then n^* increases to 0.023. Since a rise in b is accompanied by a reduction of n^*, Eq. (9.58) suggests that the effect on r^* would be ambiguous. In the range considered in the table, the net effect of b on r^* turns out to be positive.

We have assumed, thus far, a fixed relation between labor supply and population; that is, we have neglected changes in labor-force participation or in work hours and effort. In this section, we let labor supply vary for a given population by allowing for a labor/leisure choice. The changes in labor supply in this model represent some combination of variations in labor-force participation, work hours, and work effort, but the analysis does not sort out these different components of labor supply.

We carry out the analysis within the Ramsey framework by introducing leisure as an additional argument of the utility function. We use a specification of preferences that allows for transitional variations in labor supply but guarantees that the fraction of time devoted to work effort approaches a constant in the steady state. The model therefore allows us to study the transitional behavior of work effort and also to consider how changes in various parameters affect the steady-state quantity of work effort. The main conclusion, however, is that the extension to incorporate a labor/leisure choice into the Ramsey model does not alter the principal conclusions about the nature of the growth process.

9.3 LABOR/LEISURE CHOICE

Population, denoted by $N(t)$, now has to be distinguished from labor input, $L(t)$. We return to the setting in which $N(t)$ grows exogenously at the constant rate n, but $L(t)$

can now vary for given $N(t)$. Define $\ell(t)$ to be the typical person's intensity of work effort at time t, so that

$$L(t) \equiv \ell(t) \cdot N(t). \tag{9.65}$$

If $\ell(t)$ is the fraction of time spent working, then it can be measured with available data and would have a natural upper bound of 100 percent. In contrast, if $\ell(t)$ allows, as it should, for variations in work effort, then it would not be readily measurable and would not have an obvious upper bound. We do not distinguish between an increase in $\ell(t)$ that reflects a rise in effort or hours worked per year by each worker from one that reflects an expansion of labor-force participation.

We now modify the formulation of household utility from Eq. (2.1) to include a disutility of work effort:

$$U = \int_0^\infty u[c(t), \ell(t)]e^{-(\rho-n)t}dt, \tag{9.66}$$

where the partial derivatives satisfy the usual concavity conditions, including $u_c > 0$, $u_\ell < 0$, $u_{cc} < 0$, $u_{\ell\ell} \le 0$.[29] If the wage rate, w, is the amount paid per unit of labor input, then the household's budget constraint is modified from Eq. (2.2) to

$$\dot{a} = w\ell + (r - n) \cdot a - c. \tag{9.67}$$

We can proceed as usual by setting up the Hamiltonian expression,

$$J = u(c, \ell) \cdot e^{-(\rho-n)t} + \nu \cdot [w\ell + (r - n) \cdot a - c].$$

The maximization problem is the same as that in Chapter 2, except that u_c, the marginal utility of consumption, may depend on ℓ, and we have to add the new first-order condition $\partial J/\partial \ell = 0$.

The first-order condition that corresponds to Eq. (2.7) from the Ramsey model is

$$r = \rho - \left[\frac{u_{cc} \cdot c}{u_c}\right] \cdot (\dot{c}/c) - \left[\frac{u_{c\ell} \cdot \ell}{u_c}\right] \cdot (\dot{\ell}/\ell). \tag{9.68}$$

Note that we get the original formula from Chapter 2 if $u_{c\ell} = 0$. If $u_{c\ell} > 0$, then a higher value of $\dot{\ell}/\ell$ effectively subtracts from the rate of time preference, ρ, because households prefer to consume a lot in the future when ℓ will be high; that is, when they have little leisure. This effect is reversed in the introspectively more plausible case in which consumption and leisure are complements in the sense that $u_{c\ell} < 0$.

---

[29]This formulation assumes that work effort, ℓ, enters negatively into a utility function. Another approach, due to Becker (1965), assumes that time not spent at market work is used for home production. The important distinguishing feature of this alternative approach is that the productivity of home work is affected by capital accumulation and technological progress. The allocation of time between market and home work then depends on relative productivity trends and on the evolution of relative demands for market- and home-produced goods. See Greenwood and Hercowitz (1991) and Benhabib, Rogerson, and Wright (1991) for the use of this approach in dynamic contexts.

The new first-order condition, which reflects the substitution between consumption and leisure at a point in time, is

$$-u_\ell/u_c = w. \tag{9.69}$$

We would like Eq. (9.69) to be consistent with the empirical regularity that hours worked per worker—which we take as a rough proxy for ℓ—typically decline at early stages of economic development, but tend eventually to level off (see the discussion in Barro [1993, Ch. 2]). In particular, we would like the model to have a steady state in which ℓ is constant.

In the steady state of the Ramsey model, w and c grow at the same rate, x. Therefore, we want to use a form of utility function for which Eq. (9.69) implies that ℓ is constant, at least asymptotically, when w and c grow at the same rate. We also want to retain the property that the model has a steady state in which c grows at a constant rate. The appendix to this chapter shows that these conditions require the utility function asymptotically to take the form

$$u(c, \ell) = \frac{c^{1-\theta} \cdot \exp[(1 - \theta) \cdot \omega(\ell)] - 1}{1 - \theta}, \tag{9.70}$$

where $\theta > 0$, $\omega'(\ell) < 0$, and $\omega''(\ell) \leq 0$.[30] This formulation corresponds to the results in King, Plosser, and Rebelo (1988a) and Rebelo (1991).[31] The sign of $u_{c\ell}$ depends on the magnitude of θ : $u_{c\ell} \lesseqgtr 0$ as $\theta \lesseqgtr 1$. The standard iso-elastic function used in Eq. (2.8) is the special case in which $\omega(\ell) = 0$. This specification is, however, inconsistent with the choice of a finite amount of work effort.

If we use Eq. (9.70) to compute u_ℓ and u_c, then the first-order condition in Eq. (9.69) implies

$$-\omega'(\ell) = w/c. \tag{9.71}$$

The algebra for the rest of the model turns out to be cumbersome for general θ, but we can bring out the main results by considering the special case in which $\theta = 1$. The application of l'Hôpital's rule to Eq. (9.70) shows that the limit of $u(c, \ell)$ as θ approaches 1 is

$$u(c, \ell) = \log(c) + \omega(\ell); \tag{9.72}$$

that is, if utility is logarithmic in c, then the function must be separable between c and ℓ so that $u_{c\ell} = 0$. If the utility function takes the form of Eq. (9.72), then the

---

[30]These properties imply $u_c > 0$, $u_\ell < 0$, and $u_{cc} < 0$. The condition $u_{\ell\ell} \leq 0$ requires $\omega''(\ell) + (1 - \theta) \cdot [\omega'(\ell)]^2 \leq 0$, an inequality that must hold if $\theta \geq 1$.

[31]Rebelo (1991, p. 513) shows that another alternative is to specify utility as $u(c, \ell k)$, where $u(\cdot)$ is homogeneous of some positive degree, and k should now be thought of as human capital per person. The term ℓk can then be viewed as foregone leisure time, adjusted for a person's quality, as in the formulation used by Becker (1965) and Heckman (1976).

first-order condition in Eq. (9.68) reduces to the familiar expression for the growth rate of c:

$$\gamma_c = r - \rho. \tag{9.73}$$

We now define the variables per unit of effective labor to include the effect from variable work effort, ℓ; that is,

$$\hat{k} \equiv K/(\ell N e^{xt}),$$

$$\hat{c} \equiv C/(\ell N e^{xt}).$$

If we assume a closed economy and introduce firms in the usual way, then Eq. (9.73) and the conditions $r = f'(\hat{k}) - \delta$ and $a = k$ imply

$$\gamma_{\hat{c}} = f'(\hat{k}) - (\delta + \rho + x) - \gamma_\ell, \tag{9.74}$$

$$\gamma_{\hat{k}} = f(\hat{k})/\hat{k} - (x + n + \delta) - \hat{c}/\hat{k} - \gamma_\ell. \tag{9.75}$$

These results differ from the standard ones (Eqs. [2.23] and [2.24]) only because the growth rate of ℓ, γ_ℓ, adds to the growth rate of effective labor input. Since $\gamma_\ell = 0$ in the steady state, the formulas for $\hat{k}^*$ and $\hat{c}^*$ are the same as those in the Ramsey model.

We now assume that the production function is Cobb–Douglas, $f(\hat{k}) = A\hat{k}^\alpha$, and that the disutility of work takes a constant-elasticity form:

$$\omega(\ell) = -\zeta \cdot \ell^{1+\sigma}, \tag{9.76}$$

where $\zeta > 0$ and $\sigma \geq 0$. Since the wage rate is given in the Cobb–Douglas case by $w = (1 - \alpha) \cdot A\hat{k}^\alpha \cdot e^{xt}$, Eq. (9.71) becomes

$$\zeta \cdot (1 + \sigma) \cdot \ell^{1+\sigma} = (1 - \alpha) \cdot A\hat{k}^\alpha/\hat{c}. \tag{9.77}$$

(Note that the replacement of c by $\hat{c}$ on the right-hand side brings in the additional factor of ℓ on the left-hand side.) Since $\hat{y}$ is proportional to $\hat{k}^\alpha$, Eq. (9.77) implies that a high value of ℓ—little leisure—goes along with a low value of c/y. (This relation holds for a general form of $\omega(\ell)$ if $\omega'(\ell) > 0$ and $\omega''(\ell) \geq 0$.) Equation (9.77) implies that the growth rate of ℓ is given by

$$\gamma_\ell = \left(\frac{\alpha}{1+\sigma}\right) \cdot \gamma_{\hat{k}} - \left(\frac{1}{1+\sigma}\right) \cdot \gamma_{\hat{c}}. \tag{9.78}$$

If we use the Cobb–Douglas forms for $f'(\hat{k})$ and $f(\hat{k})$ and the expression for γ_ℓ from Eq. (9.78), then Eqs. (9.74) and (9.75) lead (after some algebra) to the dynamic system for $\hat{k}$ and $\hat{c}$ in the presence of variable labor supply:

$$\gamma_{\hat{k}} = A\hat{k}^{\alpha-1} - \left(\frac{1}{\alpha + \sigma}\right) \cdot [\sigma \cdot (\hat{c}/\hat{k}) + (1 + \sigma) \cdot (x + \delta) + \rho + \sigma n], \tag{9.79}$$

$$\gamma_{\hat{c}} = \alpha A\hat{k}^{\alpha-1} + \left(\frac{1}{\alpha + \sigma}\right) \cdot [\alpha \cdot (\hat{c}/\hat{k}) - (1 + \sigma) \cdot (x + \delta) - (1 + \alpha + \sigma) \cdot \rho + \alpha n].$$

$$\tag{9.80}$$

These results reduce to the standard formulas shown in Eqs. (2.36) and (2.37) if $\theta = 1$ (to get the log-utility specification that we have assumed here) and σ approaches infinity (see Eq. [9.75]). An infinite σ deters any variation in ℓ over time and therefore reproduces the results from the model with fixed labor supply.

We already mentioned that the steady-state values of $\hat{k}$ and $\hat{c}$ are the same as those in the Ramsey model, a result that can be verified by setting Eqs. (9.79) and (9.80) to 0. These steady-state values can be expressed as

$$r^* = \alpha A \cdot (\hat{k}^*)^{\alpha-1} - \delta = \rho + x,$$

$$(\hat{c}^*)/(\hat{k}^*) = (\rho + \delta + x)/\alpha - (n + x + \delta).$$

We can substitute these values into Eq. (9.77) to determine the steady-state level of work effort, ℓ^* :

$$\ell^* = \left\{ \left[\frac{1-\alpha}{\zeta \cdot (1+\sigma)} \right] \cdot \left[\frac{\rho + \delta + x}{\rho + \delta + x - \alpha \cdot (n + x + \delta)} \right] \right\}^{1/(1+\sigma)}. \tag{9.81}$$

The transitional dynamics of $\hat{k}$ and $\hat{c}$ implied by Eqs. (9.79) and (9.80) can be analyzed, as usual, with a phase diagram in $(\hat{k}, \hat{c})$ space. The system is again saddle-path stable, and we leave the construction of the phase diagram as an exercise.

If we log-linearize Eqs. (9.79) and (9.80) around the steady state in the usual manner, then the formula for the speed of convergence to the steady state turns out to be

$$2\beta = \rho - n - \left\{ (\rho - n)^2 + \left[\frac{4 \cdot (1-\alpha) \cdot (1+\sigma)}{\alpha + \sigma} \right] \cdot (\rho + \delta + x) \right.$$

$$\left. \cdot \left[\frac{\rho + \delta + x}{\alpha} - (n + x + \delta) \right] \right\}^{1/2}. \tag{9.82}$$

This formula reduces to the standard Ramsey result (Eq. [2.34] with $\theta = 1$) if we let σ approach infinity.

If we use our familiar parameter values ($\alpha = 0.75$, $x = 0.02$, $n = 0.01$. $\delta = 0.05$, $\rho = 0.02$), then the value of β implied by Eq. (9.82) is 0.030 if $\sigma = 0$. As σ rises above 0, β declines and approaches the Ramsey value—which is 0.025 with the assumed parameter values—as σ tends to infinity. Thus, the inclusion of a labor/leisure choice raises the speed of convergence, but only to a moderate extent.

The reason that the convergence coefficient is somewhat higher with variable labor supply is that ℓ declines monotonically during the transition to the steady state; that is, in this model, poor people (who expect to be richer later) work harder than rich people. We can prove this result by substituting for $\gamma_{\hat{k}}$ and $\gamma_{\hat{c}}$ from Eqs. (9.79) and (9.80) into the formula for γ_ℓ in Eq. (9.78) to get (after simplifying)

$$\gamma_\ell = \left(\frac{\alpha}{\alpha + \sigma} \right) \cdot (\chi^* - \chi),$$

where $\chi \equiv \hat{c}/\hat{k}$. It is possible to use the method developed in Appendix B of Chapter 2 to show that, if $\hat{k}(0) < \hat{k}^*$, then χ falls monotonically during the transition and, hence, $\chi > \chi^*$ applies throughout. (We leave this demonstration as an exercise.)

This result implies $\gamma_\ell < 0$; that is, ℓ falls monotonically from its initial value $\ell(0)$ to the steady-state value ℓ^*. The model therefore accords with the empirical observation that work effort declines during early stages of economic development.

We can also view the results from the perspective of Eq. (9.77). This relation shows that ℓ moves inversely with c/y and, hence, in the same direction as the gross saving rate, s. In the present model which assumes $\theta = 1$, the saving rate turns out to decrease monotonically during the transition, and ℓ falls along with the saving rate.

To eliminate the result that the saving rate falls as an economy develops—a prediction that we think conflicts with empirical evidence—we have to depart from log utility and assume a lesser willingness to substitute consumption over time; that is, $\theta > 1$ in Eq. (9.70). The problem, however, is that a value of θ that is high enough to generate a rising saving rate also generates a rising pattern for ℓ.

If the production function is Cobb–Douglas so that $\hat{w} = A \cdot (1 - \alpha) \cdot \hat{k}^\alpha$, then Eq. (9.71)—which holds for any value of θ—implies

$$-\ell \cdot \omega'(\ell) = A \cdot (1 - \alpha) \cdot \hat{k}^\alpha/\hat{c} = A \cdot (1 - \alpha)/(1 - s).$$

(Again, the transformation from c to $\hat{c}$ introduces the factor ℓ on the left-hand side.) The conditions $\omega'(\ell) < 0$ and $\omega''(\ell) \leq 0$ imply that the left-hand side is increasing in ℓ and, hence, that ℓ is positively related to s. Therefore, if we specify a value of θ that is high enough for s to rise during the transition, then ℓ must also be increasing. (This relationship holds if the production function is not Cobb–Douglas as long as the ratio $\hat{w}/\hat{c}$ is monotonically related to the ratio y/c.)

To get a transitional dynamics in which ℓ falls and s rises we have to assume a form of utility function that differs from Eq. (9.70) during the transition. We could, for example, introduce a subsistence level of consumption, $\bar{c}$ (as mentioned in Chapter 3) so that c in Eq. (9.70) is replaced by $c - \bar{c}$. (Since the original form of Eq. [9.70] still holds asymptotically, this change does not alter the steady-state properties of the model.) With this revised formulation, it would be possible to generate a transition in which s rises and ℓ declines.

APPENDIX 9A
THE FORM OF THE UTILITY FUNCTION
WITH CONSUMPTION AND WORK EFFORT

We study here the required form of the utility function, $u(c, \ell)$, in the model with a labor/leisure choice. We want the economy to have a steady state in which γ_c and ℓ are constants. Equation (9.68) implies accordingly that the elasticity of the marginal utility of consumption must be constant (just as in the Ramsey model):

$$\frac{u_{cc} \cdot c}{u_c} = -\theta, \text{ a constant.} \tag{9A.1}$$

The first-order condition in Eq. (9.69) can be written as

$$\frac{w}{c} = \frac{-u_\ell}{c \cdot u_c}.$$

We are looking for a steady state in which w and c grow at the same rate, so that w/c is constant. Therefore, if we take logs of the right-hand side and differentiate with respect to time, in the steady state,

$$(u_{\ell c} \cdot \dot{c} + u_{\ell\ell} \cdot \dot{\ell})/u_\ell - (u_{cc} \cdot \dot{c} + u_{c\ell} \cdot \dot{\ell})/u_c - \dot{c}/c = 0.$$

Since $\dot{\ell} = 0$ and $\dot{c}/c$ is generally nonzero, this condition can be rewritten as

$$\frac{c \cdot u_{\ell c}}{u_\ell} = 1 + \frac{c \cdot u_{cc}}{u_c} = 1 - \theta. \tag{9A.2}$$

Write Eq. (9A.2) as

$$\frac{1}{u_\ell} \cdot \frac{\partial(u_\ell)}{\partial c} = \frac{1 - \theta}{c}$$

and integrate with respect to c to get

$$\log(u_\ell) = (1 - \theta) \cdot \log(c) + (\text{function of } \ell).$$

Integration of this result with respect to ℓ yields

$$u(c, \ell) = c^{1-\theta} \cdot \varphi(\ell) + \psi(c), \tag{9A.3}$$

where φ and ψ are, as yet, arbitrary functions.

Equations (9A.1) and (9A.3) imply

$$\frac{u_{cc} \cdot c}{u_c} = \frac{-\theta \cdot (1 - \theta) \cdot c^{-\theta} \cdot \varphi(\ell) + c \cdot \psi''(c)}{(1 - \theta) \cdot c^{-\theta} \cdot \varphi(\ell) + \psi'(c)} = -\theta,$$

and the function $\psi(c)$ must be consistent with this equation. Therefore, $\psi(c)$ must satisfy

$$c \cdot \psi''(c) = -\theta \cdot \psi'(c).$$

If we integrate this condition twice, then we get, aside from multiplicative and additive constants,

$$\psi(c) = c^{1-\theta} \qquad \text{if } \theta \neq 1,$$

$$\psi(c) = \log(c) \qquad \text{if } \theta = 1.$$

We can substitute the result for $\psi(c)$ into Eq. (9A.3) to get the required form of $u(c, \ell)$. One way to write the result, as in Eq. (9.70), is

$$u(c, \ell) = \frac{c^{1-\theta} \cdot \exp[(1 - \theta) \cdot \omega(\ell)] - 1}{1 - \theta}. \tag{9A.4}$$

In this form, $\theta > 0$ and $\omega'(\ell) < 0$ guarantee $u_c > 0$, $u_\ell < 0$, and $u_{cc} < 0$. The condition $u_{\ell\ell} \leq 0$ requires $\omega''(\ell) + (1 - \theta) \cdot [\omega'(\ell)]^2 \leq 0$, which must hold if $\omega''(\ell) \leq 0$ and $\theta \geq 1$. An application of l'Hopital's rule shows that the function in Eq. (9A.4) approaches $\log(c) + \omega(\ell)$ as θ approaches 1.

PROBLEMS

9.1 Migration in Neoclassical Growth Models.

(a) Under what circumstances does the potential for migration raise the speed of convergence in the Solow-Swan model? What about in the Ramsey model? What are the sources of the effects on convergence?

(b) Might a government of a country that is receiving immigrants find it desirable to restrict the number that come? Might the government wish to charge a fee for immigration? Would the fee tend to vary with the immigrant's quantity of human capital?

(c) Redo part b for the case of a country that is sending emigrants.

9.2 A Model of Rural-Urban Migration (Based on Mas-Colell and Razin [1973]). Consider an economy with two productive sectors. The rural or agricultural sector, denoted A, produces output only for consumption. The urban or industrial sector, denoted I, produces output for consumption and investment. The production functions are Cobb–Douglas:

$$Y_A = (K_A)^\alpha \cdot (L_A)^{1-\alpha}; \quad Y_I = (K_I)^\lambda \cdot (L_I)^{1-\lambda},$$

where $0 < \alpha < 1, 0 < \lambda < 1$. There is no technological progress.

Each person inelastically supplies 1 unit of labor, and total population, $L = L_A + L_I$, grows at the constant rate $n \geq 0$. The natural rates of population growth are the same in the rural and urban areas. Capital, $K = K_A + K_I$, can move costlessly across sectors. People can move across sectors at some cost. The rate of migration to the urban sector is assumed to be positively related to the wage-rate differential:

$$\dot{\mu}/\mu = b \cdot (w_I - w_A)/w_A,$$

where $b > 0$ and μ is the proportion of the population employed in the urban sector.

People save a constant fraction s of income and spend the fraction η of income on industrial products for consumption purposes. Capital does not depreciate. The price of the industrial good in units of the agricultural good is denoted by p.

(a) Derive the formulas at each point in time for the capital rental rate, R; the wage rates, w_A and w_I; and the relative price of industrial output, p. What is the fraction of total capital employed in the urban sector?

(b) Construct a phase diagram in (k, μ) space, where $k \equiv K/L$. What are the steady-state levels, k^* and μ^*? Is the steady state stable?

(c) Suppose that the economy begins with $\mu < \mu^*$. Show that the migration rate into the urban sector decreases as the economy moves toward its steady state. Characterize the behavior of the relative price, p, and the growth rate of capital along the transition path. Does the model exhibit a convergence property?

9.3 Growth in an Optimizing Model of Migration (Based on Braun [1993]). Consider Braun's model of migration, which we presented in section 9.1.3. Toward the end of that section, we mentioned an extension to allow for the dynamics of the world economy. Assume that the framework of section 9.1.3 applies, including the production function in Eq. (9.27), except that the world now consists of only two economies, country 1 and country 2. The natural resources in each country, R_1 and R_2, are fixed. The populations of each country are denoted by L_1 and L_2, where $L = L_1 + L_2$ is world population. Natural population growth rates are 0 in each economy, and the initial conditions are such that the flow of migrants goes from country 2 to country 1. The cost of moving from country 2 to country 1 is still given by Eq. (9.34), except that w_{world} is replaced by w_2. The moving cost for each migrant again approaches 0 as the number of migrants goes to 0. Capital is perfectly mobile across the economies. The total capital stock, $K = K_1 + K_2$, is allocated across the economies to equalize the net marginal products of capital at each point in time. The world rate of return, r—which can now vary over time—equals the net marginal product of capital. Assume for simplicity that technological progress and depreciation are absent. Consumers in each country have Ramsey preferences with infinite horizons, as assumed in Chapter 2.

(a) Work out a dynamic system in terms of the variables k, L_2, B, and c, where B is the present value of the benefit from a permanent move from country 2 to country 1 (an analog to Eq. [9.31]) and $c \equiv C/L$ is the world's average consumption per person. Note that the state variables for the system are k and L_2; for given L, the variable L_2 determines the allocation of population between the two countries. (Hint: people who start in country 1 never move, and the path of consumption, c_1, is the same for each person. For people who start in country 2, the path of consumption, c_2, must be the same regardless of when they move to country 1 or whether they ever move. These considerations, along with the standard Ramsey formula for consumption growth, determine the behavior of c in relation to the rate of return, r.)

(b) What are the steady-state values of k, L_2, and B?

(c) Consider a log-linear approximation of the dynamic system in the neighborhood of the steady state.
    (1) Observe that, close to the steady state, a small change in L_2 has a negligible effect on wage rates in the two countries, world output, and the rate of return. Use these facts to break the four-dimensional system into two separate parts: one that applies to the world variables, k and c, and another that applies to the migration variables, L_2 and B.
    (2) Find the speed of convergence, β, for the world variables and relate the answer to the solution of the Ramsey model from Chapter 2.
    (3) Find the speed of convergence, μ, for L_2. Show how the convergence speed for per capita output in one country, y_1, depends on β and μ (see Eq. [9.45]).

9.4 Endogenous Mortality. Consider the model of fertility choice in Section 9.2.2. Suppose that the mortality rate, d, can be influenced by family or public expenditures on health.

(a) Assume that d depends on the household's current flow of expenditures on health. Determine that optimal path of these expenditures. How does d evolve as the economy develops? What are the implications for the behavior of the fertility rate, n, and the capital intensity, k?

(b) Assume now that d depends on public health expenditures per capita. Suppose that the ratio of this spending to total output is the constant g and that this spending is financed by a lump-sum tax. How do the paths of the fertility rate, n, and the capital intensity, k, depend on the choice of g? What is the government's optimal choice of g? Would it be preferable to allow g to vary over time?

9.5 Transitional Dynamics with a Labor/Leisure Choice. In Section 9.3, we worked out the dynamic conditions for a model with a labor/leisure choice. For the case of log utility and a Cobb–Douglas production function, the equations for the growth rates of $\hat{k}$ and $\hat{c}$ are given in Eqs. (9.79) and (9.80). Eq. (9.77) relates the choice of work effort, ℓ, to the variables $\hat{k}$ and $\hat{c}$.

(a) Construct the phase diagram in $(\hat{k}, \hat{c})$ space.

(b) If $\hat{k}(0) < \hat{k}^*$, then describe the transition paths for $\hat{k}$, $\hat{c}$, and ℓ.

(c) Verify that the speed of convergence, β, in the neighborhood of the steady state is given by Eq. (9.82). Why is the speed of convergence higher than that in the standard Ramsey model (Eq. [2.34])?

(d) How does the dynamic path for ℓ depend on the assumption of log utility? Is it possible to modify the model so that ℓ declines monotonically, while the gross saving rate, s, rises monotonically?

DATA ON ECONOMIC GROWTH, GROWTH ACCOUNTING

Empirical research on economic growth has used a number of data sets related to countries and regions of countries. This chapter describes some of the principal data that have been used. The final part of the chapter describes the methodology of growth accounting and discusses some of the major results.

10.1 PANEL DATA FOR COUNTRIES

Data compiled by Robert Barro and Jong-Wha Lee cover 138 countries, mostly at five-year intervals over the period 1960 to 1985 or 1990. Some variables have incomplete coverage. A detailed description and a data diskette are available from Ms. Ingrid Sayied, Economics Department, Harvard University, Cambridge MA 02138 (electronic mail: SAYIED@ HUSC3.HARVARD.EDU). The data set is broken down into seven sections: national accounts, education, population, government expenditure, price levels, political variables, and trade policy.

The material on national accounts and price levels includes the internationally comparable data provided by Robert Summers and Alan Heston (versions 5.5 and 4.0), as described in Summers and Heston (1991). The detailed figures from version 5.5 are available on diskette from the Publications Department, National Bureau of

Economic Research, 1050 Massachusetts Avenue, Cambridge MA 02138 (electronic mail: NBER@ HARVARDA.HARVARD.EDU.)

The Summers–Heston procedure begins with detailed price comparisons for countries in benchmark years for several hundred items. Benchmark studies apply to 1970, 1975, 1980, and 1985, and information from 1990 is currently being added. These figures come from the U.N. International Comparison Project (ICP). The detailed values are grouped into 150 standardized categories of goods and services. These categories break down into approximately 110 for consumption, 35 for investment, and five for government consumption. The major difficulty in ensuring comparability of prices across countries arises in the measurement of quality of services, especially general government, medical care, and education.

Summers and Heston also use standard time series data for each country on national-account aggregates, where quantities are expressed in real domestic units. (Versions 5.0 and later use the national-accounts data contained in the World Bank data set.) The benchmark-year prices for each country are combined with the national-accounts information to estimate GDP and its four broad components—private consumption, private and public gross domestic capital formation, government consumption, and the net foreign balance—in 1985 international price units for the available benchmark years. Although the final figures use the United States as a numeraire, the procedure effectively uses world weights to compute the real quantities. By 1985, 81 of the 138 countries had participated in at least one detailed benchmark study. For nonbenchmark countries, less accurate survey information on price comparisons are used.

The standard national-accounts numbers from each country are used in conjunction with the benchmark-year figures to provide time-series estimates in 1985 international prices for the four broad components of GDP. (A complicated procedure is used for countries with more than one benchmark study to ensure consistency with the time-series information.) The components of GDP are then aggregated to compute the time series of overall GDP in 1985 international prices. The data set contains information about quantities and prices for GDP and its four components.

The Barro–Lee data set also includes information distributed by the World Bank on real GDP in units of domestic base-year values. These figures can be combined with market exchange rates to make comparisons across countries.

The education data supplement the U.N. figures on school-enrollment ratios to include the measures of school attainment constructed by Barro and Lee (1994). These data apply to 129 countries, mostly at five-year intervals from 1960 to 1985. The data refer to male and female attainment of the adult population at four levels: no-schooling, primary, secondary, and higher. Census/survey information fills about 40 percent of the possible cells, and adult-literacy data provide additional estimates of the no-schooling category. School-enrollment data are then used in a perpetual-inventory framework to fill the remainder of the cells. Rough estimates of incomplete versus complete attainment are also provided at the three levels of schooling.

The population section includes data on total population, labor force, and population by age group. Also included are estimates of total fertility rates, infant mortality, and life expectancy at birth.

The government expenditure section contains Summers–Heston and World Bank figures on government consumption. Other data refer to total government expenditures, spending on defense and education, and public investment.

The political variables include measures of governmental stability, such as numbers of revolutions, coups, and assassinations. Data are also provided for indexes of political freedom and civil liberties from Gastil (various years).

The trade-policy section has information on tariff rates and nontariff barriers, country areas and distances from major exporting countries, and black-market premia on foreign exchange. This section also has data on volume of trade, terms of trade, and exchange rates.

Table 10.1 provides information for the 138 countries on a sampling of the data. (All of the tables in this chapter are grouped together, starting on p. 353.) Information from Summers–Heston version 5.5 applies to the average growth rate of real per capita GDP from 1960 to 1985; levels of real per capita GDP in 1960, 1985, and 1990; and the average ratio of real investment to real GDP from 1960 to 1985. Also reported are life expectancy at birth in 1960 and 1985, average years of school attainment for males and females in 1960 and 1985, levels of total population in 1960 and 1985, and the average growth rate of total population from 1960 to 1985.

10.2   LONG-TERM DATA ON GDP

Maddison (1991) describes long-term data on GDP and population for 16 developed countries. The figures attempt to adjust for changes in national boundaries. An unpublished September 1992 update provides annual information on per capita GDP in 1985 U.S. dollars. The conversion from domestic real GDP figures is based on Eurostat/OECD benchmark studies for 1985. These studies follow the methodology of the U.N.'s International Comparison Project (ICP), as described in section 10.1 of this chapter. One difference, however, is that Maddison uses the relative price structure of the United States—and expresses quantities in 1985 U.S. dollars—whereas the ICP uses a world average relative price structure and expresses quantities in corresponding international dollars.

The figures on real per capita GDP begin in 1870 for 13 countries (Australia, Austria, Belgium, Canada, Denmark, Finland, France, Germany, Italy, Norway, Sweden, the United Kingdom, and the United States), in 1885 for Japan, in 1899 for Switzerland, and in 1900 for the Netherlands. Data for selected years beginning in 1820 are provided in Maddison (1991, Table A.5) for the 16 countries except Canada, which starts in 1850. This source also provides data for the United Kingdom in 1700 and 1780 and for the Netherlands in 1700.

Table 10.2 shows figures at 20-year intervals starting in 1870 for GDP per capita in 1985 U.S. dollars, the corresponding ratio to the U.S. GDP per capita, and the level of population. The table also indicates the average annual growth rate over each 20-year period for real per capita GDP and population. Figures 10.1–10.4 provide a graphical description of the logarithms of real per capita GDP for these 16 countries.

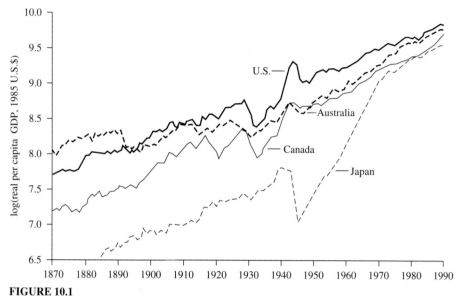

FIGURE 10.1
Real per capita GDP for U.S., Canada, Australia, and Japan.

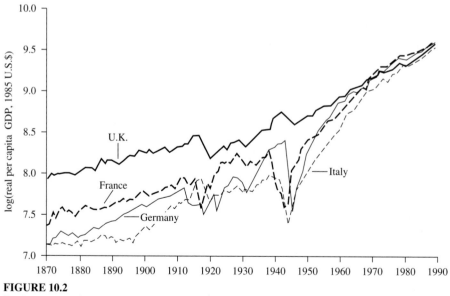

FIGURE 10.2
Real per capita GDP for France, Germany, Italy, and U.K.

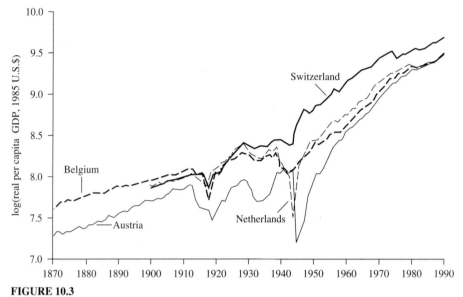

FIGURE 10.3
Real per capita GDP for Austria, Belgium, the Netherlands, and Switzerland.

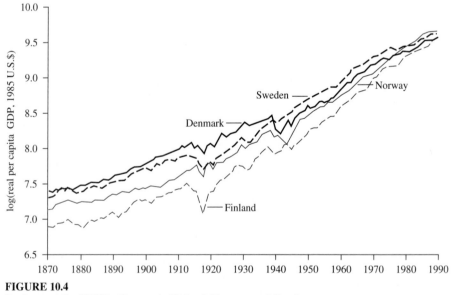

FIGURE 10.4
Real per capita GDP for Denmark, Finland, Norway, and Sweden.

Maddison (1989) provides long-term data for some additional countries. Data on real GDP indexes are presented in his Tables B–4 and B–5 for selected years from 1900 and annually for 1950-87 for nine Asian countries (Bangladesh, China, India, Indonesia, Pakistan, Philippines, South Korea, Taiwan, and Thailand) and six Latin American countries (Argentina, Brazil, Chile, Colombia, Mexico, and Peru). Population figures are in his Tables C–3 and C–4, and values of real GDP per capita are expressed in terms of 1980 international dollars in his Table A–1. Numbers are also provided for the USSR, although recent experience suggests that these values are highly inaccurate.

Table 10.3 presents the figures for the nine Asian and six Latin American countries for 1900, 1913, 1950, 1973, and 1987. The table shows real per capita GDP in 1980 international dollars, the ratio of these values to the U.S. real per capita GDP, and the level of population. Also shown are the average annual growth rates over each period of real per capita GDP and population.

Maddison (1992) describes long-term data on saving rates and investment ratios for 11 countries (Australia, Canada, France, Germany, Japan, the Netherlands, the United Kingdom, the United States, India, South Korea, and Taiwan). Figures 10.5–10.15 show the ratios to GDP of gross domestic investment and net foreign investment, all in current market prices. The data begin in 1820 for France, in 1870 for Australia, Canada, the United Kingdom, and the United States, and in later years for the other countries. Some intermediate years are missing for some of the countries, as indicated in the figures.

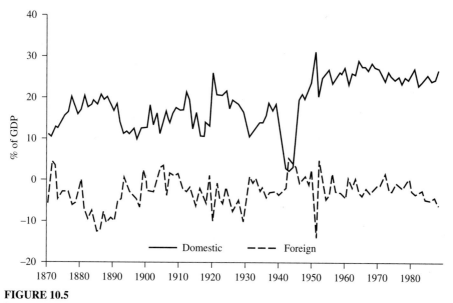

FIGURE 10.5
Investment ratios in Australia.

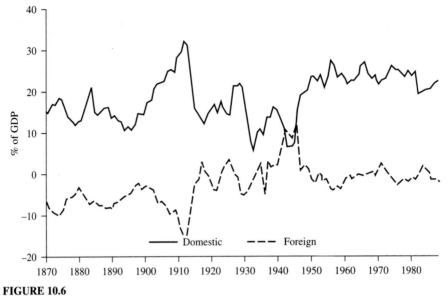

FIGURE 10.6
Investment ratios in Canada.

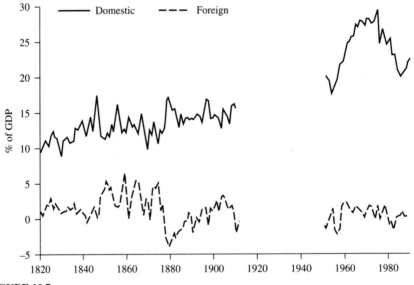

FIGURE 10.7
Investment ratios in France.

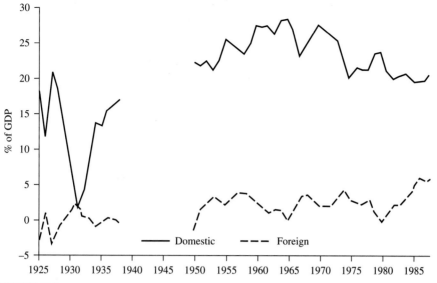

FIGURE 10.8
Investment ratios in Germany.

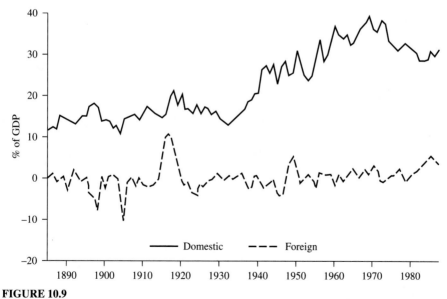

FIGURE 10.9
Investment ratios in Japan.

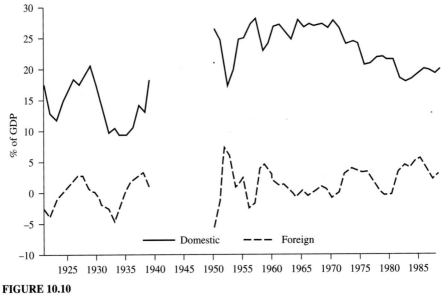

FIGURE 10.10
Investment ratios in the Netherlands.

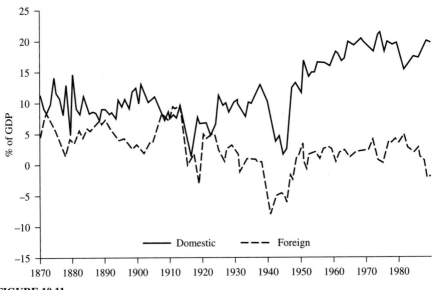

FIGURE 10.11
Investment ratios in the United Kingdom.

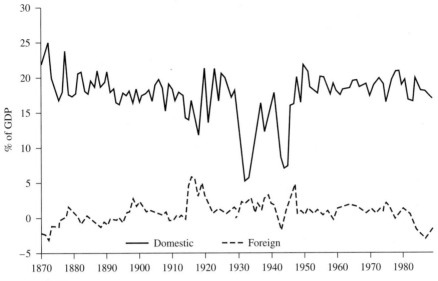

FIGURE 10.12
Investment ratios in the United States.

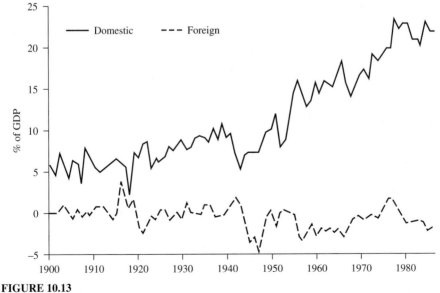

FIGURE 10.13
Investment ratios in India.

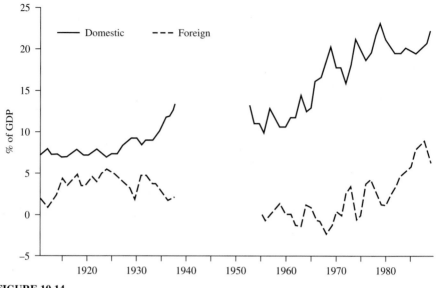

FIGURE 10.14
Investment ratios in South Korea.

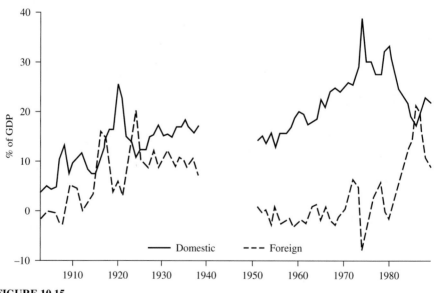

FIGURE 10.15
Investment ratios in Taiwan.

10.3 REGIONAL DATA SETS

We describe here data for the U.S. states, regions of eight European countries (Germany, the United Kingdom, Italy, France, the Netherlands, Belgium, Denmark, and Spain), provinces of Canada, and prefectures of Japan. Data for regions of other countries, such as Argentina, India, Mexico, and the USSR, are also available. Additional information is available by city and county; see, for example, Ades and Glaeser (1993).

10.3.1 Data for U.S. States

Table 10.4 shows a sampling of the data for the U.S. states (shown on the U.S. map in Fig. 10.16). Figures on nominal personal income and nominal per capita personal income are available by state since 1929 from the U.S. Commerce Department (Bureau of Economic Analysis [1989], updates appear in issues of *U.S. Survey of Current Business*). The concept of personal income used in these regional accounts corresponds to that employed in the national accounts. The numbers are reported annually, but values prior to 1965 are based on interpolations of estimates constructed at approximately five-year intervals. Data are reported with and without transfer payments. Figures on gross state product are available annually since 1963 (from issues of *U.S. Survey of Current Business*).

Reliable data on price levels are unavailable by state, although some information exists for cities. We have computed real income by dividing the nominal figures

FIGURE 10.16
Map of the continental U.S. states. The data for the U.S. states are in Table 10.4.

on personal income by the national values of the consumer price index (1982 – 84 = 1.0). (We used the figures from *Citibase* for all items except shelter since 1947. Before 1947, we used the overall index from U.S. Commerce Department, 1975, series E135.) As long as the same index is used at each date for each state, the particular index chosen does not affect the relative levels and growth rates across the states.

Earlier income figures are reported by Easterlin (1960a, 1960b) for 1920 (48 states), 1900 (48 states or territories), 1880 (47 states or territories, with Oklahoma excluded), and 1840 (29 states or territories). These data are exclusive of transfer payments, and the figures for 1840 do not cover all components of personal income. Estimates of the consumer price index for all items (U.S. Commerce Department, 1975, series E135) are used to deflate these earlier values.

For the census years since 1930, labor earnings (including those from self-employment) can be broken down into nine sectors: agriculture; mining; construction; total manufacturing; transportation and public utilities; wholesale and retail trade; finance, insurance, real estate; services; and government and government enterprises. For periods before 1930, information is available on the fraction of income originating in agriculture.

Population density is the ratio of population to total area (land plus water); the data on area are in the Bureau of the Census (1990). Net migration flows can be computed from census figures by taking the change in population over a period, subtracting the number of births, and adding the number of deaths.

10.3.2   Data for European Regions

Table 10.5 has a sampling of the data for regions of European countries (shown on the map in Fig. 10.17). We have data on GDP, population, and related variables for regions of eight European countries—Germany (11 regions), the United Kingdom (11), Italy (20), France (21), the Netherlands (4), Belgium (3), Denmark (3), and Spain (17).

For the countries other than Spain, the data on GDP and population for 1950, 1960, and 1970 are from Molle, Van Holst, and Smits (1980). Figures for 1966 (missing France and Denmark), 1970 (missing Denmark), 1974, 1980, 1985, and 1990 (missing Denmark) are from Eurostat. For Spain, data on regional income and GDP are provided for various years from 1955 to 1987 by the Banco de Bilbao (various issues). The figures on population are from INE, *Anuario Estadistico de España*, various issues. The data applied originally to 50 provinces and have been aggregated to the 17 regions shown in Table 10.5.

We do not have regional price data. In addition, the figures on GDP are sometimes provided in an index form that are not comparable across countries. We have therefore focused on regional GDP figures that are expressed as deviations from means for the respective countries. These data, shown in Table 10.5, can be used for cross-sectional analysis for regions within countries. It would be possible to use time-series data on GDP by country (as discussed in section 10.1 of this chapter) to construct figures that are meaningful across countries and over time. The underlying assumption, however, is that prices do not vary systematically across regions within a country.

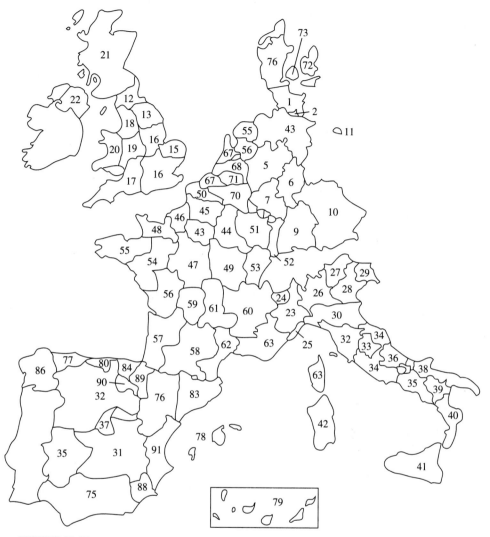

FIGURE 10.17
Map of European regions. The key for the numbers and the data for the European regions are in Table 10.5.

For the countries other than Spain, Molle, Van Holst, and Smits (1980) provide a breakdown of employment into three sectors—agriculture, industry, and services—for 1950, 1960, and 1970. For the other years, Eurostat provides a division of GDP into the same three sectors. For Spain, the breakdown of GDP into these three components for the various years is available from Banco de Bilbao (various issues).

Net migration flows are computed for the five larger countries from information on population, births, and deaths. The national sources are as follows. Germany: Statistichen Bundesamtes, *Statistiches Jahrbuch für die Bundesrepublik Deutschland*, various years. U.K.: *Population Trends 51*, Spring 1988. France:

INSEE, *Statistiques et Indicateurs des Regions Francaises,* 1978; INSEE, *Donnes de Demographie Regionale 1982,* 1986. Italy: ISTAT, *Sommario Storice di Statis-tiche Sulla Populazzione: Anni 1951–87,* 1990. Spain: INE, *Anuario Estadistico de España,* various issues.

10.3.3   Data for Canadian Provinces

Provincial data for Canada, shown in Table 10.6, were kindly provided by Frank C. Lee of Department of Finance Canada and are discussed in Coulombe and Lee (1993). A Canadian provincial map is in Fig. 10.18. Most of the data are from the official source, CANSIM, or the Canadian Conference Board.

Annual figures are available by province for population and various categories of income since 1926. (Data for Newfoundland begin after its joining with Canada in 1949, and income data for Northwest Territories and Yukon start in 1951.) Since 1961, information is available for gross provincial product and for provincial con-sumer price indexes and product deflators. Table 10.6 reports values of personal in-come in 1926 and 1992, deflated by the national value of the consumer price index. Information on interprovincial migration starts in 1950.

FIGURE 10.18
Map of Canadian provinces. The data for the Canadian provinces are in Table 10.6.

10.3.4   Data for Japanese Prefectures

Data for Japanese prefectures are in Table 10.7 (a prefectural map is shown in Fig. 10.19). The figures on income are collected since 1955 by the Economic Planning Agency (EPA) of Japan. The accounts are constructed in accordance with the "1983 standardized system of prefectural accounts," so that all figures are comparable. The aggregate of the income figures from the 47 prefectures coincides theoretically with Japan's national income. The data are collected annually and published in the

FIGURE 10.19
Map of Japanese prefectures. The key for the numbers and the data for the prefectures are in Table 10.7.

Annual Report on Prefectural Accounts. For 1930, we obtained income data by prefecture from *National Economy Studies Association.* We do not have price data by prefecture and therefore use national price indexes to deflate each region's income.

Data on population are from the Statistics Bureau at the Management and Coordination Agency. The principal source of these figures is the quinquennial population census taken by the Statistics Bureau.

Migration data are collected by the Statistics Bureau. These figures are derived from the *Basic Resident Registers* and the *Statistical Survey on Legal Migrants.* These data exclude persons without Japanese nationality.

10.4   GROWTH ACCOUNTING

10.4.1   General Setup

Following the pioneering work of Solow (1957) and predecessors discussed in Griliches (1994), the objective of growth accounting is to break down the growth rate of aggregate output into contributions from the growth of inputs, usually capital and labor, and the growth of technology. The analysis starts from a standard neoclassical production function,

$$Y(t) = A(t) \cdot F[K(t), L(t)], \tag{10.1}$$

where $A(t)$ is an index of the level of technology. In this literature, $A(t)$ is called *total factor productivity* or *TFP*.[1] Take logarithms of both sides and time derivatives to get the growth rate of aggregate output,

$$\dot{Y}/Y = \dot{A}/A + \left(\frac{AF_K}{Y}\right) \cdot \dot{K} + \left(\frac{AF_L}{Y}\right) \cdot \dot{L}.$$

Multiply and divide the expression in the first set of brackets by K and the expression in the second set of brackets by L to get

$$\dot{Y}/Y = \dot{A}/A + \left(\frac{AF_K K}{Y}\right) \cdot (\dot{K}/K) + \left(\frac{AF_L L}{Y}\right) \cdot (\dot{L}/L). \tag{10.2}$$

If the factor markets are competitive, then the marginal product of each input equals its factor price, so that AF_K equals the rental rate on capital, R, and AF_L equals the wage rate, w. Hence, the term $AF_K K/Y$ is the share of the rental payments to capital in total income, and the expression $(AF_L L)/Y$ is the share of wage payments to labor in total income.

---

[1]To simplify the algebra, we assume that technology is Hicks neutral (or output augmenting), rather than Harrod neutral (or labor augmenting). See Chapter 1 for the definitions of different types of technological progress.

Under the assumption of constant returns to scale, the capital share and the labor share add to 1. If $\alpha(t)$ is the capital share,[2] then we can rewrite Eq. (10.2) as,[3]

$$\dot{Y}/Y = \dot{A}/A + \alpha(t) \cdot (\dot{K}/K) + [1 - \alpha(t)] \cdot (\dot{L}/L). \tag{10.3}$$

In other words, the growth rate of aggregate output equals $\dot{A}/A$, the growth rate of TFP, plus a weighted average of the growth rates of the two inputs, where the weights are the corresponding input shares.

Suppose that we have data on the quantities, Y, K, and L, and on the factor prices, R and w. We can therefore compute the factor shares, $\alpha(t)$ and $1 - \alpha(t)$, as well as the growth rates, $\dot{Y}/Y$, $\dot{K}/K$, and $\dot{L}/L$. The only term in Eq. (10.3) that cannot be measured directly is the growth rate of technology, $\dot{A}/A$. We can measure $\dot{A}/A$ indirectly by reorganizing Eq. (10.3) to get

$$\dot{A}/A = \dot{Y}/Y - \{\alpha(t) \cdot \dot{K}/K + [1 - \alpha(t)] \cdot \dot{L}/L\}. \tag{10.4}$$

In other words, we can measure the TFP growth rate—or the rate of technological progress—as a residual; we subtract from $\dot{Y}/Y$ the part of this growth rate that can be accounted for by the growth rate of the inputs, K and L. The part that remains, which provides an estimate of $\dot{A}/A$, is often called the *residual*.[4]

10.4.2 Discrete Time and Variable Shares

Although the continuous-time formula in Eq. (10.4) is useful theoretically, it has to be modified for empirical purposes to apply to discrete time. Thörnqvist (1936) measures the growth rate between two points in time, t and $t + 1$, by logarithmic differences, and he uses as weights the arithmetic averages of the factor shares at times t and $t + 1$. With this approach, the TFP growth rate in discrete time is

$$\log[A(t + 1)/A(t)] = \log[Y(t + 1)/Y(t)]$$
$$- \{\overline{\alpha(t)} \cdot \log[K(t + 1)/K(t)] + [1 - \overline{\alpha(t)}] \cdot \log[L(t + 1)/L(t)]\}, \tag{10.5}$$

where $\overline{\alpha(t)} \equiv [\alpha(t) + \alpha(t + 1)]/2$ is the average share of capital over the periods t and $t + 1$.[5]

---

[2]Note that we let $\alpha(t)$ depend on time to allow for changes over time in the shares of capital and labor. For a Cobb–Douglas technology, $Y = AK^\alpha L^{1-\alpha}$, the input shares are constant at α and $1 - \alpha$, respectively.

[3]If, instead of Eq. (10.1), the production function exhibited labor-augmenting technological progress, so that $Y = F(K, AL)$, then the term $\dot{A}/A$ in equation (10.3) would be multiplied by the labor share, $[1 - \alpha(t)]$. The rest of the equation would remain the same.

[4]This methodology follows Solow (1957). Griliches (1994) describes how the concept of the residual evolved in research prior to Solow's.

[5]Equation (10.5) is only an approximation if the production function takes the general neoclassical form. Diewert (1976) shows, however, that Eq. (10.5) holds exactly if the production function has the translog specification:

$$Y = \exp\{\alpha_0 + \alpha_L \cdot \log(L) + \alpha_K \cdot \log(K) + \alpha_t t + (\beta_{kk}/2) \cdot (\log[K])^2 + (\beta_{ll}/2) \cdot (\log[L])^2$$
$$+ (\beta_{tt}/2) \cdot t^2 + \beta_{kl} \cdot \log(K) \cdot \log(L) + \beta_{kt} \cdot \log(K) \cdot t + \beta_{lt} \cdot \log^*(L) \cdot t\},$$

10.4.3 Measuring Input Shares and the Growth Rates of Inputs

CAPITAL. Ideally, we would use the flow of services of physical capital as a measure of capital input. For example, we would like to know the amount of "machine hours" used in the production process during period t. Since the available data do not usually permit this measurement, the typical procedure calculates the quantity of physical capital of a particular type and then assumes that the flow of services is proportional to the stock. Sometimes attempts are made to distinguish the outstanding stock of capital from the portion that is currently utilized in production.

Measures of the stock of physical capital come from cumulations of the figures on gross physical investment along with estimates of depreciation of existing stocks. The approach, termed the *perpetual-inventory method*, uses the relation,

$$K(t + 1) = K(t) + I(t) - \delta \cdot K(t), \tag{10.6}$$

where $K(t)$ is the stock of physical capital at time t, $I(t)$ is the flow of gross investment during period t, and δ is the constant depreciation rate.[6] If data on $I(t)$ are available and δ is known (often an unrealistic assumption), then the only other ingredient required to implement Eq. (10.6) is the initial stock of capital, $K(0)$. One way to measure $K(0)$ is to obtain a direct estimate of the stock of capital outstanding in a benchmark year. Another procedure is to make a rough guess about $K(0)$ and then use Eq. (10.6) to calculate $K(t)$ in subsequent years. The estimated stocks of capital during the first few years are sensitive to the initial guess about $K(0)$ and are therefore unreliable. However, as $K(0)$ is depreciated away, the estimated stocks become progressively more accurate. With this method, it is necessary to have data on $I(t)$ that substantially predate the interval over which the constructed series on $K(t)$ is to be used.

LABOR. If we do not consider variations in worker quality or in effort, then labor input is the sum of hours worked in a given period. Hence, it is important to take into account changing labor-force participation rates, as well as the rates of unemployment and hours per worker.

QUALITIES OF INPUTS. Early applications of the growth-accounting methodology used a weighted sum of the growth rate of capital and the growth rate of hours worked. The weights equaled the shares of each input in total income and were often assumed to be constant over time. The subtraction of the weighted sum of input

---

where the α's and β's are constants. To ensure constant returns to scale, the parameters must satisfy the restrictions $\beta_{kk} + \beta_{kl} = \beta_{ll} + \beta_{kl} = \beta_{kt} + \beta_{lt} = 0$. We leave the proof of Diewert's proposition as an exercise.

[6]This approach assumes that the contribution of each machine to the overall value of the capital stock equals the machine's replacement cost. In the language of section 3.5, this formulation neglects adjustment costs for investment and assumes, therefore, $q = 1$.

growth rates from the growth rate of aggregate output then yielded an estimate of the TFP growth rate. These studies, such as Solow (1957) and Denison (1962, 1967), usually found large residuals. In other words, a substantial fraction of the growth rate of aggregate output was not accounted for by the growth rates of measured inputs and, as a result, a substantial role was assigned to technological progress.

Jorgenson and Griliches (1967) showed that a substantial fraction of the Solow residual could be explained by changes in the quality of inputs. For example, improvements in the quality of the labor force reflect increases in average years of schooling and better health. For given quantities of capital and worker hours, improvements in the quality of labor raise output. But if labor input is measured only by worker hours, then the unmeasured quality improvements show up as TFP growth. Unmeasured improvements in the quality of capital have similar effects.

To take improvements in the quality of labor into account, worker hours can be disaggregated into many different categories based on schooling, experience, gender, and so on (see Jorgenson, Gollop, and Fraumeni [1987] for a detailed discussion and implementation of this approach). Each category is weighed in accordance with its observed average wage rate, the usual proxy for the marginal product of labor. For example, if persons with college education have higher wage rates (and are presumably more productive) than persons with high school education, then an extra worker with a college education accounts for more output expansion than would an extra worker with a high school education.

The overall labor input is the weighted sum over all categories, where the weights are the relative wage rates. For a given total of worker hours, the quality of the labor force improves—and, hence, the measured labor input increases—if workers shift toward the categories that pay higher wage rates. For example, if the fraction of the labor force that is college educated increases and the fraction with no schooling declines, then the total labor input rises even if the aggregate of worker hours does not change.

The allowance for quality change in the capital stock also requires a disaggregation into many components. The aggregate measure of capital input is the weighted sum over all types, where the weights are the relative rental rates.[7] To compute the rental rates, the usual assumption is that all investments yield the same rate of return. Under perfect foresight, the rental rate of capital is given by the arbitrage condition,

$$R_i(t) = [1 + r(t)] \cdot P_i(t) - (1 - \delta_i) \cdot P_i(t + 1), \qquad (10.7)$$

where $R_i(t)$ is the rental rate, $P_i(t)$ is the price, and δ_i is the depreciation rate for a capital good of type i, and $r(t)$ is the economy-wide real interest rate. The hope is to define categories of capital goods that are homogeneous with respect to $P_i(t)$ and δ_i. In practice, however, new varieties of a given category of goods tend to have higher quality

---

[7]Feenstra and Markusen (1992) extend this procedure to allow for the introduction of new types of capital goods. In Chapter 6, Recall that technological progress took the form of increases in the number of product varieties.

than old ones. The failure to take this quality change into account tends to understate the growth of the capital stock (and also to understate the flow of current output).

Equation (10.7) shows that, for given $P_i(t)$, the source of variation in rental rates is the rate of depreciation, δ_i. Other things equal, short-lived capital has a higher rental rate than long-lived capital. In this sense, a shift from long-lived to short-lived capital looks like an improvement in the "quality" of capital.

10.4.4 Results from Growth Accounting

Table 10.8 reports growth-accounting relationships for a number of countries over different time periods. The results come from four different studies, all of which adjust for changes in the quality of inputs by using the methodology of Jorgenson and Griliches (1967). In the table, the growth rate of real GDP is decomposed into contributions from the growth rates of capital and labor and a residual for TFP growth.

Part A of Table 10.8, from Christensen, Cummings, and Jorgenson (1980), covers Canada, France, Germany, Italy, Japan, the Netherlands, the United Kingdom, and the United States for the period 1947–73. The annual growth rates of TFP for these countries were substantial, ranging from 1.4 percent for the United States to 4.0 percent for Japan. TFP growth accounts for over one-third of the overall growth rate of real GDP in all of the countries.

Part B of the table, from Dougherty (1991), reports the decomposition of growth into the same three categories for the same OECD countries, except for the Netherlands, for a more recent period, 1960–89. One observation is that the TFP growth rates are much smaller than those found for 1947–73. The TFP growth rates in the later period range from 0.4 percent for the United States to 2.0 percent for Japan and Italy. This reduction in the worldwide growth rate of productivity is known as the *productivity slowdown*. Although the TFP growth rate fell markedly for all seven countries, the share of overall growth accounted for by TFP change remains high in some countries because the growth accounted for by changes in factor inputs also declined. For example, in the United Kingdom and Germany, TFP growth still accounts for about half of overall growth for 1960–89. However, the share of total growth accounted for by TFP change is only 11 percent in Canada and 13 percent in the United States.

Column 3 of parts A and B of Table 10.8 shows that the growth rate of labor input is virtually nil for France, Germany, Italy, and the United Kingdom for the entire period from 1947 to 1989. Note also that Japan has experienced a substantial reduction in its rate of TFP growth, from 4.0 percent per year for 1947–73 to 2.0 percent per year for 1960–89. The maintenance of a high growth rate of real GDP for 1960–89—6.8 percent per year—relied on a remarkably high contribution—3.9 percent per year—from the growth of capital input.

Part C of the table reports analogous decompositions of real GDP growth for seven Latin American countries. The results, from Elias (1990), are for Argentina, Brazil, Chile, Colombia, Mexico, Peru, and Venezuela for 1940—80. The annual growth rates of TFP range from 2.3 percent for Mexico and 1.8 percent for Brazil to 0.0 percent for Peru and 0.5 percent for Venezuela.

Finally, part D of the table shows the decomposition of the aggregate growth rate for four fast-growing East Asian countries. The results, from Young (1994), are for Hong Kong, Singapore, South Korea, and Taiwan for the period 1966–90. A surprising finding is the negative TFP growth rate for Singapore and the moderate TFP growth rates for the other three countries. In particular, these growth rates of technology are basically similar to those found for the typical OECD or Latin American country in the other parts of the table. The extremely high growth rates of real GDP for the four East Asian countries reflect remarkably high contributions from the growth of capital and labor inputs, not extraordinary improvements in total factor productivity.

10.4.5 Extensions to Include R&D

A number of studies have extended the growth-accounting framework to include an accumulated stock of R&D as an additional input. This R&D stock can be viewed as a measure of the current level of knowledge and, hence, of the level of the production function. In the theoretical models developed in Chapters 6 and 7, the R&D stock would proxy, respectively, for the number of varieties of intermediate products, N, and the aggregate quality index of goods, Q.

In the methodology described in Griliches (1973), the standard growth-accounting technique is first applied to the inputs of capital and labor to calculate the rate of TFP growth. This TFP growth rate is then regarded as determined by R&D expenditures, a trend term (to pick up exogenous technical progress), and random influences. The regression coefficient on the ratio of R&D spending to output provides an estimate of the social rate of return to R&D.

The Griliches procedure accords in a general way with the theories developed in Chapters 6 and 7. In these models, the conventional inputs—labor and nondurable intermediate goods—are paid their private marginal products, and no spillover effects are present.[8] Moreover, the sum of the payments to these inputs exhausts the total output. These results would still go through if the intermediate products had been treated as durables, so that the model would include capital goods. The usual growth-accounting approach therefore correctly assesses the contribution of changes in the standard inputs to overall growth, even though the models contain aspects of imperfect competition.

In the theories, the residual growth rate varies one-to-one with the growth rate of N or Q (see Eqs. [6.13] and [7.12]). Furthermore, the changes in N and Q are linearly related to total spending on R&D. The growth rate of N or Q is therefore proportional to the ratio of R&D spending to output (since N and Q are themselves proportional to output). The coefficient on the spending ratio gives the marginal effect of R&D on total output and therefore corresponds to the social rate of return on R&D. In the theories, this social rate of return to R&D tends to exceed the private

---

[8]In models with spillovers, such as Arrow (1962) and Romer (1986), the standard growth-accounting technique does not work because the factor prices do not equal the social marginal products.

rate of return. Hence, even if the private rate of return to R&D were observable, this number would not correctly measure the effect of the R&D spending ratio on the TFP growth rate. A regression of the TFP growth rate on the R&D ratio may work, however, because it would reflect the social rate of return to R&D.

The Griliches approach to R&D has been implemented in a number of studies for firms and industries in the United States, including Griliches and Lichtenberg (1984) and Griliches (1988). A major problem in this research is the poor quality of the data on R&D. Nevertheless, the studies tend to show high social rates of return to R&D, typically in a range of 20 to 40 percent per year.

Coe and Helpman's (1993) study of 22 OECD countries reports remarkably high rates of return to R&D within a country—around 100 percent per year. Their estimates are even higher—roughly 130 percent per year—if the spillover benefits across countries are included. One possible reason for the implausibly high estimates is the reverse linkage between productivity growth and R&D spending. The large regression coefficient may reflect the positive response of R&D spending to growth opportunities, rather than the effect of R&D on productivity growth. This potential for reverse causation also exists in the U.S. studies.

10.4.6 Limitations of Growth Accounting

To see the basic limitations of growth accounting, consider the example of a neoclassical economy in the steady state. Assume that the production function is Cobb–Douglas with exogenous, labor-augmenting technological progress at the rate x:

$$Y = AK^\alpha \cdot (Le^{xt})^{1-\alpha}.$$

Assume, for simplicity, that the aggregate labor force, L, is constant.

We found in Chapters 1 and 2 that output and the capital stock in this economy grow in the steady state at the rate x. If there was no technological progress, then output and the capital stock did not grow. If we use the growth-accounting methodology described in this section, then we attribute αx of the steady-state growth rate of output to the growth of capital at the rate x and therefore compute a TFP growth rate of $(1 - \alpha) \cdot x$. We therefore assign only the fraction $1 - \alpha$ of the growth rate of output to technological progress, whereas, in fact, no growth would have occurred without this progress. The problem is that the growth of capital at rate x is endogenous in the sense that it is driven by the technological progress at rate x. If technological progress is truly exogenous, then the reasonable economic statement is that different rates of technological change show up one-to-one in the long run as differences in growth rates of output.

Growth accounting may be able to provide a mechanical decomposition of the growth of output into growth of an array of inputs and growth of total factor productivity. Successful accounting of this sort is likely to be useful and may stimulate the development of useful economic theories of growth. Growth accounting does not, however, constitute a theory of growth because it does not attempt to explain how the changes in inputs and the improvements in total factor productivity relate to elements—such as aspects of preferences, technology, and government policies—that can reasonably be viewed as fundamentals.

TABLE 10.1
Selected variables from cross-country data set

Country	Growth rate, 60–85	GDP per capita, 1960	GDP per capita, 1985	GDP per capita, 1990	Investment ratio	Life expectancy, 1960	Life expectancy, 1985
			Africa				
Algeria	0.0220	1701	2951	2661	0.233	47.3	61.5
Angola	-0.0117	886	662	—	0.039	—	—
Benin	-0.0019	1118	1067	—	0.042	38.9	49.4
Botswana	0.0575	536	2252	—	0.234	45.7	58.3
Burkina Faso	0.0037	470	516	533	0.088	36.3	46.4
Burundi	-0.0058	589	510	522	0.050	41.8	47.9
Cameroon	0.0288	697	1432	1237	0.079	43.4	55.1
Cape Verde	0.0362	488	1205	—	0.226	—	—
Central African Republic	-0.0040	658	596	554	0.082	39.3	49.1
Chad	-0.0220	664	383	365	0.037	34.9	44.5
Comoros	0.0067	519	614	—	0.138	—	—
Congo	0.0348	1063	2540	2464	0.133	47.3	57.7
Egypt	0.0353	769	1859	1838	0.052	46.4	59.6
Ethiopia	0.0051	249	283	—	0.057	42.2	45.3
Gabon	0.0329	1786	4070	3920	0.244	40.9	51.1
Gambia	0.0089	493	616	645	0.054	32.3	42.4
Ghana	-0.0056	873	759	—	0.080	45.2	53.2
Guinea	0.0024	389	366	—	0.128	—	—
Guinea-Bissau	0.0098	482	616	656	0.207	34.8	38.7
Ivory Coast	0.0174	971	1499	1179	0.119	39.5	51.7
Kenya	0.0074	642	772	911	0.181	45.0	57.1
Lesotho	0.0461	288	912	972	0.106	47.7	54.5
Liberia	0.0055	701	805	—	0.147	41.5	53.7
Madagascar	-0.0178	1163	745	673	0.014	41.0	52.7
Malawi	0.0123	367	499	496	0.120	37.9	45.4

(continued)

353

Country	Growth rate, 60-85	GDP per capita, 1960	GDP per capita, 1985	GDP per capita, 1990	Investment ratio	Life expectancy, 1960	Life expectancy, 1985
Mali	0.0016	495	515	521	0.064	35.9	46.3
Mauritania	-0.0021	853	809	807	0.110	35.3	45.2
Mauritius	0.0153	2818	4136	5653	0.116	59.4	66.3
Morocco	0.0348	791	1889	2019	0.109	46.9	59.8
Mozambique	-0.0193	1128	697	737	0.020	35.2	47.0
Niger	0.0023	503	533	—	0.085	35.4	43.7
Nigeria	0.0174	557	860	775	0.147	39.7	50.1
Rwanda	0.0141	514	731	662	0.036	46.5	47.6
Senegal	0.0035	1017	1109	1080	0.062	39.6	46.7
Seychelles	0.0353	1258	3038	—	0.164	—	—
Sierra Leone	—	—	852	833	0.020	31.5	40.3
Somalia	-0.0126	1013	739	—	0.093	36.1	46.1
South Africa	0.0186	2107	3354	3193	0.218	49.2	59.4
Sudan	—	—	1027	959	—	38.8	49.0
Swaziland	0.0232	1207	2158	—	0.202	40.4	54.4
Tanzania	0.0148	312	452	—	0.156	40.6	52.1
Togo	0.0210	360	609	623	0.192	39.5	52.0
Tunisia	0.0369	1076	2704	2858	0.172	48.6	64.4
Uganda	-0.0151	678	465	—	0.098	43.2	47.3
Zaire	-0.0034	460	422	—	0.047	42.1	51.5
Zambia	-0.0082	950	774	700	0.279	41.8	52.1
Zimbabwe	0.0062	1010	1178	1287	0.206	45.5	57.3
North America							
Bahamas	—	—	12343	—	—	—	—
Barbados	0.0334	2703	6230	—	0.135	—	—
Canada	0.0307	7288	15695	17419	0.254	71.1	76.2
Costa Rica	0.0193	2013	3258	3616	0.172	61.9	73.4
Dominica	—	—	2440	—	—	—	—

Country	Growth rate, 60–85	GDP per capita, 1960	GDP per capita, 1985	GDP per capita, 1990	Investment ratio	Life expectancy, 1960	Life expectancy, 1985
Dominican Republic	0.0238	1145	2076	2031	0.157	52.2	65.2
El Salvador	0.0090	1379	1727	1737	0.094	50.8	60.2
Grenada	—	—	1847	2763	—	—	—
Guatemala	0.0091	1638	2056	2078	0.105	45.9	60.8
Haiti	−0.0005	871	860	—	0.058	42.4	53.9
Honduras	0.0106	999	1303	1297	0.143	46.8	63.2
Jamaica	0.0068	1794	2128	—	0.255	63.0	73.5
Mexico	0.0255	2798	5289	5376	0.183	57.3	68.1
Nicaragua	0.0033	1482	1611	—	0.125	47.3	61.9
Panama	0.0323	1504	3371	3021	0.244	60.9	71.6
St. Lucia	—	—	2213	—	—	—	—
St. Vincent	—	—	2295	—	—	—	—
Trinidad and Tobago	0.0215	5630	9642	8537	0.138	63.9	69.4
United States	0.0211	9774	16559	18399	0.240	69.8	74.9
South America							
Argentina	0.0066	3294	3887	3505	0.148	65.2	70.2
Bolivia	0.0170	1103	1688	1596	0.211	42.8	52.2
Brazil	0.0327	1745	3951	3912	0.217	54.9	64.3
Chile	0.0044	2898	3238	3988	0.147	57.3	71.3
Colombia	0.0223	1657	2893	3188	0.176	53.2	65.0
Ecuador	0.0280	1431	2885	2792	0.251	53.4	65.0
Guyana	−0.0088	1533	1230	1185	0.251	60.2	65.9
Paraguay	0.0250	1208	2258	2260	0.131	63.9	66.7
Peru	0.0099	1936	2481	2041	0.211	48.0	60.3
Suriname	0.0182	2099	3310	—	0.218	—	—
Uruguay	−0.0012	3487	3730	4281	0.185	67.3	70.8
Venezuela	−0.0009	6167	6037	5764	0.192	59.8	69.6

(continued)

TABLE 10.1 (continued)

Country	Growth rate, 60–85	GDP per capita, 1960	GDP per capita, 1985	GDP per capita, 1990	Investment ratio	Life expectancy, 1960	Life expectancy, 1985
			Asia				
Afghanistan	—	—	—	—	—	—	—
Bahrain	—	—	9452	—	—	—	—
Bangladesh	0.0132	803	1116	1206	0.046	43.6	49.9
Burma (Myanmar)	0.0256	296	561	—	0.104	—	—
China	—	—	1811	2326	—	36.3	68.8
Hong Kong	0.0627	2222	10653	14412	0.229	66.0	75.8
India	0.0121	665	899	1068	0.172	42.5	56.7
Indonesia	0.0385	621	1626	1941	0.154	41.5	58.5
Iran	0.0184	2535	4017	—	0.197	46.0	—
Iraq	0.0069	3320	3946	—	0.112	46.0	63.0
Israel	0.0343	3348	7900	8639	0.299	71.7	75.0
Japan	0.0558	2976	12004	14827	0.366	67.7	77.3
Jordan	0.0347	1141	2720	2298	0.179	47.2	65.0
Korea	0.0630	883	4267	—	0.231	54.2	68.7
Kuwait	—	—	11979	—	—	59.8	72.3
Malaysia	0.0433	1381	4073	4896	0.239	54.3	68.9
Nepal	0.0146	604	870	—	0.059	38.5	49.9
Oman	—	—	9049	—	—	40.3	54.2
Pakistan	0.0270	622	1221	1360	0.123	43.3	55.5
Philippines	0.0125	1112	1521	1750	0.163	53.1	62.8
Saudi Arabia	—	—	8691	—	—	44.7	62.4
Singapore	0.0638	1653	8153	10956	0.326	63.7	72.5
Sri Lanka	0.0212	1267	2152	—	0.157	62.3	69.8
Syria	0.0392	1530	4075	3991	0.165	50.0	64.0
Taiwan	0.0579	1359	5786	8513	0.246	65.4	72.8

TABLE 10.1 (*continued*)

Country	Growth rate, 60–85	GDP per capita, 1960	GDP per capita, 1985	GDP per capita, 1990	Investment ratio	Life expectancy, 1960	Life expectancy, 1985
Thailand	0.0386	923	2422	3526	0.187	52.7	63.8
United Arab Emirates	—	—	19627	—	—	53.4	70.1
Yemen	—	—	1267	—	—	37.4	49.9
			Europe				
Austria	0.0310	5152	11172	12849	0.283	68.8	73.7
Belgium	0.0285	5554	11324	13588	0.264	69.7	74.3
Cyprus	0.0460	2039	6442	8093	0.311	68.8	75.4
Denmark	0.0259	6748	12884	13802	0.292	72.2	74.9
Finland	0.0325	5384	12128	14216	0.385	68.5	75.0
France	0.0285	5981	12186	13931	0.297	70.4	76.6
Germany	0.0253	6660	12543	14487	0.309	69.4	74.3
Greece	0.0439	2066	6184	6678	0.288	68.8	75.9
Hungary	—	—	5309	5384	—	68.4	69.9
Iceland	0.0338	5191	12085	12960	0.320	—	—
Ireland	0.0332	3147	7215	9067	0.288	69.7	73.5
Italy	0.0340	4660	10895	12555	0.314	69.4	76.3
Luxembourg	0.0190	8269	13287	16399	0.333	—	—
Malta	0.0542	1344	5213	—	0.267	—	—
Netherlands	0.0256	6104	11570	12858	0.279	73.3	76.5
Norway	0.0369	5656	14227	14909	0.349	73.4	76.5
Poland	—	—	4204	3846	—	67.3	71.2
Portugal	0.0397	1864	5026	6520	0.261	63.7	72.9
Spain	0.0348	3165	7547	9662	0.282	68.9	76.3
Sweden	0.0229	7505	13313	14490	0.264	73.2	76.4
Switzerland	0.0183	9637	15209	17007	0.314	71.3	76.7
Turkey	0.0261	1594	3059	3711	0.232	50.5	63.1
United Kingdom	0.0215	6509	11137	13066	0.207	70.8	74.7
Yugoslavia	0.0396	1953	5250	4556	0.327	63.3	70.4

(*continued*)

357

TABLE 10.1 (continued)

Country	Growth rate, 60–85	GDP per capita, 1960	GDP per capita, 1985	GDP per capita, 1990	Investment ratio	Life expectancy, 1960	Life expectancy, 1985
			Pacific Area				
Australia	0.0220	7880	13662	14311	0.313	70.7	75.8
Fiji	0.0169	2053	3129	3728	0.209	59.2	69.8
New Zealand	0.0142	7935	11324	11534	0.268	71.0	74.4
Papua New Guinea	0.0129	1099	1519	1369	0.184	41.0	53.2
Solomon Islands	—	—	1517	—	—	—	—
Tonga	—	—	1837	—	—	—	—
Vanuatu	—	—	1694	—	—	—	—
Western Samoa	—	—	1641	1676	—	—	—

Country	Male schooling, 1960	Female schooling, 1960	Male schooling, 1985	Female schooling, 1985	Population, 1960 (1000s)	Population, 1985 (1000s)	Population growth rate, 60–85
			Africa				
Algeria	1.06	0.64	3.26	1.63	10800	21788	0.028
Angola	—	—	—	—	4816	8754	0.024
Benin	—	—	1.06	0.36	2237	3985	0.023
Botswana	1.51	1.09	4.81	2.81	481	1083	0.032
Burkina Faso	—	—	—	—	4452	7877	0.023
Burundi	—	—	—	—	2948	4731	0.019
Cameroon	—	—	2.96	1.55	5297	10051	0.026
Cape Verde	—	—	—	—	196	324	0.020
Central African Republic	—	—	1.82	0.76	1534	2646	0.022
Chad	—	—	—	—	3064	5018	0.020
Comoros	—	—	—	—	215	463	0.031
Congo	—	—	4.42	1.98	988	1939	0.027
Egypt	—	—	—	—	25922	46511	0.023

Country	Male schooling, 1960	Female schooling, 1960	Male schooling, 1985	Female schooling, 1985	Population, 1960 (1000s)	Population, 1985 (1000s)	Population growth rate, 60–85
Ethiopia	—	—	—	—	24191	43083	0.023
Gabon	—	—	—	—	486	985	0.028
Gambia	1.13	0.28	1.25	0.45	352	745	0.030
Ghana	—	—	4.29	2.20	6774	12839	0.026
Guinea	—	—	—	—	3136	4987	0.019
Guinea-Bissau	—	—	0.75	0.38	542	873	0.019
Ivory Coast	—	—	—	—	3799	9933	0.038
Kenya	1.73	0.59	4.37	1.86	8332	20096	0.035
Lesotho	2.71	2.29	3.59	3.44	870	1538	0.023
Liberia	0.87	0.27	2.76	0.91	1039	2199	0.030
Madagascar	—	—	—	—	5309	10237	0.026
Malawi	2.46	0.86	3.66	1.63	3529	7340	0.029
Mali	—	—	1.26	0.42	4375	7915	0.024
Mauritania	—	—	—	—	991	1766	0.023
Mauritius	3.00	1.92	5.52	3.69	660	1020	0.017
Morocco	—	—	—	—	11626	22025	0.026
Mozambique	0.62	0.21	1.62	0.57	7461	13711	0.024
Niger	1.40	0.33	0.84	0.27	3028	6608	0.031
Nigeria	—	—	—	—	42305	92016	0.031
Rwanda	—	—	1.526	0.19	2742	6102	0.032
Senegal	2.05	1.05	3.18	1.63	3187	6375	0.028
Seychelles	—	3.16	—	—	42	65	0.017
Sierra Leone	0.74	0.33	2.38	1.11	2241	3665	0.020
Somalia	—	—	—	—	2935	6370	0.031
South Africa	4.06	4.07	5.51	4.43	17396	31569	0.024
Sudan	0.52	0.04	1.41	0.42	11165	21822	0.027
Swaziland	1.99	1.37	4.38	3.21	326	664	0.028
Tanzania	1.77	0.94	2.87	1.74	10026	22748	0.033
Togo	0.40	0.03	3.20	1.14	1514	3028	0.028

(continued)

TABLE 10.1 (continued)

Country	Male schooling, 1960	Female schooling, 1960	Male schooling, 1985	Female schooling, 1985	Population, 1960 (1000s)	Population, 1985 (1000s)	Population growth rate, 60–85
Tunisia	0.81	0.08	3.53	1.43	4221	7261	0.022
Uganda	1.76	0.57	2.82	1.06	6562	15647	0.035
Zaire	1.20	0.14	3.44	1.15	15310	30398	0.027
Zambia	2.52	0.82	5.32	3.44	3141	7006	0.032
Zimbabwe	2.04	1.31	3.37	1.92	3812	8292	0.031
North America							
Bahamas	—	—	—	—	—	232	—
Barbados	5.93	5.20	7.57	7.41	231	253	0.004
Canada	7.93	8.22	10.49	10.25	17909	25379	0.014
Costa Rica	3.45	3.50	5.38	5.29	1236	2642	0.030
Dominica	—	3.99	—	—	—	74	—
Dominican Republic	2.57	2.17	4.44	3.90	3231	6416	0.027
El Salvador	1.95	1.46	4.13	3.08	2570	4768	0.025
Grenada	—	—	—	—	—	94	—
Guatemala	1.29	1.02	3.01	2.18	3964	7963	0.028
Haiti	1.01	0.41	1.98	1.30	3807	5889	0.017
Honduras	1.90	1.48	3.67	3.45	1935	4383	0.033
Jamaica	2.46	2.47	4.03	4.28	1629	2311	0.014
Mexico	2.69	2.13	4.80	4.06	38020	79376	0.029
Nicaragua	2.19	1.96	4.01	3.55	1493	3272	0.031
Panama	4.35	4.17	6.24	6.36	1148	2180	0.026
St. Lucia	—	3.80	—	—	—	137	—
St. Vincent	—	4.37	—	—	—	102	—
Trinidad and Tobago	4.83	4.37	6.66	6.35	843	1178	0.013
United States	8.59	8.74	11.83	11.75	180671	239283	0.011

Country	Male schooling, 1960	Female schooling, 1960	Male schooling, 1985	Female schooling, 1985	Population, 1960 (1000s)	Population, 1985 (1000s)	Population growth rate, 60–85
South America							
Argentina	5.21	4.75	6.71	6.64	20616	30331	0.015
Bolivia	4.08	2.15	5.01	3.61	3428	6371	0.025
Brazil	2.94	2.35	3.59	3.38	72594	135564	0.025
Chile	5.20	4.80	6.55	6.36	7614	12122	0.019
Colombia	2.96	2.41	4.57	4.50	15939	29879	0.025
Ecuador	3.30	2.62	5.98	5.19	4413	9317	0.030
Guyana	4.72	4.31	5.16	5.06	569	790	0.013
Paraguay	3.84	2.90	5.00	4.41	1774	3693	0.029
Peru	3.74	2.27	6.68	4.90	9931	19417	0.027
Suriname	—	—	—	—	290	383	0.011
Uruguay	4.37	4.19	6.39	6.51	2538	3008	0.007
Venezuela	2.99	2.06	5.63	5.11	7502	17317	0.033
Asia							
Afghanistan	1.63	0.30	1.89	0.18	10775	14519	0.012
Bahrain	1.64	0.80	4.76	3.73	156	429	0.040
Bangladesh	1.30	0.17	2.94	0.93	51419	101147	0.027
Burma (Myanmar)	1.361	0.67	2.53	1.53	21746	37544	0.022
China	—	—	—	—	657492	1059522	0.019
Hong Kong	7.02	3.36	8.53	6.45	3075	5456	0.023
India	2.24	0.56	4.03	2.00	442344	769183	0.022
Indonesia	1.68	0.53	3.71	3.79	96194	167332	0.022
Iran	0.59	0.31	4.24	2.31	20301	44632	0.032
Iraq	0.35	0.08	4.43	1.62	6847	15898	0.034
Israel	7.70	5.99	9.91	8.94	2114	4233	0.028
Japan	7.20	6.27	8.92	8.03	94096	120837	0.010
Jordan	2.11	0.65	5.57	3.01	1695	3407	0.028

(continued)

TABLE 10.1 (*continued*)

Country	Male schooling, 1960	Female schooling, 1960	Male schooling, 1985	Female schooling, 1985	Population, 1960 (1000s)	Population, 1985 (1000s)	Population growth rate, 60–85
Korea	4.58	2.04	9.17	6.59	25003	40806	0.020
Kuwait	1.71	1.32	5.26	5.31	278	1720	0.073
Malaysia	3.65	0.92	7.05	3.71	8140	15677	0.026
Nepal	0.07	0.07	1.27	0.44	9404	16915	0.023
Oman	—	—	—	—	505	1242	0.036
Pakistan	0.63	0.62	2.86	0.89	49955	103233	0.029
Philippines	4.26	3.32	6.66	6.31	27561	55121	0.028
Saudi Arabia	—	—	—	—	4075	11595	0.042
Singapore	4.08	1.68	5.18	3.92	1634	2558	0.018
Sri Lanka	4.10	2.61	5.80	4.94	9889	16110	0.020
Syria	1.62	0.35	5.48	2.48	4561	10458	0.033
Taiwan	4.49	1.85	8.23	5.65	10792	19258	0.023
Thailand	4.31	2.60	5.56	4.62	26392	51604	0.027
United Arab Emirates	—	—	—	—	90	1349	0.108
Yemen	—	—	1.98	0.04	4039	7621	0.025
Europe							
Austria	4.08	3.32	7.63	5.82	7048	7558	0.003
Belgium	7.62	7.12	9.55	8.79	9153	9858	0.003
Cyprus	5.49	3.19	7.38	6.89	573	665	0.006
Denmark	9.14	9.62	10.71	9.98	4581	5122	0.004
Finland	7.60	7.32	9.79	9.22	4430	4902	0.004
France	4.21	3.92	6.82	6.25	45684	55170	0.008
Germany	7.83	7.46	8.94	8.20	55433	61024	0.004
Greece	5.36	3.57	7.50	6.02	8327	9934	0.007
Hungary	7.13	6.22	11.12	10.41	9984	10657	0.003
Iceland	5.86	5.49	8.34	7.44	176	241	0.013

Country	Male schooling, 1960	Female schooling, 1960	Male schooling, 1985	Female schooling, 1985	Population, 1960 (1000s)	Population, 1985 (1000s)	Population growth rate, 60–85
Ireland	6.30	6.59	8.02	8.00	2834	3552	0.009
Italy	4.96	4.20	6.81	5.80	50200	57141	0.005
Luxembourg	—	—	—	—	314	367	0.006
Malta	5.64	4.67	7.41	6.42	329	344	0.002
Netherlands	5.63	5.12	9.12	8.05	11480	14484	0.009
Norway	5.91	5.35	10.61	10.17	3581	4153	0.006
Poland	7.38	6.18	8.91	7.97	29590	37203	0.009
Portugal	2.41	1.54	4.29	3.43	8826	10157	0.006
Spain	3.69	3.20	6.08	5.13	30455	38602	0.009
Sweden	7.70	7.46	9.65	9.25	7480	8350	0.004
Switzerland	7.28	6.49	9.91	8.35	5362	6470	0.008
Turkey	2.75	1.16	4.16	2.38	27509	50345	0.024
United Kingdom	7.71	7.76	8.77	8.54	52372	56618	0.003
Yugoslavia	5.08	3.50	8.36	6.05	18402	23124	0.009
Pacific Area							
Australia	9.01	8.85	10.12	10.36	10315	15758	0.017
Fiji	5.48	4.31	7.20	6.31	394	699	0.023
New Zealand	9.76	9.46	12.33	11.76	2372	3247	0.013
Papua New Guinea	1.87	0.77	2.14	1.14	1920	3460	0.024
Solomon Islands	—	—	—	—	—	274	—
Tonga	—	—	—	—	—	95	—
Vanuatu	—	—	—	—	—	131	—
Western Samoa	—	—	—	—	—	157	—

TABLE 10.2
Long-term data from Maddison for 16 currently developed countries

Year	GDP per capita (1985 $US)	Ratio to U.S. GDP per capita	Annual growth rate of GDP per capita	Population (1000s)	Annual growth rate of population
			Australia		
1870	3143	1.40	—	1620	—
1890	3949	1.27	0.0114	3107	0.0326
1910	4615	1.02	0.0078	4375	0.0171
1930	3963	0.70	−0.0076	6469	0.0196
1950	5970	0.69	0.0205	8177	0.0117
1970	9747	0.76	0.0245	12507	0.0212
1990	13514	0.74	0.0163	17806	0.0177
			Austria		
1870	1442	0.64	—	4520	—
1890	1892	0.61	0.0136	5394	0.0088
1910	2547	0.56	0.0149	6614	0.0102
1930	2776	0.49	0.0043	6684	0.0005
1950	2869	0.33	0.0016	6935	0.0018
1970	7547	0.59	0.0484	7467	0.0037
1990	12976	0.71	0.0271	7718	0.0017
			Belgium		
1870	2009	0.90	—	5096	—
1890	2654	0.86	0.0139	6096	0.0090
1910	3146	0.69	0.0085	7498	0.0104
1930	3855	0.68	0.0102	8076	0.0037
1950	4229	0.49	0.0046	8640	0.0034
1970	8235	0.64	0.0333	9638	0.0055
1990	13320	0.73	0.0240	9967	0.0017
			Canada		
1870	1330	0.59	—	3736	—
1890	1846	0.60	0.0164	4918	0.0137
1910	3179	0.70	0.0272	7188	0.0190
1930	3955	0.70	0.0109	10488	0.0189
1950	6112	0.71	0.0218	13737	0.0135
1970	10200	0.80	0.0256	21324	0.0220
1990	17070	0.93	0.0257	26620	0.0111
			Denmark		
1870	1543	0.69	—	1888	—
1890	1944	0.63	0.0116	2294	0.0097
1910	2856	0.63	0.0192	2882	0.0114
1930	4114	0.73	0.0182	3542	0.0103
1950	5227	0.61	0.0120	4269	0.0093
1970	9575	0.75	0.0303	4929	0.0072
1990	14086	0.77	0.0193	5140	0.0021

(continued)

TABLE 10.2 *(continued)*

Year	GDP per capita (1985 $US)	Ratio to U.S. GDP per capita	Annual growth rate of GDP per capita	Population (1000s)	Annual growth rate of population
			Finland		
1870	933	0.42	—	1754	—
1890	1130	0.36	0.0096	2364	0.0149
1910	1560	0.34	0.0161	2929	0.0107
1930	2181	0.39	0.0168	3449	0.0082
1950	3481	0.40	0.0234	4009	0.0075
1970	7838	0.61	0.0406	4606	0.0069
1990	14012	0.77	0.0290	4986	0.0040
			France		
1870	1582	0.70	—	38440	—
1890	1955	0.63	0.0106	40107	0.0021
1910	2406	0.53	0.0104	41398	0.0016
1930	3591	0.64	0.0200	41610	0.0003
1950	4176	0.49	0.0075	41836	0.0003
1970	9245	0.72	0.0397	50772	0.0097
1990	14245	0.78	0.0216	56420	0.0053
			Germany (West)		
1870	1223	0.55	—	24870	—
1890	1624	0.52	0.0142	30014	0.0094
1910	2256	0.50	0.0164	39356	0.0135
1930	2714	0.48	0.0092	44026	0.0056
1950	3542	0.41	0.0133	49983	0.0063
1970	9257	0.72	0.0480	60651	0.0097
1990	14288	0.78	0.0217	63232	0.0021
			Italy		
1870	1216	0.54	—	27888	—
1890	1352	0.44	0.0053	31702	0.0064
1910	1891	0.42	0.0168	36572	0.0071
1930	2366	0.42	0.0112	40791	0.0055
1950	2840	0.33	0.0091	47105	0.0072
1970	7884	0.62	0.0511	53661	0.0065
1990	13215	0.72	0.0258	57647	0.0036
			Japan		
1890	842	0.27	—	40077	—
1910	1084	0.24	0.0126	49518	0.0106
1930	1539	0.27	0.0175	64203	0.0130
1950	1620	0.19	0.0026	83563	0.0132
1970	8168	0.64	0.0809	104334	0.0111
1990	16144	0.88	0.0341	123540	0.0084

(continued)

TABLE 10.2 *(continued)*

Year	GDP per capita (1985 $US)	Ratio to U.S. GDP per capita	Annual growth rate of GDP per capita	Population (1000s)	Annual growth rate of population
			Netherlands		
1910	2965	0.65	—	5902	—
1930	4400	0.78	0.0197	7884	0.0145
1950	4708	0.55	0.0034	10114	0.0125
1970	9392	0.73	0.0345	13194	0.0133
1990	13078	0.72	0.0166	14947	0.0062
			Norway		
1870	1190	0.53	—	1735	—
1890	1477	0.48	0.0108	1997	0.0070
1910	1875	0.41	0.0119	2384	0.0089
1930	3086	0.55	0.0249	2807	0.0082
1950	4541	0.53	0.0193	3265	0.0076
1970	8335	0.65	0.0304	3879	0.0086
1990	15418	0.84	0.0308	4241	0.0045
			Sweden		
1870	1401	0.62	—	4164	—
1890	1757	0.57	0.0112	4780	0.0069
1910	2509	0.55	0.0178	5449	0.0065
1930	3315	0.59	0.0139	6131	0.0059
1950	5673	0.66	0.0269	7015	0.0067
1970	10707	0.84	0.0318	8043	0.0068
1990	14804	0.81	0.0162	8559	0.0031
			Switzerland		
1910	2979	0.66	—	3735	—
1930	4511	0.80	0.0207	4051	0.0041
1950	6546	0.76	0.0186	4694	0.0074
1970	12208	0.95	0.0312	6267	0.0145
1990	15650	0.86	0.0124	6796	0.0041
			United Kingdom		
1870	2693	1.20	—	29312	—
1890	3383	1.09	0.0114	35000	0.0089
1910	3891	0.86	0.0070	41938	0.0090
1930	4287	0.76	0.0048	45866	0.0045
1950	5651	0.66	0.0138	50363	0.0047
1970	8994	0.70	0.0232	55632	0.0050
1990	13589	0.74	0.0206	57411	0.0016
			United States		
1870	2244	1.0	—	40061	—
1890	3101	1.0	0.0162	63302	0.0229
1910	4538	1.0	0.0190	92767	0.0191
1930	5642	1.0	0.0109	123668	0.0144
1950	8605	1.0	0.0211	152271	0.0104
1970	12815	1.0	0.0199	205052	0.0149
1990	18258	1.0	0.0177	251394	0.0102

TABLE 10.3
Long-term data from Maddison for 15 currently less-developed countries

Year	GDP per capita (1985 $US)	Ratio to U.S. GDP per capita	Annual growth rate of GDP per capita	Population (1000s)	Annual growth rate of population
			Bangladesh		
1900	349	0.12	—	29012	—
1913	371	0.10	0.0047	31786	0.0070
1950	331	0.05	−0.0031	43135	0.0083
1973	281	0.03	−0.0071	74368	0.0237
1987	375	0.03	0.0206	102961	0.0232
			China		
1900	401	0.14	—	400000	—
1913	415	0.11	0.0026	430000	0.0056
1950	338	0.05	−0.0055	546815	0.0065
1973	774	0.07	0.0360	881940	0.0208
1987	1748	0.13	0.0582	1069608	0.0138
			India		
1900	378	0.13	—	234655	—
1913	399	0.11	0.0042	251826	0.0054
1950	359	0.05	−0.0029	359943	0.0097
1973	513	0.05	0.0155	579000	0.0207
1987	662	0.05	0.0182	787930	0.0220
			Indonesia		
1900	499	0.17	—	40209	—
1913	529	0.14	0.0045	48150	0.0139
1950	484	0.07	−0.0024	72747	0.0112
1973	786	0.07	0.0211	124189	0.0233
1987	1200	0.09	0.0302	170744	0.0227
			Pakistan		
1900	413	0.14	—	19759	—
1913	438	0.12	0.0045	20007	0.0010
1950	390	0.06	−0.0031	37646	0.0171
1973	579	0.05	0.0172	67900	0.0256
1987	885	0.07	0.0303	101611	0.0288
			Philippines		
1900	718	0.25	—	7324	—
1913	985	0.26	0.0243	9384	0.0191
1950	898	0.13	−0.0025	20062	0.0205
1973	1400	0.13	0.0193	39701	0.0297
1987	1519	0.11	0.0058	57011	0.0258

(continued)

TABLE 10.3 *(continued)*

Year	GDP per capita (1985 $US)	Ratio to U.S. GDP per capita	Annual growth rate of GDP per capita	Population (1000s)	Annual growth rate of population
Korea (South)					
1900	549	0.19	—	8772	—
1913	610	0.16	0.0081	10277	0.0122
1950	564	0.08	−0.0021	20557	0.0187
1973	1790	0.16	0.0502	34103	0.0220
1987	4143	0.31	0.0599	42512	0.0157
Taiwan					
1900	434	0.15	—	2858	—
1913	453	0.12	0.0033	3469	0.0149
1950	526	0.08	0.0040	7882	0.0222
1973	2087	0.19	0.0599	15427	0.0292
1987	4744	0.35	0.0587	19551	0.0169
Thailand					
1900	626	0.22	—	7320	—
1913	652	0.17	0.0031	8690	0.0132
1950	653	0.10	0.0000	19442	0.0218
1973	1343	0.12	0.0314	39303	0.0306
1987	2294	0.17	0.0382	53377	0.0219
Argentina					
1900	1284	0.44	—	4693	—
1913	1770	0.47	0.0247	7653	0.0376
1950	2324	0.35	0.0074	17150	0.0218
1973	3713	0.34	0.0204	25195	0.0167
1987	3302	0.24	−0.0084	31500	0.0160
Brazil					
1900	436	0.15	—	17984	—
1913	521	0.14	0.0137	23660	0.0211
1950	1073	0.16	0.0195	51941	0.0213
1973	2504	0.23	0.0368	99836	0.0284
1987	3417	0.25	0.0222	140692	0.0245
Chile					
1900	956	0.33	—	2974	—
1913	1255	0.33	0.0209	3491	0.0123
1950	2350	0.35	0.0170	6091	0.0150
1973	3309	0.30	0.0149	9899	0.0211
1987	3393	0.25	0.0018	12485	0.0166

(continued)

TABLE 10.3 *(continued)*

Year	GDP per capita (1985 $US)	Ratio to U.S. GDP per capita	Annual growth rate of GDP per capita	Population (1000s)	Annual growth rate of population
			Colombia		
1900	610	0.21	—	3998	—
1913	801	0.21	0.0210	5195	0.0201
1950	1395	0.21	0.0150	11597	0.0217
1973	2318	0.21	0.0221	22571	0.0290
1987	3027	0.22	0.0191	29496	0.0191
			Mexico		
1900	649	0.22	—	13607	—
1913	822	0.22	0.0182	14971	0.0073
1950	1169	0.17	0.0095	27376	0.0163
1973	2349	0.21	0.0303	56481	0.0315
1987	2667	0.20	0.0091	81163	0.0259
			Peru		
1900	624	0.21	—	3791	—
1913	819	0.22	0.0209	4507	0.0133
1950	1349	0.20	0.0135	7630	0.0142
1973	2357	0.21	0.0243	14350	0.0275
1987	2380	0.18	0.0007	20756	0.0264

TABLE 10.4
Data for U.S. states

State		Real per capita income, 1900 ($1000s, 82–84 base)	Real per capita income, 1990 ($1000s, 82–84 base)	Growth rate of real per capita income	Popu-lation, 1900 (millions)	Popu-lation, 1990 (millions)	Growth rate of population, 1900–1990	Net migrants, 1900–89 (millions)
AL	Alabama	1.00	9.52	0.0248	1.829	4.046	0.0088	−1.32
AZ	Arizona	3.69	10.62	0.0115	0.093	3.681	0.0409	2.03
AR	Arkansas	1.03	8.77	0.0236	1.312	2.353	0.0065	−1.14
CA	California	4.20	13.83	0.0130	1.403	29.956	0.0340	16.59
CO	Colorado	3.66	12.78	0.0137	0.529	3.302	0.0203	1.11
CT	Connecticut	3.19	17.66	0.0188	0.908	3.290	0.0143	0.76
DE	Delaware	2.52	14.18	0.0190	0.185	0.669	0.0143	0.18
FL	Florida	1.29	12.15	0.0247	0.529	13.044	0.0356	9.37
GA	Georgia	0.98	11.52	0.0271	2.222	6.504	0.0120	−0.28
ID	Idaho	2.54	9.96	0.0150	0.154	1.011	0.0209	0.04
IL	Illinois	2.99	13.73	0.0167	4.822	11.443	0.0096	−0.17
IN	Indiana	2.09	11.26	0.0185	2.516	5.554	0.0088	−0.30
IA	Iowa	2.33	11.09	0.0171	2.232	2.780	0.0024	−1.41
KS	Kansas	2.15	11.84	0.0187	1.470	2.480	0.0058	−0.65
KY	Kentucky	1.38	9.62	0.0214	2.147	3.690	0.0060	−1.54
LA	Louisiana	1.47	9.08	0.0200	1.382	4.211	0.0124	−0.52
ME	Maine	2.16	11.08	0.0180	0.694	1.231	0.0064	−0.11
MD	Maryland	2.34	14.91	0.0204	1.188	4.802	0.0155	1.26
MA	Massachusetts	3.49	14.98	0.0160	2.850	6.020	0.0083	0.14
MI	Michigan	2.13	12.02	0.0190	2.421	9.314	0.0150	0.62
MN	Minnesota	2.38	12.57	0.0183	1.737	4.390	0.0103	−0.34
MS	Mississippi	0.97	7.86	0.0230	1.551	2.574	0.0056	−1.62
MO	Missouri	2.16	11.45	0.0183	3.107	5.127	0.0056	−0.83
MT	Montana	4.77	9.18	0.0071	0.226	0.799	0.0140	−0.07
NE	Nebraska	2.43	11.54	0.0171	1.066	1.580	0.0044	−0.71
NV	Nevada	4.54	13.42	0.0118	0.035	1.224	0.0395	0.79
NH	New Hampshire	2.46	14.65	0.0196	0.412	1.111	0.0110	0.31
NJ	New Jersey	3.19	17.20	0.0185	1.884	7.735	0.0157	2.20
NM	New Mexico	1.70	9.04	0.0184	0.180	1.520	0.0237	0.16
NY	New York	3.71	14.33	0.0148	7.269	18.002	0.0101	1.13

(continued)

TABLE 10.4 *(continued)*

State		Real per capita income, 1900 ($1000s, 82–84 base)	Real per capita income, 1990 ($1000s, 82–84 base)	Growth rate of real per capita income	Popu-lation, 1900 (millions)	Popu-lation, 1990 (millions)	Growth rate of population, 1900–1990	Net migrants, 1900–89 (millions)
NC	North Carolina	0.82	10.98	0.0286	1.894	6.653	0.0140	−0.30
ND	North Dakota	2.40	9.73	0.0153	0.312	0.637	0.0079	−0.49
OH	Ohio	2.55	11.23	0.0163	4.158	10.859	0.0107	0.14
OK	Oklahoma	1.31	9.64	0.0220	0.670	3.146	0.0172	−0.19
OR	Oregon	2.85	11.12	0.0149	0.395	2.861	0.0220	1.27
PA	Pennsylvania	2.88	12.06	0.0157	6.302	11.893	0.0071	−1.99
RI	Rhode Island	3.36	12.08	0.0140	0.429	1.005	0.0095	0.05
SC	South Carolina	0.86	9.88	0.0269	1.340	3.498	0.0107	−0.75
SD	South Dakota	2.11	10.16	0.0173	0.381	0.696	0.0067	−0.43
TN	Tennessee	1.16	10.37	0.0241	2.021	4.887	0.0098	−0.46
TX	Texas	1.58	11.20	0.0215	3.049	17.055	0.0191	3.33
UT	Utah	2.11	9.36	0.0164	0.272	1.729	0.0206	0.06
VT	Vermont	2.19	11.79	0.0185	0.344	0.565	0.0055	−0.05
VA	Virginia	1.27	13.36	0.0259	1.854	6.213	0.0134	0.61
WA	Washington	3.40	12.42	0.0142	0.496	4.909	0.0255	2.16
WV	West Virginia	1.35	8.18	0.0198	0.959	1.790	0.0069	−1.10
WI	Wisconsin	2.05	11.53	0.0190	2.058	4.906	0.0097	−0.33
WY	Wyoming	3.57	11.01	0.0123	0.089	0.452	0.0181	0.03

Notes: The two-letter abbreviation (zip code) for each of the 48 states is shown before the state name.
The Census regional classifications are as follows:
Northeast: ME, NH, VT, MA, RI, CT, NY, NJ, PA.
South: DE, MD, VA, WV, NC, SC, GA, FL, KY, TN, AL, MS, AR, LA, OK, TX.
Midwest: MN, IA, MO, ND, SD, NE, KS, OH, IN, IL, MI, WI.
West: MT, ID, WY, CO, NM, AZ, UT, NV, WA, OR, CA.

TABLE 10.5
Data for European regions

Region	Real per capita GDP, 1950 proportionate deviation from country mean[a]	Real per capita GDP, 1990 proportionate deviation from country mean[b]	Growth rate of real per capita GDP deviation from country mean[c]	Popu- lation, 1950[d] (millions)	Popu- lation, 1990[e] (millions)	Growth rate of popu- lation[f]	Net migrants, various periods[g] (millions)
			Germany				
1 Schleswig-Holstein	−0.36	−0.20	0.0039	2.595	2.615	0.0002	0.31
2 Hamburg	0.54	0.42	−0.0029	1.606	1.641	0.0005	0.13
3 Niedersachsen	−0.25	−0.18	0.0019	6.797	7.342	0.0019	0.21
4 Bremen	0.34	0.20	−0.0034	0.559	0.679	0.0049	0.10
5 Nordrhein Westfalia	0.12	−0.08	−0.0049	13.207	17.248	0.0067	2.05
6 Hessen	−0.06	0.12	0.0044	4.324	5.718	0.0070	1.19
7 Rheinland-Pfalz	−0.25	−0.15	0.0023	3.005	3.735	0.0054	0.25
8 Saarland	0.17	−0.10	−0.0067	0.955	1.071	0.0029	0.00
9 Baden-Württemberg	−0.03	0.02	0.0014	6.430	9.729	0.0104	1.78
10 Bayern	−0.19	−0.01	0.0045	9.185	11.337	0.0053	1.52
11 Berlin (West)	−0.02	−0.04	−0.0005	2.147	2.118	−0.0003	0.26
			United Kingdom				
12 North	−0.07	−0.07	−0.0008	3.133	3.075	−0.0005	−0.24
13 Yorkshire-Humberside	0.11	−0.01	−0.0039	4.494	4.952	0.0024	−0.16
14 East Midlands	−0.02	0.04	0.0005	2.909	4.019	0.0081	0.21
15 East Anglia	−0.04	0.10	0.0027	1.381	2.059	0.0100	0.34
16 South-East	0.30	0.27	−0.0016	15.174	17.458	0.0035	−0.45

Region	Real per capita GDP, 1950 proportionate deviation from country mean[a]	Real per capita GDP, 1990 proportionate deviation from country mean[b]	Growth rate of real per capita GDP deviation from country mean[c]	Population, 1950[d] (millions)	Population, 1990[e] (millions)	Growth rate of population[f]	Net migrants, various periods[g] (millions)
17 South-West	-0.22	0.03	0.0056	3.238	4.667	0.0091	0.66
18 North-West	0.08	-0.02	-0.0034	6.424	6.389	-0.0001	-0.48
19 West Midlands	0.14	-0.01	-0.0045	4.422	5.219	0.0041	-0.20
20 Wales	-0.24	-0.10	0.0025	2.584	2.881	0.0027	0.08
21 Scotland	-0.03	0.00	-0.0002	5.096	5.102	0.0000	-0.45
22 Northern Ireland	-0.35	-0.22	0.0031	1.371	1.589	0.0037	-0.20
			Italy				
23 Piemonte	0.47	0.23	-0.0066	3.504	4.357	0.0054	0.87
24 Valle d'Aosta	0.53	0.31	-0.0057	0.095	0.116	0.0050	0.02
25 Liguria	0.61	0.18	-0.0106	1.555	1.723	0.0026	0.30
26 Lombardia	0.52	0.34	-0.0045	6.433	8.928	0.0082	1.25
27 Trentino-Alto Adige	0.19	0.22	0.0007	0.735	0.889	0.0048	-0.03
28 Veneto	-0.01	0.19	0.0050	3.841	4.392	0.0034	-0.35
29 Fruili-Venezia-Giulia	0.12	0.24	0.0030	1.200	1.202	0.0000	-0.58
30 Emilia-Romagna	0.17	0.28	0.0027	3.509	3.925	0.0028	0.19
31 Marche	-0.06	0.08	0.0036	1.352	1.433	0.0015	-0.13
32 Toscana	0.16	0.13	-0.0006	3.152	3.562	0.0031	0.29
33 Umbria	-0.04	0.03	0.0016	0.806	0.822	0.0005	-0.07
34 Lazio	0.21	0.17	-0.0008	3.322	5.181	0.0111	0.62
35 Campania	-0.29	-0.33	-0.0011	4.276	5.831	0.0078	-0.88
36 Abruzzi	-0.32	-0.10	0.0054	1.238	1.269	0.0006	-0.27
37 Molise	-0.49	-0.20	0.0071	0.398	0.336	-0.0042	-0.14

(continued)

TABLE 10.5 (continued)

Region	Real per capita GDP, 1950 proportionate deviation from country mean[a]	Real per capita GDP, 1990 proportionate deviation from country mean[b]	Growth rate of real per capita GDP deviation from country mean[c]	Population, 1950[d] (millions)	Population, 1990[e] (millions)	Growth rate of population[f]	Net migrants, various periods[g] (millions)
38 Puglia	−0.33	−0.26	0.0017	3.181	4.076	0.0062	−0.77
39 Basilicata	−0.47	−0.41	0.0016	0.617	0.624	0.0003	−0.25
40 Calabria	−0.48	−0.46	0.0005	1.987	2.153	0.0020	−0.79
41 Sicilia	−0.32	−0.37	−0.0012	4.422	5.185	0.0040	−1.08
42 Sardegna	−0.16	−0.27	−0.0027	1.259	1.661	0.0069	−0.23
France							
43 Region Parisienne	0.61	0.50	−0.0026	7.009	10.227	0.0094	1.02
44 Champagne-Ardenne	0.05	0.11	0.0015	1.110	1.341	0.0047	−0.06
45 Picarde	0.05	−0.05	−0.0026	1.355	1.804	0.0072	0.04
46 Haute Normandie	0.13	0.05	−0.0020	1.232	1.731	0.0085	0.03
47 Centre	−0.18	0.02	0.0049	1.758	2.363	0.0074	0.30
48 Basse Normandie	−0.14	−0.04	0.0024	1.145	1.385	0.0048	−0.10
49 Bourgogne	−0.11	−0.01	0.0025	1.376	1.602	0.0038	0.10
50 Nord-Pas de Calais	0.17	−0.09	−0.0067	3.309	3.945	0.0044	−0.39
51 Lorraine	0.24	−0.03	−0.0067	1.874	2.293	0.0050	−0.22
52 Alsace	0.19	0.14	−0.0014	1.196	1.619	0.0075	0.15
53 Franche-Comte	0.05	0.03	−0.0005	0.841	1.092	0.0065	0.02
54 Pays de la Loire	−0.11	−0.03	0.0020	2.293	3.048	0.0071	0.03
55 Bretagne	−0.20	−0.08	0.0030	2.358	2.784	0.0042	0.03
56 Poitou-Charente	−0.25	−0.11	0.0035	1.379	1.588	0.0035	−0.03
57 Aquitaine	−0.15	0.00	0.0036	2.206	2.787	0.0058	0.35
58 Midi-Pyrénées	−0.27	−0.10	0.0043	1.982	2.423	0.0050	0.29
59 Limousin	−0.05	−0.14	−0.0023	0.760	0.719	−0.0014	0.04
60 Rhône-Alpes	0.12	0.09	−0.0009	3.580	5.338	0.0100	0.77

Region	Real per capita GDP, 1950 proportionate deviation from country mean[a]	Real per capita GDP, 1990 proportionate deviation from country mean[b]	Growth rate of real per capita GDP deviation from country mean[c]	Population, 1950 (millions)[d]	Population, 1990[e] (millions)	Growth rate of population[f]	Net migrants, various periods[g] (millions)
61 Auvergne	−0.06	−0.09	−0.0009	1.261	1.314	0.0010	0.03
62 Languedoc-Roussillon	−0.18	−0.14	0.0008	1.453	2.119	0.0094	0.48
63/64 Provence-Alpes-Côtes d' Azur-Corse	0.08	−0.01	−0.0021	2.533	4.499	0.0144	1.52
Netherlands							
65 Noord	−0.10	0.04	0.0035	1.215	1.596	0.0068	—
66 Oost	−0.12	−0.13	−0.0003	1.788	3.050	0.0134	—
67 West	0.18	0.12	−0.0015	5.155	6.996	0.0076	—
68 Zuid	0.04	−0.03	−0.0016	2.007	3.306	0.0125	—
Belgium							
69 Vlaanderen	−0.14	0.09	0.0057	3.963	4.486	0.0030	—
70 Wallonie	−0.01	−0.21	−0.0049	2.841	3.251	0.0034	—
71 Brabant	0.15	0.12	−0.0008	1.849	2.248	0.0049	—
Denmark							
72 Sjalland-Lolland-Falster-Bornholm	0.08	0.19	0.0031	1.984	1.718	−0.0040	—
73 Fyn	−0.02	−0.14	−0.0034	0.396	0.586	0.0109	—
74 Jylland	−0.06	−0.05	0.0003	1.902	2.817	0.0109	—
Spain							
75 Andalucia	−0.29	−0.29	0.0002	5.621	6.920	0.0053	−1.67
76 Aragon	0.01	0.08	0.0022	1.095	1.213	0.0026	−0.12
77 Asturias	0.17	−0.06	−0.0074	0.893	1.126	0.0059	−0.02

(continued)

TABLE 10.5 (continued)

Region	Real per capita GDP, 1950 proportionate deviation from country mean[a]	Real per capita GDP, 1990 proportionate deviation from country mean[b]	Growth rate of real per capita GDP deviation from country mean[c]	Population, 1950[d] (millions)	Population, 1990[e] (millions)	Growth rate of population[f]	Net migrants, various periods[g] (millions)
78 Balears	0.08	0.34	0.0080	0.423	0.682	0.0122	0.12
79 Canaries	-0.22	-0.03	0.0059	0.800	1.485	0.0158	0.02
80 Cantabria	0.18	0.05	-0.0043	0.406	0.527	0.0067	-0.04
81 Castilla-La Mancha	-0.43	-0.26	0.0052	2.028	1.714	-0.0043	-0.91
82 Castilla-Leon	-0.13	-0.11	0.0007	2.864	2.626	-0.0022	-0.97
83 Catalunya	0.34	0.25	-0.0029	3.271	6.008	0.0156	1.42
84 Euskadi (Basque)	0.74	0.11	-0.0197	1.075	2.129	0.0175	0.43
85 Extremadura	-0.58	-0.43	0.0047	1.366	1.129	-0.0049	-0.70
86 Galicia	-0.36	-0.20	0.0050	2.604	2.804	0.0019	-0.41
87 Madrid	0.48	0.34	-0.0042	1.956	4.876	0.0234	1.40
88 Murcia	-0.35	-0.15	0.0062	0.759	1.027	0.0078	-0.16
89 Navarra	0.19	0.13	-0.0019	0.384	0.521	0.0078	0.00
90 La Rioja	0.11	0.14	0.0008	0.230	0.260	0.0032	-0.03
91 Valencia	0.05	0.10	0.0014	2.316	3.787	0.0126	0.54

[a]Difference of logarithm of per capita GDP in 1950 from country mean in 1950. Values for Spain are for 1955.

[b]Difference of logarithm of per capita GDP in 1990 from country mean in 1990. Values for Denmark are for 1985 and for Spain are for 1987.

[c]Difference of annual growth rate of per capita GDP from 1950 to 1990 from country mean growth rate. Values for Denmark are for 1950–85 and for Spain are for 1955–87.

[d]Values for Spain are for 1951.

[e]Values for Denmark are for 1986.

[f]Annual growth rate of population from 1950 to 1990. Values for Denmark are for 1950–86 and for Spain are for 1951–90.

[g]Time periods are 1954–88 for Germany, 1961–85 for the United Kingdom, 1951–87 for Italy, 1954–82 for France, and 1951–87 for Spain.

Note: The numbers for the regions correspond to those used for the map in Figure 10.17.

TABLE 10.6
Data for Canadian provinces

Province	Real per capita personal income,[a] 1926 ($1000s, 1986 base)	Real per capita personal income,[a] 1992 ($1000s, 1986 base)	Growth rate of real per capita income	Population, 1926 (millions)	Population, 1992 (millions)	Growth rate of population	Net migrants, 1950–92[b] (millions)
Alberta	3.49	17.92	0.0248	0.608	2.563	0.0218	0.200
British Columbia	3.82	18.36	0.0238	0.606	3.298	0.0257	0.713
Manitoba	3.32	15.65	0.0235	0.639	1.097	0.0082	−0.246
New Brunswick	1.98	14.35	0.0300	0.396	0.729	0.0092	−0.071
Newfoundland	—	13.62	—	—	0.578	—	−0.088
Nova Scotia	2.08	14.81	0.0297	0.515	0.906	0.0086	−0.057
Ontario	3.50	19.30	0.0259	3.164	10.099	0.0176	0.497
Prince Edward Island	1.72	13.69	0.0314	0.087	0.130	0.0061	−0.012
Quebec	2.59	16.69	0.0282	2.603	6.925	0.0148	−0.598
Saskatchewan	3.12	14.31	0.0231	0.821	0.993	0.0029	−0.335
Territories[c]	—	18.39	—	0.012	0.084	0.0296	−0.007

[a]Based on national consumer price index.

[b]Value for territories is 1951–92.

[c]Northwest Territories and Yukon.

TABLE 10.7
Data for Japanese prefectures

Prefecture	Real per capita income, 1955[a] (million yen, 1985 base)	Real per capita income, 1990 (million yen, 1985 base)	Growth rate of real per capita income[b]	Population, 1955 (millions)	Population, 1990 (millions)	Growth rate of population	Net migrants, 1955–90[c] (millions)
1 Hokkaido	0.441	2.396	0.0484	4.784	5.644	0.0030	−0.76
2 Aomori	0.326	2.045	0.0525	1.391	1.483	0.0012	−0.36
3 Iwate	0.298	2.093	0.0557	1.437	1.417	−0.0003	−0.41
4 Miyagi	0.367	2.453	0.0543	1.748	2.249	0.0046	−0.11
5 Akita	0.371	2.137	0.0500	1.362	1.227	−0.0019	−0.44
6 Yamagata	0.337	2.206	0.0537	1.370	1.258	−0.0016	−0.38
7 Fukushima	0.339	2.413	0.0561	2.120	2.104	−0.0001	−0.57
8 Niigata	0.388	2.398	0.0520	2.501	2.475	−0.0002	−0.63
9 Ibaraki	0.348	2.648	0.0580	2.099	2.845	0.0055	0.09
10 Tochigi	0.518	2.788	0.0561	1.571	1.935	0.0038	−0.13
11 Gumma	0.369	2.640	0.0562	1.624	1.966	0.0035	−0.15
12 Saitama	0.460	2.825	0.0519	2.279	6.405	0.0188	2.41
13 Chiba	0.368	2.880	0.0588	2.225	5.555	0.0166	1.93
14 Tokyo	0.811	4.238	0.0472	8.016	11.855	0.0071	0.10
15 Kanagawa	0.564	2.960	0.0474	2.901	7.980	0.0184	2.58
16 Yamanashi	0.321	2.557	0.0593	0.819	0.853	0.0007	−0.16
17 Nagano	0.374	2.633	0.0558	2.050	2.157	0.0009	−0.33
18 Shizuoka	0.452	2.883	0.0530	2.638	3.671	0.0060	−0.02
19 Toyama	0.426	2.616	0.0518	1.028	1.120	0.0016	−0.16
20 Ishikawa	0.412	2.608	0.0527	0.964	1.165	0.0034	−0.09
21 Gifu	0.441	2.551	0.0502	1.599	2.067	0.0047	−0.07
22 Aichi	0.579	2.971	0.0467	3.779	6.690	0.0104	0.86
23 Mie	0.406	2.621	0.0533	1.505	1.793	0.0032	−0.11
24 Fukui	0.395	2.429	0.0519	0.758	0.824	0.0015	−0.13
25 Shiga	0.434	2.794	0.0532	0.857	1.222	0.0065	0.09
26 Kyoto	0.531	2.664	0.0461	1.928	2.603	0.0054	0.02
27 Osaka	0.709	3.190	0.0430	4.586	8.735	0.0117	1.27
28 Hyogo	0.618	2.668	0.0418	3.660	5.405	0.0071	0.29
29 Nara	0.418	2.190	0.0473	0.777	1.375	0.0104	0.30
30 Wakayama	0.438	2.109	0.0449	1.012	1.074	0.0011	−0.15

(continued)

TABLE 10.7 (continued)

Prefecture	Real per capita income, 1955[a] (million yen, 1985 base)	Real per capita income, 1990 (million yen, 1985 base)	Growth rate of real per capita income[b]	Popu- lation, 1955 (millions)	Popu- lation, 1990 (millions)	Growth rate of popu- lation	Net migrants, 1955–90[c] (millions)
31 Tottori	0.373	2.193	0.0506	0.615	0.616	0.0000	−0.12
32 Shimane	0.336	2.121	0.0527	0.931	0.781	−0.0032	−0.26
33 Okayama	0.413	2.555	0.0521	1.716	1.926	0.0021	−0.16
34 Hiroshima	0.478	2.678	0.0492	2.180	2.850	0.0049	0.00
35 Yamaguchi	0.445	2.299	0.0469	1.619	1.573	−0.0005	−0.34
36 Tokushima	0.344	2.297	0.0542	0.898	0.832	−0.0014	−0.20
37 Kagawa	0.394	2.524	0.0531	0.951	1.023	0.0013	−0.11
38 Ehime	0.397	2.157	0.0483	1.563	1.515	−0.0006	−0.37
39 Kochi	0.367	2.025	0.0484	0.917	0.825	−0.0019	−0.18
40 Fukuoka	0.490	2.502	0.0466	3.867	4.811	0.0040	−0.28
41 Saga	0.368	2.131	0.0502	0.982	0.878	−0.0020	−0.34
42 Nagasaki	0.369	2.027	0.0487	1.795	1.563	−0.0025	−0.65
43 Kumamoto	0.326	2.294	0.0558	1.898	1.840	−0.0006	−0.47
44 Oita	0.316	2.218	0.0556	1.298	1.237	−0.0009	−0.30
45 Miyazaki	0.317	2.078	0.0537	1.155	1.169	0.0002	−0.28
46 Kagoshima	0.255	2.019	0.0591	2.084	1.798	−0.0027	−0.68
47 Okinawa	0.282	1.880	0.0542	0.801	1.222	0.0077	−0.01

[a] Value for Tochigi is for 1960.

[b] Value for Tochigi is for 1960–1990.

[c] Value for Okinawa is for 1965–1990.

Notes: The numbers for the prefectures correspond to those used for the map in Fig. 10.18.

The district classification is as follows:
district 1 (Hokkaido-Tohoku), prefectures 1–8.
district 2 (Kanto-Koshin), prefectures 9–17.
district 3 (Chubu), prefectures 18–24.
district 4 (Kinki), prefectures 25–30.
district 5 (Chugoku), prefectures 31–35.
district 6 (Shikoku), prefectures 36–39.
district 7 (Kyushu), prefectures 40–47.

TABLE 10.8
Growth accounting for a sample of 19 countries

	(1) Growth rate of GDP	(2) Contribution from capital	(3) Contribution from labor	(4) TFP growth rate
PANEL A: OECD Countries, 1947–1973				
Canada ($\alpha = 0.44$)	0.0517	0.0254 (49.2%)	0.0088 (17.0%)	0.0175 (33.9%)
France[a] ($\alpha = 0.40$)	0.0542	0.0225 (41.5%)	0.0021 (3.9%)	0.0296 (54.5%)
Germany[a] ($\alpha = 0.39$)	0.0661	0.0269 (40.6%)	0.0018 (2.8%)	0.0374 (56.6%)
Italy[b] ($\alpha = 0.39$)	0.0527	0.0180 (34.0%)	0.0011 (2.0%)	0.0337 (63.5%)
Japan[b] ($\alpha = 0.39$)	0.0951	0.0328 (34.5%)	0.0221 (23.3%)	0.0402 (42.3%)
Netherlands[c] ($\alpha = 0.45$)	0.0536	0.0247 (46.0%)	0.0042 (7.8%)	0.0248 (46.2%)
U.K.[d] ($\alpha = 0.38$)	0.0373	0.0176 (47.2%)	0.0003 (0.9%)	0.0193 (51.9%)
U.S. ($\alpha = 0.40$)	0.0402	0.0171 (42.7%)	0.0095 (23.7%)	0.0135 (33.6%)
PANEL B: G-7 Countries, 1960–1990				
Canada ($\alpha = 0.45$)	0.0410	0.0229 (55.9%)	0.0135 (32.8%)	0.0046 (11.3%)
France ($\alpha = 0.42$)	0.0350	0.0203 (58.1%)	0.0002 (0.5%)	0.0145 (41.4%)
Germany ($\alpha = 0.40$)	0.0320	0.0188 (58.7%)	−0.0025 (−8.1%)	0.0158 (49.4%)
Italy ($\alpha = 0.38$)	0.0410	0.0202 (49.3%)	0.0011 (2.8%)	0.0197 (47.9%)
Japan ($\alpha = 0.42$)	0.0681	0.0387 (56.9%)	0.0097 (14.3%)	0.0196 (28.8%)
U.K. ($\alpha = 0.39$)	0.0249	0.0131 (52.3%)	−0.0010 (−4.2%)	0.0130 (51.9%)
U.S. ($\alpha = 0.41$)	0.0310	0.0140 (45.2%)	0.0129 (41.5%)	0.0041 (13.2%)

(continued)

TABLE 10.8 (*continued*)

	(1) Growth rate of GDP	(2) Contribution from capital	(3) Contribution from labor	(4) TFP growth rate
	PANEL C: Latin American Countries, 1940–1980			
Argentina ($\alpha = 0.54$)	0.0360	0.0155 (43.1%)	0.0095 (26.4%)	0.0110 (30.5%)
Brazil ($\alpha = 0.45$)	0.0640	0.0325 (50.8%)	0.0130 (20.3%)	0.0185 (28.9%)
Chile ($\alpha = 0.52$)	0.0380	0.0130 (34.2%)	0.0100 (26.3%)	0.0150 (39.5%)
Colombia ($\alpha = 0.63$)	0.0480	0.0205 (42.7%)	0.0155 (32.3%)	0.0120 (25.0%)
Mexico ($\alpha = 0.69$)	0.0630	0.0255 (40.5%)	0.0145 (23.0%)	0.0230 (36.5%)
Peru ($\alpha = 0.66$)	0.0420	0.0285 (67.9%)	0.0135 (32.1%)	0.0000 (0.0%)
Venezuela ($\alpha = 0.55$)	0.0520	0.0295 (56.7%)	0.0175 (33.7%)	0.0050 (9.6%)
	PANEL D: East Asian Countries, 1966–1990			
Hong Kong ($\alpha = 0.37$)	0.0730	0.0309 (42.3%)	0.0200 (27.6%)	0.0220 (30.1%)
Singapore ($\alpha = 0.53$)	0.0850	0.0620 (73.1%)	0.0268 (31.6%)	−0.0040 (−4.7%)
South Korea ($\alpha = 0.32$)	0.1032	0.0477 (46.2%)	0.0435 (42.2%)	0.0120 (11.6%)
Taiwan ($\alpha = 0.29$)	0.0910	0.0368 (40.5%)	0.0362 (39.8%)	0.0180 (19.8%)

Column (1) reports the annualized growth rate of real GDP.

Column (2) is the product of the capital share, α, and the growth rate of quality-adjusted capital input. The number in parentheses is the percentage of the GDP growth rate that is explained by the growth of capital input. The average value of the capital share is reported in parentheses beneath the name of the country.

Column (3) is the product of the labor share, $1 - \alpha$, and the growth rate of quality-adjusted labor input. The number in parentheses is the percentage of the GDP growth rate that is explained by the growth of labor input.

Column (4) shows the growth rate of total factor productivity (TFP). The number in parentheses is the percentage of the GDP growth rate that is explained by TFP growth.

[a] 1950–1973

[b] 1952–1973

[c] 1951–1973

[d] 1955–1973

Source: Panel A: Christenson, Cummings, and Jorgenson (1980); panel B: Dougherty (1991); panel C: Elias (1990); panel D: Young (1994).

CHAPTER 11

EMPIRICAL ANALYSIS OF REGIONAL DATA SETS

A key property of the neoclassical growth model is its prediction of conditional convergence. An economy that starts out proportionately further below its own steady-state position tends to grow faster. We found in Chapters 1 and 2 that economies with similar tastes and technologies converge to the same steady state. In this case, absolute convergence applies; that is, poor economies tend to grow faster than rich ones.

In this chapter, we test the convergence predictions of the neoclassical growth model by looking at the behavior of regions within countries. Although differences in technology, preferences, and institutions do exist across regions, these differences are likely to be smaller than those across countries. Firms and households of different regions within a single country tend to have access to similar technologies and have roughly similar tastes and cultures. Furthermore, the regions share a common central government and therefore have similar institutional setups and legal systems. This relative homogeneity means that absolute convergence is more likely to apply across regions within countries than across countries.

Another consideration in the study of regions is that inputs tend to be more mobile across regions than across countries. Legal, cultural, linguistic, and institutional barriers to factor movements tend to be smaller across regions within a country than across countries. Hence, the assumption of a closed economy—a standard condition of the neoclassical growth model—is likely to be violated for regional data sets.

We found in Chapter 3 that the dynamic properties of economies that are open to capital movements can be similar to those of closed economies. The key element is that a fraction of the capital stock—which includes human capital—is not mobile, or cannot be used as collateral in interregional or international credit transactions. The speed of convergence is increased by the existence of capital mobility, but remains within a fairly narrow range for reasonable values of the fraction of capital that is mobile. Another result is that a technology without diminishing returns to capital—that is, some version of the AK technology—implies a zero convergence speed whether the economy is open or closed.

We also found in Chapter 9 that the allowance for migration in neoclassical growth models tends to accelerate the process of convergence. The change is, again, a quantitative modification to the speed of convergence. The main point, therefore, is that although regions within a country are relatively open to flows of capital and persons, the neoclassical growth model still provides a useful framework for the empirical analysis.

11.1 TWO CONCEPTS OF CONVERGENCE

We mentioned in Chapter 1 that two concepts of convergence appear in discussions of economic growth across countries or regions. In one view (Barro [1984, Ch. 12], Baumol [1986], DeLong [1988], Barro [1991a], Barro and Sala-i-Martin [1991, 1992a, 1992b]), convergence applies if a poor economy tends to grow faster than a rich one, so that the poor country tends to catch up with the rich one in terms of the level of per capita income or product. This property corresponds to our concept of β *convergence*.[1] The second concept (Easterlin [1960a], Borts and Stein [1964, Ch.2], Streissler [1979], Barro [1984, Ch. 12], Baumol [1986], Dowrick and Nguyen [1989], Barro and Sala-i-Martin [1991, 1992a, 1992b]) concerns cross-sectional dispersion. In this context, convergence occurs if the dispersion—measured, for example, by the standard deviation of the logarithm of per capita income or product across a group of countries or regions—declines over time. We call this process σ *convergence*. Convergence of the first kind (poor countries tending to grow faster than rich ones) tends to generate convergence of the second kind (reduced dispersion of per capita income or product), but this process is offset by new disturbances that tend to increase dispersion.

In order to make the relation between the two concepts more precise, we consider a version of the growth equation predicted by the neoclassical growth model

---

[1] This phenomenon is sometimes described as "regression toward the mean."

of Chapter 2. Equation (2.35) relates the growth rate of income per capita between two points in time to the initial level of income. We apply Eq. (2.35) here to discrete periods of unit length (say years) and we also augment it to include a random disturbance:

$$\log(y_{it}/y_{i,t-1}) = a - (1 - e^{-\beta}) \cdot \log(y_{i,t-1}) + u_{it}, \tag{11.1}$$

where the subscript t denotes the year, and the subscript i denotes the country or region. The theory implies that the intercept, a, equals $x + (1 - e^{-\beta}) \cdot [\log(\hat{y}_i^*) + x \cdot (t - 1)]$, where $\hat{y}_i^*$ is the steady-state level of $\hat{y}_i$. We assume that the random variable u_{it} has 0 mean, variance σ_{ut}^2, and is distributed independently of $\log(y_{i,t-1})$, u_{jt} for $j \neq i$, and lagged disturbances.

We can think of the random disturbance as reflecting unexpected changes in production conditions or preferences. We begin for a single cross section by treating the coefficient a as constant. This specification means that the steady-state value, $\hat{y}_i^*$, and the time trend, $x \cdot (t - 1)$, are assumed to be the same for all economies. This assumption is more reasonable for regional data sets than for international data sets; it is plausible that different regions within a country are more similar than different countries with respect to technology and preferences.

If the intercept a is the same in all places and $\beta > 0$, then Eq. (11.1) implies that poor economies tend to grow faster than rich ones. The neoclassical growth models of Chapters 1 and 2 made this prediction. The AK model discussed in Chapter 4 predicts, in contrast, a 0 value for β and, consequently, no convergence of this type. The same conclusion holds for various endogenous growth models (Chapters 6 and 7) that incorporate a linearity in the production function.[2]

Since the coefficient on $\log(y_{i,t-1})$ in Eq. (11.1) is less than 1, the convergence is not strong enough to eliminate the serial correlation in $\log(y_{it})$. Put alternatively, in the absence of random shocks, convergence to the steady state is direct and involves no oscillations or overshooting. Therefore, for a pair of economies, the one that starts out behind is predicted to remain behind at any future date. The models of leapfrogging discussed in Chapter 8 differ in this respect.

Let σ_t^2 be the cross-economy variance of $\log(y_{it})$ at time t. Equation (11.1) and the assumed properties of u_{it} imply that σ_t^2 evolves over time in accordance with the first-order difference equation,[3]

$$\sigma_t^2 = e^{-2\beta} \cdot \sigma_{t-1}^2 + \sigma_{ut}^2, \tag{11.2}$$

where we have assumed that the cross section is large enough so that the sample variance of $\log(y_{it})$ corresponds to the population variance.

---

[2]We showed, however, in Chapter 4 that β convergence would apply if the technology were asymptotically AK, but featured diminishing returns to capital for finite K.

[3]To derive Eq. (11.2), add $\log(y_{i,t-1})$ to both sides of Eq. (11.1), compute the variance, and use the condition that the covariance between u_{it} and $\log(y_{i,t-1})$ is 0.

If the variance of the disturbance, σ_{ut}^2, is constant over time ($\sigma_{ut}^2 = \sigma_u^2$ for all t), then the solution of the first-order difference Eq. (11.2) is

$$\sigma_t^2 = \frac{\sigma_u^2}{1 - e^{-2\beta}} + \left(\sigma_0^2 - \frac{\sigma_u^2}{1 - e^{-2\beta}}\right) \cdot e^{-2\beta t}, \qquad (11.3)$$

where σ_0^2 is the variance of $\log(y_{i0})$. (It can be readily verified that the solution in Eq. [11.3] satisfies Eq. [11.2].) Equation (11.3) implies that σ_t^2 monotonically approaches its steady-state value, $\sigma^2 = \sigma_u^2/(1 - e^{-2\beta})$, which rises with σ_u^2 but declines with the convergence coefficient, β. Over time, σ_t^2 falls (or rises) if the initial value σ_0^2 is greater than (or less than) the steady-state value, σ^2. Thus, a positive coefficient β (β convergence) does not imply a falling σ_t^2 (σ convergence). To put it another way, β convergence is a necessary but not a sufficient condition for σ convergence.

Figure 11.1 shows the time pattern of σ_t^2 with σ_0^2 above or below σ^2. The convergence coefficient used, $\beta = 0.02$ per year, corresponds to the estimates that we report in a later section. With this value of β, the cross-sectional variance is predicted to fall or rise over time at a slow rate. In particular, if σ_0^2 departs substantially from the steady-state value, σ^2, then it takes about 100 years for σ_t^2 to get close to σ^2.

The cross-sectional dispersion of $\log(y_{it})$ is sensitive to shocks that have a common influence on subgroups of countries or regions. These kinds of disturbances violate the condition that u_{it} in Eq. (11.1) is independent of u_{jt} for $i \neq j$. To the extent that these shocks tend to benefit or hurt regions with high or low income (that is, to the extent that the shocks are correlated with the explanatory variable), the omission of such shocks from the regressions will tend to bias the estimates of β.

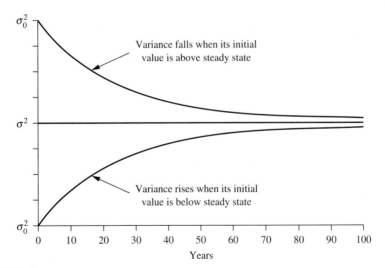

FIGURE 11.1
Theoretical behavior of dispersion. The figure shows the dispersion of per capita product, measured as the variance of the log of per capita product across economies. Although β convergence is assumed to apply, the dispersion may fall, rise, or remain constant, depending on whether it starts above, below, or at its steady-state value, σ^2. The figure assumes $\beta = 0.02$.

Examples are shocks that generate changes in the terms of trade for commodities. For the United States, an example is the sharp drop in the relative prices of agricultural goods during the 1920s. This disturbance had an adverse effect on the incomes of agricultural regions relative to the incomes of industrial regions. We can think also of the two oil price increases of the 1970s and the price decline of the 1980s. These shocks had effects in the same direction on the incomes of regions that produce oil relative to the incomes of other regions. Another example for the United States is the Civil War. This shock had a strong adverse impact on the incomes of southern states relative to the incomes of northern states.

Formally, let S_t be a random variable that represents an economy-wide disturbance for period t. For example, S_t could reflect the relative price of oil as determined on world markets. Then Eq. (11.1) can be modified to

$$\log(y_{it}/y_{i,t-1}) = a - (1 - e^{-\beta}) \cdot \log(y_{i,t-1}) + \varphi_i S_t + u_{it}, \qquad (11.4)$$

where φ_i measures the effect of the aggregate disturbance on the growth rate in region i. If a positive value of S_t signifies an increase in the relative price of oil, then φ_i would be positive for countries or regions that produce a lot of oil.[4] The coefficient φ_i would tend to be negative for economies that produce goods, such as automobiles, that use oil as an input. We think of the coefficient φ_i as distributed cross-sectionally with mean $\bar{\varphi}$ and variance σ_φ^2.

If $\log(y_{i,t-1})$ and φ_i are uncorrelated, then estimates of β in Eq. (11.4) would be unbiased when the shock is omitted from the regression. If $\log(y_{i,t-1})$ and φ_i are positively correlated, then the coefficient estimated by OLS on $\log(y_{i,t-1})$ in Eq. (11.1) would be positively or negatively biased as S_t is positive or negative. As an example, if oil producers have relatively high per capita income, an increase in oil prices will benefit the relatively rich states. Consequently, an OLS regression of growth on initial income will underestimate the true convergence coefficient. In the empirical analysis of the next sections, we hold constant proxies for S_t as an attempt to obtain unbiased estimates of the convergence coefficients.

Equation (11.4) implies that the variance of the log of per capita income evolves as

$$\sigma_t^2 = e^{-2\beta} \cdot \sigma_{t-1}^2 + \sigma_{ut}^2 + S_t^2 \cdot \sigma_\varphi^2 + 2S_t \cdot e^{-\beta} \cdot \text{cov}[\log(y_{i,t-1}), \varphi_i], \quad (11.5)$$

where the variances and covariances are conditioned on the current and past realizations of the aggregate shocks, $S_t, S_{t-1}, \ldots$. If $\text{cov}[\log(y_{i,t-1}), \varphi_i]$ equals 0—that is, if the shock is uncorrelated with initial income—then Eq. (11.5) corresponds to Eq. (11.2), except that realizations of S_t effectively move σ_{ut}^2 around over time. A

---

[4]More precisely, this shock would have a positive effect on the real income derived from the countries or regions that produce a lot of oil. This income may be owned by "foreigners" and appear as part of the net factor payments from "abroad," the term that differentiates GNP from GDP. For example, a substantial fraction of the capital inputs of Wyoming is owned by residents of other states. A positive oil shock will increase Wyoming's nominal GDP (and raise the real value of this GDP when deflated by a national price index) but not necessarily raise its GNP or personal income. For the U.S. states, this distinction is important in a few cases, notably for oil producers.

temporarily large value of S_t raises σ_t^2 above the long-run value σ^2 that corresponds to a typical value of S_t. Therefore, in the absence of a new shock, σ_t^2 returns gradually toward σ^2, as shown in Fig. 11.1.

11.2 CONVERGENCE ACROSS THE U.S. STATES

11.2.1 β Convergence

We now use the data on per capita income for the U.S. states to estimate the speed of convergence, β.[5] (The definitions and sources of the data are in Chapter 10.) Suppose, for the moment, that we have observations at only two points in time, 0 and T. Then Eq. (11.1) implies that the average growth rate over the interval from 0 to T is given by

$$(1/T) \cdot \log(y_{iT}/y_{i0}) = a - [(1 - e^{-\beta T})/T] \cdot \log(y_{i0}) + u_{i0,T}, \qquad (11.6)$$

where $u_{i0,T}$ represents the average of the error terms, u_{it}, between dates 0 and T, and the intercept is $a \equiv x + [(1 - e^{-\beta T})/T] \cdot \log(\hat{y}^*)$.

The coefficient on initial income in Eq. (11.6) is $(1 - e^{-\beta T})/T$, an expression that declines with the length of the interval, T, for a given β. That is, if we estimate a linear relation between the growth rate of income and the log of initial income, then the coefficient is predicted to be smaller the longer the time span over which the growth rate is averaged. The reason is that the growth rate declines as income increases. Hence, if we compute the growth rate over a longer time span, then it combines more of the smaller future growth rates with the initially larger growth rates. Hence, as the interval increases, the effect of the initial position on the average growth rate declines. The coefficient $[(1 - e^{\beta T}/T]$ approaches 0 as T approaches infinity, and it tends to β as T approaches 0. We obtain estimates of β from the nonlinear form of Eq. (11.6), taking account of the value of T that applies in each case. This method should generate similar estimates of β regardless of the length of the averaging interval for the data.

Table 11.1 shows nonlinear least-squares estimates in the form of Eq. (11.6) for 47 or 48 U.S. states or territories for various time periods. The rows of Table 11.1 correspond to different time periods. For example, the first row corresponds to the 110–year period between 1880 and 1990. The first column of the table refers to the equation with only one explanatory variable, the logarithm of income per capita at

---

[5]Barro and Sala-i-Martin (1992) also use the data on Gross State Product (GSP) reported by the Bureau of Economic Analysis. GSP is analogous to GDP in that it assigns the product to the state in which it has been produced. In contrast, income (like GNP) assigns the product to the state in which the owners of the inputs reside. This distinction is potentially important if the economies are open and people tend to own capital in other states, or if there is a lot of interstate commuting (people live in one state and work in another). Barro and Sala-i-Martin (1992) show that, in practice, the distinction turns out not to be that important; the estimates of the speed of convergence for GSP and personal income are similar. Since GSP data are available only starting in 1963, we limit attention in this chapter to the results that use the income data.

TABLE 11.1
Regressions for personal income across U.S. states

Period	(1) Basic equation		(2) Equations with regional dummies		(3) Equations with structural variables & regional dummies	
	$\hat{\beta}$	$R^2[\hat{\sigma}]$	$\hat{\beta}$	$R^2[\hat{\sigma}]$	$\hat{\beta}$	$R^2[\hat{\sigma}]$
1880–1990	0.0174 (0.0026)	0.89 [0.0015]	0.0177 (0.0042)	0.93 [0.0012]	—	—
1880–1900	0.0101 (0.0022)	0.36 [0.0068]	0.0224 (0.0040)	0.62 [0.0054]	0.0268 (0.0048)	0.65 [0.0053]
1900–1920	0.0218 (0.0032)	0.62 [0.0065]	0.0209 (0.0062)	0.67 [0.0062]	0.0269 (0.0075)	0.71 [0.0060]
1920–1930	−0.0149 (0.0050)	0.14 [0.0132]	−0.0122 (0.0074)	0.43 [0.0111]	0.0218 (0.0112)	0.64 [0.0089]
1930–1940	0.0141 (0.0030)	0.35 [0.0073]	0.0127 (0.0051)	0.36 [0.0075]	0.0119 (0.0072)	0.46 [0.0071]
1940–1950	0.0431 (0.0049)	0.72 [0.0078]	0.0373 (0.0053)	0.86 [0.0057]	0.0236 (0.0060)	0.89 [0.0053]
1950–1960	0.0190 (0.0035)	0.42 [0.0050]	0.0202 (0.0051)	0.49 [0.0048]	0.0305 (0.0054)	0.66 [0.0041]
1960–1970	0.0246 (0.0040)	0.51 [0.0045]	0.0135 (0.0043)	0.68 [0.0037]	0.0173 (0.0053)	0.72 [0.0036]
1970–1980	0.0198 (0.0063)	0.21 [0.0060]	0.0119 (0.0069)	0.36 [0.0056]	0.0042 (0.0070)	0.46 [0.0052]
1980–1990	0.0011 (0.0100)	0.00 [0.0104]	0.0062 (0.0084)	0.56 [0.0071]	0.0133 (0.0075)	0.75 [0.0055]
Joint, nine subperiods	0.0175 (0.0013)	— —	0.0189 (0.0019)	— —	0.0220 (0.0021)	— —
Likelihood-ratio statistic (p-value)	69.4 (0.000)		31.7 (0.000)		12.6 (0.123)	

Note: The regressions use nonlinear least squares to estimate equations of the form,

$$(1/T) \cdot \log(y_{it}/y_{i,t-T}) = a - [\log(y_{i,t-T})] \cdot [(1 - e^{-\beta T})/T] + \text{other variables},$$

where $y_{i,t-T}$ is per capita income in state i at the beginning of the interval divided by the overall CPI. T is the length of the interval, and the other variables consist of regional dummies and structural measures (see the description in the text). See Chapter 10 for a discussion of the data on the U.S. states. The samples that begin in 1880 have 47 observations. The others have 48 observations. Each column contains the estimate of β, the standard error of this estimate (in parentheses), the R^2 of the regression, and the standard error of the equation (in brackets). The estimated coefficients for constants, regional dummies, and structural variables are not reported. The likelihood-ratio statistic refers to a test of the equality of the coefficients of the log of initial income over the nine subperiods. The p-value comes from a χ^2 distribution with eight degrees of freedom.

the beginning of the period. Column two adds four regional dummies, corresponding to the four main census regions: Northeast, South, Midwest, and West (see Table 10.15 for a list of the states contained in each region). Finally, column three includes sectoral variables that are meant to capture the aggregate shocks discussed in the previous section. We already argued that the inclusion of these auxiliary variables would help to obtain accurate estimates of β.

Each cell contains the estimate of β, the standard error of this estimate (in parentheses), the R^2, and the standard error of the regression (in brackets). All equations have been estimated with constant terms, which are not reported in Table 11.1.

The point estimate of β for the long sample, 1880–1990, is 0.0174 (s.e. = 0.0026).[6] The large R^2, 0.89, can be appreciated from Figure 11.2, which provides a scatter plot of the average growth rate of income per capita between 1880 and 1990 against the log of income per capita in 1880.

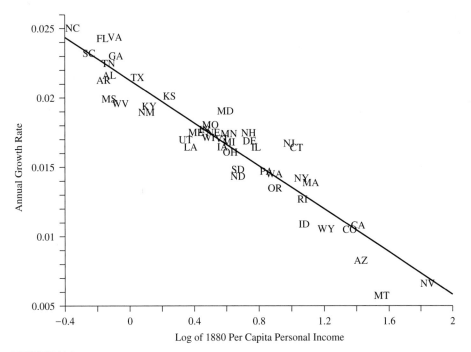

FIGURE 11.2
Convergence of personal income across U.S. states, 1880 personal income and 1880–1990 income growth. The average growth rate of state per capita income for 1880–1990, shown on the vertical axis, is negatively related to the log of per capita income in 1880, shown on the horizontal axis. Thus, absolute β convergence exists for the U.S. states. Each state is represented by its postal code (see Table 10.4).

---

[6]This regression includes 47 states or territories. Data for the Oklahoma territory are unavailable for 1880.

The second column of the first row presents the estimated speed of convergence when the four regional dummies are incorporated. The estimated β coefficient is 0.0177 (0.0042). The similarity between this estimate and the previous one suggests that the speed at which averages for the four census regions converge is not substantially different from the speed at which averages for the states within each of the regions converge. We can check this result by computing the average income for each of the four regions. The growth rate of a region's average income between 1880 and 1990 is plotted against the log of the region's average income in 1880 in Figure 11.3. The negative relation is clear (the correlation coefficient is -0.97). The estimated speed of convergence implied by this relation is 2.1 percent per year, about the same as the within-region rate shown in column 2.

The next nine rows of Table 11.1 divide the sample into subperiods. The first two are twenty years long (1880 to 1900 and 1920 to 1940), because income data for 1890 and 1910 are unavailable. The remaining seven subperiods are ten years long.

The estimated β coefficient is significantly positive—indicating β convergence—for seven of the nine subperiods. The coefficient has the wrong sign ($\beta < 0$) for only one of the subperiods, 1920–30, a time of large declines in the relative price of agricultural commodities. A likely explanation for this result is that agricultural states tended to be poor states, and the agricultural states suffered the most from

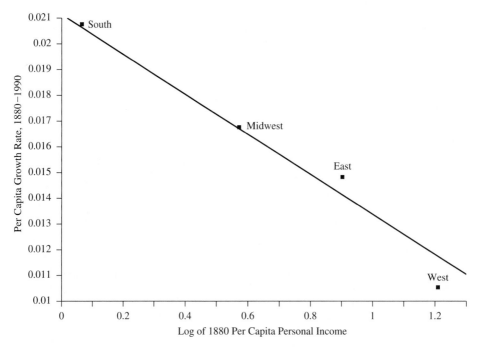

FIGURE 11.3
Convergence of personal income across U.S. regions, 1880 income and 1880–1990 income growth.
The negative relation between income growth and initial income, shown for the U.S. states in Fig. 11.2, applies in Fig. 11.3 to averages over the four main census regions.

the fall in agricultural prices. The estimated coefficient is insignificant for another subperiod, 1980–90, the interval following the oil shocks. (The 1979–81 price increase favored states that were already relatively rich, whereas the 1986 price decline had the opposite effect.)

If we constrain the β coefficients to be the same for all subperiods, then the joint estimate for the basic equation is 0.0175 (0.0013). We reject, however, the hypothesis of stability of the β coefficients over time; the likelihood-ratio statistic is 69.4, with a p-value of 0.000. (Under the null hypothesis, the likelihood-ratio statistic asymptotically follows a χ^2 distribution with eight degrees of freedom.)

Column 2 of Table 11.1 adds regional dummies, where the coefficients of these dummies are allowed to differ for each period. These regional variables capture effects that are common to all states within a region in a given period. The estimated β coefficient for the 1920s still has the wrong sign. Hence, even within regions, poor states tended to grow slower than rich states during the 1920s. The joint estimate for the nine subperiods is now 0.0189 (0.0019), similar to that for the basic regression. We again reject the hypothesis of equality of β coefficients across the subperiods; the likelihood-ratio statistic is now 31.7, with a p-value of 0.000.

Aggregate shocks that affect groups of states differentially, such as shifts in the relative prices of agricultural products or oil, might explain the instability of the estimated coefficients. Following Barro and Sala-i-Martin [1991, 1992a, 1992b], the third column of Table 11.1 adds an additional variable to the regression as an attempt to hold these aggregate shocks constant. The variable, denoted by S_{it} (for structure), is calculated as

$$S_{it} = \sum_{j=1}^{9} \omega_{ij,t-T} \cdot [\log(y_{jt}/y_{j,t-T})/T], \qquad (11.7)$$

where $\omega_{ij,t-T}$ is the weight of sector j in state i's personal income at time $t - T$, and y_{jt} is the national average of personal income per worker in sector j at time t. The nine sectors used are agriculture, mining, construction, manufacturing, trade, finance and real estate, transportation, services, and government. We think of S_{it} as a proxy for the effects reflected in the term $\varphi_i S_t$ in Eq. (11.4).

The structural variable indicates how much a state would grow if each of its sectors grew at the national average rate. For example, suppose that economy i specializes in the production of cars and that the aggregate car sector does not grow over the period between $t - T$ and t. The low value of S_{it} for this region indicates that it should not grow very fast because the car industry has suffered from the shock.

Note from Eq. (11.7) that S_{it} depends on the contemporaneous growth rates of national averages and on lagged values of state i's sectoral shares. For this reason, the variable can be reasonably treated as exogenous to the current growth experience of state i.

Because of lack of data, we can include the structural variable only for the periods after 1929. For the periods before 1929, we obtain a rough measure of S_{it} by using the share of agriculture in the state's total income.

Column three includes structural variables, as well as regional dummies, in the convergence regression. (The coefficients on the regional and structural variables are allowed to differ for each period.) One contrast with the previous results is that the estimated β coefficient for the 1920s becomes positive. The joint estimate of β for the nine subperiods is 0.022 (0.002). Unlike the previous cases, we now cannot reject at conventional critical levels the hypothesis that the coefficient is the same over the nine subperiods; the likelihood-ratio statistic is 12.6, and the p-value is 0.12.

The main conclusion is that the U.S. states tend to converge at a speed of about two percent per year. Averages for the four census regions converge at a rate that is similar to that for states within regions. If we hold constant measures of structural shocks, then we cannot reject the hypothesis that the speed of convergence is stable over time.

11.2.2   Measurement Error

The existence of temporary measurement error in income tends to introduce an upward bias in the estimate of β; that is, the elimination of measurement error over time can generate the appearance of convergence.[7] One reason for measurement error is that each state's nominal income is deflated by a national price index, because accurate indexes do not exist at the state level.

One approach to handle measurement error is to use earlier lags of the log of income as instruments in the regressions. If measurement error is temporary (and the error term is not serially correlated), then the earlier lags of the log of income would be satisfactory instruments for the log of income at the start of each period. If we reestimate column 1 of Table 11.1 with the previous lag of the log of income used as an instrument, then we get a joint estimate of β of 0.0198 (0.0016). This panel uses eight subperiods starting in 1900 because the observation for 1880–1900 is lost. The OLS estimate of β for the same eight subperiods is 0.0202 (0.0015). Hence, the use of instruments generates a minor decline in the estimate of β.

When we estimate the subperiods separately, we again find only a small difference between the instrumental-variable (IV) and OLS estimates. The largest change applies to the period 1950–60, for which the IV estimate is 0.0156 (0.0036), compared with the OLS value of 0.0190 (0.0036).

The results for columns 2 and 3 of Table 11.1 are similar. For example, for column 3, the joint IV estimate is 0.0197 (0.0026), compared with an OLS estimate of 0.0206 (0.0024). Thus, the main finding is that the instrumental procedures do not alter the basic findings on β convergence. Our conclusion is that measurement error is unlikely to be a key element in the results.

11.2.3 σ Convergence

Figure 11.4 shows the cross-sectional standard deviation for the log of per capita personal income net of transfers for 47 or 48 U.S. states or territories from 1880 to 1992. The dispersion declined from 0.54 in 1880 to 0.33 in 1920, but then rose to

---

[7]The same property holds for short-term business fluctuations. We may want to design a model in which these temporary fluctuations of output are distinguished from the kinds of transitional dynamics that appear in growth models.

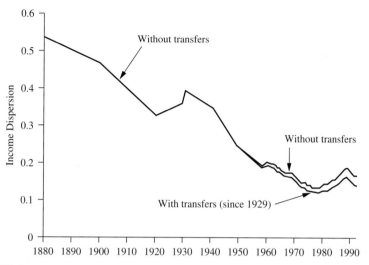

FIGURE 11.4
Dispersion of personal income across U.S. states, 1880–1992. The figure shows the cross-sectional variance of the log of per capita personal income for 47 or 48 U.S. states or territories from 1880 to 1992. This measure of dispersion declined from 1880 to 1920, rose in the 1920s, fell from 1930 to the mid-1970s, rose through 1988, and declined again through 1992.

0.40 in 1930. This rise reflects the adverse shock to agriculture during the 1920s; the agricultural states were relatively poor in 1920 and suffered a further reduction in income with the fall in agricultural prices.

After 1930, the dispersion fell to 0.35 in 1940, 0.24 in 1950, 0.21 in 1960, 0.17 in 1970, and a low point of 0.14 in 1976. The long-run decline stopped in the mid-1970s, after the first oil shock, and σ_t rose to 0.15 in 1980 and 0.19 in 1988. The rise in dispersion was reversed at the end of the 1980s (apparently as soon as Mr. Reagan was no longer President), and dispersion fell through 1992.

Figure 11.4 shows that the behavior of the cross-sectional dispersion of personal income net of transfers is similar to that of gross income of transfers. In particular, dispersion fell for both concepts of income after 1930, rose between 1977 and 1988, and fell between 1988 and 1992. Although the transfers tend to reduce the cross-state dispersion of per capita income, changes in the amount of transfers are not the main source of the long-run decline in income dispersion across the states.

11.3 CONVERGENCE ACROSS JAPANESE PREFECTURES

11.3.1 β Convergence

We now analyze the pattern of β convergence for per capita income across 47 Japanese prefectures, using the data set of Barro and Sala-i-Martin (1992b). (See Chapter 10 for the sources and definitions.) Table 11.2 reports nonlinear estimates of the convergence coefficient, β, for the period 1930–90. The setup of Table 11.2 parallels that of Table 11.1.

TABLE 11.2
Regressions for personal income across Japanese prefectures

Period	(1) Basic equation $\hat{\beta}$	$R^2[\hat{\sigma}]$	(2) Equations with district dummies $\hat{\beta}$	$R^2[\hat{\sigma}]$	(3) Equations with structural variables & district dummies $\hat{\beta}$	$R^2[\hat{\sigma}]$
1930–90	0.0279 (0.0033)	0.92 [0.0019]	0.0276 (0.0024)	0.97 [0.0012]	—	—
1930–55	0.0358 (0.0035)	0.86 [0.0045]	0.0380 (0.0037)	0.90 [0.0038]	—	—
1955–90	0.0191 (0.0035)	0.59 [0.0027]	0.0222 (0.0035)	0.81 [0.0020]	—	—
1955–1960	−0.0152 (0.0079)	0.07 [0.0133]	−0.0023 (0.0082)	0.44 [0.0111]	0.0047 (0.0118)	0.46 [0.0112]
1960–1965	0.0296 (0.0072)	0.30 [0.0108]	0.0360 (0.0079)	0.55 [0.0093]	0.0414 (0.0096)	0.56 [0.0093]
1965–1970	−0.0010 (0.0062)	0.00 [0.0097]	0.0127 (0.0067)	0.47 [0.0076]	0.0382 (0.0091)	0.62 [0.0065]
1970–1975	0.0967 (0.0100)	0.78 [0.0095]	0.0625 (0.0092)	0.87 [0.0078]	0.0661 (0.0118)	0.87 [0.0079]
1975–1980	0.0338 (0.0100)	0.23 [0.0087]	0.0455 (0.0119)	0.37 [0.0085]	0.0469 (0.0145)	0.37 [0.0086]
1980–1985	−0.0115 (0.0077)	0.04 [0.0075]	0.0076 (0.0089)	0.37 [0.0066]	0.0102 (0.0094)	0.37 [0.0067]
1985–1990	0.0007 (0.0067)	0.00 [0.0067]	0.0086 (0.0082)	0.28 [0.0061]	0.0085 (0.0085)	0.28 [0.0062]
Joint, seven subperiods	0.0125 (0.0032)	— —	0.0232 (0.0034)	— —	0.0312 (0.0040)	— —
Likelihood-ratio statistic (p-value)	94.6 (0.000)		40.6 (0.000)		26.4 (0.002)	

Note: See Chapter 10 for a discussion of the data on Japanese prefectures, and see the note to Table 11.1 for the form of the regressions. The variable $y_{i,t-T}$ is per capita income in prefecture i at the beginning of the interval divided by the overall CPI. All samples have 47 observations. The likelihood-ratio statistic refers to a test of the equality of the coefficients of the log of initial income over the seven subperiods. The p-value comes from a χ^2 distribution with six degrees of freedom.

The first row of Table 11.2 pertains to regressions for the whole period, 1930–90. The basic equation in column 1 includes only the log of initial income as a regressor. The estimated β coefficient is 0.0279 (0.0033), with an R^2 of 0.92. The good fit can be appreciated in Fig. 11.5. The strong negative correlation between the growth rate from 1930 to 1990 and the log of per capita income in 1930 confirms the existence of β convergence across the Japanese prefectures.

The estimated β coefficient is essentially the same in column 2, which incorporates dummies for the seven Japanese districts as explanatory variables. (See the notes to Table 10.18 for a listing of the prefectures contained in each district.) This

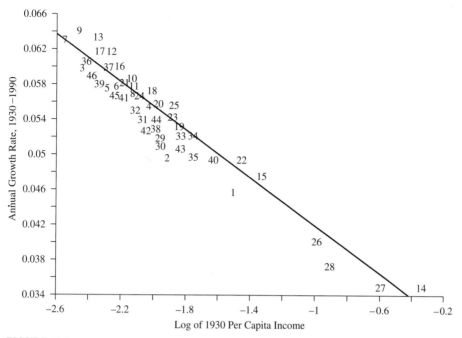

FIGURE 11.5

Convergence of personal income across Japanese prefectures, 1930 income and 1930–1990 income growth. The average growth rate of prefectural per capita income for 1930–90, shown on the vertical axis, is negatively related to the log of per capita income in 1930, shown on the horizontal axis. Thus, absolute β convergence exists for the Japanese prefectures. The numbers shown identify the prefecture (see Table 10.7).

finding suggests that the speed of convergence for prefectures within districts is similar to that across districts. This idea can be checked by running a regression that uses the seven data points for the growth and level of the average per capita income of districts. The negative relation between the growth rate from 1930 to 1990 and the log of per capita income in 1930 is displayed in Fig. 11.6. The β coefficient estimated from these observations is 0.0261 (0.0079). Hence, we confirm that the speed of convergence across districts is about the same as that within districts.

The second and third rows of Table 11.2 break the full sample into two long subperiods, 1930–55 and 1955–90. For the basic equation, the speed of convergence for the first subperiod is larger than that for the second, 0.0358 (0.0035) versus 0.0191 (0.0035). The same relation holds for the second column, which adds the district dummies as explanatory variables. (Different coefficients on the dummies are estimated for the two subperiods.) Hence, we conclude that the speed of convergence after 1955 was substantially slower than that between 1930 and 1955. The lack of sectoral data for the early period does not, however, allow us to investigate the cause of this difference. We therefore restrict the rest of the analysis to the post-1955 period.

The next seven rows of Table 11.2 break the sample into five-year subperiods starting in 1955. For three of the subperiods, the sign of the estimated β coefficient in the basic equation is opposite to the one expected. The speed of convergence is

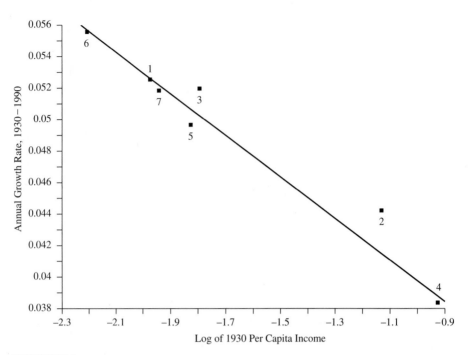

FIGURE 11.6
Convergence of personal income across Japanese districts, 1930 income and 1930–1990 income growth. The negative relation between income growth and initial income, shown for Japanese prefectures in Fig. 11.5, applies also in Fig. 11.6 to averages for the seven major districts.

positive and significant for the periods 1960–65, 1970–75, and 1975–80. The joint estimate for the seven subperiods is 0.0125 (0.0032). A test for the equality of coefficients over time is strongly rejected; the likelihood-ratio statistic is 94.6, with a p-value of 0.000.

The results with district dummies in column 2 allow for different coefficients on the dummies in each subperiod. In this case, only the estimated β coefficient for 1955–60 has the wrong sign, and it is not significant. The joint estimate is 0.0232 (0.0034). However, we still reject the equality of coefficients at the 5 percent level; the likelihood-ratio statistic is 40.6, with a p-value of 0.000.

Column 3 adds a measure of the structural variable, S_{it}, defined in Eq. (11.7). This variable is analogous to the one constructed for the U.S. states. The coefficients on the structural variable are allowed to differ for each subperiod. In contrast with the previous two columns, none of the subperiods has the wrong sign when the sectoral variable is included. The joint estimate for the seven subperiods is 0.0312 (0.0040). The likelihood-ratio statistic for the equality of coefficients over time is 26.4, with a p-value of 0.002. Therefore, although the likelihood-ratio statistic is smaller than before, we still reject the hypothesis of stability over time.

One source of instability in the estimated β coefficients is that Tokyo is an outlier in the 1980s: Tokyo was by far the richest prefecture in its district in 1980 and had the largest growth rate from 1980 to 1990, an outcome not captured by the structural variable that we have included. If we add a dummy for Tokyo for the 1980s, then we get estimated β coefficients of 0.0218 (0.0112) for 1980–85 and 0.0203 (0.0096) for 1985–90. With this dummy included, the test of equality of coefficients over the seven subperiods yields a likelihood-ratio statistic of 16.7, which implies a p-value of 0.010.

Another source of instability is the period 1970–75, for which the estimated β coefficient of 0.0661 (0.0118) is substantially higher than the others. A likely explanation for this high estimated value of β is that the oil shock of 1973 had an especially adverse impact on the richer industrial areas. The structural variable is supposed to hold constant this type of shock, but the construct that we have been able to measure does not seem to capture this effect.

As with the U.S. states, we reestimated the equations for Japanese prefectures with earlier lags of income used as instruments. The conclusion again is that the estimates are not materially affected. For example, for column 3 of Table 11.2, the joint estimate of β falls from 0.0312 (0.0040) to 0.0282 (0.0042) when the instruments are used.

11.3.2 σ Convergence across Prefectures

We want now to assess the extent to which there has been σ convergence across prefectures in Japan. We calculate the unweighted cross-sectional standard deviation for the log of per capita income, σ_t, for the 47 prefectures from 1930 to 1990. Figure 11.7 shows that the dispersion of personal income increased from 0.47 in 1930 to 0.63 in 1940. One explanation of this phenomenon is the explosion of military spending during the period. The average growth rates for districts 1 (Hokkaido–Tohoku) and

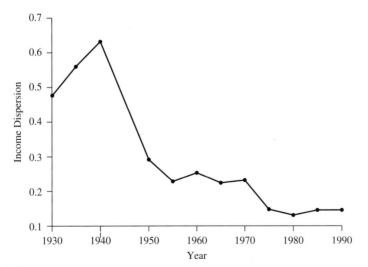

FIGURE 11.7
Dispersion of personal income across Japanese prefectures, 1930–1990. The figure shows the cross-sectional variance of the log of per capita personal income for 47 Japanese prefectures from 1930 to 1990. This measure of dispersion fell from the end of World War II until 1980.

7 (Kyushu), which are mainly agricultural, were -2.4 percent and -1.7 percent per year, respectively. In contrast, the industrial regions of Tokyo, Osaka, and Aichi grew at 3.7, 3.1, and 1.7 percent per year, respectively.

The cross-prefectural dispersion decreased dramatically after World War II: it fell to 0.29 in 1950, 0.25 in 1960, 0.23 in 1970, and hit a minimum of 0.12 in 1978. The dispersion increased slightly then: σ_t rose to 0.13 in 1980, 0.14 in 1985, and 0.15 in 1987, but has been relatively stable since 1987. Thus, the pattern is similar to that for the U.S. states.

11.4 CONVERGENCE ACROSS EUROPEAN REGIONS

11.4.1 β Convergence

We now analyze convergence for 90 regions in eight European countries: 11 in Germany, 11 in the United Kingdom, 20 in Italy, 21 in France, 4 in the Netherlands, 3 in Belgium, 3 in Denmark, and 17 in Spain. The data, described in Chapter 10, correspond to GDP per capita for the first seven countries and to income per capita for Spain.

Table 11.3 shows the estimates of β in the form of Eq. (11.6) for the period 1950–90. The regressions include country dummies for each period to proxy for

TABLE 11.3
Convergence across European regions

Period	(1) Equations with country dummies		(2) Equations with sectoral shares and country dummies	
	$\hat{\beta}$	$R^2[\hat{\sigma}]$	$\hat{\beta}$	$R^2[\hat{\sigma}]$
1950–60	0.018	0.83	0.034	0.84
	(0.006)	[0.0099]	(0.009)	[0.0094]
1960–70	0.023	0.97	0.020	0.97
	(0.009)	[0.0065]	(0.006)	[0.0064]
1970–80	0.020	0.99	0.022	0.99
	(0.009)	[0.0079]	(0.007)	[0.0077]
1980–90	0.010	0.97	0.007	0.97
	(0.004)	[0.0066]	(0.005)	[0.0064]
Joint, four subperiods	0.019	—	0.018	—
	(0.002)	—	(0.003)	—
Likelihood-ratio statistic (p-value)	4.9		8.6	
	(0.179)		(0.034)	

Note: See Chapter 10 for a discussion of the data on European regions, and see the note to Table 11.1 for the form of the regressions. The variable $y_{i,t-T}$ is an index of the per capita GDP (income for Spain) in region i at the beginning of the interval. All samples have 90 observations. The likelihood-ratio statistic refers to a test of the equality of the coefficients of the log of initial per capita GDP or income over the four subperiods. The p-value comes from a χ^2 distribution with three degrees of freedom.

differences in the steady-state values of x_i and $\hat{y}_i^*$ in Eq. (11.1) and for countrywide fixed effects in the error terms. The country dummies, which are not reported in Table 11.3, have substantial explanatory power. The first four rows of column 1 show the results for four decades. The estimates of β are reasonably stable over time; they range from 0.010 (0.004) for the 1980s to 0.023 (0.009) for the 1960s. The joint estimate for the four decades is 0.019 (0.002). The hypothesis of constant β over time cannot be rejected at conventional levels of significance; the likelihood ratio statistic is 4.9, with a p-value of 0.18.

Figure 11.8 shows for the 90 regions the relation of the growth rate of per capita GDP (income for Spain) from 1950 to 1990 (1955 to 1987 for Spain) to the log of per capita GDP or income at the start of the period. The variables are measured relative to the means of the respective countries. The figure shows the negative relation that is familiar from the U.S. states and Japanese prefectures. The correlation between the growth rate and the log of initial per capita GDP or income in Fig. 11.8 is -0.72. Since the underlying numbers are expressed relative to own-country means, the relation in Fig. 11.8 pertains to β convergence within countries, rather than between countries. The graph therefore corresponds to the estimates that include country dummies in column 1 of Table 11.3.

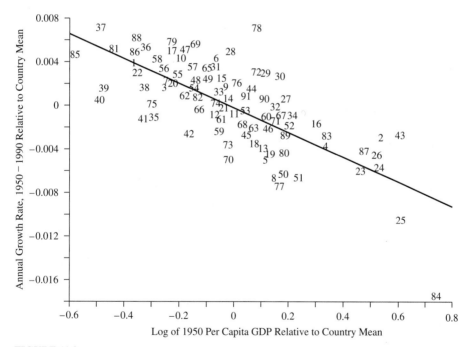

FIGURE 11.8
Growth rate from 1950 to 1990 versus 1950 per capita GDP for 90 regions in Europe. The growth rate of a region's per capita GDP for 1950–90, shown on the vertical axis, is negatively related to the log of per capita GDP in 1950, shown on the horizontal axis. The growth rate and level of per capita GDP are measured relative to the country means. Hence, this figure shows that absolute β convergence exists for the regions within Germany, the United Kingdom, Italy, France, the Netherlands, Belgium, Denmark, and Spain. The numbers shown identify the regions (see Table 10.5).

Column 2 adds the share of agriculture and industry in total employment or GDP at the start of each subperiod.[8] These share variables are as close as we can come with our present data for the European regions to measuring the structural variable, S_{it}, that appears in Eq. (11.7). The results allow for period-specific coefficients for the sectoral shares.

The joint estimate of β for the four subperiods is now 0.018 (0.003). The test of the hypothesis of stability of β across periods yields a likelihood-ratio statistic of 8.6, with a p-value of 0.034. Thus, in contrast to our findings for the United States and Japan, the inclusion of the share variables makes the β coefficients appear less stable over time. Probably, a better measure of structural composition would yield more satisfactory results.

We have also estimated the joint system for Europe with individual β coefficients for the five large countries (Germany, the United Kingdom, Italy, France, and Spain). This system corresponds to the four-period regression shown in column 2 of Table 11.3, except that the coefficient β is allowed to vary over the countries (but not over the subperiods). This system contains country dummies (with different coefficients for each subperiod) and share variables (with coefficients that vary over the subperiods but not across the countries). The resulting estimates of β are Germany (11 regions), 0.0224 (0.0067); United Kingdom (11 regions), 0.0277 (0.0104); Italy (20 regions), 0.0155 (0.0037); France (21 regions), 0.0121 (0.0061); and Spain (17 regions), 0.0182 (0.0048). Note that the individual point estimates are all close to 2 percent per year; they range from 1.2 percent per year for France to 2.8 percent per year for the United Kingdom.

The likelihood-ratio statistic for equality of the β coefficients across the five countries is 3.0, and the corresponding p-value is 0.55. Hence, we cannot reject the hypothesis that the speed of regional convergence within the five European countries is the same.

We also reestimated the European equations with earlier lags of per capita GDP or income used as instruments. This procedure necessitated the elimination of the first subperiod; hence, only the three decades from 1960 to 1990 are now included. The use of instruments had little impact on the results that included only country dummies, corresponding to column 1 of Table 11.3. The joint estimate of β goes from 0.0187 (0.0022) in the OLS case (with only three subperiods included) to 0.0165 (0.0023). If the agricultural and industrial share variables are added, however, the joint estimate of β goes from 0.0153 (0.0034) to 0.0073 (0.0038). We think that the sharp drop in the estimated β coefficient in this case reflects inadequacies in the share variables as measures of structural shifts.

11.4.2 σ Convergence

Figure 11.9 shows the behavior of σ_t for the regions within the five large countries: Germany, the United Kingdom, Italy, France, and Spain. The countries are always

---

[8]The share figures for the first three subperiods are based on employment. The values for 1980–90 are based on GDP.

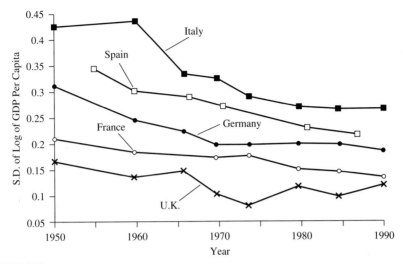

FIGURE 11.9
Dispersion of per capita GDP within five European countries. The figure shows the cross-sectional variance of the log of per capita GDP from 1950 to 1990 for 11 regions in Germany, 11 in the United Kingdom, 20 in Italy, 21 in France, and 17 in Spain. This measure of dispersion fell in most cases since 1950, but has been roughly stable in Germany and the United Kingdom since 1970.

ranked in descending order of dispersion as Italy, Spain, Germany, France, and the United Kingdom. The overall pattern shows declines in σ_t over time for each country, although little net change occurs since 1970 for Germany and the United Kingdom. The rise in σ_t from 1974 to 1980 for the United Kingdom—the only oil producer in the European sample—likely reflects the effect of oil shocks. In 1990, the values of σ_t are 0.27 for Italy, 0.22 for Spain (for 1987), 0.19 for Germany, 0.14 for France, and 0.12 for the United Kingdom.

11.5 MIGRATION ACROSS THE U.S. STATES

This section considers the empirical determinants of net migration among the U.S. states. The analysis in Section 9.1.3 suggests that m_{it}, the annual rate of net migration into region i between years $t - T$ and t, can be described by a function of the form

$$m_{it} = f(y_{i,t-T}, \theta_i, \pi_{i,t-T}; \text{variables that depend on } t \text{ but not } i), \quad (11.8)$$

where $y_{i,t-T}$ is per capita income at the beginning of the period, θ_i is a vector of fixed amenities (such as climate and geography), and $\pi_{i,t-T}$ is the population density in region i at the beginning of the period.[9] The set of variables that depends on t

---

[9]Some amenities, such as government policies with respect to tax rates and regulations, would vary over time. We do not deal with these types of variables in the present analysis.

but not on i includes any elements that influence per capita incomes and population densities in other economies. Also included are effects like technological progress in heating and air conditioning, changes that alter people's attitudes about weather and population density.

Per capita income—a proxy for wage rates—would have a positive effect on migration, whereas population density would have a negative effect. The functional form that we implement empirically is

$$m_{it} = a + b \cdot \log(y_{i,t-T}) + c_1\theta_i + c_2\pi_{i,t-T} + c_3 \cdot (\pi_{i,t-T})^2 + v_{it}, \quad (11.9)$$

where v_{it} is an error term, $b > 0$, and the form allows for a quadratic in population density, $\pi_{i,t-T}$. The marginal effect of $\pi_{i,t-T}$ on m_{it} is negative if $c_2 + 2c_3 < 0$.

Although there is an extensive literature about variables to include as amenities, θ_i, the present analysis includes only the log of average heating-degree days, denoted $\log(\text{HEAT}_i)$, which is a disamenity so that $c_1 < 0$. The variable $\log(\text{HEAT}_i)$ has a good deal of explanatory power for net migration across the U.S. states. We considered alternative measures of the weather, but they did not fit as well. It would be useful to include migration for retirement, a mechanism that likely explains outliers such as Florida. However, these kinds of modifications probably would not change the basic findings that we now present about the relation between net migration and state per capita income.

Our data on net migration for the U.S. states start in 1900 and are available for every census year except 1910 and 1930. Chapter 10 describes the sources and definitions of these data. We calculate the ten-year annual migration rates into a state by dividing the number of net migrants between dates $t - T$ and t by the state's population at date $t - T$.

Figure 11.10 shows the simple long-term relation between the migration rate and the log of initial income per capita.[10] The horizontal axis plots the log of state per capita income in 1900. The positive association is evident (correlation $= 0.51$). The main outlier is Florida, which has a lower than average initial income per capita and a very high net migration rate of 3 percent per year.

Table 11.4 shows regression results in the form of Eq. (11.9) for net migration into U.S. states. The results reported are for eight subperiods starting with 1900–20. The regressions include period-specific coefficients for $\log(y_{i,t-T})$ and for the log of heating-degree days. (The hypothesis of stability over the subperiods in the coefficients of $\log[\text{HEAT}_i]$ is rejected at the 5 percent level, although the estimated coefficients on $\log[y_{i,t-T}]$ change little if only a single coefficient is estimated for the heat variable.) Since the hypothesis that the coefficients for the population-density variables are stable over time is accepted at the 5 percent level, we estimate Eq. (11.9) with one coefficient for the density and one for the square of the density. The regressions also include period-specific coefficients for regional dummies and structural-share variables. (The estimated coefficients for the regional and structural variables are sometimes significant, but play a minor role overall.)

---

[10]The variable on the vertical axis is the average annual in-migration rate for each state from 1900 to 1987. The variable is the average for each subperiod weighted by the length of the interval.

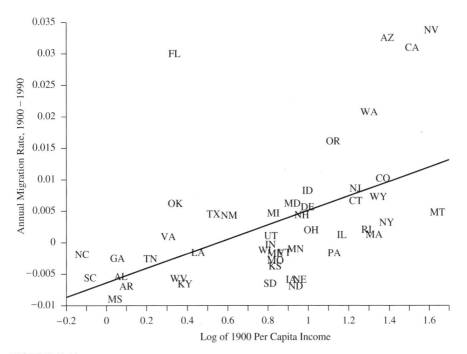

FIGURE 11.10
Migration and initial state income, 1900–1990. The average net migration rate for 48 U.S. states or territories from 1900 to 1990, shown on the vertical axis, is positively related to the log of initial per capita income, shown on the horizontal axis. Florida, Arizona, California, and Nevada have notably higher net migration rates than the values predicted by their initial levels of income.

The estimated coefficients for $\log(\text{HEAT}_i)$ in Table 11.4 are all negative and most are significantly different from 0; other things equal, people prefer warmer states. The jointly estimated coefficients for density are -0.043 (0.008) on the linear term and 0.030 (0.010) on the squared term. These point estimates imply that the marginal effect of population density on migration is negative for all states, except for the three with the highest densities: New Jersey, Rhode Island since 1960, and Massachusetts since 1970.

The coefficient on the log of initial per capita income is significantly positive for all subperiods. The joint estimate is 0.0260 (0.0023), which implies a t-value over 11. The estimated response of migration to the log of initial level is, however, not stable over time; the likelihood-ratio statistic is 17.1, with a p-value of 0.017. The main sources of instability are the unusually large coefficients on income in the 1950s and 1960s; the coefficients in these two subperiods are 0.0438 (0.0086) and 0.0435 (0.0083), respectively.

Although highly significant, the coefficient on initial income, 0.026, is small in an economic sense. The coefficient means that, other things equal, a 10 percent differential in income per capita raises net in-migration only by enough to raise the area's rate of population growth by 0.26 percent per year. Our previous results suggest that differences in per capita income tend themselves to vanish at a slow speed,

TABLE 11.4
Regressions for net migration into U.S. states, 1900–89

Period	Log of per capita income	Heating-degree days	Population density	Square of population density	$R^2[\hat{\sigma}]$
1900–20	0.0335 (0.0075)	−0.0066 (0.0037)	−0.0433 (0.0079)	0.0307 (0.0095)	0.70 [0.0111]
1920–30	0.0363 (0.0078)	−0.0124 (0.0027)	−0.0433 (0.0079)	0.0307 (0.0095)	0.61 [0.0079]
1930–40	0.0191 (0.0037)	−0.0048 (0.0014)	−0.0433 (0.0079)	0.0307 (0.0095)	0.71 [0.0041]
1940–50	0.0261 (0.0055)	−0.0135 (0.0022)	−0.0433 (0.0079)	0.0307 (0.0095)	0.82 [0.0065]
1950–60	0.0438 (0.0086)	−0.0205 (0.0031)	−0.0433 (0.0079)	0.0307 (0.0095)	0.70 [0.0091]
1960–70	0.0435 (0.0083)	−0.0056 (0.0025)	−0.0433 (0.0079)	0.0307 (0.0095)	0.70 [0.0069]
1970–80	0.0240 (0.0091)	−0.0077 (0.0024)	−0.0433 (0.0079)	0.0307 (0.0095)	0.73 [0.0072]
1980–89	0.0163 (0.0061)	−0.0066 (0.0019)	−0.0433 (0.0079)	0.0307 (0.0095)	0.72 [0.0053]
Joint, 8 subperiods	0.0260 (0.0023)	individual coefficients	−0.0427 (0.0079)	0.0300 (0.0097)	— —

Note: The likelihood-ratio statistic for a test of the equality of the income coefficients over the 8 subperiods is 17.1, with a *p*-value of 0.017 (from a χ^2 distribution with 7 degrees of freedom). The regressions use iterative, weighted least squares and take the form,

$$m_{it} = a_t + b_t \cdot \log(y_{i,t-T}) + c_{1t} \cdot \text{heat}_i + c_2 \cdot \pi_{i,t-T} + c_3 \cdot \pi_{i,t-T}^2 + c_{4t} \cdot \text{region}_i + c_{5t} \cdot S_{it},$$

where m_{it} is the net flow of migrants into state *i* between years $t - T$ and *t*, expressed as a ratio to the population at $t - T$; heat$_i$ is heating-degree days; $\pi_{i,t-T}$ is population density (thousands of persons per square mile); region$_i$ is a set of dummies for the four main census regions; and S_{it} is the structural variable described in the text. The estimates of a_t, c_{4t}, and c_{5t} are not shown. The data are discussed in Chapter 10. All samples have 48 observations. Standard errors are in parentheses.

roughly 2 percent per year. The combination of the results for migration with those for income convergence suggests that net migration rates would be highly persistent over time. The data confirm this idea: the correlation between the average migration rate for 1900–40 with that for 1940–89 is 0.70.

11.6   MIGRATION ACROSS JAPANESE PREFECTURES

Before we analyze migration across Japanese prefectures and implement Eq. (11.9) for Japan, we should mention that there is a substantial difference between the typical Japanese prefecture and the typical U.S. state in terms of area. The average size of a Japanese prefecture is 6,394 square kilometers,[11] roughly half the size of Connecticut. The largest prefecture, Hokkaido, is 83,520 km^2, or roughly the size of South Carolina. The second largest prefecture, Iwate, has an area of 15,277 km^2, a bit larger than Connecticut and a bit smaller than New Jersey. In comparison, the average U.S. state has an area of 163,031 km^2, and the area of the largest state in the continental United States, Texas, is 691,030 km^2. California, with an area of 411,049 km^2, is slightly larger than all of Japan (377,682 km^2).

The contrast in size means that Japanese prefectures resemble metropolitan areas more than states, so that daytime commuting across prefectures can be significant. Urban economists, such as Henderson (1988), think that people like to live in cities for two reasons. First, there are demand or consumption externalities. That is, cities provide amenities, such as theaters and museums, features that can be supplied only if there is a sufficient scale of demand. Second, there are production externalities, which tend to generate high wages in big cities. An offsetting force is that people want to live away from crowded cities because they tend to be associated with crime, less friendly neighborhoods, and (in equilibrium) high land and housing prices (see Roback [1982]). Thus, the decision to migrate to a city involves a tradeoff. This tradeoff can be avoided if people live in a suburb and commute to the central city. People are especially willing to pay high commuting costs when densities in the central city are extremely high.

To deal with these issues empirically, we would like to have a measure of the density of the neighboring prefectures. Conceptually, we could construct such a measure by weighting the neighbors' densities by their distance in some way. In practice, however, we observe that there are two main areas in Japan that have an abnormally high population density, Tokyo and Osaka. In 1990, Tokyo's density was 5,470 people/km^2 and Osaka's was 4,674 people/km^2, compared to an average for the other prefectures of 624 people/km^2.[12] Hence, the problems mentioned above are likely to arise in these two regions only. We can confirm this idea by considering the ratio of daytime to nighttime population, a measure of the extent of commuting.[13] A ratio smaller than one indicates that there are people who live in that prefecture but work in another, and a ratio larger than one indicates the opposite. The ratio is close to one for all prefectures except for the ones around Tokyo and Osaka: Tokyo's ratio is 1.184 and Osaka's is 1.053. The ratios for the Tokyo region are 0.872 for Saitama, 0.876 for Chiba, and 0.910 for Kanagawa. For the Osaka region, the ratios are 0.955 for Hyogo, 0.871 for Nara, and 0.986 for Wakayama.[14]

---

[11] This figure excludes Hokkaido, which is about five times as large as any of the other prefectures. The average size including Hokkaido is 8,036 km^2, two-thirds the size of Connecticut.

[12] In comparison, the U.S. state with the largest density in 1990 was New Jersey with 390 people/km^2.

[13] The source of these data is the Statistics Bureau, Management and Coordination Agency.

[14] There seems to be some commuting across prefectures in the areas surrounding Kyoto and Aichi, but the magnitudes are much smaller: Aichi's ratio is 1.016 (and its neighboring prefecture, Gifu, has a ratio of 0.977) and Kyoto's is 1.011.

We constructed a variable called "neighbor's density" by assigning the prefectures of the Tokyo area (Tokyo and its immediate neighbors, Saitama, Chiba, and Kanagawa) and the Osaka area (Osaka and its immediate neighbors, Hyogo, Nara, and Wakayama) the average density of their immediate neighbors. For other prefectures, the variable equals its own population density. We expect to find a positive relation between migration and this neighbor variable and a negative relation between migration and own density. This relation would indicate that people do not like to live in dense areas (they have to pay the congestion costs), but like to be close to these areas (so that they get the benefits of a big city).

The functional form that we estimate is

$$m_{it} = a + b \cdot \log(y_{i,t-T}) + c_1 \theta_i + c_2 \pi_{i,t-T} + c_3 \pi_{i,t-T}^{ne} + v_{it}, \qquad (11.10)$$

where v_{it} is an error term, and $\pi_{i,t-T}^{ne}$ is the population density of the surrounding prefectures. To calculate the amenity (weather) variable, we squared the difference between the maximum and average temperatures, added the square of the difference between the minimum and average temperatures, and then took the square root. Hence, this variable measures extreme temperature. A variable similar to the one used for the United States (heating-degree days) was unavailable. We experimented with other weather variables, such as maximum and minimum temperatures and average snowfall over the year. These alternative variables did not fit as well.

Figure 11.11 shows the relation between the average annual migration rate for 1955–87 and the log of income per capita in 1955. The clear positive association (simple correlation of 0.58) suggests that net migration reacts positively to income differentials. An interesting point is that the three outliers at the top of the figure are Chiba, Saitama, and Kanagawa, the prefectures surrounding Tokyo.

Table 11.5 shows the results of estimating migration equations of the form of Eq. (11.10). The first row refers to the average migration rate for the whole period, 1955–90. The coefficient on the log of initial income per capita is 0.0126 (0.0061). As expected, net migration is negatively associated with own density (-0.0049 [0.0022]) and positively associated with neighbor's density (0.0190 [0.0034]). The extreme temperature variable is insignificant.

The next seven rows in Table 11.5 show results for the five-year subperiods beginning with 1955–60. The estimated coefficient on initial income is significantly positive for all subperiods, except for 1975–80, for which the coefficient is positive, but insignificant. The joint estimate is 0.0188 (0.0019), which implies that, other things equal, a 10 percent increase in a prefecture's per capita income raises net in-migration by enough to raise that prefecture's rate of population growth by 0.19 percentage points per year. This result is close to that found for the U.S. states. A test of the stability of the income coefficients over time yields a likelihood-ratio statistic of 18.0, with a p-value of 0.006.

The own-density variable is significantly negative, except for the first subperiod, and the neighbors' density variable is positive for all subperiods (significantly so for four of the seven subperiods). The extreme weather variable is negative, but only marginally significant. Thus, weather does not seem to play an important role in the process of internal migration in Japan.

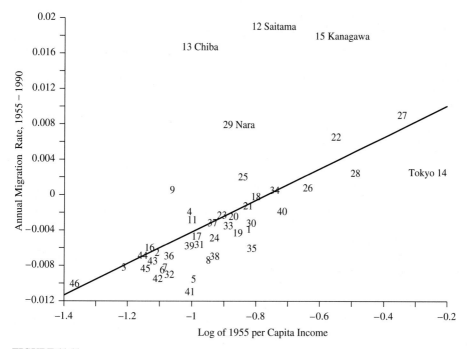

FIGURE 11.11
Migration and initial prefectural income, 1955–1990. The average net migration rate for 47 Japanese prefectures from 1955 to 1990, shown on the vertical axis, is positively related to the log of 1955 per capita income, shown on the horizontal axis. The three prefectures surrounding Tokyo—Chiba, Saitama, and Kanagawa—had substantially higher net migration rates than the values predicted by their initial levels of income.

To summarize, some main findings are that the rate of net in-migration to a prefecture is negatively related to own density and positively related to the density of neighbors. Holding other things constant, migration is positively associated with initial per capita income. A notable result is the similarity of the coefficients on income for the United States and Japan, 0.026 from the joint estimation for the U.S. states and 0.019 from the joint estimation for Japanese prefectures.

Recall that differences in per capita income tend to dissipate at a slow rate, something like 2.5 to 3 percent per year for the Japanese prefectures. Putting this result together with those for migration, the implication is that net migration rates would be highly persistent over time. The data confirm this idea: the correlation between the average migration rate for 1955–70 with that for 1970–90 is 0.60.

11.7 MIGRATION ACROSS EUROPEAN REGIONS

We now estimate the sensitivity of the net migration rate to income across the regions of the five large European countries: Germany, the United Kingdom, Italy, France, and Spain. The dependent variable is the average net migration rate for each of the

TABLE 11.5
Regressions for net migration into Japanese prefectures, 1955–90

Period	Log of per capita income	Extreme temperature	Own population density	Neighbors' population density	$R^2[\hat{\sigma}]$
1955–90	0.0126 (0.0061)	0.00014 (0.00062)	−0.0049 (0.0022)	0.0190 (0.0034)	0.62 [0.0061]
1955–60	0.0216 (0.0036)	−0.00014 (0.00012)	0.0060 (0.0013)	0.0025 (0.0019)	0.85 [0.0038]
1960–65	0.0317 (0.0058)	−0.00014 (0.00012)	−0.0019 (0.0020)	0.0147 (0.0031)	0.74 [0.0071]
1965–70	0.0344 (0.0070)	−0.00014 (0.00012)	−0.0065 (0.0017)	0.0142 (0.0025)	0.71 [0.0066]
1970–75	0.0194 (0.0060)	−0.00014 (0.00012)	−0.0064 (0.0015)	0.0114 (0.0023)	0.53 [0.0070]
1975–80	0.0060 (0.0067)	−0.00014 (0.00012)	−0.0037 (0.0011)	0.0052 (0.0014)	0.32 [0.0043]
1980–85	0.0101 (0.0044)	−0.00014 (0.00012)	−0.0023 (0.0006)	0.0037 (0.0086)	0.39 [0.0030]
1985–90	0.0148 (0.0040)	−0.00014 (0.00012)	−0.0026 (0.0006)	0.0046 (0.0084)	0.56 [0.0029]
Joint, 7 subperiods	0.0188 (0.0019)	−0.00040 (0.00015)	individual coefficients	individual coefficients	— —

Note: The likelihood-ratio statistic for the hypothesis that the income coefficients are the same is 18.0, with a p-value of 0.006. The regressions use iterative, weighted least squares to estimate equations of the form,

$$m_{it} = a_t + b \cdot \log(y_{i,t-T}) + c_1 \cdot temp_i + c_{2t} \cdot \pi_{i,t-T} + c_{3t} \cdot \pi_{i,t-T}^{ne} + c_{4t} \cdot district_i + c_{5t} \cdot S_{it},$$

where m_{it} is the net flow of migrants into prefecture i between years $t - T$ and t, expressed as a ratio to the population at time $t - T$; $temp_i$ is a measure of extreme temperature, calculated as deviations of maximum and minimum temperatures from the average temperature; $\pi_{i,t-T}$ is population density (thousands of persons per square kilometer); $\pi_{i,t-T}^{ne}$ is the population density of the neighboring prefectures (see the text); $district_i$ is a set of dummy variables for the district; and S_{it} is the structural variable described in the text. All samples have 47 observations. (See the note to Table 11.4 for additional information.)

four decades starting in 1950 (see Chapter 10 for a discussion of these data). We are missing observations for the United Kingdom in the 1950s and 1980s and for France in the 1980s.

We estimate a system of regressions similar to those used for the United States and Japan. The explanatory variables are the logarithm of per capita GDP or income at the beginning of the decade, population density at the beginning of the decade, sectoral variables (shares in employment or GDP of agriculture and industry at the start of each decade), a temperature variable, and country dummies. We estimate a system of equations for the five countries, with the density and temperature variables restricted to have the same coefficients over time and across countries, but with the coefficients of the other variables allowed to vary over time and across countries.

TABLE 11.6
Regressions for net migration into European regions, 1950–90, coefficients on the log of per capita GDP

	1950s	1960s	1970s	1980s	Total
Germany	0.0311	0.0074	0.0040	0.0024	0.0076
	(0.0121)	(0.0088)	(0.0038)	(0.0086)	(0.0014)
United Kingdom	—	0.0049	−0.0069	—	−0.0041
		(0.0011)	(0.0013)		(0.0023)
Italy	0.0182	0.0208	0.0089	0.0309	0.0117
	(0.0041)	(0.0027)	(0.0020)	(0.0106)	(0.0018)
France	0.0090	−0.0008	0.0097	—	0.0100
	(0.0056)	(0.0095)	(0.0041)		(0.0036)
Spain	0.0126	0.0135	0.0117	0.0031	0.0034
	(0.0068)	(0.0112)	(0.0063)	(0.0070)	(0.0021)
Overall	0.0107	0.0072	0.0046	0.0141	0.0064
	(0.0038)	(0.0040)	(0.0024)	(0.0070)	(0.0021)

Note: The regressions take the form,

$$m_{ijt} = a_{jt} + b_{jt} \cdot \log(y_{ij,t-T}) + c_1 \cdot \text{temp}_{ij} + c_2 \cdot \pi_{ij,t-T}$$
$$+ c_3 \cdot (\text{country dummy}) + c_{4jt} \cdot \text{AG}_{ij,t-T} + c_{5jt} \cdot \text{IN}_{ij,t-T},$$

where m_{ijt} is the net flow of migrants into region i of country j between years $t - T$ and t, expressed as a ratio to the population at time $t - T$; temp_{ij} is the average maximum temperature; $\pi_{ij,t-T}$ is population density (thousands of persons per square kilometer); $\text{AG}_{ij,t-T}$ is the share of employment or GDP (for the 1980s) in agriculture; and $\text{IN}_{ij,t-T}$ is the share in industry. All estimation is by the iterative, seemingly unrelated procedure. The table reports only the estimates of the coefficients b_{jt}. The numbers in the first five rows and first four columns apply when each country has a different coefficient for each period. The last column restricts the coefficients to be the same over time for each country. The last row restricts the coefficients to be the same across countries for each decade. The number in the intersection of the last row and column applies when all countries and time periods have a single coefficient.

Table 11.6 reports the estimated coefficients on the log of initial per capita GDP or income. The first column contains the estimates for the 1950s, the second for the 1960s, and so on. The last column restricts the coefficients to be the same over the decades. The first row is for Germany, the second for the United Kingdom, the third for Italy, the fourth for France, and the fifth for Spain. The last row restricts the coefficients to be the same for the five countries.

In contrast with the results for the United States and Japan, the coefficients on the log of per capita GDP or income are not precisely estimated for the European countries. For Germany, the estimated coefficient for the 1950s is positive and significant, 0.031 (0.012), whereas those for the other three decades are insignificant. The estimated income coefficients for Italy are significantly positive, but many of those for the United Kingdom, France, and Spain are insignificant.

If we restrict the coefficients to be the same over time, but allow them to vary across countries, then the estimated values are 0.0076 (0.0014) for Germany, −0.0041 (0.0023) for the United Kingdom, 0.0117 (0.0018) for Italy, 0.0100 (0.0036) for France, and 0.0034 (0.0021) for Spain. If we restrict the coefficients to be the same across countries, but allow them to vary over time, then the estimated values are 0.0107 (0.0038) for the 1950s, 0.0072 (0.0040) for the 1960s, 0.0046 (0.0024) for the 1970s, and 0.0141 (0.0070) for the 1980s. Finally, if we restrict the coefficients to be the same across countries *and* over time, then we get 0.0064 (0.0021). Although this estimate is significantly positive, the size of the coefficient is much smaller than the comparable values for the United States (0.026) and Japan (0.019). The main finding therefore is that the migration rate for European regions is positively related to per capita GDP or income, but the magnitude of the relation is weak, and the coefficients cannot be estimated with great precision.

11.8   MIGRATION AND CONVERGENCE

We found in Chapter 9 that the migration of workers with low human capital from poor to rich economies tends to speed up the convergence of per capita income and product. The convergence coefficients estimated in growth regressions would include this effect from migration. In this section, we attempt to estimate the effect of migration on convergence by including the net migration rate as an explanatory variable in the growth regressions. If migration is an important source of convergence— and if we can treat the migration rate as exogenous with respect to the error term in the growth equation—then the estimated convergence coefficient, β, should become smaller when migration is held constant.

We enter the contemporaneous net migration rate in growth regressions in Table 11.7. The first row reports the estimated speed of convergence, β, for the U.S. states. The sample period, 1920–90, is divided into seven ten-year subperiods. The regression includes period-specific coefficients for constant terms, dummies for the four major census regions, and the structural variable discussed before. The coefficient on the log of initial per capita income is constrained to be the same for each subperiod. This setup parallels the joint estimation shown in Table 11.1, column 3, except for the elimination of the two early subperiods.

Column 1 of the table reports the estimate of β when the migration rate is not included in the regressions. The speed of convergence is 0.0196 (0.0025), close to the familiar 2 percent per year. Column 2 adds the net migration rate as a regressor. (The coefficient on this variable is constrained to be the same for each subperiod.) The estimated coefficient on the migration rate is positive and significant, 0.093 (0.030), and the estimate of β, 0.0231 (0.0028), is actually somewhat higher than that shown in column 1. Thus, contrary to expectations, the estimate of β does not diminish when the net migration rate is held constant.

The results are likely influenced by the endogeneity of the net migration rate. Specifically, states with more favorable growth prospects (due to factors not held constant by the included explanatory variables) are likely to have higher per capita growth rates *and* higher net migration rates. We attempt to isolate exogenous shifts in migration by using as instruments the explanatory variables used to explain the net migration rate in Table 11.4. These variables include population density and the log of heating-degree days. (The assumption here is that some of these determinants of migration do not enter directly into the growth equation.) The results, contained in column 3 of Table 11.7, show an insignificant coefficient on the migration rate, -0.006 (0.048), and an estimated β coefficient, 0.0174 (0.0033), that is slightly

TABLE 11.7
Migration and convergence

	(1) Migration excluded	(2) Migration included (OLS)		(3) Migration included (IV)	
	β	β	Migration	β	Migration
United States 1920–90	0.0196 (0.0025)	0.0231 (0.0028)	0.0931 (0.0305)	0.0174 (0.0033)	−0.006 (0.048)
Japan 1955–90	0.0312 (0.0040)	0.0340 (0.0044)	0.0907 (0.0041)	0.0311 (0.0042)	−0.108 (0.112)
Germany 1950–90	0.0243 (0.0088)	0.0240 (0.0091)	−0.014 (0.235)	0.0181 (0.0093)	−0.542 (0.429)
United Kingdom 1960–80*	0.0176 (0.0132)	0.0220 (0.0203)	0.116 (0.395)	0.0261 (0.0267)	0.222 (0.570)
Italy 1950–90	0.0206 (0.0058)	0.0244 (0.0070)	0.166 (0.156)	0.0180 (0.0098)	−0.121 (0.370)
France 1950–80**	0.0224 (0.0265)	0.0172 (0.0063)	−0.038 (0.126)	0.0177 (0.0065)	−0.084 (0.178)
Spain 1950–90	0.0245 (0.0102)	0.0295 (0.0096)	−0.124 (0.102)	0.0268 (0.0119)	−0.068 (0.203)

Note: The regressions for the growth rates of per capita income or GDP are analogous to the joint estimations shown in Table 11.1, column 3 for the U.S. states; Table 11.2, column 3 for the Japanese prefectures; and Table 11.3, column 2 for the European regions (except that the five large European countries are treated separately here). The β coefficients refer to the log of initial per capita income or GDP, and the migration coefficients refer to the net migration rate. In column 1, the migration rate is not included as a regressor. In column 2, the migration rate is added, and the estimation is by OLS. In column 3, instrumental estimation is used. The instruments are the regressors included in the migration equations, as reported in Table 11.4 for the United States, Table 11.5 for Japan, and Table 11.6 for Europe.

*Two subperiods.

**Three subperiods.

lower than that in column 1. These results suggest that migration does not account for a large part of β convergence for the U.S. states.

The second row of Table 11.7 applies the same procedure to Japan. The first column reports the joint estimate of β over seven five-year periods when the migration rate is excluded as a regressor. The estimate of β, 0.0312 (0.0040), is the same as that in column 3 of Table 11.2. When the migration rate is added in column 2 of Table 11.7, the estimated coefficient on migration is positive and similar to that found for the United States, 0.0907 (0.0041), and the estimate of β increases to 0.0340 (0.0044). In column 3, which includes instruments for migration, the estimated coefficient on migration is insignificant, −0.11 (0.11), and the estimate of β, 0.0311 (0.0042), is essentially the same as that in column 1. Hence, as for the U.S. states, migration does not appear to be a major element in β convergence for the Japanese prefectures.

The last five rows of Table 11.7 apply an analogous procedure to the five large European countries. The main findings are similar to those for the United States and Japan in that the estimated β coefficients do not change a great deal when migration rates are held constant. One surprising result here is that the net migration rates are insignificant in the OLS regressions for the European regions, whereas the usual endogeneity story suggests positive coefficients. It may be that the regional net migration rates are not well measured for the European countries, a possibility that would also account for the difficulties in the estimated migration equations in these cases.

A second prediction from the migration theory in Chapter 9 is that economies with higher sensitivity of net migration to per capita income will have higher convergence coefficients, β. To check this possibility, we plot in Fig. 11.12 the estimated β coefficients against the estimated coefficients of the log of per capita GDP or income from the migration equations. The figure has seven data points, corresponding to the United States, Japan, Germany, the United Kingdom, Italy, France, and Spain. The figure shows a weak positive relation between the two coefficients; the correlation is 0.27.[15] The imprecision with which the coefficients in the migration equations are

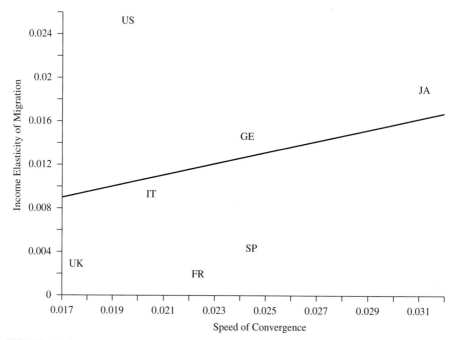

FIGURE 11.12
Income coefficient of migration and speed of convergence. The vertical axis shows the estimated coefficient on the log of per capita income or GDP from migration regressions. The horizontal axis has the estimated β convergence coefficient from growth regressions. The seven data points—for the United States, Japan, Germany, the United Kingdom, Italy, France, and Spain—exhibit a positive relation, as predicted by the theory of migration and growth.

---

[15]The β coefficients for France and the United Kingdom are those estimated over the same subperiods for which the migration data are available. The β coefficient estimated over the full sample is lower for France and higher for the United Kingdom. If we use these alternative estimates of β, then the correlation with the coefficient from the migration equations is slightly higher, 0.32.

estimated for the European countries suggests that this relation should be interpreted with caution. See Braun (1993) for further discussion of this approach.

11.9   CONCLUSIONS

We studied the behavior of the U.S. states since 1880, the prefectures of Japan since 1930, and the regions of eight European countries since 1950. The results indicate that absolute β convergence is the norm for these regional economies. That is, poor regions of these countries tend to grow faster per capita than rich ones. The convergence is absolute because it applies when no explanatory variable other than the initial level of per capita product or income is held constant.

We can interpret the results as consistent with the neoclassical growth model described in Chapters 1 and 2 if regions within a country have roughly similar tastes, technologies, and political institutions. This relative homogeneity generates similar steady-state positions. The observed convergence effect is, however, also consistent with the models of technological diffusion described in Chapter 8.

One surprising result is the similarity of the speed of β convergence across data sets. The estimates of β are around 2–3 percent per year in the various contexts. This slow speed of convergence implies that it takes 25–35 years to eliminate one-half of an initial gap in per capita incomes. This behavior deviates from the quantitative predictions of the neoclassical growth model if the capital share is close to one-third. The empirical evidence is, however, consistent with the theory if the capital share is around three-quarters.

The analysis of migration indicates that the rate of net migration tends to respond positively to the initial level of per capita product or income, once a set of other explanatory variables is held constant. This relation is clear for the U.S. states and the Japanese prefectures, but is weaker for the regions of five large European countries. We also check whether the presence of β convergence in the regional data can be explained by the behavior of net migration. The evidence here is not definitive, but suggests that migration plays only a minor role in the convergence story.

CHAPTER

12

EMPIRICAL
ANALYSIS
OF A CROSS
SECTION
OF COUNTRIES

Growth rates vary enormously across countries over long periods of time. Figure 12.1 illustrates these divergences in the form of a histogram for the growth rate of real per capita GDP for 122 countries from 1965 to 1985.[1] The mean value is 1.8 percent per year, with a standard deviation of 2.1. The lowest decile comprises 12 countries with growth rates below -0.9 percent per year, and the highest decile consists of the 12 with growth rates above 4.5 percent per year. For quintiles, the poorest performing 24 places have growth rates below 0.0 percent per year, and the best performing 24 have growth rates above 3.5 percent per year.

The difference between per capita growth at -1.0 percent per year—the average for the lowest quintile—and growth at 4.8 percent per year—the average for the highest quintile—is that real per capita GDP falls by 18 percent over 20 years in the former case and rises by 161 percent in the latter. Thus, for example, two low-growth countries, Mozambique and Nicaragua, fell from levels of real per capita GDP in 1965 of $1238 and $2081 (1985 U.S. dollars), respectively, to levels of $697 and $1611 in 1985. Over the same period, two high-growth countries, Botswana

---

[1]The GDP data are the purchasing-power adjusted values from version 5.5 of Summers and Heston (1993).

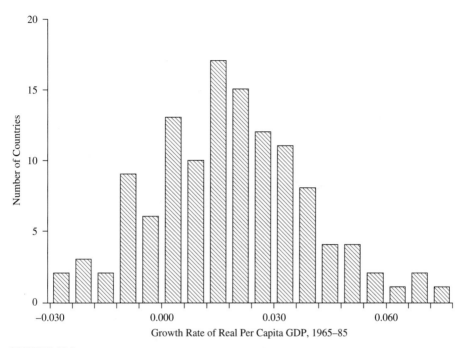

FIGURE 12.1
Histogram for growth rate. The figure shows the number of countries that lie in various ranges for the growth rate of real per capita GDP. The data are from Summers and Heston (1993). For the 122 countries, the mean growth rate is 0.018 per year and the standard deviation is 0.021. The highest growth rate is 0.073 and the lowest is –0.029.

and Korea, rose from $576 and $1035 to $2252 and $4267, respectively. Thus, even over periods as short as 20 years, the variations in growth rates made dramatic differences in the average living standards of a country's residents.

12.1 LOSERS AND WINNERS FROM 1965 TO 1985

Table 12.1 applies to loser countries, the 24 in the lowest quintile of per capita growth rates from 1965 to 1985. The countries are arranged in ascending order of growth rates, as shown in column 2. This group contains 17 countries in sub-Saharan Africa (including the islands of Madagascar and Comoros); four in Latin America (Nicaragua, Guyana, Venezuela, and Chile); and three in other regions (Afghanistan, Iraq, and Papua New Guinea). The table also shows per capita growth rates over three shorter intervals: 1965–75, 1975–85, and 1985–90.[2] The fitted values shown for the various periods will be discussed later.

---

[2] Some of the data for 1985–90 are from World Bank figures, which use market exchange rates to compare across countries.

TABLE 12.1
Details of low-growth countries

Country	(1) In sample?	(2) Growth rate 1965–85	(3) Fitted value 1965–85	(4) Growth rate 1965–75	(5) Fitted value 1965–75	(6) Growth rate 1975–85	(7) Fitted value 1975–85	(8) Growth rate 1985–90	(9) Fitted growth rate 1985–90
Mozambique	no	−0.029	—	−0.007	—	−0.051	—	0.011	—
Chad	no	−0.025	(−0.006)	−0.018	(0.003)	−0.032	(−0.014)	−0.010	—
Uganda	yes	−0.023	−0.019	−0.005	0.009	−0.041	−0.047	0.018	−0.030
Angola	no	−0.021	—	−0.039	—	−0.003	—	—	—
Madagascar	no	−0.019	(0.017)	−0.010	(0.032)	−0.028	(0.002)	−0.020	—
Zambia	yes	−0.017	−0.005	0.012	0.008	−0.046	−0.019	−0.020	−0.023
Nicaragua	yes	−0.013	0.000	0.013	0.022	−0.038	−0.022	−0.056	−0.013
Guyana	no/yes	−0.011	—	0.035	—	−0.056	−0.015	−0.007	−0.020
Zaire	yes	−0.010	−0.002	0.015	0.009	−0.035	−0.013	−0.025	0.042
Venezuela	yes	−0.010	0.019	0.000	0.026	−0.019	0.012	−0.009	0.000
Mauritania	no	−0.009	(0.001)	−0.002	(0.013)	−0.016	(−0.012)	0.000	(−0.003)
Somalia	no	−0.009	(0.002)	−0.002	(0.006)	−0.016	(−0.002)	−0.019	(0.000)
Guinea	no	−0.007	—	−0.010	—	−0.004	—	—	—
Ghana	yes	−0.007	−0.003	0.001	0.032	−0.015	−0.038	0.013	0.021
Niger	yes	−0.006	0.001	−0.001	0.007	−0.012	−0.006	−0.015	0.021
Benin	yes	−0.006	0.003	−0.013	0.002	0.001	0.004	−0.025	0.021
Afghanistan	no	−0.005	—	0.003	—	−0.012	—	—	—
Sierra Leone	no/yes	−0.004	(−0.019)	0.015	(−0.009)	−0.024	−0.029	−0.005	−0.052
Iraq	yes	−0.004	0.002	0.022	0.012	−0.029	−0.009	−0.159	−0.012
C.A.R.	yes	−0.002	0.008	0.007	0.008	−0.011	0.008	−0.015	0.026
Papua N.G.	no/yes	−0.001	—	0.012	—	−0.013	0.001	−0.021	0.030
Chile	yes	0.000	(−0.002)	−0.012	−0.013	0.011	0.009	0.042	0.031
Comoros	no	0.000	—	0.011	—	−0.011	—	−0.026	—
Liberia	yes	0.000	0.017	0.017	0.020	−0.017	0.014	—	0.025
mean		−0.010	0.001	0.002	0.011	−0.022	−0.009	−0.017	0.004
number of observations		(24)	(17)	(24)	(17)	(24)	(19)	(20)	(17)

Table 12.2 provides a parallel treatment of winners; that is, the 24 countries in the upper quintile of per capita growth rates. These countries are arranged in descending of growth rates, as shown in column 2. The winners include six countries in sub-Saharan Africa or neighboring islands (Botswana, Cape Verde, Congo, Lesotho, Seychelles, and Rwanda); one in North Africa (Tunisia); one in Latin America (Brazil); nine in East Asia (Singapore, Korea, Taiwan, Hong Kong, China, Indonesia, Japan, Malaysia, and Thailand); four in western Europe (Malta, Portugal, Norway, and Greece), and two in other regions (Yugoslavia and Syria).

The main regressions discussed below for per capita growth rates apply to two decades, 1965–75 and 1975–85. This analysis can be viewed, in part, as a determination of which characteristics make it likely that a country will end up in the losers or winners lists in Tables 12.1 and 12.2.

The first column of each table indicates whether the country is in the regression sample for growth that we use later: 12 of the 24 low-growth countries are included for 1965-75 and 14 of the 24 for 1975–85, whereas 21 of the 24 high-growth countries are included for both decades. The fitted values for 1965–75 and 1975–85 show how much of the growth rates purport to be explained by the decadal regressions. Numbers shown in parentheses are for countries that were not included in the regressions; these fitted values are based on estimates of missing data on one or more explanatory variables.

For the 20-year period, 1965–85, the average growth rate for the slow growers is -0.010 per year, and the average of the fitted values is 0.001 per year. In contrast, for the fast growers, the average growth rate is 0.048 per year, and the average of the fitted values is 0.039 per year. (It is not surprising that the residuals for the slow growers are typically negative, whereas those for the fast growers are typically positive, because the groups were selected for extreme outcomes on growth rates.) The typical fast grower therefore grew by 5.8 percentage points per year more than the typical slow grower, and 3.8 percentage points of this gap is captured on average by the fitted values. Hence, the fitted values show a wide difference between the slow and fast growers, and it is worthwhile to assess the factors that underlie the differences in the fitted growth rates between the two groups. (For all 87 countries that are included in the regressions for 1965–75 and 1975–85, the correlation between the actual and fitted growth rates for 1965–85 is 0.80.)

Tables 12.1 and 12.2 also show fitted growth rates for 1985–95. The average of these values for the slow growers is 0.004 per year, and that for the fast growers is 0.030 per year. In other words, the model predicts that the average gap between the two groups will decline from 5.8 percentage points from 1965 to 1985 to 2.6 percentage points from 1985 to 1995. Thus, the classification into slow and fast growers, based on outcomes for 1965–85, is predicted to attenuate but to persist to a significant extent.[3] The actual growth rates for 1985–90 averaged -0.017 for the losers,

---

[3]For the 87 countries that were included in the growth regressions for both decades, the correlation of the growth rate for 1965–75 with that for 1975–85 is 0.42. The correlation of the fitted value for 1985–95 with the growth rate for 1965–85 is 0.43. For 86 countries, the correlation of the growth rate for 1985–90 with that for 1975–85 is 0.53 and with that for 1965–75 is 0.36.

TABLE 12.2
Details of high-growth countries

Country	(1) In sample?	(2) Growth rate 1965–85	(3) Fitted value 1965–85	(4) Growth rate 1965–75	(5) Fitted value 1965–75	(6) Growth rate 1975–85	(7) Fitted value 1975–85	(8) Growth rate 1985–90	(9) Fitted growth rate 1985–90
Singapore	yes	0.073	0.056	0.097	0.075	0.049	0.037	0.059	0.029
Korea	yes	0.071	0.071	0.081	0.078	0.061	0.063	0.087	0.072
Botswana	yes	0.068	0.028	0.085	0.046	0.051	0.009	0.055	0.013
Malta	yes	0.064	0.052	0.074	0.073	0.054	0.032	0.053	0.028
Taiwan	yes	0.059	0.050	0.061	0.060	0.057	0.040	0.077	0.045
Hong Kong	yes	0.056	0.048	0.047	0.061	0.065	0.034	0.060	0.026
China	no	0.054	—	0.044	—	0.064	—	0.050	—
Indonesia	yes	0.051	0.035	0.046	0.039	0.055	0.032	0.035	0.032
Cape Verde	no	0.049	—	0.022	—	0.075	—	0.020	—
Japan	yes	0.049	0.043	0.064	0.055	0.034	0.032	0.042	0.036
Malaysia	yes	0.046	0.050	0.047	0.052	0.044	0.049	0.037	0.055
Congo	yes	0.045	0.024	0.046	0.026	0.044	0.021	−0.006	0.025
Lesotho	yes	0.044	0.044	0.062	0.056	0.025	0.032	0.013	0.037
Cyprus	yes	0.043	0.040	0.015	0.044	0.071	0.035	0.046	0.029
Seychelles	no	0.041	—	0.031	—	0.051	—	0.050	—

	(1)	(2)	(3)	(4)	(5)	(6)	(7)	(8)	(9)
Country	In sample?	Growth rate 1965–85	Fitted value 1965–85	Growth rate 1965–75	Fitted value 1965–75	Growth rate 1975–85	Fitted value 1975–85	Growth rate 1985–90	Fitted growth rate 1985–90
Tunisia	yes	0.040	0.036	0.050	0.041	0.030	0.031	0.011	0.040
Rwanda	yes	0.039	0.023	0.059	0.039	0.018	0.007	−0.020	0.009
Thailand	yes	0.039	0.034	0.040	0.046	0.037	0.022	0.075	0.028
Brazil	yes	0.038	0.024	0.064	0.041	0.013	0.007	−0.002	0.007
Yugoslavia	yes	0.038	0.042	0.059	0.049	0.018	0.035	−0.028	0.033
Syria	yes	0.037	0.030	0.060	0.033	0.014	0.027	−0.004	−0.005
Portugal	yes	0.037	0.026	0.059	0.039	0.014	0.013	0.052	0.028
Norway	yes	0.035	0.036	0.035	0.037	0.036	0.035	0.009	0.026
Greece	yes	0.035	0.034	0.053	0.043	0.017	0.025	0.015	0.033
mean		0.048	0.039	0.054	0.049	0.042	0.029	0.033	0.030
number of observations	(24)	(21)	(24)	(21)	(24)	(21)	(24)	(21)	(21)

Notes to Tables 12.1 and 12.2: The countries selected are those in the lowest and highest quintiles for growth rates of real per capita GDP from 1965 to 1985, according to Summers–Heston (1993), version 5.5. The classification "in sample" refers to countries included in the growth regressions for the decades 1965–75 and 1975–85, as discussed later. The designation "no/yes" means that the country is in the second decadal sample but not the first. Growth rates for 1965–85, 1965–75, and 1975–85 are for real per capita GDP, as reported in Summers and Heston version 5.5. The fitted values are from the regressions discussed later. The projected growth rates for 1985–95 are also based on these regressions. The actual growth rates for 1985–90 are from Summers and Heston version 5.5 or the World Bank data files. Figures shown in parentheses are based in part on approximations of missing data.

compared to 0.033 for the winners, so that the actual spread remained at 5.0 percentage points over this period.

12.2   THE EMPIRICAL ANALYSIS OF GROWTH RATES

This section considers the empirical determinants of growth; that is, the regression results that underlie the fitted values shown in Tables 12.1 and 12.2. The sample of 97 countries, listed in the appendix in Table 12A.1, covers a broad range of experience from developing to developed countries. The included countries were determined by the availability of data. The main analysis deals with growth rates over two decades, 1965–75 and 1975–85, and thereby contains a limited amount of time-series variation.

One hypothesis from the Solow–Swan and Ramsey models of Chapters 1 and 2 is absolute convergence: poorer countries typically grow faster per capita and tend thereby to catch up to the richer countries. This hypothesis implies that the growth rate of real per capita GDP from 1965 to 1985 would tend to be inversely related to the level of real per capita GDP in 1965. Figure 12.2 shows that this proposition fares badly in terms of the cross-country data: for 119 countries, the growth rate from 1965 to 1985 is basically unrelated to the log of per capita GDP in 1965. (The correlation is actually slightly positive, 0.17.) Thus, any hope of reconciling the convergence hypothesis with the data has to rely on the concept of conditional convergence. We have to examine the relation between the growth rate and the starting position after holding constant some variables that distinguish the countries.

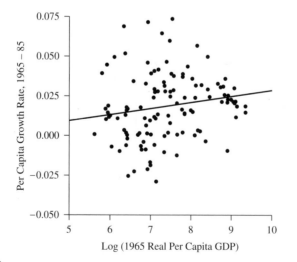

FIGURE 12.2
Per capita growth rate versus initial per capita GDP. The growth rate of real per capita GDP from 1965 to 1985 is plotted against the logarithm of real per capita GDP in 1965. The data are from Summers and Heston (1993). For the 119 countries, the correlation between the two variables is 0.17.

We use an empirical framework that relates the real per capita growth rate to two kinds of variables: first, initial levels of state variables, such as the stock of physical capital and the stock of human capital in the forms of educational attainment and health; and second, control or environmental variables (some of which are chosen by governments or private agents), such as the ratio of government consumption to GDP, the ratio of domestic investment to GDP, the black-market premium on foreign exchange (intended as a proxy for market distortions), movements in the terms of trade, the fertility rate, measures of political instability and the rule of law, the amounts of political freedom and civil liberties, tariff rates, and so on.

One of the state variables that we use is school attainment at various levels, as constructed by Barro and Lee (1993). We use standard U.N. numbers on life expectancy at birth to represent the initial level of health. The available data on physical capital seem unreliable, especially for developing countries and even relative to the measures of human capital, because they depend on arbitrary assumptions about depreciation and also rely on inaccurate measures of benchmark stocks and investment flows. As an alternative to using the limited data that are available on physical capital, we assume that, for given values of schooling and health, a higher level of initial real per capita GDP reflects a greater stock of physical capital per person (or a larger quantity of natural resources).

We can write a function for a country's per capita growth rate in period t, Dy_t, as

$$Dy_t = F(y_{t-1}, h_{t-1}; \ldots), \qquad (12.1)$$

where y_{t-1} is initial per capita GDP and h_{t-1} is initial human capital per person (based on measures of educational attainment and health). The omitted variables, denoted by $\ldots$, comprise an array of control and environmental influences. These variables would include preferences for saving and fertility, government policies with respect to spending and market distortions, and so on.

12.2.1   Effects from State Variables

The Solow–Swan and Ramsey models predict that, for given values of the environmental and control variables, an equiproportionate increase in y_{t-1} and h_{t-1} would reduce Dy_t in Eq. (12.1). That is, because of diminishing returns to reproducible factors, a richer country—with higher levels of y and h—tends to grow at a slower rate. The environmental and control variables determine the steady-state level of output per "effective" worker in these models. A change in any of these variables, such as the saving rate or a government policy instrument, affects the growth rate for given values of the state variables. For example, a higher saving rate or a lower tax rate on capital income tends to increase Dy_t in Eq. (12.1) for given values of y_{t-1} and h_{t-1}.

The model with human and physical capital in Chapter 5 predicts some influences on growth from imbalances between physical and human capital. In particular, for given y_{t-1}, a higher value of h_{t-1} in Eq. (12.1) tends to raise the growth rate.

This situation applies, for example, in the aftermath of a war that destroys primarily physical capital. Thus, although the influence of y_{t-1} on Dy_t in Eq. (12.1) would be negative, the effect of h_{t-1} tends to be positive.

Empirically, we enter the initial level of per capita GDP into the growth equation in the form $\log(y_{t-1})$ so that the coefficient on this variable represents the rate of convergence; that is, the responsiveness of the growth rate, Dy_t, to a proportional change in y_{t-1}.[4] In the basic regressions, the variable h_{t-1} is represented by average years of school attainment at various levels and by the logarithm of life expectancy at birth.

Theories of technological diffusion usually assume that more human capital raises the ability to absorb new technologies. (See Nelson and Phelps [1966].) In the model of Chapter 8, this process would operate if an increase in human capital lowers the cost of imitating the ideas that were discovered elsewhere. This effect means that a higher level of human capital raises the responsiveness of the growth rate to reductions in the initial level of per capita GDP. That is, the speed of convergence— the reaction of Dy_t to $\log(y_{t-1})$—is greater the higher h_{t-1}. We capture this effect empirically by including in the regressions not only the level variables, $\log(y_{t-1})$ and h_{t-1}, but also the interaction term, $\log(y_{t-1}) \cdot h_{t-1}$. (Benhabib and Spiegel [1993] consider an analogous variable.) A negative coefficient on the interaction term means that a higher h_{t-1} speeds up convergence; that is, raises the responsiveness of Dy_t to a fall in $\log(y_{t-1})$.

12.2.2 Control and Environmental Variables

In the basic regression that we consider below, the control and environmental variables are public expenditures on education as a ratio to GDP, denoted by $G\text{-}educ./Y$; the ratio of real gross domestic investment to real GDP, I/Y; the ratio of government consumption (measured net of spending on defense and education) to GDP, $G\text{-}cons./Y$; the black-market premium on foreign exchange; a measure of political instability (a linear combination of revolutions and per capita political assassinations per year); and the growth rate of the terms of trade. We take account of the likely endogeneity of these variables by using lagged values as instruments. These lagged variables may be satisfactory because the error term in the equation for the per capita growth rate turns out to display little serial correlation. (The per capita growth rate is itself not highly serially correlated; for the 87 countries in the main sample, the correlation of the growth rate for 1975–85 with that for 1965–75 is 0.42.)

In the neoclassical growth models of Solow–Swan and Ramsey, the effects of the control and environmental variables on the growth rate correspond to their

---

[4]This identification would be exact if the length of the observation interval for the data were negligible. Suppose that the data are observed at interval T, convergence occurs continuously at the rate β, and all right-hand side variables other than $\log(y)$ do not change over time. In this case, Eq. (2.35) from Chapter 2 implies that the coefficient on $\log(y_{t-T})$ in a regression for the average growth rate, $(1/T) \cdot \log(y_t/y_{t-T})$, is $-(1 - e^{-\beta T})/T$. This expression tends to β as T tends to 0 and tends to 0 as T approaches infinity.

influences on the steady-state position. For example, an exogenously higher value of I/Y raises the steady-state level of output per effective worker; the growth rate, Dy_t, tends accordingly to increase for given values of the state variables. Similarly, a government-induced distortion of markets tends to depress the steady-state level of output per effective worker and thereby reduce the growth rate for given values of the state variables.

In neoclassical growth models, a change in a control or environmental variable affects the steady-state level of output per effective worker, but not the long-term per capita growth rate. The long-run or steady-state growth rate is given by the rate of exogenous technological progress. In contrast, in the endogenous-growth models of Chapters 6 and 7, variables that affect R&D intensity also influence long-term growth rates. However, even in the Solow–Swan and Ramsey models, if the adjustment to the new steady-state position takes a long time—as seems to be true empirically—then the growth effect of a variable such as the investment ratio or a government policy instrument lasts for a long time.

The measures of educational attainment that we use are based on years of schooling and do not adjust for variations in school quality. The educational spending variable, $G\text{-}educ./Y$, is a crude proxy for this quality (although it pertains to the current flow of schooling, rather than to the accumulated stock). We therefore expect to find a positive link between $G\text{-}educ./Y$ and the growth rate for given values of the state variables.

We assume that the variable $G\text{-}cons./Y$ includes expenditures that do not directly affect productivity, but that entail distortions of private decisions. These distortions can reflect the governmental activities themselves and also involve the adverse effects from the associated public finance.[5] A higher value of $G\text{-}cons./Y$ leads to a lower steady-state level of output per effective worker and, hence, to a lower growth rate for given values of the state variables.

We view the black-market premium on foreign exchange as a proxy for market distortions. (The black-market premium is also an attractive variable because it is objectively measurable and widely available.) Thus, we anticipate that a higher black-market premium, like other governmental distortions, lowers the steady-state level of output per effective worker and therefore reduces the growth rate for given values of the state variables.

We view an increase in political instability as equivalent to a decline in the security of property rights. As with an increase in tax rates or other governmental distortions, the worsening of property rights tends to lower the steady-state level of output per effective worker and, consequently, to reduce the growth rate for given values of the state variables. The measure that we use is the average over each decade of the number of revolutions (successful and unsuccessful) per year and the number of political assassinations per million inhabitants. The equal weighting of these two variables is somewhat arbitrary, but does correspond to the regression coefficients

---

[5] We would hold constant the tax effects directly, but the available data on public finance are inadequate for this purpose. See Easterly and Rebelo (1993) for attempts to measure the relevant marginal tax rates.

in a prediction equation for numbers of revolutions.[6] That is, we can interpret the political-instability variable as a measure of the probability of a dislocation in the form of a revolution.

We include also the growth rate over each decade of the terms of trade, where the terms of trade is defined as the ratio of export prices to import prices. We view this variable as determined on world markets and therefore exogenous to the behavior of an individual country. An improvement in the terms of trade raises a country's real income and tends thereby to increase its consumption. An effect on production, GDP, depends, however, on a response of allocations or effort to the shift in relative prices. If an increase in the relative price of the goods that a country produces tends to generate more output, that is, a positive response of supply, then the effect of this variable on the growth rate would be positive. One effect of this type is that an increase in the relative price of oil—an import for most countries—would reduce the production of goods that use oil as an input.

12.3   REGRESSION RESULTS FOR GROWTH RATES

12.3.1   A Basic Regression

Table 12.3 contains the regression results for the growth rate of real per capita GDP. For the basic formulation, 87 countries are included for 1965–75 and 97 countries for 1975–85. Table 12A.2 in the appendix shows the means and standard deviations for the variables that are included in the various regressions. The variables are described in detail in the data set of Barro and Lee (1994).

Column 1 of Table 12.3 shows estimates that are obtained by the seemingly unrelated (SUR) technique. This procedure allows for country random effects that are correlated over time. Note, however, that the correlation of the residuals from the growth-rate equations across the two time periods is small; the AR(1) coefficient in this column is 0.21. This finding applies to the various cases that we consider.

Column 2 is the same as column 1, except that instrumental variables are employed. The instruments comprise some of the original variables and lags of the other variables; lag values are reasonable candidates as instruments because the correlation of the residuals in the growth regressions between the two decades is never substantial. We focus on the instrumental results, as shown in column 2, but indicate the instances in which substantial differences arise from the SUR estimates in column 1.

---

[6]A least-squares regression of average number of revolutions per year for 1975-85 shows an estimated coefficient of 0.45 (0.10) on the 1965–75 value of average number of revolutions per year and 0.47 (0.16) on the 1975–85 number of average political assassinations per million population per year. Alesina and Perotti (1993) use instead a principal-component measure, based on several indicators of political instability.

TABLE 12.3
Regressions for growth rate of real per capita GDP, part 1

	(1)	(2)	(3) INST (difference between coefficients of low & high income groups)	(4)	(5)	(6)
Estimation method	**SUR**	**INST**	**INST**	**INST**	**INST**	**INST**
log(GDP)	−0.0254 (0.0028)	−0.0261 (0.0031)	0.004 (0.0075)	−0.0262 (0.0032)	−0.0267 (0.0031)	−0.0259 (0.0031)
male secondary education	0.0134 (0.0056)	0.0164 (0.0058)	0.011 (0.0243)	0.0223 (0.0068)	0.0164 (0.0058)	0.0172 (0.0061)
female secondary education	−0.0551 (0.0068)	−0.0090 (0.0070)	−0.0202 (0.0295)	−0.0154 (0.0081)	−0.0102 (0.0071)	−0.0098 (0.0082)
male higher education	0.055 (0.029)	0.050 (0.030)	−0.138 (0.174)	0.044 (0.030)	0.053 (0.030)	0.048 (0.031)
female higher education	−0.085 (0.039)	−0.079 (0.040)	0.167 (0.220)	−0.076 (0.041)	−0.071 (0.036)	−0.078 (0.043)
log (life expectancy)	0.058 (0.013)	0.064 (0.014)	0.111 (0.050)	0.048 (0.016)	0.076 (0.015)	0.061 (0.016)
log(GDP)* human capital	−0.315 (0.097)	−0.290 (0.107)	0.168 (0.316)	−0.307 (0.107)	−0.209 (0.097)	−0.309 (0.130)
G-educ./Y	0.062 (0.085)	0.229 (0.109)	−0.309 (0.219)	0.227 (0.114)	0.205 (0.108)	0.234 (0.107)
I/Y	0.074 (0.020)	0.024 (0.025)	0.030 (0.050)	0.022 (0.028)	0.026 (0.026)	0.024 (0.026)
G-cons./Y	−0.060 (0.023)	−0.113 (0.028)	0.070 (0.080)	−0.134 (0.032)	−0.104 (0.028)	−0.118 (0.030)
log(1+black-market premium)	−0.0309 (0.0047)	−0.0299 (0.0083)	0.0502 (0.0181)	−0.0292 (0.0086)	−0.0312 (0.0078)	−0.0314 (0.077)
political instability	−0.0286 (0.0094)	−0.0329 (0.0183)	0.0392 (0.0313)	−0.0324 (0.0182)	−0.0270 (0.0178)	−0.0341 (0.0182)
growth rate, terms-of-trade	0.130 (0.036)	0.108 (0.038)	0.042 (0.076)	0.091 (0.039)	0.112 (0.037)	0.110 (0.039)
male primary education	—	—	—	−0.0035 (0.0030)	—	—
female primary education	—	—	—	0.0046 (0.0032)	—	—
change in male secondary school	—	—	—	—	0.0066 (0.0065)	—
change in female secondary school	—	—	—	—	−0.0128 (0.0083)	—

(continued)

TABLE 12.3 *(continued)*

Estimation method	(1) SUR	(2) INST	(3) INST (difference between coefficients of low & high income groups)	(4) INST	(5) INST	(6) INST
change in male higher school	—	—	—	—	0.018 (0.019)	—
change in female higher school	—	—	—	—	−0.028 (0.034)	—
change in log (life expectancy)	—	—	—	—	—	−0.0001 (0.0009)
R^2 (number of observations)	0.65 (87) 0.54 (97)	0.62 (87) 0.51 (97)	0.66 (87) 0.54 (97)	0.63 (81) 0.50 (96)	0.64 (87) 0.53 (96)	0.62 (87) 0.50 (94)
serial correlation coefficient	0.21	0.21	0.28	0.22	0.16	0.23
p-values for joint hypothesis	—	—	0.08	0.35	0.22	—

TABLE 12.3
Regressions for growth rate of real per capita GDP, part 2

Estimation method	(7) INST	(8) INST	(9) INST	(10) INST	(11) INST	(12) INST
	(0.0033)	(0.0031)	(0.0031)	(0.0031)	(0.0031)	(0.0033)
male secondary education	0.0147 (0.0065)	0.0149 (0.0061)	0.0160 (0.0059)	0.0152 (0.0061)	0.0166 (0.0060)	0.0170 (0.0057)
female secondary education	−0.0027 (0.0084)	−0.0103 (0.0077)	−0.0093 (0.0072)	−0.0103 (0.0079)	−0.0091 (0.0071)	−0.0098 (0.0070)
male higher education	0.026 (0.038)	0.051 (0.033)	0.055 (0.031)	0.038 (0.034)	0.050 (0.030)	0.068 (0.032)
female higher education	−0.011 (0.063)	−0.086 (0.046)	−0.081 (0.041)	−0.084 (0.048)	−0.079 (0.040)	−0.089 (0.040)
log(life expectancy)	0.059 (0.015)	0.047 (0.013)	0.059 (0.015)	0.045 (0.012)	0.063 (0.015)	0.045 (0.015)
log(GDP)* human capital	−0.438 (0.112)	−0.473 (0.151)	−0.328 (0.117)	−0.526 (0.157)	−0.299 (0.107)	−0.321 (0.121)
G-educ./Y	0.178 (0.108)	0.231 (0.104)	0.231 (0.108)	0.235 (0.102)	0.220 (0.108)	0.119 (0.118)
I/Y	0.033 (0.025)	0.016 (0.025)	0.022 (0.025)	0.013 (0.025)	0.025 (0.025)	0.028 (0.023)

(continued)

TABLE 12.3 *(continued)*

Estimation method	(7) INST	(8) INST	(9) INST	(10) INST	(11) INST	(12) INST
G-cons./Y	−0.118 (0.030)	−0.128 (0.029)	−0.118 (0.029)	−0.128 (0.028)	−0.114 (0.028)	−0.101 (0.029)
log(1+black-market premium	−0.0333 (0.0082)	−0.0286 (0.0083)	−0.0283 (0.0085)	−0.0302 (0.0083)	−0.0310 (0.0082)	−0.0292 (0.0084)
political instability	−0.0616 (0.0177)	−0.0230 (0.0178)	−0.0322 (0.0174)	−0.0203 (0.0176)	−0.0353 (0.0186)	−0.0368 (0.0170)
growth rate, terms-of-trade	0.106 (0.037)	0.114 (0.037)	0.114 (0.038)	0.103 (0.037)	0.108 (0.038)	0.114 (0.041)
male secondary enrollment	0.013 (0.012)	—	—	—	—	—
female secondary enrollment	−0.030 (0.021)	—	—	—	—	—
male higher enrollment	0.071 (0.063)	—	—	—	—	—
female higher enrollment	−0.118 (0.095)	—	—	—	—	—
log(FERT)	—	−0.0165 (0.0059)	—	−0.0316 (0.0101)	—	—
growth rate of population	—	—	−0.21 (0.19)	−0.63 (0.33)	—	—
change in population share < 15	—	—	—	—	0.007 (0.075)	—
tariff rate	—	—	—	—	—	−0.0176 (0.0081)
R^2 (number of observations)	0.61 (87) 0.51 (94)	0.62 (87) 0.53 (97)	0.62 (87) 0.52 (97)	0.63 (87) 0.54 (97)	0.62 (87) 0.51 (97)	0.63 (74) 0.58 (82)
serial correlation coefficient	0.30	0.17	0.19	0.18	0.21	0.00
p-values for joint hypothesis	0.21	—	—	0.003	—	—

TABLE 12.3
Regressions for growth rate of real per capita GDP, part 3

Estimation method	(13) INST	(14) INST	(15) INST	(16) INST	(17) INST	(18) INST
log(GDP)	−0.0259 (0.0032)	−0.0286 (0.0033)	−0.0263 (0.0030)	−0.0251 (0.0034)	−0.0274 (0.0031)	−0.0278 (0.0032)
male secondary education	0.0161 (0.0058)	0.0148 (0.0058)	0.0147 (0.0061)	0.0165 (0.0058)	0.0158 (0.0058)	0.176 (0.0058)
female secondary education	−0.0087 (0.0069)	−0.0097 (0.0082)	−0.0075 (0.0077)	−0.0098 (0.0069)	−0.0074 (0.0071)	−0.0098 (0.0069)

(continued)

TABLE 12.3 *(continued)*

Estimation method	(13) INST	(14) INST	(15) INST	(16) INST	(17) INST	(18) INST
male higher education	0.051 (0.029)	0.054 (0.031)	0.059 (0.032)	0.046 (0.029)	0.040 (0.030)	0.061 (0.030)
female higher education	−0.080 (0.039)	−0.063 (0.044)	−0.080 (0.042)	−0.071 (0.038)	−0.076 (0.040)	−0.090 (0.039)
log (life expectancy)	0.064 (0.015)	0.051 (0.013)	0.059 (0.014)	0.063 (0.016)	0.067 (0.014)	0.066 (0.014)
log(GDP)* human capital	−0.275 (0.106)	−0.524 (0.122)	−0.351 (0.106)	−0.235 (0.124)	−0.300 (0.107)	−0.294 (0.097)
G-educ./Y	0.224 (0.108)	0.221 (0.102)	0.189 (0.120)	0.148 (0.110)	0.268 (0.114)	0.226 (0.107)
I/Y	0.023 (0.025)	0.030 (0.025)	0.022 (0.025)	0.034 (0.026)	0.025 (0.025)	0.021 (0.025)
G-cons./Y	−0.112 (0.028)	−0.129 (0.031)	−0.127 (0.031)	−0.117 (0.029)	−0.106 (0.029)	−0.098 (0.029)
log(1+black-market premium)	−0.0300 (0.0083)	−0.0250 (0.0078)	−0.0270 (0.0091)	−0.0214 (0.0086)	−0.0341 (0.0088)	−0.0281 (0.0082)
political instability	−0.0307 (0.0187)	−0.0254 (0.0180)	−0.0363 (0.0170)	−0.0285 (0.0193)	−0.0303 (0.0181)	−0.0327 (0.0177)
growth rate, terms-of-trade	0.106 (0.038)	0.134 (0.037)	0.104 (0.038)	0.148 (0.110)	0.107 (0.037)	0.113 (0.037)
political rights	−0.0008 (0.0015)	—	—	—	—	—
civil liberties	0.0010 (0.0018)	—	—	—	—	—
rule of law	—	0.0042 (0.0011)	—	—	—	—
G-def./Y	—	—	0.001 (0.048)	—	—	—
war dummy	—	—	−0.0061 (0.0039)	—	—	—
public investment/ total investment	—	—	—	−0.0032 (0.0082)	—	—
log(working-age population)	—	—	—	—	0.0018 (0.0011)	—
log(GDP, bordering)	—	—	—	—	—	0.0025 (0.0014)
R^2 (number of observations)	0.63 (87) 0.51 (97)	0.67 (81) 0.60 (88)	0.63 (87) 0.51 (97)	0.63 (83) 0.48 (92)	0.64 (87) 0.51 (97)	0.63 (87) 0.53 (96)
serial correlation coefficient	0.20	0.03	0.20	0.26	0.20	0.21
p-values for joint hypothesis	0.86	—	0.24	—	—	—

TABLE 12.3
Regressions for growth rate of real per capita GDP, part 4

Estimation method	(19) INST	(20) INST	(21) INST (GDP growth rate from World Bank data)	(22) INST (GDP growth and level from World Bank data)	(23) INST uses same sample as [22], with Summers–Heston data	(24) 2SLS (one cross section)
log(GDP)	−0.0235 (0.0033)	−0.0262 (0.0032)	−0.0258 (0.0033)	−0.0141 (0.0023)	−0.0258 (0.0031)	−0.0226 (0.0038)
male secondary education	0.0177 (0.0060)	0.0070 (0.0067)	0.0171 (0.0063)	0.0329 (0.0072)	0.0249 (0.0061)	0.0238 (0.0086)
female secondary education	−0.0093 (0.0071)	0.0026 (0.0084)	−0.0109 (0.0073)	−0.0336 (0.0083)	−0.0165 (0.0075)	−0.0160 (0.0124)
male higher education	0.041 (0.031)	0.056 (0.031)	0.046 (0.030)	0.016 (0.037)	0.038 (0.032)	0.035 (0.046)
female higher education	−0.056 (0.039)	−0.104 (0.043)	−0.078 (0.040)	−0.047 (0.050)	−0.070 (0.042)	−0.047 (0.068)
log (life expectancy)	0.056 (0.016)	0.060 (0.014)	0.082 (0.016)	0.046 (0.014)	0.052 (0.014)	0.051 (0.024)
log(GDP)* human capital	−0.301 (0.110)	−0.407 (0.114)	−0.251 (0.107)	−0.277 (0.092)	−0.416 (0.116)	−0.391 (0.224)
G-educ./Y	0.126 (0.113)	0.178 (0.109)	0.281 (0.118)	0.558 (0.145)	0.332 (0.111)	0.187 (0.196)
1/Y	0.003 (0.029)	0.014 (0.025)	0.037 (0.027)	0.024 (0.035)	0.031 (0.027)	−0.015 (0.044)
G-cons./Y	−0.091 (0.030)	−0.110 (0.027)	−0.070 (0.031)	−0.120 (0.040)	−0.139 (0.031)	−0.096 (0.046)

(continued)

TABLE 12.3 (*continued*)

Estimation method	(19) INST	(20) INST	(21) INST (GDP growth rate from World Bank data)	(22) INST (GDP growth and level from World Bank data)	(23) INST uses same sample as [22], with Summers–Heston data	(24) 2SLS (one cross section)
log(1 + black-market premium)	−0.0281 (0.0080)	−0.0363 (0.0079)	−0.0249 (0.0100)	−0.0452 (0.0097)	−0.0369 (0.0090)	−0.0360 (0.0196)
political instability	−0.0233 (0.0197)	−0.0227 (0.0178)	−0.0239 (0.0190)	−0.0429 (0.0196)	−0.0339 (0.0163)	−0.0709 (0.0458)
growth rate, terms-of-trade	0.143 (0.038)	0.084 (0.037)	0.068 (0.041)	0.025 (0.047)	0.094 (0.038)	0.135 (0.064)
liquid liabilities ratio	0.0157 (0.0071)	—	—	—	—	—
Sub-Saharan Africa	—	−0.0074 (0.0045)	—	—	—	—
Latin America	—	−0.0139 (0.0040)	—	—	—	—
East Asia	—	0.0014 (0.0048)	—	—	—	—
R^2 (number of observations)	0.57 (72) 0.56 (88)	0.63 (87) 0.57 (97)	0.62 (79) 0.47 (92)	0.62 (57) 0.34 (88)	0.74 (57) 0.51 (88)	0.63 (87) —
serial correlation coefficient	0.06	0.12	0.31	0.39	0.47	—

Note: The estimation for column 1 uses the SUR (seemingly-unrelated) technique, which allows the error term to be correlated across the two ten-year periods and to have a different variance in each period. Columns 2–23 modify the SUR procedure to use instrumental variables, as discussed in the text. Column 24 uses two-stage least squares. The dependent variable is the growth rate of real per capita GDP, based on Summers–Heston (1993), except for columns 21 and 22, which use World Bank data to measure the growth rate. The dependent variable is observed for each country (where data are available) for 1965–75 and 1975–85. In column 24, the growth rate refers to 1965–85 on those for 1965–75. Standard errors of coefficients are shown in parentheses. The serial correlation coefficient is the AR(1) value in a regression of the residuals for 1975–85 on those for 1965–75. The p-values for joint hypotheses refer in column 3 to the hypothesis that the coefficients are the same for the two groups of countries and in other columns to the hypothesis that the coefficients of the newly entered variables are all equal to 0.

INITIAL PER CAPITA GDP. The variable log(GDP) is an observation of the log of real per capita GDP for 1965 in the 1965–75 regression and for 1975 in the 1975–85 regression. Earlier values—for 1960 and 1970, respectively—are used as instruments. This instrumental procedure lessens the tendency to overestimate the convergence rate because of temporary measurement error in GDP. (For example, if log[GDP] in 1965 were low due to temporary measurement error, then the growth rate from 1965 to 1975 would tend to be high because the observation for 1975 would tend not to include the same measurement error.)

The estimated coefficient on log(GDP) in column 2, -0.026 (s.e. $= 0.003$), shows the conditional convergence that has been reported in various studies, such as Barro (1991a) and Mankiw, Romer, and Weil (1992). The convergence is conditional in that it predicts higher growth in response to lower starting GDP per person only if the other explanatory variables (some of which are highly correlated with GDP per person) are held constant. The magnitude of the coefficient implies that convergence occurs at the rate of 3.0 percent per year.[7]

EDUCATIONAL ATTAINMENT. The school-attainment variables that tend to be significantly related to subsequent growth are average years of male secondary and higher schooling and average years of female secondary and higher schooling, all observed at the start of each decade, 1965 and 1975. Since these variables are predetermined, they enter as their own instruments in the regressions. The explanatory power for growth rates is greater in this form—which distinguishes years of attainment at the secondary and higher levels—than with an alternative nonlinear specification in terms of total years of schooling. Attainment at the primary level turns out not to be significantly related to growth rates, as discussed later.

The estimated coefficients on male secondary and higher attainment are 0.016 (0.006) and 0.050 (0.030), respectively. A test for the joint significance of the two male schooling variables has a p-value of 0.000; hence, the variables are jointly highly significant. The estimated coefficients mean, for the 1965–75 sample, that a one-standard-deviation increase in male secondary schooling (0.68 years, see Table 12A.2) raises the growth rate by 1.1 percentage points per year, whereas a one-standard-deviation increase in male higher schooling (0.091 years) raises the growth rate by 0.5 percentage points per year.

A puzzling finding is that the initial levels of female secondary and higher education tend to enter negatively in the growth-rate equations; the estimated coefficient is -0.009 (0.007) for secondary and -0.079 (0.040) for higher. Although secondary schooling is insignificant and higher schooling is only marginally significant, a test for the joint significance of the two female schooling variables has a p-value of only 0.007. Thus, the female schooling variables are jointly highly significant. One possible explanation for the negative estimated coefficients is that a large spread between

---

[7]This result uses the formula from footnote 4. The result is correct, however, only if the other right-hand side variables do not change as per capita GDP varies.

male and female attainment is a good measure of backwardness; hence, less female attainment—especially at the higher level—signifies more backwardness and accordingly higher growth potential through the convergence mechanism.

The hypothesis that all four schooling variables do not enter into the growth equation is rejected with a p-value of 0.000. The corresponding p-values for the exclusion of the two secondary-attainment variables is 0.004, whereas that for the two higher-schooling variables is 0.14.

LIFE EXPECTANCY. We measure life expectancy at birth by an average of values prevailing over the five years prior to the start of each decade: 1960–64 in the first case and 1970–74 in the second. (The results are essentially the same if the values reported for 1965 and 1975 are used instead.) The variable is entered in the form log(life expectancy) and is used as its own instrument. This variable is highly significant in the growth regressions; the estimated coefficient is 0.064 (0.014). The result means that a one-standard-deviation increase in life expectancy (which is equivalent to 13 years for 1965–75) is estimated to raise the growth rate by 1.4 percentage points per year.

It is likely that life expectancy has such a strong, positive relation with growth because it proxies for features other than good health that reflect desirable performance of a society. For example, higher life expectancy may go along with better work habits and a higher level of skills (for given measured values of per capita product and years of schooling).

THE INTERACTION BETWEEN GDP AND HUMAN CAPITAL. The interaction term between initial per capita GDP and human capital appears as the initial value of log(GDP) (expressed as a deviation from the sample mean for the relevant decade) multiplied by the sum of the five variables for school attainment and life expectancy (where each variable enters as a deviation from its sample mean). This sum weights each of the five variables by the regression coefficient on the level of the variable. In other words, the concept of human capital that has a direct impact on growth (which can be interpreted in terms of the imbalance effect discussed in Chapter 5) is assumed to be the same as the one that matters for the interaction with initial per capita GDP (which can be viewed in terms of the technological-diffusion effect considered in Chapter 8). The instrumental variables include the values of log(GDP) for 1960 and 1970 (expressed as deviations from sample means) multiplied by each of the human-capital variables (also expressed as deviations from sample means).

The estimated coefficient on the interaction term is significantly negative, -0.29 (0.11). The negative coefficient means that the growth rate is more sensitive to log(GDP) when overall human capital—the total effect from educational attainment and life expectancy—is higher. Quantitatively, if we consider a one-standard-deviation band of the human-capital variable, then the effect of log(GDP) on the growth rate has a range from -0.021 (for relatively low human-capital places) to -0.031 (for relatively high human-capital places), with an average effect of -0.026.

We can relax the constraint that the human-capital variables enter into the interaction term in the same way that they appear as level effects in the growth equation. The regressions were carried out with the coefficients in the interaction term freed up, that is, with four new coefficients to estimate. A likelihood-ratio test (Wald test) of the restrictions yields a statistic of 4.1, which is distributed asymptotically under the null hypothesis as a χ^2 statistic with 4 degrees of freedom. The corresponding p-value is 0.39; hence, the null hypothesis that the human-capital variables appear in the same way in the two parts of the model is accepted at conventional significance levels.

PUBLIC SPENDING ON EDUCATION. The variable *G-educ./Y* is the average value over each 10-year period of the ratio of nominal government spending on education to nominal GDP. The corresponding instrument is the average value of the ratio over the preceding five years (1960–64 and 1970–74). The estimated coefficient in column 2 is significantly positive, 0.23 (0.11). The coefficient means that a one-standard-deviation increase in *G-educ./Y* (by 1.5 percentage points for 1965–75) raises the growth rate by 0.3 percentage points per year. This result can be viewed as modifying the effects from years of schooling to include a rough proxy for the quality of schooling.

INVESTMENT RATIO. The ratio of real gross domestic investment (private plus public) to real GDP, *I/Y*, enters into the regressions as decade averages for 1965–75 and 1975–85. (The data are from Summers and Heston [1993].) The corresponding instrument is the average value of the ratio over the preceding five years (1960–64 and 1970–74). The estimated coefficient in column 2 is positive, but statistically insignificant, 0.024 (0.025). This result provides the most striking contrast with the results from the SUR regression in column 1. In that case, the estimated coefficient on *I/Y* is significantly positive, 0.074 (0.020), as is typical of growth regressions. (See, for example, Levine and Renelt [1992], Mankiw, Romer, and Weil [1992], and DeLong and Summers [1991].)

The results suggest that the principal reason for the positive partial association between growth and investment in column 1 reflects reverse causation from growth to investment, rather than from investment to growth. (Similar conclusions appear in research by Blomström, Lipsey, and Zejan [1993]). In particular, once the other explanatory variables have been held constant, "exogenous" shifts in the investment ratio (that is, shifts captured by the relation of the current investment ratio to the past investment ratio and the other instruments) are not significantly related to growth. The result applies even though lagged investment is a "good" instrument for current investment in the sense that the two are closely related: a regression of the average value of *I/Y* for 1965–75 on a constant and the average of *I/Y* for 1960–64 has an R^2 of 0.82. The corresponding R^2 for a regression of the 1975–85 ratio on the value for 1970–74 is 0.76.

One possible reason for the low explanatory power of *I/Y* for growth is that the measure of investment in the data is inappropriate. In particular, the concept includes public and private spending; we consider later a separation into public and private components, but find that the conclusions do not change very much. In any case, most researchers who detect an important effect of the investment ratio on growth use the same kind of investment data that we employ.[8]

The main reasons that the results about investment differ from some previous findings are, first, we hold constant some additional explanatory variables—notably life expectancy at the start of each period—that turn out to diminish the role of the investment ratio, and, second, we use earlier investment ratios as instruments. If we eliminate the life-expectancy variable from the regressions, then the estimated coefficient (from the instrumental procedure) on I/Y becomes 0.058 (0.026). If, in addition, we use the SUR technique, then the coefficient on I/Y becomes 0.099 (0.020). This last result—in which the t-statistic for the estimated coefficient of I/Y is 4.9—is similar to findings reported by other researchers.

GOVERNMENT CONSUMPTION. The variable G-$cons./Y$ is the average over each decade of the Summers and Heston (1993) ratio of real government consumption to real GDP less the ratio of nominal spending on defense and non-capital expenditures on education to nominal GDP. (We do not have deflators available for spending on defense and education.) The elimination of expenditures for defense and non-capital outlays for education—categories of spending that are included in standard measures of government consumption—was made because these items are not properly viewed as consumption. In particular, they are likely to have direct effects on productivity or the security of property rights. (We have entered total educational spending separately into the growth equation, as already discussed, and we consider later a possible role for defense spending.) The associated instrument for G-$cons./Y$ is the average value prevailing in the five years previous to each 10-year period (1960–64 and 1970–74).

The estimated coefficient of G-$cons./Y$ in column 2, -0.11 (0.03), is significantly negative. The result means that a one standard-deviation increase in G/Y (by 6.5 percentage points in the 1965–75 period) is associated with a fall in the growth rate by 0.7 percentage points per year. It is possible that the estimated effect on growth is so strong because the G-$cons./Y$ variable proxies for political corruption or other aspects of bad government, as well as for direct effects of nonproductive public expenditures and taxation. We discuss later some results that use direct measures of the quality of political institutions; the estimated coefficient on G-$cons./Y$ turns out not to be much affected by the addition of these variables.

BLACK-MARKET PREMIUM ON FOREIGN EXCHANGE. The variable $\log(1 +$ black-market premium$)^9$ is an average for each decade. We think of this variable as a proxy for government distortions of markets, and we therefore expect to find a

---

[8]DeLong and Summers (1991) argue that the producer-durables component of investment is especially important, but they also report significant effects from total investment.

[9]These data are from Wood (1988), updated with information from International Currency Analysis (1991).

negative relation with the growth rate (for given values of the state variables). It is also likely that poor economic outcomes generate changes in policies that could be reflected as changes in the black-market premium. We attempt to isolate the relation between the black-market premium and growth by using the average value of the premium over the preceding five years (1960–64 and 1970–74) as an instrument.

The estimated coefficient of the black-market premium in column 2 is significantly negative, −0.030 (0.008). The black-market premium is zero for countries that had no restrictions on the foreign-exchange rate (24 out of 87 for 1965–75 and 22 out of 97 for 1975–85), and the overall mean is 0.15 for 1965–75 and 0.22 for 1975–85. The estimated effect implies that a one-standard-deviation increase in the variable (by 0.20 in the 1965–75 period) is estimated to reduce the growth rate by 0.6 percentage points per year.

POLITICAL INSTABILITY. The political-instability variable is the average over each decade of revolutions per year and political assassinations per million inhabitants per year.[10] We view this variable as representing the probability of threats to property rights through political turmoil; thus, greater instability lowers the incentive to invest in various activities. We therefore expect that more instability will lower the growth rate for given values of the state variables. It is also likely that lower economic growth increases political instability, an effect stressed by Londregan and Poole (1990). We attempt to isolate the influence of instability on growth by using as an instrument the average value of political instability in the five years prior to each decade.

The estimated coefficient on political instability in column 2 is negative and marginally significant, −0.033 (0.018). An inverse relation between political instability and growth has also been reported in Barro (1991a) and Alesina and Perotti (1993), among others. For many countries, the instability variable takes on the value zero (30 out of 87 in the first decade and 33 out of 97 in the second).[11] Overall, the mean is 0.076 in 1965–75 and 0.097 in 1975–85. The estimated coefficient means that a one-standard-deviation increase in political instability (a rise by 0.12 in the 1965–75 period) lowers the growth rate by 0.4 percentage points per year.

THE TERMS OF TRADE. The growth rate of the terms of trade is viewed as exogenous and therefore enters as its own instrument. The estimated coefficient of this variable in column 2 is significantly positive, 0.11 (0.04). The result means that a one-standard-deviation increase in the growth rate of the terms of trade (by 3.6 percentage points per year in the 1965–75 period) raises the growth rate by 0.4 percentage points per year.

---

[10]The data are described in Banks (1979) and cover the period 1960–85 for most countries. If a country's observations were missing for part of the period (typically for the early years), then we used the average for the years that were available.

[11]For 1965–75, 50 of 87 countries had 0 revolutions and 40 had 0 political assassinations. For 1975–85, 46 of 97 countries had 0 revolutions and 53 had 0 political assassinations.

CONSTANT TERMS. The regressions also include separate constant terms for each decade. One notable result is that the excess of the constant for the first period over that of the second period is 0.013 with a t-value of 5.0. Thus, for given values of the explanatory variables, the estimated growth rate for 1975–85 is lower than that for 1965–75 by 1.3 percentage points per year.[12]

12.3.2   Tests of Stability of Coefficients

Column 3 of Table 12.3 shows results when countries with 1960 per capita GDP below the median ($1500 in 1985 prices) are separated from those above the median. The numbers shown are the differences between the coefficients estimated for the low-income and high-income groups. Standard errors for the differences between the coefficients are shown in parentheses. A likelihood-ratio test (Wald test) of equality for the coefficients of the two groups yields a statistic of 22.0, which is distributed asymptotically under the null hypothesis as a χ^2 variable with 14 degrees of freedom. The p-value is 0.08; hence, the hypothesis that low- and high-income countries can be included together would be accepted at the 5 percent critical level but not at the 10 percent level. This result suggests that it does not do great violence to the data to incorporate a broad range of country experience into a single, simple empirical model.

We can also allow for an array of different coefficients for the two time periods. (In the initial estimation, only the constant terms differed across the periods.) A likelihood-ratio test of the hypothesis that the coefficients (other than the constant), are the same for the two decades yields a statistic of 14.5, which is distributed under the null as a χ^2 variable with 13 degrees of freedom. The p-value is 0.34; hence, the hypothesis of stability in the coefficients over time is accepted at usual significance levels.

12.3.3   Additional Explanatory Variables

Columns 4–20 of Table 12.3 show the effects from some additional explanatory variables, most of which have been proposed by previous researchers.

PRIMARY SCHOOLING. Column 4 adds average years of male and female attainment at the primary level. These variables enter as levels and also in the overall human-capital term that interacts with log(GDP). The estimated coefficients on primary attainment are individually insignificant and are also jointly insignificant (p-value = 0.35). The lack of a role for primary education in the determination of growth is surprising. The small magnitude of the estimated coefficients for years of primary schooling is, however, consistent with the finding that the magnitude found

---

[12]The mean growth rate for each decade also depends on the mean values of the regressors. For the 87 countries included in the regressions for both decades, the average growth rate in the first period exceeds that in the second period by 1.7 percentage points per year.

for more advanced level years of schooling is greater at the higher level than at the secondary level. The result would suggest a convex relation between human capital and years of schooling, except that the signs of the coefficients at the secondary and higher levels are positive only for male attainment.

CONTEMPORANEOUS CHANGES IN SCHOOLING AND LIFE EXPECTANCY. The results discussed thus far include only initial levels of the human-capital variables. Column 5 adds the contemporaneous changes of male and female secondary and higher schooling over each decade. These variables, rather than the initial levels, would appear in growth-accounting exercises (see, for example, Benhabib and Spiegel [1993]). The exogeneity of the growth rates of attainment can be questioned, although they are largely predetermined by prior years of school enrollment. In any event, the results use the changes in years of attainment as their own instruments.

The estimated coefficients in column 5 show the familiar pattern of positive effects for male attainment and negative effects for female attainment. However, none of the estimated coefficients are individually significant, and a joint test for significance has a p-value of 0.22. The result in column 6, which adds the change in the log of life expectancy to the basic regression, shows similarly that the change in this health measure is insignificant. Thus, we cannot detect contemporaneous effects from shifts in the human-capital variables on the growth rate. Benhabib and Spiegel (1993) reached similar conclusions for educational variables. One possible explanation for these findings is that the changes in school attainment and health have too much measurement error—including inaccuracies in the timing of the relation between human capital and production—to isolate the effects.

SCHOOL-ENROLLMENT RATIOS. Column 7 shows the results when male and female secondary and higher school-enrollment ratios are added to the basic regressions. These variables have been used frequently by previous researchers who did not have access to data on stocks of school attainment. In the regression shown in column 7, the enrollment ratios are entered as levels and also as part of the human-capital term that interacts with log(GDP).

The inclusion of the enrollment variables reduces the estimated effect of the attainment variables, but does not otherwise have much effect on the results. The enrollment variables are themselves individually and jointly insignificant; the p-value for the significance of these four variables is 0.21. The point estimates of coefficients show the same pattern as the attainment variables in that the male coefficients are positive, the female coefficients are negative, and the magnitude of the effect from higher schooling is greater than that for secondary schooling.

FERTILITY RATE AND POPULATION GROWTH. Column 8 adds the U.N. measure of total fertility rates (the typical woman's prospective number of live births over her lifetime), a variable that has a negative effect on the steady-state level of output per effective worker in neoclassical growth models with exogenous population growth. In these models, an exogenously higher fertility rate tends to reduce the growth rate of per capita output for given values of the state variables.

The analysis is more complicated in the models of endogenous fertility discussed in Chapter 9. If fertility is higher at given values of per capita income and human capital because people like children more, then the cross-sectional relation between fertility and per capita growth would tend to be negative. In contrast, if higher fertility reflects lower costs of raising children, then the relation could be positive.

Column 8 includes the decade average of the log of the total fertility rate, with the log of the fertility rate at the start of each decade (1965 or 1975) used as an instrument. The estimated coefficient is significantly negative, -0.016 (0.006). The coefficient implies that a one-standard-deviation increase in the fertility rate (in the 1965–75 sample) lowers the per capita growth rate by 0.7 percentage points per year.

Column 9 uses the growth rate of population over each decade instead of the fertility rate. This variable enters as its own instrument. The estimated coefficient is negative, but statistically insignificant.

Column 10 includes simultaneously the fertility rate and the growth rate of population. The estimated coefficient on fertility is significantly negative, whereas that on the population growth rate is significantly positive. For given fertility, a higher population growth rate signals higher net immigration or lower mortality, elements that would plausibly be positively related to growth. (Population growth would, however, also depend on age structure and the ages at which mothers typically have children.)

Column 11 includes as an alternative demographic variable the change in the share of the population that is under age 15 (from U.N. data). An increase in this share would be expected to lower the per capita growth rate partly because of the increase in the number of persons of nonworking age and partly because the work effort of adults would be directed more toward child rearing. (These effects have been stressed by Sarel [1992].) The population-share variable turns out, however, to be statistically insignificant in the regressions.

TARIFF RATE. Lee (1993) estimated growth equations that included a measure of tariff rates on capital goods and intermediate products. Column 12 includes this variable, which is observed only for the single year 1980 for each country. The variable serves as its own instrument, mainly because we have available no satisfactory instruments. The estimated coefficient is significantly negative. (Because of the limited availability of the tariff-rate data, the sample is reduced to 74 countries in the first period and 82 countries in the second period.) This result brings out another channel through which distortions of markets can reduce the growth rate.

We also considered the effects of nontariff barriers, as measured by the United Nations (basically by counting lines of regulations). This measure, available only for 1980, turned out to be insignificantly related to the growth rate.

DEMOCRACY. We have already included government-policy variables that relate to spending on education and consumption, market distortions, and political instability. Governments can also influence economic performance by altering the extent of democratic rights, such as freedom of speech and the press, freedom to run for office and vote, and so on. Gastil (1987 and other issues) provides measures since 1972 of these kinds of civil liberties and political rights in the form of subjective indexes for each country from one (most freedom) to seven.

Column 13 adds to the regressions the indexes for political rights and civil liberties. (The value for the first decade refers to 1972–74, and the value for the second decade to 1975–85.) These variables are used as their own instruments, although the exogeneity of political freedoms and civil liberties with respect to economic growth can be questioned. The result is that the variables are individually and jointly insignificant (p-value = 0.86). Thus, once the other explanatory variables are held constant, variations in political freedoms and civil liberties are not systematically related to the rate of economic growth. If one wants to argue that democracy is good for growth, then the channel of effects has to operate indirectly from democracy to some of the independent variables, such as educational attainment and market distortions.

THE RULE OF LAW AND THE QUALITY OF POLITICAL INSTITUTIONS. The Gastil (1987) data do not refer specifically to economic freedoms, such as aspects of government that directly affect property rights or the ability to carry out business transactions. Knack and Keefer (1994) have compiled information on these aspects of government from the International Country Risk Guide, a publication by a private firm that provides consulting services to international investors. The data are subjective measures of the quality of political institutions with respect to implications for the riskiness of investments. Although the data represent only the informed opinions of experts, one argument for their reliability is that clients are willing to pay substantial fees to acquire the information.

Data from the International Country Risk Guide are available for 111 countries on five measures of institutional quality,[13] described in the appendix to Knack and Keefer's paper as follows: *rule of law* (the extent to which institutions provide effectively for implementation of laws, adjudication of disputes, and orderly succession of power); *corruption in government* (related to the frequency of bribes in areas such as international trade, taxation, and police protection); *quality of the bureaucracy* (including the degree of autonomy from political pressure); *expropriation risk* (assessment of risks of outright confiscation and forced nationalization); and *repudiation of contracts by government* (including risks of repudiation or modification due to changes in government). The first three variables are measured on a scale of

---

[13] Knack and Keefer (1994) also provide information from a second source, Business Environmental Risk Intelligence, but for only 55 countries. These data do, however, go back to the early 1970s. Wheeler and Mody (1992) and Mauro (1993) use data from a third firm, Business International. This source has observations for 68 countries in the 1980s. Less complete information is available for the 1970s for 57 countries.

0 to 6, with 6 indicating the most favorable environment. The final two variables are on a scale of 0 to 10, with 10 the most favorable. The data used by Knack and Keefer are for the earliest year of availability, usually 1982, but for some countries it is 1984 or 1985. It would be possible to assemble time-series information, but only starting in the early 1980s.

The Knack–Keefer variable that turns out to have the most explanatory power for growth in our framework is the measure of the rule of law. Since only the single observation from the early 1980s is available for each country, the same value of the variable is used for the 1965–75 and 1975–85 periods, and the variable is used as its own instrument. The estimated coefficient, shown in column 14 of Table 12.3, is positive and significant: 0.0042 (0.0011). This coefficient means that an increase in the measure of the rule of law by one standard deviation (a rise by 2 along the scale from 0 to 6) raises the growth rate by 0.8 percent per year.

The inclusion of the rule-of-law variable does not have a large effect on most of the other estimated coefficients. For variables that might proxy for the effectiveness of government, the impacts on the estimated coefficients of G-cons./Y and the black-market premium variable are minor, but the estimated coefficient on political instability falls in magnitude.

If the rule-of-law variable is included, then none of the other Knack–Keefer variables from the International Country Risk Guide are statistically significant. If the corruption measure is added, then its coefficient is -0.0002 (0.0013),[14] while that on rule of law becomes 0.0042 (0.0012). For quality of the bureaucracy, the coefficient is 0.0017 (0.0018), while that on rule of law is 0.0028 (0.0016). In this case, the high correlation (0.92) between the two explanatory variables causes both estimated coefficients to be individually insignificant. For risk of expropriation, the coefficient is -0.0014 (0.0012), and that on rule of law is 0.0053 (0.0014). Finally, for risk of repudiation, the coefficient is -0.0013 (0.0012), and that on rule of law is 0.0049 (0.0013).

We would like to interpret the coefficient on the rule-of-law variable as an estimate of the effect of the legal and political framework on the growth rate. The results might, however, reflect the reverse impact of growth on the propensity to maintain the rule of law. We do not have good instruments available—not even earlier values of the rule-of-law variable—to make this distinction. One finding, however, is that the results are similar in separate estimations for the two decades, 1965–75 and 1975–85. The estimated coefficient on the rule-of-law variable is 0.0059 (0.0017) for the first period and 0.0063 (0.0027) for the second period. Since the variable applies to the early 1980s, we would have anticipated different effects for the two periods if the main direction of causation were from growth to the maintenance of the rule of law, rather than vice versa. Thus, the results provide some indication that a better legal and political framework is conducive for growth.

---

[14]The theoretical effect of corruption is unclear; in some cases, the economy would operate more efficiently if governmental rules can be readily overcome by cash payments. See Shleifer and Vishny (1993) for a theoretical discussion.

WAR AND DEFENSE EXPENDITURES. We have already discussed the growth effects of political instability, measured by revolutions and political assassinations. Economies are also affected, usually adversely, by wars and threats of conflicts with other countries. It is difficult to get accurate measures of war intensities for lots of countries, and we use here a variable that is a dummy for countries that participated in at least one external war over the period 1960–85 (see Barro [1991b]). For the 87 countries in the 1965–75 sample, 39 percent of the countries were involved in at least one war.

We also add to the regressions the average ratio of nominal defense expenditures to GDP over each decade. This variable, denoted $G\text{-}def./Y$, reflects the pressures from actual and threatened military conflicts and, in this respect, would be expected to have a negative relation with growth for given values of the state variables. An exogenous increase in $G\text{-}def./Y$—that is, one not related to greater military threats from neighbors—might, however, generate an increase in national security. In this case, the improvement in property rights would tend to favor economic growth. Thus, the overall effect of $G\text{-}def./Y$ on the growth rate is ambiguous.

Column 15 shows the results when the war dummy and $G\text{-}def./Y$ are included in the regressions. Earlier values of the defense-spending ratio (for 1960–64 and 1970–74) are used as instruments (and the war dummy enters as its own instrument). The result is that the estimated coefficient of $G\text{-}def./Y$ is essentially 0, whereas that on the war dummy is negative, but not statistically significant (-0.0061 [0.0039]). We think that the failure to isolate important growth effects from external wars involves the poor quality of the data, rather than the unimportance of war.

PRIVATE VERSUS PUBLIC INVESTMENT. As already mentioned, the investment ratio, I/Y, is based on the standard concept of investment from international systems of accounts, a concept that includes public and private expenditures. One possibility is that the failure to detect important positive effects of investment on growth in column 2 is that the productivity of public investment differs from that of private investment.

We have some information on the breakdown of investment into public and private parts, but the data are problematic in several respects. First, the concept of public is not precise, and the standard measures classify most capital expenditures of public enterprises as private investment.[15] Second, the coverage across countries is incomplete and begins in most places only in 1970. Finally, we lack deflators for the components of public and private investment that are comparable to the Summers-Heston deflators for total investment.

We have constructed the average ratio of public to total investment for the two sample periods, 1965–75 and 1975–85. For the 1965–75 period, we have to rely

---

[15] Easterly and Rebelo (1993) consider in detail the breakdown of public investment into its various components. They find that expenditures on transport and communications are positively related to growth. Using U.S. time-series data, Aschauer (1985) argues that this kind of infrastructure investment enhances productivity.

on the information on public investment for 1970–75. Also, the procedure assumes implicitly that the deflators for public and private investment are the same. Table 12A.2 shows that the mean ratio of public to total investment is 0.29 for the first decade and 0.35 for the second decade.

Column 16 includes the ratio of public to total investment in the regressions. Since we lack information prior to 1970, we cannot use prior values of this ratio as instruments (at least for the 1965–75 sample). The results shown in column 16 use the ratio of public to total investment in each period as its own instrument. The estimated coefficient is statistically insignificant, −0.003 (0.008). Also, the estimated coefficient on I/Y, 0.034 (0.026), is only slightly higher than that shown in column 2. Thus, the division of investment into public and private components does not materially affect the results.

SCALE EFFECTS. The theories of endogenous growth developed in Chapters 6–8 imply some benefits from larger scale. In particular, if there are significant setup costs at the country level for inventing or adapting new products or production techniques, then larger economies would, on this ground, perform better. We test for the existence of this countrywide scale effect by adding to the regressions the log of the working-age population (total population less those under 15 or 65 and older).[16] Since we hold fixed the log of initial per capita GDP and the measures of human capital for the average person, this population variable would have a positive effect on growth if the scale effect at the country level is important. The variable log(working-age population) pertains to the start of each decade (1965 and 1975) and enters as its own instrument.

Column 17 shows that the estimated coefficient is positive, 0.0018 (0.0011), but not statistically significant at usual critical levels. The magnitude of the coefficient means that a one-standard-deviation increase in working-age population (an increase in the log of population by 1.4 in the 1965–75 period) would raise the per capita growth rate by 0.2 percentage points per year. Thus, the cross-country data are consistent with a weak positive linkage between scale and per capita growth, but this relation would not account for much of the cross-country variation in growth rates.

SPILLOVER EFFECTS FROM NEIGHBORING COUNTRIES. Chua (1993) has argued that countries can benefit from increased economic activity in their close geographical neighbors. The benefits could come from increased supplies of technological knowledge, managerial talent, skilled labor, and capital. Examples that have been offered include the role of South Africa in Botswana, Lesotho, and Swaziland, and the effects of Hong Kong on southern China. (Ades and Chua [1993] also point out that the spillover effects can be negative if they involve military threats and the spread of political instability.)

---

[16]We use this measure because the data on labor force have major problems of measurement, especially for the poorer countries. The results are essentially the same if we use total population instead of working-age population.

We measure the economic effect from geographic neighbors in column 18 by adding the weighted average of the log of per capita GDP for a country's immediate geographical neighbors. The variable pertains to 1965 for the first period and to 1975 for the second, and the instruments employed are the values for 1960 and 1970. The result is that the estimated coefficient is positive and marginally significant, 0.0025 (0.0014). Quantitatively, the result means that a one-standard-deviation increase in the log(GDP) of bordering countries (by 1.3 in 1965) raises the growth rate by 0.3 percentage points per year. Thus, this finding provides some support for the spillover effect proposed by Chua.

THE STATE OF FINANCIAL DEVELOPMENT. King and Levine (1993) have stressed the beneficial effects on investment and growth from the existence of sophisticated financial markets. To a large extent, however, the development of these markets is endogenous in the sense of being a regular part of the process of economic growth. Improvements in transportation, communications, and other sectors are similar in this context. It is possible, however, that exogenous variations in the financial sector play a special role in the growth process.

Column 19 adds one of King and Levine's preferred proxies for the state of financial development, the ratio of a measure of liquid liabilities to GDP. The regressions include the average of this ratio over each decade, and the instruments are the values of the ratio at the start of each decade. The result is that the estimated coefficient is significantly positive, 0.016 (0.007). (Note that data limitations on the financial variable reduce the sample size to 72 countries in the first decade and 88 countries in the second decade.) The coefficient means that a one-standard-deviation increase in the liquid/liabilities ratio (by 0.26 in the 1965–75 period) raises the per capita growth rate by 0.4 percentage points per year.

It is unclear whether the relation between growth and financial sophistication isolates the effect of an exogenous improvement in the financial system on the growth rate, or, in reverse, reflects the impact of good growth prospects on the incentive to develop the financial sector. This reverse-causation story works if growth rates are, to some extent, predictable by agents from information that is not included in the regressions. This type of argument could, however, also have been raised in the context of some of the other results.

REGIONAL DUMMY VARIABLES. Column 20 includes regional dummy variables for sub-Saharan Africa, Latin America, and East Asia. The interpretation of the estimated coefficients on these variables is somewhat problematic, however, because the choice of which regions to assign dummies is endogenous. Basically, we selected regions for which previous researchers have observed that growth rates are surprisingly low or high. (For the countries included in the regressions, the average per capita growth rate in sub-Saharan Africa is 0.008 below the mean in 1965–75 and 0.013 below the mean in 1975–85. The corresponding values for Latin America are 0.006 and 0.014. For the East Asian countries, the average per capita growth rate is 0.027 above the mean in 1965–75 and 0.026 above the mean in 1975–85.) In any case, our perspective is that, if we have already included enough explanatory variables to explain why growth was below expectations in sub-Saharan Africa and Latin America and above expectations in East Asia, then the estimated coefficients of the dummy variables would differ insignificantly from 0.

In column 20, the estimated coefficient of the Latin American dummy is significantly negative, -0.0139 (0.0040), that for sub-Saharan Africa is negative but not significant at usual critical values, -0.0074 (0.0045), and that for East Asia is positive but insignificant, 0.0014 (0.0048). Thus, the included regressors explain well the strong growth performance in East Asia and also do reasonably well in accounting for the weak performance in sub-Saharan Africa.

One possibility is that part of the slow growth in Latin America reflects adverse effects of government policies, such as corruption and market distortions, that have not been adequately captured by the other variables that are included in the regressions. If the rule-of-law variable (see column 14) is included along with the continent dummies, then the Latin-America dummy becomes smaller in magnitude (-0.0102 [0.0037]) but remains statistically significant. The other continent dummies are still insignificant in this case (-0.0041 [0.0045] for sub-Saharan Africa and -0.0011 [0.0044] for East Asia).

12.3.4 World Bank Data on GDP

The results described thus far use the Summers–Heston (1993) data to compute levels and growth rates of real GDP. This source attempts to adjust for cross-country differences in the cost of living by using observed prices of goods and services (see Chapter 10 for a discussion). An alternative, more standard, procedure uses domestic GDP figures and market exchange rates to compare the values of GDP across countries. The nature of the Summers–Heston calculations implies that the differences between the two approaches will be more substantial for comparisons of levels of real GDP than for comparisons of growth rates over ten- or twenty-year periods.

Column 21 shows the results in the form of the basic regressions when the dependent variable, the growth rate of real per capita GDP, is computed from World Bank figures that rely on domestic data. A comparison of column 21 with column 2 shows that, although the sample of countries differs somewhat, the results on estimated coefficients are essentially the same. Thus, as anticipated, the two approaches to measuring GDP do not differ materially with respect to the computation of growth rates over the two decades. (The correlation between the World Bank and Summers–Heston per capita growth rates for 79 countries for 1965–75 is 0.90, whereas that for 92 countries for 1975–85 is 0.95.)

Column 22 shows the results when the World Bank's exchange-rate based figures on GDP are used to measure the independent variable, log(GDP). (The alternative measure of log[GDP] appears as a level variable and also in the interaction term with the human-capital variables.) The Summers–Heston data continue to be used, however, in the construction of the ratio variables I/Y and G-cons./Y.

The estimated coefficients in column 22 indicate some substantial differences from those in column 2, which are based on the Summers–Heston data. Since the sample of countries in column 2 differs from that in column 21, we can isolate the effects from the change in the measure of GDP by refitting the equations with the Summers–Heston data, but with the sample the same as the one used in column 22. These results are in column 23: the only difference between columns 22 and 23 is that the former uses World Bank data on GDP, whereas the latter uses Summers–Heston data. (The results in column 23 are, in any case, similar to those in column 2.)

The most striking difference between columns 22 and 23 is that the estimated coefficient on log(GDP)—which determines the rate of convergence—is much smaller in magnitude when World Bank data are used: 0.014 versus 0.026. The estimated coefficient is highly significant in either case—the "t-statistic" is 6.1 in column 22 and 8.3 in column 23—but the Summers–Heston figures show nearly twice the rate of convergence.

The likely explanation for the different estimates is that poor countries tend to have relatively low prices for nontraded goods; that is, for poor countries, the Summers–Heston price deflator for GDP tends to be low relative to the market exchange rate. This pattern means that the World Bank GDP figures (based on exchange rates) show much greater cross-sectional variation. For instance, for the 79 countries included for the 1965–75 sample in column 21, the standard deviation of the log of Summers–Heston GDP is 0.97, whereas that for the World Bank is 1.41 (see Table 12A.2). Similarly, for 92 countries for 1975–85, the standard deviations are 0.96 and 1.45, respectively. The greater spread in the World Bank data accounts for the smaller magnitude of the estimated coefficient on log(GDP) in column 22 than in column 23.

We can also include simultaneously as regressors the values of log(GDP) from Summers–Heston and the World Bank. If we use the World Bank version of the growth rate to measure the dependent variable, then the result is that the estimated coefficient on the World Bank log(GDP) is -0.001 (0.003), whereas that on the Summers–Heston log(GDP) is -0.026 (0.005).[17] The results are virtually the same if the Summers–Heston version of the growth rate is the dependent variable; the estimated coefficients are then 0.004 (0.003) for World Bank log(GDP) and -0.029 (0.005) for Summers–Heston log(GDP). Thus, in either case, the regressions strongly prefer the Summers–Heston version of the level of real GDP. These results therefore provide indirect evidence that Summers and Heston have actually succeeded in obtaining more accurate representations of each country's per capita output.

12.3.5   Results from a Single Cross Section

Column 24 replicates the framework from Barro (1991a) in that the data consist of only a single cross section of countries. The growth rate applies to 1965–85, the state variables—for initial GDP and the human-capital variables—still pertain to

---

[17]The regressions also include two interactions terms with the human-capital variables, one based on World Bank log(GDP) and the other based on Summers–Heston log(GDP).

the start of the sample, and the other variables are averages from 1965 to 1985. The instruments are the same as those used before for the 1965–75 sample, primarily averages of observations from 1960 to 1964 (or the value in 1960 in the case of log[GDP]).

The estimated coefficients in column 24 are similar to those estimated for the two decades in column 2. The main difference is that the standard errors of the estimated coefficients tend to be greater with the single cross section, because of the loss of information.

The magnitude of the estimated coefficient on the log of initial GDP is 0.0226 (0.0038) in column 24, compared with 0.0261 (0.0031) in column 2. The value from column 24 corresponds to growth rates averaged over 20 years, whereas that from column 2 corresponds to growth rates averaged over 10 years. Therefore, the theory predicts that the estimated coefficient would be smaller in magnitude in column 24 than in column 2 (see the formula in footnote 4). In fact, both estimates imply a rate of convergence of 3.0 percent per year (see footnote 7).

12.4 SOURCES OF GROWTH FOR SLOW AND FAST GROWERS

The basic equation in column 2 of Table 12.3 is the source of the fitted values for 1965–75 and 1975–85 for the slow and fast growers that are shown in Tables 12.1 and 12.2. The fitted growth rates for 1985–95 come from the same estimated model, where the values of the explanatory variables are those applying in 1985 for log(GDP) and secondary and higher schooling; as averages for 1980–84 for log(life expectancy), *G-educ./Y*, and political instability; and as averages for 1985–89 for *I/Y* and *G-cons./Y*. The growth rate of the terms of trade is the fitted value based on the experience for 1975–85. (The results for 1965–75 and 1975–85 show that this growth rate exhibits significantly positive serial correlation.)[18] We already noted that the fitted values for 1965–75 and 1975–85 explain a substantial part of the observed differences in per capita growth rates between the slow and fast growers. Therefore, although the remaining residual errors in individual country growth rates are also substantial, it is worthwhile to examine the differences in the explanatory variables that generate the differences in the fitted growth rates.

We can break down the fitted values of growth rates into the contributions from each of the explanatory variables that appear in the basic model shown in Table 12.3, column 2. This exercise provides a form of growth accounting in which the determining variables are, unlike the growth rates of factor inputs, arguably exogenous influences. One observation from this exercise is that the fitted growth rates depend on the combined influence of several factors, rather than from one or two key

---

[18]The fitted growth rates for 1985–95—but not the deviations of these values from sample means—also depend on the constant term. We used the average of the constants estimated for 1965–75 and 1975–85 to construct the fitted growth rates shown in Tables 12.1 and 12.2. The subsequent discussion deals with deviations from means and therefore does not depend on the constant term.

elements. To bring out some general tendencies, we combine the results into regional groups of slow- or fast-growing countries in Table 12.4. The contributions of the explanatory variables to the fitted growth rate are averaged for five groups. For the slow growers (from Table 12.1), we examine 17 sub-Saharan African countries and 4 Latin American countries. For the fast growers (from Table 12.2), we consider six sub-Saharan African countries, nine East Asian countries, and four western European countries.

To ease the presentation, Table 12.4 combines the contributions from the initial values of log(GDP), male and female secondary and higher schooling, life expectancy, and the interaction term between log(GDP) and the human-capital variables into a net convergence effect. That is, this variable shows the contribution to the fitted growth rate (as a deviation from the sample mean) for initial per capita GDP, when conditioned on the initial values of human capital per person. The table shows separately the contributions to the fitted growth rate from *G-educ./Y*, *I/Y*, *G-cons./Y*, the black-market premium, political instability, and the growth rate of the terms of trade. The sum of the individual contributions gives the fitted growth rate (as a deviation from the sample mean), as shown in the next to last column of the table. The final column shows the actual average growth rate for the group (also as a difference from the sample mean).

Begin with the 17 slow-growing sub-Saharan African countries in the period 1965–75. The net convergence effect is close to 0; that is, the positive effect on growth from the low starting value of per capita GDP is roughly canceled on average by the negative effects from low school attainment and life expectancy. The negative value for fitted growth (relative to the sample mean) of −0.019 reflects the contributions from high government consumption (−0.010), low investment (−0.003), low educational spending (−0.002), and moderate distortions as reflected in the black-market premium (−0.002). The average of the actual growth performance, −0.032, is worse than that indicated by the fitted value.

In the 1975–85 decade, the net convergence term becomes positive (0.003), because levels of per capita GDP fell in the previous decade in relation to school attainment and life expectancy. The negative contributions from *G-cons./Y*, *I/Y*, and *G-educ./Y* are about the same as in the previous period, but the black-market premium becomes much more adverse (−0.014). This change likely reflects an increase in governmental distortions. Political instability also becomes a negative contributor (−0.003). Note, however, that contrary to some popular views about the situation in sub-Saharan Africa, the terms-of-trade variable is not an important element in either decade. The overall fitted growth rate for 1975–85 is −0.027 (relative to the sample mean), which conforms well with the actual value of −0.033.

For 1985–95, the convergence term becomes even more favorable (0.009), and the black-market premium becomes less adverse (−0.008). The overall fitted value of −0.014 compares to an actual value for 1985–90 of −0.020.

The clearest contrast for the group of 14 slow-growing sub-Saharan African countries is the group of 9 fast-growing East Asian economies. Table 12.4 shows that the contribution from the net convergence term is substantially positive (0.021) for the East Asian group in 1965–75. In other words, although the fast-growing East Asian countries began in 1965 with higher per capita GDP than the slow-growing

TABLE 12.4
Sources of growth for groups of countries

Group	Period	Convergence effect (net)	G − educ./Y	I/Y	G − cons/Y	Black-market premium	Political instability	Terms of trade	Fitted growth	Actual growth
17 sub-Saharan African slow growers	1965–75	−0.001	−0.002	−0.003	−0.010	−0.002	−0.001	−0.001	−0.019	−0.032
	1975–85	0.003	−0.002	−0.003	−0.009	−0.014	−0.003	0.001	−0.027	−0.033
	1985–95	0.009	−0.002	−0.002	−0.008	−0.008	−0.004	0.000	−0.014	−0.020
4 Latin American slow growers	1965–75	−0.014	0.000	0.000	−0.001	−0.008	0.001	0.003	−0.020	−0.021
	1975–85	−0.002	0.001	−0.001	−0.002	−0.008	−0.003	−0.002	−0.016	−0.037
	1985–95	0.006	0.002	0.000	−0.001	−0.025	−0.002	−0.001	−0.019	−0.018
6 sub-Saharan African fast growers	1965–75	0.020	0.002	−0.001	−0.005	0.000	−0.001	−0.002	0.012	0.021
	1975–85	0.007	0.004	0.000	−0.008	0.001	0.000	0.002	0.005	0.033
	1985–95	0.002	0.004	0.000	−0.009	0.004	0.001	0.004	0.005	0.008
9 East Asian fast growers	1965–75	0.021	−0.001	0.001	0.004	0.003	0.001	0.000	0.028	0.028
	1975–85	0.013	−0.002	0.002	0.006	0.006	0.001	0.000	0.027	0.040
	1985–95	0.004	−0.001	0.002	0.006	0.007	0.002	0.000	0.020	0.048
4 European fast growers	1965–75	0.008	0.000	0.003	0.003	0.004	0.000	−0.001	0.018	0.025
	1975–85	0.002	0.000	0.002	0.003	0.005	0.002	0.001	0.015	0.019
	1985–95	−0.004	−0.001	0.002	0.002	0.007	0.003	0.000	0.010	0.022

Note: The groups of countries refer to those shown in Tables 12.1 and 12.2. Each entry shows the average contribution of the indicated variable to the fitted growth rate of real per capita GDP (expressed relative to the sample mean). The contributions are averages for the designated group of countries and time period. The net convergence effect is the combined impact from the initial values of log(GDP), male and female secondary and higher school attainment, log(life expectancy), and the interaction term between log(GDP) and the human-capital variables. The fitted growth rate is the sum of the contributions shown separately. The actual growth rate refers to the average deviation from the sample mean for the indicated group of countries and time period.

sub-Saharan African countries ($2009 versus $836), the initial levels of real per capita GDP in the East Asian group were low on average relative to the levels of school attainment and life expectancy. Other notable positive contributions for the East Asian countries come from *G-cons./Y* (0.004) and the black-market premium (0.003). Thus, there were favorable growth effects from markedly low government consumption and a lack of distortions as indicated by a low or zero black-market premium. The overall fitted growth rate for the East Asian fast growers in 1965–75 is 0.028 (relative to the sample mean), and the actual value is the same.

For 1975–85, the contribution from the net convergence term for the East Asian countries falls to 0.013, because per capita GDP rose over the previous decade in relation to the levels of school attainment and life expectancy. An offsetting force is that three of the other variables become more favorable: the contributions are now 0.006 from *G-cons./Y*, 0.006 from the black-market premium, and 0.002 from *I/Y*. The overall fitted growth rate of 0.027 is below the actual value of 0.040.

Finally, the fitted growth rates for the East Asian countries for 1985–95 continue the previous pattern: the net convergence effect becomes smaller (0.004), but the other terms maintain or enhance their contributions. Consequently, the overall fitted growth rate for 1985–95 remains at the high value of 0.020 (relative to the sample mean). The actual performance for 1985–90 is notably better, 0.048.

Another natural comparison is between the 17 slow-growing sub-Saharan African countries and the 6 fast-growing sub-Saharan African countries. Table 12.4 shows for 1965–75 that the 17 African slow growers differ from the 6 fast growers most clearly in the net convergence term, which is −0.001 for the former group and 0.020 for the latter.[19] That is, the fast growers have particularly low values of initial per capita GDP in relation to their levels of schooling and life expectancy. The fast growers also get better contributions from *G-cons./Y* (−.005 versus −0.010), *G-educ./Y* (0.002 versus −0.002), the black-market premium (0.000 versus −0.002), and *I/Y* (−0.001 versus −0.003). In other words, the fast growers tend to have less government consumption and market distortions and more educational spending and investment.

Similar comparisons apply for the 1975–85 and 1985–95 periods, except that *G-cons./Y* becomes less favorable for the fast growers and the difference between the groups in the black-market premium becomes more pronounced. We should note that the model does not explain much of the good growth performance for the African fast growers in the 1975–85 period: the fitted value of 0.005 (relative to the sample mean) compares with an actual value of .033. The fitted value for 1985–95, 0.005, is, however, close to the actual value for 1985–90 of 0.008.

Table 12.4 also allows a comparison of the 17 sub-Saharan African slow growers with 4 Latin American slow growers (Nicaragua, Venezuela, Guyana, and Chile).

---

[19]The convergence term for one of the fast growers, Rwanda (0.027), would be too high if its true real per capita GDP for 1965 were greater than the remarkably low reported value of $337 (1985 U.S. prices), compared with $514 in 1960 and $625 in 1970. If Rwanda is excluded from the group of fast-growing sub-Saharan African countries, then the mean contribution from the net convergence effect falls from 0.020 to 0.017 for 1965–75.

For 1965–75, the overall fitted value for the Latin American group (-0.020) is nearly the same as that for Africa. The main places in which the Latin American countries perform worse is in the net convergence term (-0.014)—because these countries start with high values of per capita GDP in relation to schooling and health—and the black-market premium (-0.008). The Latin-American countries do better in the cases of *G-cons./Y*, the terms of trade, *I/Y*, and *G-educ./Y*.

In 1975–85, the model does not explain well the extremely low growth rates in the badly-performing Latin American countries; the fitted value is -0.016 and the actual is -0.037. This outcome, extended to the full set of Latin American countries, underlies the significance of the Latin American dummy variable in Table 12.3, column 20.

For 1985–95, the striking change is the increase in the magnitude of the black-market premium, to -0.025. This element, which tends to reflect market distortions, underlies the low value of fitted growth, -0.019, which nearly matches the low value of actual growth for 1985–90, -0.018.

One of the slow-growing Latin American countries is Chile, which had a fitted growth rate (relative to the sample mean) for 1965–75 of -0.043 and an actual value of -0.042. The contribution of the black-market premium for this period was -0.027. For 1975–85, the fitted value improved to -0.002 and the actual to 0.000; a major reason was the improvement of the black-market premium (reflecting a reduction of distortions) to 0.003. This process continued for 1985–95, where the fitted value rose to 0.012, but the actual value for 1985–90 improved even more, to 0.031.

Brazil, a country on the fast-growers list, provides an interesting contrast. The fitted growth rates (relative to sample means) are 0.010 in 1965–75, -0.005 in 1975–85, and -0.011 in 1985–95, and the actual values are 0.034, -0.005, and -0.013 (for 1985–90). One source of change for Brazil is that the contribution from the black-market premium goes from 0.002 in 1965–75 to -0.006 in 1985–95. Thus, while Chile has apparently moved away from market distortions and low growth, Brazil's policies and outcomes have moved in the opposite direction.

Finally, Table 12.4 includes four fast-growing western European countries. In 1965–75, the net convergence effect is positive (0.008), because the relatively high levels of initial per capita GDP are more than offset by the relatively high values of school attainment and life expectancy. The other main positive contributions to growth are from low distortions as reflected in low or zero black-market premia (0.004), high *I/Y* (0.003), and low *G-cons./Y* (0.003). Overall, the fitted growth rate is 0.020 (relative to the sample mean), compared with an actual value of 0.025.

In 1975–85, the net convergence term for the four European countries falls to 0.002, because per capita GDP rose over the previous decade in relation to human capital. The contribution from *I/Y* declines, but that from low distortions (small or 0 black-market premia) rises slightly. Overall, the fitted growth rate is now 0.015 above the sample mean, compared to an actual value of 0.019.

For 1985–95, the rise in GDP in relation to schooling and life expectancy reduces the net convergence term to -0.004. This change lowers the average fitted growth rate to 0.010 above the sample mean. The actual value for 1985–90, 0.022, is, however, notably better.

12.5 EMPIRICAL ANALYSIS OF THE INVESTMENT RATIO

Table 12.5 shows regressions for investment ratios. The first column uses the ratio for total investment, I/Y, whereas the second column uses the ratio for private investment, I-private/Y. The forms are the same as the one used for the growth rate in Table 12.3 (except that the investment ratios do not appear as independent variables). The dependent variables are the average values of the investment ratios for 1965–75 and 1975–85. In the second column, we estimated the ratio of private investment to GDP by using the available information since 1970 on the division of total investment into public and private components.

TABLE 12.5
Regressions for investment ratio

Dependent variable	I/Y	I-private/Y
log(GDP)	0.0036 (0.0121)	−0.0026 (0.0104)
male secondary education	0.040 (0.016)	0.028 (0.010)
female secondary education	−0.052 (0.017)	−0.034 (0.011)
male higher education	−0.011 (0.059)	0.006 (0.034)
female higher education	0.022 (0.084)	0.034 (0.050)
log(life expectancy)	0.274 (0.052)	0.288 (0.045)
log(GDP)* human capital	0.086 (0.127)	0.360 (0.095)
G-educ./Y	0.00 (0.38)	−0.19 (0.30)
G-cons./Y	−0.130 (0.101)	−0.069 (0.078)
log(1+black-market premium)	−0.036 (0.024)	−0.058 (0.018)
political instability	−0.109 (0.065)	−0.019 (0.049)
growth rate, terms of trade	−0.032 (0.120)	−0.164 (0.092)
R^2 (number of observations)	0.58 (87) 0.62 (97)	0.68 (83) 0.71 (92)
serial correlation coefficient	0.42	0.52

Notes: Estimation is by three-stage least squares. Standard errors of coefficients are shown in parentheses. The instruments are the same as those used in the growth-rate regressions. See also the note to Table 12.3.

For the first column, which uses I/Y, one result is that the estimated coefficient on log(GDP) is essentially 0, 0.004 (0.012). This finding does not mean, however, that I/Y does not change as an economy develops, the basic assumption in the Solow–Swan model. Some of the right-hand side variables—notably educational attainment and life expectancy—rise systematically with the level of development, and these changes would be associated with increases in I/Y.

For secondary schooling, the estimated coefficient of male attainment is significantly positive, 0.040 (0.016), and that for female attainment is significantly negative, –0.052 (0.017). This pattern resembles the one found before for the growth rate. In the case of the investment ratio, however, the estimated coefficients of the higher-attainment variables are individually and jointly insignificantly different from 0. The estimated coefficient on log(life expectancy) is significantly positive, 0.27 (0.05), and the effect from the interaction between log(GDP) and human capital is insignificant, 0.086 (0.127). The overall conclusion is that a greater initial stock of human capital—more schooling and more health—generates a higher investment ratio. That is, the negative effect from more female secondary schooling tends to be more than offset by the positive influences from male secondary schooling and life expectancy.

The effects of the human-capital variables imply that I/Y tends to rise as school attainment and, especially, life expectancy increase. This mechanism accounts for the strong positive correlation between I/Y and log(GDP) (0.66 between I/Y for 1965–75 and log[GDP] for 1965, 0.69 between I/Y for 1975–85 and log[GDP] for 1975), even though the estimated coefficient on log(GDP) in the first column of Table 12.5 is essentially 0.

The results also show negative relations between the market-distortion variables and I/Y: the estimated coefficients are –0.13 (0.10) on *G-cons./Y*, –0.036 (0.024) on the black-market premium, and –0.109 (0.065) on political instability. None of these variables are individually significant at the 5 percent level, but the p-value for the joint significance of the three is 0.052. Thus, there is an indication that a greater amount of market distortions reduces the incentive to invest and thereby lowers I/Y.

For *I-private/Y* in the second column of Table 12.5, the main differences in the results are, first, the interaction term between log(GDP) and human capital has a significantly positive coefficient, 0.36 (0.10); second, the black-market premium has a significantly negative coefficient, –0.058 (0.018); and third, the growth rate of the terms of trade has a coefficient that is negative and nearly significant, –0.16 (0.09). Political instability and *G-cons./Y* have weaker negative effects than before. The effect from the black-market premium indicates more clearly the adverse effect from distortions on the incentive to invest.

12.6 EMPIRICAL ANALYSIS OF FERTILITY AND HEALTH

This section considers the determinants of the fertility rate and of two health indicators, life expectancy at birth and the infant mortality rate. A particular concern is the effect of educational attainment on fertility and health. Previous discussions of these kinds of effects in developing countries appear in Behrman (1990) and Schultz (1989).

TABLE 12.6
Regressions for fertility and health

Dependent variable	(1) Log(fertility) 1965, 1985	(2) Log(life expectancy) 1965, 1985	(3) Infant mortality 1965, 1985
log(GDP)	0.93 (0.31)	0.603 (0.099)	−0.134 (0.028)
log(GDP) squared	−0.070 (0.020)	−0.0330 (0.0064)	0.0071 (0.0018)
male primary education	0.094 (0.036)	0.0163 (0.0118)	−0.0071 (0.0033)
female primary education	−0.194 (0.038)	0.0225 (0.0123)	−0.0034 (0.0034)
male secondary and higher education	−0.191 (0.060)	0.0288 (0.0180)	−0.0054 (0.0050)
female secondary and higher education	0.155 (0.067)	−0.0215 (0.0201)	0.0032 (0.0056)
R^2 (number of observations)	0.68 (90) 0.81 (102)	0.77 (89) 0.84 (99)	0.73 (88) 0.82 (100)
serial correlation coefficient	0.61	0.43	0.43

Note: Estimation is by the SUR technique. Standard errors of coefficients are shown in parentheses. The variables are observed (where data are available) in 1965 and 1985. The dependent variable in column 1 is the log of the total fertility rate. In column 2, it is the log of life expectancy at birth, and in column 3, the infant mortality rate. The serial correlation coefficient is the AR(1) value in a regression of the residuals for 1985 on those for 1965.

12.6.1   Results for Fertility

The first column of Table 12.6 shows an estimated model for the log of the fertility rate. The system consists of two equations that are widely spaced in time; the variables are observed in 1965 and 1985. The wide spacing is advisable because much of the reported movement over time in the fertility rate—as well as in life expectancy and infant mortality—appears to be interpolation (see Bos, Vu, and Stephens [1992] for a discussion of the health data). For the 20-year interval between 1965 and 1985, it is likely that much of the reported changes in fertility and health represent actual changes, rather than measurement error. The independent variables are log(GDP) and its square, male and female primary attainment, and male and female secondary and higher attainment (entered as the sum of years of schooling at these two advanced levels).

The estimated relation between fertility and log(GDP)—0.93 (0.31) on the linear term and –0.070 (0.020) on the squared term—is positive at very low levels of per capita GDP and negative at higher levels. The implied break point at which the relation switches from positive to negative is at a value of real per capita GDP of $767 (1985 U.S. dollars). In 1965, 12 of the 90 countries in the regression sample for fertility were below this critical level, and in 1985, 13 of the 102 countries were below it.

The results suggest that the Malthusian positive linkage between per capita income and fertility operates for the least well-off countries. From the perspective of theories of fertility choice, as in Chapter 9, this relation would be expected when the goods costs of raising children dominates over costs that depend on the value of time or on levels of human capital per person. The negative relation between per capita income and fertility—which holds for all but the poorest countries—is predicted when the dominant effect comes from child-rearing costs that depend positively on wage rates or per capita stocks of human capital.

The sign of the estimated relation between schooling and fertility depends on gender and the level of schooling. For females, the effect of primary schooling is significantly negative, –0.19 (0.04), whereas that of advanced schooling is significantly positive, 0.16 (0.07).[20] For males, the pattern is reversed; the coefficient on primary schooling is significantly positive, 0.09 (0.04), and that of higher schooling is significantly negative, –0.19 (0.06). We can interpret the difference by gender from the observation that women typically play the key role in child rearing, especially in developing countries. The effects from primary schooling suggest that more female attainment affects primarily the value of time devoted to raising children; hence, the effect on fertility is negative. In contrast, an increase in male primary attainment has mainly a positive income effect on the demand for children; therefore, the effect on fertility is positive.[21] These patterns reverse, however, for schooling at the higher levels.

12.6.2   Results on Health

Columns 2 and 3 of Table 12.6 shows regressions for life expectancy at birth and the infant mortality rate. Thus, these measures of health attainment are viewed as determined by levels of per capita income and school attainment.

For the log of life expectancy, the estimated relation with log(GDP) shows a positive linear term, 0.60 (0.10), and a negative squared term, –0.033 (0.006). Hence, the positive linkage between per capita GDP and life-expectancy diminishes as per capita GDP rises. The implied relation remains positive as long as real per capita GDP is less that $9287 (1985 U.S. dollars), a condition that holds for 87 of the 89 countries in the regression sample for life expectancy in 1965 and for 79 of the 99 countries in the sample in 1985. The property that the relation between per capita GDP and life expectancy becomes negative for the highest-income countries is likely an artifact of the quadratic approximation to the true nonlinear form. Probably, the true relation asymptotes to a 0 relation, rather than a negative one.

---

[20]If secondary and higher attainment are entered separately, then a test of the hypothesis that the coefficients are the same at these two levels (for females and males) is accepted with a p-value of 0.68.

[21]The regressions already hold constant the levels of real per capita GDP. It is likely, however, that higher levels of school attainment imply positive long-run income effects, holding constant the current value of per capita GDP.

For the schooling variables, the main effect is the positive interaction between life expectancy and primary attainment. Although the estimated coefficients on male and female primary schooling shown in column 2 are individually only marginally significant (0.016 [0.012] on male primary and 0.022 [0.012] on female primary) the joint effect is highly significant: the p-value is 0.000. Thus, there is a strong indication that more primary schooling goes along with greater life expectancy. In contrast, the two advanced-level schooling variables are jointly insignificant, with a p-value of 0.22.

The results are similar for the infant mortality rate in column 3. The nonlinear form in log(GDP) implies that infant mortality declines with per capita GDP as long as per capita GDP is less than $12539 (1985 U.S. dollars). This condition holds for all 88 countries in the regression sample for the mortality rate in 1965 and for 92 of the 100 countries in the sample in 1985. The results imply that the inverse relation between infant mortality and per capita GDP attenuates as per capita GDP rises. The true effect likely asymptotes to 0, rather than the positive effect implied by the quadratic approximation.

The main interplay with the schooling variables involves the negative interaction between the mortality rate and primary schooling. The two estimated coefficients for primary attainment are jointly highly significant, with a p-value of 0.000. The two coefficients for attainment at the advanced levels are jointly insignificant, with a p-value of 0.41.

12.7 SUMMARY AND CONCLUSIONS ABOUT GROWTH

Differences in per capita growth rates across countries are large and relate systematically to a set of quantifiable explanatory variables. One element of this set is a net convergence term, the positive effect on growth when the initial level of real per capita GDP is low relative to the starting amount of human capital in the forms of educational attainment and life expectancy. There is also evidence that countries with higher initial human capital converge faster to their steady-state positions.

The empirical findings on conditional convergence are consistent with the neoclassical growth model of Chapters 1 and 2 and with the imbalance effect for physical and human capital that was described in Chapter 5. The convergence effect also appears, however, in the models of technological diffusion that were described in Chapter 8. In addition, these diffusion models predict that higher initial human capital will speed up convergence, another relation that appears in the data.

For given values of per capita GDP and human capital, growth depends negatively on variables that reflect distortions and the size of government: the ratio of government consumption to GDP, the black-market premium on foreign exchange, and political instability. In contrast, if governments provide more effective maintenance of the rule of law, then growth appears to be enhanced. These effects from government actions are consistent with the neoclassical growth model, but would also arise in theories of endogenous growth.

Growth increases with favorable movements in the terms of trade and declines with increases in the fertility rate. The relation with fertility is predicted by the Solow–Swan model of Chapter 1 and can also arise in the theory of endogenous fertility from Chapter 9.

The relation between growth and the investment ratio is weak when the variables already mentioned are held constant and if the lagged investment ratio is used as an instrument. Thus, there is some indication that the observed positive correlation across countries between growth and the investment ratio reflects primarily the influence of growth on the propensity to invest.

TABLE 12A.1
List of countries included in growth-rate regressions

1. Algeria	57. Haiti	95. Nepal
3. Benin	58. Honduras	97. Pakistan
4. Botswana	59. Jamaica	98. Philippines
7. Cameroon	60. Mexico	100. Singapore
9. Central African Republic	61. Nicaragua	101. Sri Lanka
12. Congo	62. Panama	102. Syria
13. Egypt*	65. Trinidad & Tobago*	103. Taiwan
16. Gambia*	66. United States	104. Thailand
17. Ghana	67. Argentina	106. Yemen (North Arab Republic)*
21. Kenya	68. Bolivia	107. Austria
22. Lesotho	69. Brazil	108. Belgium
23. Liberia	70. Chile	109. Cyprus
25. Malawi	71. Colombia	110. Denmark
26. Mali	72. Ecuador	111. Finland
28. Mauritius*	73. Guyana*	112. France
31. Niger	74. Paraguay	113. Germany
33. Rwanda	75. Peru	114. Greece
34. Senegal	77. Uruguay	117. Ireland
36. Sierra Leone*	78. Venezuela	118. Italy
38. South Africa	81. Bangladesh	120. Malta
39. Sudan	84. Hong Kong	121. Netherlands
40. Swaziland*	85. India	122. Norway
41. Tanzania	86. Indonesia	124. Portugal
42. Togo	87. Iran	125. Spain
43. Tunisia	88. Iraq	126. Sweden
44. Uganda	89. Israel	127. Switzerland
45. Zaire	90. Japan	128. Turkey
46. Zambia	91. Jordan	129. United Kingdom
47. Zimbabwe	92. Korea	130. Yugoslavia
49. Barbados*	94. Malaysia	131. Australia
50. Canada		133. New Zealand
51. Costa Rica		134. Papua New Guinea*
53. Dominican Republic		
54. El Salvador		
56. Guatemala		

Note: The countries listed here are included in the growth-rate regressions. Those marked with an asterisk are included for 1975–85 but not for 1965–75. The numbers shown are those used by Summers and Heston (1993) and Barro and Lee (1994).

TABLE 12A.2
Means and standard deviations

Variable	(1) Mean 1965–75 sample (87 observations)	(2) Standard deviation 1965–75 sample (87 observations)	(3) Mean 1975–85 sample (97 observations)	(4) Standard deviation 1975–85 sample (97 observations)
growth rate of per capita GDP	0.030	0.023	0.011	0.026
log(GDP), 1965, 1975	7.56	0.94	7.83	0.96
log(GDP), 1985	—	—	7.95	1.04
per capita GDP, 1965, 1975	2943	2838	3873	3556
per capita GDP, 1985	—	—	4597	4404
male secondary school, 1965, 1975	0.74	0.68	1.05	0.94
male secondary school, 1985[a]	—	—	1.42	1.08
female secondary school, 1965, 1975	0.52	0.64	0.78	0.91
female secondary school, 1985[a]	—	—	1.10	1.04
male higher school, 1965, 1975	0.11	0.12	0.18	0.20
male higher school, 1985	—	—	0.27	0.25
female higher school, 1965, 1975	0.053	0.091	0.089	0.133
female higher school, 1985	—	—	0.16	0.19
male primary school, 1965, 1975[b]	3.17	1.84	3.28	1.84
male primary school, 1985[b]	—	—	3.80	1.69
female primary school, 1965, 1975[b]	2.53	2.04	2.66	2.05
female primary school, 1985[b]	—	—	3.12	1.96
change in male secondary school[a]	0.34	0.49	0.37	0.36
change in female secondary school[a]	0.28	0.42	0.32	0.33
change in male higher school[a]	0.076	0.123	0.093	0.103
change in female higher school[a]	0.044	0.073	0.070	0.077

Variable	(1) Mean 1965–75 sample (87 observations)	(2) Standard deviation 1965–75 sample (87 observations)	(3) Mean 1975–85 sample (97 observations)	(4) Standard deviation 1975–85 sample (97 observations)
male secondary enrollment, 1965, 1975[c]	0.33	0.25	0.46	0.27
male secondary enrollment, 1985[d]	—	—	0.54	0.29
female secondary enrollment, 1965, 1975[c]	0.25	0.24	0.39	0.29
female secondary enrollment, 1985[d]	—	—	0.50	0.33
male higher enrollment, 1965, 1975[c]	0.077	0.085	0.127	0.120
male higher enrollment, 1985[d]	—	—	0.161	0.135
female higher enrollment, 1965, 1975[c]	0.040	0.055	0.082	0.094
female higher enrollment, 1985[d]	—	—	0.129	0.136
male primary enrollment, 1965, 1975[c]	0.851	0.202	0.887	0.174
male primary enrollment, 1985[c]	—	—	0.930	0.146
female primary enrollment, 1965, 1975[c]	0.748	0.293	0.797	0.253
female primary enrollment, 1985[c]	—	—	0.864	0.222
log(life expectancy), 1960–64, 1970–74	4.00	0.21	4.05	0.20
log(life expectancy), 1980–84	—	—	4.12	0.18
life expectancy, 1960–64, 1970–74	55.7	11.7	58.6	11.2
life expectancy, 1980–84	—	—	62.4	10.8
interaction term, 1965, 1975	0.014	0.016	0.016	0.018
G-educ./Y	0.038	0.015	0.045	0.017
I/Y	0.199	0.099	0.193	0.085
G-cons./Y	0.092	0.065	0.101	0.072
log(1+black-market premium)	0.15	0.20	0.22	0.36
political instability	0.076	0.123	0.097	0.144
revolutions	0.124	0.217	0.154	0.210
political assassinations per million inhabitants	0.029	0.088	0.041	0.142

(continued)

TABLE 12A.2 *(continued)*

Variable	(1) Mean 1965–75 sample (87 observations)	(2) Standard deviation 1965–75 sample (87 observations)	(3) Mean 1975–85 sample (97 observations)	(4) Standard deviation 1975–85 sample (97 observations)
growth rate of terms of trade	0.000	0.036	−0.013	0.035
log(fertility rate)	1.53	0.45	1.37	0.53
fertility rate, 1965, 1985	5.3	1.8	4.2	2.1
infant mortality rate, 1965, 1985[e]	0.092	0.055	0.060	0.046
population growth rate	0.021	0.010	0.020	0.011
change in population share under age 15	−0.011	0.024	−0.020	0.026
population fraction under 15, 1965, 1985	0.390	0.083	0.362	0.103
population fraction 65 & over, 1965, 1985	0.052	0.032	0.060	0.042
political rights	4.1	2.2	3.8	2.0
political rights, 1991	—	—	3.3	2.1
civil liberties	3.8	1.9	3.8	1.8
civil liberties, 1991	—	—	3.3	1.8
rule of law[f]	3.2	2.0	3.1	2.0
G-def./Y	0.032	0.035	0.038	0.042
war dummy	0.39	—	0.36	—
public investment/total investment	0.29	0.20	0.35	0.19
tariff rate, 1980[g]	0.17	0.18	0.17	0.17
log(working-age population), 1965, 1975	8.36	1.40	8.39	1.50
working-age population, 1965, 1975 (millions)	16093	41834	14724	39847
log(GDP), bordering countries, 1965, 1975[a]	7.34	1.26	7.79	0.97
liquid/liabilities ratio[h]	0.35	0.26	0.42	0.26
sub-Saharan African dummy	0.25	—	0.27	—
Latin American dummy	0.23	—	0.24	—
East Asian dummy	0.10	—	0.10	—
growth rate, 1985–90[i]	—	—	0.011	0.033

Variable	(1) Mean 1965–75 sample (87 observations)	(2) Standard deviation 1965–75 sample (87 observations)	(3) Mean 1975–85 sample (97 observations)	(4) Standard deviation 1975–85 sample (97 observations)
World Bank per capita GDP growth rate[j]	0.029	0.023	0.012	0.025
log(GDP), World Bank, 1965, 1975[j]	7.03	1.41	7.25	1.45
log(GDP), World Bank, 1985[k]	—	—	7.37	1.51
GDP, World Bank, 1965, 1975[j]	2871	2965	3606	4854
GDP, World Bank, 1985[k]	—	—	4350	5997

Notes: The table shows unweighted means and standard deviations for each variable. Columns 1 and 2 refer to the 87 countries that are in the sample for the 1965–75 period. The values pertain to 1965–75 or to 1965, as indicated. The footnotes below indicate when the sample is less than 87 countries. Columns 3 and 4 refer to the 97 countries that are in the sample for the 1975–85 period. The values pertain to 1975–85, 1975, or 1985, as indicated. The footnotes indicate when the sample is less than 97 countries.

Real per capita GDP is measured in 1985 U.S. dollars. The school-attainment variables are in years. The enrollment rates refer to fractions of the relevant population. Life expectancy is in years. The interaction term is the product of log(GDP) (relative to the sample mean) and the five human-capital variables included in the regressions (see the text). Political instability is the average of revolutions per year and political assassinations per million population per year. The fertility rate is the number of live births per woman over her lifetime. The infant mortality rate is the fraction of children who do not survive beyond age one. Political rights and civil liberties are the Gastil (1987) indices, where one indicates the most rights and seven the least. Rule of law, from Knack and Keefer (1994), is a survey measure taken from the International Country Risk Guide. The variable is intended to gauge the extent to which institutions allow for implementation of laws, adjudication of disputes, and an orderly succession of power. The figures range from 0 to 6, with 6 indicating the most effective institutions. War dummy equals 1 if the country experienced an external war between 1960 and 1985. The tariff rate is the weighted average rate on imports of capital goods and intermediates from Lee (1993). The working-age population is total population less those under 15 or 65 and over. GDP for bordering countries is the population-weighted average of real per capita GDP for adjacent countries. The liquid/liabilities ratio is the ratio of a measure of liquid liabilities to GDP from King and Levine (1993).

[a] 96 observations for 1975–85 sample.
[b] 81 observations for 1965–75 sample, 95 observations for 1975–85 sample.
[c] 94 observations for 1975–85 sample.
[d] 89 observations for 1975–85 sample.
[e] 86 observations for 1965–75 sample, 95 for 1975–85 sample.
[f] 81 observations for 1965–75 sample, 88 for 1975–85 sample.
[g] 74 observations for 1965–75 sample, 82 for 1975–85 sample.
[h] 77 observations for 1965–75 sample, 89 for 1975–85 sample.
[i] 95 observations for 1975–85 sample.
[j] 79 observations for 1965–75 sample, 92 for 1975–85 sample.
[k] 92 observations for 1975–85 sample.

APPENDIX
ON MATHEMATICAL
METHODS

TABLE OF CONTENTS

1.1 Differential Equations

    1.1.1 Introduction

    1.1.2 First-Order Ordinary Differential Equations

        Graphical Solutions

         Constructing the diagram

         Stability

        Analytical Solutions

         Linear, first-order differential equations with constant coefficients

         Linear, first-order differential equations with variable coefficients

    1.1.3 Systems of Linear Ordinary Differential Equations

        Phase Diagrams

         Diagonal systems

         A nondiagonal example

         A nonlinear example

        Analytical Solutions of Linear, Homogeneous Systems

        The Relation between the Graphical and Analytical Solutions

        Stability

        Analytical Solutions of Linear, Nonhomogeneous Systems

        Linearization of Nonlinear Systems

        The Time-Elimination Method for Nonlinear Systems

1.2 Static Optimization
    1.2.1 Unconstrained Maxima
    1.2.2 Classical Nonlinear Programming: Equality Constraints
    1.2.3 Inequality Constraints: The Kuhn–Tucker Conditions
1.3 Dynamic Optimization in Continuous Time
    1.3.1 Introduction
    1.3.2 The Typical Problem
    1.3.3 Heuristic Derivation of the First-Order Conditions
    1.3.4 Transversality Conditions
    1.3.5 The Behavior of the Hamiltonian over Time
    1.3.6 Sufficient Conditions
    1.3.7 Infinite Horizons
    1.3.8 Example: The Neoclassical Growth Model
    1.3.9 Transversality Conditions in Infinite-Horizon Problems
    1.3.10 Summary of the Procedure to Find the First-Order Conditions
    1.3.11 Present-Value and Current-Value Hamiltonians
    1.3.12 Multiple Variables
1.4 Useful Results in Matrix Algebra: Eigenvalues, Eigenvectors,
    and Diagonalization of Matrices
1.5 Useful Results in Calculus
    1.5.1 Implicit Function Theorem
    1.5.2 Taylor's Theorem
    1.5.3 L'Hôpital's Rule
    1.5.4 Integration by Parts
    1.5.5 Fundamental Theorem of Calculus
    1.5.6 Rules of Differentiation of Integrals
        Differentiation with Respect to the Variable of Integration
        Leibniz's Rule for Differentiation of Definite Integrals

This appendix discusses the main mathematical methods that are used in the text. We consider differential equations, static optimization, dynamic optimization, some results in matrix theory, and a few results from calculus.

1.1 DIFFERENTIAL EQUATIONS

1.1.1 Introduction

A differential equation is an equation that involves derivatives of variables. If there is only one independent variable, then it is called an *ordinary differential equation* (ODE). The *order* of the ODE is that of the highest derivative; that is, if the highest derivative in an ODE is of order n, then it is an nth-order ODE. When the functional form of the equation is linear, then it is a *linear ODE*. most of the differential equations that we encounter in the book involve derivatives of functions with respect to *time*.

An example of a differential equation is

$$a_1 \cdot \dot{y}(t) + a_2 \cdot y(t) + x(t) = 0, \tag{A.1}$$

where the dot on top of $y(t)$ represents the derivative of $y(t)$ with respect to time, $\dot{y}(t) \equiv dy(t)/dt$; a_1 and a_2 are constants; and $x(t)$ is a known function of time. The function $x(t)$ is sometimes called the *forcing function*. Equation (A.1) is a first-order linear ODE with constant coefficients. If $x(t) = a_3$, a constant, then the equation is called *autonomous*. (An equation is autonomous when it depends on time only through the variable $y[t]$.) If $x(t) = 0$, then the equation is called *homogeneous*.

A second-order, linear ODE with constant coefficients takes the form,

$$a_1 \cdot \ddot{y}(t) + a_2 \cdot \dot{y}(t) + a_3 \cdot y(t) + x(t) = 0, \tag{A.2}$$

where a_1 and a_2 are constants and $\ddot{y}(t) \equiv d^2 y(t)/dt^2$. The equation

$$a_1 \cdot \dot{y}(t) + a_2(t) \cdot y(t) + x(t) = 0, \tag{A.3}$$

where $a_2(t)$ is a known function of time, is a first-order, linear ODE with *variable coefficients*. The equation

$$\log[\dot{y}(t)] + 1/y(t) = 0 \tag{A.4}$$

is a *nonlinear first-order ODE*.

The goal when solving a differential equation is to find the behavior of $y(t)$. The first solution method that we use is *graphical*, a technique that can be used for nonlinear, as well as linear, differential equations. The disadvantage is that it can be used only for autonomous equations. The second method is *analytical*. In some circumstances, we will be able to find an extract formula for $y(t)$, even when the equation is not autonomous. The drawback of the analytical approach is that it can be used only with a limited set of functional forms. One of them, however, is the linear function in Eq. (A.1). When we encounter nonlinear differential equations, we will often approximate the solution by linearizing the equation by means of a Taylor-series expansion. (See Section 1.5.2 of this chapter.)

A third method for solving differential equations relies on numerical analysis. Most modern mathematical computer packages contain subroutines that solve differential equations numerically. Matlab, for example, has the subroutines ODE23 and ODE45, and Mathematica has the command NDSOLVE.

1.1.2   First-Order Ordinary Differential Equations

GRAPHICAL SOLUTIONS.

Constructing the diagram. Consider an autonomous ordinary differential equation of the form,

$$\dot{y}(t) = f[y(t)], \tag{A.5}$$

where $f(\bullet)$ is a known function. Equation (A.5) is autonomous because the function $f(\bullet)$ does not depend on time independently of y. The function $f(\bullet)$ may or may not be linear.

To solve Eq. (A.5) graphically, we plot $f(\bullet)$ as a function of y in Fig. A.1a,b,c. The horizontal axis shows the value of y, and the vertical axis has $f(\bullet)$ and $\dot{y}$. Positive values of $f(\bullet)$ correspond to positive values of $\dot{y}$, in accordance with Eq. (A.5). Since $\dot{y}$ is the derivative of y with respect to time, positive values of $\dot{y}$ correspond to increasing values of y. To reflect this relation, we draw arrows pointing east (increasing y) when $f(\bullet)$ lies above the horizontal axis and pointing west (decreasing y) when $f(\bullet)$ lies below the horizontal axis. The arrows reveal the direction in which y moves over time and therefore provide a qualitative solution to the differential equation.

Sometimes the differential equation is expressed in terms of the difference of two functions, for example,

$$\dot{y}(t) = f[y(t)] - g[y(t)].$$

Instead of graphing $f(\bullet) - g(\bullet)$, we can graph $f(\bullet)$ and $g(\bullet)$ separately. The rate of change of $y(t)$, $\dot{y}(t)$, is given in this case by the vertical distance between $f(\bullet)$ and $g(\bullet)$. For values of y where $f(\bullet)$ lies above $g(\bullet)$, $\dot{y}(t)$ is positive and therefore $y(t)$ is increasing over time. The opposite is true when $f(\bullet)$ lies below $g(\bullet)$. The steady state is given by the point(s) at which the curves $f(\bullet)$ and $g(\bullet)$ cross.

As an example, consider a linear form for $f(\bullet)$:

$$\dot{y}(t) = f[y(t)] = a \cdot y(t) - x, \tag{A.6}$$

where a and x are constants, with $a > 0$. The graph of $f(\bullet)$ is a straight line with positive slope. This line, depicted in Fig. A.1a, intercepts the vertical axis at $\dot{y} = -x$ and crosses the horizontal axis at $y^* = x/a$. For values of y above y^*, the function lies

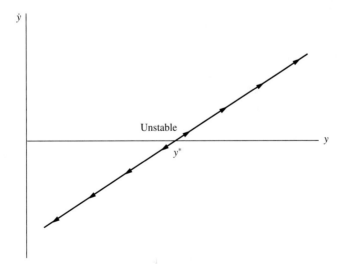

FIGURE A.1a
Linear ODE. If the coefficient a in Eq. (A.6) is positive, then the differential equation for y is unstable.

above the horizontal axis. Thus, $\dot{y}$ is positive and y is increasing. Hence, to the right of y^*, we draw arrows pointing northeast (see Fig. A.1a). The opposite conditions apply to the left of y^*, and we draw arrows pointing southwest.

If the initial value, $y(0)$, equals y^*, then Eq. (A.6) implies that $\dot{y}$ equals 0, so that y does not change over time. It follows that $y(t)$ remains forever at y^*. The value y^* is called the *steady-state* value of y.

If $y(0) > y^*$, then $\dot{y} > 0$, so that y grows over time. Conversely, if $y(0) < y^*$, then $\dot{y} < 0$, so that y decreases over time. The qualitative dynamics of $y(t)$ are fully determined in Fig. A.1a: once the initial value, $y(0)$, is specified, the arrows show how y moves as time evolves. An interesting point is that unless $y(0) = y^*$, the dynamics of the equation when $a > 0$ move y away from the steady state. This behavior applies for initial values below and above y^*. In this case, we say that the differential equation is *unstable*.

Imagine now that $a < 0$. The graph of $f(\cdot)$ is then a downward-sloping straight line, depicted in Fig. A.1b, which intercepts the vertical axis at $\dot{y} = -x$ and the horizontal axis at $y^* = -x/a$. To the left of y^*, $\dot{y}$ is positive, so that y increases over time. Correspondingly, the arrows in the figure point southeast. The opposite relation applies to the right of y^*. Note that regardless of the initial value, $y(0)$, the dynamics of the equation brings $y(t)$ back to the steady state, y^*. In this case, we say that Eq. (A.6) is *stable*.

This graphical approach can be used to analyze the dynamics of more complicated nonlinear functions. Consider, for example, the differential equation

$$\dot{y}(t) = f[y(t)] = s \cdot [y(t)]^{\alpha} - \delta \cdot y(t), \tag{A.7}$$

where s, δ, and α are positive constants and $\alpha < 1$. Chapter 1 shows that the fundamental equation of the Solow–Swan growth model takes the form of Eq. (A.7),

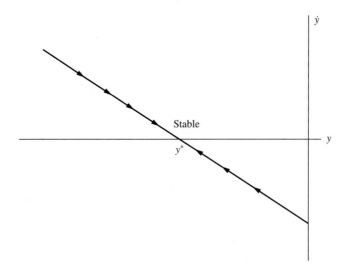

FIGURE A.1b
Linear ODE. If the coefficient a in Eq. (A.6) is negative, then the differential equation for y is stable.

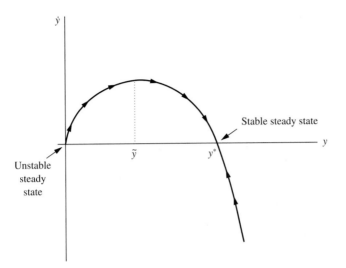

FIGURE A.1c
Nonlinear ODE. In Eq. (A.7), the slope of $f(\bullet)$ with respect to y is initially positive and is subsequently negative. The steady state at 0 is unstable, whereas that at y^* is stable.

where $y(t)$ is the capital stock. Under this interpretation, Eq. (A.7) says that the net increase in the capital stock equals the difference between total saving and total depreciation. Total saving is assumed to be the constant fraction, s, of output, y^α, and total depreciation is proportional to the existing capital stock.

Since only nonnegative values of the capital stock are economically meaningful, we look only at the first quadrant in Fig. A.1c. For low values of y, the function $f(\bullet)$ is upward sloping. It reaches a maximum when $s\alpha \tilde{y}^{\alpha-1} = \delta$, and it becomes downward sloping for higher values of y. The function $f(\bullet)$ crosses the horizontal axis at two points, $y = 0$ and $y = y^* = (\delta/s)^{1/(\alpha-1)}$.

To the right of y^*, $\dot{y}$ is negative, so that y is falling. Hence, we draw arrows pointing west. To the left of y^*, $\dot{y}$ is positive, so that y is rising, and we draw arrows pointing east. It follows that the equation has two steady states. The first one is y^* and is stable in that, for any positive initial value, $y(0)$, the dynamics of the equation moves $y(t)$ toward y^*. The second steady state, 0, is unstable; if $y(0) > 0$, then the dynamics moves $y(t)$ away from 0.

Stability. The preceding discussion suggests that if $f(\bullet)$ slopes upward at the steady-state value, y^*, then the steady state is unstable. That is, if $y(0) \neq y^*$, then $y(t)$ moves away from y^*. The reason is simple: if $f(\bullet)$ is upward sloping when $f(y^*) = 0$, then, for $y > y^*$, $f(y) > 0$. Hence, $\dot{y} > 0$ and y increases over time. On the other hand, for $y < y^*$, $f(y) < 0$, $\dot{y} < 0$, and y decreases over time. The conclusion is that y increases when it is already too large and falls when it is already too small, an indication of instability.

Conversely, if $f(\bullet)$ is downward sloping at the steady-state value, y^*, then the equation is stable. In this case, if $y(0) \neq y^*$, then $y(t)$ approaches y^* over time.

To summarize, if we are interested in the stability of the differential equation in the neighborhood of a steady state, then all we have to do is compute the derivative of $f(\cdot)$ and evaluate it at the steady-state value, y^*:

$$\text{if } \partial\dot{y}/\partial y\Big|_{y^*} > 0, \text{ then } y \text{ is locally unstable,}$$

(A.8)

$$\text{if } \partial\dot{y}/\partial y\Big|_{y^*} < 0, \text{ then } y \text{ is locally stable.}$$

Although nonlinear differential equations may have more than one steady state, the local stability properties of each of these steady states will still be determined by the condition in Eq. (A.8).

ANALYTICAL SOLUTIONS. The solution to some equations is almost immediate because the equation can be integrated. For instance, the solution to $\dot{y}(t) = a$ is obviously $y(t) = b + at$, where b is an arbitrary constant.

Equations that involve polynomial functions of time are equally easy to solve, for example,

$$\dot{y}(t) = a_0 + a_1 t + a_2 \cdot t^2 + \cdots + a_n \cdot t^n$$

has the solution

$$y(t) = b + a_0 t + a_1 \cdot (t^2/2) + \cdots + a_n \cdot [t^{n+1}/(n+1)].$$

In general, the functional forms that we work with will not be this simple. We now derive the general solution for linear, first-order ODEs.

Linear, first-order differential equations with constant coefficients. The general form of the linear, first-order ODE with constant coefficients is

$$\dot{y}(t) + a \cdot y(t) + x(t) = 0,$$

(A.9)

where a is a constant and $x(t)$ is a known function of time. The easiest way to solve this equation is to carry out the following steps.

First, put all the terms involving y and its derivatives on one side of the equation and the rest on the other side:

$$\dot{y}(t) + a \cdot y(t) = -x(t).$$

Second, multiply both sides of the equation by e^{at} and integrate:

$$\int e^{at} \cdot [\dot{y}(t) + a \cdot y(t)] \cdot dt = -\int e^{at} \cdot x(t) \cdot dt.$$

(A.10)

The term e^{at} is called the *integrating factor*. The reason for multiplying by the integrating factor is that the term inside the left-hand side integral becomes the derivative of $e^{at} \cdot y(t)$ with respect to time:

$$e^{at} \cdot [\dot{y}(t) + a \cdot y(t)] = (d/dt)[e^{at} \cdot y(t) + b_0],$$

where b_0 is an arbitrary constant. Note that the integral on the left-hand side of Eq. (A.10) is the integral of the derivative of some function and therefore equals the function itself (see Section 1.5.6). Hence, the term on the left-hand side of Eq. (A.10) equals $e^{at} \cdot y(t) + b_0$.

Third, compute the integral on the right-hand side of Eq. (A.10), making sure to add another constant term b_1. Note that this integral is a function of t. Call the result $\text{INT}(t) + b_1$. Since $x(t)$ is a known function of time, $\text{INT}(t)$ is also a known function of time.

Fourth, multiply both sides by e^{-at} to get $y(t)$:

$$y(t) = -e^{-at} \cdot \text{INT}(t) + be^{-at}, \tag{A.11}$$

where $b = b_1 - b_0$ is an arbitrary constant. Equation (A.11) is the general solution to the ODE in Eq. (A.9).

Consider the differential equation

$$\dot{y}(t) - y(t) - 1 = 0. \tag{A.12}$$

In this example, the forcing function $x(t)$ is a constant, -1. To solve this equation, we follow the steps outlined above. First, put all the terms involving $y(t)$ and its derivatives on the left-hand side of the equation and all the other terms on the right-hand side. Then multiply both sides by e^{-t} and integrate:

$$\int e^{-t}[\dot{y}(t) - y(t)] \cdot dt = \int e^{-t}dt. \tag{A.13}$$

The term inside the integral on the left-hand side is the derivative of $e^{-t} \cdot y(t) + b_0$ with respect to time. Hence, the integral on the left-hand side equals $e^{-t} \cdot y(t) + b_0$. The right-hand side equals $-e^{-t} + b_1$. Hence, the solution to Eq. (A.12) is

$$y(t) = -1 + be^{t}, \tag{A.14}$$

where $b = b_1 - b_0$ is an arbitrary constant. We can verify that Eq. (A.14) satisfies Eq. (A.12) by taking derivatives with respect to time to get $\dot{y}(t) = be^{t} = y(t) + 1$.

The result in Eq. (A.11) is the *general solution* to Eq. (A.9); to get a *particular* or *exact solution*, we have to specify the arbitrary constant of integration, b. To pin down which of the infinitely many possible paths applies, we need to know a value of $y(t)$ for at least one point in time. This *boundary condition* will determine the unique solution to the differential equation.

Figure A.2 shows an array of solutions to the ODE in the example of Eq. (A.12). To choose among them, imagine that we know that $y(t) = 0$ when $t = 0$. This type of boundary condition is called an *initial condition* because it pins down the path by specifying the value of $y(t)$ at the initial date. In our example, we can substitute $t = 0$ and $y(0) = 0$ in Eq. (A.14) to find that $y(0) = -1 + be^{0} = 0$, which implies $b = 1$. We can therefore plug $b = 1$ into Eq. (A.14) to get the particular solution,

$$y(t) = -1 + e^{t}. \tag{A.15}$$

This equation, which determines a unique value of y at every point in time, corresponds to the time path labeled A in Fig. A.2.

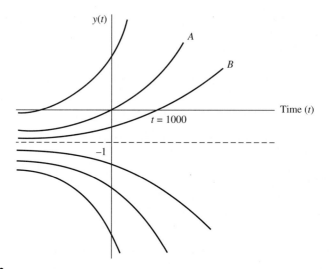

FIGURE A.2
Solutions to a differential equation. The figure shows an array of solutions to the differential Eq.
(A.12).

Instead of knowing the initial value of the function, we may know the value
at some terminal date, that is, we could have a *terminal condition.*[1] As an example,
suppose that the terminal date is $t_1 = 1000$, and the value of $y(t)$ at that time is 0.
Thus, $y(1000) = -1 + b \cdot e^{1000} = 0$. The solution, $b = e^{-1000}$, implies

$$y(t) = -1 + (e^{-1000}) \cdot e^t. \tag{A.16}$$

This result corresponds to path B in Fig. A.2.

Linear, first-order differential equations with variable coefficients. Consider
now the differential equation

$$\dot{y}(t) + a(t) \cdot y(t) + x(t) = 0, \tag{A.17}$$

where $a(t)$ is a known function of time, but is no longer a constant. We can follow
the same steps as before. The difference is that the integrating factor is now $e^{\int_0^t a(\tau)d\tau}$,
so that the left-hand side becomes the derivative of $y(t) \cdot e^{\int_0^t a(\tau)d\tau}$.[2] Again, when we

---

[1] When we deal with growth models with infinite horizons, we may know the limiting value of a variable
as time tends to infinity. This information will provide us with a terminal condition.

[2] The lower limit of integration can be an arbitrary constant. Leibniz's rule for differentiation of definite
integrals says that $d[\int_0^t f(\tau)d\tau]/dt = f(t)$. Note that we are taking the derivative with respect to the
upper limit of integration. See Section 1.5.6.

integrate the derivative of a function, we get back the original function. Using this information, we find that the solution to the ODE is

$$y(t) = -e^{-\int_0^t a(\tau)d\tau} \cdot \int e^{\int_0^t a(\tau)d\tau} \cdot x(t) \cdot dt + b \cdot e^{-\int_0^t a(\tau)d\tau}, \qquad (A.18)$$

where b is an arbitrary constant of integration. To find the particular or exact solution, we again have to make use of a boundary condition.

1.1.3 Systems of Linear Ordinary Differential Equations

We now study a system of linear, first-order ODEs of the form

$$\dot{y}_1(t) = a_{11}y_1(t) + \cdots + a_{1n}y_n(t) + x_1(t),$$

$$\cdots$$

$$\dot{y}_n(t) = a_{n1}y_1(t) + \cdots + a_{nn}y_n(t) + x_n(t).$$

In matrix notation, the system is

$$\dot{y}(t) = A \cdot y(t) + x(t), \qquad (A.19)$$

where $y(t)$ is a column vector of n functions of time, $\begin{bmatrix} y_1(t) \\ \vdots \\ y_n(t) \end{bmatrix}$, $\dot{y}(t)$ is the column vector of the n corresponding derivatives, A is an $n \times n$ square matrix of constant coefficients, and $x(t)$ is a vector of n functions.

We consider three procedures for solving this system of differential equations. The first one is a graphical device called a *phase diagram*, similar to the one that we used for a single differential equation. The advantage of a phase diagram is that it is simple and provides a qualitative solution. Furthermore, this technique works for nonlinear, as well as linear, systems. The drawbacks of phase diagrams are that they work only for 2×2 systems and only for autonomous equations with steady states.

The second procedure is *analytical*. The advantages of the analytical approach are that it gives quantitative answers and can be used in larger systems. The disadvantage is that it works, in general, only for linear equations. Later in this section, however, we use linear approximations to nonlinear systems.

The third procedure is *numerical*. Later in this section, we describe the time-elimination method for solving nonlinear systems numerically.

PHASE DIAGRAMS.

Diagonal systems. Start with the simple case in which A is a 2×2 *diagonal* matrix and the equations are homogeneous; that is, the components of the vector $x(t)$ are 0. The system can then be rewritten as

$$\dot{y}_1(t) = a_{11} \cdot y_1(t),$$

$$\dot{y}_2(t) = a_{22} \cdot y_2(t), \qquad (A.20)$$

where a_{11} and a_{22} are real numbers.

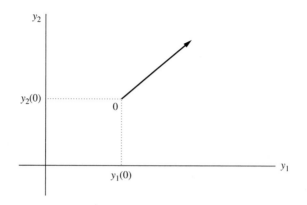

FIGURE A.3
Directions of motion. The figure shows the directions of motion for y_1 and y_2 in the diagonal system given in Eq. (A.20).

A phase diagram is a graphical tool, similar to the one used in the previous section, which allows us to visualize the dynamics of the system. In Fig. A.3, y_1 is on the horizontal axis, and y_2 is on the vertical axis. Each point in the space represents the position of the system (y_1, y_2) at a given moment in time. Imagine that, at time 0, we are at the point labeled "0" in the figure; that is, y_1 equals $y_1(0)$ and y_2 equals $y_2(0)$. If we want to see what the position of the economy will be at the "next instant," then we could have a third dimension to represent time. More conveniently, we can represent the dynamics with arrows that point in the direction of motion, just as in Section 1.1.2. For instance, an arrow that points northeast at point "0" signifies that the variables y_1 and y_2 are each growing over time. If the arrow points north, then y_2 grows and y_1 is stationary, and so on.

The object of a phase diagram is to translate the dynamics implied by the two differential equations into a system of arrows that describe the qualitative behavior of the economy over time. As a simple example, consider the diagonal system that we studied before. The dynamics depend on the signs of the two diagonal elements of A. We now consider three cases.

Case 1, $a_{11} > 0$ and $a_{22} > 0$: To construct the phase diagram, follow the following steps:

(*a*) Start in Fig. A.4a by plotting the locus of points for which $\dot{y}_1$ equals 0, called the $\dot{y}_1 = 0$ *schedule*. In this case, the locus corresponds to the points for which $\dot{y}_1(t) = 0$; that is, the vertical axis.

(*b*) Analyze the dynamics of y_1 in each of the two regions generated by the $\dot{y}_1 = 0$ schedule. For positive y_1, (that is, to the right of the $\dot{y}_1 = 0$ schedule), $\dot{y}_1$ is positive because $a_{11} > 0$ and $y_1 > 0$. Hence, the arrows point east. The opposite is true to the left of the vertical axis because in that region, $\dot{y}_1$ is given by the product of a positive number, $a_{11} > 0$, and a negative number, $y_1 < 0$. Therefore, the arrows point west.

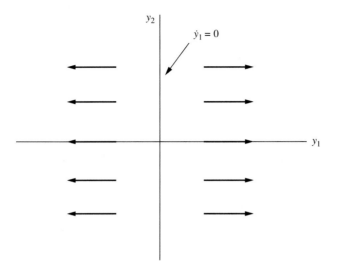

FIGURE A.4a
The $\dot{y}_1 = 0$ locus. The figure shows the $\dot{y}_1 = 0$ schedule (the vertical axis in this example) for the system in Eq. (A.20) when $a_{11} > 0$. The arrows show the direction of motion for y_1.

      (*c*) Repeat the procedure for $\dot{y}_2$. In the present example, the $\dot{y}_2 = 0$ schedule is the horizontal axis shown in Fig. A.4b. For positive y_2, $\dot{y}_2$ is the product of two positive numbers and is therefore positive. Hence, y_2 is increasing and, correspondingly, the arrows point north. Similarly, the arrows point south for negative y_2.

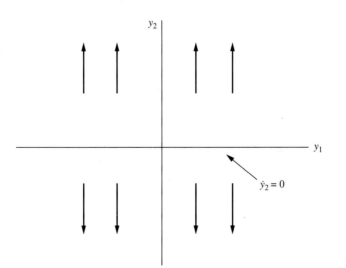

FIGURE A.4b
The $\dot{y}_2 = 0$ locus. The figure shows the $\dot{y}_2 = 0$ schedule (the horizontal axis in this example) for the system in Eq. (A.20) when $a_{22} > 0$. The arrows show the direction of motion for y_2.

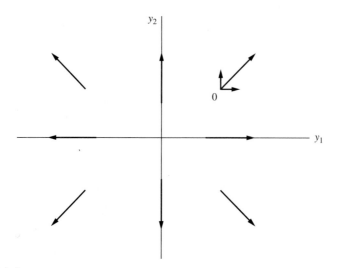

FIGURE A.4c
The phase diagram in an unstable case. The results from Figs. A.4a and A.4b are joined to generate a simple phase diagram. The arrows show the directions of motion for y_1 and y_2 when $a_{11} > 0$ and $a_{22} > 0$. This system is unstable.

   (*d*) Join the two pictures in Fig. A.4c. The two schedules divide the space into four regions. (In this simple case, the regions correspond to the four quadrants, a result that is not general.) In the first quadrant, one arrow points east and the other points north. We combine the two into an arrow that points northeast. This construction means that, if the economy is in this region, then y_1 and y_2 are increasing. The combined arrows for the second, third, and fourth quadrants point northwest, southwest, and southeast, respectively. Along the vertical axis, the arrows point north for positive y_2 and south for negative y_2. On the horizontal axis, the arrows point east for positive y_1 and west for negative y_1. Finally, at the origin, $\dot{y}_1$ and $\dot{y}_2$ are 0. Hence, if the economy happens to be at the origin, then it remains there forever. This point is the *steady state*. It is *unstable* in that if the initial position deviates from the origin by a small amount in any direction, then the dynamics of the system (the arrows) take it away from the steady state.
   (*e*) Use the boundary conditions to see which one of the many paths depicted in the picture constitutes the exact solution. Imagine, for example, that, at time zero, the value of y_1 is 1 and the value of y_2 is 2. (In this case, the two boundary conditions are initial conditions, but, in other cases that we consider, we may have one initial condition and one terminal condition or two terminal conditions.) The initial conditions imply that the system starts at point "0" in Fig. A.4c. The subsequent behavior of y_1 and y_2 is given by the path going through "0," as depicted in Fig. A.4c.
   Case 2, $a_{11} < 0$ and $a_{22} < 0$: Arguments similar to those of the previous section imply that the $\dot{y}_1 = 0$ schedule is again the vertical axis, and the $\dot{y}_2 = 0$ schedule is again the horizontal axis. We follow the same steps as before to find in Fig. A.5 that the arrows point southwest in the first quadrant, southeast in the second, northeast in the third, and northwest in the fourth. The steady state is the origin and,

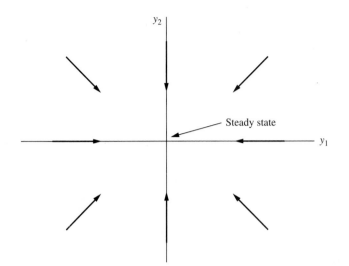

FIGURE A.5
The phase diagram in a stable case. In this example, $a_{11} < 0$ and $a_{22} < 0$ apply in Eq. (A.20). This system is stable.

unlike the previous case, this position is *stable*. For any initial values of y_1 and y_2, the dynamics of the system takes it back to the steady state.

    Case 3, $a_{11} < 0$ and $a_{22} > 0$: As in the previous cases, the $\dot{y}_1 = 0$ schedule is the vertical axis, and the $\dot{y}_2 = 0$ schedule is the horizontal axis. The dynamics in this third case, shown in Fig. A.6, are, however, more complicated than before. The arrows point northwest in the first quadrant, northeast in the second, southeast

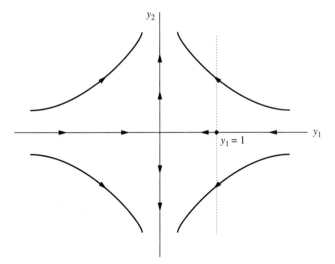

FIGURE A.6
The phase diagram in a case of saddle-path stability. In this example, $a_{11} < 0$ and $a_{22} > 0$ apply in Eq. (A.20). This system is saddle-path stable.

in the third, and southwest in the fourth. The arrows point toward the origin along the horizontal axis and away from it along the vertical axis. The origin is, again, the steady state.

The new element is that the system is neither stable nor unstable. If the system starts at the steady state, then it remains there. If it starts along the horizontal axis, then the dynamics of the system takes it back to the steady state. But if the system starts at any point off the horizontal axis, no matter how close to it, then the dynamics takes it away from the steady state. The system explodes in the sense that y_2 approaches infinity as t tends to infinity.

This case is called *saddle-path stable*. The reason for this name is the analogy with a marble left on top of a saddle. There is one point on the saddle where, if left there, the marble does not move. This point corresponds to the steady state. There is a trajectory on the saddle with the property that if the marble is left at any point on that trajectory, then it rolls toward the steady state. But if the marble is left at any other point, then the marble falls to the ground.

Two results about the dynamic paths shown in Fig. A.6 are worth highlighting. First, none of the paths cross each other. Second, there are only two paths going through the steady state, one is the saddle path that we just mentioned, and the other is the unstable path that corresponds to the vertical axis. These paths are called the *stable arm* and the *unstable arm*, respectively. All two-dimensional systems of ODEs that exhibit saddle-path stability have one stable arm and one unstable arm, each going through the steady state.

Figure A.6 shows the dynamics of the economy for all possible points. The particular path followed depends on two boundary conditions, which have to be specified. As an example, suppose that the initial condition is $y_1(0) = 1$, and the terminal condition is $\lim_{t \to \infty}[y_2(t)] = 0$. The initial condition says that the economy starts anywhere on the vertical line $y_1 = 1$ (see Fig. A.6). Among all the possible points on this line, only the one on the horizontal axis has the property that y_2 approaches 0 as time goes to infinity. Hence, the terminal condition ensures that the starting point for this economy is $y_2(0) = 0$, right on the stable arm.

By symmetry, the case in which $a_{11} > 0$ and $a_{22} < 0$ also displays saddle-path stability. The only difference is that now the horizontal axis is unstable, whereas the vertical axis is stable.

The key lesson in this section is that if the matrix associated with the system of ODEs is diagonal, then its stability properties depend on the signs of the coefficients. If both are positive, then the system is unstable. If both are negative, then the system is stable. If they have opposite signs, then the system is saddle-path stable.

A nondiagonal example. When the system of ODEs is nondiagonal, we follow the same steps to construct the phase diagram. As an example, consider the case

$$\dot{y}_1(t) = 0.06 \cdot y_1(t) - y_2(t) + 1.4,$$
$$\dot{y}_2(t) = -0.004 \cdot y_1(t) + 0.04,$$
(A.21)

with the boundary conditions $y_1(0) = 1$ and $\lim_{t \to \infty}[e^{-0.06t} \cdot y_1(t)] = 0$.

The $\dot{y}_1 = 0$ locus is the upward-sloping line $y_2 = 1.4 + 0.06 \cdot y_1$. If we start at a point on the $\dot{y}_1 = 0$ schedule and increase y_1 a bit, then the right-hand side of the expression for $\dot{y}_1$ in Eq. (A.21) increases. Hence, $\dot{y}_1$ becomes positive and y_1 is increasing in that region. The arrows in this region therefore point east. A symmetric argument implies that the arrows point west for points to the left of the $\dot{y}_1 = 0$ schedule.

The $\dot{y}_2 = 0$ locus is given by $y_1 = 10$, a vertical line; that is, this locus is independent of y_2. The expression for $\dot{y}_2$ in Eq. (A.21) implies that if y_1 rises, then $\dot{y}_2$ decreases. Hence, to the right of the $\dot{y}_2 = 0$ locus, $\dot{y}_2$ is negative, and the arrows point south. The reverse is true to the left of the locus.

The two loci divide the space into four regions, labeled 1 through 4 in Fig. A.7a. The steady state is the point at which the two loci cross, a condition that corresponds in this case to $y_1^* = 10$ and $y_2^* = 2$. In region 1, the combined arrows point southwest; in region 2, northwest; in region three, northeast; and in region four, southeast.

To assess the stability properties of the system, we can ask the following question: From how many of the four regions do the arrows allow the system to move toward the steady state? If the answer is two, then the system is saddle-path stable, and the saddle path is located in these two regions.

Figure A.7a shows that the system can move toward the steady state if and only if it starts in regions 1 and 3. Therefore, the system is saddle-path stable. The saddle path, located in regions 1 and 3, goes through the steady state. If the system starts on this path, then it converges to the steady state. If it starts slightly above the saddle path in region 3—say at point x_0 in Fig. A.7a—then it follows the arrows northeast for a while. The path eventually crosses the $\dot{y}_1 = 0$ locus, and the system then moves northwest, away from the steady state. We can also show readily that the

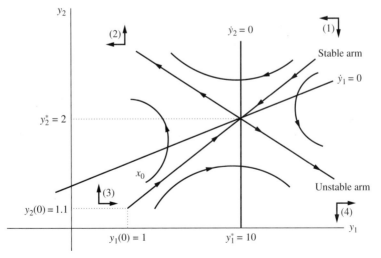

FIGURE A.7a
The phase diagram in a nonlinear example with saddle-path stability. The figure shows the phase diagram for the system in Eq. (A.21). This system is saddle-path stable.

system diverges from the steady state if it starts below the stable arm in region 3. In fact, the system diverges from the steady state if it begins at any point that is not on the stable arm.

The exact path along which the system evolves depends on the boundary conditions. This example specifies one initial and one terminal condition. The initial condition says that the system starts somewhere on the vertical line $y_1 = 1$. The terminal condition says that the product of y_1 and a term that goes to 0 at a rate of 0.06 per year goes to 0 as t goes to infinity. If the system ends up in the steady state, then y_1 will be constant, so that the product of a constant and a term that approaches zero will be zero. Hence, the terminal condition will be satisfied if y_1 approaches a constant in the long run. If the system does not end up in the steady state, then y_1 will increase or decrease at an ever increasing rate. (The arrows move the economy away from the $\dot{y}_1 = 0$ axis, and y_1 grows in magnitude at an increasing rate.) Since the product of a factor that decreases at rate of 0.06 per year and a factor whose absolute value grows at ever increasing rates is not 0, the terminal condition requires the system to end up at the steady state. It follows that because $y_1(0)$ is not at the steady state, the corresponding value $y_2(0)$ must be the one that puts the system on the stable arm, as shown in Fig. A.7a.

Suppose that we erase the normal axes and the $\dot{y}_1 = 0$ and $\dot{y}_2 = 0$ schedules, as shown in Fig. A.7b. We are then left with the stable arm (with arrows pointing toward the steady state) and the unstable arm (with arrows pointing away from the steady state). These two lines divide the space into four regions with the corresponding dynamics as represented by the arrows. Note the similarity between Fig. A.7b and Fig. A.6. We can, in fact, think of Fig. A.7b as a distorted version of Fig. A.6. This perspective will allow us to interpret the analytical solution to these systems.

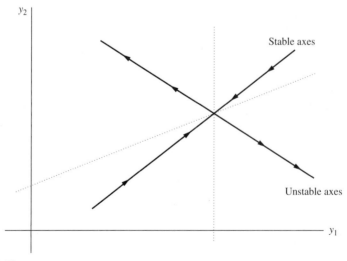

FIGURE A.7b
The stable arm and the unstable arm. This figure is generated by erasing the $y_1 = 0$ and $y_2 = 0$ schedules and the normal axes in Fig. A.7a. We are left with the stable arm and the unstable arm.

A nonlinear example. We conclude this section on phase diagrams with a nonlinear example. Consider the following system:

$$\dot{k}(t) = k(t)^{0.3} - c(t), \tag{A.22}$$

$$\dot{c}(t) = c(t) \cdot [0.3 \cdot k(t)^{-0.7} - 0.06], \tag{A.23}$$

with boundary conditions $k(0) = 1$ and $\lim_{t \to \infty}[e^{-0.06t} \cdot k(t)] = 0$. The main difference between this system and the ones already considered is that the functional forms are now nonlinear. However, to construct a phase diagram for nonlinear systems, we follow exactly the same steps as before.

The $\dot{k} = 0$ locus is given from Eq. (A.22) by $c = k^{0.3}$. If we put k on the horizontal axis and c on the vertical, then this locus is an upward-sloping and concave curve, as shown in Fig. A.8. Consider a point slightly to the right of the $\dot{k} = 0$ locus; that is, with slightly higher k and the same c. Equation (A.22) implies that the new point has a larger right-hand side; hence, $\dot{k}$ must be positive. Therefore, k rises to the right of the $\dot{k} = 0$ schedule and the arrows point east. A symmetric argument shows that the arrows point west to the left of the $\dot{k} = 0$ schedule.

The $\dot{c} = 0$ schedule is given from Eq. (A.23) by $k = 10$, a vertical line (see Fig. A.8). Consider a point to the right of the $\dot{c} = 0$ locus; that is, with the same c and higher k. Equation (A.23) implies $\dot{c} < 0$; hence, the arrows point south. By a similar argument, the arrows to the left of the $\dot{c} = 0$ schedule point north.

We can now combine the dynamics for k and c. The steady state is the point at which the $\dot{k} = 0$ and $\dot{c} = 0$ loci cross, a condition that corresponds to $k^* = 10$ and $c^* = 2$. Figure A.8 shows that the arrows are such that the system approaches the steady state only from regions 1 and 3. We conclude that the system is saddle-path

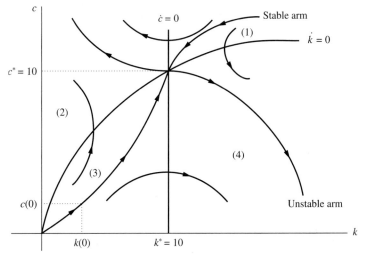

FIGURE A.8
The phase diagram for a nonlinear model. The figure shows the phase diagram for the system in Eqs. (A.22) and (A.23). This system is saddle-path stable.

stable. The stable arm in this case is *not* a linear function. It is still true, however, that the stable arm runs between regions 1 and 3 and goes through the steady state. The unstable arm moves between regions 2 and 4.

We can again use the boundary conditions to select the path that the system will follow. In this example, the boundary conditions ensure that the system begins on the stable arm and therefore approaches its steady state over time.

ANALYTICAL SOLUTIONS OF LINEAR, HOMOGENEOUS SYSTEMS. We now consider the analytical solution to systems of linear ODEs. We start with the homogeneous case because the solution to the general case is intensive in notation. The $x(t)$ vector in Eq. (A.19) is then set to 0, so the system becomes

$$\dot{y}(t) = A \cdot y(t), \tag{A.24}$$

where $y(t)$ is an $n \times 1$ column vector of functions of time, $y_i(t)$, A is an $n \times n$ matrix of constant coefficients, and $\dot{y}(t)$ is the vector of time derivatives corresponding to $y(t)$.

Imagine that there is an $n \times n$ matrix V with the property that if we premultiply A by V^{-1} and postmultiply by V, then we get a diagonal $n \times n$ matrix:

$$V^{-1}AV - D, \tag{A.25}$$

where D is a square matrix in which all the off-diagonal elements are 0. Section 1.4 shows that V and D may exist: they are, respectively, the matrix of eigenvectors and the diagonal matrix of eigenvalues associated with A.[3]

We can define the variables $z(t)$ as

$$z(t) = V^{-1} \cdot y(t).$$

Since V^{-1} is a matrix of constants, $\dot{z}(t) = V^{-1} \cdot \dot{y}(t)$. We can therefore rewrite the system from Eq. (A.24) in terms of the transformed $z(t)$ variables:

$$\dot{z}(t) = V^{-1} \cdot \dot{y}(t) = V^{-1}A \cdot y(t) = V^{-1}AVV^{-1} \cdot y(t) = D \cdot z(t) \tag{A.26}$$

This system consists of n one-dimensional differential equations:

$$\dot{z}_1(t) = \alpha_1 \cdot z_1(t),$$
$$\dot{z}_2(t) = \alpha_2 \cdot z_2(t),$$
$$\cdots \tag{A.27}$$
$$\dot{z}_n(t) = \alpha_n \cdot z_n(t).$$

We showed in Section 1.1.2 that the solution for each of these differential equations takes the form $z_i(t) = b_i \cdot e^{\alpha_i t}$, where each b_i is an arbitrary constant of integra-

---

[3] A sufficient condition for the matrix A to be diagonalizable is for all the eigenvalues to be different. In this case, the eigenvectors are linearly independent, so that $\det(V) \neq 0$ and V^{-1} exists.

tion that is determined by the boundary conditions (see Eq. [A.11]). We can express this result in matrix notation as

$$z(t) = Eb, \tag{A.28}$$

where E is a diagonal matrix with $e^{\alpha_i t}$ in the ith diagonal term, and b is a column vector of the constants b_i.

We can transform the solution for the z variables back to the y variables by using the relation $y + Vz$. The solution for y is

$$y = VEb,$$

or, in nonmatrix notation,

$$y_i(t) = v_{i1}e^{\alpha_1 t} \cdot b_1 + v_{i2}e^{\alpha_2 t} \cdot b_2 + \cdots + v_{in}e^{\alpha_n t} \cdot b_n. \tag{A.29}$$

In summary, the general method to solve a system of equations of the form of Eq. (A.24) is

1. Find the eigenvalues of the matrix A and call them $\alpha_1, \ldots, \alpha_n$.
2. Find the corresponding eigenvectors and arrange them as columns in a matrix V.
3. The solution takes the form of Eq. (A.29).
4. Use the boundary conditions to determine the arbitrary constants of integration (b_i).

THE RELATION BETWEEN THE GRAPHICAL AND ANALYTICAL SOLU-TIONS. We now relate the graphical and analytical approaches to each other. Remember that when we constructed the phase diagram, we suggested that if we erase the axes and the $\dot{y}_i = 0$ loci and look at the remaining picture in Fig. A.7b, we get a distorted version of the picture in Fig. A.6, for which the matrix A was diagonal. We saw also that the analytical solution involved a diagonal matrix of eigenvalues. The similarities in the two approaches are no coincidence: when we diagonalize a matrix we implicitly find a set of axes (or vector basis) on which the linear application represented by A can be written as a diagonal matrix (see Section 1.4). The new axes are the eigenvectors, and the elements in the corresponding diagonal matrix are the eigenvalues.

The graphical solution to the system of equations is basically the same thing. The stable and unstable arms correspond to the two eigenvectors. If we think of these two arms as a new set of axes—that is, if we erase the old axes and the $\dot{y}_i = 0$ schedules—then the old matrix A can be represented by the diagonal eigenvalue matrix. The phase diagram for the nondiagonal case looks accordingly like a distorted version of the diagonal one.

STABILITY. Recall that the stability properties of the diagonal examples depend on the signs of the diagonal elements. Not surprisingly, therefore, the stability properties of the nondiagonal system depend on the signs of its eigenvalues. Several possibilities arise:

(*a*) The two eigenvalues are *real* and *positive*. In this case, the system is unstable.

(*b*) The two eigenvalues are *real* and *negative*. In this case the system is stable.

(*c*) The two eigenvalues are *real* with *opposite signs*. In this case, the system is saddle-path stable. Furthermore, when the system is saddle-path stable, the *stable arm corresponds to the eigenvector associated with the negative eigenvalue*.[4] Similarly, the unstable arm corresponds to the eigenvector associated with the positive eigenvalue. The intuition is again that the axes associated with the diagonal matrix are given by the eigenvectors. As we saw in the examples, when the system is diagonal, the axis associated with the negative component of the diagonal matrix is the stable arm, and the axis associated with the positive component is the unstable arm.

(*d*) The two eigenvalues are *complex* with *negative real parts*. The system converges in this case to the steady state in an oscillating manner (Figure A.9a).

(*e*) The two eigenvalues are *complex* with *positive real parts*. The system is unstable and oscillating, as depicted in Fig. A.9b.

(*f*) The two eigenvalues are *complex* with *zero real parts*. The trajectories are then ellipses around the steady state, as shown in Fig. A.9c.

(*g*) The two eigenvalues are *equal*. In this case, the matrix of eigenvectors cannot be inverted, and the analytical solution outlined earlier in this section cannot be applied. The solution in this case takes the form

$$y_i(t) = (b_{i1} + b_{i2} \cdot t) \cdot e^{\alpha t},$$

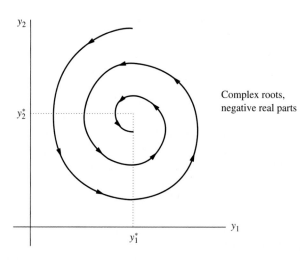

FIGURE A.9a
Stable, oscillating dynamics. If the two eigenvalues are complex with negative real parts, then the system converges to the steady state in an oscillating manner.

---

[4]Throughout the book we will use interchangeably the terms eigenvector associated with negative eigenvalue and negative eigenvector.

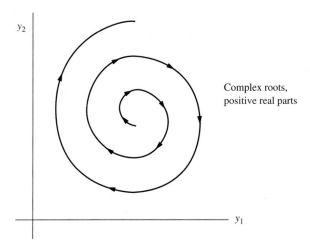

FIGURE A.9b
Unstable, oscillating dynamics. If the two eigenvalues are complex with positive real parts, then the system diverges from the steady state in an oscillating manner.

where b_{i1} and b_{i2} are functions of the constants of integration and the coefficients in A, and α is the unique eigenvalue. The solution is stable if $\alpha < 0$ and unstable if $\alpha > 0$.

We should mention that in nonlinear systems, there is one more type of equilibrium called a *limit cycle*. A stable limit cycle is one toward which trajectories converge, and an unstable limit cycle is one from which trajectories diverge.

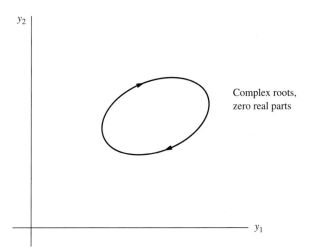

FIGURE A.9c
Oscillating dynamics. If the two eigenvalues are complex with 0 real parts, then the trajectories are ellipses around the steady state. This system neither converges nor diverges.

The stability properties of systems with higher dimensions are similar. If all eigenvalues are positive, then the system is unstable. If all the eigenvalues are negative, then the system is stable. If the eigenvalues have different signs, then the system is saddle-path stable. Since, as argued before, the stable arm corresponds to the eigenvector(s) associated with the negative eigenvalue(s), the dimension of the stable arm is the number of negative eigenvalues. For instance, in a 3×3 system with one negative eigenvalue, the stable arm is a line going through the steady state and corresponding to the negative eigenvector. If there are two negative eigenvalues, then the stable manifold is a plane going through the steady state. This plane is generated by the two negative eigenvalues. In an $n \times n$ system, the stable arm (sometimes called the *stable manifold*) is a hyperplane generated by the associated eigenvectors, with dimension equal to the number of negative eigenvalues.

ANALYTICAL SOLUTIONS OF LINEAR, NONHOMOGENEOUS SYSTEMS.
Consider now the nonhomogeneous system of differential equations,

$$\dot{y}(t) = A \cdot y(t) + x(t), \tag{A.30}$$

where $y(t)$ is an $n \times 1$ vector of functions of time, $\dot{y}(t)$ is the corresponding vector of time derivatives, A is an $n \times n$ matrix of constants, and $x(t)$ is an $n \times 1$ vector of known functions of time, where these functions can be constants. The procedure to find the solutions to Eq. (A.30) parallels the one that we used for the homogeneous case. Begin again with the matrix V, composed of the eigenvectors of A, such that $V^{-1}AV$ generates a diagonal matrix D, which contains the eigenvalues of A. Transform the system by premultiplying all terms by V^{-1} and then define $z \equiv V^{-1}y$ to get

$$\dot{z} = V^{-1}\dot{y} = V^{-1} \cdot (Ay + x) = V^{-1}AVV^{-1}y + V^{-1}x = Dz + V^{-1}x.$$

This matrix equation defines a system of n linear differential equations of the form

$$\dot{z}_i(t) = \alpha_i \cdot z_i(t) + V_i^{-1} \cdot x(t),$$

where V_i^{-1} is the ith row of V^{-1}. As we saw in Section 1.1.2, the solution to each of these linear ODEs with fixed coefficients takes the form of equations (A.11):

$$z_i(t) = e^{\alpha_i t} \cdot \int e^{-\alpha_i \tau} \cdot V_i^{-1} \cdot x(\tau) \cdot d\tau + e^{\alpha_i t} \cdot b_i,$$

for $i = 1, \ldots, n$, where b_i is again an arbitrary constant of integration. We can write these solutions in matrix notation as

$$z = E\hat{X} + Eb, \tag{A.31}$$

where, again, E is a diagonal matrix of terms $e^{\alpha_i t}$, $\hat{X}$ is a column vector with integrals of the form $\int e^{-\alpha_i \tau} \cdot V_i^{-1} \cdot x(\tau) \cdot d\tau$ as each of its elements, and b is a column vector of arbitrary constants. Once the time path of z is known, we can find the time path of y by premultiplying z by V.

As an example, consider the system of ODEs in Eq.(A.21). In matrix notation, this system can be written as

$$\begin{bmatrix} \dot{y}_1(t) \\ \dot{y}_2(t) \end{bmatrix} = \begin{bmatrix} 0.06 & -1 \\ -0.004 & 0 \end{bmatrix} \begin{bmatrix} y_1(t) \\ y_2(t) \end{bmatrix} + \begin{bmatrix} 1.4 \\ 0.04 \end{bmatrix}, \tag{A.32}$$

with the boundary conditions $y_1(0) = 1$ and $\lim_{t\to\infty}[e^{-0.06 \cdot t} \cdot y_1(t)] = 0$. In this example, x is a vector of constants. In Section 1.4, we show how to find the eigenvalues and eigenvectors associated with a matrix A. We find that the diagonal matrix of eigenvalues, D, and the matrix of eigenvectors, V, are given by

$$D = \begin{bmatrix} 0.1 & 0 \\ 0 & -0.4 \end{bmatrix}, \quad V = \begin{bmatrix} 1 & 1 \\ -0.04 & 0.1 \end{bmatrix},$$

where $V^{-1} = \begin{bmatrix} 0.1/0.14 & -1/0.14 \\ 0.04/0.14 & 1/0.14 \end{bmatrix}$.

Define $\begin{bmatrix} z_1 \\ z_2 \end{bmatrix} = V^{-1} \begin{bmatrix} y_1 \\ y_2 \end{bmatrix}$. The system in terms of the new variables can be written as

$$\dot{z}_1 = 0.1 \cdot z_1 + 10/14,$$

$$\dot{z}_2 = -0.04 \cdot z_2 + 9.6/14,$$

a system of two differential equations that we know how to solve (see Section 1.1.2):

$$z_1(t) = 100/14 + b_1 e^{0.1 \cdot t},$$

$$z_2(t) = 240/14 + b_2 e^{-0.04 \cdot t},$$

where b_1 and b_2 are constants of integration, which have to be pinned down by the boundary conditions. We can transform the solution for z_1 and z_2 into a solution for y_1 and y_2 by premultiplying z by V^{-1} to get

$$y_1(t) = 10 + b_1 e^{0.1 \cdot t} + b_2 e^{-0.04 \cdot t}, \tag{A.33}$$

$$y_2(t) = 2 - 0.04 \cdot b_1 e^{0.1 \cdot t} + 0.1 \cdot b_2 e^{-0.04 \cdot t}. \tag{A.34}$$

We now need to determine the values of the constants, b_1 and b_2. The initial condition $y_1(0) = 1$ implies $b_1 + b_2 = -9$. We can multiply both sides of Eq. (A.32) by $e^{-0.06 \cdot t}$, take limits as t goes to infinity, and use the terminal condition, $\lim_{t\to\infty}[e^{-0.06 \cdot t} \cdot y_1(t)] = 0$, to get

$$\lim_{t\to\infty}[e^{-0.06 \cdot t} \cdot y_1(t)] = \lim_{t\to\infty}[10 \cdot e^{-0.06 \cdot t} + b_1 e^{0.04 \cdot t} + b_2 e^{-0.1 \cdot t}] = 0.$$

The first and third terms in the middle expression go to 0 as t goes to infinity, but the second term approaches infinity unless b_1 equals 0. Hence, the condition for the whole expression to equal 0 is $b_1 = 0$, which implies $b_2 = -9$. The exact solution to the system of ODEs is therefore

$$y_1(t) = 10 - 9 \cdot e^{-0.04 \cdot t},$$

$$y_2(t) = 2 - 0.9 \cdot e^{-0.04 \cdot t}.$$

Note that $y_1(t)$ equals 1 at $t = 0$, increases over time, and asymptotes to its steady-state value, $y_1^* = 10$ (see Fig. A.10a). The variable y_2 equals 1.1 at $t = 0$, increases over time, and asymptotes to its steady-state value, $y_2^* = 2$ (see Fig. A.10b). In other words, the boundary conditions select the initial value of y_2 that causes the system to end up at its steady state. In terms of Fig. A.7a, the value $y_2(0)$ is chosen

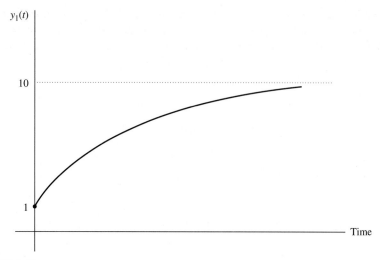

FIGURE A.10a
Solution for $y_1(t)$. The figure shows the solution for $y_1(t)$ in the system in Eq. (A.32).

so as to put the system on the stable arm. At the initial point, $\begin{bmatrix} y_1(0) \\ y_2(0) \end{bmatrix} = \begin{bmatrix} 1 \\ 1.1 \end{bmatrix}$, the vector going toward the steady state is $\begin{bmatrix} 9 \\ 0.9 \end{bmatrix}$ or, by normalizing the first element to unity, $\begin{bmatrix} 1 \\ 0.1 \end{bmatrix}$, the negative eigenvector. Hence, as noted before, the stable arm goes through the steady state and corresponds to the eigenvector associated with the negative eigenvalue.

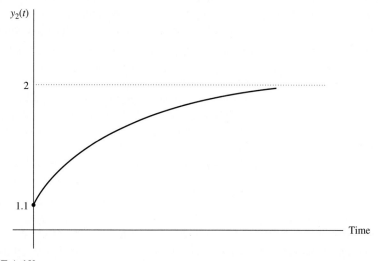

FIGURE A.10b
Solution for $y_2(t)$. The figure shows the solution for $y_2(t)$ in the system in Eq. (A.32).

LINEARIZATION OF NONLINEAR SYSTEMS. Many of the systems of ODEs that we encounter in the book are nonlinear. In this case, we can use the phase-diagram techniques that we discussed before, or alternatively, we can approximate the equations linearly by means of Taylor-series expansions.

Consider the following system of ODEs:

$$\dot{y}_1(t) = f^1[y_1(t), \ldots y_n(t)],$$
$$\dot{y}_2(t) = f^2[y_1(t), \ldots y_n(t)],$$
$$\cdots$$
$$\dot{y}_n(t) = f^n[y_1(t), \ldots y_n(t)],$$
(A.35)

where the functions $f^1(\bullet)$, $f^2(\bullet)$, ..., $f^n(\bullet)$ are nonlinear. We can use a Taylor-series expansion to study the system's dynamics in the neighborhood of its steady state. (Taylor's Theorem is in Section 1.5.2.) The first-order expansion can be written as

$$\dot{y}_1(t) = f^1(\bullet) + (f^1)_{y_1}(\bullet) \cdot (y_1 - y_1^*) + \cdots + (f^n)_{y_n}(\bullet) \cdot (y_n - y_n^*) + R_1,$$
$$\cdots$$
(A.36)
$$\dot{y}_n(t) = f^n(\bullet) + (f^n)_{y_1}(\bullet) \cdot (y_1 - y_1^*) + \cdots + (f^n)_{y_n}(\bullet) \cdot (y_n - y_n^*) + R_n,$$

where $f^1(\bullet)$, ..., $f^n(\bullet)$ are the values of the functions $f^1(\bullet)$, ..., $f^n(\bullet)$ at the steady state, and $(f^1)_{y_i}(\bullet)$, ..., $(f^n)_{y_i}(\bullet)$ are the partial derivatives with respect to y_i at the steady state. The terms R_i are the Taylor residuals. If the system is close to its steady state, then these residuals are small and can be neglected. The convenience of linearizing around the steady state is that by definition of a steady state, the first element in each of the equations—$f^1(\bullet), \cdots, f^n(\bullet)$—is 0; that is, the steady-state value of $\dot{y}_i$ is zero for all i.

The linearized system in Eq. (A.36) can be written in matrix notation as

$$\dot{y} = A \cdot (y - y^*),$$
(A.37)

where A is an $n \times n$ matrix of constants corresponding to the first partial derivatives evaluated at the steady state. This linear system is similar to those analyzed in previous sections.

Consider the system of nonlinear equations that we have already studied graphically,

$$\dot{k} = k^{0.3} - c,$$
(A.22)

$$\dot{c} = c \cdot (0.3 \cdot k^{-0.7} - 0.06),$$
(A.23)

with the boundary conditions $k(0) = 1$ and $\lim_{t \to \infty}[e^{-0.06t} \cdot k(t)] = 0$. The steady-state values are $k^* = 10$ and $c^* = 2$. We can linearize this system as follows:

$$\dot{k} = 0.3 \cdot (k^*)^{-0.7} \cdot (k - k^*) - (c - c^*) = 0.06 \cdot k - c + 1.4,$$
(A.38)

$$\dot{c} = c^* \cdot [0.3 \cdot (-0.7) \cdot (k^*)^{-1.7}] \cdot (k - k^*) - 0 \cdot (c - c^*) = -0.004 \cdot k + 0.04.$$

We know how to solve this linear system; in fact, we have already solved it! If we relabel k and c as y_1 and y_2, respectively, then it coincides with the system in Eq. (A.32).

As a graphical intuition, consider the phase diagram that we constructed for the nonlinear system defined by Eqs. (A.22) and (A.23), as depicted in Fig. A.8. The loci in this figure are nonlinear. Around the steady state, however, the $\dot{c} = 0$ locus is vertical, and the $\dot{k} = 0$ locus is upward sloping. We can approximate these two loci with a vertical line and an upward-sloping line going through the same steady state. When the system is close to its steady state, this approximation is good. The approximation deteriorates as we move away from the steady state because the $\dot{k} = 0$ schedule is strictly concave. The dynamics of the nonlinear system is similar to that of the linear system in the vicinity of the steady state. In fact, at the steady state, the nonlinear stable arm corresponds to the negative eigenvector of the linearized system. Qualitatively, we see by comparing Figs. A.7a and A.8 that the two systems have similar dynamic properties.

THE TIME-ELIMINATION METHOD FOR NONLINEAR SYSTEMS. In Section 1.1.3, we saw that one way to get a qualitative solution to a system of nonlinear differential equations was to use a phase diagram. The problem with this graphical approach is that it does not allow us to evaluate the model quantitatively. Later in that section, we worked out an analytical solution to a linearized version of the system. The problem with this approach is that the quantification is local, valid only as an approximation in the neighborhood of the steady state. This section describes a method to find global numerical solutions to a system of ODEs. This method provides accurate results for a given configuration of parameters.

Consider again the system on nonlinear equations defined by Eqs. (A.22) and (A.23):

$$\dot{k}(t) = k(t)^{0.3} - c(t), \tag{A.22}$$

$$\dot{c}(t) = c(t) \cdot [0.3 \cdot k(t)^{-0.7} - 0.06], \tag{A.23}$$

with the boundary conditions $k(0) = 1$ and $\lim_{t \to \infty} [e^{-0.06t} \cdot k(t)] = 0$. The phase diagram for this system is in Fig. A.8. If we knew the initial values, $c(0)$ and $k(0)$, then standard numerical methods for solving differential equations would allow us to solve out for the entire paths of c and k by integrating Eqs. (A.22) and (A.23) with respect to time.[5]

The problem is that $c(0)$ is unknown. Instead, we are given the transversality condition, a restriction that forces the initial value of c to be on the stable arm. The challenge is to express this condition in terms of the required value of $c(0)$. The usual solution involves a method called *shooting*. Start with a guess about $c(0)$, and

---

[5]When the boundary conditions of a problem take the form of a set of values for all the variables at a single point in time, then we call it an *initial-value problem*. For instance, the problem above would be an initial-value problem if we replaced the transversality condition, $\lim_{t \to \infty} [e^{-0.06t} \cdot k(t)] = 0$, with some value for $c(0)$. In contrast, for a *boundary-value problem*, the boundary conditions apply at different points in time. The system given above is a *boundary-value problem* because we are given an initial condition, $k(0) = 1$, which applies at $t = 0$, and a terminal condition, $\lim_{t \to \infty} [e^{-0.06t} \cdot k(t)] = 0$, which applies at $t = \infty$. Initial-value problems are much easier to solve numerically.

then work out the time paths implied by the differential Eqs. (A.22) and (A.23). Then check whether the time paths approach the steady state and therefore satisfy the transversality condition. If the paths miss—as is almost sure to be true on the first guess—then the system eventually diverges from the steady state. In this case, adjust the guess accordingly; reduce the conjectured value of $c(0)$ if the prior guess is too high, and vice versa. An approximation to the correct $c(0)$ can be found by iterating many times in this manner.

Mulligan and Sala-i-Martin (1991) worked out a much more efficient numerical technique called the *time-elimination method*. The key to this method is to eliminate time from the equations, just as we do when we construct a phase diagram. Recall that the stable arm shown in Fig. A.8 expresses c as a function of k. In dynamic programming, this function is sometimes called the *policy function*. Imagine for a moment that we had a closed-form solution to this policy function, $c = c(k)$. In this case, we could use Eq. (A.22) to express $\dot{k}$ as a function of k: $\dot{k} = k^{0.3} - c(k)$. Since we know $k(0)$, we could use standard numerical methods to solve this first-order differential equation in k. Once we knew the path for k, we could determine the path for c (since we know the policy function, $c[k]$).

The time-elimination method provides a numerical technique for working out the policy function, $c = c(k)$. The trick is to note that the slope of this function is given by the ratio of $\dot{c}$ to $\dot{k}$:

$$dc/dk = c'(k) = \dot{c}/\dot{k} = \frac{c(k) \cdot [0.3 \cdot k^{-0.7} - 0.06]}{k^{0.3} - c(k)}, \qquad (A.39)$$

where we used the formulas for $\dot{k}$ and $\dot{c}$ from Eqs. (A.22) and (A.23). Time does not appear in Eq. (A.39); hence, the name time-elimination method.

Note that Eq. (A.39) is a differential equation in c, where the derivative, dc/dk, is with respect to k rather than to t. To solve this equation numerically by standard methods, we need one boundary condition; that is, we have to know one point, (c, k), that lies on the stable arm. Although we do not know the initial pair, $[c(0), k(0)]$, we know that the policy function goes through the steady state, (c^*, k^*). We can therefore start from this point and then solve Eq. (A.39) numerically to determine the rest of the policy function.[6] Note that, by eliminating time, we transformed a difficult *boundary-value problem* into a much easier *initial-value problem*.

Before we implement this method, there is one more problem that must be addressed. The slope of the policy function at the steady state is

$$c'(k^*) = (\dot{c})^*/(\dot{k})^* = 0/0,$$

which is an indeterminate form. There are two ways to solve this problem. The first one uses l'Hôpital's rule for evaluating indeterminate forms (see Section 1.5.3). In this example, the application of l'Hôpital's rule yields

---

[6]We might have considered starting from the steady state and going backwards in time to solve the original system of two differential equations numerically. This idea does not work, however, because $\dot{k}$ and $\dot{c}$ are 0 at the steady state. Therefore, if we start at the steady state, then we do not know how to move backwards in time; that is, we cannot tell from where we came.

$$c'(k^*) = \left[c^* \cdot (-0.21) \cdot (k^*)^{-1.7} \right] / \left[0.3 \cdot (k^*)^{-0.7} - c'(k^*) \right],$$

which implies a quadratic equation in $c'(k)$:

$$[c'(k^*)]^2 - [0.3 \cdot (k^*)^{-0.7}] \cdot c'(k^*) - 0.21 \cdot c^* \cdot (k^*)^{-1.7} = 0.$$

This equation has two solutions for $c'(k^*)$:

$$c'(k^*) = [0.3 \cdot (k^*)^{-0.7} - \left\{ [0.3 \cdot (k^*)^{-0.7}]^2 - 4 \cdot (0.21) \cdot c^* \cdot (k^*)^{-1.7} \right\}^{1/2}]/2, \quad \text{(A.40)}$$

$$c'(k^*) = [0.3 \cdot (k^*)^{-0.7} + \left\{ [0.3 \cdot (k^*)^{-0.7}]^2 - 4 \cdot (0.21) \cdot c^* \cdot (k^*)^{-1.7} \right\}^{1/2}]/2. \quad \text{(A.41)}$$

There are two solutions because there are two trajectories that go through the steady state: the stable arm and the unstable arm. The phase diagram in Fig. A.8 suggests that the stable arm is upward sloping and the unstable arm is downward sloping. Since the slope of the stable arm at the steady state is positive, it must be given by the solution in Eq. (A.41).

The second way to compute the steady-state is to realize that at the steady state, the policy function corresponds to the negative eigenvector. In other words, the slope of the negative eigenvector coincides with the steady-state slope of the policy function. Hence, we can use this value as the initial slope and then use Eq. (A.39) to compute the whole policy function. The advantage of the eigenvalue method over the l'Hôpital's rule method is that it does not require prior qualitative information about the sign of the steady-state slope.

The time-elimination method can be readily extended to systems of three differential equations with two controls and one state variable (see Mulligan and Sala-i-Martin [1991, 1993]). Consider a nonlinear system of equations,

$$\dot{c}(t) = c[c(t), u(t), k(t)],$$
$$\dot{u}(t) = u[c(t), u(t), k(t)], \qquad \qquad \text{(A.42)}$$
$$\dot{k}(t) = k[c(t), u(t), k(t)],$$

where $c(t)$ and $u(t)$ are control variables, and $k(t)$ is the state variable. Imagine that we are given the initial value $k(0)$ and two transversality conditions (which apply at $t = \infty$). Suppose that the steady-state values are c^*, u^*, and k^*. Again, if we knew $c(0)$ and $u(0)$, then we could find the solution to Eq. (A.42) by integrating with respect to time. The problem, however, is that $c(0)$ and $u(0)$ are unknown.

Imagine for the moment that we had closed-form expressions for $c(k)$ and $u(k)$, the policy functions for the problem. In this case, we could plug these two functions into the $\dot{k}$ equation to get a single differential equation in k. Since we know $k(0)$, the whole time path for $k(t)$ could be found by integrating this differential equation with respect to time. Once we knew the path for k, we could determine the paths for c and u by plugging $k(t)$ into the two functions $c(k)$ and $u(k)$.

The time-elimination method provides a simple way to find $c(k)$ and $u(k)$ numerically. Use the chain rule of calculus to eliminate time from Eq. (A.42) to get the slopes of $c(k)$ and $u(k)$ as follows:

$$dc/dk = c'(k) = \dot{c}/\dot{k} = \frac{c[c(k), u(k), k]}{k[c(k), u(k), k]},$$

(A.43)

$$du/dk = u'(k) = \dot{u}/\dot{k} = \frac{u[c(k), u(k), k]}{k[c(k), u(k), k]}.$$

We can solve this system numerically by using the steady state, (c^*, u^*, k^*), as the initial condition. The steady-state slopes can be found by using l'Hôpital's rule or by computing the slope of the eigenvector associated with the negative eigenvalue.

1.2 STATIC OPTIMIZATION

1.2.1 Unconstrained Maxima

Consider a univariate real function $u(\cdot)$. We say that a function $u(x)$ has a local maximum at $\bar{\bar{x}}$ if for all x in the neighborhood of $\bar{\bar{x}}$ (that is, for all x in the interval $[x - \epsilon, x + \epsilon]$, where ϵ is some positive number), $u(\bar{\bar{x}}) \geq u(x)$. We say that $u(x)$ has an absolute maximum[7] at $\bar{\bar{x}}$ if for all x in the domain of u, $u(\bar{\bar{x}}) \geq u(x)$.

Let $u(x)$ be twice continuously differentiable in the closed interval $[a, b]$ and let $\bar{\bar{x}}$ in the interior of $[a, b]$ be a local maximum. A *necessary condition* for $\bar{\bar{x}}$ to be an *interior local maximum* is for the first derivative of $u(\cdot)$ evaluated at $\bar{\bar{x}}$ to be 0, $u'(\bar{\bar{x}}) = 0$, and for the second derivative to be nonpositive, $u''(\bar{\bar{x}}) \leq 0$. If $u'(\bar{\bar{x}}) = 0$ and $u''(\bar{\bar{x}}) \leq 0$, then $\bar{\bar{x}}$ is an interior local maximum. That is, if the objective function is strictly concave (a negative second derivative), then the necessary condition $u'(\bar{\bar{x}}) = 0$ is also a *sufficient condition*.

For practical purposes, if we want to find the maximum of a function in some interval, we compute the first derivative of that function and find the values of x that satisfy the equation $u'(\bar{\bar{x}}) = 0$. This condition gives us some candidate points, often called *critical points*. We then compute the second derivative of $u(\cdot)$ and evaluate it at the critical points. If it is negative, then the critical point is a local maximum. We then compare the values $u(\bar{\bar{x}})$ with the value of the function at each of the corners a and b. The absolute maximum of $u(\cdot)$ in the interval $[a, b]$ occurs at one of the $\bar{\bar{x}}$, a, or b, depending on which has the largest image.

The multidimensional case is similar to the unidimensional case that we just described. Consider a function $u : R^n \to R$, twice continuously differentiable. A necessary condition for $u(x)$ to have an interior local maximum at $\bar{x}$ (where x is now an n-dimensional vector, $x \equiv [x_1, \ldots, x_n]$) is for all the partial derivatives to vanish when evaluated at $\bar{\bar{x}}$. In other words, just as in the unidimensional case, functions are "flat at the top."

---

[7] A function $u(\cdot)$ achieves a minimum at point $\bar{\bar{x}}$ if $-u(\cdot)$ achieves a maximum at that point. Hence, to analyze minima of the function $u(\cdot)$, we can analyze maxima of $-u(\cdot)$.

These necessary conditions are not sufficient, however, because local minima and saddle points also satisfy them. As a parallel to the unidimensional case, a sufficient condition is for the function u to be strictly concave at the critical point.[8]

1.2.2 Classical Nonlinear Programming: Equality Constraints

Suppose that we want to find the maximum of the function $u : R^n \to R$, subject to the constraint that the chosen point lie along a plane generated by the restriction $g(x) = a$, where $g : R^n \to R$, and x is an n-dimensional vector, $x \equiv (x_1, \ldots, x_n)$. That is, the problem is

$$\max_{x_1 \ldots x_n} [u(x_1, \ldots, x_n)], \text{ subject to}$$
$$g(x_1, \ldots, x_n) = a. \qquad (A.44)$$

We assume that $u(\cdot)$ and $g(\cdot)$ are twice continuously differentiable. One easy way to solve this problem is to realize that the restriction describes an implicit function for x_1, $x_1 = \tilde{x}_1(x_2, \ldots, x_n)$. (We assume here that the restriction uniquely determines x_1 for given values of $x_2, \ldots, x_n$.) We can plug the result for x_1 into $u(x)$ to get an unconstrained function of $(x_2, \ldots, x_n)$:

$$u[x_1(x_2, \ldots, x_n), (x_2, \ldots x_n)] \equiv \tilde{u}(x_2, \ldots, x_n). \qquad (A.45)$$

As just mentioned, the necessary condition for an unconstrained maximum of a function is for all the partial derivatives to vanish. When taking partial derivatives of $u(\cdot)$ with respect to each of the arguments x_i, $i = 2, \ldots, n$, we have to realize that $u(\cdot)$ depends on x_i directly and also indirectly through the dependence of x_1 on x_i. Hence, the necessary condition for a constrained maximum is

$$\partial \tilde{u}(\cdot)/\partial x_i = [\partial u(\cdot)/\partial x_1] \cdot \partial \tilde{x}_1/\partial x_i + \partial u(\cdot)/\partial x_i = 0 \qquad (A.46)$$

for $i = 2, \ldots, n$. We can calculate the partial derivatives $\partial \tilde{x}_1/\partial x_i$ from the implicit function theorem (Section 1.5.1), $\partial \tilde{x}_1/\partial x_i = -[\partial g(\cdot)/\partial x_i]/[\partial g(\cdot)/\partial x_1]$. By plugging this expression into Eq. (A.46) we get

$$\frac{\partial g(\cdot)/\partial x_i}{\partial g(\cdot)/\partial x_1} = \frac{\partial u(\cdot)/\partial x_i}{\partial u(\cdot)/\partial x_1}. \qquad (A.47)$$

---

[8] One way to check strict concavity is to determine the definiteness of the Hessian, the matrix of second derivatives: if the Hessian is negative definite, then the function u is strictly concave. A matrix is *negative definite* if and only if all its eigenvalues are strictly negative. A matrix is *negative semidefinite* if and only if all its eigenvalues are nonpositive. A matrix is *positive definite* if and only if all its eigenvalues are positive. A matrix is *positive semidefinite* if and only if all its eigenvalues are nonnegative. A matrix is not definite if its eigenvalues do not all have the same signs. As we argued in a previous section, if we want to know the signs of the eigenvalues, then we do not necessarily have to calculate them. For instance, in the 2×2 case, if the determinant of a matrix is negative, then the eigenvalues must have opposite signs, because the determinant of the matrix equals the product of its eigenvalues.

Another way to write down the same conditions is for each of the partial derivatives of g with respect to x_i to be proportional to the partial derivative of u with respect to x_i, where the constant of proportionality μ is the same for all i. This set of conditions can be written in matrix notation as

$$Du(\overline{\overline{x}}) = \mu \cdot Dg(\overline{\overline{x}}), \qquad (A.48)$$

where $\overline{\overline{x}}$ is an n-dimensional vector, and Dg and Du are the vectors of partial derivatives of g and u with respect to each of their arguments ($Dg \equiv [\partial g(\bullet)/\partial x_1, \ldots, \partial g(\bullet)/\partial x_n]$, and analogously for Du). The vectors Dg and Du are called the *gradients* of g and u, respectively. The gradient of a function $u(\bullet)$ evaluated at a point $\overline{\overline{x}}$ is a vector perpendicular to the tangent line of the function at that point (see Fig. A.11). Equation (A.48) says that a necessary condition for $\overline{\overline{x}}$ to be a maximum of the constrained problem is for the gradient of the restriction to be proportional to the gradient of the objective function at that point. The factor of proportionality is often called the *Lagrange Multiplier, μ*.

If we think of $u(\bullet)$ as a utility function and $g(\bullet) = a$ as a budget constraint (total spending, $g[\bullet]$, equals total income, a), then Eq. (A.48) is the familiar equality between marginal rates of substitution and marginal rates of tansformation (or relative prices).

A convenient device for the derivation of these first-order conditions is the *Lagrangian*, which adds to the objective function a constant μ times the constraint:

$$L(\bullet) = u(x_1, \ldots, x_n) + \mu \cdot [a - g(x_1, \ldots, x_n)]. \qquad (A.49)$$

The first-order conditions in Eq. (A.48) are found by taking derivatives of the Lagrangian with respect to each of its arguments. Note that the derivative with respect to the Lagrange multiplier, μ, recovers the constraint.

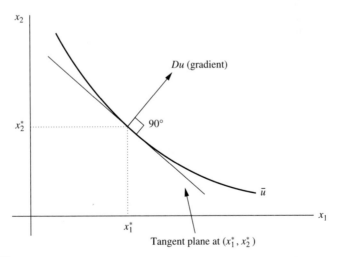

FIGURE A.11
Solution to a maximization problem subject to equality constraints. The figure illustrates the solution from Eq. (A.48), which involves a Lagrange Multiplier, μ.

To give an economic interpretation to the Lagrange multiplier, consider the change in utility, $u(\cdot)$, when income, a, changes. The total change in utility is given by

$$du(\cdot)/da = \sum_{i=1}^{n}[\partial u(\cdot)/\partial x_i] \cdot \partial \bar{\bar{x}}_i/\partial a,$$

where $\partial \bar{\bar{x}}_i/\partial a$ is the change in the optimal quantity of good x_i when the constraint is relaxed by the amount ∂a. We can use the first-order conditions in Eq. (A.48) to rewrite this expression as

$$du(\cdot)/da = \sum_{i=1}^{n} \mu \cdot [\partial g(\cdot)/\partial x_i] \cdot \partial \bar{\bar{x}}_i/\partial a. \tag{A.50}$$

If we totally differentiate the budget constraint with respect to a, then we get

$$dg(\cdot)/da = \sum_{i=1}^{n}[\partial g(\cdot)/\partial x_i] \cdot \partial x_i/\partial a = 1.$$

Substitution of this result into Eq. (A.50) implies

$$du(\cdot)/da = \mu. \tag{A.51}$$

In other words, the Lagrange multiplier, μ, represents the extra utility that the agent gets when the constraint is relaxed by one unit. The Lagrange multiplier is therefore often referred to as the *shadow price* or *shadow value of the constraint*. This interpretation is important and will be used throughout the book.

1.2.3   Inequality Constraints: The Kuhn–Tucker Conditions

Imagine now that an agent faces m inequality restrictions of the form $g_i(x_1, \ldots, x_n) \le a_i$ for $i = 1, \ldots, m$. All the functions $g_i(\cdot)$ are assumed to be twice continuously differentiable, and each a_i is constant. The problem can be written as

$$\max_{x_i \ldots x_n}[u(x_1, \ldots, x_n)], \text{ subject to}$$
$$g_1(x_1, \ldots, x_n) \le a_1,$$
$$\ldots \tag{A.52}$$
$$g_m(x_1, \ldots, x_n) \le a_m.$$

Most economic constraints take the form shown in Eq. (A.52). For example, a budget constraint does not require an agent to spend all of his income but says that he cannot spend more than his income.

An easy way to solve the problem in Eq. (A.52) is to use the Kuhn–Tucker (1951) theorem. The theorem says that if $\bar{\bar{x}} = (\bar{\bar{x}}_1, \ldots, \bar{\bar{x}}_n)$ is a solution to Eq. (A.52),[9] then there exists a set of m Lagrange multipliers such that

---

[9]An additional condition is that the "constraint qualification" be satisfied. This condition requires the gradients of the constraints to be linearly independent.

$$(a) \quad Du(\bullet) = \sum_{i=1}^{m} \mu_1 \cdot [Dg_i(\bullet)], \tag{A.53}$$

$$(b) \quad g_i(\bullet) \le a_i, \mu_i \ge 0,$$

$$(c) \quad \mu_i \cdot [a_i - g_i(\bullet)] = 0.$$

Condition (a) in Eq.(A.53) says that the gradient of the objective function must be a linear combination of the gradients of the restrictions. The weights in this linear combination are the Lagrange Multipliers. In the particular case when there is only one restriction, $m = 1$, this condition is equivalent to Eq. (A.48). Condition (b) in Eq. (A.53) says that for $\bar{\bar{x}}$ to be an optimum, the constraints have to be satisfied and the shadow prices must be nonnegative. That is, $Du(\bullet)$ must lie on the cone generated by the $Dg_i(\bullet)$.

Condition (c) in Eq. (A.53) is often called the *complementary-slackness condition*. It says that the product of the shadow price and the constraint is 0. This condition means that if the constraint $g_i(\bullet) - a_i$ is not binding (if it is not satisfied with strict equality), then the shadow price must be 0. That is, $Dg_i(\bullet)$ receives no weight in the linear combination that generates $Du(\bullet)$. In contrast, if the price is strictly positive, then the constraint associated with it must be binding.[10]

Consider the example in Fig. A.12. There are two constraints, $g_1(\bullet) \le a_1$ and $g_2(\bullet) \le a_2$. The first constraint restricts the set of points in the space to lie between the curve labeled g_1 and the origin. Similarly, the second constraint restricts to the

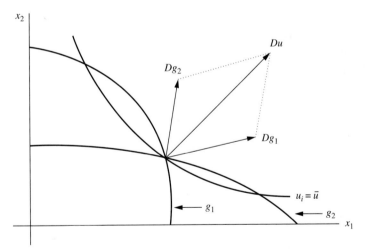

FIGURE A.12
Solution to a maximization problem subject to inequality constraints. The figure illustrates the solution to a maximization problem of the form of Eq. (A.53) with two inequality constraints.

---

[10]In economic terms, the complementary-slackness condition says that if a constraint is not binding (that is, if it is unimportant) and we relax it by one unit, then the attained utility does not change.

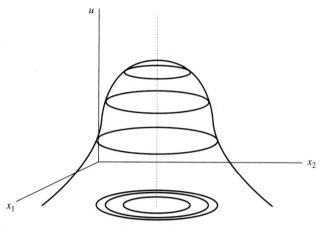

FIGURE A.13a
Preferences over two goods. The indifference curves for x_1 and x_2 are assumed to take the form of a bell.

space between the curve labeled g_2 and the origin. The objective function can be represented by a set of indifference curves labeled u_i, which increase in the northeast direction. The gradients of the two constraints (which point in the direction perpendicular to the tangent at that particular point) are labeled Dg_1 and Dg_2. Condition (a) says that if $\overline{\overline{x}}$ is to be an optimum, then the gradient of $u(\cdot)$ must be a linear combination of the two gradients Dg_1 and Dg_2. Condition (b) says that the linear combination must involve nonnegative weights. Graphically, this means that the gradient of u must lie on the cone described by the gradients of the two constraints.

To understand the meaning of the complementary-slackness condition, imagine that the preferences for a pair of goods takes the form of a bell (Fig. A.13a). The indifference curves are circles around a point that yields maximum utility. (This point would correspond to a level of satiation beyond which agents would not like to go, no matter what the prices are.) Suppose that the budget constraint lies to the left of this satiation point (see Fig. A.13b). The agent would like to consume more of both goods, but the budget constraint does not permit this. Hence, the constraint is binding. The Kuhn–Tucker theorem says that the gradient of the objective function at the optimum is proportional to the gradient of the constraint. Since the gradient is perpendicular to the function, this condition means that the maximum occurs at the tangency point.

Consider now what happens when the satiation point is fully inside the budget set (Fig. A.13c). The individual clearly achieves maximum utility by remaining inside the budget set. In other words, since the constraint is not binding, the agent behaves as if he were not constrained. The Kuhn–Tucker Theorem says that at the optimum, the gradient of the objective function is proportional to the gradient of the constraint. The complementary-slackness condition says that when the constraint is not binding, the factor of proportionality is 0. Hence, the gradient of the objective function must equal 0, the condition for an unconstrained maximum. To summarize, the complementary-slackness condition says that if a constraint is not binding, then it will not affect the optimal choice.

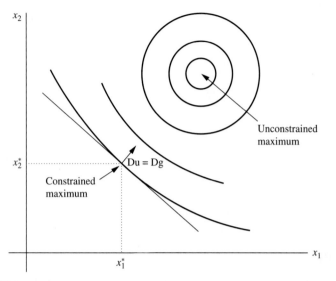

FIGURE A.13b
Maximizing utility subject to a binding inequality constraint. In this example, the budget constraint for x_1 and x_2 is binding.

The Kuhn–Tucker conditions can be read another way by writing the Lagrangian function as

$$L(x_1, \ldots, x_n; \mu_1, \ldots, \mu_m) = u(x_1, \ldots, x_n) + \sum_{i=1}^{m} \mu_i \cdot [a_i - g_i(x_1, \ldots, x_n)]. \quad \text{(A.54)}$$

Condition (a) in Eq. (A.53) says that a necessary condition for the vector $\overline{\overline{x}}$ to be a maximum of the constrained problem is for it to be a maximum of the associated

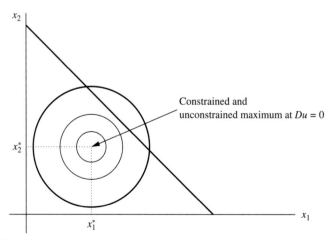

FIGURE A.13c
Maximizing utility subject to a nonbinding inequality constraint. In this example, the budget constraint for x_1 and x_2 is not binding.

Lagrangian. Conditions (*b*) and (*c*) in Eq. (A.53) say that at the optimum, the Lagrangian has a minimum with respect to the vector $\mu \equiv (\mu_1, \ldots, \mu_m)$. (Condition [*b*] says that the two components in [*c*] are nonnegative; hence, the product of the two is minimized at 0.) Taken together, conditions (*a*)–(*c*) in Eq. (A.53) say that a necessary condition for $\bar{\bar{x}}$ to be an optimum is for the Lagrangian to have a saddle point at $(\bar{\bar{x}}, \mu)$; that is, a maximum with respect to x and a minimum with respect to μ.

Conditions (*a*)–(*c*) in Eq. (A.53) are the set of necessary conditions of the Kuhn–Tucker theorem; if a point is to be an optimum, it must satisfy them. If the objective function $u(\bullet)$ is concave and the constraints from a convex set, then the necessary conditions are also sufficient.[11]

1.3 DYNAMIC OPTIMIZATION IN CONTINUOUS TIME

1.3.1 Introduction

Mathematicians have long worried about dynamic problems. It is commonly thought that the first person to solve one of these problems was Bernoulli in 1696. Euler and Lagrange also worked with dynamic problems. Most applications of their theoretical findings were in physics, especially as related to Hamilton's principle or the principle of least action. Economists have been interested in dynamic problems since at least the work of Hotelling and Ramsey in the 1920s. It was not until the 1960s, however, that dynamic mathematical techniques were widely introduced into economics, mainly in the work of the neoclassical growth theorists. These techniques are now part of the toolbox of most modern economists.

The methodology that classical mathematicians used to solve dynamic problems is known as the *calculus of variations*. This approach has since been generalized in two ways. First, Richard Bellman, an American mathematician, developed the method of *dynamic programming* in the 1950s. This method is especially suited to discrete-time problems and is particularly useful for stochastic models. Second, also in the 1950s, a team of Russian mathematicians led by L. Pontryagin developed the *maximum principle of optimal control*. (The first English translation of this work did not appear, however, until 1962.)

In this chapter, we demonstrate how to use Pontryagin's technique. The Maximum Principle is a generalization of the classical calculus of variations in that it provides solutions to problems in which one or more of the constraints involve the derivatives of some of the state variables. This type of constraint is central to the theory of economic growth.

---

[11]A slightly less restrictive set of sufficient conditions is given by Arrow and Enthoven (1961); they require the objective function to be quasi-concave, that is, to exhibit convex upper-level sets.

Our goal in this chapter is not to prove the Maximum Principle but, rather, to provide a heuristic derivation along with a description of the procedure that we follow to use the solutions. This approach will provide us with a set of tools that will allow us to solve the various dynamic models that will be encountered in the book.[12]

1.3.2 The Typical Problem

The typical problem that we want to solve takes the following form. The agent chooses or controls a number of variables, called *control variables,*[13] so as to maximize an objective function subject to some constraints. These constraints are dynamic in that they describe the evolution of the state of the economy, as represented by a set of *state variables,* over time. The problem is given by

$$\max_{c(t)} V(0) = \int_0^T v[k(t), c(t), t] \cdot dt, \text{ subject to} \qquad (A.55)$$

$$(a) \quad \dot{k}(t) = g[k(t), c(t), t],$$

$$(b) \quad k(0) = k_0 > 0, \text{ given,}$$

$$(c) \quad k(T) \cdot e^{-\bar{r}(T) \cdot T} \geq 0,$$

where $V(0)$ is the value of the objective function as seen from the initial moment 0, $\bar{r}(t)$ is an average discount rate that applies between dates 0 and t, and T is the terminal planning date, which could be finite or infinite. We discuss the difference between a finite and an infinite horizon in Section 1.3.7.

The variable $k(t)$—which appears with an overdot in Eq. (A.55a)—is the *state variable* and the variable $c(t)$ is the *control variable*. Each of these variables are functions of time. The objective function in Eq. (A.55) is the integral of instantaneous felicity functions, $v(\bullet)$,[14] over the interval from 0 to T. These felicity functions depend, in turn, on the state and control variables, $k(t)$ and $c(t)$, and on time, t.

The accumulation constraint in Eq. (A.55a) is a differential equation in $k(t)$; this constraint shows how the choice of the control variable, $c(t)$, translates into a pattern of movement for the state variable, $k(t)$. The expression for $\dot{k}(t)$ is called the *transition equation* or *equation of motion*. Although we write down only one transition equation, there is a continuum of constraints, one for every point in time between 0 and T.[15]

---

[12] A full proof of the Maximum Principle is in Pontryagin, et al. (1962).

[13] Pontryagin, et al. (1962) call these control variables "steering variables."

[14] Examples of felicity functions are utility functions of consumers, profit functions of firms, and objective functions of governments. To fix ideas, in this chapter we identify them with utility functions.

[15] This accumulation equation could be cast as an inequality restriction, $\dot{k} \leq g(\bullet)$. Typically, individuals will not find it optimal to satisfy this restriction with strict inequality because it will be advantageous to increase $c(t)$ to raise the current flow of utility or to increase $k(t)$ to raise the future flows of utility. We therefore leave the restriction as an equality.

The initial condition in Eq. (A.55b) says that the state variable, $k(t)$, begins at a given value, k_0. The final constraint, in Eq. (A.55c), says that the chosen value of the state variable at the end of the planning horizon, $k(t)$, discounted at the rate $\bar{r}(T)$, must be nonnegative. For finite values of T, this constraint implies $k(T) \geq 0$, as long as the discount rate $\bar{r}(T)$ is positive and finite. If $k(t)$ represents a person's net assets and T is the person's lifetime, then the constraint in Eq. (A.55c) precludes dying in debt. If the planning horizon is infinite, then the condition says that net assets can be negative and grow forever in magnitude, as long as the rate of growth is less than $\bar{r}(t)$. This constraint rules out chain letters or Ponzi schemes for debt.

An economic example of a dynamic problem of this kind is a growth model in which $v(\bullet)$ is an instantaneous utility function that depends on the level of consumption and is discounted by a time-preference factor,

$$ v(k, c, t) = e^{-\rho t} \cdot u[c(t)]. \tag{A.56} $$

In this example, $v(\bullet)$ does not depend on the capital stock, $k(t)$, and depends directly on time only through the discount factor, $e^{-\rho t}$. The constraint describes the accumulation of the variable $k(t)$. If we think of $k(t)$ as physical capital, then an example of such a constraint is

$$ \dot{k} = g[k(t), c(t), t] = f[k(t), t] - c(t) - \delta \cdot k(t), \tag{A.57} $$

where δ is the fraction of the capital stock that depreciates at every instant. Equation (A.57) says that the increase in the capital stock (net investment) equals total saving minus depreciation. Total saving, in turn, equals the difference between output, $f(\bullet)$, and consumption, $c(t)$. The dependence of production on t, for given $k(t)$, could reflect the state of technology or knowledge at a given point in time.

1.3.3   Heuristic Derivation of the First-Order Conditions

A formal proof of the Maximum Principle is outside the scope of this book; we will instead provide a heuristic derivation. Readers who are interested only in the procedure for finding the first-order conditions, and not in the derivation, can skip Sections 1.3.3–1.3.9 and go directly to Section 1.3.10.

The starting point is the static method for solving nonlinear optimization problems, the Kuhn–Tucker Theorem. This theorem, described in Section 1.2.3, suggests the construction of a Lagrangian of the form,

$$ L = \int_0^T v[k(t), c(t), t] \cdot dt + \int_0^T \left\{ \mu(t) \cdot \left(g[k(t), c(t), t] - \dot{k}(t) \right) \right\} \cdot dt $$
$$ + \nu \cdot k(T) \cdot e^{-\bar{r}(T) \cdot T}, $$

$$ \tag{A.58} $$

where $\mu(t)$ is the Lagrange multiplier associated with the constraint in Eq. (A.55a), and ν is the multiplier associated with the constraint in Eq. (A.55c).[16] Since there is a continuum of constraints (a), one for each instant t between 0 and T, there is a corresponding continuum of Lagrange multipliers, $\mu(t)$. The $\mu(t)$ are called *costate variables* or *dynamic Lagrange multipliers*. Following the parallel with the static case, these costate variables can be interpreted as shadow prices: $\mu(t)$ is the price or value of an extra unit of capital stock at time t in units of utility at time 0. Since each of the constraints, $g(\bullet) - \dot{k}$, equals 0, each of the products, $\mu(t) \cdot [g(\bullet) - \dot{k}]$, also equals 0. It follows that the "sum" of all of the constraints equals 0:

$$\int_0^T \left\{ \mu(t) \cdot \left(g[k(t), c(t), t] - \dot{k}(t) \right) \right\} \cdot dt = 0.$$

This expression appears in the middle of Eq. (A.58).

To find the set of first-order necessary conditions in a static problem, we would maximize L with respect to $c(t)$ and $k(t)$ for all t between 0 and T. The problem with this procedure is that we do not know how to take the derivative of $\dot{k}$ with respect to k. To avoid this problem, we can rewrite the Lagrangian by integrating the term $\mu(t) \cdot \dot{k}(t)$ by parts to get[17]

$$L = \int_0^T (v[k(t), c(t), t] + \mu(t) \cdot g[k(t), c(t), t]) \cdot dt \tag{A.59}$$
$$+ \int_0^T \dot{\mu}(t) \cdot k(t) \cdot dt + \mu(0) \cdot k_0 - \mu(T) \cdot k(T) + \nu \cdot k(T) \cdot e^{-\bar{r}(T) \cdot T}.$$

The expression inside the first integral is referred to as the *Hamiltonian* function,

$$K(k, c, t, \mu) \equiv v(k, c, t) + \mu \cdot g(k, c, t). \tag{A.60}$$

The Hamiltonian function has an economic interpretation (see Dorfman [1969]). At an instant in time, the agent consumes $c(t)$ and owns a stock of capital $k(t)$. These two variables affect utility through two channels. First, the direct contribution of consumption, and perhaps capital, to utility, is captured by the term $v(\bullet)$ in Eq. (A.60). Second, the choice of consumption affects the change in the capital stock in accordance with the transition equation for $\dot{k}$ in Eq. (A.55a). The value of this change in the capital stock is the term $\mu \cdot g(\bullet)$ in Eq. (A.60). Hence, for a given value of the shadow price, μ, the Hamiltonian captures the total contribution to utility from the choice of $c(t)$.

---

[16]We would also have the constraints $c(t) \geq 0$, but commonly assumed forms of the utility function imply that these constraints will not be binding. We therefore ignore these inequality restrictions in the present discussion.

[17]To integrate $\int_0^T (\dot{k}) \cdot \mu dt$ by parts, start with $(d/dt)(\mu k) = \dot{\mu} k + \dot{k} \mu$. Integrate both sides of this expression between 0 and T and note that $\int_0^T (d/dt)(k\mu) \cdot dt = k(T) \cdot \mu(T) - k(0) \cdot \mu(0)$. From this expression, subtract the integral of $k\dot{\mu}$ to get $\int_0^T (\dot{k}) \cdot \mu dt = k(T) \cdot \mu(T) - k(0) \cdot \mu(0) - \int_0^T (\dot{\mu}) \cdot k dt$, which is the expression used to compute Eq. (A.59). See Sections 1.5.4 and 1.5.5 for further discussion.

Rewrite the Lagrangian from Eq. (A.59) as

$$L = \int_0^T \left(H[k(t), c(t), t] + \dot{\mu}(t) \cdot k(t) \right) \cdot dt + \mu(0) \cdot k_0 - \mu(T) \cdot k(T) + v \cdot k(T) \cdot e^{-\bar{r}(T) \cdot T}.$$

$$(A.61)$$

Let $\bar{\bar{c}}(t)$ and $\bar{\bar{k}}(t)$ be the optimal time paths for the control and state variables, respectively. If we perturb the optimal path $\bar{\bar{c}}(t)$ by an arbitrary perturbation function, $p_1(t)$, then we can generate a neighboring path for the control variable,

$$c(t) = \bar{\bar{c}}(t) + \epsilon \cdot p_1(t).$$

When $c(t)$ is thus perturbed, there must be a corresponding perturbation to $k(t)$ and $k(T)$ so as to satisfy the budget constraint:

$$k(t) = \bar{\bar{k}}(t) + \epsilon \cdot p_2(t),$$

$$k(T) = \bar{\bar{k}}(T) + \epsilon \cdot dk(T).$$

If the initial paths are optimal, then $\partial L/\partial \epsilon$ should equal 0. Before we compute such a derivative, it will be convenient to rewrite the Lagrangian in terms of ϵ:

$$\bar{\bar{L}}(\cdot, \epsilon) = \int_0^T \left(H[k(\cdot, \epsilon); c(\cdot, \epsilon)] + \dot{\mu}(\bullet) \cdot k(\cdot, \epsilon) \right) \cdot dt$$

$$+ \mu(0) \cdot k_0 - \mu(T) \cdot k(T, \epsilon) + v \cdot k(T, \epsilon) \cdot e^{-\bar{r}(T) \cdot T}.$$

We can now take the derivative of the Lagrangian with respect to ϵ and set it to 0:

$$\partial \bar{\bar{L}}/\partial \epsilon = \int_0^T [\partial H/\partial \epsilon + \dot{\mu} \cdot \partial k/\partial \epsilon] \cdot dt + [v - \mu(T)] \cdot \partial k(T, \epsilon)/\partial \epsilon = 0.$$

The chain rule of calculus implies $\partial H/\partial \epsilon = [\partial H/\partial c] \cdot p_1(t) + [\partial H/\partial k] \cdot p_2(t)$ and $\partial k(T, \epsilon)/\partial \epsilon = dk(T)$. Use these formulas and rearrange terms in the expression for $\partial \bar{\bar{L}}/\partial \epsilon$ to get

$$\partial L/\partial \epsilon = \int_0^T \left\{ [\partial H/\partial c] \cdot p_1(t) + [\partial H/\partial k + \dot{\mu}] \cdot p_2(t) \right\} \cdot dt$$

$$+ [v \cdot e^{-\bar{r}(T) \cdot T} - \mu(T)] \cdot dk(T) = 0. \quad (A.62)$$

Equation (A.62) can hold for all perturbation paths, described by $p_1(t)$, $p_2(t)$, and $dk(T)$, only if each of the components in the equation vanishes, that is,

$$\partial H/\partial c = 0, \quad (A.63)$$

$$\partial H/\partial k + \dot{\mu} = 0, \quad (A.64)$$

$$v \cdot e^{-\bar{r}(T) \cdot T} = \mu(T). \quad (A.65)$$

The first-order condition with respect to the control variable in Eq. (A.63) says that if $\bar{\bar{c}}(t)$ and $\bar{\bar{k}}(t)$ are a solution to the dynamic problem, then the derivative of the Hamiltonian with respect to the control c equals 0 for all t. This result is called the *Maximum Principle*. Equation (A.64) says that the partial derivative of the Hamiltonian with respect to the state variable equals the negative of the derivative of the multiplier, $-\dot{\mu}$. This result and the transition equation in Eq. (A.55a) are often called the Euler Equations. Finally, Eq. (A.65) says that the costate variable at the terminal date, μ, equals ν, the static Lagrange multiplier associated with the non-negativity constraint on k at the terminal date, discounted at the rate $\bar{r}(T)$.

1.3.4 Transversality Conditions

Section 1.2.3 showed that the Kuhn–Tucker necessary first-order conditions include a complementary-slackness condition associated with the inequality constraints. In the static problem, these conditions say that if a restriction is not binding, then the shadow price associated with it is 0. In the present dynamic problem, there is an inequality constraint that says that the stock of capital left at the end of the planning period, discounted at the rate $\bar{r}(T)$, cannot be negative, $k(T) \cdot e^{-\bar{r}(T) \cdot T} \geq 0$. The condition associated with this constraint requires $\nu \cdot k(T) \cdot e^{-\bar{r}(T) \cdot T} = 0$, with $\nu \geq 0$. Equation (A.65) implies that we can rewrite this complementary-slackness condition as

$$\mu(T) \cdot k(T) = 0. \tag{A.66}$$

This boundary condition is often called the *transversality condition*. It says that if the quantity of capital left is positive, $k(T) > 0$, then its price must be 0, $\mu(T) = 0$. Alternatively, if capital at the terminal date has the positive value, $\mu(T) \geq 0$, then the agent must leave no capital, $k(T) = 0$. We discuss later the meaning of Eq. (A.66) when T is infinite.

1.3.5 The Behavior of the Hamiltonian over Time

To see how the optimal value of the Hamiltonian behaves over time, take the total derivative of H with respect to t to get

$$dH(k, c, \mu, t)/dt = [\partial H/\partial k] \cdot \dot{k} + [\partial H/\partial c] \cdot \dot{c} + [\partial H/\partial \mu] \cdot \dot{\mu} + \partial H/\partial t. \tag{A.67}$$

The first-order condition in Eq. (A.63) implies that, at the optimum, $\partial H/\partial c = 0$; hence, the second term on the right-hand side of Eq. (A.67) equals 0. Equation (A.64) requires $\partial H/\partial k = -\dot{\mu}$. Since $\partial H/\partial \mu = -\dot{k}$, the first and third terms on the right-hand side of Eq. (A.67) cancel. Hence, at the optimum, the total derivative of the Hamiltonian with respect to time equals the partial derivative, $\partial H/\partial t$. If the problem is autonomous—that is, if neither the objective function nor the constraints depend directly on time—then the derivative of the Hamiltonian with respect to time is 0. In other words, the Hamiltonian associated with autonomous problems is constant at all points in time. These results on the behavior of the Hamiltonian will be used later in this chapter.

1.3.6 Sufficient Conditions

In a static, nonlinear maximization problem, the Kuhn–Tucker necessary conditions are also sufficient when the objective function is concave and the restrictions generate a convex set. Mangasarian (1966) extends this result to dynamic problems and shows that if the functions $v(\cdot)$ and $g(\cdot)$ in Eq. (A.55) are both concave and k and c, then the necessary conditions are also sufficient. This sufficiency result is easy to use but is somewhat restrictive.

More general sufficiency conditions are given by Arrow and Kurz (1970). Define $H^0(k, \mu, t)$ to be the maximum of $H(k, c, \mu, t)$ with respect to c, given k, μ, and t. The Arrow–Kurz theorem says that if $H^0(k, \mu, t)$ is concave in k, for given μ and t, then the necessary conditions are also sufficient. Concavity of $v(\cdot)$ and $g(\cdot)$ is sufficient, but not necessary, for the Arrow–Kurz condition to be satisfied. The disadvantage of this more general result is that checking the properties of a derived function, such as H^0, tends to be harder than checking the properties of $v(\cdot)$ and $g(\cdot)$.

1.3.7 Infinite Horizons

Most of the growth models we discuss in the book involve economic agents with infinite planning horizons. The typical problem takes the form

$$\max_{c(t)} V(0) = \int_0^\infty v[k(t), c(t), t] \cdot dt, \text{ subject to} \tag{A.68}$$

$$(a) \quad \dot{k}(t) = g[k(t), c(t), t],$$

$$(b) \quad k(0) = k_0 > 0, \text{ given,}$$

$$(c) \quad \lim_{t \to \infty}[k(t) \cdot e^{-\bar{r}(t) \cdot t}] \geq 0.$$

The only difference between Eqs. (A.68) and (A.55) is that the planning horizon—the number on top of the integral—in Eq. (A.68) is infinity, rather than $T < \infty$. The first-order conditions for the infinite-horizon problem are the same as those for the finite horizon case, Eqs. (A.63) and (A.64). The key difference is that the transversality condition, shown in Eq. (A.66), applies not to a finite T, but to the limit as T tends to infinity. In other words, the transversality condition is now

$$\lim_{t \to \infty}[\mu(t) \cdot k(t)] = 0. \tag{A.69}$$

The intuitive explanation for the new condition is that the value of the capital stock must be asymptotically 0, otherwise something valuable would be left over. If the quantity, $k(t)$, remains positive asymptotically, then the price, $\mu(t)$, must approach 0 asymptotically. If $k(t)$ grows forever at a positive rate—as occurs in some of the models that we study in this book—then the price $\mu(t)$ must approach 0 at a faster rate so that the product, $\mu(t) \cdot k(t)$, goes to 0.

Although Eq. (A.69) has intuitive appeal as the limiting version of Eq. (A.66), there is disagreement over the conditions under which Eq. (A.69) is actually a necessary condition for the infinite-horizon problem in Eq. (A.68). Recall that the only argument we gave for its validity was the analogy to the transversality condition in the finite-horizon case. Some researchers have found counter examples in which Eq. (A.69) is not a necessary condition for optimization. In Section 1.3.9, we discuss one of these examples.

One transversality condition that always applies was found by Michel (1982). He argues that the transversality condition requires the value of the Hamiltonian to approach 0 as t goes to infinity:

$$\lim_{t \to \infty}[H(t)] = 0. \tag{A.70}$$

We can derive this transversality condition if we follow Michel and think of the infinite-horizon case as a setting in which the agent chooses the terminal date, T. If we perturb the terminal date T in Eq. (A.61) by $\epsilon \cdot dT$, then we find that the limit of integration now depends on ϵ. When we take derivatives of the Lagrangian with respect to ϵ, we find that one of the terms in Eq. (A.62) is $H(T) \cdot dT$. This term comes from taking the derivative of the limit of integration, $T(\epsilon)$, with respect to ϵ. As with all of the terms in Eq. (A.62), this one will have to be 0 at the optimum. If the terminal date is fixed, so that $dT = 0$, then $H(T)$ can take on any value. But if the terminal date is variable, so that dT is nonzero, then $H(T)$ must vanish. If we take the limit as T goes to infinity, then we get the transversality condition in Eq. (A.70). This condition is redundant in most of the models that we study in the book because it will be satisfied whenever Eq. (A.69) is satisfied. Thus, in most cases, we can use Eq. (A.69) and ignore Eq. (A.70).

1.3.8 Example: The Neoclassical Growth Model

Assume that economic agents choose the path of consumption, $c(t)$, and capital, $k(t)$, so as to maximize the objective function,

$$U(0) = \int_0^\infty e^{-\rho t} \cdot \log[c(t)] \cdot dt, \text{ subject to} \tag{A.71}$$

(a) $\dot{k}(t) = [k(t)]^\alpha - c(t) - \delta \cdot k(t),$

(b) $k(0) = 1,$

(c) $\lim_{t \to \infty}[k(t) \cdot e^{-\bar{r}(t) \cdot t}] \geq 0,$

where α is a constant with $0 < \alpha < 1$. The interest rate, $r(t)$, equals the net marginal product of capital, $\alpha \cdot k(t)^{\alpha-1} - \delta$, and the average interest rate, $\bar{r}(t)$, equals $(1/t) \cdot \int_0^t r(v) \cdot dv$. This example is a simple version of the neoclassical growth model, which is examined in detail in Chapter 2.

The agent can be thought of as a household-producer who wants to maximize utility, represented as the present discounted value of a stream of instantaneous felicities. Each of these felicities depends on the instantaneous flow of consumption. The felicity function is assumed in Eq. (A.71) to be logarithmic. The discount rate is $\rho > 0$. The agent has access to the technology (The Cobb–Douglas form described in Chapter 1) that transforms capital into output according to $y(t) = [k(t)]^\alpha$. The accumulation constraint in Eq. (A.71a) says that total output has to be divided between consumption, $c(t)$; depreciation, $\delta \cdot k(t)$; and capital accumulation, $\dot{k}(t)$. The initial condition in Eq. (A.71b) says that the capital stock at time 0 is 1. The restriction in

Eq. (A.71c) says that the capital stock left over at the "end of the planning horizon," when discounted at the average interest rate, $\bar{r}(t)$, is nonnegative. (If $k[t]$ represents household assets, then this condition precludes chain-letter policies in which debt accumulates forever at a rate at least as high as the interest rate.)

To solve the optimization problem, set up the Hamiltonian,

$$H(c, k, t, \mu) = e^{-\rho t} \cdot \log(c) + \mu \cdot (k^\alpha - c - \delta k). \tag{A.72}$$

Equations (A.63) and (A.64) imply that the first-order conditions are

$$H_c = e^{-\rho t} \cdot (1/c) - \mu = 0, \tag{A.73}$$

$$H_k = \mu \cdot (\alpha k^{\alpha-1} - \delta) = -\dot{\mu}, \tag{A.74}$$

and Eq. (A.69) implies that the transversality condition is

$$\lim_{t \to \infty}[\mu(t) \cdot k(t)] = 0. \tag{A.75}$$

Equation (A.74) and the transition relations in Eq. (A.71a) form a system of ODEs in which $\dot{\mu}$ and $\dot{k}$ depend on μ, k, and c. Equation (A.73) relates μ to c, so that we can eliminate one of these two variables from the system. If we eliminate μ and take logs and time derivatives of Eq. (A.73), then we get

$$-\rho - \dot{c}/c = \dot{\mu}/\mu.$$

We can substitute this result into equation (A.74) to eliminate $\dot{\mu}/\mu$ to get

$$\dot{c}/c = (\alpha k^{\alpha-1} - \rho - \delta). \tag{A.76}$$

This condition says that consumption accumulates at a rate equal to the difference between the net marginal product of capital, $\alpha k^{\alpha-1} - \delta$, and the discount rate, ρ.

Equations (A.71a) and (A.76) form a system of non-linear ODEs in k and c. In the steady state, the term $\alpha k^{\alpha-1}$ equals $\rho + \delta$, which determines the steady-state capital stock as $k^* = [(\rho + \delta)/\alpha]^{-1/(1-\alpha)}$. Equation (A.71a) then determines the steady-state level of consumption as $c^* = (k^*)^\alpha - \delta k^*$. Equation (A.74) implies that, as t goes to infinity, $\dot{\mu}/\mu$ tends to $-\rho$, so that $\mu(t)$ tends to $\mu(0) \cdot e^{-\rho t}$. The transversality condition in equation (A.75) can therefore be expressed as

$$\lim_{t \to \infty}[e^{-\rho t} \cdot k(t)] = 0. \tag{A.77}$$

Equation (A.77) provides a terminal condition, which, together with the initial condition $k(0) = 1$, yields the exact solution to the system of ODEs.

If we set $\rho = 0.06$, $\delta = 0$, and $\alpha = 0.3$, then this system corresponds to the nonlinear system that we studied in Section 1.1.3 with Eq. (A.22) and (A.23) and linearized later in that section with Eq. (A.38). We know from before that this system exhibits saddle-path stability, and the initial and terminal conditions ensure that the economy starts exactly on the stable arm. We use more complicated versions of this model in the text.

Finally, we can verify that the above conditions imply that the steady-state value of the Hamiltonian is 0, as implied by Eq. (A.70):

$$\lim_{t\to\infty}[H(t)] = \lim_{t\to\infty}\left(e^{-\rho t} \cdot \log[c(t)]\right) + \lim_{t\to\infty}\left(\mu(t) \cdot [k(t)^\alpha - c(t) - \delta \cdot k(t)]\right) =$$

$$\log(c^*) \cdot \lim_{t\to\infty}[e^{-\rho(t)}] + 0 \cdot \lim_{t\to\infty}[\mu(t)] = 0 + 0 = 0.$$

Hence, although Eq. (A.70) is a necessary condition for optimization, it is already implied by the other conditions.

1.3.9 Transversality Conditions in Infinite-Horizon Problems

The transversality condition in Eq. (A.75) is not universally accepted as a necessary condition for the infinite-horizon problem. Halkin (1974) provides an example in which the optimum does not satisfy the transversality condition.[18] An even more famous counterexample is the neoclassical growth model of Ramsey (1928). The difference between the original Ramsey model and the one described in the last section is that Ramsey assumed no discounting. His version of the model is

$$\max U(0) = \int_0^\infty \log[c(t)] \cdot dt, \text{ subject to} \tag{A.78}$$

(a) $\dot{k}(t) = [k(t)]^\alpha - c(t) - \delta \cdot k(t),$

(b) $k(0) = 1,$

(c) $\lim_{t\to\infty}[k(t)] \geq 0.$

The only difference between Eq. (A.78) and Eq. (A.71) is that in the former ρ has been set to 0. An immediate problem with Eq. (A.78) is that if $c(t)$ asymptotically approaches a constant (as in the previous problem), then utility is not bounded. To solve this problem, Ramsey rewrote the integrand as the deviation from a "bliss point." This revised specification will result in bounded utility if the deviation from the bliss point approaches 0 at a fast enough rate.

We found in the previous section that steady-state consumption converged to a constant, given by $c^* = (k^*)^\alpha - \delta k^*$, where k^* satisfied $\alpha \cdot (k^*)^{\alpha-1} = (\rho + \delta)$. We therefore begin with the conjecture that steady-state consumption in the present model will be $\tilde{c} = \tilde{k}^\alpha - \delta\tilde{k}$, where $\tilde{k}$ satisfies $\alpha\tilde{k}^{\alpha-1} = \delta$. The corresponding Ramsey-like objective function is

$$U(0) = \int_0^\infty (\log[c(t)] - \log[\tilde{c}]) \cdot dt. \tag{A.79}$$

To solve the problem of maximizing $U(0)$, set up the Hamiltonian,

$$H(c, k, \mu) = (\log(c) - \log[\tilde{c}]) + \mu \cdot (k^\alpha - c - \delta k). \tag{A.80}$$

---

[18]This example was first presented in Arrow and Kurz (1970, p. 46). They mention, however, that the idea came from Halkin, who published the result later in *Econometrica*.

The first-order conditions are

$$H_c = 1/c - \mu = 0, \qquad (\text{A.81})$$

$$H_k = \mu \cdot [\alpha k^{\alpha-1} - \delta] = -\dot{\mu}, \qquad (\text{A.82})$$

which correspond to Eq. (A.73) and (A.74).

If c tends to $\tilde{c}$ as t approaches infinity, then Eq. (A.81) implies

$$\lim_{t \to \infty}[\mu(t)] = 1/\tilde{c} > 0. \qquad (\text{A.83})$$

Since $\lim_{t \to \infty}[k(t)] = \tilde{k} > 0$, it follows that $\lim_{t \to \infty}[\mu(t) \cdot k(t)] \neq 0$; hence, the usual transversality condition in Eq. (A.75) is violated.

The literature has a number of examples of this sort in which the standard transversality condition is not a necessary condition for optimization. Pitchford (1977) observes that all known cases involve no time discounting. Weitzman (1973) shows that for discrete-time problems, a transversality condition analogous to Eq. (A.75) is necessary when there is time discounting and the objective function converges. Benveniste and Scheinkman (1982) show that this result holds also in continuous time.

All of the models discussed in this book feature time discounting and an objective function that converges. We therefore assume that the transversality condition in Eq. (A.75) is a necessary condition for optimization in our infinite-horizon problems.

1.3.10   Summary of the Procedure to Find the First-Order Conditions

Instead of going through the whole derivation every time we encounter a dynamic problem, we shall use the following cookbook procedure.

Step one: Construct a Hamiltonian function by adding to the felicity function, $v(\bullet)$, a Lagrange multiplier times the right-hand side of the transition equation:

$$H = v(k, c, t) + \mu(t) \cdot g(k, c, t). \qquad (\text{A.84})$$

Step two: Take the derivative of the Hamiltonian with respect to the control variable and set it to 0:

$$\partial H/\partial c = \partial v/\partial c + \mu \cdot \partial g/\partial c = 0. \qquad (\text{A.85})$$

Step three: Take the derivative of the Hamiltonian with respect to the state variable (the variable that appears with an overdot in the transition equation) and set it to equal the negative of the derivative of the multiplier with respect to time:

$$\partial H/\partial k \equiv \partial v/\partial k + \mu \cdot \partial g/\partial k = -\dot{\mu}. \qquad (\text{A.86})$$

Step four (transversality condition):

Case 1: Finite horizons. Set the product of the shadow price and the capital stock at the end of the planning horizon to 0:

$$\mu(T) \cdot k(T) = 0. \qquad (\text{A.87})$$

Case 2: Infinite horizons with discounting. The transversality condition is

$$\lim_{t \to \infty}[\mu(t) \cdot k(t)] = 0. \tag{A.88}$$

Case 3: Infinite horizons without discounting. The Ramsey counter example shows that Eq. (A.88) need not apply. In this case, we use Michel's condition,

$$\lim_{t \to \infty}[H(t)] = 0. \tag{A.89}$$

If we combine Eq. (A.85) and (A.86) with the transition equation from Eq. (A.55a), then we can form a system of two differential equations in the variables μ and k. Alternatively, we can use Eq. (A.85) to transform the ODE for $\dot{\mu}$ into an ODE for $\dot{c}$. For the system to be determinate, we need two boundary conditions. One initial condition is given by the starting value of the state variable, $k(0)$. One terminal condition is given by the transversality condition, Eq. (A.87), (A.88), or (A.89), depending on the nature of the problem.

1.3.11   Present-Value and Current-Value Hamiltonians

Most of the models that we deal with in this book have an objective function of the form,

$$\int_0^T v[k(t), c(t), t] \cdot dt = \int_0^T e^{-\rho t} \cdot u[k(t), c(t)] \cdot dt, \tag{A.90}$$

where ρ is a constant discount rate, and $e^{-\rho t}$ is a discount factor. Once the discount factor is taken into account, the instantaneous felicity function does not depend directly on time. If the constraints are the ones assumed before, then we can solve the problem by constructing the Hamiltonian,

$$H = e^{-\rho t} \cdot u(k, c) + \mu \cdot g(k, c, t).$$

In this formulation, the shadow price $\mu(t)$ represents the value of the capital stock at time t in units of time-zero utils.

It is sometimes convenient to restructure the problem in terms of current-value prices; that is, prices of the capital stock at time t in units of time-t utils. To accomplish this restructuring, rewrite the Hamiltonian as

$$H = e^{-\rho t} \cdot [u(k, c) + q(t) \cdot g(k, c, t)],$$

where $q(t) \equiv \mu(t) \cdot e^{\rho t}$. The variable $q(t)$ is the *current-value shadow price*. Define $\hat{H} = He^{\rho t}$ to be the *current-value Hamiltonian:*

$$\hat{H} \equiv u(k, c) + q(t) \cdot g(k, c, t). \tag{A.91}$$

The first-order conditions are still $H_c = 0$ and $H_k = -\dot{\mu}$. They can be expressed, however, in terms of the current-value Hamiltonian and current-value prices as

$$\hat{H}_c = 0, \tag{A.92}$$

$$\hat{H}_k = \rho q - \dot{q}. \tag{A.93}$$

The transversality condition, $\mu(T) \cdot k(T) = 0$, can be expressed as

$$q(T) \cdot e^{-\rho T} \cdot k(T) = 0. \qquad (A.94)$$

An interesting point about Eq. (A.93) is that it looks like an asset-pricing formula: q is the price of capital in terms of current utility, $\hat{H}_k$ is the dividend received by the agent (the marginal contribution of capital to utility), $\dot{q}$ is the capital gain (the change in the price of the asset), and ρ is the rate of return on an alternative asset (consumption). Equation (A.93) says that at the optimum, the agent is indifferent between the two types of investments because the overall rate of return to capital, $(\hat{H}_k + \dot{q})/q$, equals the return to consumption, ρ.

1.3.12   Multiple Variables

Consider now a more general dynamic problem with n control and m state variables. Choose $c_1(t), c_2(t), \ldots, c_n(t)$ to maximize

$$\int_0^T u[k_1(t), \ldots, k_m(t); c_1(t), \ldots, c_n(t); t] \cdot dt, \text{ subject to}$$

$$\dot{k}_1(t) = g^1[k_1(t), \ldots, k_m(t); c_1(t), \ldots c_n(t); t],$$
$$\dot{k}_2(t) = g^2[k_1(t), \ldots, k_m(t); c_1(t), \ldots c_n(t); t],$$
$$\ldots$$
$$\dot{k}_m(t) = g^m[k_1(t), \ldots, k_m(t); c_1(t), \ldots c_n(t); t], \qquad (A.95)$$
$$k_1(0) > 0, \ldots, k_m(0) > 0, \text{ given,}$$
$$k_1(T) \geq 0, \ldots, k_m(T) \geq 0, \text{ free.}$$

The solution is similar to that for one control variable and one state variable, as analyzed above. The Hamiltonian is

$$H = u[k_1(t), \ldots, k_m(t); c_1(t), \ldots, c_n(t); t] + \sum_{i=1}^m \mu_i \cdot g^i(\bullet). \qquad (A.96)$$

The first-order necessary conditions for a maximum are

$$\partial H/\partial c_i(t) = 0, i = 1, \ldots, n, \qquad (A.97)$$
$$\partial H/\partial k_i(t) = -\dot{\mu}_i, i = 1, \ldots, m, \qquad (A.98)$$

and the transversality conditions are

$$\mu_i(T) \cdot k_i(T) = 0, i = 1, \ldots, m. \qquad (A.99)$$

1.4   USEFUL RESULTS IN MATRIX ALGEBRA: EIGENVALUES, EIGENVECTORS, AND DIAGONALIZATION OF MATRICES

Given an n-dimensional square matrix A, can we find the values of a scalar α and the corresponding nonzero column vectors v, such that

$$(A - \alpha I) \cdot v = 0, \qquad (A.100)$$

where I is the n-dimensional identity matrix? Note that Eq. (A.100) forms a system of n homogeneous linear equations (that is, the constant term is 0 for all equations). If we want nontrivial solutions, so that $v \neq 0$, then the determinant of $(A - \alpha I)$ must vanish:

$$\det(A - \alpha I) = 0. \tag{A.101}$$

Equation (A.101) defines a polynomial equation of nth degree in α and is called the *characteristic equation*. Typically, there will be n solutions to this equation. These solutions are called *characteristic roots* or *eigenvalues*.

By construction and through rearrangement of Eq. (A.101), each eigenvalue, α_i, is associated with a vector v_i (determined up to a scalar multiple) that satisfies

$$Av_i = v_i \alpha_i, i = 1, \ldots, n. \tag{A.102}$$

The vector v_i is called the *characteristic vector* or *eigenvector*. For every α_i, Eq. (A.102) determines and $n \times 1$ column vector (A is $n \times n$, v_i is $n \times 1$, and α_i is 1×1). We can arrange these column vectors into an $n \times n$ matrix V to get

$$AV = VD, \tag{A.103}$$

where V is the $n \times n$ matrix of eigenvectors, and D is an $n \times n$ diagonal matrix with the eigenvalues as diagonal elements.

If $\det(V) \neq 0$, a condition that holds if the eigenvectors are linearly independent, then V can be inverted and Eq. (A.103) can be rewritten as

$$V^{-1}AV = D. \tag{A.104}$$

In other words, if we premultiply A by the inverse of V and postmultiply it by V, then we get a diagonal matrix with the eigenvalues as diagonal elements. This procedure is called *diagonalization* of the matrix A. This result is useful for solving systems of differential equations.

Intuitively, when we diagonalize a matrix, we find a set of axes (a *vector basis*) for which the linear application represented by A can be expressed as a diagonal matrix. The new axes correspond to the eigenvectors. The linear application in these transformed axes is given by the diagonal matrix of eigenvalues.

We can state two useful results. First, if all the eigenvalues are different, then the matrix of eigenvectors is nonsingular; that is, $\det(V) \neq 0$. In this case, V^{-1} exists and, hence, the matrix A can be diagonalized.

A second interesting theorem states that the determinant and trace (the sum of the elements on the main diagonal) of the diagonal matrix equal, respectively, the determinant and trace of the original matrix. This result will be useful in situations in which we want to know the signs of the eigenvalues. Suppose, for example, that A is a 2×2 matrix and we want to know whether its two eigenvalues have the same sign. If the determinant of A is negative, then the determinant of D will be negative. But since D is diagonal, its determinant is just the product of the two eigenvalues. Hence, the two eigenvalues must have opposite signs.

As an example, consider the eigenvalues, eigenvectors, and diagonal matrix associated with $A = \begin{bmatrix} 0.06 & -1 \\ -0.004 & 0 \end{bmatrix}$. Start by constructing the system of equations,

$$(A - \alpha I) \cdot v = \begin{bmatrix} 0.06 - \alpha & -1 \\ -0.004 & 0 - \alpha \end{bmatrix} \begin{bmatrix} v_1 \\ v_2 \end{bmatrix} = 0. \qquad (A.105)$$

To get a nontrivial solution, where $v \neq 0$, we must have

$$\begin{vmatrix} 0.06 - \alpha & -1 \\ -0.004 & 0 - \alpha \end{vmatrix} = 0.$$

This equality determines the characteristic equation, $\alpha^2 - 0.06 \cdot \alpha - 0.004 = 0$, which is satisfied for two values of α: $\alpha_1 = 0.1$ and $\alpha_2 = -0.04$. The diagonal matrix associated with A is therefore

$$D = \begin{bmatrix} 0.1 & 0 \\ 0 & -0.04 \end{bmatrix}.$$

To find the eigenvector associated with the positive eigenvalue, $\alpha_1 = 0.1$, substitute α_1 into Eq. (A.105):

$$\begin{bmatrix} 0.06 - .1 & -1 \\ -0.004 & -0.1 \end{bmatrix} \begin{bmatrix} v_{11} \\ v_{21} \end{bmatrix} = 0.$$

This equation imposes two conditions on the relation between v_{11} and v_{21}: $-0.04 \cdot v_{11} - v_{21} = 0$ and $-0.004 \cdot v_{11} - 0.1 \cdot v_{21} = 0$. The second condition is linearly dependent on the first and can be ignored. The resulting solution for v_{11} and v_{21} will therefore be unique only up to an arbitrary scalar multiple of each value. If we normalize v_{11} to 1, then we get $v_{21} = -0.04$. The first eigenvector is therefore $\begin{bmatrix} 1 \\ -0.04 \end{bmatrix}$.

If we repeat the procedure for $\alpha_2 = -0.04$, then we find a relation between v_{12} and v_{22}: $0.1 \cdot v_{12} - v_{22} = 0$. If we normalize v_{12} to 1, then we get $v_{22} = 0.1$, and the second eigenvector is $\begin{bmatrix} 1 \\ 0.1 \end{bmatrix}$. The two eigenvectors are linearly independent, and the matrix of normalized eigenvectors is

$$V = \begin{bmatrix} 1 & 1 \\ -0.04 & 0.1 \end{bmatrix}.$$

We can now check that, indeed, $V^{-1}AV = D$ by calculating the inverse of V:

$$V^{-1} = \begin{bmatrix} 0.1/0.14 & -1/0.14 \\ 0.04/0.14 & 1/0.14 \end{bmatrix}.$$

It is then easy to verify that $V^{-1}AV$ is the diagonal matrix D shown above.

1.5 USEFUL RESULTS IN CALCULUS

1.5.1 Implicit Function Theorem

Let $f(x_1, x_2)$ be a bivariate *function* in the real space. Assume that $f(\cdot)$ is twice continuously differentiable. Let $\phi(x_1, x_2) = 0$ be an *equation* that involves x_1 and x_2 only through $f(x_1, x_2)$ and that implicitly defines x_2 as a function of x_1: $x_2 = \tilde{x}_2(x_1)$.

An example is $\phi(x_1, x_2) = f(x_1, x_2) - a = 0$, where a is a constant. The implicit function theorem says that the slope of the implicit function, $\tilde{x}_2(x_1)$, is

$$\frac{d\tilde{x}_2}{dx_1} = -\frac{\partial f(x_1, x_2)/\partial x_1}{\partial f(x_1, x_2)/\partial x_2}. \tag{A.106}$$

This result holds whether or not an explicit or closed-form solution exists for $\tilde{x}_2(x_1)$.

As an example, consider the function $f(x_1, x_2) = 3x_1^2 - x_2$ and the equation $\phi(x_1, x_2) = 3x_1^2 - x_2 - 1 = 0$. In this case, we can find an explicit function $\tilde{x}_2(x_1) = 3x_1^2 - 1$. If we apply the implicit function theorem from Eq. (A.106), then we get

$$d\tilde{x}_2/dx_1 = -(6x_1)/(-1) = 6x_1.$$

In this example, we do not need the implicit function theorem to compute $d\tilde{x}_2/dx_1$, because we can differentiate $\tilde{x}_2(x_1) = 3x_1^2 - 1$ directly to get $6x_1$. The theorem is useful, however, when no closed-form solution exists for $\tilde{x}_2(x_1)$.

As another example, consider $f(x_1, x_2) = \log(x_1) + 3 \cdot (x_1)^2 \cdot x_2 + e^{x_2}$ and the equation $\phi(x_1, x_2) = \log(x_1) + 3.(x_1)^2 \cdot x_2 + e^{x_2} - 17 = 0$, which implicitly defines x_2 as a function of x_1. An explicit function $\tilde{x}_2(x_1)$ cannot be found. We can, however, compute the derivative of this function by using the implicit function theorem,

$$d\tilde{x}_2/dx_1 = -[(1/x_1) + 6x_1x_2]/(3 \cdot (x_1)^2 + e^{x_2}).$$

A multivariate version of the implicit function theorem is also available. Let $f(x_1, \ldots, x_n)$ be an n-variate function in the real space. Assume that $f(\cdot)$ is twice continuously differentiable. Let $\phi(x_1, \ldots, x_n) = 0$ be an equation that involves $x_1, \ldots, x_n$ only through $f(x_1, \ldots, x_n)$ and that implicitly defines x_n as a function of $x_1, x_2, \ldots, x_{n-1}$: $x_n = \tilde{x}_n(x_1, \ldots, x_{n-1})$. The implicit function theorem gives the derivatives of the implicit function $\tilde{x}_n(x_1, \ldots, x_{n-1})$ as

$$\frac{\partial \tilde{x}_n}{\partial x_i} = -\frac{\partial f(\cdot)/\partial x_i}{\partial f(\cdot)/\partial x_n}, i = 1, \ldots, n - 1. \tag{A.107}$$

1.5.2 Taylor's Theorem

Let $f(x)$ be a univariate function in the real space. Taylor's theorem says that we can approximate this function around the point x^* with a polynomial of degree n as follows:

$$f(x) = f(x^*) + (df/dx)\big|_{x^*} \cdot (x - x^*) + (d^2 f/dx^2)\big|_{x^*} \cdot (x - x^*)^2 \cdot (1/2!)$$
$$+ (d^3 f/dx^3)\big|_{x^*} \cdot (x - x^*)^3 \cdot (1/3!) +$$
$$\cdots + (d^n f/dx^n)\big|_{x^*} \cdot (x - x^*)^n \cdot (1/n!) + R_n, \tag{A.108}$$

where $(d^n f/dx^n)\big|_{x^*}$ is the nth derivative of f with respect to x evaluated at the point x^*, $n!$ is the factorial of n ($n! = n \cdot [n-1] \cdot \ldots \cdot 2 \cdot 1$), and R_n is a residual. The expression in Eq. (A.108)—with R_n omitted—is the *Taylor-Series expansion* of $f(x)$ around x^*.

The presence of the residual R_n in the equation indicates that the Taylor expansion is not an exact formula for $f(x)$. The content of the theorem is that it describes conditions under which the approximation gets better as n increases.

We can check on the accuracy of the Taylor formula—that is, on the size of R_n—by computing the approximation to a polynomial. If the formula is useful, then it should reproduce the exact polynomial. For example, if we use a polynomial of degree 3 to approximate x^3 around 1, then we get

$$x^3 = 1^3 + (3 \cdot 1^2) \cdot (x - 1) + (6 \cdot 1) \cdot (x - 1)^2/2 + 6 \cdot (x - 1)^3/6 + R_3$$

$$= 1 + (3x - 3) + 3 \cdot (x^2 - 2x + 1) + (x^3 - 3x^2 + 3x - 1) + R_3 = x^3.$$

The residual, R_3 is 0 in this case.

As another example, we can use a polynomial of order 4 to approximate the nonlinear function e^x around 0:

$$e^x = e^0 + e^0 \cdot x + e^0 \cdot (x^2/2) + e^0 \cdot (x^3/6) + e^0 \cdot (x^4/24) + R_4$$

$$= 1 + x + (x^2/2) + (x^3/6) + (x^4/24) + R_4.$$

The approximation (the formula with R_n omitted) gets better the higher the value of n.

If we use a polynomial of order 1 to approximate a function around a point x^*, then we say that we *linearize* the function around x^*. We can also *log-linearize* a function $f(x)$ by using a first-order Taylor expansion of $\log(x)$ around $\log(x^*)$. Log-linearizations are used frequently in this book and are often useful for empirical analyses.

The two-dimensional version of Taylor's theorem is as follows. Let $f(x_1, x_2)$ be a twice continuously differentiable real function. We can approximate $f(x_1, x_2)$ around the point (x_1^*, x_2^*) with a second-order expansion as follows:

$$f(x_1, x_2) = f(x_1^*, x_2^*) + f_{x_1}(\bullet) \cdot (x_1 - x_1^*) + f_{x_2}(\bullet) \cdot (x_2 - x_2^*) + (1/2) \cdot [f_{x_1 x_1}(\bullet)$$
$$\cdot (x_1 - x_1^*)^2 + 2 \cdot f_{x_1 x_2}(\bullet) \cdot (x_1 - x_1^*) \cdot (x_2 - x_2^*) + f_{x_2 x_2}(\bullet) \cdot (x_2 - x_2^*)^2] + R_2,$$

$$\text{(A.109)}$$

where $f_{x_i}(\bullet)$ is the partial derivative of $f(\bullet)$ with respect to x_i evaluated at (x_1^*, x_2^*), and $f_{x_i x_j}(\bullet)$ is the second partial derivative of $f(\bullet)$ with respect to x_i and x_j evaluated at (x_1^*, x_2^*). The linear approximation of $f(\bullet)$ around (x_1^*, x_2^*) is given by the first three terms of the right-hand side of Eq. (A.109).

1.5.3 L'Hôpital's Rule

Let $f(x)$ and $g(x)$ be two real functions twice continuously differentiable. Suppose that the limits of both functions as x approaches x^* are 0; that is, $\lim_{x \to x^*}[f(x)] = \lim_{x \to x^*}[g(x)] = 0$. Imagine that we are interested in the limit of the ratio, $f(x)/g(x)$, as x approaches x^*. In this case, the ratio takes on the indeterminate form 0/0 as x tends to x^*. L'Hôpital's rule is

$$\lim_{x \to x^*} \left(\frac{f(x)}{g(x)} \right) = \lim_{x \to x^*} \left(\frac{f'(x)}{g'(x)} \right), \tag{A.110}$$

provided that the limit on the right-hand side exists. If the right-hand side still equals 0/0, then we can apply l'Hôpital's rule again, until we get a result that is hopefully not an indeterminate form. L'Hôpital's rule applies to the indeterminate form 0/0 and also works for the indeterminate form ∞/∞. The rule does not apply, however, if $f(x)/g(x)$ tends to infinity as x approaches x^*.

As an example, consider $f(x) = 2x$ and $g(x) = x$. The limit of the ratio $f(x)/g(x)$ as x tends to 0 is

$$\lim_{x \to x^*} \left(\frac{f(x)}{g(x)} \right) = \frac{0}{0} = \lim_{x \to x^*} \left(\frac{f'(x)}{g'(x)} \right) = \frac{2}{1} = 2.$$

1.5.4 Integration by Parts

To integrate a function by parts, note that the formula for the derivative of a product of two functions of time, $v_1(t)$ and $v_2(t)$, implies

$$d[v_1 v_2] = v_2 \cdot dv_1 + v_1 \cdot dv_2,$$

where $dv_1 = v_1'(t) \cdot dt$ and $dv_2 = v_2'(t) \cdot dt$. Take the integral of both sides of the above equation to get

$$v_1 v_2 = \int v_2 \cdot dv_1 + \int v_1 \cdot dv_2.$$

Rearrange to get the formula for integration by parts:

$$\int v_2 \cdot dv_1 = v_1 v_2 - \int v_1 \cdot dv_2. \tag{A.111}$$

As an example, compute the integral $\int te^t \, dt$. Define $v_1 = t$ and $dv_2 = e^t \, dv$. By integrating dv_2 we get $v_2 = e^t$. Take the derivative of v_1 to get $dv_1 = 1$. Use the formula for integration by parts in Eq. (A.111) to get

$$\int te^t dt = te^t - \int e^t dt = e^t \cdot (t - 1).$$

1.5.5 Fundamental Theorem of Calculus

Let $f(t)$ be continuous in $a \le t \le b$. If $F(t) = \int f(t) \cdot dt$ is the indefinite integral of $f(t)$, so that $F'(t) = f(t)$, then the definite integral is

$$\int_a^b f(t)dt = \int_a^b F'(t)dt = F(b) - F(a). \tag{A.112}$$

An interpretation of a definite integral is that it represents the area below the function $f(t)$ and between the points a and b (see Fig. A.14).

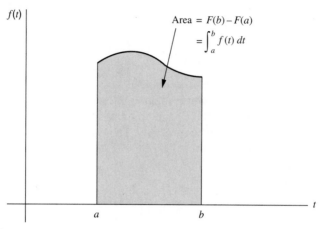

FIGURE A.14
The definite integral. The definite integral corresponds to the area under a curve between the limits of integration.

1.5.6 Rules of Differentiation of Integrals

DIFFERENTIATION WITH RESPECT TO THE VARIABLE OF INTEGRATION.
The condition $F'(t) = f(t)$ implies that the derivative of an indefinite integral with respect to the variable of integration, t, is the function $f(t)$ itself:

$$\frac{\partial}{\partial t}\left(\int f(t)dt\right) = \frac{\partial}{\partial t}[F(t)] = F'(t) = f(t). \tag{A.113}$$

LEIBNIZ'S RULE FOR DIFFERENTIATION OF DEFINITE INTEGRALS. Let $F(a, b, c)$ be the function describing the definite integral of $f(c, t)$, where a and b are, respectively, the lower and upper limits of integration, and c is a parameter of the function $f(\cdot)$:

$$F(a, b, c) = \int_a^b f(c, t) \cdot dt. \tag{A.114}$$

We assume that $f(c, t)$ has a continuous partial derivative with respect to c, $f_c(\cdot) \equiv \partial f(\cdot)/\partial c$. The derivative of $F(\cdot)$ with respect to c is

$$\frac{\partial F(\cdot)}{\partial c} = \int_a^b f_c(c, t)dt. \tag{A.115}$$

The derivatives of $F(\cdot)$ with respect to the limits of integration are

$$\frac{\partial F(\cdot)}{\partial b} = \frac{\partial}{\partial b}\left(\int_a^b f(c, t)dt\right) = f(c, t)\bigg|_{t=b} = f(c, b), \tag{A.116}$$

$$\frac{\partial F(\cdot)}{\partial a} = \frac{\partial}{\partial a}\left(\int_a^b f(c, t)dt\right) = -f(c, t)\bigg|_{t=a} = -f(c, a). \tag{A.117}$$

We can combine Eqs. (A.115–(A.117) to get Leibniz's rule of integration. Suppose that a and b are functions of c:

$$F(c) = \int_{a(c)}^{b(c)} f(c, t) \cdot dt. \qquad (A.118)$$

Leibniz's rule is

$$\frac{dF(c)}{dc} = \int_{a(c)}^{b(c)} f_c(c, t) \cdot dt + f\big(c, b[c]\big) \cdot b'(c) - f\big(c, a[c]\big) \cdot a'(c). \qquad (A.119)$$

REFERENCES

Abel, Andrew and Olivier Blanchard (1983). "An Intertemporal Equilibrium Model of Saving and Investment," *Econometrica*, 51, 3 (May), 675–692.

Ades, Alberto F. and Edward L. Glaeser (1993). "Trade and Circuses: Explaining Urban Growth," unpublished paper, Harvard University, November.

Ades, Alberto and Hak B. Chua (1993). "Regional Instability and Economic Growth: Thy Neighbor's Curse?" unpublished paper, Harvard University.

Aghion, Philippe and Peter Howitt (1992). "A Model of Growth through Creative Destruction," *Econometrica*, 60, 2 (March), 323–351.

Alesina, Alberto and Roberto Perotti (1993). "Income Distribution, Political Instability, and Investment," NBER Working Paper no. 4486, October.

Arrow, Kenneth J. (1962). "The Economic Implications of Learning by Doing," *Review of Economic Studies*, 29 (June), 155–173.

Arrow, Kenneth J., Hollis B. Chenery, Bagicha S. Minhas, and Robert M. Solow (1961). "Capital-Labor Substitution and Economic Efficiency," *Review of Economics and Statistics*, 43 (August), 225–250.

Arrow, Kenneth J. and Mordecai Kurz (1970). *Public Investment, the Rate of Return, and Optimal Fiscal Policy*, Baltimore, Johns Hopkins Press.

Arrow, Kenneth J. and Alain C. Enthoven (1961). "Quasiconcave Programming," *Econometrica*, 29 (October), 779–800.

Aschauer, David A. (1985). "Fiscal Policy and Aggregate Demand," *American Economic Review*, 75, 1 (March), 117–127.

Asher, H. (1956). *Cost-Quantity Relationships in the Airframe Industry*, R-291, Santa Monica, The Rand Corporation.

Banco de Bilbao (various issues). *Renta Nacional de España y su Distribucion Provincial*, Bilbao, Banco de Bilbao-Vizcaya.

Banks, Arthur S. (1979). *Cross-National Time-Series Data Archive*, Center for Social Analysis, State University of New York, Binghamton.

Barro, Robert J. (1974). "Are Government Bonds Net Wealth?" *Journal of Political Economy*, 81, 6 (December), 1095–1117.

518

Barro, Robert J. (1984). *Macroeconomics*, first edition, New York, Wiley.

Barro, Robert J. (1987). "Government Spending, Interest Rates, Prices, and Budget Deficits in the United Kingdom, 1701–1918," *Journal of Monetary Economics*, 20, 2 (September), 221–247.

Barro, Robert J. (1990a). "The Stock Market and Investment," *The Review of Financial Studies*, 3, 1, 115–130.

Barro, Robert J. (1990b). "Government Spending in a Simple Model of Endogenous Growth," *Journal of Political Economy*, 98, 5 (October), part II, S103–S125.

Barro, Robert J. (1991a). "Economic Growth in a Cross Section of Countries," *Quarterly Journal of Economics*, 106, 2 (May), 407–443.

Barro, Robert J. (1991b). "A Cross Country Study of Growth, Saving, and Government," in B. Douglas Bernheim and John B. Shoven, eds., *National Saving and Economic Performance*, Chicago, University of Chicago Press.

Barro, Robert J. (1993). *Macroeconomics*, fourth edition, New York, Wiley.

Barro, Robert J. and Gary S. Becker (1989). "Fertility Choice in a Model of Economic Growth," *Econometrica*, 57, 2 (March), 481–501.

Barro, Robert J. and Jong-Wha Lee (1993). "International Comparisons of Educational Attainment," *Journal of Monetary Economics*, 32, 3 (December), 363–394.

Barro, Robert J. and Jong-Wha Lee (1994). "Sources of Economic Growth," *Carnegie–Rochester Conference Series on Public Policy*.

Barro, Robert J. and Xavier Sala-i-Martin (1991). "Convergence across States and Regions," *Brookings Papers on Economic Activity*, no. 1, 107–182.

Barro, Robert J. and Xavier Sala-i-Martin (1992a). "Convergence," *Journal of Political Economy*, 100, 2 (April), 223–251.

Barro, Robert J. and Xavier Sala-i-Martin (1992b). "Regional Growth and Migration: A Japan–United States Comparison," *Journal of the Japanese and International Economies*, 6 (December), 312–346.

Barro, Robert J. and Xavier Sala-i-Martin (1992c). "Public Finance in Models of Economic Growth," *Review of Economic Studies*, 59, 4 (October), 645–661.

Barro, Robert J., N. Gregory Mankiw, and Xavier Sala-i-Martin (1992). "Capital Mobility in Neoclassical Models of Growth," NBER Working Paper no. 4206, November.

Baumol, William J. (1986). "Productivity Growth, Convergence, and Welfare: What the Long-Run Data Show," *American Economic Review*, 76, 5 (December), 1072–1085.

Becker, Gary S. (1965). "A Theory of the Allocation of Time," *Economic Journal*, 75 (September), 493–517.

Becker, Gary S. (1991). "The Demand for Children," chapter 5 in *A Treatise on the Family*, Cambridge MA, Harvard University Press.

Becker, Gary S. and Robert J. Barro (1988). "A Reformulation of the Economic Theory of Fertility," *Quarterly Journal of Economics*, 103, 1 (February), 1–25.

Becker, Gary S., Kevin M. Murphy, and Robert Tamura (1990). "Human Capital, Fertility, and Economic Growth," *Journal of Political Economy*, 98, 5 (October), part II, S12–S37.

Behrman, Jere R. (1990). "Women's Schooling and Nonmarket Productivity: A Survey and a Reappraisal," unpublished paper, University of Pennsylvania.

Benhabib, Jess and Roger E.A. Farmer (1991). "Indeterminacy and Increasing Returns," unpublished paper, New York University, November.

Benhabib, Jess and Mark M. Spiegel (1993). "The Role of Human Capital and Political Instability in Economic Development," unpublished paper, New York University, March.

Benhabib, Jess, Richard Rogerson, and Randall Wright (1991). "Homework in Macroeconomics: Household Production and Aggregate Fluctuations," *Journal of Political Economy*, 99, 6 (December), 1166–1187.

Benveniste, Lawrence M. and Jose A. Scheinkman, "Duality Theory for Dynamic Optimization Models of Economics: The Continuous Time Case," *Journal of Economic Theory*, 27, 1 (June), 1–19.

Bernheim, B. Douglas and Kyle Bagwell (1988). "Is Everything Neutral?" *Journal of Political Economy*, 96, 2 (April), 308–338.

Blanchard, Olivier (1985). "Debt, Deficits, and Finite Horizons," *Journal of Political Economy*, 93, 2 (April), 223–247.

Blanchard, Olivier and Stanley Fischer (1989). *Lectures on Macroeconomics*, Cambridge MA, MIT Press.

Blanchard, Olivier, Changyong Rhee, and Lawrence H. Summers (1993). "The Stock Market, Profit, and Investment," *Quarterly Journal of Economics*, 108, 1 (February), 115–136.

Blomström, Magnus, Robert E. Lipsey, and Mario Zejan (1993). "Is Fixed Investment the Key to Economic Growth?" NBER Working Paper no. 4436, August.

Boldrin, M. and A. Rustichini (1993). "Growth and Indeterminacy in Dynamic Models with Externalities," unpublished paper, Northwestern University.

Borjas, George J. (1992). "Ethnic Capital and Intergenerational Mobility," *Quarterly Journal of Economics*, 107, 1 (February), 123–150.

Borjas, George J., Stephen G. Bronars, and Stephen J. Trejo (1992). "Self-Selection and Internal Migration in the United States," *Journal of Urban Economics*, 32, 2 (September), 159–185.

Borts, George H. and Jerome L. Stein (1964). *Economic Growth in a Free Market*, New York, Columbia University Press.

Bos, Eduard, My T. Vu, and Patience W. Stephens (1992). "Sources of World Bank Estimates of Current Mortality Rates," Policy Research Working Paper Series, Washington D.C., The World Bank.

Bowman, Larry W. (1991). *Mauritius: Democracy and Development in the Indian Ocean*, Boulder CO, Westview.

Brainard, William C. and James Tobin (1968). "Pitfalls in Financial Model Building," *American Economic Review*, 58, 2 (May), 99–122.

Braun, Juan (1993). *Essays on Economic Growth and Migration*, Ph.D. dissertation, Harvard University.

Brezis, Elise, Paul Krugman, and Daniel Tsiddon (1993). "Leapfrogging in International Competition: A Theory of Cycles in National Technological Leadership," *American Economic Review*, 83, 5 (December), 1211–1219.

Brock, William A. (1975). "A Simple Perfect Foresight Monetary Model," *Journal of Monetary Economics*, 1, 2 (April), 133–150.

Caballe, Jordi and Manuel S. Santos (1993). "On Endogenous Growth with Physical and Human Capital," *Journal of Political Economy*, 101, 6 (December), 1042–1067.

Caballero, Ricardo J. and Adam B. Jaffe (1993). "How High are the Giants' Shoulders: an Empirical Assessment of Knowledge Spillovers and Creative Destruction in a Model of Economic Growth," in *NBER Macroeconomics Annual 1993*, Cambridge MA, MIT Press, 15–74.

Cass, David (1965). "Optimum Growth in an Aggregative Model of Capital Accumulation," *Review of Economic Studies*, 32 (July), 233–240.

Chamley, Christophe (1992). "The Last Shall Be First: Efficient Constraints on Foreign Borrowing in a Model of Endogenous Growth," *Journal of Economic Theory*, 58, 2 (December), 335–354.

Chiang, Alpha C. (1984). *Fundamental Methods of Mathematical Economics*, third edition, New York, McGraw-Hill.

Chiang, Alpha C. (1992). *Dynamic Optimization*, New York, McGraw-Hill.

Chiswick, Barry R. (1978). "The Effect of Americanization on the Earnings of Foreign-born Men," *Journal of Political Economy*, 86, 5 (October), 897–921.

Christensen, Laurits R., Dianne Cummings, and Dale W. Jorgenson (1980). "Economic Growth, 1947–1973: An International Comparison," in John W. Kendrick and Beatrice Vaccara, eds., *New Developments in Productivity Measurement and Analysis*, NBER Conference Report, Chicago, University of Chicago Press.

Chua, Hak B. (1993). *Regional Spillovers and Economic Growth*, Ph.D. dissertation, Harvard University.

Coase, Ronald W. (1960). "The Problem of Social Cost," *Journal of Law and Economics*, 3 (October), 1–44.

Coe, David T. and Elhanan Helpman (1993). "International R&D Spillovers," NBER Working Paper No. 4444, August.

Cohen, Daniel and Jeffrey Sachs (1986). "Growth and External Debt under Risk of Debt Repudiation," *European Economic Review*, 30, 3 (June), 526–560.

Collins, Susan M. and Won Am Park (1989). "External Debt and Macroeconomic Performance in South Korea," in Jeffrey D. Sachs, ed., *Developing Country Debt and the World Economy*, Chicago, University of Chicago Press, 121–140.

Coulombe, Serge and Frank C. Lee (1993). "Regional Economic Disparities in Canada," unpublished paper, University of Ottawa, July.

DeLong, J. Bradford (1988). "Productivity Growth, Convergence, and Welfare: Comment," *American Economic Review*, 78, 5 (December), 1138–1154.

DeLong, J. Bradford and Lawrence H. Summers (1991). "Equipment Investment and Economic Growth," *Quarterly Journal of Economics*, 106, 2 (May), 445–502.

Denison, Edward F. (1962). "Sources of Growth in the United States and the Alternatives Before Us," Supplement Paper 13, New York, Committee for Economic Development.

Denison, Edward F. (1967). *Why Growth Rates Differ*, Washington D.C., The Brookings Institution.

Denison, Edward F. (1974). *Accounting for United States Economic Growth, 1929-1969*, Washington D.C., The Brookings Institution.

Diamond, Peter (1965). "National Debt in a Neoclassical Growth Model," *American Economic Review*, 55, 5 (December), 1126–1150.

Diewert, W. Erwin (1976). "Exact and Superlative Index Numbers," *Journal of Econometrics*, 4, 2 (May), 115–146.

Dixit, Avinash K. and Joseph E. Stiglitz (1977). "Monopolistic Competition and Optimum Product Diversity," *American Economic Review*, 67, 3 (June), 297–308.

Dolado, Juan, Alessandra Goria, and Andrea Ichino (1993). "Immigration, Human Capital, and Growth in the Host Country: Evidence from Pooled Country Data," unpublished paper, Bank of Spain, April.

Domar, Evsey D. (1946). "Capital Expansion, Rate of Growth, and Employment," *Econometrica,* 14, (April), 137–147.

Dorfman, Robert (1969). "An Economic Interpretation of Optimal Control Theory," *American Economic Review*, 59, 5 (December), 817–831.

Dougherty, Christopher (1991). *A Comparison of Productivity and Economic Growth in the G-7 Countries*, Ph.D. dissertation, Harvard University.

Dowrick, Steve and Duc Tho Nguyen (1989). "OECD Comparative Economic Growth 1950–85: Catch-Up and Convergence," *American Economic Review*, 79, 5 (December), 1010–1030.

Easterlin, Richard A. (1960a). "Regional Growth of Income: Long-Run Tendencies," in Simon Kuznets, Ann Ratner Miller, and Richard A. Easterlin, eds., *Population Redistribution and Economic Growth, United States, 1870–1950. II: Analyses of Economic Change*, Philadelphia, The American Philosophical Society.

Easterlin, Richard A. (1960b). "Interregional Differences in Per Capita Income, Population, and Total Income, 1840–1950," in *Trends in the American Economy in the Nineteenth Century*, Princeton, Princeton University Press.

Easterly, William (1993). "How Much Do Distortions Affect Growth?" *Journal of Monetary Economics*, 32, (November), 187–212.

Easterly, William and Sergio Rebelo (1993). "Fiscal Policy and Economic Growth: An Empirical Investigation," *Journal of Monetary Economics*, 32 (December), 417–458.

Elias, Victor J. (1990). *Sources of Growth: A Study of Seven Latin American Economies*, San Francisco, ICS Press.

Ethier, Wilfred J. (1982). "National and International Returns to Scale in the Modern Theory of International Trade," *American Economic Review*, 72, 3 (June), 389–405.

Faig, Miguel (1991). "A Simple Economy with Human Capital: Transitional Dynamics, Technology Shocks and Fiscal Policies," University of Toronto, May.

Feenstra, Robert C. and James R. Markusen (1992). "Accounting for Growth with New Inputs," NBER Working Paper no. 4114, July.

Fischer, Stanley (1979). "Anticipations and the Nonneutrality of Money," *Journal of Political Economy*, 87, 2 (April), 225–252.

Fisher, I. (1930). *The Theory of Interest*, New York, Macmillan.

Galor, Oded and David N. Weil (1993). "The Gender Gap, Fertility, and Growth," NBER Working Paper no. 4550, November.

Galor, Oded and Harl E. Ryder (1989). "Existence, Uniqueness, and Stability of Equilibrium in an Overlapping-Generations Model with Productive Capital," *Journal of Economic Theory*, 49, 2 (December), 360–375.

Gastil, Raymond D. (1987). *Freedom in the World*, Westport CT, Greenwood Press.

Geary, Robert C. (1950–51). "A Note on 'A Constant Utility Index of the Cost of Living'," *Review of Economic Studies*, 18, 1, 65–66.

Greenwood, Jeremy and Zvi Hercowitz (1991). "The Allocation of Capital and Time over the Business Cycle," *Journal of Political Economy*, 99, 6 (December), 1188–1214.

Greenwood, Michael J. (1975). "Research on Internal Migration in the United States: A Survey," *Journal of Economic Literature*, 13, 2 (June), 397–433.

Griliches, Zvi (1957). "Hybrid Corn: An Exploration in the Economics of Technological Change," *Econometrica*, 25, 4 (October), 501–522.

Griliches, Zvi (1973). "Research Expenditures and Growth Accounting," in B.R. Williams, ed., *Science and Technology in Economic Growth*, New York, Macmillan.

Griliches, Zvi (1988). "Productivity Puzzles and R&D: Another Explanation," *Journal of Economic Perspectives*, 2, 4 (Fall), 9–21.

Griliches, Zvi (1994). "The Residual, Past and Present: A Personal View," unpublished paper, Harvard University.

Griliches, Zvi and Frank Lichtenberg (1984). "R&D and Productivity Growth at the Industry Level: Is there Still a Relationship," in Zvi Griliches, ed., *R&D, Patents, and Productivity*, Chicago, University of Chicago Press.

Grossman, Gene M., and Elhanan Helpman (1991). *Innovation and Growth in the Global Economy*, Cambridge MA, MIT Press.

Gulhati, Ravi, and Raj Nallari (1990). "Successful Stabilization and Recovery in Mauritius," EDI Development Policy Case Series, Analytical Case Studies, no. 5, Washington D.C., The World Bank.

Halkin, Hubert (1974). "Necessary Conditions for Optimal Control Problems with Infinite Horizons," *Econometrica*, 42, 2 (March), 267–272.

Harrod, Roy F. (1939). "An Essay in Dynamic Theory," *Economic Journal*, 49 (June), 14–33.

Harrod, Roy F. (1942). *Toward a Dynamic Economics: Some Recent Developments of Economic Theory and their Application to Policy*, London, Macmillan.

Hart, Peter E. (1994). "Galtonian Regression Across Countries and the Convergence of Productivity," unpublished paper, University of Reading.

Hatton, Timothy J. and Jeffrey G. Williamson (1992). "What Drove the Mass Migration from Europe in the Late Nineteenth Century," unpublished paper, Harvard University, October.

Hayashi, Fumio (1982). "Tobin's Marginal q and Average q: A Neoclassical Interpretation," *Econometrica*, 50, 1 (January), 213–224.

Heckman, James J. (1976). "A Life-Cycle Model of Earnings, Learning, and Consumption," *Journal of Political Economy*, 84, 4 (August), Part 2, S11–S44.

Henderson, J. Vernon (1988). *Urban Development: Theory, Fact, and Illusion*, Oxford, Oxford University Press.

Hicks, John (1932). *The Theory of Wages*, London, Macmillan.

Hirshleifer, Jack (1987). *Economic Behavior in Adversity*, Chicago, University of Chicago Press.

Inada, Ken-Ichi (1963). "On a Two-Sector Model of Economic Growth: Comments and a Generalization," *Review of Economic Studies*, 30 (June), 119–127.

International Currency Analysis (1991). *World Currency Yearbook 1988–89*, Brooklyn.

International Monetary Fund (1991). *International Financial Statistics Yearbook*, Washington D.C., International Monetary Fund.

Jones, Larry E. and Rodolfo E. Manuelli (1990). "A Convex Model of Equilibrium Growth: Theory and Policy Implications," *Journal of Political Economy*, 98, 5 (October), pp. 1008–1038.

Jorgenson, Dale W. and Zvi Griliches (1967). "The Explanation of Productivity Change," *Review of Economic Studies*, 34 (July), 249–280.

Jorgenson, Dale W., Frank M. Gollop, and Barbara M. Fraumeni (1987). *Productivity and U.S. Economic Growth*, Cambridge MA, Harvard University Press.

Jovanovic, Boyan and Yaw Nyarko (1994). "The Bayesian Foundations of Learning by Doing," unpublished paper, New York University, February.

Jovanovic, Boyan and Saul Lach (1991). "The Diffusion of Technological Inequality Among Nations," unpublished paper, New York University.

Judd, Kenneth L. (1985). "On the Performance of Patents," *Econometrica*, 53, 3 (May), 567–585.

Judson, Ruth (1993). "Do Low Human Capital Coefficients Make Sense? A Puzzle and Some Answers," unpublished paper, MIT, October.

Kaldor, Nicholas (1963). "Capital Accumulation and Economic Growth," in Friedrich A. Lutz and Douglas C. Hague, eds., *Proceedings of a Conference Held by the International Economics Association*, London, Macmillan.

Kamien, Morton I. and Nancy L. Schwartz (1991). *Dynamic Optimization, The Calculus of Variations and Optimal Control in Economics and Management*, second edition, Amsterdam, North Holland.

Kendrick, John W. (1976). *The Formation and Stocks of Total Capital*, New York, Columbia University Press.

Kimball, Miles S. (1987). "Making Sense of Two-Sided Altruism," *Journal of Monetary Economics*, 20, 2 (September), 301–326.

King, Robert G. and Ross Levine (1993). "Finance, Entrepreneurship, and Growth: Theory and Evidence," *Journal of Monetary Economics*, 32 (December), 513–542.

King, Robert G. and Sergio Rebelo (1993). "Transitional Dynamics and Economic Growth in the Neoclassical Model," *American Economic Review*, 83, 4 (September), 908–931.

King, Robert G., Charles I. Plosser, and Sergio Rebelo (1988a). "Production, Growth and Business Cycles: I. The Basic Neoclassical Model," *Journal of Monetary Economics*, 21, 2/3 (March/May), 195–232.

King, Robert G., Charles I. Plosser, and Sergio Rebelo (1988b). "Production, Growth and Business Cycles: II. New Directions," *Journal of Monetary Economics*, 21, 2/3 (March/May), 309–341.

Knack, Stephen and Philip Keefer (1994). "Institutions and Economic Performance: Cross-Country Tests Using Alternative Institutional Measures," unpublished paper, American University, February.

Knight, Frank H. (1944). "Diminishing Returns from Investment," *Journal of Political Economy*, 52 (March), 26–47.

Koopmans, Tjalling C. (1965). "On the Concept of Optimal Economic Growth," in *The Econometric Approach to Development Planning*, Amsterdam, North Holland, 1965.

Kremer, Michael (1993). "Population Growth and Technological Change: One Million B.C. to 1990," *Quarterly Journal of Economics*, 108, 3 (August), 681–716.

Kremer, Michael and James Thomson (1993). "Why Isn't Convergence Instantaneous?" unpublished paper, MIT, November.

Krugman, Paul (1979). "A Model of Innovation, Technology Transfer, and the World Distribution of Income," *Journal of Political Economy*, 87, 2 (April), 253–266.

Krugman, Paul (1991). "History Versus Expectations," *Quarterly Journal of Economics*, 106, 2 (May), 651–667.

Kuhn, Harold W. and Albert W. Tucker, (1951). "Nonlinear Programming," in J. Neyman, ed., *Proceedings of the Second Berkeley Symposium on Mathematical Statistics and Probability*, Berkeley, University of California Press, 481–492.

Kurz, Mordecai (1968). "The General Instability of a Class of Competitive Growth Processes," *Review of Economic Studies*, 35 (April), 155–174.

Kuznets, Simon (1973). "Modern Economic Growth: Findings and Reflections," *American Economic Review*, 63, 3 (June), 247–258.

Kuznets, Simon (1981). "Modern Economic Growth and the Less Developed Countries," *Conference on Experiences and Lessons of Economic Development in Taiwan*, Taipei, The Institute of Economics, Academia Sinica.

Kydland, Finn E. and Edward C. Prescott (1982). "Time to Build and Aggregate Fluctuations," *Econometrica*, 50, 6 (November), 1345–1370.

Lee, Jong-Wha (1993). "International Trade, Distortions, and Long-Run Economic Growth," *IMF Staff Papers*, 40 (June), 299–328.

Leontief, Wassily (1941). *The Structure of the American Economy: 1919–1929*, Cambridge MA, Harvard University Press.

Levine, Ross and David Renelt (1992). "A Sensitivity Analysis of Cross-Country Growth Regressions," *American Economic Review*, 82, 4 (September), 942–963.

Lewis, William Arthur (1954). "Economic Development with Unlimited Supplies of Labor," *Manchester School of Economics and Social Studies*, 22 (May), 139–191.

Londregan, John B. and Keith T. Poole (1990). "Poverty, the Coup Trap, and the Seizure of Executive Power," *World Politics*, 42, 2 (January), 151–183.

Lucas, Robert E., Jr. (1988). "On the Mechanics of Development Planning," *Journal of Monetary Economics*, 22, 1 (July), 3–42.

Maddison, Angus (1982). *Phases of Capitalist Development*, Oxford, Oxford University Press.

Maddison, Angus (1989). *The World Economy in the Twentieth Century*, Paris, OECD.

Maddison, Angus (1991). *Dynamic Forces in Capitalist Development*, Oxford, Oxford University Press.

Maddison, Angus (1992). "A Long-Run Perspective on Saving," *Scandinavian Journal of Economics*, 94, 2, 181–196.

Malthus, Thomas R. (1798). *An Essay on the Principle of Population*, London, W. Pickering, 1986.

Mangasarian, O.L. (1966). "Sufficient Conditions for the Optimal Control of Nonlinear Systems," *SIAM Journal of Control*, 4 (February), 139–152.

Mankiw, N. Gregory, David Romer, and David N. Weil (1992). "A Contribution to the Empirics of Economic Growth," *Quarterly Journal of Economics*, 107, 2 (May), 407–437.

Mansfield, Edwin (1985). "How Rapidly Does New Industrial Technology Leak Out?" *Journal of Industrial Economics*, 34, 2 (December), 217–223.

Mansfield, Edwin, Mark Schwartz, and Samuel Wagner (1981). "Imitation Costs and Patents: An Empirical Study," *Economic Journal*, 91 (December), 907–918.

Mas-Colell, Andreu and Assaf Razin (1973). "A Model of Intersectoral Migration and Growth," *Oxford Economic Papers*, 25 (March), 72–79.

Matsuyama, Kiminori (1991). "Increasing Returns, Industrialization, and the Indeterminacy of Equilibrium," *Quarterly Journal of Economics*, 106, 2 (May), 617–650.

Mauro, Paolo (1993). "Corruption, Country Risk and Growth," unpublished paper, Harvard University, November.

McCallum, Bennett T. (1984). "Are Bond-Financed Deficits Inflationary? A Ricardian Analysis," *Journal of Political Economy*, 92, 1 (February), 123–135.

McCallum, Bennett T. (1989). "Real Business Cycle Models," in Robert J. Barro, ed., *Modern Business Cycle Theory*, Cambridge MA, Harvard University Press.

Michel, Philippe (1982). "On the Transversality Condition in Infinite Horizon Optimal Problems," *Econometrica*, 50, 4 (July), 975–985.

Molle, Willem, Bas Van Holst, and Hans Smit (1980). *Regional Disparity and Economic Development in the European Community*, Westmead, England, Saxon House.

Mulligan, Casey B. (1993). "On Intergenerational Altruism, Fertility, and the Persistence of Economic Status," Ph.D. dissertation, University of Chicago.

Mulligan, Casey B. and Xavier Sala-i-Martin (1991). "A Note on the Time-Elimination Method for Solving Recursive Economic Models," NBER Technical Working Paper no. 116, November.

Mulligan, Casey B. and Xavier Sala-i-Martin (1993). "Transitional Dynamics in Two-Sector Models of Endogenous Growth," *Quarterly Journal of Economics*, 108, 3 (August), 737–773.

Murphy, Kevin M. and Finis Welch (1990). "Empirical Age-Earnings Profiles," *Journal of Labor Economics*, 8, 2 (April), 202–229.

Murphy, Kevin M., Andrei Shleifer, and Robert W. Vishny (1989). "Industrialization and the Big Push," *Quarterly Journal of Economics*, 106, 2 (May), 503–530.

Nelson, Richard R. and Edmund S. Phelps (1966). "Investment in Humans, Technological Diffusion, and Economic Growth," *American Economic Review*, 56, 2 (May), 69–75.

Ohyama, Michihiro and Ronald W. Jones (1993). "Technology Choice, Overtaking and Comparative Advantage," unpublished paper, University of Rochester, December.

Phelps, Edmund S. (1962). "The New View of Investment: A Neoclassical Analysis," *Quarterly Journal of Economics*, 76, 4 (November), 548–567.

Phelps, Edmund S. (1966). *Golden Rules of Economic Growth*, New York, Norton.

Pitchford, John D. (1977). *Applications of Control Theory to Economic Analysis*, Amsterdam, North Holland.

Pontryagin, Lev S., et al. (1962). *The Mathematical Theory of Optimal Processes*, New York, Interscience Publishers.

Quah, Danny (1993). "Galton's Fallacy and Tests of the Convergence Hypothesis," *Scandinavian Journal of Economics*, 95, 4, 427–443.

Ramsey, Frank (1928). "A Mathematical Theory of Saving," *Economic Journal*, 38 (December), 543–559.

Rapping, Leonard (1965). "Learning and World War II Production Functions," *Review of Economics and Statistics*, 47 (February), 81–86.

Rebelo, Sergio (1991). "Long-Run Policy Analysis and Long-Run Growth," *Journal of Political Economy*, 99, 3 (June), 500–521.

Reinganum, Jennifer F. (1989). "The Timing of Innovation: Research, Development, and Diffusion," in Richard Schmalensee and Robert D. Willig, eds., *Handbook of Industrial Organization*, volume I, New York, North Holland.

Ricardo, David (1817). *On the Principles of Political Economy and Taxation*, Cambridge, Cambridge University Press, 1951.

Rivera-Batiz, Luis A. and Paul M. Romer (1991). "Economic Integration and Endogenous Growth," *Quarterly Journal of Economics*, 106, 2 (May), 531–555.

Roback, Jennifer (1982). "Wages, Rents, and the Quality of Life," *Journal of Political Economy*, 90, 6 (December), 1257–1278.

Robinson, Joan (1938). "The Classification of Inventions," *Review of Economic Studies*, 5 (February), 139–142.

Romer, Paul M. (1986). "Increasing Returns and Long-Run Growth," *Journal of Political Economy*, 94, 5 (October), 1002–1037.

Romer, Paul M. (1987). "Growth Based on Increasing Returns Due to Specialization," *American Economic Review*, 77, 2 (May), 56–62.

Romer, Paul M. (1990). "Endogenous Technological Change," *Journal of Political Economy*, 98, 5 (October), part II, S71–S102.

Romer, Paul M. (1992). "Two Strategies for Economic Development: Using Ideas and Producing Ideas," in The World Bank, *Annual Conference on Economic Development*, Washington D.C.

Romer, Paul M. (1993). "Idea Gaps and Object Gaps in Economic Development," *Journal of Monetary Economics*, 32, (December), 543–573.

Rybczynski, T.M. (1955). "Factor Endowments and Relative Commodity Prices," *Economica*, N.S., 22 (November), 336–341.

Saint-Paul, Gilles (1992). "Fiscal Policy in an Endogenous Growth Model," *Quarterly Journal of Economics*, 107, 4 (November), 1243–1259.

Sala-i-Martin, Xavier (1990). *On Growth and States*, Ph.D. dissertation, Harvard University.

Sala-i-Martin, Xavier (1992). "Transfers," NBER Working Paper no. 4186, October.

Samuelson, Paul A. (1954). "The Pure Theory of Public Expenditure," *Review of Economics and Statistics*, 36 (November), 387–389.

Samuelson, Paul A. (1958). "An Exact Consumption-Loan Model of Interest with or without the Social Contrivance of Money," *Journal of Political Economy*, 66, 6 (December), 467–482.

Sarel, Michael (1992). "Demographic Dynamics and the Empirics of Economic Growth," unpublished paper, Harvard University.

Schmookler, Jacob (1966). *Invention and Economic Growth*, Cambridge MA, Harvard University Press.

Schultz, T. Paul (1989). "Returns to Women's Education," PHRWD Background Paper 89/001, The World Bank, Population, Health, and Nutrition Department, Washington D.C.

Schumpeter, Joseph A. (1934). *The Theory of Economic Development*, Cambridge MA, Harvard University Press.

Searle, Allan D. (1946). "Productivity Changes in Selected Wartime Shipbuilding Programs," *Monthly Labor Review*.

Segerstrom, Paul S. (1991). "Innovation, Imitation, and Economic Growth," *Journal of Political Economy*, 99, 4 (August), 807–827.

Shell, Karl (1967). "A Model of Inventive Activity and Capital Accumulation," in Karl Shell, ed., *Essays on the Theory of Optimal Economic Growth*, Cambridge MA, MIT Press, 67–85.

Sheshinski, Eytan (1967). "Optimal Accumulation with Learning by Doing," in Karl Shell, ed., *Essays on the Theory of Optimal Economic Growth*, Cambridge MA, MIT Press, 31–52.

Shleifer, Andrei and Robert W. Vishny (1993). "Corruption," *Quarterly Journal of Economics*, 108, 3 (August), 599–617.

Sidrauski, Miguel (1967). "Rational Choice and Patterns of Growth in a Monetary Economy," *American Economic Review*, 57, 2 (May), 534–544.

Smith, Adam (1776). *An Inquiry into the Nature and Causes of the Wealth of Nations*, New York, Random House, 1937.

Solow, Robert M. (1956). "A Contribution to the Theory of Economic Growth," *Quarterly Journal of Economics*, 70, 1 (February), 65–94.

Solow, Robert M. (1957). "Technical Change and the Aggregate Production Function," *Review of Economics and Statistics*, 39 (August), 312–320.

Solow, Robert M. (1969). "Investment and Technical Change," in Kenneth J. Arrow, et al., eds., *Mathematical Methods in the Social Sciences*, Palo Alto, Stanford University Press.

Spence, Michael (1976). "Product Selection, Fixed Costs, and Monopolistic Competition," *Review of Economic Studies*, 43, 2 (June), 217–235.

Srinivasan, T.N. (1964). "Optimal Savings in a Two-Sector Model of Growth," *Econometrica*, 32 (July), 358–373.

Stone, Richard (1954). "Linear Expenditure Systems and Demand Analysis: An Application to the Pattern of British Demand," *Economic Journal*, 64 (September), 511–527.

Streissler, Erich (1979). "Growth Models as Diffusion Processes: II," *Kyklos*, 32, 3, 571–586.

Summers, Lawrence H. (1981). "Taxation and Corporate Investment: A q-Theory Approach," *Brookings Papers on Economic Activity*, no. 1, 67–127.

Summers, Robert and Alan Heston (1991). "The Penn World Table (Mark 5): An Expanded Set of International Comparisons, 1950–1988," *Quarterly Journal of Economics*, 106, 2 (May), 327–368.

Summers, Robert and Alan Heston (1993). "Penn World Tables, Version 5.5," available on diskette from the National Bureau of Economic Research, Cambridge MA.

Swan, Trevor W. (1956). "Economic Growth and Capital Accumulation," *Economic Record*, 32 (November), 334–361.

Teece, David J. (1977). "Technological Transfer by Multinational Firms: The Resource Cost of Transferring Technological Know-How," *Economic Journal*, 87 (June), 242–261.

Temple, Robert (1986). *The Genius of China*, New York, Simon and Schuster.

Thompson, Earl A. (1976). "Taxation and National Defense," *Journal of Political Economy*, 82, 4 (August), 755–782.

Thörnqvist, Leo (1936). "The Bank of Finland's Consumption Price Index," *Bank of Finland Monthly Bulletin*, no. 10, 1–8.

U.S. Department of Commerce, Bureau of the Census (1975). *Historical Statistics of the United States, Colonial Times to 1970*, Washington D.C., U.S. Government Printing Office.

U.S. Department of Commerce, Bureau of the Census (1989). *State Personal Income: 1929–87*, Washington D.C., U.S. Government Printing Office.

U.S. Department of Commerce, Bureau of the Census (1990). *Statistical Abstract of the United States*, Washington D.C., U.S. Government Printing Office.

Uzawa, Hirofumi (1961). "Neutral Inventions and the Stability of Growth Equilibrium," *Review of Economic Studies*, 28 (February), 117–124.

Uzawa, Hirofumi (1964). "Optimal Growth in a Two-Sector Model of Capital Accumulation," *Review of Economic Studies*, 31 (January), 1–24.

Uzawa, Hirofumi (1965). "Optimal Technical Change in an Aggregative Model of Economic Growth," *International Economic Review*, 6 (January), 18–31.

Uzawa, Hirofumi (1968). "Time Preference, the Consumption Function, and Optimum Asset Holdings," in J.N. Wolfe, ed., *Value, Capital, and Growth*, Chicago, Aldine.

Ventura, Jaume (1993). "Patterns of Growth," unpublished paper, Harvard University, December.

Ventura, Jaume (1994). "Growth and Interdependence," unpublished paper, Harvard University, April.

Von Furstenberg, George M. (1977). "Corporate Investment: Does Market Valuation Matter in the Aggregate?" *Brookings Papers on Economic Activity*, no. 2, 347–397.

Von Neumann, John (1937). "Über ein Ökonomisches Gleichungssystem und eine Verallgemeinerung des Brouwerschen," *Ergebnisse eines Mathematische Kolloquiums*, 8, translated by Karl Menger as "A Model of General Equilibrium," *Review of Economic Studies* (1945), 13, 1–9.

Wahl, Jenny Bourne (1985). *Fertility in America: Historical Patterns and Wealth Effects on the Quantity and Quality of Children*, Ph.D. dissertation, University of Chicago.

Weil, Philippe (1987). "Love Thy Children: Reflections on the Barro Debt Neutrality Theorem," *Journal of Monetary Economics*, 19, 3 (May), 377–391.

Weil, Philippe (1989). "Overlapping Families of Infinitely Lived Agents," *Journal of Public Economics*, 38, 2 (March), 183–198.

Weitzman, Martin L. (1973). "Duality Theory for Infinite Horizon Convex Models," *Management Science*, 19, 783–789.

Wheeler, David and Ashoka Mody (1992). "International Investment Location Decisions: The Case of U.S. Firms," *Journal of International Economics*, 33 (August), 57–76.

Wood, Adrian (1988). "Global Trends in Real Exchange Rates, 1960 to 1984," World Bank Discussion Paper no. 35, Washington D.C., The World Bank.

Wright, Theodore P. (1936). "Factors Affecting the Cost of Airplanes," *Journal of the Aeronautical Sciences*, 3, 122–128.

Xie, Danyang (1992). *Three Essays on Economic Growth and Development*, Ph.D. dissertation, University of Chicago.

Yaari, Menahem E. (1965). "Uncertain Lifetime, Life Insurance, and the Theory of the Consumer," *Review of Economic Studies*, 32 (April), 137–150.

Young, Allyn (1928). "Increasing Returns and Economic Progress," *Economic Journal*, 38 (December), 527–542.

Young, Alwyn (1989). *Hong Kong and the Art of Landing on Ones's Feet: A Case Study of a Structurally Flexible Economy*, Ph.D. dissertation, Fletcher School, Tufts University, May.

Young, Alwyn (1990). "Invention and Bounded Learning by Doing," paper presented at NBER growth conference, Cambridge MA, November.

Young, Alwyn (1992). "A Tale of Two Cities: Factor Accumulation and Technical Change in Hong Kong and Singapore," in Olivier J. Blanchard and Stanley Fischer, eds., *NBER Macroeconomics Annual 1992*, Cambridge MA, MIT Press, 13–54.

Young, Alwyn (1994). "The Tyranny of Numbers: Confronting the Statistical Realities of the East Asian Growth Experience," unpublished paper, MIT, February.

INDEX

A

Abel, A., 126, 138
Ades, A. F., 341, 442
Aghion, P., 12, 41, 241, 242n
AK model, 39–42, 141–144
  government and growth in, 152–161
Alesina, A., 424n
Altruism, 135–137
Analysis, empirical:
  of international data, 414–461
  of regional data, 382–413
Anuario Estadistico de España, 342
Arrow, K. J., 11, 12, 40, 42, 146, 147, 351n
Aschaur, D. A., 441n
Asher, H., 147
Assets, behavior of a small economy's, 99

B

β (beta) (*see* Convergence coefficient)
Bagwell, K., 60n
Banks, A. S., 435n
Barro, R. J., 6, 7, 60n, 95, 101n, 106n, 108, 122n, 153, 158, 170, 291, 293, 308–311, 315, 323, 330, 331, 383, 387n, 391, 393, 421, 424, 431, 441, 445
Baumol, W. J., 7, 383

Becker, G. S., 309–311, 313, 315, 322n
Behrman, J. R., 308, 452
Benhabib, J., 199n, 322n, 437
Bequests, 135–137
Bernheim, B. D., 60n
Births, 312
Black-market premium on foreign exchange, 434–435
Blanchard, O., 61n, 91n, 109, 110, 111, 115, 122n, 126n, 128, 138, 139, 295
Blomström, M., 433
Boldrin, M., 199n
Borjas, G. J., 292, 293
Borts, G. H., 383
Bos, E., 453
Bowman, L. W., 267
Braun, J., 291, 300, 306, 307, 308, 328
Braun model:
  of migration and growth, 300–308
Brezis, E., 255n, 279, 280
Brock, W. A., 94
Bronars, S. G., 293
Budget, family, 313–314
Bureau of Economic Analysis, 341
Bureaucracy, quality of, 439

C

Caballe, J., 208
Caballero, R. J., 271n

529

Capital:
   accumulation, golden rule of, 19–22
   effect of on population growth,
      348–350
   growth rate of, 188–190
   human, 432–433
   human and physical, one-sector model
      with, 172–179
   human in two-sector models of
      endogenous growth, 171–210
   mobility, 308
   physical and human, 101–108
    one-sector model with, 144–146
   share, 24
   stock, behavior of a small economy's,
      98–99
   stock, fundamental dynamic equation
      for, 17–18
   stock, the path of, 79–80
Cass, D., 11, 12, 59
CES (*see* Constant-elasticity-of-
      substitution production functions)
Chamley, C., 199n
Chenery, H. B. (with Arrow), 42
Child-rearing costs, 312–313
Chiswick, B. R., 292
Christensen, L. R., 5, 350
Chua, H. B., 46n, 275n, 442, 443
CIES, 65
Citibase, 342
Closed economy, 102–103
Coase, R. W., 261
Cobb–Douglas:
  example of a model with learning-by-
    doing and knowledge spillovers,
    150–151
  example of transitional dynamics in
    an endogenous growth model,
    161–164
  function, 17
  model, 40
    with learning-by-doing and knowl-
      edge spillovers, 150–151
  production function, 10
    convergence speed of, 36–38
  technology, 25–26
Coe, D. T., 7, 352
Coefficients, stability of, 436
Cohen, D., 101, 138

Collins, S. M., 107
Congestion model of productive govern-
    ment services, 158–161
Constant intertemporal elasticity substitu-
    tion (CIES), 65
Constant-elasticity-of-substitution
    production functions (CES),
    42–46
  example of transitional dynamics in
    an endogenous growth model,
    164–166
Consumer variety, compared with
    producer variety, 236–237
Consumption:
  behavior of a small economy's, 99
  function, in Ramsey's model, 66–67
  growth rate of, 188
Convergence, 383–387
  absolute, 26–29
  β, 7, 383
    across European regions, 398–400
    across Japanese prefectures,
      393–397
    across the U.S. states, 387–392
  coefficient, β, 53–54, 105
  conditional, 10, 26, 28–30
  and the dispersion of per capita
    income, 31–32
  across European regions, 398–401
  across Japanese prefectures, 393–398
  and migration, 410–413
  in model of technological diffusion,
    274–276
  in the Ramsey model, 83
  σ, 383
    across European regions, 400–401
    across Japanese prefectures,
      397–398
    across the U.S. states, 392–393
  in the Solow–Swan model with
    migration, 290–294
  speed of, 36–38
    log-linear approximations of, 80–82
  across the U.S. states, 387–393
Corruption in government, 439
Coulombe, S., 344
Countries included in growth-rate
    regressions, 457
Cummings, D., 5, 350

D

Data, 330–346, 353–381
  empirical analysis of international,
    414–461
  empirical analysis of regional,
    382–413
  growth accounting, 380–381
  international, 342–346
    education, 358–363
    GDP, 332–334, 353–358, 364–369,
      372–376
    growth, 416–419
    income, 377–379, 394
    investment ratio, 335–340,
      353–358
    life expectancy, 353–358
    migration, 372–376
    population, 358–369, 372–379
  U.S., 341–342
    education, 360
    GDP, 333, 341–342, 355, 366,
      370–371
    income, 370–371, 388–389
    investment ratio, 355
    life expectancy, 355, 360
    migration, 370–371
    population, 366, 370–371
  World Bank, on GDP, 444–445
Death, as the termination of a family
    dynasty, 110, 312
Debt, in the Ramsey model, 62
Defense expenditures, 441
DeLong, J. B., 7, 383, 433, 434n
Democracy, 438–439
Denison, E. F., 5, 38, 349
Diagonalization of matrices, 511–512
Diamond, P., 109, 115, 128
Diewert, W. E., 347n
Differential equations, 463–491
  first-order ordinary, 464–471
  systems of linear ordinary, 471–491
Dispersion, 383–387
  across the U.S. states, 392–393
Dixit, A. K., 213, 240
Dolado, J., 292
Domar, E. D., 10, 47
Dougherty, C., 5, 350
Dowrick, S., 383

Dynamic efficiency, and the golden rule,
    133–134
Dynamics (*see* Transitional dynamics)

E

Easterlin, R. A., 342, 383
Easterly, W., 423n, 441n
Ectoplasm, 15
Education, 431–432, 436–437
  data (*see* Data, international; Data, U.S.)
  public spending on, 433
Eigenvalues, 510–512
Eigenvectors, 510–512
Elias, V. J., 5, 350
Emigration (*see* Migration)
End-of-the-world model, 93
Endogenous growth models, 12, 38–48
Equilibrium:
  in the *AK* model, 142
  market, in models with improvements
    in product quality, 252–254
  in models with learning-by-doing
    and knowledge spillovers,
    148–149
  in overlapping-generations models
    (closed economy), 130–131
  in Ramsey's model, 70–71
  world, 100–101
Ethier, W. J., 213
Euler equation, 63
Expropriation, 439

F

Faig, M., 208
Farmer, R. E. A., 199n
Feenstra, R. C., 349n
Fertility:
  choice, 308–321
  empirical analysis of, 452–455
  rates, 9, 437–438
Firms:
  behavior of, in the *AK* model, 141–142
  behavior of, in models with improve-
    ments in product quality, 242–252
  market value of, 252
  in overlapping-generations models, 130
  in Ramsey's model, 67–70

Fiscal policy in the Ramsey model, 95
Fischer, S., 61n, 94
Fisher, I., 10
Foreign exchange, black-market premium
    on, 434–435
Fraumeni, 5, 38, 349

G

Galor, O., 50, 313n
Galton's fallacy, 32
Gastil, R. D., 332, 439, 461n
GDP (*see* Gross domestic product)
Geary, R. C., 109
General Agreement on Tariffs and Trade
    (GATT), 277
Glaeser, E. L., 341
Golden rule, the:
    and dynamic efficiency, 133–134
    modified, 74n
Gollop, F. M., 5, 38, 349
Goria, A., 292
Government:
    consumption, 434
    and growth in the *AK* model, 152–161
    and growth in the Ramsey model, 95
    policy, effect of on growth, 7–8
    the public-goods model of productive
        government services, 152–158
    repudiation of contracts by, 439
Greenwood, J., 293
Greenwood, M. J., 322n
Griliches, Z., 269, 346, 347n, 349, 350,
    351, 352
Gross domestic product (GDP):
    growth of, in various countries,
        1–5
    long-term data on, 332
    World Bank data on, 444–445
Gross state product (GSP), 387n
Grossman, G. M., 12, 231, 235, 242n,
    245, 266n
Growth:
    accounting, 346–352
        data, 380–381
        extensions to include R&D,
            351–352
    consequences of small differentials
        over long periods, 1–3
    empirical regularities about, 5

endogenous:
    conditions for in the one-sector
        model, 167–169
    conditions for in the Uzawa–Lucas
        model, 198–200
    models of, 38–48
    with transitional dynamics, 41–42
rates:
    determinants of, in the *AK* model,
        143–144
    determinants of, in models with
        technological change, 220
    empirical analysis of international,
        420–424
    regression results, 457–461
    regression results, international,
        424–446
    recent losers and winners, 415–420
    source of, for slow and fast growers,
        446–450
    theory, history of, 9–13
GSP, 387n
Gulhati, R., 267

H

Hamiltonian:
    behavior over time, 503
    current value, 509–510
    present-value, 63, 509–510
Harrod, R. F., 10, 33, 47
Harrod–Domar controversy,
    46–48
Harrod neutral, 33
        Hart, P. E., 32
Hatton, T. J., 292, 293
Health, empirical analysis of, 452–455
Helpman, E., 7, 12, 231, 235, 242n, 245,
    266n, 352
Henderson, J. V., 405
Hercowitz, Z., 322n
Heston, A., 26n, 330–332, 414n, 415,
    420, 430n, 433, 434, 444, 445,
    457n
Hicks, J., 33
Hicks neutral, 33
Hirshleifer, J., 178
Households, 60–67
    behavior of, in the *AK* model,
        141

in models with improvements in
product quality, 252–254
in models with technological change,
218–219
in overlapping-generations models,
128–129
Howitt, P., 12, 41, 241, 242n

I

Ichino, A., 292
ICP, 331–332
Imitation, 268–271
and innovation, mutual, 276
variations in the cost of, 272–274
Immigration (*see* Migration)
Implicit function theorem, 512–513
Inada, K-I., 16
Inada conditions, 16–17
Income:
data (*see* Data, international; Data, U.S.)
Japanese, 394–397
per capita, dispersion of, and
convergence, 31–32
U.S., 388–389
Inefficiency, dynamic, golden rule of,
19–22
Infinite horizons, 135–137, 504–505
Inflation in the Ramsey model, 94
Innovation:
and imitation, mutual, 276
imitators of in following countries,
268–271
incentive for, 246–251
in the leading country, 254–259,
267–268
R&D included in growth accounting,
351–352
Instability, political, 435
Intensive form, 17
Interest rate, equilibrium with a given,
122–125
International Comparison Project (ICP),
331–332
International data (*see* Data, international)
Inventions:
classification of, 32–33
(*See also* Innovation; Technological
change)

Investment:
adjustment costs for, 119–127
behavior of firms, 119
data (*see* Data, international; Data,
U.S.)
foreign, 276–279
gross, inequality restrictions on, in the
Uzawa–Lucas model, 194–196
irreversibility of in the Ramsey model,
93
non-negative gross, 175–179
private versus public, 441–442
ratio, 433–434
empirical analysis of, 451–452

J

Jaffe, A. B., 271n
Jones, L. E., 41, 161
Jones, R. W., 280n, 283
Jorgenson, D. W., 5, 38, 349, 350
Jovanovic, B., 266n, 271n, 280n
Judd, K. L., 223n
Judson, R., 87

K

Kaldor, N., 5, 87, 104
Keefer, P., 439, 440, 461n
Kendrick, J. W., 180
Kimball, M. S., 136
King, R. G., 86, 323, 443, 461n
Knack, S., 439, 440, 461n
Knight, F. H., 12, 39n, 9
Koopmans, T. C., 11, 12, 59, 61n
Kremer, M., 125n, 151
Krugman, P., 199n, 255n, 266n, 279,
280
Kurz, M., 41n
Kuznets, S., 5n
Kydland, F. E., 216

L

Labor:
effect of on population growth, 348–350
effective (amount of), 35
leisure choice, 321–326
supply, 285–327
Lach, S., 266n, 271n

Land in the Ramsey model, 94
Law, rule of, 439–440
Leader-follower model, 266–276
Leapfrogging, 279–281
Learning-by-doing, 146–152
Lee, F. C., 344
Lee, Jong-Wha, 308, 330, 331, 421, 424, 438, 461n
Leisure/labor choice, 321–326
Leontief, W., 46
Leontief production function, 46–48
Levine, R., 433, 443, 461n
Lichtenberg, F., 352
Life expectancy, 432
L'Hôpital's rule, 514–515
Linear, homogeneous systems, 480–481
Linear, nonhomogeneous systems, 484–486
Linearization of nonlinear systems, 487–488
Lipsey, R. E., 433
Loans, in the Ramsey model, 62
Londregan, J. B., 435
Lucas, R. E., 12, 152, 172, 182, 198, 211

M

McCallum, B. T., 95, 216
Maddison, A., 5, 6, 8, 38, 87, 332, 335
Malthus, Thomas R., 9, 13, 308–309
Mankiw, N. G., 7, 57, 101n, 106n, 431, 433
Mansfield, E., 269, 271n
Manuelli, R. E., 41, 161
Market equilibrium, 70–71
  in models with improvements in product quality, 252–254
  in models with technological change, 218–219
Market value of firms, 252
Markusen, J. R., 349n
Mas-Colell, A., 328
Matsuyama, K., 199n
Mauro, P., 439n
Migration:
  in the Braun model, 300–308
  and convergence, 410–413
  data (*see* Data, international; Data, U.S.)
  across European regions, 407–410

function, 288–289
  across Japanese prefectures, 404–407
  in models of economic growth, 285–308
  in the Ramsey model, 294–300
  in the Solow–Swan models, 286–294
  across the U.S. states, 401–404
Minhas, B. S. (with Arrow), 42
Models:
  AK, 39–42, 141–144
    government and growth in, 152–161
  Braun, of migration and growth, 300–308
  Cobb–Douglas, 40
  Cobb–Douglas, with learning-by-doing and knowledge spillovers, 150–151
  congestion, of productive government services, 158–161
  with different technologies for production and education, 179–198
  End-of-the-world, 93
  of endogenous growth, 12, 38–48
  endogenous growth, transitional dynamics in, 161–166
  with finite horizons, 110–119
  finite-horizon, of a closed economy, 114–116
  finite-horizon, of an open economy, 116–119
  government and growth in the *AK* model, 152–161
  leader-follower, 266–276
  with learning-by-doing and knowledge spillovers, 146–152
  neoclassical, 16
  one-sector:
    of endogenous growth, 140–169
    transitional dynamics with inequality restrictions on gross investment, 201–203
    with physical and human capital, 144–146, 172–179
  overlapping-generations (OLG), 109, 128–137
  with poverty traps, 48–52
  Ramsey's:
    behavior of the saving rate in, 77–79
    with a constraint on international credit, 101–108

with consumer optimization, 59–92
the consumption function in, 66–67
convergence in, 84
dynamic paths in, 85
equilibrium in, 70–71
firms in, 67–70
fiscal policy in, 94
government and growth in, 95
inflation in, 94
irreversibility of in, 92
land in, 94
log-linearization of, 87–89
with migration, 294–300
numerical solutions of, 82–87
open-economy version, 96–101
steady state in, 72–74
Romer's, of technological change,
 226–230
Solow–Swan, 14–58
 convergence coefficient in,
  53–54
 dynamics of, 23
 with labor augmenting technological
  progress, 34
 migration in, 286–294
technological change:
 in expansion of variety, 212–238
 in improvement of quality, 240–263
two-sector, of endogenous growth,
 171–210
with two sectors of production,
 179–182
Uzawa–Lucas, 182–196
 generalized, 196–198
 with reversed factor intensities,
  197–198
 solution of, 204–208
with a variety of consumer products,
 231–237
with a variety of producer products,
 213–230
Mody, A., 439n
Molle, W., 342, 343
Monopoly:
 power, erosion of, 223–226
 profit, 246–249
 researcher, technological leader as,
  255–259
Murphy, K. M., 116, 313n

N

Nallari, R., 267
Nelson, R. R., 269, 422
Neoclassical, defined, 16
Neoclassical production functions, 52–53
Nguyen, D. T., 383
Numerical solutions of the nonlinear
 system (Ramsey's model),
 82–87
Nyarko, Y., 280n

O

OECD (*see* Organization for Economic
 Cooperation and Development)
Ohyama, M., 280n, 283
OLG (*see* Overlapping-generations
 model)
One-sector model:
 of endogenous growth, 140–169
 with physical and human capital,
  144–146, 172–179
 transitional dynamics with inequality
  restrictions on gross investment,
  201–203
Open economy, 103–108
Optimality (*see* Pareto optimality)
Organization for Economic Cooperation
 and Development (OECD), 27
Output:
 behavior of a small economy's, 98–99
 growth rate of, 190–193
 path of, 79–80
Overlapping-generations model (OLG),
 109
Oversaving, 169

P

Pareto nonoptimality, in models with
 learning-by-doing and knowledge
 spillovers, 149–150
Pareto optimality, 259–262
 in models with technological change,
  220–222
Park, W. A., 107
Perotti, R., 424n
Phase diagram, 74–76
 of a finite-horizon, closed economy, 114

Phase diagram (*continued*)
  of a finite-horizon, open economy,
    117
  when migration is a choice variable,
    305
  for a model with fertility choice,
    317
  for the one-sector model when
    $\omega < \omega^*$, 203
  for the one-sector model when
    $\omega > \omega^*$, 202
  for the open economy model with
    adjustment costs, 123
  of the Ramsey model, 73
  of the Ramsey model with migration,
    299
  of transitional dynamics in a CES
    endogenous growth model, 166
  of transitional dynamics in an endoge-
    nous growth model, 163
Phelps, E. S., 20, 266*n*, 269, 422
Plosser, C. I., 323
Policy:
  experiments, 24–25
  function, 76
  government, effect of on growth, 7
  implications in models with learning-
    by-doing and knowledge
    spillovers, 149–150
Political institutions, the quality of,
  439–440
Poole, K. T., 435
Population, 285–327
  data (*see* Data, international; Data,
    U.S.)
  growth, 437–438
Population Trends, 51, 343
Poverty traps, 49–52
Preference, variation in parameters of,
  108–110
Prescott, E. C., 216
Producer variety, compared with con-
  sumer variety, 236–237
Production functions:
  Cobb–Douglas, 10
  constant-elasticity-of-substitution
    (CES), 42–46, 55–56
  Leontief, 46–48
  neoclassical, 16, 52–53

Productivity slowdown, 6
Proof that γ_K declines monotonically
    if the economy starts from
    $k(0) < k$, 90–92
Public services (*see* Services, public)
Putty, 15

Q

q, average and marginal, 122
Quah, D., 32
Quality index, aggregate, 251–252

R

R&D (*see* Research and development)
R&D effort, determination of in models
    with improvements in product
    quality, 249–251
Ramsey, F., 9, 10, 59, 61*n*
Ramsey's intertemporally separable util-
    ity function, 10
Ramsey's model:
  behavior of the saving rate in, 77–79
  with a constraint on international
    credit, 101–108
  with consumer optimization, 59–92
  the consumption function in, 66–67
  convergence in, 83
  dynamic paths in, 85
  equilibrium in, 70–71
  firms in, 67–70
  fiscal policy in, 95
  government and growth in, 95
  inflation in, 94
  irreversibility of in, 93
  land in, 94
  log-linearization of, 88–89
  with migration, 294–300
  numerical solutions of, 82–87
  open-economy version, 96–101
  steady state in, 72–74
Rapping, L., 147
Razin, A., 328
Rebelo, S., 12, 86, 179, 323, 423*n*, 441*n*
Reinganum, J. F., 226, 247*n*
Renelt, D., 433
Research and development (R&D), 7, 32
  (*See also* Technological change)

Rhee, C., 122n
Ricardo, David, 9
Rivera-Batiz, L. A., 216, 227
Roback, J., 405
Robinson, J., 33
Rogerson, R., 322n
Romer, P. M., 7, 11, 12, 38, 40, 41, 57,
    146, 147, 170, 213, 216n, 226,
    227, 267, 272, 351n, 431, 433
Romer's model of technological change,
    226–230
Rustichini, A., 199n
Rybczinski, T. M., 138
Ryder, H. E., 50

S

Sachs, J., 101, 138
Saint-Paul, G., 169
Sala-i-Martin, X., 101n, 106n, 108, 158,
    170, 291, 293, 383, 387n, 391, 393
Samuelson, P. A., 109, 128, 153
Santos, M. S., 208
Sarel, M., 438
Saving, national, 9
Saving, Ramsey's rule of optimal, 63
Saving rates:
    behavior of, 89–90
        in the Cobb–Douglas case, 78
        in the Ramsey model, 77–79
        in the Uzawa–Lucas model, 193
    exogenous, 14–58
    fixed, equilibrium for a closed econ-
        omy with, 125–127
Sayied, Ingrid, 330
Scale effects, 442
    of a model with learning-by-doing and
        knowledge spillovers, 151–152
    in the public-goods model of
        productive government services,
        157–158
Schmookler, J., 147
Schmoos, 15
Schultz, T. P., 308, 452
Schumpeter, Joseph A., 9, 241
Schwartz, M., 269, 271n
Searle, A. D., 147
Seemingly unrelated (SUR) technique,
    424

Segerstrom, P. S., 266n
Services, public, 158–159
    as an influence on property rights,
        159–161
Sheshinski, E., 11, 12, 147
Shleifer, A., 440n
Sidrauski, M., 94
Smith, Adam, 9
Smits, H., 342, 343
Social planner, benevolent, 71
Social planning, 157, 220–222, 259–262
Solow neutral, 33
Solow, R. M., 10, 15, 17, 33, 346, 347n,
    349
Solow, R. M. (with Arrow), 42
Solow–Swan model, 14–58
    convergence coefficient in, 53–54
    dynamics of, 23
    with labor augmenting technological
        progress, 34
    migration in, 286–294
Spence, M., 213, 231, 240
Spiegel, M. M., 437
Spillover effects, 442–443
Srinivasan, T. N., 179, 195
Standards of living, 4
Static optimization, 491–498
*Statistiches Jahrbuch für die Bundes-
    republik Deutschland,* 343
Steady state:
    in the Braun model with migration,
        304–308
    defined, 19
    in a model with fertility choice,
        316–321
    of the overlapping-generations model,
        131–133
    in Ramsey's model, 72–74
    in the Ramsey model with migration,
        297–300
    in the Solow–Swan model with migra-
        tion, 289–290
    of the Uzawa–Lucas model, 183–184
Stein, J. L., 383
Stephens, P. W., 453
Stiglitz, J. E., 213, 240
Stock, capital, fundamental dynamic
    equation for, 17–18
Stone, R., 109

Stone–Geary form, 109
Stone–Geary preferences, 93
Streissler, E., 383
Subsidies, 222–223
Summers, L. H., 122n
Summers, R., 26n, 122n, 330–332, 414n,
    415, 420, 430n, 433, 434, 444,
    445, 457n
SUR, 424
Swan, T. W., 10, 15, 17

T

Tamura, R., 313n
Tariff rate, 438
Taylor's theorem, 513–514
Technology, 146–148
    capital and labor augmenting, 33
    capital and labor saving, 33
    change in, 32–36
    change in models with an expanding
        variety of products, 212–238
    change in models with improvement in
        quality of products, 240–263
    change in Romer's model of, 226–230
    the diffusion of, 265–281
    labor augmenting, 54–55
    leadership, 254–259
Teece, D. J., 269, 277
Temple, R., 281n
Thompson, E. A, 125n
Thomson, J., 125n
Thörnqvist, L., 347
Time-elimination method for nonlinear
    systems, 83, 488–491
Trade, terms of, 435
Transitional dynamics, 22, 74–87
    in the AK model, 142–143
    in the Braun model with migration,
        304–308
    in an endogenous growth model,
        161–166
    with inequality restrictions on gross
        investment, 201–203
    in a model with fertility choice,
        316–321
    of the overlapping-generations model,
        134–135
    in the Ramsey model with migration,
        297–300
    in the Solow–Swan model with migra-
        tion, 290–294
    speed of, 36–38
    of the Uzawa–Lucas model,
        184–194
Transversality condition, 65–66,
    503
    in infinite-horizon problems,
        507–508
Trejo, S. J., 293
Tsiddon, D., 255n, 279, 280

U

U.S. data (see Data, U.S.)
U.S. Survey of Current Business, 341
Utility function:
    form of, with consumption and work
        effort, 326–327
    Ramsey's intertemporally separable,
        10
Uzawa, H., 12, 33, 108, 109, 172, 179n,
    182, 195
Uzawa–Lucas model, 182–196
    generalized, 196–198
    with reversed factor intensities,
        197–198
    solution of, 204–208

V

Van Holst, B., 342, 343
Variety, consumer compared with
    producer, 236–237
Ventura, J., 137, 179n
Vishny, R. W., 440n
Von Furstenberg, G. M., 122n
Von Neumann, John, 39n
Vu, M. T., 453

W

Wagner, S., 269, 271n
Wahl, J. B., 308
Wald test, 433
War expenditures, 441
Weil, P., 114, 136, 295
Weil, D. N., 7, 57, 313n, 431,
    433
Welch, F., 116

Wheeler, D., 439n
Williamson, J. G., 292, 293
Wood, A., 434n
World Bank, 444–445
World economy:
    with a constraint on international
        credit, 101–108
    dynamics of, in the Braun model,
        306–308
World equilibrium, 100–101
Wright, R., 322n
Wright, T. P., 147

X

Xie, D., 199n

Y

Yaari, M. E., 111
Young, Allyn, 9
Young, Alwyn, 5, 6, 266, 267, 281n, 351

Z

Zejan, M., 433